# Frommer's®

# Texas

## *6th Edition*

## by David Baird, Eric Peterson & Neil E. Schlecht

Wiley Publishing, Inc.

Published by:
**WILEY PUBLISHING, INC.**
111 River St.
Hoboken, NJ 07030-5774

ISBN 978-1-118-00284-1 (paper); ISBN 978-1-118-10190-2 (ebk); ISBN 978-1-118-10191-9 (ebk);
ISBN 978-1-118-10192-6 (ebk)

Editor: Shelley Bance with Cate Latting
Production Editor: Katie Robinson
Cartographer: Nick Trotter
Photo Editor: Richard Fox
Production by Wiley Indianapolis Composition Services
Front cover photo: Pepperweed in bloom with El Capitan in distance, Guadalupe Mountains National Park,
Texas ©Tim Fitzharris / Minden Pictures
Back cover photo: Austin: Historical wall murals on Congress Avenue ©Witold Skrypczak / Lonely Planet
Images

For information on our other products and services or to obtain technical support, please contact our
Customer Care Department within the U.S. at 877/762-2974, outside the U.S. at 317/572-3993 or fax
317/572-4002.

Wiley also publishes its books in a variety of electronic formats. Some content that appears in print may
not be available in electronic formats.

Manufactured in the United States of America

5   4   3   2   1

# CONTENTS

List of Maps  vi

## 1  THE BEST OF TEXAS  1

The Best Luxury & Historic Hotels  1

The Best Bed & Breakfasts &
  Boutique Hotels  3

The Best Hotel Bargains  4

The Best Restaurants  5

The Best Texan Dining  6

The Best Lone Star Experiences  7

The Best Museums  8

The Best Shopping  9

The Best Places for
  Boot-Scootin'  10

The Best of Natural Texas  11

The Best Historical Attractions  12

The Best Family Adventures  13

The Best of Texas Online  14

## 2  TEXAS IN DEPTH  16

Texas Today  17

Looking Back: Texas History  17

GLOSS'RY: HOW TO TALK LIKE A TEXAN  20

Texas in Pop Culture  22

Eating & Drinking  29

When to Go  31

TEXAS CALENDAR OF EVENTS  33

Responsible Travel  35

Tours  37

## 3  SUGGESTED TEXAS ITINERARIES  40

The Regions in Brief  40

Texas in 1 Week  44

Texas in 2 Weeks  46

Texas for Families  48

Exploring the Hill Country  49

## 4  DALLAS  52

Orientation  53

THE NEIGHBORHOODS IN BRIEF  57

FAST FACTS: DALLAS  62

Where to Stay  63

FAMILY-FRIENDLY HOTELS  71

Where to Dine  71

FAMILY-FRIENDLY RESTAURANTS  77

PICNIC PLACES  80

Exploring Dallas  80

DOWNTOWN DALLAS'S OUTDOOR
  SCULPTURE  84

Shopping  92

Big D After Dark  95

Arlington  99

# 5 FORT WORTH 102

Orientation 103
*THE NEIGHBORHOODS IN BRIEF* 103
*FAST FACTS: FORT WORTH* 105
Where to Stay 106
*FAMILY-FRIENDLY HOTELS* 113
Where to Dine 114
*FAMILY-FRIENDLY RESTAURANTS* 116

Exploring Fort Worth 121
*CHRISTMAS IN THE STOCKYARDS* 121
*THE GRAPEVINE VINTAGE RAILROAD* 123
Shopping 131
Fort Worth After Dark 132
*GRAPEVINE* 135

# 6 HOUSTON & EAST TEXAS 137

Orientation 138
*THE NEIGHBORHOODS IN BRIEF* 141
Getting Around 147
*FAST FACTS: HOUSTON* 148
Where to Stay 149
*FAMILY-FRIENDLY HOTELS* 157
Where to Dine 159
*FAST FOOD À LA HOUSTON* 161

*FAMILY-FRIENDLY RESTAURANTS* 166
Seeing the Sights 169
Sports & Outdoor Activities 178
Shopping 180
Houston After Dark 182
Side Trips to East Texas 186
*RACE RELATIONS IN EAST TEXAS* 188
*TEXAS STATE RAILROAD* 190

# 7 THE TEXAS GULF COAST 192

Galveston 192
*HURRICANE IKE & AFTERMATH* 194
*THE GREAT STORM* 196
Brazosport 199
*BIRDING ALONG THE TEXAS COAST* 201
*TEXAS'S MOST DESERTED BEACH* 204
Corpus Christi 205
Rockport 211

*WHOOPING CRANES: BACK FROM THE
    BRINK OF EXTINCTION* 212
Port Aransas 216
Padre Island National Seashore 219
*THE RACE TO SAVE THE SEA TURTLES* 221
South Padre Island 223
*FACE TO FACE WITH A SEA TURTLE* 227

# 8 SAN ANTONIO 231

Orientation 232
*THE NEIGHBORHOODS IN BRIEF* 234
Getting Around 235
*FAST FACTS: SAN ANTONIO* 237
Where to Stay 237
*FAMILY-FRIENDLY HOTELS* 247
Where to Dine 250
*FAMILY-FRIENDLY RESTAURANTS* 258
Seeing the Sights 259

Sports & Outdoor Activities 267
Shopping in San Antonio 268
San Antonio After Dark 270
*CONJUNTO: AN AMERICAN CLASSIC* 273
Small-Town Texas 274
Hill Country Side Trips from
    San Antonio 277
*A TASTE OF ALSACE IN TEXAS* 278
*THE HILL COUNTRY WINE TRAIL* 280

# 9 AUSTIN 283

Orientation 283

*THE NEIGHBORHOODS IN BRIEF* 285

Getting Around 286

*FAST FACTS: AUSTIN* 287

Where to Stay 288

*IT PAYS TO STAY* 296

*FAMILY-FRIENDLY HOTELS* 298

Where to Dine 299

*GROCERY STORE DINING* 303

*FAMILY-FRIENDLY RESTAURANTS* 305

*FOOD TRUCKS PARK IN AUSTIN* 308

Seeing the Sights 309

*GOING BATTY* 310

Staying Active 317

Shopping 319

*FIRST THURSDAYS* 320

Austin After Dark 321

Hill Country Side Trips from
Austin 324

# 10 WEST TEXAS 331

El Paso 331

*FAST FACTS: EL PASO* 336

*EL PASO'S ALLIGATOR ART* 338

*THE COPPER CANYON* 348

Small Towns of Central
West Texas 349

*A SIDE TRIP TO CANDELARIA* 353

*MARFA'S MYSTERY LIGHTS* 356

*GALLERY HOPPING IN THE BIG BEND* 357

Midland & Odessa 360

*MIDLAND'S FAMOUS SON, GEORGE* 361

San Angelo 365

Del Rio & Amistad National
Recreation Area 371

*THE LEGEND OF ROY BEAN* 375

# 11 BIG BEND & GUADALUPE MOUNTAINS NATIONAL PARKS 379

Big Bend National Park 379

Guadalupe Mountains National
Park 393

A Side Trip to Carlsbad Caverns
National Park 399

# 12 THE PANHANDLE PLAINS 407

Amarillo 408

*UNANTICIPATED REWARDS* 413

Canyon & Palo Duro Canyon
State Park 420

*OLD ROUTE 66* 422

Lubbock 424

*A DIFFERENT KIND OF TEXAS TEA* 429

# 13 PLANNING YOUR TRIP TO TEXAS 434

Getting There 434

Getting Around 435

*TEXAS: GATEWAY TO MEXICO* 438

Tips on Accommodations 440

*FAST FACTS: TEXAS* 441

Airline Websites 453

Index 454

# LIST OF MAPS

The Regions in Brief   42

The Best of Texas in 1 Week   45

The Best of Texas in 2 Weeks   47

Texas for Families   49

Exploring the Hill Country   50

Dallas–Fort Worth   54

Downtown & Deep Ellum Accommodations, Dining & Attractions   58

Uptown & Oak Lawn Accommodations & Dining   61

Fort Worth Stockyards National Historic District   105

Downtown Fort Worth   107

Fort Worth Cultural District   109

Houston   139

Central Houston Accommodations   142

Central Houston Dining & Attractions   144

East Texas   187

The Texas Gulf Coast   193

Galveston   195

Corpus Christi   207

South Padre Island   225

South-Central Texas   233

Greater San Antonio Accommodations, Dining & Attractions   238

Central San Antonio Accommodations   241

Central San Antonio Dining & Attractions   251

Greater Austin Accommodations, Dining & Attractions   290

Central Austin Hotels, Dining & Attractions   293

West Texas   333

El Paso   334

Big Bend National Park   381

Guadalupe Mountains National Park   395

Carlsbad Caverns National Park   401

The Panhandle Plains   409

Amarillo   411

Lubbock   425

Texas Driving Times & Distances   437

## ABOUT THE AUTHORS

**David Baird** is a writer, editor, and translator based in Austin, Texas.

**Eric Peterson** lives in Denver, Colorado, and writes about all sorts of subjects, including but not limited to travel, business, politics, music, skiing, and environmental issues. He is the author of several Frommer's guides and *Ramble Texas* (Fulcrum Books, 2010). Peterson's byline has appeared in such publications as the New York *Daily News, High Country News, Westwood,* and *ColoradoBiz.*

**Neil E. Schlecht** was reared in North Dallas. He attended Plano Senior High School, returned for graduate school at the University of Texas at Austin, and married a fellow Texan. Now living in northwestern Connecticut, he is the author and co-author of more than a dozen travel guides, including *Frommer's Peru,* and is the author and photographer of *Buenos Aires Day by Day* and *Mallorca & Menorca Day by Day.* His Texas heroes are Ann Richards, Stevie Ray Vaughan, and Jimmie Dale Gilmore.

## HOW TO CONTACT US

In researching this book, we discovered many wonderful places—hotels, restaurants, shops, and more. We're sure you'll find others. Please tell us about them, so we can share the information with your fellow travelers in upcoming editions. If you were disappointed with a recommendation, we'd love to know that, too. Please write to

*Frommer's Texas,* 6th Edition
Wiley Publishing, Inc. • 111 River St. • Hoboken, NJ 07030-5774
frommersfeedback@wiley.com

## ADVISORY & DISCLAIMER

Travel information can change quickly and unexpectedly, and we strongly advise you to confirm important details locally before traveling, including information on visas, health and safety, traffic and transport, accommodation, shopping and eating out. We also encourage you to stay alert while traveling and to remain aware of your surroundings. Avoid civil disturbances, and keep a close eye on cameras, purses, wallets and other valuables.

While we have endeavored to ensure that the information contained within this guide is accurate and up-to-date at the time of publication, we make no representations or warranties with respect to the accuracy or completeness of the contents of this work and specifically disclaim all warranties, including without limitation warranties of fitness for a particular purpose. We accept no responsibility or liability for any inaccuracy or errors or omissions, or for any inconvenience, loss, damage, costs or expenses of any nature whatsoever incurred or suffered by anyone as a result of any advice or information contained in this guide.

The inclusion of a company, organization or Website in this guide as a service provider and/or potential source of further information does not mean that we endorse them or the information they provide. Be aware that information provided through some Websites may be unreliable and can change without notice. Neither the publisher or author shall be liable for any damages arising herefrom.

## FROMMER'S STAR RATINGS, ICONS & ABBREVIATIONS

Every hotel, restaurant, and attraction listing in this guide has been ranked for quality, value, service, amenities, and special features using a **star-rating system.** In country, state, and regional guides, we also rate towns and regions to help you narrow down your choices and budget your time accordingly. Hotels and restaurants are rated on a scale of zero (recommended) to three stars (exceptional). Attractions, shopping, nightlife, towns, and regions are rated according to the following scale: zero stars (recommended), one star (highly recommended), two stars (very highly recommended), and three stars (must-see).

In addition to the star-rating system, we also use seven feature icons that point you to the great deals, in-the-know advice, and unique experiences that separate travelers from tourists. Throughout the book, look for:

**special finds**—those places only insiders know about

**fun facts**—details that make travelers more informed and their trips more fun

**kids**—best bets for kids and advice for the whole family

**special moments**—those experiences that memories are made of

**overrated**—places or experiences not worth your time or money

**insider tips**—great ways to save time and money

**great values**—where to get the best deals

The following abbreviations are used for credit cards:

| AE | American Express | DISC | Discover | V | Visa |
|----|------------------|------|----------|---|------|
| DC | Diners Club | MC | MasterCard | | |

## TRAVEL RESOURCES AT FROMMERS.COM

Frommer's travel resources don't end with this guide. Frommer's website, **www.frommers. com**, has travel information on more than 4,000 destinations. We update features regularly, giving you access to the most current trip-planning information and the Best airfare, lodging, and car-rental bargains. You can also listen to podcasts, connect with other Frommers. com members through our active-reader forums, share your travel photos, read blogs from guidebook editors and fellow travelers, and much more.

# THE BEST OF TEXAS

by David Baird, Eric Peterson & Neil Edward Schlecht

I n this chapter, we've put together lists of our favorite experiences, destinations, and services to help you plan your own Texas travels.

## THE best LUXURY & HISTORIC HOTELS

- **The Adolphus Hotel** (Dallas; ✆ 800/221-9083 or 214/742-8200): This landmark Beaux Arts hotel, built by beer baron Adolphus Busch, looks and feels like a European château. Revel in the luxury of darkwood parlors, baroque art and antiques, and an opulent dining room, one of Big D's best restaurants. Rooms are English country style, and a three-course English tea is served every afternoon. See p. 64.
- **Rosewood Mansion on Turtle Creek** (Dallas; ✆ 888/ROSEWOOD [767-3966] or 214/599-2100): Repeatedly named one of the top five hotels in the United States, the Mansion draws movie stars, princes, presidents, and luxury mavens. Formerly the grand estate of a cotton magnate in the 1920s and 1930s, the Mansion is refined and supremely elegant throughout, with service to match. The revamped restaurant has again vaulted to the top of the heap. See p. 66.
- **Stoneleigh Hotel & Spa** (Dallas; ✆ 800/921-8498 or 214/871-7111): A spectacular updating of a landmark 1923 Dallas fixture, this swank Uptown Art Deco hotel, with richly colored rooms, feels more like an intimate boutique hotel than a large, impersonal business hotel. The Bolla Bar and upstairs penthouse, occupying an entire floor, drip with style. See p. 68.
- **Omni Fort Worth Hotel** (Fort Worth; ✆ 888/444-OMNI [6664] or 817/535-6664): Fort Worth's newest and sleekest hotel has plenty of Texan touches to go with its grand public rooms, great spa, rooftop terrace pool and bar, and onsite Bob's Steak & Chop House. The views from upper floors are the best in town. See p. 110.
- **Stockyards Hotel** (Fort Worth; ✆ 800/423-8471 or 817/625-6427): Over-the-top luxury would be gauche in the old Stockyards, so this extremely comfortable and authentic slice of the Old West qualifies as a Fort Worth indulgence: cowboy luxury. Outlaws on the run, cowpokes and their madames, and the country-and-western elite have all propped up their boots here. Cowtown's cattle-ranching and railroad past are effortlessly evoked in the rooms, each of which is different. See p. 108.

- **Four Seasons Hotel Houston** (Houston; ✆ **800/819-5053** or 713/650-1300): With lots of space to stretch out in and lots of service so you don't have to stretch too far, this hotel surpasses all others in amenities and services. Within a few blocks are the baseball park, the basketball arena, a shopping mall, and the convention center. A bit beyond these are the city's theater and nightlife hubs. See p. 149.

- **Hotel Derek** (Houston; ✆ **866/292-4100** or 713/961-3000): Here is the most comfortable and fun place to stay in Houston's highly popular Uptown/Galleria area. The Derek offers a rare combination of practicality and style, making it a perfect choice for the business traveler or the vacation shopper. Service is smooth, and there's always something happening there. See p. 155.

- **Lancaster Hotel** (Houston; ✆ **800/231-0336** or 713/228-9500): Personal service, charming rooms, and a great location are the keys to this hotel's success. If there's one hotel that makes having a car unnecessary in Houston, this is it. Within easy walking distance are the symphony, the opera, three theaters, the ballet, and several restaurants and clubs. See p. 150.

- **Omni Corpus Christi Hotel** (Corpus Christi; ✆ **800/843-6664** or 361/887-1600): The two towers of the Omni overlook Corpus Christi Bay, and the floor-to-ceiling windows of the 20-story Bayfront Tower afford spectacular views of the Gulf, particularly from its upper floors. Pamper yourself with a massage from the in-house massage therapist or relax in the whirlpool. See p. 210.

- **Isla Grand Beach Resort** (South Padre Island; ✆ **800/292-7704** or 956/761-6511): From the high-ceilinged lobby to the beautiful landscaping around the swimming pools, this resort spells luxury. Many rooms have grand views of the ocean. See p. 228.

- **Omni La Mansión del Río** (San Antonio; ✆ **800/292-7300** or 210/518-1000): Occupying what was once the local seminary, this hotel has kept the local feel of the building, with architectural features such as beamed ceilings and stone balconies. La Mansión is not a high-rise, and it enjoys a wide frontage along the River Walk. It is, in short, the best hotel for experiencing San Antonio. See p. 243.

- **Mokara Hotel & Spa** (San Antonio; ✆ **866/605-1212** or 210/396-5800): If relaxation and pampering are what you seek, the Mokara should be your choice in San Antonio. From the moment you step foot into the lobby, everything is taken care of effortlessly. The hotel has a great location on the River Walk, but the rooms are so attractive and comfortable, the service so personal, and the spa so easy to enjoy that you may never leave. See p. 242.

- **The Driskill** (Austin; ✆ **800/252-9367** or 512/474-5911): If you want to play cattle baron, you can't do better than stay in this opulent 1886 hotel, restored to its former glory at the end of the 20th century. See p. 289.

- **Four Seasons Austin** (Austin; ✆ **800/332-3442** or 512/478-4500): With panoramic views of the lake, the wonderful service for which this chain is known, and a spa that consistently wins high praise, nothing is lacking here. Rooms are large and comfortable and come with all the amenities. Right outside the door is Austin's popular hike-and-bike trail, which rings the lake, and Austin's comfortable and fun downtown. See p. 289.

- **Lake Austin Spa Resort** (Austin; ✆ **800/847-5637** or 512/372-7300): This spa resort gets more write-ups than any other lodging in Austin, and has been selected best destination spa in the country by the readers of *Condé Nast Traveler*. Nothing spells luxury better than the pampering spa treatments for which this place is known. But you can also find it in the beauty and serenity that surround the place. See p. 297.

- **Cibolo Creek Ranch** (Shafter; ✆ **866/496-9460** or 432/229-3737): Tucked under the Chinati Mountains in some of the most wide-open country in all of Texas, this is a getaway for the most special of occasions, and accordingly priced. The idyllic setting plays host today to a first-class resort, featuring beautiful guest rooms with red-tile floors, adobe walls, and sumptuous border decor. The recreational opportunities are as impressive as the scenery. See p. 355.
- **Gage Hotel** (Marathon; ✆ **800/884-GAGE** [4243] or 432/386-4205): Located 50 miles north of Big Bend National Park, the historic Gage Hotel opened in 1927 as the social hub for area ranchers and miners, but fell into shambles under the desert sun in the ensuing decades. But that period is long over: The current owners restored the old redbrick's many charms in the early 1980s, melding history and an eye for Texas chic. The historic rooms have cow-skin rugs, hardwood floors, Navajo blankets, and oodles of personality. See p. 391.

# THE best BED & BREAKFASTS & BOUTIQUE HOTELS

- **Bailey's Uptown Inn** (Dallas; ✆ **214/720-2258**): A welcome oddity in Uptown Dallas, this well-managed, impeccable inn with just five rooms is the perfect antidote to large, impersonal hotels. From the downstairs living room, with a fireplace and piano, to color-coded rooms with private balconies, it's the kind of place that will appeal to those who fear frilly B&Bs. See p. 68.
- **Hôtel St. Germain** (Dallas; ✆ **214/871-2516**): Ever wanted to stay with your spouse at a plush bordello? This intimate boutique hotel with its elegant, prix-fixe restaurant is about as close as you'll come to that fantasy. A gorgeous mix of early-20th-century France and New Orleans, the seven suites are so swank, with such pampering features as wood-burning fireplaces, draped Napoléon sleigh beds, bidets, and soaking tubs, that you may not want to leave. See p. 128.
- **The Ashton Hotel** (Fort Worth; ✆ **866/327-4866** or 817/332-0100): Just off Sundance Square, this boutique hotel—Fort Worth's only small luxury hotel—offers plush rooms and smooth service, as well as one of the best restaurants in north Texas: Six 10 Grille. See p. 110.
- **La Colombe d'Or** (Houston; ✆ **713/524-7999**): Have a four-course French dinner served in your suite's separate dining room. With such personal service and with only five suites, there's no way you'll get lost in the shuffle. Occupying a mansion built for an oil tycoon in the 1920s, the hotel has uncommon architectural features, and is furnished with antiques. Its location in Houston's Montrose District puts it squarely in the middle of the hippest part of town. See p. 153.
- **George Blucher House Bed & Breakfast Inn** (Corpus Christi; ✆ **866/884-4884** or 361/884-4884): This wonderful B&B combines the ambience of an elegant historic home—it was built in 1904—with modern amenities. Breakfasts are served by candlelight, and you're just across the street from a prime bird-watching area. See p. 209.
- **Oge House—Inn on the Riverwalk** (San Antonio; ✆ **800/242-2770** or 210/223-2353): The King William area abounds with B&Bs, but the Oge House stands out as much for its professional service as for its gorgeous mansion and lovely rooms. See p. 246.

o **Bonner Garden** (San Antonio; ✆ 800/396-4222 or 210/733-4222): The former home of artist Mary Bonner is a fascinating structure of concrete and stone, beautifully proportioned and richly trimmed in carved wood. Fanciful murals make visitors smile, and the garden and rooftop sitting areas are sheer pleasure. See p. 247.

o **Mansion at Judges Hill** (Austin; ✆ 800/311-1619 or 512/495-1800): Guest rooms in the original mansion evoke a more relaxed and gracious era, especially those on the second floor with large and inviting porches, tempting one to linger and enjoy the view. The friendly and helpful service reinforces the feeling. See p. 296.

o **Kimber Modern** (Austin; ✆ 512/912-1046): Nothing looks sharper than modern design brilliantly set in natural surroundings. It makes the common terrace of this small hotel an uncommonly beautiful place to linger on a lazy afternoon. The rooms are equally inviting. See p. 295.

o **Hotel Saint Cecilia** (Austin; ✆ 512/852-2400): This new hotel captures the feel for what's fun about the Austin scene. It also takes comfort to an entirely new level: Sleep deeply on a handmade Swedish mattress; greet the morning with your favorite crepes; lounge on the private deck or patio of your room; or spin some vinyl on your in-room turntable. See p. 295.

# THE best HOTEL BARGAINS

o **Belmont Hotel** (Dallas; ✆ 866/870-8010 or 214/393-2000): Dallas usually goes gaga over mirrored glass and brand-spanking-new buildings, so it's a refreshing change to find this vintage 1940s motor lodge in Oak Cliff transformed into a stylish, retro boutique hotel. With its cool lounge bar and midcentury-modern decor, it's a dollop of Palm Springs with the attitude of Austin and views of the Dallas skyline—all for very affordable rates. See p. 65.

o **Hyatt Summerfield Suites Dallas/Lincoln Park** (Dallas; ✆ 866/974-9288 or 214/696-1555): This straightforward, residential-style hotel primarily targets businesspeople, but is also superb for other travelers and families. The spacious suites have fully equipped kitchens, and there is a pool and small spa, an exercise room, and a business center. See p. 70.

o **Stonehouse Hotel** (Fort Worth; ✆ 817/626-2589): If bargain to you means a dirt-cheap place to sleep, this "cowboy hotel"—once a boarding house for ropers—in the Stockyards District will appeal. I'm not saying this is luxurious, but weekdays, rooms (full of Western paraphernalia) are half-price, and one room with bunk beds goes for just $25 a head. See p. 110.

o **Lovett Inn** (Houston; ✆ 800/779-5224 or 713/522-5224): This B&B offers attractive, comfortable rooms with private balconies for a low price. Add a pool and a central location that is handy but quiet, and you have a winning combination. See p. 154.

o **Best Western Sunset Suites—Riverwalk** (San Antonio; ✆ 866/560-6000 or 210/223-4400): Enjoy low room rates, lots of free perks, and a convenient location near downtown—not to mention superattractive rooms in a historic structure. See p. 245.

o **Austin Motel** (Austin; ✆ 512/441-1157): Look for the classic neon sign in Austin's hip SoCo area. The rooms have been individually furnished, many in fun and funky styles, but the place retains its 1950s character and its lower-than-1990s prices. See p. 296.

- **Travelodge Hotel—La Hacienda Airport** (El Paso; ☎ 800/772-4231 or 915/772-4231): Some roadside motels surprise you with their attention to detail; this is definitely one of them. We like the eight Jacuzzi rooms, with picture windows separating the tubs from the bedrooms, and the spacious, amusingly decorated family suites. See p. 344.

# THE best RESTAURANTS

- **Fearing's** (Dallas; ☎ 214/922-4848): Cowboy boot–clad chef Dean Fearing made his name as an innovator of Southwestern cuisine at the Mansion on Turtle Creek. At long last, he opened his own place within the swanky new Ritz-Carlton uptown. Named *Esquire* magazine's New Restaurant of the Year in 2008, it may just eclipse the fancy-pants hotel that hosts it. See p. 78.
- **Neighborhood Services Bar & Grill** (Dallas; ☎ 214/368-1101): The name makes it plain: this is a neighborhood eatery, even if true neighborhoods don't really exist in Dallas. But the kitchen of this newcomer aims much higher, with comfort food so perfectly executed that the restaurant has won a place among flashier, and pricier, company. See p. 76.
- **Stephan Pyles Restaurant** (Dallas; ☎ 214/580-7000): Dallas's other celebrity chef in boots, the man who created the legendary Star Canyon, Stephan Pyles now rules over the Arts District. This refined restaurant turns out the expected, stellar steaks, but also ventures into more adventurous Southwestern and Latin American territory. See p. 72.
- **Brownstone** (Fort Worth; ☎ 817/332-1555): With a chef granted star status on TV's "Top Chef" in the kitchen, this newcomer has brought a sophisticated, farm-to-table approach to downtown Cowtown. The restaurant is sleek and comfortable, the Southern cooking delectable. See p. 116.
- **Lanny's Alta Cocina Mexicana** (Fort Worth; ☎ 817/850-9996): The great-grandson of the man behind Fort Worth's standard for Tex-Mex, Joe T. Garcia's, has struck out on his own with this sensational fine-dining take on Mediterranean cooking with Mexican sensibilities. Sophisticated but unfussy, it's *the* place to dine in downtown Fort Worth. See p. 118.
- **Mark's** (Houston; ☎ 713/523-3800): No fussy French nouvelle here, and no boring steak and potatoes either. Mark's serves up dishes that satisfy while they fulfill our eternal quest for something new and creative. This is New American cooking as it should be. See p. 162.
- **Reef** (Houston; ☎ 713/526-8282): Chef Brian Caswell has been racking up honors and awards from both the local and national press with his popular seafood restaurant. Set in a former Chrysler dealership, the dining experience is welcoming and relaxing. The food comes fresh out of the Gulf and is prepared in ways that highlight that freshness. See p. 160.
- **Cafe Annie** (Houston; ☎ 713/840-1111): No other restaurant in Houston garners the attention that this place does from foodies and food critics alike. With innovative Southwestern cooking, the best wine list in the city, and a master sommelier (the only "master" in Texas), the restaurant has its credentials. Chef/owner Robert Del Grande offers up wonderful dishes that show just how fertile the cross-breeding of Mexican and American cooking can be. See p. 168.
- **Sandbar** (San Antonio; ☎ 210/222-2426): Variety and freshness are on display here every day. Choose from a dozen different varieties of oysters. Eat your fish

raw, marinated, or cooked. Keep it simple or make it elaborate. Opt for a traditional method of preparation or go for something original. There are no poor choices. See p. 256.

o **Uchi** (Austin; ✆ 512/916-4808): Don't think of this restaurant as just a good place for sushi and Japanese cuisine. It's a great restaurant, period, with creative cooking that transcends its humble roots. The setting, in a beautifully revamped 1930s house, is transcendent, too. See p. 301.

o **Café Central** (El Paso; ✆ 915/545-2233): Well worth the splurge, Café Central is a sleek urban bistro serving sophisticated international cuisine. The menu changes daily, but always offers a wide range of standout fare—most notably creative Southwestern interpretations of traditional Continental dishes. The wine list is one of the city's best, and desserts include the best *leches* (Mexican milk cakes) in all of Texas. See p. 346.

# THE best TEXAN DINING

o **Sonny Bryan's Smokehouse** (Dallas; ✆ 214/357-7120): Sonny Bryan's has been turning out sweet barbecue since 1910, and the little smoke shack has acquired legendary status. Salesmen perch on their car hoods with their sleeves rolled up and wolf down hickory-smoked brisket, sliced-beef sandwiches, and succulent onion rings. Thinner sorts squeeze into tiny one-armed school desks and get ready to douse their brisket with superb, tangy sauce. A classic. See p. 79.

o **Bob's Steak & Chop House** (Dallas; ✆ 214/528-9446): Bob's will satisfy the steak connoisseur—the real Texan—in you. With a clubby but relaxed mahogany look and behemoth wet-aged prime beef and sirloin filets, this is a place for the J. R. crowd. Even the accompaniments—"smashed" potatoes and honey-glazed whole carrots—are terrific. And the meat-shy need not fear: The chophouse salad is a meal in itself. Cigar aficionados should keep their noses trained for Bob's cigar dinners: Every course is served with a different cigar. See p. 74.

o **Lonesome Dove Western Bistro** (Fort Worth; ✆ 817/740-8810): This friendly and eclectic restaurant challenges Cowtown to broaden its horizons. The Southwestern menu at this Stockyards eatery successfully stretches the popular theme in new ways, adding unique Texas touches that are both avant-garde and comforting. Pop in for the inexpensive Stockyards lunch special or dive into a blowout dinner. See p. 114.

o **Angelo's Barbecue** (Fort Worth; ✆ 817/332-0357): Fort Worth's classic Texas barbecue joint is as unpretentious as they come: Its wood paneling, mounted deer and buffalo heads, metal ceiling fans, and Formica tables might have come from a Jaycees lodge. That's kitschy cool to some, meaningless to everyone else. What is important is the fantastic hickory-smoked barbecue. See p. 119.

o **Fiesta Loma Linda** (Houston; ✆ 713/924-6074): When the bubble of a perfectly puffed tortilla smothered in chili con queso bursts, anticipation meets realization in the Tex-Mex experience. The aroma, the texture, the taste . . . words fail us. You can scour the borderlands a long time before coming up with an old-fashioned Tex-Mex joint like this one. The restaurant even has its own special tortilla maker for producing these puffed-up beauties. See p. 162.

o **Gaidos** (Galveston; ✆ 409/762-9625): Proud of its traditional cooking as practiced on the Texas Gulf Coast, Gaidos is the keeper of the flame for seafood devoid of fads and trends. The family has been serving up stuffed snapper, gumbo, and fried oysters for four generations. See p. 199.

○ **La Playa** (Corpus Christi; ✆ **361/980-3909**): For a Tex-Mex restaurant to be considered truly great, it must, of course, do a good job with the traditional enchiladas in chili gravy, have excellent fajitas, and pay attention to the details in cooking the rice and beans. It helps if it has a signature dish or two. In this case, it's deep-fried avocados. See p. 211.

○ **La Playa** (Port Aransas; ✆ **361/749-0022**): This place is in no way connected to La Playa of Corpus Christi. But the cooking is just as local, with Tex-Mex-style seafood dishes such as *campechana* cocktails and fish tacos. The margaritas transcend cultures. La Playa has that homey, welcoming feel that is as much Texas as anything else. See p. 218.

○ **Mi Tierra** (San Antonio; ✆ **210/225-1262**): Some people dismiss this cafe as touristy. Not so. It is the practitioner of old San Antonio cooking traditions. Order any of the Tex-Mex specialties and sit back and enjoy the ambience—both the food and the decor are expressions of local tastes when celebrating is called for. And travelers may celebrate once they've hit upon this gem. See p. 254.

○ **Shady Grove** (Austin; ✆ **512/474-9991**): This is the most quintessentially Austin restaurant in town. It offers a laid-back Texan menu, a huge outdoor patio, and an "unplugged" music series. See p. 303.

○ **L&J Café** (El Paso; ✆ **915/566-8418**): An El Paso landmark since 1927, the L&J is inexpensive and offers some of the best Tex-Mex food you'll find anywhere. The chicken enchiladas, overflowing with fluffy meat and buried under chunky green chile and jack cheese, approach perfection. It doesn't hurt that the salsa is spicy, the beer is cold, and the service is quick and friendly, even when the place is filled to capacity—as it is most of the time. See p. 347.

○ **Starlight Theatre** (Terlingua; ✆ **432/371-4300**): A 1930s movie palace abandoned when the mines in Terlingua went bust, the Starlight Theatre was reborn as an eatery and watering hole in 1991. The stage is still here, but the silver screen takes a back seat to the food (especially the trademark chili and filet mignon), drink (namely Texas beers and prickly pear margaritas), and desserts (including a very good *tres leches*). See p. 391.

# THE best LONE STAR EXPERIENCES

○ **Hopping Aboard the Grapevine Vintage Railroad:** The Old West comes alive aboard the Tarantula Railroad. A nostalgic train (when running, a restored 1896 steam locomotive called "Puffy" by locals) rumbles along the track from Stockyards Station in Fort Worth, tracing the route of the Chisholm Trail, to the Cotton Belt Depot in historic Grapevine, Texas, a town with 75 restored turn-of-the-20th-century buildings. See p. 123.

○ **Lassoing the Fort Worth Stock Show & Rodeo:** Fort Worth ain't called Cowtown for nothing. In late January and early February, the Southwestern Exposition and Livestock Show, as it's officially called, recalls the glory cowboy days with horse shows, auctions, and livestock from beef cattle to llamas and swine. The nightly rodeos are big draws. See p. 127.

○ **Attending a Mariachi Mass at Mission San José:** The Alamo may be more famous, but hearing a congregation of San Antonians raise their voices in spirited prayer reminds you that the city's Spanish missions aren't just, well, history. See p. 263.

o **Tubing on the River:** In central Texas, upstream from the town of Gruene, is a stretch of the Guadalupe River that Texans love to float down "leisurely like" in tubes (one tube per person and one for the ice chest). During the late spring and early summer, the air is hot, the water is cold, and the "tuber" (tube-potato?) finds life most agreeable. There is no shortage of outfitters who can set you up with a tube. See p. 329.

o **Explore the Borderlands:** There are nearly 800 miles of Texas-Mexico border, and the Rio Grande from the Gulf of Mexico to El Paso is a fascinating region. We are big fans of Ciudad Acuña, across the river from Del Rio, and the amazing canyons in Big Bend National Park, but the entire "borderlands" region is more attractive and diverse than most visitors realize. See chapters 10 and 11.

o **Exploring Big Bend National Park:** Vast and wild, this rugged terrain harbors thousands of species of plants and animals—some seen practically nowhere else on earth. A visit can include a hike into the sun-baked desert, a float down a majestic river through the canyons, or a trek among high mountains where bears and mountain lions rule. See "Big Bend National Park," in chapter 11.

# THE best MUSEUMS

o **Nasher Sculpture Center** (Dallas): This world-class collection of modern sculpture is in the downtown Dallas Arts District. Ray Nasher and his wife, Patsy, spent 4 decades assembling what has been called the finest private collection in the world (it includes superlative works by Miró, David Smith, Brancui, Moore, Giacometti, Picasso, Matisse, Calder, and many more). Designed by Renzo Piano, it has a gorgeous open-air sculpture garden with landscape design by Peter Walker. See p. 83.

o **Meadows Museum of Art** (Dallas): In a building with plenty of room to show off the greatest collection of Spanish masters outside Spain, the Meadows was built by a Dallas oilman fascinated with Spanish art. The museum proudly displays a wealth of works by Velázquez, Goya, Ribera, Murillo, Zurbarán—just about all the biggies from Spain's golden era as well as the 20th-century masters Picasso, Dalí, and Miró. See p. 87.

o **Kimbell Art Museum** (Fort Worth): Probably the country's finest small museum, this masterwork by Louis Kahn is a joyous celebration of architecture and a splendid collection of art to boot. Kahn's graceful building, a wonder of technology and natural light, is now a chapter in architectural studies worldwide. The small permanent collection ranges from prehistoric Asian and pre-Columbian pieces to European old masters, Impressionists, and modern geniuses. The Kimbell also gets some of the world's most important traveling shows. See p. 126.

o **Modern Art Museum of Fort Worth** (Fort Worth): In a modernist building designed by Japanese architect Tadao Ando, the Modern—actually the oldest art museum in Texas—is the nation's second largest dedicated to contemporary and modern art. The permanent collection includes works by Picasso, Rothko, Warhol, Rauschenberg, and Pollock. See p. 127.

o **Amon Carter Museum of Western Art** (Fort Worth): This museum has one of the finest collections of Western and American art in the country, including the most complete group of works by Frederic Remington and Charles M. Russell, two behemoths of Western art. It also possesses a great photography collection and important paintings by Georgia O'Keeffe and others. See p. 125.

- **Menil Collection** (Houston): One of the great private collections of the world, it could very well have ended up in Paris or New York, but was graciously bestowed by the collectors on their adopted city. To experience the Menil is pure delight; very little comes between the viewer and the art, which includes works by many of the 20th-century masters, classical works from the ancients, and tribal art from around the world. See p. 175.

- **Museum of Fine Arts, Houston** (Houston): With the addition of the Audrey Jones Beck Building, this museum has doubled its exhibition space and has put its collection of Impressionist and baroque art in the best possible light. The museum has several satellite facilities and attracts major touring exhibitions. See p. 174.

- **The Center for the Arts & Sciences** (Brazosport): The center is one of those rare entities that does a lot of things exceptionally well, including a terrific natural history museum, a delightful small planetarium, an attractive art gallery, two theaters for a variety of performing arts events, and a nature trail. See p. 201.

- **San Antonio Museum of Art** (San Antonio): Almost as impressive for its architecture as for its holdings, this museum combines several castlelike buildings of the 1904 Lone Star Brewery. The Nelson A. Rockefeller Center for Latin American Art is the most comprehensive collection of its kind in the United States. See p. 261.

- **Marion Koogler McNay Art Museum** (San Antonio): A beautiful collection beautifully located and beautifully displayed. This small museum is a delight to visit, especially for fans of modern art, who will devour its collection of works by the modern masters. See p. 262.

- **McDonald Observatory** (northwest of Fort Davis): McDonald Observatory is considered one of the world's best astronomical research facilities. Twice a day, visitors can glimpse sunspots, flares, and other solar activity. Nighttime "Star Parties" are held 3 evenings a week, during which visitors can view constellations and celestial objects through the observatory's high-powered telescopes. See p. 350.

- **Panhandle-Plains Historical Museum** (Canyon): The largest history museum in Texas, this excellent institution is anything but a dusty collection of spurs and bits. Well thought out, engaging, and informative, it is largely hands-on—you can sit in a Ford Mustang and listen to Buddy Holly tunes or try out a sidesaddle. There are also comprehensive exhibits on the region's history in terms of petroleum, art, transportation, Western heritage, and paleontology/geology. See p. 421.

# THE best SHOPPING

- **Neiman Marcus** (Dallas): Established in 1907, Neiman Marcus is intimately identified with Big D and its shopaholics. The luxury purveyor's annual holiday catalog, with his-and-her fantasies for the rich, has become an institution. The downtown store is classy and retro cool, the best place in north Texas to drape yourself in Prada and Chanel. See p. 93.

- **NorthPark Center** (Dallas): Dallas loves to shop, and while there are more malls than most people (except Dallasites) know what to do with, NorthPark is the most traditional and elegant (even with a recent expansion that doubled its size). The graceful layout outclasses its more garish competitors. Rotating pieces from Ray Nasher's spectacular collection of modern sculpture are on display throughout. See p. 94.

- **Stockyards National Historic District** (Fort Worth): In Cowtown, looking the part is important. Pick up Western duds—suits and shirts with elegant piping and embroidered yokes that would have made you a star in the Old West, plus cowboy boots and other Western paraphernalia—just steps away from the old Stockyards livestock pens. On the main drag is Maverick, which has upscale Western wear and a bar serving up Lone Star longnecks. M. L. Leddy's is a family-owned shop with a big boot sign out front and top-quality hats, hand-tooled belts, and custom-made boots. And just down the street, plunk down the cash for exquisite custom cowboy boots at Ponder Boot Company. See chapter 5.

o **Uptown** (Houston): In this relatively small district, you can find Houston's Galleria (with over 300 retailers, including Saks, Neiman Marcus, Tiffany's, and Versace) and four other malls fronting Post Oak (with such retailers as Cartier and FAO Schwarz). See "Shopping," in chapter 6.

o **Paris Hatters** (San Antonio): Pope John Paul II, Prince Charles, Jimmy Smits, and Dwight Yoakam have all had Western headgear made for them by Paris Hatters, in business since 1917 and still owned by the same family. About half of the sales are special order, but the shelves are stocked with high-quality ready-to-wear hats, too. See p. 270.

o **Heritage Boots** (Austin): The handmade boots of this little store on South Congress, will adjust to your feet the way mass-produced boots will never do. Spend just a bit of time in this store, and you'll come out with an entirely altered view of what a good boot should be. See p. 321.

o **Fredericksburg** (Texas Hill Country): It's hard to say how a town founded by German idealists ended up being a magnet for Texas materialists, but Fredericksburg's main street is chockablock with boutiques. This is the place to come for everything from natural chocolate mint–scented room deodorizer to handmade dulcimers. See p. 324.

o **Gallery Hopping in the Big Bend** (Marfa, Alpine, Marathon, Terlingua): Besides being remote, this is one of the most artsy corners of the state, with a wide range of artists and galleries throughout these small towns. See p. 357.

# THE best PLACES FOR BOOT-SCOOTIN'

o **Adair's Saloon** (Dallas): Deep Ellum's down-and-dirty honky-tonk is unfazed by the discos, rock clubs, and preppy SMU students in its midst. It sticks with its down-to-earth style, knee-slapping country and redneck rock bands, cheap beer, and tables and walls blanketed in graffiti. See p. 97.

o **Gilley's Dallas** (Dallas): The original Gilley's is where John Travolta rode a bucking bronco in *Urban Cowboy*, and now Big D has a branch of the famous Houston honky-tonk. If bigger is better, this one's right up there with the best of them: It's got 90,000 square feet of dance floor, bars, and stages, and even if it primarily draws tourists, it's still a good time. See p. 97.

o **Billy Bob's Texas** (Fort Worth): Kind of like a big-tent country theme park, Billy Bob's has it all: 40 bars, a huge dance floor for two-stepping, pro bull riding, and live performances by big names in country music. Of course, it also has dance lessons: Shuffle and two-step like a Texan after a few hours with instructor Wendell Nelson. See p. 134.

o **Pearl's Dancehall & Saloon** (Fort Worth): Perhaps a tad less down-and-dirty than when it was called Big Balls of Cowtown, Pearl's is still a winner. In the shadow of

Billy Bob's, it's an intimate spot for live Western swing and honky-tonk and dance lessons every Wednesday. See p. 134.

- **Blanco's** (Houston): This is a genuine honky-tonk where you go for music and dancing, and not for dressing up in Western duds. It's strictly come as you are, and this place attracts 'em from all walks of life, from bankers to oil field workers. The small venue gets some of the best of Texas's country music bands. See p. 185.

- **Floore's Country Store** (San Antonio): Not much has changed since the 1940s when this honky-tonk, boasting the largest dance floor in south Texas (half an acre), opened up. Boots, hats, and antique farm equipment hang from the ceiling of this typical Texas roadhouse. There's always live music on weekends; Willie Nelson, Dwight Yoakam, Robert Earl Keen, and Lyle Lovett have all played here. See p. 272.

- **Texas Hill Country** (San Antonio and Austin): The Texas Hill Country has some of the best honky-tonks in the state. In Gruene, just outside of New Braunfels, Gruene Hall is the oldest country-and-western dance hall in Texas and still one of the mellowest places to listen to music. Arkey Blue's Silver Dollar Bar is a genuine spit-and-sawdust cowboy honky-tonk on the Main Street of Bandera. When there's no live music, plug a quarter in the old jukebox and play a country ballad by owner Arkey. And look for the table where Hank Williams, Sr., carved his name. See the sections on Hill Country Side Trips in chapters 8 and 9.

- **Broken Spoke** (Austin): This is the gen-u-ine item, a Western honky-tonk with a wood-plank floor and a cowboy-hatted, two-steppin' crowd. Still, it's in Austin, so don't be surprised if the band wears Hawaiian shirts, or if tongues are planted firmly in cheeks for some songs. See p. 323.

# THE best OF NATURAL TEXAS

- **The Dallas Arboretum & Botanical Garden:** Who knew Dallas had more than dust, concrete, steel, and glass? This surprising oasis on the edge of White Rock Lake is a great spot to duck the Texas sun. Relax on 70 acres of groomed gardens and natural woodlands, interspersed with a handful of historic homes. The gardens are especially colorful in spring and fall. See p. 84.

- **Fort Worth Botanic Gardens:** A rambling, spacious showcase of 2,500 native and exotic species of plants on 100-plus acres, this is the oldest botanical garden in Texas, created back in the late 1920s. The Texas Rose Garden, with 3,500 roses that bloom in late April and October, and the beautiful Japanese Garden are terrific places to hide out from the world. Bring a picnic, a book, and a flying disk. See p. 125.

- **Big Thicket National Preserve:** It has been called "the American Ark" for its incredibly rich variety of plants and wildlife, all packed into 100,000 acres of watery bottomland in deepest east Texas. Explore the area on foot or in a canoe, and see how the woods grow so thickly here that they all but blot out the sun, and make trailblazing almost impossible. See "Side Trips to East Texas," in chapter 6.

- **Aransas National Wildlife Refuge:** A mecca for birders, with some 300 species sighted here, the refuge is also home to snakes, turtles, lizards, mammals, and a variety of frogs and other amphibians. Aransas has become famous for being the main winter home of the near-extinct whooping crane, the tallest bird in America—5 feet high with an 8-foot wingspan. See "Rockport," in chapter 7.

- **Mustang Island State Park:** This barrier island has more than 5 miles of wide, sandy beach, with fine sand, few rocks, and broken shells, and almost enough waves for surfing. The park is one of the most popular of Texas state parks, and is especially busy on summer weekends. See "Port Aransas," in chapter 7.
- **Lady Bird Johnson Wildflower Center:** Few people remember that Lady Bird Johnson started a program to beautify America's highways—and she began practicing it in her home state. This flower-powered research center is a natural outgrowth of this first lady's lifelong efforts to beautify the state. See p. 311.
- **McKittrick Canyon:** The canyon is forested with conifers and deciduous trees. In autumn, the maples, oaks, and other hardwoods burst into color, painting the world in bright colors set off by the rich variety of the evergreens. See "Guadalupe Mountains National Park," in chapter 11.
- **Palo Duro Canyon State Park:** This 60-mile canyon, sculpted by the Prairie Dog Town Fork of the Red River over the past 90 million years, is a grand contrast to the ubiquitous, treeless plains of the Texas Panhandle. Its 800-foot cliffs, striped with orange, red, and white rock and adorned by groves of juniper and cottonwood trees, present an astoundingly stark beauty. See "Canyon & Palo Duro Canyon State Park," in chapter 12.
- **The Canyons on the Rio Grande:** Santa Elena, Boquillas, and Mariscal canyons in Big Bend National Park and Colorado Canyon in Big Bend Ranch State Park have some of the state's best scenery, an unparalleled blend of rock, air, and sky. See "River Running" in chapter 11.

# THE best HISTORICAL ATTRACTIONS

- **The Sixth Floor Museum at Dealey Plaza** (Dallas): The events of November 22, 1963, shook the world. John F. Kennedy's assassination in Dallas is remembered by everyone old enough to remember, and argued over still. Visitors can tour the sixth floor of the Texas School Book Depository, from where the Warren Commission concluded that a single sniper, Lee Harvey Oswald, felled the president. The museum also examines the life, times, and legacy of the Kennedy presidency, making it a place to revisit not only the tragic episode but also an era. See p. 81.
- **The Stockyards National Historic District** (Fort Worth): Still looking the part, this area north of downtown was once the biggest and busiest cattle, horse, mule, hog, and sheep marketing center in the Southwest. Put on your boots and best Western shirt and tour the Livestock Exchange Building; Cowtown Coliseum (the world's first indoor rodeo arena); former hog and sheep pens now filled with Western shops and restaurants; and Billy Bob's Texas, the "world's largest honky-tonk." Then grab a longneck beer at the White Elephant saloon—the oldest bar in Fort Worth and the site of the city's most famous gunfight in 1897—and check in at the historic Stockyards Hotel. Finally, check out the "longhorn cattle drive" that rumbles down Exchange Avenue daily—or take the Vintage Train into Grapevine. See chapter 5.
- **San Jacinto Monument** (Houston): Here on the battlefield of San Jacinto, a small army of Texans led by General Sam Houston charged the much larger, better equipped Mexican army and dealt them a crushing blow. The victory gave Texas its independence. A monument and museum occupy the battlefield to honor and explain the history of the battle and its significance. See p. 170.

- **USS *Lexington* Museum on the Bay** (Corpus Christi): Exploring this huge World War II–era aircraft carrier offers non-naval persons the opportunity to get an idea of what it was like to live for sometimes months in the claustrophobic conditions of such a limited area. In addition to sleeping, dining, and cooking areas, the ship provided a hospital, a rec room, and, of course, numerous necessary working areas. See p. 206.

- **The Alamo** (San Antonio): It's smaller than you might expect, and it sits smack in the heart of downtown San Antonio; but the graceful mission church that's come to symbolize the state is a must-see, if only to learn what the fuss is all about. See p. 259.

- **San Antonio Missions National Historical Park:** It's impossible not to remember the Alamo when you're in San Antonio; more difficult to recall is that the Alamo was originally just the first of five missions established by the Franciscans along the San Antonio River. Exploring the other four missions that make up this national park, built uncharacteristically close to each other, will give you a glimpse of the city's early Spanish and Indian history. See p. 263.

- **State Capitol** (Austin): The country's largest state capitol, second only in size to the U.S. Capitol—but 7 feet taller—underwent a massive renovation and expansion in the 1990s, which left it more impressive than ever. See p. 309.

- **New Braunfels:** Trying to decide which of the Hill Country towns is the most representative of the area's rich German heritage is tough, but the *gemütlich* inns, history-oriented museums, and sausage-rich restaurants—not to mention the major celebration of Oktoberfest—make New Braunfels a standout. See "Hill Country Side Trips from Austin," in chapter 9.

- **El Paso Mission Trail:** Established in the 17th and 18th centuries, these three historic Spanish missions provide a link to El Paso's colonial past. They are among the oldest continually active missions in the country and warrant a visit for their architectural and historic merit. Especially impressive is the large Presidio Chapel San Elceario, near the site of "The First Thanksgiving," said to have taken place in 1598, 23 years before the Plymouth Thanksgiving. See p. 337.

# THE best FAMILY ADVENTURES

- **Dallas Heritage Village** (Dallas): Modern Dallas gleams with skyscrapers and a love for newness, but its Western heritage lives on in this museum-like facsimile of the Old West, a 13-acre park of historic buildings. Mounted like a late-19th-century village, it has a redbrick Main Street, Victorian homes, a train depot, general store, one-room church, schoolhouse, and bank. The "Living Farmstead" re-creates a 19th-century prairie with actors in period garb. See p. 85.

- **The Stockyards** (Fort Worth): Far from a dry old historic district, the Stockyards come alive with the flavor of the Old West. Kids will adore the twice-daily "cattle drive" of the Fort Worth Herd, which rumbles down the cobbled main drag, led by cowhands in 19th-century duds. They'll also love to find their way around the Cowtown Cattlepen Maze, a human maze made to look like old cattlepens. See "Exploring Fort Worth," in chapter 5.

- **Fort Worth's Children's Museums** (Fort Worth): The Fort Worth Museum of Science and History is large and multifaceted, with a domed IMAX theater, a planetarium, and great hands-on science displays. The National Cowgirl Museum and Hall of Fame teaches little cowgirls and cowboys about pioneering women of the American West, but in a way that really brings the culture to life: Jukeboxes pump out country tunes, and kids can ride a simulated bucking bronco, see the film of their adventure on the museum's website, and get their pictures superimposed on Old West film posters. The Fort Worth Zoo is one of the best in the country. See "Exploring Fort Worth," in chapter 5.

- **Arlington:** Sandwiched between Dallas and Fort Worth is a kids' suburban dream world: Stumble from the roller coasters at Six Flags Over Texas to the water slides at Hurricane Harbor, visit Ripley's Believe It or Not and the Palace of Wax, and catch a game at the Rangers Ballpark, one of the best-designed baseball stadiums in the country. See "Arlington," in chapter 4.

- **Space Center Houston** (Houston): Always the most popular attraction in the city, NASA's Space Center Houston is a joint effort powered by NASA technology and Disney know-how. It is the epitome of interactive display and simulation that manages to fascinate both kids and parents. During your visit, check out what's going on at the Johnson Space Center through a tram ride and video feeds. See p. 172.

- **The Gulf Side of South Padre Island:** Fine white sand and warm water lapping at your toes—what more do you want? Although the shore is lined with hotels and condos, the beaches are public and open to everyone. See "Padre Island National Seashore," in chapter 7.

- **Six Flags Fiesta Texas** (San Antonio): Major thrill rides, a huge swimming pool shaped like Texas, and entertainment/food areas with Texas history themes— there's something for every family member at this theme park, and it's even slightly educational. See p. 264.

- **The Austin Bats:** Most adults and kids tend to finds bats a bit creepy—until they learn more about them, that is. From March to November, you can watch thousands of bats emerge in smoky clouds from under the Congress Avenue Bridge, and find out why Austinites adore the little critters. See "Going Batty" on p. 310.

- **Balmorhea State Park:** This is one of the crown jewels of the Texas state parks and also one of the smallest, at 45 acres. The main attraction is the massive 1¾-acre swimming pool—3.5 million gallons of water at a fairly constant 74°F (23°C). Not your usual swimming pool, it's teeming with small fish and laden with rocks. Swimming, snorkeling, and scuba diving are all popular. At a reconstructed *cienega* (desert wetland) you may spot native wildlife such as a Texas spiny soft-shell turtle, a blotched water snake, or a green heron. See "Small Towns of Central West Texas," in chapter 10.

# THE best OF TEXAS ONLINE

- **The Handbook of Texas Online** (www.tshaonline.org/handbook/search): The Handbook is an encyclopedia with concise entries that explain who's who, what's what, and where's where in Texas. It's easy to use and has information on just about everything, from the locations of towns and counties to explanations of some of the state's legends, to biographical data on the many characters who left their mark on Texas history.

- **Texas Department of Transportation** (www.traveltex.com): The state's official tourism website is practically the only one you'll need—everything else will be a link. We especially like the section that offers easily printable discount coupons, primarily for lodgings and attractions.

o **Texas Outside** (www.texasoutside.com): This is a great resource for planning outdoor activities for just about anywhere in the state. It breaks Texas down into different regions and has separate pages for Texas's largest cities. You'll find maps and information on all sorts of outdoor sports, such as hiking, hunting, fishing, biking, and canoeing.

o **Dallas–Fort Worth Area Official Visitors' Website** (www.dfwandbeyond.com): For purely practical matters, this bureaucratic-sounding address gives you the lowdown on area events and even allows you to download coupons good for saving a few bucks at museums, theme parks, and other local attractions.

o **Guidelive.com:** The entertainment Web page of the *Dallas Morning News,* north Texas's major newspaper, contains the most current events listings, as well as restaurant, movie, music, and show reviews for both Dallas and Fort Worth. It even has a shopping blog that promises the inside guide to the best local finds and deals.

o **MySanAntonio.com:** The website of the city's only mainstream newspaper, the *San Antonio Express-News,* not only provides the daily news, but also links to local businesses such as dry cleaners and florists and to movie, nightlife, and dining listings and reviews.

o **Austin 360** (www.austin360.com): Movie times, traffic reports, restaurant picks, homes, jobs, cars . . . this site, sponsored in part by the *Austin-American Statesman,* the city's main newspaper, is a one-stop clicking center for a variety of essentials. It's easy to navigate, too.

o **Texas Cooking Online** (www.texascooking.com): We all know the Internet's best for purely personal and marginal interests, so once you're done with your trip planning, check out this website out for authentic Texas cooking, including recipes and discussions of mysteries such as the Texas fruitcake subculture conspiracy.

# TEXAS IN DEPTH

by Neil Edward Schlecht

Texas looms large in American culture, and Texans are a unique bunch, unapologetic in their swaggering embrace of the place they call home. "It's flat and dry," you say. "Yup, parts are," they reply. "It's hot," you say. "Hotter 'n hell," they confirm. "Texans talk funny," you say. "Y'all do too," they retort. Self-confident and independent almost to a fault, Texas seems to embody all that's good, bad, and especially big about the United States. The former independent Republic of Texas—which shook off the landlord claims of Spain, Mexico, France, and even the U.S.—has die-hards who still wish Texas would suck it up and secede.

---

Texans don't seem to mind too much if outsiders get caught up in the myths and clichés about Texas (that way, they get to keep the truth to themselves). A 10-gallon hat doesn't hold 10 gallons of anything, nor is Texas flat, dry, and featureless, filled with cowboys on the range, oilmen watching their backyard gushers spit up black gold, and helmet-haired beauty queens. But it's hard to compete with the state's image, the canvas for 100 Western flicks. The big-sky frontier of Texas and the West is the quintessential American landscape, and the mythic cowboy leading his longhorn cattle on long drives is a heroic figure. The outlaws who thumbed their noses at authority (behind the barrel of a gun) and the boomtown gamblers who struck it rich are also part of the romantic tale of Texas.

Once a separate nation, and today bigger than England and France combined, Texas is a place that dreams big and walks tall, where the sky and ranches—and, Texans hope, the possibilities—are massive. The history of Texas is laced with events and heroes large and legendary, many of which have catapulted into state and national lore. In many ways, Texas has come to symbolize the nation's westward expansion, its complicated struggle for independence, and the dearly held mystique of a land of opportunity and wide-open spaces. Texas's complex settlement pattern—the territory was claimed by Spain, France, and Mexico before becoming an independent republic and then the 28th state in the Union in 1845—supports its mythic status. "Six flags" really did famously fly over the state from the 16th to the 19th century, during which time there were eight changes of government. Even though the state has increasingly become one of immigrants from other states and other nations south of the border, Texans continue to exhibit a fiercely independent streak. The pages that follow explore the state's history and provide a primer on its unique culture.

# TEXAS TODAY

The legendary cowboy still exists, but Texas is now decidedly more urban than rural and home to three of the nation's 10 largest cities: Houston, Dallas, and San Antonio. Texas today is as much a leader of high-tech industries as it is an agricultural and ranching state. There are world-class art museums and collections in Houston, Fort Worth, and Dallas, where local philanthropists have used their money and influence to import the world's most celebrated architects to build some of the nation's most talked-about museums. Although Texas is, by and large, a conservative place, Austin has long supported thriving hippie and renegade musician communities, and Dallas is nipping at its heels with a thriving music scene. The state is a melting pot with pockets of Czech, German, and Irish communities; bilingual populations in the lower Rio Grande Valley and border towns; and more than four million people of Hispanic descent.

This enormous state also has immense geographical diversity: desert plains in the Texas Panhandle, the Piney Woods in east Texas, beaches in the Gulf Coast, north Texas prairies, scenic wildflowers and lakes in central Texas Hill Country, desert canyons in Big Bend National Park, and the rugged Guadalupe Mountains.

Still, some of the clichés are true. Texas, the second-largest state in the United States in both landmass and population, is larger than any country in Europe. You can set out from Amarillo in your car and drive south for 15 hours and still not reach Mexico. And everything is bigger in Texas, of course: the ranches, the steaks, and the bigger and badder cars—Cadillacs with longhorns on the grille and monster pickup trucks with gun racks—really do exist. In Texas, you can carry a concealed handgun—even in church—and the state is known as the capital punishment capital of the world. "Don't Mess with Texas" is more than an effective anti-litter campaign.

Despite the bluster, Texans are startlingly friendly and hospitable folks. Deals are still completed with handshakes, and adults say "yes, ma'am" and "nossir" to each other. Also, Texans love their sports, especially football. This is a place where entire towns pack the bleachers for Friday-night high-school games and preachers mention the game in their sermons, praying for victory in a kind of gridiron holy war.

Former Texas governor and owner of the Texas Rangers baseball team—and now former president—George W. Bush maintains a sprawling ranch in Crawford, Texas (outside of Waco), to which he regularly retreated during his presidency. Today, he calls Dallas home.

As the Bush presidency perhaps unwittingly illustrated, it's hard for most people—whether in other parts of the U.S. or abroad—to be indifferent about Texas. It's a place to romanticize and ridicule, to dream about and dismiss. Texans can leave the state, but sooner or later they'll admit their weaknesses for Texas dance halls and Old West saloons, Tex-Mex and barbecue, cowboy boots, and country music. From the big sky and flat plains and the Hill Country highways lined by Texas bluebonnets to the larger-than-life personalities like LBJ, Anne Richards, Lance Armstrong, and Willie Nelson, Texas stays with you.

# LOOKING BACK: TEXAS HISTORY

Texas's roots stretch back to some 30,000 different Native American tribes—including the Caddos, Coahuiltecans, Tonkawans, Apaches, and Comanches—who occupied the land long before European settlers arrived in the 16th century. Indeed, the name "Texas" can be traced to Native American tribes: *Tejas* is thought to be the Spanish pronunciation of the Caddo word for "friend." Some of that Native American legacy can still be seen, in the form of pictographs and petroglyphs, at **Lubbock Lake Landmark,** an archaeological and natural history preserve. The **Panhandle Plains Historical Museum** in Canyon, the largest history museum in the state, has an excellent section on paleontology and geology.

Six Flags Over Texas is more than the name of an amusement park. The flags of six different nations have flown over Texas: Spain, France, Mexico, the Republic of Texas, the Confederate States of America, and the United States of America. Texas is not only immense, but it's a state with a complicated and colorful history.

**EUROPEAN CONQUEST**   Spain was the first European country to claim the territory, and France also ruled over a short-lived colony in Texas. In 1519, the Spanish explorer Alonso Álvarez de Piñeda made a map of the Texas coast, establishing the basis for the first claim to the land. Just like other Spaniards elsewhere in the Americas, Alvar Núñez Cabeza de Vaca was in search of cities of gold when he landed in Galveston in 1528.

In 1598, the explorer Juan de Oñate formally claimed Texas for Spain, but the first permanent settlement and official mission, Corpus Christi de la Isleta (near El Paso), didn't come for another 84 years. Spain eventually held Texas for 300 years. The 1749 adobe **Spanish Governor's Palace** (the seat of government when San Antonio served as the capital of the Spanish province of Texas), the **El Paso Missions Trail** (including the **Presidio Chapel of San Elceario**, where the "first Thanksgiving" is said to have taken place in 1598), the four Franciscan missions of **San Antonio Missions National Historic Park**, and the **Meadows Museum of Art** in Dallas (with a fine collection of Spanish old masters) are good places to relive the state's Spanish heritage.

In 1690, Spaniards quickly responded to a French territorial claim and settlements in Texas and Louisiana by establishing their own mission, San Francisco de los Tejas, in east Texas. Just 3 decades later, the Mission of San Antonio de Valero—known to all as the **Alamo**—led to the founding of the city of San Antonio (which became the seat of Spanish government in Texas in 1772). The brief French period of rule is evoked at Austin**'s French Legation Museum,** built in 1841 for France's representative to the Republic of Texas.

**MEXICO'S TURN**   After winning independence from Spain in 1821, Mexico turned its sights north and granted authorization to Stephen F. Austin to settle in southeast Texas with a colony of 300 families (the "Texas Original 300"). The new colony, made up mostly of people from Tennessee, marked the official beginning of a fast-growing Anglo-American colonization. Austin would become known as the "Father of Texas."

American settlers were forced to accept both Mexican citizenship and Roman Catholicism to remain in Texas. Mexico did little to protect its colony or define the state's rights, however. As more Americans settled there, Texas took on the shape of a U.S. outpost, despite the Mexican flag flying over it. Stephen Austin organized a militia (which would become the famous Texas Rangers) to protect the colony. As tensions grew, Mexico denied the entry of additional American settlers in 1830, and further religious, political, and cultural clashes prompted the self-proclaimed president of Mexico, Gen. Antônio López de Santa Anna, to bolster his troops in Texas. Texans requested the status of an independent Mexican state. When their diplomatic initiative failed, Texans declared independence from Mexico on March 2, 1836.

Texas forces attacked San Antonio. Gen. Santa Anna and his troops vastly outnumbered and then ruthlessly crushed the valiant Texans, led by Davy Crockett and Jim Bowie, at the Alamo in a 2-week battle in March 1836. Mexican troops slaughtered more than 300 Texas prisoners at Goliad only days later, unwittingly giving rise to the battle cry of independence: "Remember the Alamo! Remember Goliad!" (Today, of course, the second defeat has been largely wiped from memory.) The Texans, led by Gen. Sam Houston's army, rebounded with a stunning and decisive victory over Gen. Santa Anna at the Battle of San Jacinto, winning their independence from Mexico on April 21, 1836.

Besides seeing the famous **Alamo,** visitors interested in reliving the period of Mexican rule over Texas can check out the **San Jacinto Monument,** where Houston's small band of Texans defeated the Mexican army, and the **San Fernando Cathedral,** the oldest cathedral sanctuary in the U.S., from which Gen. Santa Anna raised the flag of "no quarter." Mexican (-American) culture lives on at the mariachi Masses at the **Mission San José** in San Antonio.

**THE REPUBLIC OF TEXAS, STATEHOOD & CIVIL WAR** The Lone Star flag flew over the Republic of Texas from 1836 to 1845. The new nation was officially recognized by the United States and Europe, but not Mexico. Six different sites served as the Texas capital, until the town of Austin became the permanent capital in 1839 (visitors can tour the country's largest **state capitol,** built in 1888). The republic's government was based on the U.S. model, with a president, senate, house of representatives, and an army, navy, and militia. Yet the new republic faced daunting problems, including boundary disputes, debt, and continual concerns about Mexican attack. Texas joined the United States as the 28th state in 1845, ceding some western lands (parts of modern-day Oklahoma, New Mexico, and Colorado) to the Union. The state's annexation precipitated the Mexican-American War in 1846, which concluded with Mexico's surrender to the United States 2 years later. The Treaty of Guadalupe Hidalgo rejected Mexican claims on Texas and the Southwest.

That wasn't the end of tensions and division, however. As a slave state, Texas joined the southern Confederate States of America and seceded from the United States in January 1861. About 90,000 Texans saw military service, and the war devastated the Texas economy. At the end of the Civil War, Texas rejoined the Union in 1870.

**THE WILD WEST & TEXAS OIL** Texas formed part of the Wild West, and most settlers lived a frontier life. A war-ravaged economy and abundant longhorn cattle in southern Texas led to the great Texas trail drives to northern markets in the 1860s. The drives north from Texas to Kansas City, such as the famous Chisholm Trail, brought prosperity to ranchers and particularly the city of Fort Worth, which became known as "Cowtown" as the site of cattle auctions and shipping companies. Commerce grew exponentially as railroads reached Texas at the end of the 19th century. In 1873, the Houston and Texas Central Railway reached the Red River, where it connected with the Missouri, Kansas and Texas Railroad to establish the first rail route from Texas to St. Louis (and the East). The boomtown environment attracted opportunistic entrepreneurs and the Wild West drew outlaws, among them Wild Bill Hickok, John Wesley Hardin, and Billy the Kid (and later, Texas-born Bonnie Parker and Clyde Barrow, who hid out at the Stockyards Hotel in Fort Worth and were later gunned down by Texas Rangers).

But progress was apparent across the state. By 1883, the University of Texas had begun classes in Austin, and in 1888, the current **state capitol** was dedicated. At the turn of the 20th century, the Texas oil and gas boom exploded with the discovery of

# GLOSS'RY: HOW TO talk LIKE A TEXAN

It may be true that Texans talk differently, but it's tough to pin down a true Texas accent—a reality evident in virtually any Hollywood movie about the place. Most Texans don't speak with the Southern drawl of the deep South. It's more of a Western twang. And because Texas is such a big place, influenced by the language of adventurers heading west and newly arrived immigrants (Yankees from the north, Mexicans from south of the border), Texans have adopted a rich vocabulary and colorful manner of speaking.

It's not just how they say it, but what they say that makes Texans stand out. Their folksy language and homespun hyperbole seem to come effortlessly. Longtime CBS news anchor Dan Rather, a native of Wharton, Texas, was both ridiculed and celebrated for his colorful language; on one election night, he described a candidate who "tore through Dixie like a big wheel through a cotton field." Evocative phrases, such as "that dawg don't hunt," also spilled effortlessly from the sharp tongue of the late former Texas governor Ann Richards, who famously chided George Bush, Sr., for having been born "with a silver foot in his mouth." Another tried-and-true method of talkin' Texan is to sprinkle in Spanish words and Anglicize the Spanish names of towns and streets. Even non-Hispanic Texans liberally toss around phrases like "Hola," "Qué pasa?" and "Adiós, amigo" in their everyday patter. Keep an ear out for things like "Guada-loop" (for Guadalupe) and "Man-shack" (for Manchaca).

Here are some common Texas terms you might hear during your stay:

- **All the fixin's**  Accompaniments—beans, mashed potatoes, gravy, and the like—to go with chicken-fried steak. The plate should groan under their weight.
- **Awl**  Texas's largest industry. As in, awl 'n' gas.
- **Big ol'**  Large; esteemed.

- **Buffalo chip**  What cowboys kick around out in the fields—cow dung.
- **Coke**  Generic term for soft drink. Dr. Pepper, Pepsi, RC Cola—they're all just "Coke" to Texans.
- **Dadgummit** and **dadburnit**  Common expletives.
- **Fixin' to**  A general state of preparedness or intent to carry out an act ("I'm fixin' to eat that chicken-fried steak of yours").
- **Gimme cap**  Freebie baseball caps, with logos of awl 'n' gas and other companies on the bill; redneck uniform to be worn as an alternative to cowboy hat. The name is derived from the frequent request, "Gimme one them thar caps."
- **Give a holler**  A plea to call, write, or e-mail.
- **Good ol' boy**  A true Texan.
- **Gussied up**  The look necessary for going out; dolled up 'n' pretty.
- **Hook 'em**  The cry and hand signal (index finger and pinkie raised like horns) of University of Texas graduates everywhere—as in, "Hook 'em, horns."
- **Howdy, y'all**  The one-size-fits-all greeting—singular, plural, who cares? Y'all is a contraction of "you all," but is actually just Texan for "you." Howdy is pronounced "high-dee."
- **I reckon**  The act of thinking out loud.
- **Kicker**  Cowboy who puts his pointy-toed boots to good use.
- **Over yonder**  Where you'll likely be when you give a holler.
- **Yankee**  A Northerner; outsider; opponent of Texas statehood.
- **Yes, ma'am**  The polite way to respond to any woman over 20.
- **Yessir** and **nossir**  The polite way to respond to a Texan man.

the Spindletop oil field near Beaumont, transforming the agricultural economy and bringing riches to many other Texans. The discovery of "black gold" produced new Texas boomtowns, drawing an influx of workers—known as wildcatters and mavericks—looking for rapid wealth. Additional oil fields were discovered in East and West Texas, as well as beneath the Gulf of Mexico.

You can explore more of the Lone Star state's Western heritage in Fort Worth at the **Stockyards National Historic District** (including daily longhorn cattle drives, the Stockyards Museum, and vintage railroad to Grapevine), **Texas Cowboy Hall of Fame, National Cowgirl Museum and Hall of Fame,** and **Log Cabin Village.** In Dallas, visit **Old City Park** for a living museum of a late-19th-century village. Some of the finest Western art in the U.S. is found at the **Amon Carter Museum of Western Art** in Fort Worth.

**THE 20TH CENTURY TO TODAY**   Though Texas suffered through the Great Depression along with the rest of the country, the state quickly became the largest producer of oil in the country. The good times were enhanced at **Gruene Hall** in the Hill Country near Austin, the oldest country-and-western dance hall in Texas; and **Floore's Country Store** in San Antonio, a 1940s roadhouse with a half-acre dance floor. Visitors today can relive the early–20th century and enjoy outstanding live music at both establishments.

The 1960s were an especially event-filled and tumultuous time in Texas. In 1962, **NASA** opened the Manned Spacecraft Center in Houston (later renamed Lyndon B. Johnson Space Center). But the next real watershed event in Texas was a tragic one. On November 22, 1963, President John F. Kennedy was assassinated as his motorcade passed through downtown Dallas. The presumed assassin, Lee Harvey Oswald, was gunned down on national television by local businessman Jack Ruby. See the grassy knoll and visit the excellent **Sixth Floor Museum at Dealey Plaza,** housed in the infamous Texas School Book Depository, for exhibits that not only detail the assassination, but bring to life the times and legacy of the Kennedy presidency.

Kennedy's vice president, Texas's own Lyndon B. Johnson, was sworn in as the 36th president aboard the presidential plane at Dallas's Love Field airport. LBJ's wife, Lady Bird Johnson, would later create her own lasting legacy with a dedication to beautifying Texas with wildflowers on the sides of highways and throughout the Hill Country; visitors today can ramble the gardens at the **Lady Bird Johnson Wildflower Center** in Austin. In 1966, a gunman, Charles Whitman, terrorized the University of Texas in Austin, killing 17 people with a rifle from the observation deck of the campus tower. By the end of the decade, President Kennedy's mission to go to the moon was accomplished; the Apollo 11 astronaut Neil Armstrong uttered his memorable first words after landing on the moon: "Houston, the Eagle has landed." Visit the **Space Center Houston** for an interactive display of NASA technology.

In 1988, the transplanted Houstonian (also a U.S. congressman with a background in the Texas oil business) **George H.W. Bush** was elected president of the United States. Bush's son, George W. Bush, was elected the 43rd president of the United States in 2000 after a controversial decision by the U.S. Supreme Court, and he served two terms in office.

Throughout the late–20th century, the urban areas of Texas continued their explosive growth. Houston, San Antonio, and Dallas rank among the 10 largest cities in the United States. Texas's Hispanic growth also continues, with more than one-third of Texas residents now of Hispanic origin. The major cities and fast-growing, formerly suburban communities successfully attracted firms that relocated their headquarters

## The Lore of Texas Types

- **The Wildcatter:** An independent oil-man, a gambler at heart whose fortunes rise and fall with the oil and gas industry.
- **The Roughneck:** A laborer who operates the oil rigs. Often itinerant or immigrant—down-and-dirty and flush with cash. A Texas sailor.
- **The Maverick:** It originally denoted an unbranded calf, but came to be understood as a Texas archetype: the nonconformist, independent-thinking man (or woman!).

from around the country. Texas is now a leader in the technology industry. The capital, Austin, has been transformed from a government and university town to one of the nation's most important clusters of high-tech corporations and computer-chip makers (including the local Dell, a computer company founded by a University of Texas student in his dorm room). Other high-tech and cutting-edge Texas companies include Texas Instruments, EDS, and Whole Foods. Austin (home to the South by Southwest Music + Film conference and one of the country's most vibrant music scenes), Dallas, Fort Worth, and Houston are today among the highest-ranked and most popular cities in the country for young people looking for jobs and a better quality of life.

Sadly, Texas also has become associated with controversy and scandal. In 1993, the Branch Davidians, a sect led by David Koresh, sequestered themselves inside the Mount Carmel Center outside Waco; after a 50-day standoff, the storming of the compound by the US ATF (as well as FBI and Texas National Guard) resulted in the deaths of Koresh and 73 other men, women, and children (both followers and agents). In 1998, an African-American man, James Byrd, was dragged to his death by a truck in Jasper, Texas; three white young men were indicted in the racist murder, which prompted the passing of a hate crimes law in Texas. In 2001, the Houston-based Enron Corporation became a national symbol of corporate greed and corruption when it was discovered to have perpetrated a complex accounting fraud that enriched executives while bankrupting employees and investors. In 2008, an arsonist, possibly a member of a local anarchist group, launched a gasoline bomb and heavily damaged the Governor's Mansion in Austin.

But despite its setbacks, the Lone Star state still triumphs: In 2011, despite record snowfall and ice storms, Dallas hosted Super Bowl XLV at the Cowboys' new $1.3 *billion* stadium in Arlington, Texas. That may seem like an incredible amount for a sports stadium, but in Texas, of course, it's hardly scandalous.

# TEXAS IN POP CULTURE

**MUSIC** The role that Texas musicians have played in creating a particularly American idiom of popular music, from country to blues, jazz, and rock, is impossible to overestimate. Neither country and western nor the blues originated in Texas, but both genres of roots music have been indelibly shaped by talented Texans. The state ranks alongside Tennessee or Louisiana for contributions to the Americana music scene, and the number of individual music greats spawned in Texas is astonishing.

They've come from such big cities as Houston, Austin, and Dallas, of course, but most remarkable is how many have rolled out of Lubbock. The barren lands of West Texas have proved incredibly fertile for the creation of homespun music. Texas has spawned so many musicians that a museum honoring their contributions to pop culture is in the works, most likely to be housed in Houston.

Most listeners think of country music when they think of Texas sounds, and the state was certainly instrumental in the form's early development, a product of cowboy songs and folk contributions from new immigrants. **Bob Wills and the Texas Playboys,** who emerged from Lubbock in the 1920s, introduced Western swing (or Texas swing), a combustible mix of hillbilly tunes, fiddle music, jazz, polka, cowboy ballads, and Mexican ranchero music. Texas artists such as **George Jones** in the 1950s popularized honky-tonk, characterized by steel guitars, fiddles, and plaintive vocals. Jones, one of country's finest voices, became a balladeer and top-10 hit maker. Like **Kenny Rogers** of Conroe, Texas, he was more closely identified with Nashville than with Texas.

With characteristic independence, Texas musicians developed their own kind of country. Progressive and outlaw country fused hard-core honky-tonk, folk, rock, and blues. With country music reaching a national audience in the 1970s with the blandly orchestrated Nashville sound, a gang of Texas outlaws, led by **Willie Nelson, Waylon Jennings, Jerry Jeff Walker** (not a native Texan, but closely identified with the scene), and **Kris Kristofferson** seized the stage with a gritty, maverick rejection of the slicker country being produced in Nashville. Waylon and Willie's "Luckenbach, Texas," a song about a town with two dozen people, became a state anthem. Nelson, the braided, bandanna-wearing iconoclast of Texas country, has evolved into one of Texas's most beloved contemporary figures. He began his career as a songwriter of hits for Patsy Cline ("Crazy") and others before positioning himself as a cult artist and finally a crossover country star, daring to dabble in all genres, from traditional country and ballads ("Blue Eyes Cryin' in the Rain") to potent country poetry and even reggae. Nelson is currently into alternative fuels (marketing a biodiesel fuel called "BioWillie," which is available in eight states, including 16 locations in Texas) as much as he is into exploring new musical genres.

Other Texas singer-songwriters, such as **Guy Clark** and **Townes Van Zandt,** less prone to the outlaw lifestyle but still resolutely independent, mined a territory of lyrical country-folk music. These unjustly overlooked artists laid the foundation for the current generation of Texas songwriters, including **Lyle Lovett, Jimmie Dale Gilmore,** and **Steve Earle,** musicians at home in country as well as in rock, gospel, and the blues. Western swing has undergone a couple of rounds of revival, in the 1970s and again in the early 1990s. **Asleep at the Wheel,** a multipiece band that has gone through innumerable changes in lineup, has been present for both revivals. Current stars among Texas singer-songwriters with a touch of twang include **Nanci Griffith, Michelle Shocked,** and **Kelly Willis.** Expanding the horizons of Texas music are Dallas-area rockabilly bar-burners **Reverend Horton Heat;** Texas polka aficionados **Brave Combo,** originally from Denton; and Austin's rootsy **the Gourds.**

Texas blues began with such legendary figures as **Blind Lemmon Jefferson** (whose "Black Snake Moan" struck quite a chord in the 1920s) and **Blind Willie Johnson,** both of whom played the area around Deep Ellum in Dallas. **Robert Johnson** may have been from Mississippi, but he made his only known recordings in Dallas and San Antonio in the 1930s. **Sam "Lightning" Hawkins,** of Houston, created a blistering blues guitar style that influenced generations of rockers. Other notable Houston blues musicians include **B. B. King, Albert Collins,** and **Clarence "Gatemouth" Brown.**

Port Arthur's **Janis Joplin**'s raw vocals and blues-inflected rock (not to mention her heroin overdose and posthumous hit, "Me and Bobby McGee") made her an icon of the 1960s. **Stevie Ray Vaughan,** an incendiary guitar wizard from south Dallas, also became a blues-rock star before his light went out prematurely in a helicopter crash in 1990. Austin club regulars **Angela Strehli, Lou Ann Barton,** and **Toni Price** continue the Texas blues tradition.

Texas has produced its share of rock-'n'-roll pioneers, too. Lubbock's **Buddy Holly,** the bespectacled proto-rocker who with his band, the Crickets, influenced Elvis, the Beatles, and countless new-wavers with tunes like "Peggy Sue" and "That'll Be the Day," went down in a 1959 plane crash after just a couple of years at the top. **Roy Orbison,** from Vernon, Texas, began his career in rockabilly, but his high, haunting voice propelled a number of memorable mainstream hits in the 1960s, like "Only the Lonely" and "In Dreams." **ZZ Top,** from Houston, started out in swaggering blues-rock territory, singing about "Tush" and "LaGrange" before their belly-length beards and songs like "Legs" and "Tube Steak Boogie" made them MTV darlings. Current Texas faves on the alternative scene include the intellectual pop of **Spoon** (from Austin); the dusty, Neil Young–like **Centro-Matic** (Denton); the trippy, postrock instrumentalists **Explosions in the Sky** (Midland), whose music is the soundtrack to the football-oriented TV show *Friday Night Lights* and the epic film *Australia;* and the costumed, unwieldy collective **the Polyphonic Spree** (Dallas).

With its Latino roots and large Hispanic population, Texas has given rise to yet another genre that reflects cross-cultural fertilization: Tex-Mex border sounds. Conjunto, *norteña,* and Tejano are all slightly different takes on this definitive Tex-Mex style, anchored by the accordion and 12-string Mexican guitar. The megastar **Selena** (Corpus Christi) brought Tejano to national Latino audiences before her death (she was murdered by the founder of her fan club), and reached a wider audience through films and books about her life. **Flaco Jiménez** is the leading conjunto proponent today. Another cross-cultural musical phenomenon in Texas is zydeco, a Creole stew that combines Afro-Caribbean, blues, and Cajun rhythms, and is especially popular in the Houston and Galveston areas (as well as Louisiana). **Los Lonely Boys,** three Mexican-American brothers from San Angelo, had a huge hit in 2004 with "Heaven" and their radio-friendly brand of Latino-tinged blues pop, which some have labeled "Texican."

In large part, Texas has proved such fecund musical ground because of its strong tradition of live performance. For a couple of decades now, Austin has immodestly declared itself the "Live Music Capital of the World," and its rollicking clubs have presented nightly diverse lineups of homegrown and imported live music acts. From Armadillo World Headquarters to Club Foot and Liberty Lunch, Austin has embraced a disproportionate share of legendary, beloved, and now-defunct live music venues. **Gilley's** and **Billy Bob's,** two huge, slick honky-tonks still going strong in Houston and Fort Worth, are important national showcases for traditional country and redneck rock bands, while classic small-town Texas dance halls such as **Gruene Hall** (in Gruene, pronounced "green," located south of Austin, smack in the middle of New Braunfels) keep the flame burning. Dancing to country music is a true Texas art, and while the popularity of individual dances—the Two-Step, Cotton-Eyed Joe, and line dancing (a kind of kickers' aerobics)—rises and falls with the latest hits, in Texas they have amazing staying power. The dance floors of local honky-tonks pack in young Billy Ray Cyrus look-alikes and single rodeo queens in tight jeans as well as nimble older folks boot-scootin' like there's no tomorrow.

For rock and alternative music lovers, two of the biggest music festivals in the country are held annually in Austin: South by Southwest (SXSW), in March, and the outdoors Austin City Limits Festival (cruelly held in Sept, at the tail end of the brutal central Texas summer).

**FILM**  Texas—with its larger-than-life characters and mythic representation of the Southwest—has been featured very prominently in films, both popular blockbusters and serious art films. Foremost among them, of course, were Westerns starring John Wayne, many of which were placed in Texas, including *The Alamo, Red River,* and *Three Texas Steers.* John Ford's 1956 *The Searchers*—also starring Wayne—is generally considered one of the greatest Westerns ever filmed. *Giant* (also from 1956) is expansive like Texas itself, set on a massive ranch location under a huge sky with Rock Hudson as a ranch baron who wins over Elizabeth Taylor. In 1969's *Easy Rider,* Peter Fonda and Dennis Hopper take a motorcycle road trip through Texas and meet up with Jack Nicholson.

More recent, mainstream movies include *Terms of Endearment,* an Oscar winner based on Larry McMurtry's book, set in Houston and starring Jack Nicholson (as a former astronaut), Debra Winger, and Shirley McLaine; *The Best Little Whorehouse in Texas,* with Dolly Parton as a madam running the Chicken Ranch (which sold neither chickens nor eggs) in a small Texas town; *Urban Cowboy,* more or less *Saturday Night Fever* relocated from NYC to Houston's honky-tonks, complete with John Travolta in a 10-gallon hat; and the football-themed *Friday Night Lights,* based on the book by H. G. Bissinger.

The art film category is well represented by *No Country for Old Men,* the Oscar-winning Coen Brothers film based on the violent Cormac McCarthy novel of the same name; *The Last Picture Show,* Peter Bogdanovich's film (based on another McMurtry novel) about high-school seniors in Anarene, a nowheresville Texas town; *Tender Mercies,* Bruce Bereford's 1983 movie starring Robert Duvall as a drifter and former country singer who finds redemption in the hands of a widow on the Texas plains; *Paris, Texas,* about another Texas drifter (played by Harry Dean Stanton), though this time made by a German, Wim Wenders; and *Days of Heaven,* by the Texan Terrence Malick, about a steel worker who flees to the wheat fields of Texas and finds conflict and tragedy when confronted by a wealthy landowner. If that's all too bleak and grown-up, how about *The Texas Chainsaw Massacre,* or Richard Linklater's homages to Austin, *Slacker* and *Dazed and Confused?*

Movies are increasingly being filmed in Texas. Austin has emerged as the "Third Coast" alternative to Los Angeles and New York City as a filmmaker's haven. Texas filmmakers include legendary director Terrence Malick (*The Thin Red Line, Days of Heaven, Badlands, The New World*) and young moviemakers creating an Austin school of sorts: Richard Linklater (*Before Sunrise, Waking Life, School of Rock, Fast Food Nation*) and Robert Rodriguez (*El Mariachi, Spy Kids*). Several well-known actors make their homes in Austin, too, including Matthew McConaughey and Sandra Bullock.

**TELEVISION**  Surely the most famous television series set in Texas was the long-running nighttime soap *Dallas,* which gave rise to the national mantra "Who shot J.R.?" and made people across the globe believe that Texans had oil rigs in their backyards. *Lonesome Dove,* based on the novel by Texan Larry McMurtry, was a hugely successful miniseries in 1989, featuring Robert Duvall and Tommy Lee Jones and filmed at several Texas ranches. *Walker, Texas Ranger* starred Chuck Norris in a Western police drama, with plenty of martial arts and a partner who was a former Dallas Cowboy. More recently, the critically acclaimed series adapted from the book and film of the same name, *Friday Night Lights,* beautifully explored a small West Texas town where the weekly ritual, the high school football game, is an obsession (the show was shot in Austin). *King of the Hill,* an animated series from Mike Judge, an Austinite by way of Garland, was set in the fictional small Texas town of Arlen. PBS's *Austin City Limits* is a legendary, long-running, live-music program featuring diverse artists from all over the country and globe.

**BOOKS** Fans of James Michener will appreciate his historical novel *Texas.* Although wordy and a bit tedious, Michener was an excellent storyteller as well as historian, and his book (exhaustively) brings the state and its people to life. (It's a big state, but couldn't he have done it in fewer than 1,344 pages?)

Two authors who share a "Mc" in their surnames dominate the subject of contemporary fiction set in Texas: Larry McMurtry and Cormac McCarthy. These two writers are much more than an introduction to both the real and mythical Texas. The contributions of McMurtry to the Texas canon are many. *Lonesome Dove* (1985) won the Pulitzer Prize for its depiction of ex–Texas Rangers on a cattle drive. Other significant works by McMurtry about or set in Texas, many delving into the lives of cowboys and ranchers, include *Leaving Cheyenne; Terms of Endearment; The Last Picture Show; Horseman, Pass By; In a Narrow Grave: Essays on Texas;* and *All My Friends Are Going to Be Strangers.* Cormac McCarthy, who is not a Texan, is also a Pulitzer Prize winner; his works of the past 25 years have been some of the best received in American literature. The Western and Southern Gothic themes, and depiction of brutal violence, hone in on weighty matters of life and death, and McCarthy is frequently compared to William Faulkner. His masterworks are *Blood Meridian* (concerning the 19th-c. travels of "the kid," largely in Texas, and often cited as one of the greatest American novels of the 20th c.) and *All the Pretty Horses* (about a young cowboy and his friend from West Texas who venture to Mexico). McCarthy's *No Country for Old Men* is also set in southwestern Texas, along the Mexico border.

Annie Proulx's *That Old Ace in the Hole* is set in the Panhandle. Texas author Sandra Cisneros's short stories, such as *Women Hollering Cree,* are powerful and critically acclaimed. *The Gates of the Alamo,* by Stephen Harrigan, is a gripping, fictionalized version of Texas's most famous battle. Among fiction and nonfiction with somewhat more mass appeal is *Friday Night Lights,* for many readers one of the finest sports books written, chronicling the football obsession of a small West Texas town; and *Semi-Tough,* a novel by Dan Jenkins about two Fort Worth football studs, one of the funniest books written. Jenkins's *Baja Oklahoma* offers a funny, poignant, and somewhat raunchy look at what we might call classic modern Texans, at least the Fort Worth trailer-trash variety.

Even readers who don't cook will enjoy *The Only Texas Cookbook,* by Linda West Eckhardt. Interspersed among its 300 recipes—including classics such as Fuzzy's Fantastic South Texas Road Meat Chili and Bad Hombre Eggs—are numerous humorous anecdotes on food-related subjects. Those who savor biting political humor—and don't mind seeing every Texas Republican mercilessly skewered—will thoroughly enjoy any book of essays by the late newspaper columnist Molly Ivins, who is credited with bestowing the nickname "Dubya" on George W. Bush.

**FAMOUS TEXANS** You may already know that outsize personalities such as outlaws Bonnie Parker and Clyde Barrow, rock stars Buddy Holly and Janis Joplin, and former president Lyndon B. Johnson hail from Texas. But there are plenty of other famous folks with Texan roots, some of whom might surprise you.

**Lance Armstrong** (Plano). Heroic cycling champion—record-holding all-time champion of the Tour de France—and inspirational survivor of testicular cancer. Wore a Texas Lone Star on his helmet and one of those ubiquitous "LIVESTRONG" yellow bracelets on his wrist. He lives in Austin.

**Gene Autry** (Tioga). A singin' cowboy and A-list film star who made it big with "The Yellow Rose of Texas" in the 1930s.

**George W. Bush** (Midland). He wasn't born on the prairies of Texas (rather, in blue-state Connecticut), but the former governor clings hard to his Texas heritage, with a ranch in Crawford, outside Waco. He grew up in the midst of the oil business, tried his hand at that, failed, and then owned the Texas Rangers baseball team before becoming governor of Texas and then president of the United States. His core of closest advisors, including Karl Rove and Karen Hughes, were also Texans.

**Joan Crawford** (San Antonio). Hollywood's "Mommie Dearest," from deep in the heart of Texas.

**Michael Dell** (Austin). This Houston-born whiz kid and billionaire (one of the richest men in America) started Dell Computer Corporation, which today is one of the largest tech companies in the world, in his dorm room at UT in Austin. Though he dropped out of UT, Dell later gave the university $50 million.

**Farrah Fawcett** (Corpus Christi). 1970s bathing suit pinup, Charlie's hottest angel—the woman who created the wings hairstyle—and UT grad.

**Phyllis George** (Denton). Former Miss America, former morning show host, and former wife of a Kentucky governor.

**Howard Hughes** (Houston). Eccentric billionaire industrialist as famous for his reclusive and weirdo tendencies as his moneymaking prowess, which included planes, movies, and tools.

**Steve Martin** (Waco). Wild-and-crazy comedian turned occasionally serious author (*Shopgirl*) and art collector.

**Meat Loaf** (Houston). Monster of a man with a big voice who recorded "Bat Out of Hell." He later translated his music video experience into an acting career (in *The Rocky Picture Horror Show* and B-grade action films) before slimming down and cutting his stringy locks.

**Bill Moyers** (Marshall). From student of religion to LBJ press secretary to soft-spoken but contentious PBS journalist who investigated such weighty matters as philosophy, ironmen, and dying.

**Madalyn Murray O'Hair** (Austin). Strident atheist who roared tirelessly for the separation of church and state.

**Roy Orbison** (Wink). The man with the growl in his classic '60s song "Pretty Woman." Dark specs, amazing angelic voice, and even more amazing hair.

**Dan Rather** (Wharton). Serious newsman who made anchorman, with a penchant for odd signature sign-offs, down-home aphorisms, and bizarre episodes in his personal life.

**Ginger Rogers** (Fort Worth). Fred's favorite dance partner hailed from Cowtown; I bet she did a mean two-step.

**Jaclyn Smith** (Houston). Another Charlie's angel, and Kmart spokesperson.

**Liz Smith** (Fort Worth). Gossip queen and columnist.

**Sissy Spacek** (Quitman). Sometimes brilliant actress who went from *Badlands* to a *Coal Miner's Daughter* to *Missing*.

**Lee Trevino** (Dallas). Pro golfer—and serious rival of Nicklaus and Palmer—whose folksy language and links style made Tex-Mex cool in the mid-'70s.

**Van Cliburn** (Kilgore). Accomplished pianist (winner of Tchaikovsky competition in 1958) and namesake of international piano competition held annually in Fort Worth's Bass Performance Hall.

**TEXAN STYLE** Some Yankees and coastal snob types might be inclined to think that "Texan style" is an oxymoron. And it's true, Texans are probably better known as world-class shoppers than arbiters of taste. But style? Texans have plenty of their own. Beyond oil, championship sports teams, and roots music, Texas's greatest export is the classic Western cowboy style that it embodies. Everybody from Ralph Lauren to Madonna seems to have adopted cowboy duds as the very symbol of American cool and rugged independence. Outsiders may not pull it off with as much natural ease as Texans, but the basics of cowboy style aren't hard to master.

There's the fundamental **ranch-hand style,** which depends on clothes tough enough to withstand the demands of life on the range: long, snug-fitting, boot-cut jeans (preferably Wrangler or Lee) that bunch up at the bottom, worn with a belt featuring a big ol' buckle, scuffed-up calfskin cowboy boots, a crisp Western shirt, and a cowboy hat (straw in summer, felt in winter). Taking the basic elements, you can gussy up the look as much as you wish. The **drugstore cowboy** or **rodeo queen** look adopts fun and fancy embellishments such as embroidered yokes and sterling silver collar tips. **Urban cowboys** in oil and banking simply throw more money at the basics, and don boots and hats with their pinstripes for business (and ranch-style gabardine twill pants in place of jeans on the weekends). The boots aren't made of regular old calfskin leather, but of such exotic skin as alligator, ostrich, or eel, preferably handmade and with elaborate uppers. The hat will be a top-of-the-line number from a classic Western outfitter such as M. L. Leddy's in Fort Worth. The belt buckle (along with the tip and keeper) is sterling silver.

For a certain kind of woman in Texas—the kind that will wear a Western shirt only if it is expensively studded with rhinestones and rubies—the classic look has long been the one created by upscale Dallas and Houston shopping mavens: big salon-coifed and frosted hair, a wide pearly smile, and an overly precious designer outfit, accented by a cornucopia of fur and jewelry. The Robert Altman film *Dr. T & the Women* got the Dallas upper-class look of professional shoppers down to a T.

**Cowboy boots** date from the riding boots worn by the Spanish conquistadors and *vaqueros* (cowboys). They're the most fundamental element of the cowboy look, and almost everyone in Texas owns at least one pair. Real cowboys have everyday boots and dress-up or dance-floor boots. The basics are plain old black or brown calfskin boots, with either a roper (low heel) or a riding or semiwalking (high heel) style. The toes can be pointed, squared off, or gently rounded. The sharp pointed toe is the most authentic, though today many younger ropers go with the rounded style. The tops, which are generally calf high, can be either V-shaped or straight, but should always have stitched-on pull straps. Boot stores stock a bewildering array of leathers: Besides basic (but smooth, rugged, and inexpensive) calfskin, you'll find showy and more delicate (and often vastly more expensive) exotic skins, such as lizard, eel, alligator, ostrich, snake, stingray, water buffalo, and kangaroo. Generally, the most expensive boots are horned-toe crocodile; a pair of those babies will set you back a couple of grand. Boot design can be no nonsense or elaborately styled, with contrasting uppers, fancy stitching, and piping.

Even more important than look, though, is fit: A boot has to fit properly. It should be snug, requiring you to pull on with both straps and yank off with a touch of difficulty, but not tight. Your heel should snap into place but allow for a little movement. A good boot seller can help you determine the right fit. Don't buy unless you're sure. Look for Texas brands such as Lucchese, Nocona, Justin, and Tony Lama.

**Cowboy hats** are serious business. They're worn at all times and not taken off indoors; if you don't think so, check out a Western dance hall on a Friday night, where you'll find cowboys twirling about the dance floor with their best hats firmly in place. The classic Stetson, like the one LBJ wore on the ranch, dates from the 1850s. A cowboy's proper "beaver" dress hat can run $1,000 or more. The key to your new hat is getting it formed, or creased, for that perfect range or courthouse look. A real-life roper retires his white straw hat at the end of summer, opting for a sturdy felt sombrero for autumn and winter—a seasonal fashion dictum not unlike the one that demands New Englanders banish white from their wardrobes after Labor Day.

Most traditional and urban cowboys go for heavy, pressed-cotton **Western shirts** in plaids or solids. Fancy Western swing shirts with pearl snaps, contrasting yokes, and little "smile" or "arrow" pockets aren't that easy to find these days. If you want a singing cowboy or fancy honky-tonk shirt, you'll need to either go vintage or shell out big bucks for a high-end designer, such as Manuel of Hollywood (who dresses Dolly Parton and other flashy country-music stars). At its most basic, though, the Western shirt should have a reinforced Western yoke, flap pockets, a full cut, and snapped cuffs. The shirttail is always worn tucked in.

The most important **Western accessories** are belt buckles, belts, hatbands, bolo ties, and bandannas. For Texan males, hand-tooled belts (often with the wearer's name embossed), hatbands, and especially buckles—which range from obscenely large Texas state seals, oil derricks, and Jack Daniel's emblems to simple, elegant silver buckles, tips, and keepers—allow him to express himself. A real Texan never buys a leather belt that comes with a buckle. Bolo ties, though still worn in some parts, are a little passé for the average Joe trying to adopt the cowboy look.

# EATING & DRINKING

Texans are famous for their love of artery-clogging steaks the size of Volkswagens. Amarillo's Big Texan Steak Ranch restaurant features a 72-ouncer (eat it in under an hour and get it free). Locals are rabidly fond of **chicken-fried steak.** This oddity is a thick slab of inexpensive beef beaten until tender and dipped in batter, deep-fried like chicken, buried under a puddle of cream gravy, doused with pepper, and served with a glob of mashed potatoes (skins on). Home-style veggies such as okra and black-eyed peas are also worthy accompaniments. A good chicken-fried steak—crisp, light, and tender—is weirdly enjoyable, but an inferior one can be like gnawing on an old tire. Note to Yankees who don't want to get laughed out of town: Don't specify "medium" or "medium rare" when ordering a chicken-fried steak. It comes only one way: cooked.

But steak—whether broiled or chicken fried—is only part of the story. The real holy trinity of Texas eats consists of three down-home staples that no true Texan can do without for long: chili, barbecue, and Tex-Mex.

**CHILI** A bowl of Texas red (beef chili without beans), hot or hotter than hell, is often thought of as Mexican or Tex-Mex. But it's as Texan as they come, with its origins in San Antonio in the late 1800s. Chili (not *chile,* which is Spanish for pepper) should be thick, meaty, and spicy, and served unadorned. Real Texas chili is made with beef (or occasionally rabbit or venison), but not beans. This standard has been relaxed, though, and plenty of Texans like pinto beans (never kidney beans) in their chili. There are annual chili cook-offs across the state; the most famous is held in the border town of Terlingua. Degrees of fire are usually designated as one-, two-, or three-alarm or indicated by an X, XX, or XXX. Four Xs means that the bowl of devil's soup is guaranteed to scorch your tongue, lips, and entire digestive tract.

Weird food item: **Frito pie,** which is meaty chili, cheese, and diced onions poured over a plate of (or into a bag of) Frito's corn chips. Frito pie is a staple in Texas school cafeterias (or at least it was when I was growing up).

**BARBECUE (BBQ)** Vying with chili and chicken-fried steak for the honor of state dish is barbecue (though Texans didn't invent it; the word comes from the Spanish, *barbacoa,* and the style originated in Spain and evolved in the Caribbean and Latin America). Still, the art of roasting meats over an open fire distinguishes Texans from, say, lesser humans. Texans slow-cook (smoke) beef brisket and ribs (and, to a lesser extent, pork, chicken, turkey, sausage, and *cabrito,* young goat) in pits over mesquite or hickory wood. The slow roasting and wood give it the unique, revered flavor. Texas barbecue, unlike its worthy regional competitors in such places as Memphis and the Carolinas, is almost wholly focused on beef, and it tends to be tangier and spicier than the sweeter pork popular in those places. A plate of brisket or ribs is served with heaps of tangy barbecue sauce (which is often also employed as a basting sauce), and side dishes such as potato salad, pinto beans, and coleslaw. A proper Texas barbecue will be either a down-and-dirty, ramshackle joint such as Sonny Bryan's in Dallas and Angelo's in Fort Worth, or a rustic place in the country with long picnic tables and a huge barbecue pit in full view, such as the Salt Lick in Driftwood, outside of Austin.

**TEX-MEX** Neither identifiably Mexican nor strictly Texan, Tex-Mex is, as the name indicates, a hybrid menu of simple dishes. A Texan gets homesick for authentic Tex-Mex cooking just as fast as she does for barbecue or chili. No Texan has ever had good Tex-Mex except in Texas; both barbecue and chili seem a bit easier to reproduce over state lines. Not spicy or intricate like authentic Mexican food, Tex-Mex is greasy, filling, tasty, and cheap, a step above addictive junk food. There is little distinction between dishes and ingredients. Almost all involve corn or flour tortillas, lots of white and yellow cheese, chili, hot sauce, and rice and refried beans—meaning that a good plate of Tex-Mex will lack for color. It will be essentially a uniformly muddy, yellow-brown hue. Tex-Mex dishes can be spiced up with Tabasco sauce or scorcher jalapeño peppers, which young Texans learn to gobble up like pickles.

All Tex-Mex meals begin with tortilla chips and salsa (hot sauce) and guacamole for dipping. Enchiladas, chiles rellenos, *tacos al carbón,* and burritos have long been the standard-bearers for Tex-Mex, but in the past couple of decades, **fajitas**—grilled beef or skirt steak rolled in flour tortillas and dolled up with guacamole, pico de gallo, and cilantro—have become the most popular dish. Less than authentic, but wildly popular, is the substitution of strips of barbecued chicken breast for beef.

**BEVERAGES** Texans wash down chili and barbecue with plastic glasses of **ice tea** (it's the rare Texan who says *iced* tea) the size of small oil drums, and **Texas beer,** preferably longnecks of Lone Star, Pearl, and Shiner Bock, drunk straight from the bottle. Beverage choices shift slightly in Tex-Mex restaurants. While pitchers of ice tea are fine, the beer should be ice-cold *cerveza,* Mexican beer such as Corona,

Tecate, Dos Equis, or Bohemia, usually served with a wedge of lime squeezed into the bottle or can. And the number-one libation for washing down a plate of Tex-Mex is the **margarita,** a tart concoction of tequila, lime juice, and triple sec, either served on the rocks or frozen. Most margaritas use cheap well tequila, but connoisseurs opt for "top-shelf" margaritas (served on the rocks), made with 100% blue agave tequilas. And the connoisseurs of connoisseurs drink aged tequilas—called *reposado* or *añejo*—straight, followed by a "tequila chaser," like the one served at Javier's restaurant in Dallas: a shot glass of orange juice, lemon juice, V8, pepper, salt, and Tabasco.

Texas also has a surprisingly robust roster of **wineries,** many in the central Texas Hill Country around Fredericksburg and the High Plains near Lubbock. Llano Estacado and Pheasant Ridge are national award winners.

# WHEN TO GO

High season is summer, when the kids are out of school, and winter the low season, though beaches along the Gulf Coast are busiest in winter—even if seldom really crowded. The Texas heat (see below) makes summer a less desirable time to travel, if it can be avoided (though, of course, Texans are famous for their omnipresent air-conditioning). Unless you're looking for some rowdy spring-break action, you should avoid all resort areas, including the beaches and national parks, during March and early April, when students from colleges across the country descend upon the Gulf Coast. Outside of that, midspring and midautumn are generally the best times to visit, with moderate temperatures and fewer crowds (especially at big sights such as the Alamo).

One real draw in spring is the Texas wildflowers (including the famous bluebonnets) that bloom along roadsides in Hill Country during late March and early April. The South by Southwest Music + Film Conference (SXSW) takes over Austin for more than a week in March, so if you're an indie rock fan, that's the week to go; if not, that's one to avoid. The Texas State Fair takes place in late September/early October.

## Weather

The weather in Texas is especially mercurial and subject to extremes, following the oft-heard dictum: "If you don't like the weather, wait 5 minutes and it'll change." Although the unprecedented snowfall and ice storm in Dallas that marred Super Bowl XLV in 2011 was odd even for this state, you should expect unusual weather. For the most part, though, Texas weather is mild most of the year, with 200 days of sunshine and an average temperature of 73°F (23°C). Of course, in a state as big as Texas, with such a variety of physiography, climate varies by location, sometimes dramatically, making it difficult to generalize. It can be snowing in one area such as the northern Panhandle, while at the same time folks are swimming at South Padre Island.

With its immense size, Texas ranks first in the U.S. for the number of tornadoes, with an average of about 130 a year. Like the rest of the Gulf Coast states, Texas experiences its share of hurricanes (and lesser tropical storms) on the coast during the summer and autumn.

**Spring** is mild for most of the state. Frequent, intense thunderstorms, which experts say can "move in squall lines," hit throughout Texas in late spring. The north, central, and east areas of Texas experience the greatest rainfall in May. **Summer** is very hot across the state, making air-conditioning a necessity everywhere. High temperatures average in the 90s (30s Celsius) across most of the state in July and August.

The heat is most excruciating in the upper Rio Grande (including Big Bend National Park), where high temperatures climb well above 100°F (38°C). South Texas also sees triple-digit highs from late May to late September. Summer is extremely arid in the west, but very humid in the east and south of Texas. Areas within 100 miles of the Gulf Coast have significant rainfall during the late summer.

**Autumn** is mostly moderate in temperature, although the remnants of the Texas summer heat can extend well into early fall. Though most parts of the state are considerably drier than spring, early autumn is extremely wet along the Gulf Coast, which experiences tropical weather disturbances. **Winter** can be much colder than most visitors expect, especially in north Texas. Few areas in the state escape freezing temperatures. Snowfall occurs at least once every winter in the northern half of Texas (though accumulations of more than a couple of inches are rare, except in the High Plains), and freezing rain and ice are common. The Dallas–Fort Worth area usually gets a dusting of snow once or twice a winter (with average snowfall just over 2 inches annually), but in February 2011, it suffered the worst storm in 15 years. The area received an unprecedented amount of snow—as much as 11 to 14 inches combined with ice and bitterly cold temperatures—that threatened Super Bowl traffic and dampened commerce.

## Average Monthly High/Low Temperatures & Precipitation

| | JAN | FEB | MAR | APR | MAY | JUNE | JULY | AUG | SEPT | OCT | NOV | DEC |
|---|---|---|---|---|---|---|---|---|---|---|---|---|
| **Dallas** | | | | | | | | | | | | |
| Temp. (°F) | 54/34 | 60/38 | 68/45 | 76/55 | 83/63 | 92/71 | 96/75 | 96/74 | 88/67 | 79/56 | 66/45 | 58/37 |
| Temp. (°C) | 12/1 | 15/3 | 20/8 | 24/13 | 28/17 | 33/21 | 36/23 | 36/23 | 31/19 | 26/13 | 19/7 | 14/2 |
| Precip. (in.) | 1.9 | 2.2 | 2.6 | 3.8 | 5.0 | 2.9 | 2.2 | 2.0 | 3.0 | 3.5 | 2.2 | 1.9 |
| **Houston** | | | | | | | | | | | | |
| Temp. (°F) | 61/41 | 66/44 | 73/51 | 79/58 | 85/65 | 91/71 | 94/73 | 93/73 | 89/68 | 82/59 | 72/50 | 65/44 |
| Temp. (°C) | 17/6 | 18/7 | 24/12 | 26/16 | 29/19 | 32/23 | 33/24 | 33/24 | 31/22 | 27/16 | 22/12 | 18/7 |
| Precip. (in.) | 3.9 | 2.9 | 3.5 | 3.6 | 5.6 | 5.1 | 3.4 | 3.7 | 4.3 | 4.7 | 3.7 | 3.6 |
| **San Antonio** | | | | | | | | | | | | |
| Temp. (°F) | 62/39 | 66/43 | 74/50 | 80/58 | 86/66 | 92/72 | 95/74 | 95/74 | 90/69 | 82/59 | 71/48 | 64/42 |
| Temp. (°C) | 16/3 | 19/5 | 23/10 | 27/14 | 29/19 | 33/23 | 35/24 | 35/23 | 32/21 | 28/15 | 22/9 | 17/5 |
| Precip. (in.) | 1.2 | 1.7 | 1.9 | 1.6 | 2.6 | 4.2 | 3.6 | 1.9 | 2.5 | 3.2 | 2.1 | 1.7 |
| **Corpus Christi** | | | | | | | | | | | | |
| Temp. (°F) | 66/46 | 69/49 | 75/56 | 81/63 | 86/70 | 91/74 | 93/75 | 93/75 | 90/72 | 84/64 | 75/55 | 69/49 |
| Temp. (°C) | 18/7 | 21/9 | 24/13 | 28/17 | 30/21 | 32/23 | 34/24 | 34/24 | 32/22 | 29/18 | 24/13 | 20/9 |
| Precip. (in.) | 1.7 | 1.6 | 1.9 | 1.2 | 2.0 | 3.2 | 1.9 | 3.2 | 5.4 | 3.4 | 1.6 | 1.7 |
| **Amarillo** | | | | | | | | | | | | |
| Temp. (°F) | 49/22 | 53/26 | 61/32 | 71/42 | 79/52 | 88/61 | 91/66 | 89/64 | 82/57 | 72/45 | 59/32 | 51/24 |
| Temp. (°C) | 9/-6 | 12/-3 | 17/1 | 22/6 | 26/11 | 31/16 | 33/19 | 32/18 | 28/13 | 23/7 | 16/0 | 10/-4 |
| Precip. (in.) | 0.5 | 0.6 | 0.9 | 1.1 | 2.8 | 3.5 | 2.8 | 3.0 | 1.9 | 1.3 | 0.6 | 0.5 |

## Holidays

Banks, government offices, post offices, and many stores, restaurants, and museums are closed on the following legal national holidays: January 1 (New Year's Day), the third Monday in January (Martin Luther King, Jr., Day), the third Monday in February (Presidents' Day), the last Monday in May (Memorial Day), July 4 (Independence Day), the first Monday in September (Labor Day), the second Monday in October (Columbus Day), November 11 (Veterans' Day/Armistice Day), the fourth Thursday in November (Thanksgiving Day), and December 25 (Christmas). The Tuesday after the first Monday in November is Election Day, a federal government holiday in presidential-election years (held every 4 years, and next in 2012).

# Texas Calendar of Events

For an exhaustive list of events beyond those listed here, check http://events.frommers.com, where you'll find a searchable, up-to-the-minute roster of what's happening in cities all over the world.

## JANUARY

**AT&T Cotton Bowl Classic (& Parade),** Dallas. This annual college football bowl game is somewhat less prestigious than it once was, but it's still important in pigskin circles. Call ✆ **214/634-7525.** January 1.

**River Walk Mud Festival,** San Antonio. Each year, the horseshoe bend of the San Antonio River Walk is drained for maintenance, and San Antonians cheer up by electing a king and queen to reign over such events as Mud Stunts Day and the Mud Pie Ball. Call ✆ **210/227-4262.** Mid-January.

**Super Bull,** Amarillo. Don't come expecting football—this is a bull-riding event at the Amarillo Civic Center. Call ✆ **800/692-1338** or 806/376-7767. Mid-January.

**Southwestern Exposition and Livestock Show and Rodeo,** Fort Worth. Fort Worth's famous rodeo and livestock show is the nation's oldest, drawing nearly one million people to Will Rogers Memorial Center for 30 rodeo performances. It's kicked off by the All-Western Parade, the biggest horse-drawn parade in the world. Call ✆ **817/877-2400.** Mid-January to early February.

## FEBRUARY

**Stock Show and Rodeo,** San Antonio. San Antonio hosts more than 2 weeks of rodeo events, livestock judging, country-and-western bands, and carnivals at the AT&T Center. Call ✆ **210/225-5851.** Early February.

**Mardi Gras,** Galveston. The city's biggest party of the year, with parades, masked balls, and a live-entertainment district around the Strand. Call ✆ **888/425-4753.** Late February to early March.

## MARCH

**Houston Livestock Show and Rodeo,** Houston. Billed as the largest event of its kind, the rodeo includes all the usual events like bull riding and calf roping, plus performances by famous country-and-western artists. A parade downtown kicks off the celebration. Call ✆ **713/791-9000.** First 3 weeks of March.

**South by Southwest,** Austin. The Austin Music Awards kick off this huge conference, with hundreds of concerts at more than two dozen city venues. Keynote speakers have included Johnny Cash. Now with film and new media components. Call ✆ **512/467-7979.** Mid-March (during spring break at the University of Texas).

**Dyeing o' the River Green and Pub Crawl,** San Antonio. Are leprechauns responsible for turning the San Antonio River into the green River Shannon? Irish dance and music fill the Arneson River Theatre from the afternoon into the night. Call ✆ **210/227-4262.** March 17.

## APRIL

**Texas Hill Country Wine and Food Festival,** Austin. Book a month in advance for the cooking demonstrations; beer, wine, and food tastings; and celebrity chef dinners. For the food fair, just turn up hungry. Call ✆ **512/329-0770.** First weekend after Easter.

**San Jacinto Festival and Texas History Day,** West Columbia. Highlights include a parade, talent show, arts and crafts show, and barbecue cook-off. The talent show, where you never know what's going to happen next, is the fun part. Call ✆ **800/938-4853** or 979/265-2508. Mid-April.

**International Festival,** Houston. This festival highlights the culture, food, music, and heritage of a different country every year. Call ✆ **713/926-6368.** Last 2 weekends in April.

**Fiesta San Antonio,** San Antonio. What started as a modest marking of Texas's independence more than 100 years ago is now a huge event, with an elaborately costumed royal court presiding over 10 days of revelry: parades, balls, food fests, sporting events, concerts, and art shows all over town. Call ☎ **877/SA-FIESTA** (723-4378) or 210/227-5191. Mid- to late April.

## MAY

**Art Car Parade and Ball,** Houston. The parade of decorated cars is marvelous and hilarious and attracts participants from around the country. The ball—held in a large downtown parking garage—is always a spirited event. Call ☎ **713/926-6368.** Second weekend in May.

**Tejano Conjunto Festival,** San Antonio. This festival celebrates the lively and unique blend of Mexican and German music born in south Texas. The best conjunto musicians perform at the largest event of its kind in the world. Call ☎ **210/271-3151.** Mid-May.

**Return of the Chili Queens,** San Antonio. An annual tribute to chili, with music, dancing, crafts demonstrations, and, of course, chili aplenty. Bring the Tums. Call ☎ **210/207-8600.** Memorial Day weekend.

## JUNE

**American Institute of Architects Sandcastle Competition,** Galveston. More than 80 architectural and engineering firms from around the state build sand castles and sand sculptures, taking this pastime to new heights. Call ☎ **713/520-0155.** Early June.

**Juneteenth Festival,** statewide. News of the Emancipation Proclamation didn't reach Texas until June 19, 1865—nearly 3 years after Lincoln signed it. This day is celebrated with blues, jazz, and gospel music, family reunions, and a variety of events. Houston has a major celebration; call ☎ **713/284-8352** for more information. Weekend nearest June 19.

## JULY

**Gran Fiesta de Fort Worth,** Fort Worth. An outdoor festival celebrating Texas's Hispanic culture with Latin music, art, food, and parades. Call ☎ **214/855-1881.** Third week in July.

**Great Texas Mosquito Festival,** Clute. A joyous celebration to divert everyone from the annoying pest. Call ☎ **800/938-4853** or 979/265-2508. Late July.

**Miss Texas USA Pageant,** Lubbock. This annual beauty contest takes place at Lubbock Municipal Coliseum and area hotels. Call ☎ **800/692-4035** or 806/747-5232. Last week in July.

## AUGUST

*Austin Chronicle* **Hot Sauce Festival,** Austin. The largest hot-sauce contest in the world features more than 300 salsa entries, judged by celebrity chefs and food editors. The music at this superparty is hot, too. Call ☎ **512/454-5766.** Last Sunday in August.

## SEPTEMBER

**Marfa Lights Festival,** Marfa. Celebration of the lights that inexplicably appear on the horizon just east of town. Expect street dances, live music, parades, and lots of food. Call ☎ **800/650-9696** or 915/729-4942. Labor Day weekend.

**Grapefest,** Fort Worth. Yes, Texas makes wine—some of it pretty decent. It flows freely at this, one of the country's biggest wine festivals. There's also live music and other entertainment. Call ☎ **817/410-3185.** Early September.

**Fiestas Patrias,** Houston. One of the largest community-sponsored parades in the Southwest celebrating Mexico's independence from Spain. Houston's several *ballet folklórico* troupes twirl their way through downtown streets in a pageant of color and traditional Mexican music. Call ☎ **713/926-2636.** Mid-September (around the 16th).

**Pioneer Days,** Fort Worth. A festival commemorating Fort Worth's early pioneer and cattle rancher heritage with country music, rodeos, and Wild West shows. Call ☎ **817/336-8791** or 625-7005. Mid-September.

**Bayfest!,** Corpus Christi. This huge festival fills Shoreline Drive from I-37 down to Bayfront Park with music, games, food, arts and crafts, and fireworks over the bay. Call ☎ **800/678-6232** or 361/881-1888. Late September.

**State Fair of Texas,** Dallas. The nation's biggest state fair, held at the fairgrounds built in 1936 in grand Art Deco style. Call ☎ **214/565-9931.** Late September to third week of October.

## OCTOBER

**Commemorative Air Force Annual AIR-SHO,** Midland. Come see vintage aircraft on display and strutting their stuff in flight. Call ☏ **800/624-6435** or 915/683-3381. First weekend in October.

**Wings over Houston Airshow,** Houston. This thrilling event usually features displays of current military aircraft and performances of aerial acrobatics. Call ☏ **281/531-9461.** Mid-October.

**Texas Jazz Festival,** Corpus Christi. This free and popular festival attracts hundreds of big-name musicians from across the United States. Call ☏ **800/678-6232** or 361/881-1888. Mid- to late October.

**Halloween,** Austin. About 100,000 costumed revelers take over 7 blocks of historic 6th Street. Call ☏ **800/926-2282.** October 31.

## NOVEMBER

**South Padre Island Kite Festival,** South Padre Island. What could be more fun than flying a kite above blue waters? Or prettier to watch? For all those still young at heart. Call ☏ **800/678-6232** or 361/881-1888. Early November.

**Lighting Ceremony and River Walk Holiday Parade,** San Antonio. Trees and bridges along the river are illuminated by some 80,000 lights, and Santa Claus arrives on a boat during this floating river parade. Call ☏ **210/227-4262.** Friday after Thanksgiving.

## DECEMBER

**Christmas in the Stockyards,** Fort Worth. Cowtown's classic Old West corner is lit up even more than usual for holiday shopping and caroling with a Texas accent. Call ☏ **817/626-7921.** Throughout December.

**Fiestas Navideñas,** San Antonio. The Mexican market hosts piñata parties, a blessing of the animals, and surprise visits from Pancho Claus. Call ☏ **210/207-8600.** Weekends in December.

**Zilker Park Tree Lighting,** Austin. The lighting of a magnificent 165-foot tree is followed by the Trail of Lights, a mile-long display of life-size holiday scenes. Call ☏ **512/499-6700.** Sundays through December 24.

**Harbor Lights Celebration,** Corpus Christi. The harbor is decked out for the holidays. There's an illuminated boat parade, fireworks, entertainment, and a visit from Santa Claus. Call ☏ **800/678-6232** or 361/881-1888. First weekend in December.

**Dickens on the Strand,** Galveston. This street party in the city's historic district features revelers dressed up in Victorian costume, parades, street vendors, and lots of entertainment. Call ☏ **409/765-7834.** First weekend in December.

**Las Posadas,** San Antonio. Children carrying candles lead a procession along the river, reenacting the search for lodging in a moving multifaith rendition of the Christmas story. Call ☏ **210/224-6163.** Second Sunday in December.

# RESPONSIBLE TRAVEL

Traveling "green," seeking sustainable tourism options, is a concern in almost every part of the world today. Texas, with its large expanses of nature and the massive resources consumed in its major cities—among the biggest with some of the most congested road systems in the country—is no different. Although one could argue that any vacation that includes an airplane flight can't be truly "green," you can still go on holiday and contribute positively to the environment. Travelers can choose to take certain steps toward responsible travel. Go with forward-looking companies that embrace responsible development practices and work with local communities to help preserve destinations for the future. An increasing number of sustainable tourism initiates can help you plan a family trip and leave as small a "footprint" as possible on the places you visit.

The 2010 BP Gulf oil spill—the worst on record in U.S. waters—had an impact on the Texas Gulf Coast, though ultimately less severe that the devastation it wrought on Louisiana and other coastal states. Tar balls were discovered on beaches around Galveston, and the spill certainly affected the tourist and seafood trade along the Gulf Coast and in cities such as Houston. Long-term environmental damage hasn't been fully assessed, and the debate goes on regarding the continued presence of oil and its impact on coastal fisheries, wildlife, and other aspects of the environment. Home to big oil, big cars and trucks, and arctic air-conditioned shopping malls, Texas may not qualify as the greenest state in the Union. Still, there are certainly pockets of progressive environmental attitudes in the state, beginning with Austin.

Most of Texas's eco-tourism activities consist of do-it-yourself trips to state and national parks. The **Big Bend Country** region, including Guadalupe Mountains National Park and Big Bend National Park (p. 379), is the big draw in Texas for naturalists. **Road Scholar (Elderhostel)** (𝒞 **800/454-5768;** www.roadscholar.org) organizes a number of guided tours for naturalists and outdoors types. Birding is of growing interest, particularly along the Gulf Coast and in other parts of south Texas, and some travel operators now offer birding trips.

**WWOOF**, the World-Wide Opportunities on Organic Farms exchange program (𝒞 **949/715-9500;** www.wwoofusa.org), facilitates opportunities to work on farms and learn about organic farming practices and sustainable living. Its participating "host" members are 45 farms in or near Dallas, Houston, and Austin in particular. Opportunities range from growing vegetables and working with animals to constructing farm buildings and winemaking. It's a terrific experience for families.

The small town of **Bastrop** (near Austin) is highlighted as one of the National Trust for Historic Preservation's "Dozen Distinctive Destinations" (www.preservation nation.org/travel-and-sites/sites/southwest-region/bastrop-texas.html): Downtown farmers markets and independently owned local restaurants support the area's farmers and producers through the "Go Texan" restaurant program. In addition, Bastrop's green zone along the Colorado River is great for watersports and two state parks allow for hiking and biking on nature trails.

Texas Parks and Wildlife devotes part of its literature and website to **Great Texas Wildlife Trails** (www.tpwd.state.tx.us/huntwild/wild/wildlife_trails), which include birding trails. For information on the 51 **Wildlife Management Areas (WMA) of Texas,** where ecosystems are carefully managed but sustainable outdoor recreational opportunities are encouraged, visit www.tpwd.state.tx.us/huntwild/hunt/wma. For WMA nature tours, permits ($12) are required. You can find eco-friendly travel tips, statistics, and touring companies and associations—listed by destination under "Travel Choice"—at the International Ecotourism Society (TIES) website, **www.ecotourism.org**. Also, check out **Conservation International** (www.conservation.org)—which, with *National Geographic Traveler,* annually presents **World Legacy Awards** to those travel tour operators, businesses, organizations, and places that have made a significant contribution to sustainable tourism. **Ecotravel. com** is part online magazine and part eco-directory that lets you search for touring companies in several categories (water based, land based, spiritually oriented, and so on). In addition to the resources for Texas listed above, see www.frommers.com/planning for more tips on responsible travel.

# TOURS

## Academic Trips & Language classes

**Road Scholar (Elderhostel)** ★★★ (© 800/454-5768; www.roadscholar.org) offers more than three dozen organized, educational Texas trips, many with a naturalist's bent. They include **"San Antonio: Conversational Spanish and Culture in the Alamo City";** astronomy in the Davis Mountains of West Texas; the "Great Texas Coastal Birding Trail"; hiking in Big Bend; "Stories, and Cowboy Poetry of the West"; and history and politics in the capital and Texas Hill Country.

## Adventure & Wellness Trips

The massive expanse of Texas is dotted with lakes and has numerous rivers, almost 700 miles of Gulf Coast, plenty of forestland, and several mountain ranges. Its two national parks provide many opportunities for hiking and there are also scenic canyons, spectacular caves, and vast areas of rugged desert. Though the state hasn't quite caught on with most of the major national adventure-travel companies, if you're nonetheless keen on adventure travel in Texas, check out **GORPtravel** (© 877/440-**GORP** [4677] or 303/516-1153; http://gorptravel.away.com). It offers several Texas trips, from rafting or canoeing the Rio Grande to Old West dude ranch vacations, where you get to play cowboy when you're not busy fishing, swimming, or just loafing. Another good national company that offers bicycling and walking tours in Texas Hill Country, Big Bend, Davis Mountains, and Texas Wine Country, as well as multisport adventures in Texas, is **Planet Earth Adventures** ★ (© 800/923-4453; www. planetearthadventures.com). See also the variety of outdoors and educational trips offered by **Road Scholar,** the program arm of Elderhostel (see above).

You can obtain information on the state's outdoors outfitters, including numerous hunting and fishing guides, from the **Texas Outfitters and Guides Association,** P.O. Box 33141, Kerrville, TX 78029-3141 (© 830/238-4207).The **official state vacation guide** (see "Visitor Information," p. 452) is a good source of information for those planning outdoor recreation in the state. Information on fishing, hunting, and the numerous state parks in Texas is available from the **Texas Parks and Wildlife Department** (© 800/792-1112 or 512/389-8950; www.tpwd.state.tx.us). Reservations for camping at state parks can be made through the department's website or by calling © 512/389-8900. General outdoor recreation information is also online at **www.texasoutside.com**.

Additionally, the **World Birding Center** (www.worldbirdingcenter.org) is located in the lower Rio Grande Valley, and it offers a wealth of information on birding events, tours, and sites, such as the 50-acre **South Padre Island Birding and Nature Center** (© 956/761-3005). Another resource is **www.traveltex.com**, where you can search under "Attractions" for a mixed bag of "Outdoor" events, tours, and activities, including nature preserves and wildlife refuges (such as the 24,000-acre San Bernard National Wildlife Refuge, on the Gulf Coast, home to herons and blue geese, and Enchanted Rock State Natural Area, near Fredericksburg). There's also a section devoted to "Ranches and Rodeos," with information on ranch and orchard tours, horseback riding on the beach, and more.

Among spa and wellness destinations, one stands out for the total luxury rejuvenation package: **Lake Austin Spa Resort** ★★★ (© 800/847-5637; www.lake austin.com), named the top destination spa in North America by readers of Condé

Nast Traveler in 2010. This spectacular spot, in the Hill Country just outside the capital, has a 25,000-square-foot LakeHouse spa; indoor and outdoor pools; classes on dreams, painting, dog training, gardening, and healthy cooking; book discussions; a full slate of yoga, fitness, and meditation activities; and excellent spa dining.

## Food & Wine Trips

The amusingly named **Texas Toast Culinary Tours** ★★ (© 817/239-1634; www.texastoastculinarytours.com), a Fort Worth–based culinary tour group founded by a restaurant critic, leads culinary-themed road trips to Marfa and the Big Bend region of West Texas, and to Austin, San Antonio, and the Hill Country, as well as wine-tasting tours, "Beer and BBQ" bus tours, and "Feeding Frenzy" restaurant outings. **Texas Wine Tours** (© 877/839-9463; www.texas-wine-tours.com) takes trips to 14 Hill Country wineries, including stops in Fredericksburg and occasional events in places such as Luckenbach. Wine tours in white stretch limos are the focus of **Wine Tours of Texas** (© 877/693-0800 or 512/458-5466; www.winetoursof texas.com). For bicycling tours of Texas Wine Country, complete with gourmet picnics, check out **Planet Earth Adventures** ★ (© 800/923-4453; www.planetearth adventures.com).

## Guided Tours

**Gray Line Tours** (© 800/803-5073; www.grayline.com), one of the largest tour operators in the world, organizes a number of escorted bus trips, package tours, and day trips in Dallas, Fort Worth, Austin, Houston/Galveston, San Antonio, and South Padre Island—though most trips are in Dallas and Fort Worth.

**Sí Texas Tours,** in Bandera (© 888/748-3927 or 830/460-4565; www.sitexas tours.com), offers escorted tours and chartered bus trips to San Antonio, the Texas Hill Country, and south Texas.

At **InfoHub** (www.infohub.com/travel/sit/sit_pages/texas.html), you'll find links to a number of other themed trips and package tours (such as cycling the Hill Country and hiking in Big Bend).

## Volunteer & Working Trips

**Together Green,** in association with the National Audubon Society, has a number of environmental volunteer opportunities and events organized by state; check out the current roster of Texas volunteer gigs at **www.togethergreen.org**.

If you want to work in Texas while on vacation, what could be more appropriate than working on a real Texas dude ranch? Okay, it's more like playing cowboy, and these jobs are ultimately more about vacation than work, but you'll still get the chance to observe and participate in roping and roundups, herding cattle, going on trail rides, and getting your fill of Texas longhorns. Some dude ranches that offer working vacations are: **Beaumont Ranch** ★★ (© 888/864-6935; www.beaumontranch.com), an 800-acre ranch in Grandview, near Dallas; **Dixie Dude Ranch** ★ (© 880/375-YALL [9255] or 830/796-7771; www.dixieduderanch.com), a 725-acre ranch in Bandera, northwest of San Antonio; **Mayan Dude Ranch** ★ (© 830/796-3312; www.mayanranch.com), a family-owned ranch near Bandera, with plenty of leisure activities; and **Running-R Guest Ranch** (© 830/796-3984), also in Bandera.

## Walking Tours

The official **Texas State Travel Guide** has a new, handy feature with podcast walking tours (downloadable to your MP3 player) of Dallas, Houston, San Antonio, Corpus Christi, Fort Worth, and Austin. Visit **www.traveltex.com/multimedia/ podcast-walking-tours**.

**Planet Earth Adventures** ★ (© 800/923-4453; www.planetearthadventures. com) focuses primarily on bicycling tours, but it also plans to offer walking tours of the Texas Hill Country and more.

Also, see chapter 3 for tours exploring various regions of the state.

# SUGGESTED TEXAS ITINERARIES

**3**

When Texas became a state in 1845, the relevant legislation included a clause allowing it to split into five distinct states if the state legislature approved it. Likewise, planning a Texas road trip can be something like planning a road trip across five states—for example, El Paso is closer to Tucson, Arizona (319 miles away), than it is to Dallas (634 miles away). There is a lot of ground to cover: big cities; beautiful, wide-open spaces; and miles and miles of highway in between. With all of the acreage, it's important not to stretch yourself too thin. It's easy to spend too much time behind the wheel in Texas. As always, tailor your itinerary to your interests. If you like cowboy culture, Fort Worth and Amarillo might be focal points; hikers and paddlers will want to beeline to Big Bend National Park; city slickers might head to Dallas and Houston; and music lovers should flock to Austin. During your time on the Texas road, take the opportunity to explore places off the beaten path, and take a gander at those wide-open spaces. This big state has a lot to offer, so take advantage of as much as you can.

## THE REGIONS IN BRIEF

You can plan your trip to Texas in a couple of ways. If you're interested in a particular activity, such as birding, you might choose two or three locations and divide your time among them. Conversely, you could first select a destination, such as one of the state's major cities or national parks, and then decide what to do while you're there.

This book is organized geographically, and because this is such a large state, many visitors will limit their Texas vacation to one or two regions. We've summarized our coverage of the state to help you decide what kind of Texas experience you want to have.

**THE DALLAS–FORT WORTH METROPLEX**   Made famous by both a TV show about a Texas oil family and a football team, and infamous by the assassination of JFK, Dallas is a center of commerce and the headquarters for numerous banks, insurance companies, and other businesses. Big D, as it's known to locals, is one of the most sophisticated cities in Texas, with excellent restaurants, glitzy shopping, swank hotels, and a continually expanding arts scene. Dallas's unpretentious sister, Fort Worth, is equal parts Old West and "Museum Capital of the Southwest." Longhorns still rumble through the Stockyards National Historic District, while the city attracts art lovers to its top-notch museums. Both cities make good bases for outdoor recreation, children's activities, and professional sports outings. The city of Arlington, sandwiched between Dallas and Fort Worth, is home to several theme parks and the Texas Rangers baseball team.

**HOUSTON & EAST TEXAS**   The state's largest city (and the fourth-most-populous city in the United States), Houston is the heart of the nation's oil and gas industry. Although not considered a primary tourist destination, Houston has an abundance of attractions, including several excellent museums, performing arts such as the city's outstanding symphony orchestra, and a variety of outdoor activities. NASA's Johnson Space Center made Houston famous and is the city's most popular attraction. Nearby Galveston combines small-town easiness with a good mix of museums and children's activities, plus beaches that draw hordes of springbreakers and families throughout the warm months. East Texas, along the Louisiana border, is a prime destination for anglers, boaters, and other outdoor recreationists.

**THE TEXAS GULF COAST**   A world removed from the rest of the state, the coastal areas fronting the Gulf of Mexico have beach activities as well as good boating and even some surfing (okay, it's no Hawaii, but you *can* surf here). The Texas Gulf Coast is among the nation's top bird-watching regions, and also has superb fishing. You'll also find a handful of good museums and an active art scene.

**SAN ANTONIO**   The delightful, Latin-inflected city of San Antonio hosts the most famous historic site in Texas: the Alamo, where in 1836 Davy Crockett and about 187 other Texas freedom fighters died at the hands of the much larger Mexican army. San Antonio also has numerous other historic sites, a charming River Walk, fine cultural attractions, and a madcap schedule of festivals that make it a popular party spot. West and north of the city, the Texas Hill Country is one of the prettiest areas of Texas, dotted with hills (of course!), lakes, rivers, wildflowers, and picturesque small towns with authentic Texas flavor. There are numerous historic inns, antiques stores, small museums, and opportunities for watersports and other outdoor activities.

**AUSTIN**   The state capital, Austin is a laid-back but sophisticated and suddenly bustling large city with a distinct personality—a little unusual, a bit intellectual, and a lot different from other Texas cities of its size. It's a place where you'll see bumper stickers that read KEEP AUSTIN WEIRD, even though it's experienced a technology-based boom and a huge influx of money and new residents from California and elsewhere across the nation. In addition to museums, historic sites, and a wide range of outdoor activities, you'll find the best nightlife in the state, with live music practically everywhere, any night of the week—from country to blues to rock to swing. To the west, the Hill Country is easily accessible via day trips.

**WEST TEXAS**   Though Texas is largely urban, if you grew up watching TV and movie Westerns, you'd more likely believe the plains of West Texas are the real Texas, a land of dusty roads, weathered cowboys, and huge cattle ranches. Although the shootouts are now staged and the cattle drives are by truck and rail, this region retains much of the small-town Old West flavor, and even the region's biggest city, El Paso, is in many ways just an overgrown cow town. The area's history comes alive at numerous museums and historic sites, such as the combination courtroom and saloon used in the late 1800s by Judge Roy Bean, the self-styled "Law West of the Pecos." West Texas also has the 67,000-acre Lake Amistad, a national recreation area along the U.S.-Mexico border.

# The Regions in Brief

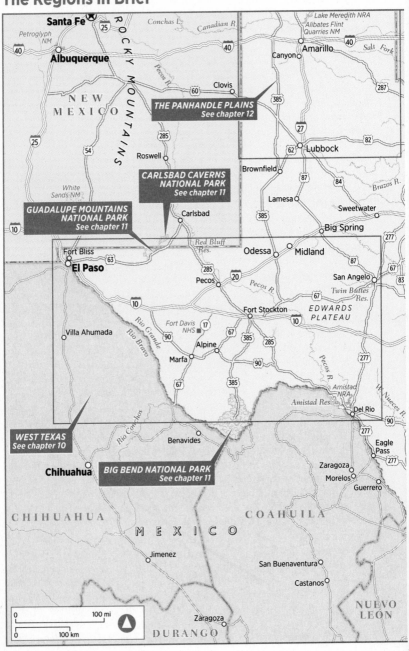

Santa Fe

Petroglyph NM

Albuquerque

NEW MEXICO

ROCKY MOUNTAINS

Conchas L.

Canadian R.

Pecos R.

Clovis

**THE PANHANDLE PLAINS**
See chapter 12

Lake Meredith NRA
Alibates Flint
Quarries NM

Canyon

Amarillo

Salt Fork

Lubbock

Roswell

White Sands NM

**CARLSBAD CAVERNS NATIONAL PARK**
See chapter 11

Brownfield

Lamesa

Sweetwater

Brazos R.

**GUADALUPE MOUNTAINS NATIONAL PARK**
See chapter 11

Carlsbad

Red Bluff Res.

Big Spring

Fort Bliss

El Paso

Odessa

Midland

San Angelo

Pecos

Pecos R.

Twin Buttes Res.

Villa Ahumada

Rio Grande

Rio Bravo

Fort Davis NHS

Fort Stockton

EDWARDS PLATEAU

Alpine

Marfa

Pecos R.

W. Nueces R.

Amistad NRA

Amistad Res.

Del Rio

**WEST TEXAS**
See chapter 10

Rio Conchos

Benavides

Eagle Pass

**BIG BEND NATIONAL PARK**
See chapter 11

Chihuahua

Zaragoza

Morelos

Guerrero

CHIHUAHUA

COAHUILA

MEXICO

Jimenez

San Buenaventura

Castanos

NUEVO LEON

0    100 mi
0    100 km

Zaragoza

DURANGO

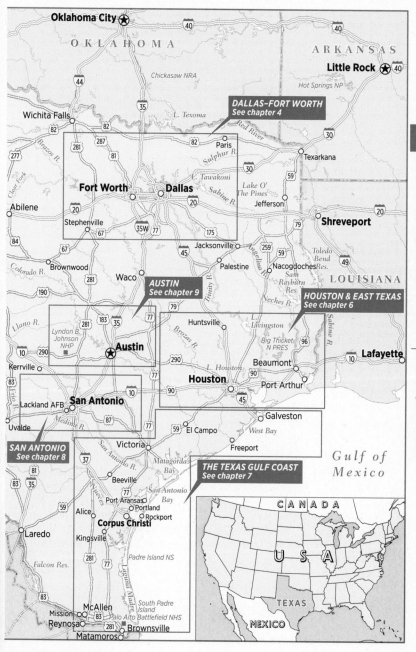

**BIG BEND & GUADALUPE MOUNTAINS NATIONAL PARKS** Among America's lesser visited national parks, Big Bend and Guadalupe Mountains contain rugged mountain scenery, the likes of which is found nowhere else in Texas, or even in surrounding states. There are spectacular and inspiring views from dizzying peaks, as well as hiking, rafting, and other outdoor activities. And Carlsbad Caverns National Park is just over the state line in New Mexico, an easy side trip for those visiting Guadalupe Mountains National Park.

**THE PANHANDLE PLAINS** A mix of terrain and varied experiences await visitors to this vast, rugged region that occupies the northern reaches of Texas. Close to an entire day's drive from the coast, it's where you'll find small-town charm, good museums, fascinating historic sites, and one of the most outrageous steakhouses in Texas. The main cities—just big towns, actually—are Amarillo and Lubbock, each with comfortable lodgings and good eats. The region has plenty to do and see, with watersports on Lake Meredith National Recreation Area, and hiking, horseback riding, and some of the area's most spectacular scenery at Palo Duro Canyon State Park. This is also home to a monument to rock-'n'-roll pioneer Buddy Holly and a display of old Cadillacs, noses buried in the ground with their unmistakable fins pointed skyward.

# TEXAS IN 1 WEEK

This route brings you to the four major metro areas in Texas—Dallas–Fort Worth, Austin, San Antonio, and Houston—while diverting for a Gulf Coast getaway on Padre Island National Seashore.

## Day 1: Arrive in Dallas-Fort Worth

The Dallas–Fort Worth area is a good starting point for any Texas trip. Rent a car if you don't already have one, and pick lodging accessible to the attractions you want to see in either city and get your bearings. Visit the **John F. Kennedy Memorial** (p. 81) and the **Sixth Floor Museum at Dealey Plaza** ★★ (p. 81), and, if you have time, make an excursion to **Fair Park** ★ (p. 86). After dinner at **Sonny Bryan's Smokehouse** ★ (p. 79) or another Dallas dining staple, check out **Lower Greenville**'s nightlife (p. 97).

## Day 2: Explore Dallas-Fort Worth

Split time between the artistic highlights of Dallas and Fort Worth, hitting the Arts District in Dallas (be sure to visit the **Nasher Sculpture Center** ★★★ [p. 83]), but leave plenty of time to roam in Fort Worth's incomparable **Cultural District** (p. 124), where the **Modern Art Museum of Fort Worth** ★★★ (p. 127) and **Kimbell Art Museum** ★★★ (p. 126) are mustsees. In the evening, have dinner in the **Stockyards National Historic District** ★★ before paying a visit to **Billy Bob's Texas** ★★★ (p. 134), a mega–country club, or taking in live music at another one of the city's many honky-tonks.

## Day 3: Explore Austin

Get going early for the 200-mile drive to Austin. If it's hot, head immediately to **Barton Springs Pool** ★★ (p. 310), for a dip to cool off. Visit the new **Blanton Museum of Art** ★ (p. 311) in the afternoon, then make it to the **Congress Avenue Bridge** for the sundown bat exodus (p. 310). Have dinner downtown

# The Best of Texas in 1 Week

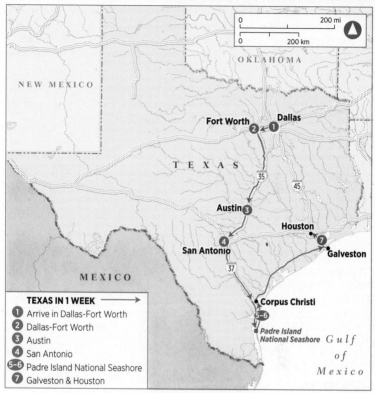

0          200 mi
0          200 km

OKLAHOMA

NEW MEXICO

Fort Worth ② ← ① Dallas

TEXAS

35

45

Austin ③

Houston ●

④ ⑦

San Antonio ● Galveston

37

MEXICO

● Corpus Christi

⑤–⑥

■ Padre Island
National Seashore     *Gulf*

*of*

*Mexico*

**TEXAS IN 1 WEEK** →
① Arrive in Dallas-Fort Worth
② Dallas-Fort Worth
③ Austin
④ San Antonio
⑤–⑥ Padre Island National Seashore
⑦ Galveston & Houston

**3**

SUGGESTED TEXAS ITINERARIES | Texas in 1 Week

and explore the famed **Austin music scene** in the Warehouse District, on Sixth Street, on Red River, or in South Austin. Stay either downtown or on South Congress at the **Austin Motel ★** (p. 396) or the **Hotel San José ★★** (p. 295).

## Day 4: Explore San Antonio

It's an 80-mile drive south from Austin to San Antonio. Park downtown and visit the **Alamo ★★** (p. 259), **HemisFair Park,** and the **San Antonio Museum of Art ★★**. Alternatively, you could spend the afternoon visiting the four lesser known missions that compose the **San Antonio Missions National Historical Park ★★** (p. 263). Return downtown for some time on the **River Walk ★★★** (p. 361), culminating in dinner at one of the many restaurants in the vicinity.

## Days 5 & 6: Explore Padre Island National Seashore

From San Antonio, head down to Padre Island Seashore, a 180-mile drive, and take your time unwinding from the hectic urban pace of the first 4 days of the trip. Explore **Padre Island National Seashore ★** (p. 219). Take time to

45

wander the beach, surf, fish, swim, or simply read a book and nap in the sun. Stay in **Corpus Christi** (p. 205), or—if you are up for more driving—head farther down the Gulf Coast to **South Padre Island** (p. 223). But, as it's a 410-mile drive to Galveston, you might want to start heading north sometime in the afternoon of Day 6.

## Day 7: Explore Galveston & Houston

From Corpus Christi, it's about 150 miles to **Galveston,** where you can spend more time on the beach or delve into the city's fascinating history. Drive back east into Houston for the afternoon to visit **Space Center Houston ★★★** (p. 172) before dining at one of Houston's many terrific eateries.

# TEXAS IN 2 WEEKS

Start with the first 3 days of the preceding 1-week itinerary, then divert to West Texas and Big Bend Country for a week before working your way back to San Antonio for Day 11, and then continue with the final 3 days of the preceding 1-week itinerary before heading back home.

## Day 4: Drive to Del Rio & Explore

From San Antonio, it is only 154 miles to **Del Rio** (p. 372), so you'll have time to get a late start and spend more time in the former city. Or you can get going early, take the scenic drive from Junction to Rocksprings on U.S. 377 to Del Rio, and visit **Amistad National Recreation Area ★** (p. 374), the **Whitehead Memorial Museum ★** (p. 373), or **Seminole Canyon State Park** (p. 377) in the area. Then drive west and stay in **Marathon** (p. 391) or **Alpine** (p. 358) to get a jump on exploring Big Bend.

## Days 5–7: Explore Big Bend National Park & Vicinity

From Del Rio, drive west toward **Big Bend National Park ★★** (p. 379). There is plenty to see along the way: You can stop at the Pecos River for a dramatic view or visit Langtry and learn a bit about Judge Roy Bean, and the **Seminole Canyon** (p. 377) is also a worthwhile diversion. Do some hiking and exploring before stopping at the **Gage Hotel ★★** in Marathon (p. 391) for the night of Day 5. You can also drive to Terlingua or Study Butte as a base for your Big Bend excursions. Another option is camping in Big Bend National Park or staying in park limits at **Chisos Mountains Lodge ★** (p. 389). Make plans to go on day hikes or do a rafting trip on the Rio Grande, a 2-day trip if possible. There are also interesting sights, stores, and restaurants in **Terlingua** (p. 391) and plenty of cultural history along the river in and outside of the park.

## Days 8 & 9: Explore Big Bend Ranch State Park & Marfa

From Big Bend, drive the Wild and Scenic River portion of FM 170 to Presidio, taking time to get out on a few hikes in **Big Bend Ranch State Park ★★** (p. 379). From Presidio, take U.S. 67 to **Marfa** (p. 354). Stay and eat in Marfa

# The Best of Texas in 2 Weeks

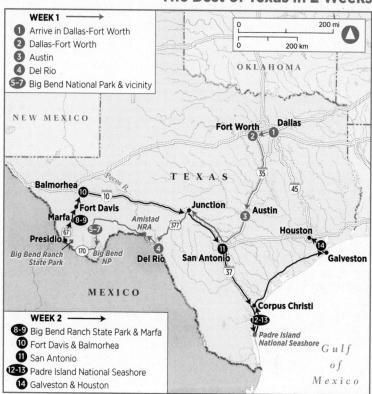

**WEEK 1**

1. Arrive in Dallas-Fort Worth
2. Dallas-Fort Worth
3. Austin
4. Del Rio
5-7. Big Bend National Park & vicinity

**WEEK 2**

8-9. Big Bend Ranch State Park & Marfa
10. Fort Davis & Balmorhea
11. San Antonio
12-13. Padre Island National Seashore
14. Galveston & Houston

or **Alpine** (p. 358). On Day 9, check out the **Chinati Foundation**'s ★★ (p. 355) avant-garde installations (it requires your time 10am–4pm for a guided tour) and downtown Marfa while the sun is up. Once it goes down, take U.S. 90 east 9 miles to see **Marfa's Mystery Lights** (p. 356), or else head north to the **McDonald Observatory** ★ (p. 350) if there's a Star Party that night. If Marfa's accommodations are booked, Alpine is a great alternative, as it has some noteworthy galleries and the **Museum of the Big Bend** ★ (p. 359).

## Day 10: Explore Fort Davis & Balmorhea

Spend your final day in West Texas, before heading east for the Gulf Coast, by exploring **Fort Davis National Historic Site** ★ (p. 350) or **Davis Mountains State Park** (p. 351). You can stay in Fort Davis, or continue—stopping at the oasis of a swimming pool at **Balmorhea State Park** ★★ (p. 353) if it's hot—and cut down on the drive to the Gulf Coast. After bunking in Balmorhea or somewhere off I-10 for the night, continue with Day 5 from the 1-week itinerary for the last 3 days of your trip.

# TEXAS FOR FAMILIES

Texas is a good choice for a family vacation, but because of its sheer size, it's best to pare back the car time from your itinerary. The major cities have plenty of kid-friendly attractions and pursuits, so adjust your time in each place accordingly: Families with budding astronauts will want to dedicate a whole day to Space Center Houston; other families might want to spend more time in the attraction-packed suburb of Arlington.

## Day 1: Arrive in Dallas

As we mentioned above in the 1-week itinerary, Dallas is a good starting point for any Texas trip. Rent a car if you don't already have one, and pick lodging accessible to the attractions you want to see in either city and get your bearings. In Dallas, visit **Heritage Village** ★ (p. 85) and make an excursion to **Fair Park** ★ (p. 86). Eat at **Fireside Pies** ★ (p. 79) or **Sonny Bryan's Smokehouse** ★ (p. 79), both family-friendly mainstays in Big D.

## Day 2: Explore Arlington & Fort Worth

**Arlington** (p. 99) is a top Texas family destination, located roughly midway between Dallas and Fort Worth. The suburb is home to such attractions as **Six Flags Over Texas** (p. 100) and the **Legends of the Game Baseball Museum** at the **Texas Rangers Ballpark** (p. 100). You can combine the day with some time in Fort Worth, or bypass Arlington altogether if your kids are old enough to appreciate the fantastic art museums in Fort Worth. The **Cowtown Cattlepen Maze** (p. 122) and the **Fort Worth Zoo** ★★★ are good bets for kids of all ages. That night, stay in Fort Worth after dining at **Joe T. Garcia's Mexican Dishes** (p. 115).

## Days 3 & 4: Explore Houston

Get a good start on your drive to Houston, because there is plenty to see and do in the 2 days you'll spend there: **Space Center Houston** ★★★ (p. 172), the **Children's Museum of Houston** ★★ (p. 172), the **Orange Show** ★★ (p. 171), the **Downtown Aquarium** (p. 169), the **Kemah Boardwalk** (p. 171), and the **Health Museum** ★★★ (p. 173) are all worthy destinations. **Lupe Tortilla** (p. 166) is a reliable kid-friendly restaurant in town.

## Days 5 & 6: Explore the Gulf Coast & Padre Island National Seashore

Drive down the Gulf Coast from Houston to Corpus Christi and spend time at **Padre Island National Seashore** ★ (p. 123), a great spot to spend a couple of days and burn off some steam swimming, fishing, flying kites, and otherwise playing in the surf and sun.

## Day 7: Explore Austin or San Antonio

To cap off your Texas family vacation, take your pick of the **Alamo** ★★ (p. 259) and **HemisFair Park** (p. 265) in San Antonio or **Zilker Park** ★ (p. 316), the **Texas State Capitol** ★★ (p. 309), and the **Austin Children's Museum** ★★ (p. 316) in Austin. If you can extend your trip by a few days, you can do both cities better justice.

**3**

Map legend:
1. Dallas
2. Arlington & Fort Worth
3-4 Houston
5-6 Gulf Coast & Padre Island National Seashore
7. Austin or San Antonio

# EXPLORING THE HILL COUNTRY

The rolling green hills of central Texas, flanked by Austin to the east and San Antonio to the south, punctuated by crystalline rivers and limestone bluffs, make up one of the prettiest spots in the state. Besides the small towns and big cities, there is plenty in this region alone to keep a road trip going for a week—or more.

## Day 1: Arrive in Austin

The capital of the Lone Star State, **Austin** is also the state's intellectual and cultural center, thanks to the presence of the University of Texas. This also makes it a point of civic pride and the subject of an entire campaign to "Keep Austin Weird." Rife with terrific museums, great parks, and one of the liveliest bar scenes in the country, this is just the place to start your Hill Country excursion. **Curra's Grill ★★** (p. 301) is a great choice for dinner.

## Days 2 & 3: Explore Austin

Central Austin is very good for a walking tour, but you'll need to drive to many of the attractions. In Austin, visit the **state capitol ★★** (p. 309), the **Lady**

49

# Exploring the Hill Country

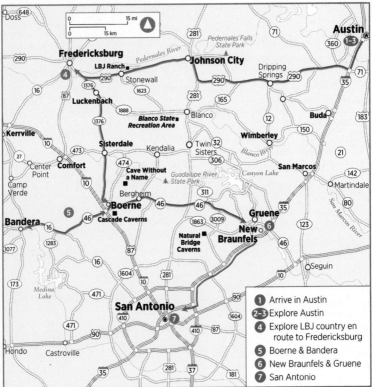

Map legend:
1. Arrive in Austin
2-3. Explore Austin
4. Explore LBJ country en route to Fredericksburg
5. Boerne & Bandera
6. New Braunfels & Gruene
7. San Antonio

**Bird Johnson Wildflower Center ★★★** (p. 311), and the **Barton Springs Pool ★★** (p. 310), paradise on a hot day. If you're a night owl, be sure to check out some of the city's terrific venues for live music of every imaginable genre, or just go bar-hopping on Sixth Street. If it's between March and October, be sure to check out the nightly exodus of over one million bats from the Congress Avenue Bridge at dusk.

## Day 4: Explore LBJ Country en route to Fredericksburg

From Austin, take U.S. 290 west to **Lyndon B. Johnson State and National Historic Parks at LBJ Ranch ★** (p. 327) for a few hours of exploration before continuing on your way to historic **Fredericksburg ★** (p. 324). If you have time, check out **Enchanted Rock State Natural Area ★★** (p. 325), 18 miles north of town.

## Day 5: Boerne & Bandera

From Fredericksburg, backtrack east on U.S. 290 and head south on FM 1376 to Boerne via Luckenbach. Wander downtown **Boerne** (p. 277) or tour the

**Cave Without a Name** (p. 277) before checking into a B&B or guest ranch in the area. If you're up for it, go boot-scootin' that night in Bandera at **Arkey's** (p. 282), a colorful and authentic honky-tonk.

## Day 6: New Braunfels & Gruene

After breakfast, take Tex. 46 east about 45 miles to **New Braunfels** (p. 328). If time and weather permit, rent an inner tube and float the Guadalupe River or hit **Schlitterbahn ★**, the largest water park in the state. If not, visit the **Museum of Texas Handmade Furniture ★** (p. 329). Check in to the **Gruene Mansion Inn** (p. 330) and take in a rollicking show at **Gruene Hall ★★** (p. 330), the oldest country-and-western dance hall in Texas.

## Day 7: San Antonio

From New Braunfels, head south on I-35 about 40 miles to **San Antonio** (p. 231). Spend the day ambling the **River Walk ★★★** (p. 261), enjoying some Mexican food, and shopping the import stalls at **Market Square ★** (p. 261). Take a tour of one of the famous local attractions, such as the **Alamo ★★** (p. 259) or the **San Antonio Missions National Historical Park ★★** (p. 263). It's only an 80-mile drive north on I-35 back to Austin.

# DALLAS

by Neil Edward Schlecht

Known to locals as simply "Big D," Dallas is the north Texas city that doesn't lack for confidence. Dallasites, like most Texans who are given to hyperbole when talking about their state, are proud to declare that their city is nicknamed "Big D" because, well, everything's bigger and better in Dallas.

However, Americans and people around the world have grown up with images of Dallas as a city that's sometimes bigger, but not necessarily better. A sniper gunned down President John F. Kennedy as his motorcade snaked through downtown Dallas in 1963; while the nation mourned, a local nightclub owner murdered the presumed assassin, Lee Harvey Oswald, right under the noses of local police. The Dallas Cowboys, a football club whose supporters had the audacity to call it "America's Team," won five Super Bowls and made scantily clad cheerleaders with big hair a required accessory alongside professional sports teams. Bonnie and Clyde began their wanton spree of lawlessness in Dallas. J. R. Ewing presided over an oil empire in the TV soap opera *Dallas,* and propagated an image of tough-talking businessmen who wore cowboy boots with pinstriped suits and had oil rigs pumping in their backyard. The irascible H. Ross Perot—remember him?—made a fortune in technology and thought he deserved to run the country. His place in pop culture has now been taken over by Mark Cuban, the high-tech billionaire and owner of the NBA's Dallas Mavericks.

Dallas has come to symbolize the kind of place where such larger-than-life characters live out the American dream, even if their versions are slightly skewed. Big D is about dreaming big, so the city, not much more than 400 square miles of flat prairie land broken up by shiny skyscrapers and soaring suburban homes, adopts all things big. Big cars. Big hair. Big belt buckles. Big attitude.

With 1.3 million inhabitants, Dallas is only the third-largest city in Texas, though it ranks number nine in the United States. Flat and featureless, it has little in the way of natural gifts or historical precedents that might have predicted its growth. Yet the city grew from a little Republic of Texas pioneer outpost in the mid–19th century into a major center for banking, finance, and oil. It is a largely conservative city, and its residents' biggest passions seem to be making money and spending it, often ostentatiously. In the city that spawned Neiman Marcus, shopping is a religion, and megamalls fan out in every direction, part of an endless commercial sprawl.

Dallas, host of Super Bowl XLV, is fiercely passionate about big-time sports, too, and not only the Cowboys. Just about every professional sports league has a franchise in Dallas, and there's also rodeo and the Texas Motor Speedway. This is a place where the top high school football teams routinely sell out playing fields that seat 20,000 and schedule their playoff games in Cowboys Stadium, to accommodate a fan base that reaches far beyond parents and teachers.

Dallas is also a place where Southern Baptist churches pack in nearly as many people for Sunday services, and, for the most part, conservative politics reign supreme. The George W. Bush Presidential Center, to open in 2013, will include an institute, presidential library, and museum. It will be located at Dallas's top university, Southern Methodist University (SMU), the alma mater of George's wife, Laura. Dallas is also the post–White House residence of the Bushes.

Dallas ranks as the top business and leisure destination in Texas (and the second-most-popular convention site in the country). The city is more cosmopolitan than ever before, and a great deal of effort and resources have gone into establishing a cultural life on a par with business opportunities. A recent burst of arts philanthropy—and hiring virtually every renowned international architect in the book to build up the Arts District—has catapulted Dallas into the big leagues. Slick and newly sophisticated Dallas has plenty to entertain visitors, many of whom come on business and stay around to play a bit: great hotels, eclectic restaurants, a thriving nightlife, and even a robust alternative music scene—and, lest we forget, the enduring appeal of nonstop shopping.

# ORIENTATION

## Arriving

### BY PLANE

**DALLAS/FORT WORTH INTERNATIONAL AIRPORT (DFW)**   Most visitors will arrive via **DFW Airport** (© 972/574-6000; www.dfwairport.com), located midway between the two cities and one of the largest airports in the nation. It's the world's third-busiest airport and larger than the island of Manhattan, with four terminals connected by a "people mover." **DFW Airport Visitor Information** (© 972/574-3694) provides hotel, sightseeing, and transportation information, and the **Airport Assistance Center** (© 972/574-4420) offers crisis counseling, foreign language assistance, and car-seat rental. Currency exchange booths and ATMs are in terminals A, B, D (International, the newest terminal), and E. All the major car-rental companies have representatives here (but note that if you're returning a car, the rental terminal is a good 5 miles away, so allow extra time before your departure). Transportation between terminals is quick and easy on Skylink, the world's largest airport train.

Ground transportation to Dallas, Fort Worth, or the surrounding area is by **Dallas Area Rapid Transit (DART)** bus, airport shuttle, private car, charter limo, courtesy car, or taxi. Many hotels offer courtesy transportation to and from the airport; check to see if yours does. Transport by bus is the cheapest option, but the best value is taking the airport shuttle. For more about ground transportation, call © 972/574-5878 or visit www.dfwairport.com/transport/index.php.

**DART** (© 214/979-1111; www.dart.org) offers two principal means of public transportation between DFW Airport and downtown Dallas: the **Trinity Railway Express (TRE)** and **DART.** The **TRE** operates Monday through Saturday (**Note:** not Sun); the 202 express bus runs hourly, 7 days a week, from 6am to 11pm. The single-ride fare east of DFW is $5; west of DFW, it's $3.50. An express 1-day pass costs $7 and is good for unlimited rides on DART and the T (including your return trip) until 3am the next day. For more information, call © 817/215-8600 or visit

# Dallas–Fort Worth

www.trinityrailwayexpress.org. Passenger terminals at DFW Airport are served by two **DART** shuttles serving terminals A and C and terminals B and E; both operate from CentrePort/DFW Airport Station. **Express route 310** (to/from remote north parking) or **408** (to/from remote south parking). The fare is $1.75 one-way. For more information, call ✆ **214/979-1111** or visit www.dart.org.

Another convenient mode of transportation to and from the airport is **Super Shuttle DFW** (✆ **800/BLUE-VAN** [258-3826] or 817/329-2000; www.supershuttle.com), which can be reached 24 hours a day. A typical fare to Dallas is $17 to $32, and to Fort Worth, $17 to $26. The **Yellow Checker Shuttle "Airporter"** (✆ **817/267-5150** or 972/222-2000) operates shuttle services between DFW and Fort Worth; the cost to or from the Airporter Park & Ride lot at 1000 E. Weatherford St. in downtown Fort Worth is $15, and to downtown hotels, $19.

Taxis are on hand at airport arrival gates. You can also make airport transportation reservations by calling **Yellow Checker** (✆ **214/426-6262** or 817/426-6262) or **Cowboy Cab** (✆ **214/428-0202**). If you prefer limousine service, try **ExecuCar** (✆ **800/410-4444**), **Agency Limousine** (✆ **800/277-LIMO** [5466] or 817/284-7575), or **DFW Towncars** (✆ **214/956-1880**). The flat-rate taxi fare to downtown Dallas is $40, downtown Fort Worth, $43; limo service is about $55 and $60, respectively.

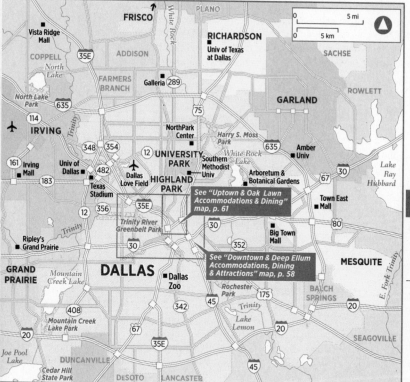

**DRIVING FROM DFW AIRPORT** International Parkway connects directly to major freeways serving both Dallas and Fort Worth (Hwy. 114 and 635 north, and 183 and 360 south). Signs clearly indicate the route; each city is 18 miles from the airport. Despite that seemingly short distance, the drive to downtown Dallas or Fort Worth in peak times takes about an hour.

**LOVE FIELD** Love Field (© **214/670-6073;** www.dallas-lovefield.com) is just 7 miles from downtown Dallas. After DFW Airport was built, Love Field became primarily a private plane and cargo airport for DHL and Federal Express. Southwest Airlines has continued to operate out of it, and it has been resurrected as a commercial airport, with Delta and Continental Express building or revamping terminals. While you're hanging around in the Southwest terminal, drop in on the **Frontiers of Flight Museum** (© **214/350-1651;** www.flightmuseum.com), open Monday through Saturday from 10am to 5pm, and Sunday from 1 to 5pm. Admission costs $8 for adults, $6 seniors, $5 for children 3 to 17.

All major car-rental companies have locations here. The same ground transportation services for DFW Airport also travel to Love Field. A taxi downtown costs about $18; the Super Shuttle to downtown Dallas is $17.

## BY CAR

You'll almost surely need a car to get around Dallas and Fort Worth (unless you stick to the downtown areas), so it's not a bad idea to arrive in one. The major roads into Dallas are **I-635** (better known as LBJ Fwy.), which goes from DFW Airport east to Dallas; **I-20,** which joins I-635 and heads west to Fort Worth; **I-35,** north-south from the border towns in south Texas, through San Antonio, Austin, and Dallas, and all the way to Oklahoma; and **U.S. 75** (the Central Expwy.), which runs north-south from downtown Dallas to the northern suburbs. From Houston, the drive to Dallas (or Fort Worth) is about 5 hours; from Austin, 4 hours. Dallas is about an hour from Fort Worth.

## BY TRAIN

Amtrak's Texas Eagle serves Dallas's **Union Station,** 400 S. Houston St. (✆ **214/ 653-1101**), and Fort Worth's **Intermodal Transportation Center (ITC)** in the southeast corner of the city at 1001 Jones St. and 9th Street (✆ **817/332-2931**). Trains arrive from Chicago, St. Louis, Little Rock, San Antonio, and Los Angeles; Heartland Flyer trains serve Oklahoma City and Fort Worth. For more information and reservations, contact Amtrak at ✆ **800/USA-RAIL** (872-7245) or visit www.amtrak.com or www.texaseagle.com.

The **Trinity Railway Express (TRE)** travels back and forth between Dallas and Fort Worth (day pass, $7; single fare, $5); for more information, call ✆ **214/979-1111** or 817/215-8600 (www.trinityrailwayexpress.org).

## Essentials

### VISITOR INFORMATION

The **Dallas Convention & Visitors Bureau** (✆ **800/CDALLAS [232-5527];** www.visitdallas.com) operates a comprehensive website (with online hotel and airfare arrangements) and the **Dallas Tourist Information Center,** located in the historic Old Red Courthouse downtown, 100 S. Houston St. (✆ **214/571-1301,** 24-hr. events hotline; Mon–Fri 8am–5pm, Sat–Sun 9am–5pm). It has Internet terminals and touch-screen computer information kiosks.

---

### DFW: The Metroplex

North Texas's two biggest cities, Dallas and Fort Worth, are often referred to as "DFW"—or, in a term that could only have been devised by so-called marketing geniuses, the "Metroplex"—as though they were closely intertwined twin cities. Although unrelenting development has filled the flat land gaps between them and created a greater population of some four million (and a ranking in the top five in the country for urban sprawl), the two cities remain 30 miles apart and, perhaps more important, worlds apart culturally. Slick and glitzy Dallas, home of the NFL's Cowboys—also known as America's Team—thrives on an identity of banking and big business; it's "where the East peters out," in the words of Will Rogers. Fort Worth, the "Cowtown" of the legendary cattle drives and now the cultural capital of north Texas, has long identified itself quite differently as being where the West begins. More laid-back than Dallas, Fort Worth might be considered comparatively pokey, were it not for its surprising roster of world-class museums, progressive civic-mindedness, good-natured downtown nightlife, and enduring Western character.

To get an immediate handle on what's happening in Dallas, check out the *Dallas Morning News* "Weekend Guide" (guidelive.com) or *Dallas Observer* (www.dallas observer.com), a free weekly paper with arts, entertainment, and dining information.

## CITY LAYOUT

Dallas is extremely spread out, covering nearly 400 square miles. Traditionally, most people have worked in the downtown central business district and commuted to their homes in residential districts primarily north and east (but also south and west) of the city. New business attracted to the city has resulted in many more offices in outlying areas, particularly the corridor from Richardson to Plano, north of Dallas along U.S. 75 (Central Expwy.) and west of the city in Carrollton and Irving/Las Colinas.

The West End Historic District, financial center, and Arts District are all downtown, just west of Central Expressway (though Deep Ellum, also part of downtown, is on the east side of U.S. 75). Central, in fact, divides east and west Dallas. LBJ Freeway, or I-635, runs through far north Dallas. It connects to I-20, which runs a loop south of the city. Irving, Grand Prairie, and Arlington are all due west, between Dallas and Fort Worth. I-30 leads directly west to Fort Worth.

# The Neighborhoods in Brief

In addition to the six major neighborhoods discussed below, the city is surrounded by concentric rings of ever-expanding suburbs. In addition to ever-bigger homes, these areas, especially north of the city, are marked by scores of megamalls, minimalls, and strip malls of chain stores and restaurants that make the new developments very difficult to distinguish from one another. New stadiums and shopping and entertainment facilities are drawing more and more people to Plano, McKinney, and Frisco.

**Downtown Dallas** This area encompasses the **Dallas Arts District,** the nexus of downtown Dallas's fine and performing arts, including the Dallas Museum of Art, Nasher Sculpture Center, Meyerson Symphony Center, Crow Collection of Asian Art, and others; the **West End Historic District,** a former warehouse district and one of the oldest parts of the city transformed into a popular hotel, restaurant, nightlife, and shopping scene; and the core of downtown offices that extend east from **Reunion Arena** and **Dealey Plaza,** where the flagship Neiman Marcus is the sole remaining department store. Though some urban-minded professionals are finally beginning to renovate residential loft spaces, downtown Dallas remains pretty much a ghost town after 6pm (except for West End). Still, it has a number of major hotels and makes a good place to drop anchor, especially for visiting businesspeople.

**Deep Ellum** Located east of downtown and bounded by Elm, Main, Commerce, and Canton streets, is Deep Ellum. This area once was Big D's best impersonation of Austin, the live-music capital of the Southwest. Unfortunately, Deep Ellum has experienced an eruption of violence, gang related and otherwise, so the nightlife scene here is not what it once was, though there are still a number of nightclubs and bars. Simultaneously ragged and chic, the former industrial district is home to alternative, blues, rock, and other music clubs interspersed with discos, honky-tonks, art galleries, furniture and secondhand shops, and upscale restaurants. The area is dead during the day, but it gets pretty rowdy at night and on weekends. The name is said to be a Southern drawl pronunciation of the main street, Elm.

**Uptown & Oak Lawn** Located northeast of downtown and promoted as "Uptown," **McKinney Avenue, Knox-Henderson,** and **Victory Park** are destinations with chic restaurants, shopping meccas, and *in* places to live. The pace has slowed a bit, but chic, modern condos continue to go up even in the face of housing slowdowns. McKinney Avenue, once the site of elegant old homes, is now the center of the Dallas

# Downtown & Deep Ellum Accommodations, Dining & Attractions

**ACCOMMODATIONS** ■
The Adolphus Hotel **13**
Belmont Hotel **1**
The Corinthian B&B **20**
The Magnolia **14**
Spring Hill Suites Dallas
Downtown West End **8**

Dallas-Fort Worth Int'l Airport
Dallas Love Field
35E
114
75
635
67
30
360
35E
**DALLAS**
30
67
45
175
35E

**Area of detail**

0 ——————— 1/2 mi
0 ——————— 0.5 km

Blackburn St.

**TURTLE CREEK PARK**

**CENTRAL EXPRESSWAY**

75

R.E. LEE PARK

**UPTOWN**

Harry Hines Blvd.

**MARKET CENTER**

35E

Dallas North Tollway

Oak Lawn Ave.

Maple Ave.

**REVERCHON PARK**

Market Center Blvd.

Oak Lawn Ave.

McKinnon St.

Harry Hines Blvd.

Cedar Springs Rd.

**GREENWOOD CEMETERY**

McKinney Ave.

366

Woodall Rogers Freeway

345

Industrial Blvd.

Stemmons Freeway

Trinity River

2

4  3  Pearl St.
6  5
7
**ARTS DISTRICT**
Ross Ave.

Continental St. Viaduct

8
**WEST END**
35E
9
10  11  12
**DEALEY PLAZA**

Pacific Ave.
Elm St.
Main St.
Commerce St.
13  14
13
**DOWNTOWN**
Young St.
Elm St.
Griffin St.
Lamar St.

Central Expwy.
Pearl Expwy.

1

31

Commerce St. Viaduct

Reunion Blvd.

Houston St.

**REUNION PARK**

**Dallas Convention Center**

17

260
←**BISHOP ARTS DISTRICT**

30

Beckley Ave.

**TRINITY RIVER GREENBELT PARK**

Houston St. Viaduct

Jefferson Blvd. Viaduct

15

16
35E

Industrial Blvd.

Lamar St.

Corinth St.

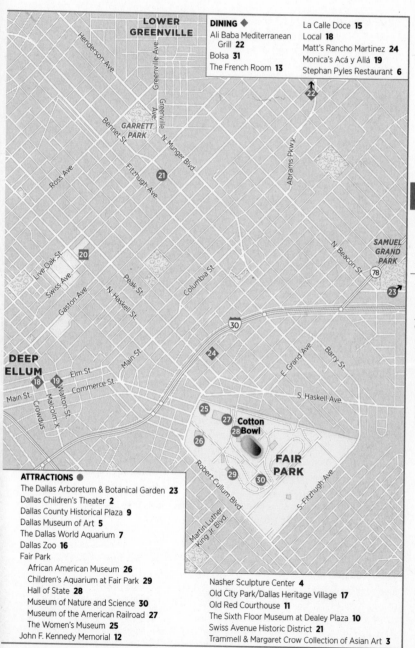

LOWER GREENVILLE

**DINING ◆**
Ali Baba Mediterranean Grill **22**
Bolsa **31**
The French Room **13**
La Calle Doce **15**
Local **18**
Matt's Rancho Martinez **24**
Monica's Acá y Allá **19**
Stephan Pyles Restaurant **6**

GARRETT PARK

SAMUEL GRAND PARK

DEEP ELLUM

Cotton Bowl

FAIR PARK

**ATTRACTIONS ●**
The Dallas Arboretum & Botanical Garden **23**
Dallas Children's Theater **2**
Dallas County Historical Plaza **9**
Dallas Museum of Art **5**
The Dallas World Aquarium **7**
Dallas Zoo **16**
Fair Park
  African American Museum **26**
  Children's Aquarium at Fair Park **29**
  Hall of State **28**
  Museum of Nature and Science **30**
  Museum of the American Railroad **27**
  The Women's Museum **25**
John F. Kennedy Memorial **12**

Nasher Sculpture Center **4**
Old City Park/Dallas Heritage Village **17**
Old Red Courthouse **11**
The Sixth Floor Museum at Dealey Plaza **10**
Swiss Avenue Historic District **21**
Trammell & Margaret Crow Collection of Asian Art **3**

art gallery scene, while Knox-Henderson is split right down the middle between trendy restaurants and upscale home-furnishings stores. Some of the hottest shopping and nightlife spots are in **West Village** in Uptown. **Victory Park,** the site of new luxury hotels and the American Airlines Center, hasn't quite taken off as an entertainment enclave, as once envisioned. **Oak Lawn, Cedar Springs,** and **Turtle Creek,** the heart of artsy and gay Dallas, are home to some of its finest hotels, restaurants, shops, and the original Dallas Theater Center, built by Frank Lloyd Wright.

**Greenville Avenue & East Dallas** The high point of Dallas nightlife, as it has been for decades, is this long strip located northeast of downtown Dallas, from LBJ Freeway south to Ross Avenue. Upper Greenville draws a slightly older and sophisticated crowd, while Lower Greenville (below Mockingbird) swims with nightclubs, bars both shabby and snooty, bohemian restaurants, vintage clothing stores, and resale furniture shops. East Dallas is home to the party district of Deep Ellum, the Lakewood residential neighborhood, and old Dallas sites like the Cotton Bowl and Texas fairgrounds.

**Park Cities** The traditional haunt of the Dallas elite, Park Cities encompasses one of America's wealthiest residential districts, **Highland Park,** as well as the not-too-shabby **University Park** and the city's major university, preppy SMU, where the George W. Bush Presidential Center will be located. Park Cities is north of downtown and west of Central Expressway. Plenty of Dallasites tend to refer to the entire zone as Highland Park, if only to use the best-known district as shorthand.

**North Dallas** The area along the northern edge of the city and southern edge of the suburbs is where the hard-core shopping begins (in places such as the Galleria, Valley View, and Prestonwood malls in Addison). It is also home to an ever-growing contingent of hotels and restaurants away from the downtown business scene.

**Oak Cliff** For decades, this neighborhood on the other side of I-30 was considered the wrong side of the tracks. But in the last decade (though truly only in the last 2 or 3 years), it has become a hotbed of indie cool. The Bishop Arts District has some of the coolest restaurants, bars, and shops—Dallas's own version of Austin hipness.

## GETTING AROUND
### By Public Transportation

Until the early 2000s, Dallas was a typical Southern city covering a huge area where there wasn't a lick of public transportation. Things have really improved with the addition of **Dallas Area Rapid Transit (DART) buses and light rail** (℃ 214/979-1111; www.dart.org), and its coverage is constantly expanding out from the downtown area. Pick up a map at any visitor information center or at most hotels and major attractions. Single-ride fare (no transfers) is $1.75 (85¢ for seniors, students, and children). Day passes are available for $4 ($2 for seniors, students, and children); for premium routes (serving the suburbs), the 1-day pass is $7 ($2 discounted). You can purchase single tickets and day passes from the new ticket vending machines (TVMs) on all rail station platforms.

Of particular interest to visitors (especially kids) in the downtown area is the free **McKinney Avenue Streetcar Service** (also called the **M-Line Trolley**), which travels from the Dallas Arts District to Cityplace Station and the West Village (it goes along McKinney Ave. from Uptown's Allen St. to downtown's Ross Ave. and St. Paul Ave., next to the Dallas Museum of Art). The vintage trolleys are from 1906, 1913, and 1920, and operate year-round between 7am and 10pm Monday through Friday, 10am and 10pm Saturday and Sunday (every 15 min. during peak and lunch hours, every half-hour during off-peak hours and Sat–Sun). The trolley is perfect for bar,

# Uptown & Oak Lawn Accommodations & Dining

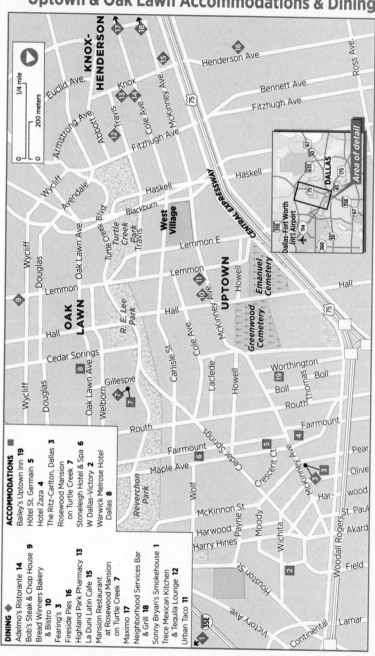

**DINING ◆**

Adelmo's Ristorante **14**
Bob's Steak & Chop House **9**
Bread Winners Bakery
 & Bistro **10**
Fearing's **3**
Fireside Pies **16**
Highland Park Pharmacy **13**
La Duni Latin Cafe **15**
Mansion Restaurant
 at Rosewood Mansion
 on Turtle Creek **7**
Maximo **17**
Neighborhood Services Bar
 & Grill **18**
Sonny Bryan's Smokehouse **1**
Trece Mexican Kitchen
 & Tequila Lounge **12**
Urban Taco **11**

**ACCOMMODATIONS ■**

Bailey's Uptown Inn **19**
Hôtel St. Germain **5**
Hotel Zaza **4**
The Ritz-Carlton, Dallas **3**
Rosewood Mansion
 on Turtle Creek **7**
Stoneleigh Hotel & Spa **6**
W Dallas-Victory **2**
Warwick Melrose Hotel
 Dallas **8**

## Real Highway Names

To get around Dallas, you'll need to know and adopt the colloquial names of the major local thoroughfares. As a general rule, numbers give way to proper names.

| Official Name | Real-Folks Name |
|---|---|
| U.S. 75 | Central Expressway ("Central") |
| I-635 | LBJ Freeway ("LBJ") |
| Northwest Highway | Loop 12 |
| I-35E | Stemmons |
| I-35/U.S. 77/I-635/I-30 | R. L. Thornton |

gallery, and restaurant shopping in Uptown, and great for getting from hotels in the area to the Arts District downtown.

*Note:* Nearby DART light rail stations are included in the listings in this chapter, but only when one is within a 20-minute walk of the hotel, restaurant, or attraction. For additional route and fare information for DART, call © **214/979-1111,** or log on to www.dart.org.

### By Car

You can now actually get around Dallas without a car, if you stick to the major downtown sights, hotels, and restaurants. However, if you want to visit shopping centers in North Dallas or outlying areas, like Arlington and Fort Worth, you'll probably be better off with an automobile. Be advised, though, that if your hotel doesn't have parking, street parking can be an expensive hassle in the downtown area.

The major car-rental agencies, which have outlets at DFW and Love Field airports and at several addresses throughout the Metroplex, include **Alamo** (© 800/462-5266; www.alamo.com), **Avis** (© 800/230-4898; www.avis.com), **Budget** (© 800/527-0700; www.budget.com), **Dollar** (© 800/800-3665; www.dollar.com), **Enterprise** (© 800/736-8222; www.enterprise.com), **Hertz** (© 800/654-3131; www.hertz.com), **National** (© 800/227-7368; www.nationalcar.com), and **Thrifty** (© 800/847-4389; www.thrifty.com).

*Note:* Yellow lights do little to slow down drivers in Dallas; even the running of red lights seems to have become epidemic in recent years, so be very careful before proceeding when the light turns green.

### By Taxi

Don't expect to hail a cab as you would in midtown Manhattan, though you will find taxis parked in front of the bigger, upscale hotels and at the airports. Mostly, though, you'll need to call a cab. Among the more than a dozen taxi companies are **Cowboy Cab Company** (© 214/428-0202) and **Yellow Checker** (© 214/426-6262).

Fares are $2.25 (initial drop) and 20¢ each additional ⅑ mile. Extras include a $2 extra passenger charge, a $3.60 airport exit fee, and a $2.60 airport drop-off fee.

# [Fast FACTS] DALLAS

**American Express** There are offices at 8317 Preston Center Plaza

(© **800/363-0214;** Mon–Fri 9am–6pm), and **Jim's Travel Link,** 1250 W.

Mockingbird Lane, Ste. 160 (© **214/**720-1000; Mon–Fri 8:30am–5pm).

**Babysitters** If your hotel doesn't provide baby-sitting, contact **Baby Sitters of Dallas** (© 214/692-1354; www.babysittersof dallas.com) for child care.

**Dentists** To find a local dentist, call © 800/DEN-TIST (336-8478).

**Doctors** The **Doctor Directory** at University of Texas Southwestern/St. Paul Medical Center, 5509 Harry Hines Blvd. (© 214/645-8300) is a physician's referral service that can direct you to an appropriate health professional or specialist.

**Drugstores** There are 24-hour **CVS** drugstores located at 10455 N. Central Expwy. at Meadow (© 214/369-3872), and 703 Preston Forest Center (© 214/363-1571). Others include **Kroger,** 17194 Preston Rd. at Campbell Road (© 972/931-9371), and **Albertsons,** 7007 Arapaho Rd. (© 972/387-8977).

**Hospitals** Major hospitals include the **Baylor University Medical Center,** 3500 Gaston Ave. (© 880/4BAYLOR [422-9567], or for 24-hr. emergency, 214/820-2501; www.baylor health.com); the **Children's Medical Center of Dallas,** 1935 Motor St. (© 214/456-7000; www.childrens.com); and **Presbyterian Hospital of Dallas,** 8200 Walnut Hill Lane, at Greenville Avenue

(© 214/345-6789; www.texashealth.org).

**Internet Access** The **Visitor Information Office** (© 214/571-1301; www.visitdallas.com) at the Old Red Courthouse (Houston, Main, and Commerce sts.) has computers with Internet access for an hourly fee. Decidedly hipper is **Main Street Internet,** 2656 Main St. (© 214/237-1121); it's got a full bar, overstuffed couches, and occasional live music.

**Maps** The Visitor Information Offices at DFW Airport and the Old Red Courthouse (at Houston, Main, and Commerce sts.) have several maps of varying detail of Dallas and the surrounding area. If that's not enough, contact **MAP Dallas/Fort Worth** (© 817/949-2225), which provides free street maps and visitor guides.

**Newspapers & Magazines** Both the *Dallas Morning News* "Weekend Guide" (which comes out on Fri; guidelive.com) and the *Dallas Observer* (www.dallasobserver.com), a free weekly, have plenty of current information on the arts, entertainment, and dining. *D Magazine,* a local monthly, has similar listings, as well as restaurant reviews. *Dallas Voice* is a free weekly serving Dallas's gay and

lesbian community, with listings of upcoming events.

**Police** For a police emergency, dial © 911; for nonemergencies, call © 214/742-1519 or 972/574-4454. The main precinct headquarters is located at 334 S. Hall, in the central business district (© 214/670-5840).

**Post Office** The central post office, 400 N. Ervay St. (© 800/275-8777 or 214/760-4700), is open Monday through Saturday from 8:30am to 5pm.

**Safety** In most areas during the day, Dallas is as safe as any big American city. You should exercise particular care, though, around Fair Park and after 7pm in downtown. Gay and lesbian travelers should exercise caution in the Oak Lawn section; though this area has the greatest concentration of gay residents and establishments, harassment has historically been a problem.

**Taxes** The general sales tax is 8.25%, hotel tax is 15%, and restaurant tax is 7%.

**Transit Information** For public transportation questions, call © 214/979-1111.

**Weather** For weather information, call © 214/787-1111; for current time and temperature, call © 214/844-6611.

# WHERE TO STAY

If you're in Dallas for a business trip or just a brief vacation, or are hoping to avoid too much time on Dallas freeways, you'll do well to choose your hotel according to neighborhood. Some of the city's best hotels are downtown near the central business area and Dallas Arts District, and in the fashionable area called Uptown, but many more hotels (especially more affordable chains) are nestled in North Dallas and near Irving. For most people, the latter locations will involve considerably more highway time, because Dallas is so spread out.

Dallas has a bundle of excellent lodgings at the top end, many chic and modern, but some with a surprisingly old-world feel. The majority of hotels in the city are large, well run, and aimed squarely at business travelers, though some very appealing boutique hotels have also taken root. The best of the cheaper lodgings are all-suite hotels. *Note:* Reservations in Dallas are toughest to come by when conventions take over the city. Check as early as possible with the **Dallas Convention & Visitors Bureau** (see "Visitor Information," earlier in this chapter) to find out if your visit coincides with major business traffic to the city.

Virtually all hotels offer some deals, especially on weekends when their business clientele dries up; check the individual hotels' websites for special online offers. The hotel occupancy tax in Dallas is 15%.

## DOWNTOWN
### Expensive

**The Adolphus Hotel** ★★    Built in 1912 by the Missouri beer baron Adolphus Busch, the grande dame of Dallas hotels exudes luxury and refinement. In the midst of the financial district, just a couple of blocks from another, more contemporary landmark—Neiman Marcus—this Beaux Arts hotel is a world of baroque splendor and deep pampering: dark-wood parlors, beautiful art and antiques such as 17th-century Flemish tapestries and crystal chandeliers, a grand ballroom, and an opulent dining room. Rooms are very large and tastefully appointed in English country-house style, with marble bathrooms and separate sitting and dining areas. The suites are Texas large. The graceful, old-world style of the Adolphus is epitomized by the three-course English tea served in the lobby living room on Saturday from 3 to 5pm. The longtime favorite **French Room** (p. 72), serving classic French cuisine, remains one of Dallas's finest restaurants; it is about as baroque a dining room as you'll find in town.

1321 Commerce St. (at Akard), Dallas, TX 75202. ℰ **800/221-9083** or 214/742-8200. Fax 214/651-3563. www.hoteladolphus.com. 422 units. $159–$299 double; from $219 suite. Special theme packages available. AE, DC, DISC, MC, V. Valet parking $24. DART: Akard. Pets 30 lbs. and under accepted with $50 fee. **Amenities:** 2 restaurants, including the French Room; bar/grill; free airport transfers; concierge; exercise room; access to nearby health club; room service. *In room:* A/C, TV, TV/DVD (in some), Wi-Fi (free).

**The Magnolia** ★    Located in the city's most famous building, the landmark 1922 headquarters of Magnolia (later Mobil) Oil—known by its illuminated rooftop sign sculpture of Pegasus, the winged horse—this hotel is one of the most prized properties leading a renaissance in the heart of downtown. Many of the building's original architectural details have been lovingly preserved. The hotel is refined and state of the art, with a terrific fitness center and business facilities. Rooms are quite a bit larger than most and handsomely designed in contemporary style, with leather club chairs and sleek desks, and many are two-bedroom suites with full kitchens, perfect for families or longer business stays. The Magnolia Room, which occupies the entire second floor, is a great place to unwind: It has a stocked library, billiards, TV, bar, and Wi-Fi, and a breakfast buffet, evening cocktails, and bedtime milk and cookies (all complimentary) are served there. Shoppers will be happy to discover that the original Neiman Marcus is just down the block.

1401 Commerce St., Dallas, TX 75201. ℰ **888/915-1110** or 214/915-6500. Fax 214/253-0053. www. magnoliahoteldallas.com. 330 units. $199–$279 double; $329–$500 suite. Rates include breakfast buffet. Weekend packages available. AE, DC, DISC, MC, V. Valet parking $22. DART: Akard. **Amenities:** Coffee shop; bar/lounge; babysitting; concierge; health club and spa; room service. *In room:* A/C, TV, hair dryer, minibar, Wi-Fi (free).

## Moderate

**Belmont Hotel** ★★★ 🍴  Though retro chic is all the rage, no place in Dallas does it more authentically than this hipster boutique hotel at the edge of Oak Cliff (a 5-min. drive from downtown). Rising from the ashes of a 1946 motor lodge, and from a bluff with panoramic views of downtown Dallas, it's a great spot for arts-, architecture-, and design-conscious individuals to stay—and feel like they're not in Dallas. It does midcentury modern with real style, but without the heavy dose of glamour that other new hotels insist on. It's cozy and comfortable, with a variety of rooms spread out over four distinctly different buildings, including garden rooms, two-story loft suites, and bungalow rooms. Accommodations echo the spare aesthetic of the period, but add nice doses of warmth and color. Bonuses include flatscreen TVs, plush robes, Kiehl's products, and SMOKE, a cool barbecue restaurant, making this nifty little place an excellent value. An outdoor terrace and lounge area frame the Big D skyline at sunset, and the lounge bar, BarBelmont, has become the watering hole of choice for the cognoscenti fleeing the slick Uptown scene.

901 Fort Worth Ave. (Oak Cliff, 1 block north of the I-30/Sylvan Rd. exit), Dallas, TX 75208. ☎ **866/870-8010** or 214/393-2000. www.belmontdallas.com. 64 units. $109–$160 double; $179–$240 suite. AE, DC, DISC, MC, V. Valet parking $15; self-parking free. **Amenities:** Restaurant; bar; health club; outdoor heated pool; room service. *In room:* A/C, TV, hair dryer, minibar, Wi-Fi (free).

**The Corinthian Bed and Breakfast** ★★ 🎁  B&Bs aren't much of a Dallas thing, and, in truth, the Corinthian is closer to a boutique hotel than a traditional B&B. As such, it's a great alternative in Big D. On the east side of Central Expressway, north of Deep Ellum and near Swiss Avenue, the house is an exceedingly handsome 1905 structure—which once served as a boardinghouse for young ladies and was converted to a B&B in 2001—with a formal dining room, a handsome parlor (complete with the original fireplace and antique grand piano), a grand staircase, and a modern carriage house backing the backyard. The rooms are ample, cozy and very tastefully decorated with antique pieces, elegant without trying too hard. Gourmet breakfasts are a source of pride.

4125 Junius St., Dallas, TX 75246. ☎ **866/598-9988** or 214/818-0400. Fax 214/818-0401. www.corinthianbandb.com. 5 units. $129–$219 double. AE, DC, DISC, MC, V. Free parking. *In room:* A/C, TV, hair dryer, Wi-Fi (free).

**SpringHill Suites Dallas Downtown/West End** 🍴  If you want to be right in the thick of it—within walking distance of the restaurants and rowdy bars of the West End, the Sixth Floor Museum and Dealey Plaza, the Arts District, and downtown's business district—but don't want to burn through your savings or the company per diem, this Marriott property (formerly an AmeriSuites hotel) is a good, safe, and convenient choice. The good-size, comfortable suites have basic kitchenettes and sleeper sofas—nothing fancy, but solid accommodations. Visiting businesspeople should find the business center to their liking, while more leisure-oriented visitors should take to the second-floor outdoor pool, which, though small, has privileged views of the Big D skyline.

1907 N. Lamar St. (at Corbin), Dallas, TX 75202. ☎ **888/287-9400** or 214/999-0500. Fax 214/999-0501. www.marriott.com. 148 units. $149–$189 double. Rates include breakfast buffet. AE, DC, DISC, MC, V. Valet parking $22. DART: West End. **Amenities:** Concierge; exercise room; heated outdoor pool; room service. *In room:* A/C, TV, fridge, Wi-Fi (free).

## UPTOWN & OAK LAWN
### Very Expensive

**Hôtel St. Germain** ★★★   The St. Germain is blissfully out of place in Dallas. The tiny, intimate boutique hotel and restaurant, a Relais & Châteaux property, envelops guests in old-world luxury and romance, with a library, parlors, and sumptuous style that borders on bordello. The seven suites are individually decorated with antiques from late-19th-century France and New Orleans, and pampering features include wood-burning fireplaces, tapestries, draped Napoleon sleigh beds, bidets, and Jacuzzis and soaking tubs. Indulgence is rarely cheap and, of course, it isn't here (though the two largest and most expensive suites really skew the price range); but you get a lot of refined white-glove treatment for the price of admission. The romantic restaurant, which overlooks an ivy-covered garden courtyard and serves a seven-course, prix-fixe candlelight gourmet dinner (Tues–Sat for $85 per person), is ideal for a special occasion (jackets required) or merely a superior meal. The parlorlike Champagne Bar achieves the impossible by feeling like Paris in Dallas.

2516 Maple Ave. (at Mahon St.), Dallas, TX 75201. ℂ **214/871-2516.** Fax 214/871-0740. www.hotelst germain.com. 7 units. $290–$650 suite. Rates include continental breakfast. AE, DC, DISC, MC, V. Valet parking $25. DART: Pearl. **Amenities:** Restaurant; concierge; nearby health club; room service. *In room:* A/C, TV/DVD/VCR, hair dryer, minibar, Wi-Fi (free).

**The Ritz-Carlton, Dallas** ★★   The boom predicted for the Victory Park area, marketed as a spiffier Dallas version of Times Square, rides as much on new, buzzed-about, five-star luxury properties like the Ritz as it does on the district's centerpiece, the American Airlines Center. The good news, then, is that this high-rise hotel and condo building does not disappoint. With amenities like Dean Fearing's ballyhooed restaurant **Fearing's** (p. 75), a 12,000-square-foot spa, a rooftop pool and deck, a massive ballroom, and expansive views, it pretty much defines what a luxury hotel in Dallas should be. Rooms (occupying the first eight floors; those reaching to the 21st floor are private residences) are huge and elegantly appointed, with rich fabrics, Frette linens, and Bulgari bath products. While it's the perfect place for well-heeled guests whose tastes do not run to the chic modern minimalism so popular in new designer hotels, it's not overdone or stuffy, either. Rather, it feels gently contemporary.

2121 McKinney Ave., Dallas, TX 75201. ℂ **214/922-0200.** Fax 214/922-4707. www.ritzcarlton.com. 218 units. $399–$519 double; from $569 suite. AE, DC, DISC, MC, V. Valet parking $15 day, $25 overnight. DART: Pearl. Pets 25 lbs. and under accepted with $125 fee. **Amenities:** Restaurant (Fearing's); 2 bars; lounge; concierge; concierge-level rooms; exercise room; outdoor heated pool; room service; spa. *In room:* A/C, TV/DVD, CD player, hair dryer, minibar, Wi-Fi (free).

**Rosewood Mansion on Turtle Creek** ★★★   As a place where movie stars, princes, and presidents stay, and the rest of us paupers merely dream about, the hilltop Mansion, usually lauded as the most desirable hotel in Dallas, is luxury personified. Whereas the Adolphus (see above) has an old-world moneyed feel, the Mansion has a brasher new-money atmosphere. It is perhaps the top place in the state for a blowout splurge. If it feels like a home—albeit a very grand and showy one—that's because it was the spectacular residence of a Texas cotton magnate in the 1920s and 1930s. The Mansion, now a Rosewood hotel, is all marble floors, inlaid wood ceilings, and stained-glass windows. Regular rooms are gargantuan, as are the beds and bathrooms, and the suites ridiculously so. The hotel's recent restyling of rooms, adding more sedate colors and a contemporary look, is an unqualified success. Service is faultless across-the-board. The **Mansion Restaurant** (p. 75), which received a makeover after the departure of chef Dean Fearing, no longer focuses on Southwestern fare, but it continues to be one of Dallas's finest hotel dining experiences.

2821 Turtle Creek Blvd. (off Cedar Springs Rd.), Dallas, TX 75219. © **888-ROSEWOOD** (767-3966) or 214/599-2100. Fax 214/528-4187. www.mansiononturtlecreek.com. 143 units. $375–$550 double; from $695 suite. Weekend rates and other packages available. AE, DC, DISC, MC, V. Valet parking $25. Small pets allowed with surcharge. **Amenities:** Restaurant; bar; babysitting; concierge; exercise room; health club; outdoor heated pool; room service. *In room:* A/C, TV/DVD, hair dryer, minibar, MP3 docking station, Wi-Fi.

**W Dallas-Victory** ★   This splashy property, part of the ever-expanding W chain, rises with glass-happy hubris on the Big D skyline, and it's received oodles of attention from locals hip to the newest big thing on the scene. Principal among its attractions are the trendy Ghostbar and the local incarnation of Craft, a New York City restaurant that's taken up residence in the W. The hotel, near downtown and the chic shopping and restaurant destinations of Uptown, is a striking, 15-story tower (including pricey residential condos) with a 16th-floor infinity pool. Inside, it's stylishly minimalist, if noticeably self-conscious. Rooms have plenty of rich, spare style, with colored tile bathrooms, swank furnishings and fabrics, and large windows. Accommodations aren't merely double or deluxe units; they're called "spectacular rooms," "wonderful rooms," "fabulous rooms," "mega rooms," and, not to be outdone by adjectives, "wow suites" and "extreme wow suites." That may strike some as just a little too precious; for much less dough, I'd haul my bags over to the Palomar (p. 69) if contemporary styling at a reasonable price is what you want. But visitors with toy dogs in tow (yes, pets are welcome) will undoubtedly be happy here; the Ghostbar even comes with its own helipad, and there's a 10,000-square-foot Bliss Spa for all the required pampering.

2440 Victory Park Lane (next to the American Airlines Center), Dallas, TX 75219. © **877/WHOTELS** (946-8357) or 214/397-4100. Fax 214/397-4105. www.whotels.com/dallas. 252 units. $309–$599 double; from $429 suite. AE, DC, DISC, MC, V. Valet parking $20. DART: Victory. Pets accepted for $25 per day plus $100 cleaning fee. **Amenities:** 2 restaurants; bar; state-of-the-art exercise room; outdoor heated infinity pool; room service; spa. *In room:* A/C, TV, DVD/CD player, hair dryer, minibar, MP3 docking station, Wi-Fi ($10 per day).

## Expensive

**Hotel ZaZa** ★   Dallas's former "it" hotel now has a host of competitors as the place to be seen, but the ZaZa remains confident and brash, its style appealing to the young and fabulous, fashionable, and merely wealthy. The ZaZa is like a cocktail of Vegas and Los Angeles as served up in Dallas, but with the friendliness common in Texas. If you're tired of bland upscale hotels, check out this wildly unique, four-story boutique lodging at the southern end of McKinney Avenue. A business hotel for many in the arts-and-entertainment world, it's a (pet-friendly) pleasurefest of exclusive style. Standard rooms are decorated with plush fabrics and relatively understated good taste. But the real stars are the spacious, over-the-top Concept suites, with themed decor (ranging from Out of Africa and Erotica to the expected Texas and, no lie, the Shag-a-delic suite) and balconies, and massive Magnificent Seven suites, which are more like apartments. The eye-popping Dragonfly restaurant and cocktail lounge are fixtures in the Big D nightlife firmament, and the Zen-like ZaSpa continues the hotel's sybaritic overtures. Some guests will definitely feel like the place is trying too hard to be cool, and customer service often leaves something to be desired.

2332 Leonard St. (at McKinney), Dallas, TX 75201. © **800/597-8399** or 214/468-8399. Fax 214/468-8397. www.hotelzaza.com. 145 units. $225–$300 double; $350–$1,000 suite. Special packages available. AE, DC, DISC, MC, V. Valet parking $20. DART: Pearl. Pets accepted with $50 fee. **Amenities:** Restaurant; bar; babysitting; concierge; exercise room; outdoor pool; room service; spa. *In room:* A/C, TV hair dryer, minibar, Wi-Fi (free).

**Stoneleigh Hotel & Spa** ★★★ A fixture of Dallas since 1923, the new Stoneleigh is hardly recognizable after a $36-million renovation—and that's a good thing. The once run-down hotel was lovingly brought back to its original grandeur in 2008, and it has style to burn, with the welcoming feel of a large, luxury boutique hotel. The makeover hasn't erased the hotel's Art Deco foundations, thankfully, most evident in public rooms and the Studio Suites, my favorite rooms here. The Stoneleigh explodes with vibrant color and rich surfaces, including deep-red or grass-green walls and shiny black marble sink countertops in some bathrooms. For a real treat, ask for a tour of the Penthouse, a historic apartment that's one of Dallas's grandest spaces. Featuring bold original art by Texas artists, a 5,000-square-foot spa, and a swank Art Deco–style Bolla Bar, the hotel is a haven for business travelers and vacationing hipsters alike. In a quieter section of Uptown, this place has a uniquely intimate and exclusive feel for a large hotel, and can even be quite a good deal—check online for significantly discounted prices.

2927 Maple Ave. (at Randall St.), Dallas, TX 75201. ② **800/921-8498** or 214/871-7111. www.stoneleigh hotel.com. 170 units. $259–$480 double; $550–$650 suite. AE, DC, DISC, MC, V. Valet parking $20. **Amenities:** Restaurant; bar; babysitting; state-of-the-art exercise room; concierge; room service; spa. *In room:* A/C, TV, hair dryer, Wi-Fi (free).

## Moderate

**Bailey's Uptown Inn** ★★ 🏨 Although bigger is usually thought better in Dallas, this is a case where smaller—at least for those who appreciate the intimacy of a small inn—is more delightful. Innkeeper Andrea Freidheim has fashioned a terrific boutique retreat in the midst of happening Uptown. In an attractive two-story townhouse are just five elegantly designed, spacious rooms (named for their color scheme), which are sedate and filled with handsome antique pieces and personality, without veering into precious B&B territory. The two rooms on the second floor have their own private balconies, but decorwise I'm partial to the chocolate room (either the power of suggestion or a nod to my chocolate Labrador). The living room downstairs has a lovely fireplace and piano, and makes a great place to meet others or gather if you're with a group. A nice feature is that if you're not a breakfast person, you can skip it and get a cheaper rate. (A full breakfast is served only on weekends, anyway.) This is a great little find, with plenty of personality that corporate Dallas often lacks.

2505 Worthington St., Dallas, TX 75204. ② **214/720-2258.** Fax 214/292-9557. www.baileysuptowninn. com. 5 units. $179–$219 double. AE, DISC, MC, V. Free parking. *In room:* A/C and fan, TV, Wi-Fi (free).

**Warwick Melrose Hotel Dallas** ★ This is another one of Dallas's upscale hotels with an old-world, rather than an Old West, atmosphere. In the heart of the Oak Lawn neighborhood, near the nightlife of Cedar Springs and Turtle Creek, the midsize Melrose feels like a gracious old neighbor. Built in 1924, the eight-floor hotel was once a favorite of artists and entertainers such as Arthur Miller, Elizabeth Taylor, and Luciano Pavarotti. The revamped hotel today is a model of refined taste and caters mostly to executives and couples on weekend getaways. No two rooms are alike, though they are uniformly luxurious and inviting, with 10-foot ceilings, crown molding, antiques, and marble-tiled bathrooms. The renovated Landmark restaurant consistently wins accolades, and the stately Library Bar is a terrific spot for a nightcap.

3015 Oak Lawn Ave. (at Cedar Springs Rd.), Dallas, TX 75219. ② **214/521-5151.** Fax 214/521-2470. www. warwickmelrosedallas.com. 184 units. $179–$249 double; $349 suite. Weekend and Internet-only rates available. AE, DC, DISC, MC, V. Valet parking $24. **Amenities:** Restaurant; bar; concierge; exercise room; nearby health club; room service. *In room:* A/C and fan, TV, hair dryer, minibar, MP3 docking station, Wi-Fi ($11 per day).

## NORTH & EAST DALLAS
### Expensive

**The Guest Lodge at Cooper Aerobics Center** ★ ⛺ Worried that every time you go on vacation you seem to put on a few pounds? Then I've got the place for you. This inviting retreat at one of the nation's foremost health facilities, the Cooper Clinic, is set on 30 acres of trees, trails, and duck ponds in North Dallas. The small hotel—called the "second-healthiest hotel in the country" by *USA Today*—remains a well-kept secret, a place to unwind and work off stress and pounds. The spacious, comfortable rooms have French doors that open onto private balconies. But the best part is that guests have complimentary access to the Cooper Fitness Center, which is connected to the famous sports clinic named for Dr. Kenneth Cooper, the author of a dozen fitness books and one of the most influential figures in American fitness training and diagnostics. The facilities include a 40,000-square-foot health club, lighted tennis courts, pools, and a running track, as well as a Mediterranean-style spa for all manner of relaxing body treatments. You can't very well stay at a place like this without eating healthfully, so most guests take full advantage of the complimentary full continental breakfast and "heart-healthy" fare at the Colonnade Room restaurant.

12230 Preston Rd. (at Churchill), Dallas, TX 75230. ⒸⓅ **800/444-5187** or 972/386-0306. Fax 972/386-2942. www.cooperaerobics.com. 62 units. $189–$269 double; $399–$505 suite. Rates include continental breakfast. All-inclusive spa packages available. AE, DC, DISC, MC, V. Free parking. **Amenities:** Restaurant; babysitting; health club and spa; heated outdoor pool; room service; tennis court (lighted). *In room:* A/C, TV, hair dryer, minibar, Wi-Fi (free).

**Palomar Dallas** ★★★ A superb reimagining of a '60s-era Hilton has created one of Dallas's most fashionable hotels. Respecting just enough of its midcentury bones, the Palomar struts its stuff with chic retro glamour. This Kimpton hotel not only competes with, but even upstages, some of the big boys on the scene. Public areas exude midcentury-modern cool, while rooms feel contemporary, with brightly colored accents and elegant furnishings and bedding. Executive king rooms, usually occupying corner locations, are especially spacious and comfortable. Unusual for a hotel of this class, pets are very welcome (there were about a half-dozen dogs on hand for morning coffee during my last visit). Amenities include a chic outdoor infinity pool, a plush Exhale Spa with yoga classes, and a restaurant and bar, Central 214, which looks like an updated, swank Palm Springs hangout. Service throughout the hotel is impeccable and very friendly, and special needs are met very well, such as the "Bone Appetite" package that welcomes four-legged guests.

5300 E. Mockingbird Lane (at Central Expwy.), Dallas, TX 75206. ⒸⓅ **888/253-9030** or 214/520-7969. Fax 214/520-8025. www.hotelpalomar-dallas.com. 198 units. $269–$309 double; $369–$489 suite. AE, DC, DISC, MC, V. Valet parking $20. DART: Mockingbird. Pets accepted. **Amenities:** 2 restaurants; bar; concierge; exercise room; outdoor heated infinity pool; room service; spa. *In room:* A/C, TV/DVD, CD player, hair dryer, minibar, MP3 docking stations, Wi-Fi (free).

### Moderate

**Embassy Suites Dallas—Park Central Area** ☺ ⚡ In far North Dallas, on the edge of the bedroom community Richardson (my hometown), this hotel recently underwent a multimillion-dollar restoration. It's equally comfortable for families and business travelers (especially those with Texas Instruments and the telecom businesses along the corridor just north on Central Expwy.). Rooms, built around a huge, airy atrium, are all suites; they're more comfortable, warmer, and less generic than many at this price, and they have separate living areas and sleeper sofas. The indoor pool and Jacuzzi are an unexpected bonus.

13131 N. Central Expwy. (just north of LBJ Fwy.), Dallas, TX 75243. © **888/254-0637** or 972/234-3300. Fax 972/437-9863. www.embassysuites1.hilton.com. 279 units. $119–$189 double. Rates include full breakfast and manager's reception. Special discounts available. AE, DC, DISC, MC, V. Free parking. Pets 25 lb. or under accepted with $25 fee. **Amenities:** Restaurant; bar; state-of-the-art exercise room; Jacuzzi; indoor pool; room service. *In room:* A/C, TV, fridge, hair dryer, Internet ($10 per day), minibar.

**Hotel Lumen ★ 👔**   An unexpected delight in the Park Cities area, right next to the SMU campus, this stylish, discreet boutique hotel has plenty of contemporary panache and confidence, with luxurious midcentury-modern-inspired rooms and a dark, swanky bar and restaurant, Social. Though it targets a hip crowd of upscale business, media, and arts patrons, it's also well priced, and it's even pet-friendly (pets stay for no extra charge). Accommodations, done in rich chocolates and creams, feature angular desks, plasma TVs, plush linens, and cool tiled bathrooms. The most enticing rooms, the Spectra studios, are very spacious and have large picture windows with LED lighting facing Hillcrest Avenue and SMU. Though the Lumen's larger sister hotel, the Palomar (see above), is a cut above, this small hotel is a good choice for anyone looking for a quiet stay in chic surroundings.

6101 Hillcrest Ave. (just north of Mockingbird Lane), Dallas, TX 75205. © **214/219-2400.** Fax 214/219-2402. www.hotellumen.com. 52 units. $179–$229 double; $239–$279 suite. AE, DC, DISC, MC, V. Valet parking $13. Pets accepted. **Amenities:** Restaurant; bar; concierge; access to nearby fitness center; room service. *In room:* A/C, TV/DVD, movie library, CD player, hair dryer, kitchenette (in suites), minibar, Wi-Fi (free).

**Hyatt Summerfield Suites Dallas/Lincoln Park ★ ☺ 🏷**   Recently acquired by Hyatt, this residential-style hotel remains a very good value, popular with business visitors who often stay for a week or more. The colorful and spacious suites have fully equipped kitchens, and look like apartments as decorated by West Elm. (There are three different floor plans to choose from, but for most visitors, the least expensive room is sufficient.) The attractive outdoor pool is a nice bonus for families. Conveniently located in the Park Cities district, off Central Expressway and near NorthPark Center and Northwest Highway, the hotel is just 10 minutes from downtown (unless you catch rush hour) and even nearer to the nightlife options of Greenville and McKinney avenues. There are four other Summerfield Suites locations in the Dallas area, including in Uptown.

8221 N. Central Expwy. (U.S. 75 at Northwest Hwy.), Dallas, TX 75225. © **866/974-9288** or 214/696-1555. Fax 214/696-1550. www.hyatt.com/hyatt/summerfield. 155 units. $109–$159 1-bedroom suite; $219–$249 2-bedroom suite. Rates include breakfast buffet. Weekend rates available. AE, DISC, MC, V. Parking $6. Pets accepted with $250 fee. **Amenities:** Exercise room; Jacuzzi; outdoor pool. *In room:* A/C, TV/DVD, hair dryer, Internet (free), kitchen, minibar.

## NEAR THE AIRPORT
### Very Expensive

**Four Seasons Resort and Club at Las Colinas ★★ ☺**   Plenty of visitors come to Dallas to work, but at the Four Seasons, they also come to play, and seriously. With one of the top golf courses in the area (off limits to nonguests), this is the place to stay if you have to play golf and just any old course won't do. The pros show up to play the PGA Byron Nelson Classic here every May, and the course consistently wins accolades as one of the best in the nation. Other sports enthusiasts will also be happy: The laid-back, but luxurious property was a top-of-the-line sports club before it became a resort hotel, and there are tennis courts, pools, tracks, and a full-service European spa on the 400-acre grounds. Guest rooms are large, airy, and elegant; golf villa rooms have terraces overlooking the 18th green or the handsomely landscaped

# FAMILY-FRIENDLY hotels

**Embassy Suites Dallas–Park Central Area** (p. 69)   Large and airy, with glass elevators that stream up the interior of a huge central atrium, this hotel welcomes the whole family—even pets. Distractions include a nice pool, complimentary full breakfasts, and racquetball courts. For parents, there are free cocktails every evening.

**Four Seasons Resort and Club at Las Colinas** (p. 70)   Your kids don't have to be golfers, but if they're into

any sports at all, this resort should seem like an amusement park to them, with tennis courts, three outdoor pools, and one indoor pool, as well as a host of complimentary children's programs.

**Hyatt Summerfield Suites Dallas/Lincoln Park** (p. 70)
Conveniently located near North Park, this residential-style hotel has suites that are like apartments and a nice little outdoor pool where you can cool off.

pool garden. Families will appreciate the "Kids for All Seasons" program with activities and special attention for younger guests. The hotel is only about 15 minutes from DFW Airport.

4150 N. MacArthur Blvd. (at Mills Lane), Irving, TX 75038. ℭ **800/819-5053** or 972/717-0700. Fax 972/717-2550. www.fourseasons.com/dallas. 431 units. $295–$395 double; from $750 suite. Rates include use of sports club and spa; greens fees $195. Weekend rates, sports and other packages available. AE, DC, DISC, MC, V. Valet parking $20. **Amenities:** 2 restaurants; bar; lounge; babysitting; children's programs; concierge; golf course; exercise room; 1 indoor/3 outdoor pools; room service; spa; 8 lit outdoor/4 indoor tennis courts; *In room:* A/C, TV, CD player, hair dryer, minibar, Wi-Fi ($10 per day).

### Inexpensive

**Comfort Suites DFW Airport** 🖢   As its name makes clear, this agreeable chain hotel offers convenience to travelers on their way in or out of Dallas, including free airport transportation. What you'll find are good, standard-size rooms (though some are a bit tight), and a range of services and amenities, including a small outdoor pool and fitness center, designed to make your short stay hassle-free. One-bedroom suites feature extra sofa sleepers in the living room and large work desks, while executive rooms sport cathedral ceilings and skylights, and some are equipped with whirlpool tubs. If you're not inclined to stay in your room and work, you can take advantage of the free breakfast.

4700 W. John Carpenter Fwy. (just south of I-114, btw. Esters and International Pkwy.), Irving, TX 75063. ℭ **877/424-6423** or 972/929-9097. Fax 972/929-9247. www.comfortsuites.com. 101 units. $64–$99 double; $110 suite. Rates include full breakfast. AE, DC, DISC, MC, V. Free parking. **Amenities:** Free airport transfers; exercise room; Jacuzzi; outdoor pool. *In room:* A/C, TV, fridge, hair dryer, Internet (free).

# WHERE TO DINE

It wasn't that long ago that the Dallas dining scene was pretty unexciting: It was mostly run-of-the-mill Mexican and Tex-Mex, with undistinguished steakhouses and halfhearted Southwestern themes. That has changed dramatically, and today the Dallas restaurant scene has exploded and become as sophisticated as anywhere in the country. While you can still get home cooking, Tex-Mex, and barbecue in abundance, Dallas has suddenly become resolutely cosmopolitan, with chic and sophisticated Pan-Asian, Italian, and Southwestern newcomers injecting life into the local dining scene, with a vigor that has even jolted the old stalwarts. Some of the hippest spots are in fashionable hotels, including the excellent **Fearing's** at the Ritz-Carlton Dallas; **Central 214** at Palomar Dallas; and **Craft** at W Dallas-Victory (see hotel reviews above). The Dallas Visitors Bureau once claimed there were four times more restaurants per capita in Dallas than in New York City; since I'm from the former and spend much of my time in the latter, I'm more than a bit dubious about such a claim, but it's certain that you won't suffer from lack of choice.

## DOWNTOWN & DEEP ELLUM
### Very Expensive

**The French Room** ★★ FRENCH/CONTINENTAL    Dinner here is the closest thing in Dallas to a state dinner at Versailles. This is the restaurant that will make the biggest impression on your dining companions (and perhaps, though not necessarily, on your credit card statement). The grand French Room—under an elaborate vaulted ceiling and crystal chandeliers in the historic Adolphus Hotel (p. 64)—is a standout, even if at times the food isn't quite the equal of the surroundings. Formal but not stuffy, with impeccable service, it's a place to feel like king and queen for a day. The three-course prix fixe and the five-course Chef's Tasting menu actually represent pretty good values for such a setting and all-around elegance and quality. From beef tenderloin with a black truffle-potato terrine to miso-marinated Alaskan halibut with baby shiitake and sweet potatoes in carrot-ginger sauce, the menu is superb throughout. Dessert may be a crème brûlée trio or, even better, the soufflé of the day (flavors change daily). As you might expect, the wine list is pricey, but there are also less expensive options. The ambience is formal: Jackets are required for men; no jeans or tennis shoes permitted.

In the Adolphus Hotel, 1321 Commerce St. (at Akard St.). ✆ **214/742-8200.** www.hoteladolphus.com/dining. Reservations required. Prix-fixe dinners $80–$150. AE, DC, DISC, MC, V. Tues–Sat 6–10pm. DART: Akard.

**Stephan Pyles Restaurant** ★★ NEW SOUTHWESTERN/INTERNATIONAL The local celebrity chef Stephan Pyles, a fifth-generation Texan, made his name with Southwestern cooking at Routh Street Café and then, most famously, Star Canyon, before taking a long hiatus. A few years ago, he returned to Dallas with a heap of fanfare and critical raves, establishing his eponymous restaurant downtown in the Arts District. Large, but not overwhelming in size, and flashy, but not ridiculously so, the restaurant is refined and cosmopolitan—a little like Dallas itself. It features exposed brick and Texas stone, an O'Keeffe-like stick chandelier, a copper-covered bar and dividing curtain, comfortably spaced tables, and semicircular leather-clad booths.

The main attraction of the dining room, though, is the huge, glass-enclosed kitchen. From it spills forth a delectable roster of Southwestern, Latin, and international dishes, opening with eight types of ceviche (available individually or in tasting groups), iced gazpacho shooters, and spit-roasted suckling pig and apple-pecan empanadas. Main courses boast similarly interesting twists, but don't try too hard to be cutting-edge. The boneless barbecued beef short rib, served with a salsa of tamal, criollo, and chipotle, is perfection, and a Star Canyon favorite, the bone-in cowboy rib-eye with red-chile onion rings and mushroom ragout, will also satisfy traditionalists. The wine list is about as good as it gets in Dallas, with an emphasis on lesser known finds from around the world as well as big-spender California cabernets and Bordeaux. Since dinner is a pricey endeavor, diners looking for value should check out lunch, which locals know to be a real bargain, with most main courses under $15.

1807 Ross Ave., Ste. 200 (at St. Paul St.). ✆ **214/580-7000.** www.stephanpyles.com. Reservations required. Main courses $29–$49. AE, DC, DISC, MC, V. Mon–Fri 11:30am–2pm; Mon–Wed 6–10:30pm; Thurs–Sat 6–11pm. DART: Akard.

## Expensive

**Local ★★** 🏨 NEW AMERICAN   With an arty, intimate, minimalist design that would be perfectly at home in Manhattan or San Francisco, this tiny but chic eatery inhabits Deep Ellum's Boyd Hotel, built in 1908 and the oldest standing hotel in Dallas. Though the neighborhood, once the hip spot downtown, has had a rough time of it, chef-owner Tracy Miller's Local continues to excel. Original walls (one with painted period outdoor advertising that reads TAKE CARDUI THE WOMAN'S TONIC) and hardwood floors have been preserved, adding a warm feel to the Eames chairs and black leatherette booths. With just 50 seats, the restaurant caters to the cognoscenti among Dallas diners, though the food has a decidedly homespun and laid-back angle. The well-executed menu is composed of "tall order" and "short order" dishes, with innovative twists on comfort food, including items such as hazelnut-mustard-crusted halibut, a buffalo burger basket, and mascarpone mac-and-cheese. The wine list has some hard-to-find selections from boutique producers. The chef's tasting menu, seven courses for $70, is a superb deal.

2936 Elm St. (at Malcolm X Blvd.). ℂ **214/752-7500.** www.localdallas.com. Reservations required. Main courses $20–$34. AE, DC, DISC, MC, V. Tues–Sat 6–10pm.

## Moderate

**Bolsa ★★** 🍴 NEW AMERICAN   In an airy, converted body shop in Oak Cliff, just west of the hip Bishop Arts District, this excellent new restaurant is emblematic of the new Dallas. Focusing on fresh farm-to-table, local organic ingredients and small plates in simple but urban-industrial-chic surroundings, this is far from the glitzy and glib Dallas of power lunches and steakhouse dinners. The fresh menu, which often features some unusual entries such as quail and sweetbreads, changes daily, but always has great salads, flatbreads, and bruschetta. The fantastic house cocktails and sweet outdoor patio make Bolsa a place to come back to again and again. The killer $10 lunch deal is one of the best in town, and the thoughtfully selected wine list featuring small producers tops out at $50.

614 W. Davis St. (Oak Cliff). ℂ **214/367-9367.** www.bolsadallas.com. Reservations recommended. Main courses $10–$24. AE, DC, DISC, MC, V. Mon–Fri 11am–10:30pm; Sat 11am–12am; Sun 11am–9pm.

**La Calle Doce ★** ☺ 🍴 MEXICAN/SEAFOOD   This cozy Mexican joint, in a modest old blue house in Oak Cliff, south of Dallas, has been one of the best home-style Mexican restaurants in the area for more than 25 years. A cult favorite, it deserves to be much better known. The extensive menu focuses on *nuevo* Mexican fish dishes, such as superb ceviche (fish and shrimp marinated with lime), Mexican seafood (such as octopus) cocktails, mahimahi tacos, and other main courses such as *chile relleno de mariscos* (poblano pepper stuffed with shrimp, scallops, octopus, and fish). They even do respectable Spanish paella, or you can opt for the more standard Tex-Mex plates. The soups, such as *sopa de pescado* (fish soup) and *caldo Xochitl* (Oaxacan-style chicken soup) make wonderful appetizers. The margaritas are among the best in town. If your kids like Mexican and Tex-Mex, they should feel like they're eating at Grandma's house—that is, if they call Grandma *abuela*.

415 W. 12th St. (btw. Zang and Tyler sts., west of I-35 E.). ℂ **214/941-4304.** www.lacalledoce-dallas.com. Reservations recommended. Main courses $8–$17. AE, DC, DISC, MC, V. Mon–Fri 11am–9:30pm; Sat 11am–10:30pm; Sun 11am–9pm.

**Monica's Acá y Allá ★** 🍴 TEX-MEX   Tex-Mex in a funky Deep Ellum setting— part restaurant, part bar, part dance floor—is the ticket at "Monica's Here and There," now in its second decade of consistent popularity. The inviting space is big on atmosphere, with deep-red bordello walls, a long pale-yellow banquet, and funky sconces, the perfect venue for high-volume salsa music and dressed-up margaritas (which are excellent, by the way). The creative menu offers new twists on Tex-Mex such as Mexican lasagna, snapper *verde* (in a green tomatillo sauce), and sirloin noir, as well as more traditional Mexican City specialties. If the food makes you want to get up and dance, feel free. Friday and Saturday nights, the place heats up like a loud nightclub; but Sunday afternoons and early evenings are quieter, and there are free Latin dance lessons. The inexpensive Sunday brunch (with $1 house margaritas) is rightly popular, and weeknight specials include half-price entrees on Tuesday and 75¢ margaritas on Wednesday. But one of the best bargains in the city is the daily lunch special for just $5. If you like Monica's, you'd be wise to check its sister restaurant, the more refined and upscale **Ciudad**, 3888 Oak Lawn Ave. in Turtle Creek Village (© **214/219-3141**); some locals have proclaimed it the finest Mexican eatery in town.

2914 Main St. © **214/748-7140.** www.monicas.com. Reservations recommended. Main courses $9–$17. AE, DISC, MC, V. Tues–Fri 11am–2pm; Tues–Thurs 5–10pm; Fri–Sat 5pm–midnight; Sat 11am–3pm; Sun 9am–3pm and 6–11pm.

## GREENVILLE AVENUE & EAST DALLAS
### Moderate

**Ali Baba Mediterranean Grill** 🌶 LEBANESE/MIDDLE EASTERN   Family-owned (two brothers and their mom, by way of Syria), Ali Baba—which has moved from its longtime Lower Greenville address to a spot near the Lakewood Theater—still draws crowds for its good, cheap Middle Eastern fare during limited dining hours. Don't be surprised to find a line of customers clamoring to get in. This plain, tiny place packs them in for great rich hummus, marinated beef, grilled chicken, falafel, and Syrian and Lebanese dishes like stuffed kibbe. The tabbouleh and signature rice dish, made with vermicelli and sautéed in seasoned olive oil, are standouts. If you find yourself in North Dallas rather than downtown, check out the newer, larger, and more upscale-looking **Ali Baba** in Richardson at 2103 N. Central Expwy. (© **972/437-1222**).

1901 Abrams Pkwy. © **214/823-8235.** www.alibabacafe.com. Main courses $10–$18. Tues–Sat 11:30am–2pm and 5:30–9pm.

**Matt's Rancho Martinez** ☺ 🌶 TEX-MEX   In the gently bohemian Lakewood neighborhood east of downtown, Matt's is a Tex-Mex favorite—the real deal. Simple and relaxed, with a nice patio deck, it's Texan to the core, and laid-back as can be (though it can get pretty noisy when the margarita-drinking hordes descend). Start with great chips and salsa, of course (or the renowned Bob Armstrong *queso* dip—stir the ingredients), and move on to the chiles rellenos topped with green sauce, raisins, and pecans. If you're not big into Tex-Mex, try the chicken-fried steak: Matt's version of the classic Texas dish even found its way into the pages of *Gourmet* magazine. Matt's has 10 different types of fajitas, grilled specials such as quail, and a dozen daily lunch specials, bargains at $7.25 (Mon–Sat and all day Tues).

6332 La Vista Dr. (at Gaston; Lakewood Theater Plaza). © **214/823-5517.** www.mattstexmex.com. Reservations recommended on weekends. Main courses $8–$20. AE, DISC, MC, V. Mon–Thurs 11am–10pm; Fri–Sat 11am–11pm.

## UPTOWN/OAK LAWN/NORTH DALLAS
### Very Expensive

**Bob's Steak & Chop House** ★★ STEAK   Consistently ranked one of the top steakhouses in the country, Bob's has the requisite masculine look down: dark and clubby with mahogany booths and crisp white table linens. But its USDA Prime steaks set it apart. Bob Sambol serves monster portions of wet-aged (a difference that steak connoisseurs will recognize), corn-fed Midwestern prime beef and sirloin filets. They're accompanied by "smashed" potatoes, heavy on butter, bits of chopped onion, and a honey-glazed whole carrot. That adds up to a ton of food. The porterhouse weighs in at 28 ounces; the signature, though, is a 20-ounce, bone-in prime rib broiled like a steak. Other entrees worth considering include a perfect rack of lamb, veal chop, and lobster. The chophouse salad—mixed greens with cucumber, tomato, bell pepper, onion, bacon, and hearts of palm—is splendid. Bob's is a bit homier than other big-time steakhouses; even though it gets plenty of businessmen in suits and boots, if you're not wearing a jacket, you won't feel out of place—especially in the back room, where diners wear denim. Serious cigar smokers are in luck, especially if they catch one of Bob's cigar dinners in which every course is served with a different cigar. Popular outposts of Bob's are now located in Plano (North Dallas) and even—heaven forbid!—San Francisco.

4300 Lemmon Ave. (at Wycliff Ave.). © **214/528-9446.** www.bobs-steakandchop.com. Reservations required. Main courses $22–$49. AE, DISC, MC, V. Mon–Thurs 5–10pm; Fri–Sat 5–11pm.

**Fearing's** ★★★ SOUTHWESTERN/NEW AMERICAN   Dean Fearing made a name for himself—perhaps the most famous name among Dallas chefs—in 21 years at the Mansion on Turtle Creek, where he was one of the kingpins of haute Southwestern cooking. When he left that comfortable home for his own, eponymous and exceedingly elegant restaurant ensconced within the sparkling new Ritz-Carlton hotel, it was obvious he was aiming high. His aim has proved sharper than ever, and Fearing's is the most talked-about restaurant in town, with plenty of expected Texan swagger. Two bars have become destinations: Rattlesnake Bar, the more old-money watering hole, and the outdoor Live Oak bar, a magnet for younger movers and shakers. There are four distinct dining areas, each with its own flavor and flair: the bustling Dean's Kitchen; the more refined Gallery; the charming, glass-walled Sendero, beneath a gorgeous Murano chandelier; and the outdoor Ocaso patio (diners' wishes are generally accommodated). Some of Fearing's Southwestern standards made the trip, including his famed tortilla soup. But some Asian-inflected menu items, including a scrumptious soy-glazed black cod, and inventive ones, like Nilgai antelope on a sauté of black truffles, cabbage, and wild boar sausage, also signal that Fearing's isn't about the past. It's about one of the most spectacular dining experiences in Big D, even if only part of that is about the food.

2121 McKinney Ave. (in the Ritz-Carlton, Dallas). © **214/922-4848.** www.fearingsrestaurant.com. Reservations required. Main courses $26–$48. AE, DC, DISC, MC, V. Mon–Fri 11:30am–2:30pm; Sat 11am–3pm; Mon–Thurs 6–10:30pm; Fri–Sun 6–11pm; Sun brunch 11:15am–3pm. DART: Akard.

**Mansion Restaurant at Rosewood Mansion on Turtle Creek** ★★ NEW AMERICAN/INTERNATIONAL   The Mansion—which has undergone several important changes in recent years, including adding a mouthful of a name—remains one of Dallas's biggest and best splurges. But it must now compete with the likes of Southwestern star chefs Stephan Pyles and Dean Fearing (formerly at the helm here) for the attention of the local and visiting glitterati. The high-end, signature Southwestern cuisine of a few years back is, for the most part, gone, too. The restaurant is now more cosmopolitan; the four sleekly contemporary dining areas, a product of a massive interior renovation, reflect the change in outlook (but the Mansion remains the priciest restaurant in town). Fresh seafood flown in daily is a focus, as are fresh local ingredients. Meat lovers will be happy to find a roasted veal chop and a prime filet with duck-fat fries. Committed foodies should opt for the chef's seasonal tasting menu (the six-course prix fixe is a comparatively good deal). Once rather stuffy, the Mansion's new, relaxed attitude is evident in the dress code: Jeans are now welcome. The blowout brunch remains a Dallas fixture.

2821 Turtle Creek Blvd. (off Cedar Springs Rd.). © 214/443-4747. www.mansiononturtlecreek.com/ dine1.cfm. Reservations required. Main courses $42–$55; prix-fixe tasting menu $115. AE, DC, DISC, MC, V. Mon–Sat 11:30am–2pm; Sun 11:10am–2:30pm; Sun–Thurs 6–10pm; Fri–Sat 6–11pm.

## Expensive

**Adelmo's Ristorante** 🏠TUSCAN   If Dallas gets to feel a little too slick and taken with newness, try this charming, traditional, and down-to-earth Italian eatery occupying a cute two-story house tucked into a nexus of high-end design and furnishings shops. Family-owned Adelmo's is a refreshing and unexpected find in the Knox-Henderson corridor. Adelmo's may not be fashionable, but it is as cozy and friendly as it looks, with excellent, personal service, and a good value to boot. In old-school fashion, entrees come with a dinner salad. Classic dishes include homemade pastas, of course, and *osso buco* (braised veal shanks). I dined on stuffed mushrooms and gnocchi, pork loin medallions Florentine, and a Gorgonzola-crusted buffalo rib-eye. The wine list has some delightful finds and good deals. Dallas has plenty of restaurants hoping to be the next big thing, but Adelmo's is content to be cool in its own skin.

4537 Cole Ave. (at Knox St.). © 214/559-0325. www.adelmos.com. Reservations recommended. Main courses $18–$39. AE, DC, DISC, MC, V. Mon–Fri 11:30am–2pm; Mon–Sat 6–10pm.

**Maximo** ★★ ☺ MEXICAN   Although this large but cozy North Dallas restaurant, specializing in exquisitely prepared and reasonably priced Mexico City specialties, has a devoted following, I'm always surprised how many people don't know about it. I can't help but think that if they did, it would easily displace their other go-to Mexican restaurants in the city. Among the standout dishes from across Mexico, including Puebla, Oaxaca and the Yucatán, are *aguja al cazo* (spicy braised short rib served with chipotle mac-and-cheese) and *pollo cocinado dos veces* (twice-cooked chicken in a corn husk). A great way to start the meal, and ideal for sharing, is the fresh guacamole or ceviche prepared at your table. The decor is clubby and sophisticated, with touches of Mexican silver and bursts of rich color, but without being self-conscious. The house margaritas are superb, but the Maximo Heat, with muddled fresh jalapeños, may be the top margarita in the state. Sunday's brunch buffet is a delicious steal at $16.

5301 Alpha Rd. (near the Galleria mall). © 972/233-5656. www.maximodallas.com. Reservations recommended. Main courses $14–$27. AE, DISC, MC, V. Mon–Thurs 11am–10pm; Fri–Sat 11am–11pm; Sun 10:30am–3pm and 5–9pm.

**Neighborhood Services Bar & Grill** ★★★ STEAK   There is just one thing that's frustrating about this wildly successful, clubby neighborhood eatery (in the parking lot of a shopping center) that executes everything with aplomb: It doesn't take reservations, and after being named by *D Magazine* as the city's Best New Restaurant in 2010, it takes some patience and even willpower to get a table. But the wait is well worth it. One of three restaurants in Dallas, all similarly named, by Nick Badovinus, it's the kind of place where you could easily become a regular—if it weren't for that pesky competition to sit down. This is surefire comfort food: It doesn't try too hard, other than aim for and achieve consistent, good-value pleasure. The big salads are spectacular; main courses such as carmelized Nantucket sea scallops and handmade pastas (among the dishes that change nightly) are delightful; cocktails are great, and the wine list is interesting and affordable. Although the indoor booths are nice, I usually angle for a table on the covered patio, which is a little less frenetic.

# FAMILY-FRIENDLY restaurants

**Fireside Pies** (p. 79) In a funky, energetic atmosphere, parents and kids can enjoy pecan wood–fired pies made from a creative list of fixin's and cheeses.

**Highland Park Pharmacy** (p. 79) This old-time soda fountain and lunch counter serves the food that kids and nostalgic parents should love: grilled-cheese sandwiches and chicken salad, followed by a milkshake or root beer float.

**La Calle Doce** (p. 73) This cheery, brightly painted Mexican home is sure to delight the kids. The parents can sample affordable but well-prepared seafood dishes, while the kids pig out on enchiladas and other familiar Tex-Mex.

**La Duni Latin Cafe** (p. 78) Latin American *tortas* and more are offered at this eclectic spot. Save room for dessert— the sweets are excellent.

**Matt's Rancho Martinez** (p. 74) Tex-Mex the way it was meant to be—simple and relaxed. The kids can start with the chips and salsa while Mom and Dad sip a margarita on the patio.

**Maximo** (p. 76) Parents can get sophisticated Mexican gourmet cuisine, including inventive cocktails, at reasonable prices, but it's not too adventuresome for families who want to branch out from run-of-the-mill Tex-Mex.

**Peggy Sue BBQ** (p. 79) An inexpensive, down-home, 1950s-style barbecue joint in a stylish neighborhood, Park Cities (near SMU). It has a more varied menu than most barbecue places, with a terrific salad bar and veggies.

**Sonny Bryan's Smokehouse** (p. 79) Kids may wonder if they're really on vacation when they sit down to eat at a one-armed school desk at this atmospheric little shack, but the beef sandwich with barbecue sauce, a heckuva sloppy Joe, should keep them from squirming.

**Urban Taco** (p. 78) Though it's a hipster location for good, authentic Mexico City tacos, this is also a stylish, family-friendly place to dabble in Mexican rather than Tex-Mex food.

10720 Preston Rd., Ste. 101. © **214/368-1101.** www.neighborhoodservicesdallas.com. Reservations not accepted. Main courses $17–$29. AE, DISC, MC, V. Mon–Sat 5–11pm.

**Trece Mexican Kitchen & Tequila Lounge** ★ MEXICAN This modern and sleek uptown restaurant and tequila bar—with more than 120 different tequilas on offer, including several on tap—cultivates a buzz among fashionable locals, but there's more to Trece than meets the eye. There's plenty to look at, including the patrons, but the sophisticated haute Mexican/Latin American cuisine and specialty cocktails aim higher than the restaurant's superficial appeal. Indulge or ignore the nightclub ambience, whichever your preference, and focus on the food, including delectable ceviche, guacamole prepared at your table, and chipotle-braised short ribs. Dishes more than stand up to the color-shifting LED screens, wenge wood, and high decibels. But a sedate evening this will not be. If it gets too noisy, ask for the tequila menu and join the fun.

4513 Travis St. © **214/780-1900.** www.trecerestaurant.com. Reservations required. Main courses $12–$25. AE, DISC, MC, V. Mon–Wed 5–10pm; Thurs–Sat 5:30pm–midnight; Sun 11am–10pm.

## Moderate

**Bread Winners Bakery & Bistro** ✦ AMERICAN/BAKERY With tables outside under trees on a relaxed patio and a display case full of scrumptious desserts just inside the door, it would be easy to think of this charming Uptown neighborhood joint as a place for a quick lunch or dessert and coffee. But step back into the series of dining rooms and you'll find a more serious restaurant, one specializing in well-executed American dishes with very fresh ingredients. In the warrenlike house that was once the legendary Andrew's (where I had a memorable first date with my wife eons ago), built around an enclosed courtyard, the restaurant is transformed into a romantic, easygoing dinner affair—still a great spot for a date after all these years. The pulled pork or fish tacos are excellent, and vegetarians will be pleased by a veggie menu (on request) as well as a long roster of pastas and salads. Of course, if all you want is a burger (okay, smoked-apple-bacon-Gorgonzola burger) or any of the couple of dozen sandwiches for lunch, or one of those diet-busting desserts, Bread Winners is a winner at that, too, and the weekend brunch is a perennial favorite. Check out the New Orleans–style Quarter Bar upstairs and its rooftop deck. Additional locations are at Inwood Village, 5560 W. Lover's Lane (© **214/351-3339**), and 4021 Preston Rd. (© **972/312-9300**) in Plano.

3301 McKinney Ave. (at Hall). © **214/754-4940**. www.breadwinnerscafe.com. Reservations recommended on weekends. Main courses $11–$25. AE, DC, DISC, MC, V. Mon–Sat 7am–4pm; Sun 9am–3pm; Wed–Sun 5–10pm. DART: Cityplace.

**La Duni Latin Cafe** ★ ☺ LATIN AMERICAN/BAKERY   How cool is a restaurant that has its own "artisan" car wash next door? One of my favorite spots to take my mom in Dallas, this popular place trots out fresh, carefully prepared, and tasty versions of favorites from across the Americas. Although it may be best known among diners with a sweet tooth for its sinful desserts and pastries, it's also a terrific spot for lunch and dinner (and brunch on weekends). Good appetizers include the stuffed *arepa* (cornmeal dough patty) and *empanadas criollas* (stuffed turnover pastries). Great for lunch is the array of yummy *tortas* (Latin sandwiches). And classic entrees include *pollo al aljibe,* quite a bit fancier than I've had in Cuba, and grilled *asado* (chimichurri-marinated beef). Desserts are not to be missed; the sweet and moist *cuatro leches* cake is nearly famous, but I'm just as fond of the cupcakes and triple-chocolate truffle cake. La Duni's fantastic cocktails, such as the famed margarinha and the *mojito,* also draw aficionados and give it a bit of a bar scene in the evening. Children will feel at home in the relaxed atmosphere, and they'll surely enjoy some of the simpler items on the menu, such as chicken-and-cheese enchiladas and quesadillas. But their eyes will really light up when they see the dessert counter. Look for the new La Duni Latin Kitchen in NorthPark Center, a great pit stop during shopping excursions.

4620 McKinney Ave. (just north of Knox). © **214/520-7300**. www.laduni.com. Reservations recommended. Main courses $7.50–$24. AE, DC, DISC, MC, V. Tues–Fri 11am–5pm; Sat–Sun brunch 9am–3pm; Tues–Sun tea 3–5pm; Sun–Thurs 5–9:30pm; Fri–Sat 5–10:30pm.

**Urban Taco** ★ ☺ 🦐 MEXICAN/TACOS   This smart, colorful and cleanly modern little restaurant is deceptive: Yes, it's technically a taco joint, but it also serves subtle and sophisticated Mexico City cooking, such as ceviche and inspired seafood dishes, including red snapper Acapulco. The guacamole and salsa—surely the barometer of any good *taquería*—are splendid (you can sample all the creative salsas, such as jalapeño avocado or poblano-pepita pesto, for just 25¢ each). The house specialty is, of course, tacos—of the gourmet, soft variety. The spicy ahi tuna tacos, as well as unexpected entries like potato-zucchini tacos, are all excellent. The tostadas of Dos XX beer–braised beef are a personal favorite, and the margaritas are worthy of a cool cocktail bar.

3411 McKinney Ave. © **214/240-9344**. www.urban-taco.com. Reservations not accepted. Main courses $9–$19. AE, DISC, MC, V. Sun–Thurs 11am–10pm; Fri–Sat 11am–11pm. DART: Cityplace.

## Inexpensive

**Fireside Pies** ★★ ☺ PIZZA   While Fireside serves up the best New York–style pizza in Dallas, locals talk about this funky and energetic place in the revered tones usually used for fine dining—which means it's packed every night. They don't take reservations, so that often means you're in for a wait. But hang in there and have a beer, because the wait is worth it. The hand-stretched pies (baked in a custom pecan wood–fired oven) are spectacularly fresh and scrumptious, as well as monstrous in size. They use a "heavy-handed" cheese blend of mozzarella, fontina, Fontinella, and Parmegiano Reggiano. Picking favorites from the creative list is hugely difficult, though the Peta Pie (goat cheese, portobello mushrooms, arugula, roasted red peppers, and roasted pinyon nuts) has my name all over it. There are also great fresh salads (also huge) and grinders, and beer by the pitcher, a compact wine list, and a full range of cocktails and soda floats. Whether you're inside the plant-filled main room or out on the patio, you'll be in good company, with a crowd of cheerful regulars. Its success has led to expansion, and there are now locations at 7709 Inwood Rd. (📞 **214/357-3800**) and in Plano at 5717 Legacy Dr. (📞 **972/398-2700**).

2820 N. Henderson Ave. (east of Central Expwy.). 📞 **214/370-3916**. www.firesidepies.com/home.asp. Reservations not accepted. Main courses $9–$15. AE, DISC, MC, V. Daily 5pm–midnight.

**Highland Park Pharmacy** ☺ 🍴 LIGHT FARE/BREAKFAST/BRUNCH   It's sad that most places like this have disappeared across the country. Amazingly, this one, in Dallas since 1912, is still here, blissfully out of place with all the home-goods stores and high-end restaurants that surround it. An authentic slice of Americana, this old-time soda fountain and lunch counter (and, yes, pharmacy) has stood its ground, even as everything around it has become an ultra-chic bar, restaurant, or home-furnishings store. If you've got a hankering for a grilled pimento cheese sandwich, homemade chicken salad, or a limeade, chocolate milkshake, or root beer float, this is the place; just grab a bar stool. It's a good spot for breakfast, too. Just don't ask the soda jerk for a latte or other fancy fixin's.

3229 Knox St. (at Travis St.). 📞 **214/521-2126**. Reservations not accepted. Dishes $3–$9. AE, MC, V. Mon–Fri 7am–6pm; Sat 9am–5:30pm.

**Peggy Sue BBQ** ☺ 🍴 BARBECUE   Though this comfy, casual, cheery place looks like it's been around forever, it only opened in 1989 (albeit on the spot where a local barbecue haunt did exist since the 1940s). If it looks and feels like a neighborhood spot—though somewhat incongruous in fancy Park Cities—stuck in midcentury mode, well, that's exactly the way the owners would have it. With meats smoked on the premises, and a salad bar and full roster of delicious fresh vegetables (choose three for a meal), it's a perfect place to bring hungry carnivores, the kids, and even vegetarians. Parents will appreciate the inexpensive kids' menu, which comes with a veggie the kids may even eat. Brisket quesadillas and onion rings are great starters for the table; adventurous sorts can try the Texas Torpedoes (cream cheese filled, batter-fried jalapeños). Terrific sandwiches include the chopped brisket and Piggy Soo (pulled pork), while full-meal standards (served with two veggies) worth a bet are the smoky baby back ribs and Polish kielbasa sausage. If you can make it to dessert, '50s-style heaven awaits: fried pies, peach cobbler, and root beer floats.

6600 Snider Plaza (at Hillcrest). 📞 **214/987-9188**. www.peggysuebbq.com. Reservations recommended. Main courses $5.25–$15. AE, DC, DISC, MC, V. Sun–Thurs 11am–9pm; Fri–Sat 11am–10pm.

**Sonny Bryan's Smokehouse** ★ ☺ 🍴 BARBECUE   Barbecue is serious business down here. Everybody's got a favorite, whose merits they'll defend like it was the

Alamo, but just about all Dallasites agree that legendary Sonny Bryan's is the original, the one barbecue spot you've got to visit before leaving Dallas. Serving patrons since 1958 in the ramshackle little building in a humble section of Oak Lawn, this place is so popular that even on scorching hot days, you'll see businesspeople with their sleeves rolled up, leaning against their cars, trying in vain not to get barbecue sauce all over themselves. Inside the smoke shack, there are just two rows of tiny one-armed school desks, under signs that read RESERVED, PHYLLIS, or LITTLE JERRIE. Place your order for hickory-smoked brisket, meaty ribs, sliced beef sandwiches, and juicy "handmade" onion rings at the counter. Then grab a bottle of sauce in a mini Mexican beer bottle and a fistful of napkins, and squeeze into a desk—or grab a spot at one of the picnic tables in the parking lot (or, heck, jump on the hood of your car). Come early, though; Sonny's is open only until the food runs out, which is apt to happen before the stated closing time. If you can't make it to the atmospheric original, there are more consumer-friendly branches of Sonny Bryan's serving up the same great and sloppy barbecue across Dallas and the suburbs, but while they're good for fast barbecue, they don't have anywhere near the authentic appeal of the original place.

2202 Inwood Rd. (near Harry Hines Blvd.). 📞 **214/357-7120.** Reservations not accepted. Dishes $5–$14. AE, DISC, MC, V. Daily 10am–8pm. DART: Medical/Market Center.

# EXPLORING DALLAS

Dallas has long been better known for its business and banking instincts than its cultural treasures and must-see attractions. Fort Worth still gallops ahead of it on the cultural radar, though the playing field is nearly leveled with the world-class Nasher Sculpture Center and other prominent local collectors donating valuable works to the city, as well as the stunning new, $340-million **AT&T Performing Arts Center,** which includes the **Wyly Theater** and **Winspear Opera House** (designed by Rem Koolhaas and Norman Foster, respectively). Of course, plenty of visitors simply come to Dallas and go native: Shop during the day, eat, drink, and attend big-time sporting events at night and on weekends. Big D, a relatively young city, can certainly entertain visitors for a few days or more through its infamous Kennedy legacy (which it has reluctantly embraced), revitalized state fairgrounds, a growing arts scene, and a handful of parks and enjoyable places for the kids—and, of course, loads of shopping.

## THE TOP ATTRACTIONS
### Historic Downtown Dallas

**Dallas County Historical Plaza**   Just a couple of blocks from the spot where JFK's motorcade slowly rolled by the Texas School Book Depository is the heart of historic downtown Dallas—though nothing of permanence was built here until the 1890s. In the middle of the plaza is a reminder of Dallas's recent origins as a Western outpost: **John Neely Bryan Cabin,** a replica of the one-room log structure built by the Tennessee-born attorney credited with founding the city in 1841. The original cabin stood on the banks of the Trinity River.

Across Main Street is the **John F. Kennedy Memorial,** funded by private donations and designed by the famed architect Philip Johnson in 1970. The open-roofed square room, made of limestone, is a "cenotaph" (an empty tomb), according to Johnson. Unfortunately, the memorial is also empty of emotion—not the moving testament to a president and event that so marked the American national psyche. Inside the four solemn walls is a black marble slab, which looks like a low coffee table, engraved with the words JOHN FITZGERALD KENNEDY. Johnson's intent was for the open roof to symbolize the "freedom of spirit of JFK," but I doubt that many visitors will feel their own spirits soar here.

 A Dollar Saved . . .

Look for $1 and $2 coupons for museums and other attractions in the *Dallas/Fort Worth Area Visitors Guide* and other tourism board publications (available free at the CVB office in the Old Red Courthouse, as well as at some hotels and restaurants in Dallas).

Just west of the Kennedy Memorial, across Record Street, is the **Old Red Courthouse,** built in self-important Romanesque Revival style in 1890 on the site of the original log courthouse (property donated by city founder John Neely Bryan). The blue granite and red sandstone building today houses the **Dallas Visitors Center** (which has Internet access, along with sightseeing, hotel, and restaurant information).

Occasionally, true nonbelievers still hang around the Texas School Book Depository trumpeting far-fetched, wacky, and occasionally plausible tales about the JFK assassination to anyone who will listen.

Junction of Main, Market, Elm, and Record sts. No admission fees for memorial. Memorial open year-round daily 24 hr. DART: West End.

**The Sixth Floor Museum at Dealey Plaza** ★★ ☺   November 22, 1963, is a day Dallas can't live down and the world can't forget. A sniper assassinated the nation's 35th president, John Fitzgerald Kennedy, in Dallas as his motorcade traveled west on Elm Street. Whether or not there was a single shooter or more camped out on the grassy knoll below, and whether or not the Cubans or the Russians or the CIA were involved, the Warren Commission concluded that 24-year-old Lee Harvey Oswald fired his rifle at least three times from a window perch on the sixth floor of the Texas School Book Depository, killing JFK and critically injuring the Texas governor, John Connally. (Oswald had days earlier secured a menial job at the School Book offices.)

The redbrick building overlooks Dealey Plaza, an otherwise unremarkable spot that is ingrained in the memory of most Americans and people across the globe. The museum, the top draw in north Texas, preserves the spot where Oswald crouched and fired his rifle (now encased in Plexiglas), but it also examines the life, times, and legacy of the Kennedy presidency. The exhibit provides a moment-by-moment account of the day of the assassination and a day-by-day recollection of that harrowing November

Dominating the Big D skyline is sphere-topped **Reunion Tower** (© 214/651-1234; DART light rail: Union), the top of which is lit up like a giant pin cushion at night. The tower, located in Reunion Park at Reunion Boulevard, rises 50 stories, and the dome rotates very slowly (completing a single rotation in just under an hour), though imperceptibly to the naked eye. Take an exterior elevator to an observation deck for panoramic views of the city and surrounding plains, or have a drink or dinner at the Dome cocktail lounge or the restaurant **Five Sixty**, where you can blame your spinning head on something other than the libations in front of you.

week. The display, which includes documentary film footage and more than 400 photos, summons the "Camelot" White House before getting to the event that put Dallas on the quivering lips of people across the globe. On view are images from the famous Zapruder film, whose frames have been isolated and examined more than any footage in history. However, there is no original evidence on display; everything examined by the Warren Commission forms part of the National Archives in Washington, D.C. The JFK assassination has been so hashed over and occupies such a place in pop culture that few visitors are likely to discover much in the way of new information. It is, however, a place to revisit the tragic episode, as children's drawings from the period and visitor remarks inscribed in "Memory Books" at the museum's exit attest. Unless the information here is new to you or you want to relive the episode in great detail, spending no more than a couple of hours here should be plenty. Newly opened in 2010 is the **Museum Store + Café** (with yummy treats from La Duni), across the street at 501 Elm St.

**Dealey Plaza,** which draws two million curious visitors annually, remains a stark public square at the junction of a triple underpass, virtually unchanged from 4 decades ago. A red X marks the spot on the asphalt of Elm Street where Kennedy was struck; incredibly, many visitors to Dallas feel compelled to dodge traffic and have their pictures taken while standing on the X as cars hurtle by. Unless you really want to follow in the footsteps of JFK, however, I strongly advise against such reckless participation in our nation's history.

411 Elm St. at Houston (entrance on Houston St.). © **214/747-6660.** www.jfk.org. Admission (including audio guide) $14 adults; $13 seniors, students, and children 7–18; free for children 6 and under. Tues–Sun 10am–6pm; Mon noon–6pm. Closed Thanksgiving and Dec 25. DART: West End.

### The Arts District

Art lovers will want to spend the better part of a morning or afternoon in the Arts District, though you could do a drive-by through a couple of the museums in a little over an hour. To get there via public transport, take DART light rail to Pearl or St. Paul station.

**Dallas Museum of Art** ★   Though always considered a notch below a world-class institution, the Dallas Museum of Art (DMA) significantly improved its standing within the art world when it received the undeniably world-class modern and contemporary art collections of three prominent local collectors (the Hoffmans, the Rachofskys, and the Roses); the collections, gifted together in an unprecedented deal, totaled more than 800 works as well as future acquisitions. The I. M. Pei–designed museum also contains impressive collections of international art, especially from the Americas, Africa, and Asia and the Pacific. The Arts of the Americas section is the largest and most impressive, with valuable contributions from pre-Columbian lost civilizations of the Aztec, Maya, and Nazca peoples and Spanish colonial arts. The more limited Art of Europe gallery exhibits a handful of works by the biggies—Van Gogh, Monet, Cézanne, Gauguin, and Degas—while the small 20th-century collection includes Picasso, Mondrian, and Giacometti, among others.

The contemporary collection includes works by Mark Rothko, Jackson Pollock, the Texan Robert Rauschenberg, and Jasper Johns. In the Wendy & Emery Reves Collection is a curious re-creation of Coco Chanel's French summer home, complete with her collection of furnishings and paintings by such French Impressionists as Monet, Toulouse-Lautrec, and Degas. The DMA mounts interesting occasional shows, including "Van Gogh's Sheaves of Wheat" and the blockbuster "Splendors of China's Forbidden City" exhibit. In the atrium hangs a gorgeous, monumental blown-glass sculpture by Dale Chihuly. Live jazz combos can be enjoyed there on Thursdays from 5 to 9pm, along with cocktails and dinner. A couple of hours at this museum should be sufficient, unless you're a dedicated art hound.

1717 N. Harwood (at Ross St.). ℂ **214/922-1200.** www.dallasmuseumofart.org. Admission $10 adults, $7 seniors, $5 students, free for children 11 and under, free to all 1st Tues of month. Joint admission tickets to the Dallas Museum of Art and the Nasher Sculpture Center $16 adults, $12 seniors, $8 students. Tues–Wed and Fri–Sun 11am–5pm; Thurs 11am–9pm; 3rd Fri of month 11am–midnight. Guided tours Sat–Sun 2pm; gallery talks Wed 12:15pm; art talks Thurs 7pm. Closed Thanksgiving, Dec 24–25, and Jan 1.

**Nasher Sculpture Center** ★★★ ☺ Despite its status as the principal art museum in a city of considerable wealth, the rather modest permanent collection of the Dallas Museum of Art is proof that either north Texans don't collect much great art or they don't donate it on a grand scale to local institutions. One notable exception to that rule is Raymond Nasher, one of the world's foremost collectors of contemporary sculpture. A local businessman, by way of New York, who made his banking and real estate fortune in Dallas (with the shopping mall NorthPark Center, among other properties), Nasher decided, after years of being wooed by the Dallas Museum of Art as well as such major institutions as the Guggenheim Museum in New York and the National Gallery of Art in Washington, D.C., to establish a public sculpture garden in his adopted city. The $50-million project was entirely funded by the private Nasher Foundation.

The Nasher Sculpture Center opened in 2003 on a 2½-acre site adjacent to the Dallas Museum of Art, in a glass-and-marble structure infused with natural light, designed by the renowned architect Renzo Piano. The center should change the way art aficionados think about Dallas and should make it an art destination. The collection, which includes high-quality pieces by virtually all of the great modern masters and was amassed over 4 decades by Ray and his wife, Patsy, is considered by some art experts to be the finest private sculpture collection in the world. The tasteful 54,000-square-foot center, a place of quiet refuge in downtown Dallas, features an outdoor sculpture garden landscaped by Peter Walker, with pieces from Nasher's immense collection exhibited both indoors and out. The collection includes some of the finest individual works from the likes of Pablo Picasso, Auguste Rodin, Joan Miró, David Smith, Constantin Brancusi, Henry Moore, Alberto Giacometti, Henri Matisse, Alexander Calder, Isamu Noguchi, Richard Serra, Mark di Suvero, Magdalena Abakanowicz, Joseph Beuys, Roy Lichtenstein, and many others.

# DOWNTOWN DALLAS'S outdoor SCULPTURE

Fans of monumental contemporary sculpture, after visiting the Nasher Center and the outdoor sculpture garden at the Dallas Museum of Art, should pick up the *Walking Sculpture* brochure (available at the Visitors Center), which details 33 outdoor public sculptures in the downtown area. Along the way, you'll find works by Richard Serra, Ellsworth Kelly, Mark di Suvero, and Henry Moore. On the first Saturday of each month, a guided walking tour is offered, departing from the Crow Collection of Asian Art (see above) at 10:30am. Call ✆ **214/953-1977** for required reservations and more information.

Among the monumental pieces in the open-air museum, there are too many highlights to mention, though James Turrell's "skyspace" *Tending (Blue)* perhaps deserves special recognition as a site-specific piece commissioned for the museum. Set at the back of the garden, near the bathrooms, it is a walk-in box open to the sky, with optical effects and an unexpected perspective. One of the most recent acquisitions in the Sculpture Garden is Jonathan Borofsky's 2004 *Walking to the Sky*, which depicts seven life-size figures defying gravity and climbing a 100-foot pole that reaches toward the clouds. Although the Nasher Sculpture Center—which has some of the biggest names in art and architecture attached to it—opened with big publicity and truly ought to be one of Dallas's most highly prized treasures, it has had some difficulty attracting visitors, especially locals. If you're at all a fan of modern art, or even of contemporary architecture, don't miss the opportunity to see this spectacular museum. Allow 1 or 2 hours for a visit here.

2001 Flora St. (btw. Harwood and Olive sts.). ✆ **214/242-5100**. www.nashersculpturecenter.org. Admission (includes audio tour) $10 adults, $7 seniors, $5 students, free for children 12 and under, free for all 1st Sat of month. Joint admission tickets to Nasher Sculpture Center and Dallas Museum of Art $16 adults, $12 seniors, $8 students. Tues–Sun 11am–5pm. Closed July 4, Thanksgiving, Dec 24–25, and Jan 1.

**Trammell & Margaret Crow Collection of Asian Art ★** This exceptionally displayed collection is the product of a fascination with the arts of Japan, China, and India by one of Dallas's best-known real estate developers. The 500 pieces on display (taken from a collection of more than 7,000 objects) range from 1000 B.C. to the 20th century. The first floor is dedicated to the arts of Japan; its galleries hold Japanese scrolls and screens, as well as ceramics and bronzes. The Chinese galleries focus mostly on painting, sculpture, and decorative arts from the last Chinese empire, the Qing dynasty (1644–1911). Across a sky bridge is the third gallery, dedicated to Indian culture, with Hindu sculptures and features of Indian architecture, including a large residence facade in elaborately carved red limestone. There are also sculptures from Cambodia—a standout is the pre-Khmer 7th-century figure of Vishnu—and Nepalese and Tibetan objets d'art. Allow an hour or two to see it all.

Crow's non-Asian sculpture collection is on display at the **Trammell Crow Center,** located at 2001 Ross Ave. at Harwood. It includes 19th- and 20th-century French bronzes (by Rodin and Maillol) throughout the office building and in the garden.

2010 Flora St. (btw. Harwood and Olive sts.). ✆ **214/979-6430**. www.crowcollection.com. Free admission. Tues–Thurs 10am–9pm; Fri–Sun 10am–6pm. Free guided public tours Thurs 6:30pm and Sat 1pm.

## The Outskirts of Downtown: Historic Parks, Fairgrounds & Museums

**The Dallas Arboretum & Botanical Garden** ★ ☺   Dallas may not be celebrated for its cool green beauty, but the area around White Rock Lake, and more specifically the Dallas Arboretum and Botanical Garden, is a welcome oasis. Just 15 minutes from the gleaming skyscrapers of downtown Dallas are nearly 70 acres of carefully planted and groomed gardens and natural woodlands, interspersed with a handful of historic residences, that meander along the banks of the lake. The Jonsson Color Garden features one of the nation's largest collections of azaleas, which bloom spectacularly in spring, and nearly 6 acres of chrysanthemums in the fall. While north Texas is not exactly New England, it's as ablaze in color during October and November as anywhere else in this neck of the woods. If you find yourself in Dallas during the torrid summer (or spring and fall) months, the Palmer Fern Deli is a secluded, shady spot where mist-sprayers drop the temperature at least 10° to 15°—reason enough for a visit here. An hour is probably enough time to see most of the gardens, though it's a fine place to linger, read, and relax.

8525 Garland Rd. ☏ **214/515-6500.** www.dallasarboretum.org. Admission $12 adults, $10 seniors, $8 children 3–12, free for children 2 and under. Daily 9am–5pm. Closed Thanksgiving, Dec 25, and Jan 1.

**Dallas Heritage Village** ★ ☺   Dallas's Old West heritage is on self-conscious display in this downtown 13-acre park of three dozen historic buildings. The complex re-creates a late-19th-century village, complete with a redbrick Main Street, Victorian homes, a log cabin dating from 1847, and Old West standards such as a train depot, general store, one-room church, schoolhouse, bank (said to have been robbed by Bonnie and Clyde in the 1930s), and law offices. All have been transported from their original locations in and around Dallas, immaculately restored, and reconstructed on the attractive grounds, which have the glittering city skyline as a backdrop. On guided tours, visitors are escorted inside several buildings, including the Living Farmstead, a re-creation of a north Texas farm (ca. 1860). On selected dates during the first 2 weeks of December, the village celebrates Candlelight at Old City Park, a popular Victorian holiday celebration; Candlelight admission tickets are $3 more than regular prices.

A pretty good restaurant, Brent Place, occupies an 1876 "architecture-catalog" farmhouse (kit house ordered by mail and shipped via rail to rural areas) and serves lunch Tuesday through Saturday from 11am to 3pm; call ☏ **212/421-3057** for reservations. Visitors are allowed to picnic on the grounds. Plan to spend 1½ hours or so here.

### Fair Park Passport

Get in to seven Fair Park Museums for a single price, a savings of 40% over retail admission prices, with the newly inaugurated **Fair Park Passport,** available by calling ☏ **214/428-5555** or logging on to www.fairpark.org. Tickets are $24 for adults and $14 for children ages 3 to 12. Participating museums are the African American Museum, the Hall of State, the Museum of the American Railroad, the Science Place, the Dallas Aquarium at Fair Park, Texas Discovery Gardens, the Museum of Nature and Science, and the Women's Museum.

1515 S. Harwood. ☏ **214/421-5141.** www.dallasheritagevillage.org. Admission $7 adults, $5 seniors, $4 children 3–12. Tues–Sat 10am–4pm; Sun noon–4pm. DART: Cedars.

**Fair Park ★ ☺** Fair Park, a classic conglomeration of Art Deco buildings and spacious grounds built for the 1936 Texas Centennial Exposition, is undergoing a renaissance. Built to commemorate the Republic of Texas's independence from Mexico, it is the only intact and unaltered, pre-1950s World's Fair site in the United States. Recognized as a National Historic Landmark for its architecture (the only such landmark in Dallas), Fair Park is an attraction year-round, but especially so during the annual State Fair of Texas (last weekend of Sept and first 3 weeks of Oct).

The 277-acre grounds include several museums and performance and sporting facilities like the State Fair Coliseum, Cotton Bowl, Fair Park Bandshell, and Starplex Amphitheater, one of the city's top concert venues. The two major areas are the Esplanade and the Lagoon. There's much to see and do at Fair Park, so depending on your time, you may have to pick and choose. Plan on 2 or 3 hours minimum, and a full day during the State Fair of Texas. Below are the highlights:

The **Women's Museum: An Institute for the Future ★**, 3800 Parry Ave. (**©** 214/915-0860; www.thewomensmuseum.org), is a huge coup for Dallas. The pet project of a trio of Texas women and designed by Wendy Joseph, the chief designer behind the Holocaust Museum in Washington, D.C., this exciting $25-million museum is an ambitious, high-tech architectural feast, audacious enough to encompass the accomplishments of women over the past century.

The museum presents two dozen mostly interactive exhibits, with a clear predilection for engaging the visitor with technological wizardry. Audio guides (hand-held cellphones) feature the voices of "mentors" Connie Chung, Gladys Knight, and the late Texas governor Ann Richards. "It's Amazing" is a glass labyrinth of female stereotypes, behind which are revealed several women who defied convention; "Mothers of Invention" showcases popular inventions by women (such as Liquid Paper, conceived by a Dallas secretary, and the brown paper bag). The museum is open Tuesday through Sunday from noon to 5pm. Admission is $5 for adults, $4 for seniors and students ages 13 to 18, and $3 for children ages 5 to 12.

The **Hall of State,** 3939 Grand Ave. (**©** 214/421-4500; www.hallofstate.com; Tues–Sat 9am–5pm, Sun 1–5pm; free admission), is the centerpiece and principal Art Deco legacy at Fair Park. Inside is a Texan's dream, the Hall of Heroes, with larger-than-life stalwarts of the Republic of Texas, including Sam Houston and Stephen F. Austin. Venture into the four-story-high Great Hall, yet more proof that bigger is always better in Texas.

Trains evoke nostalgic feelings of travel and exploration in just about everyone; the collection at the **Museum of the American Railroad,** 1105 Washington St. (**©** 214/428-0101; www.dallasrailwaymuseum.com), including 28 locomotives, steam-era Pullman passenger cars, and Dallas's oldest surviving train depot, is sure to feed such impulses in visitors of all ages. The entry in the "Bigger in Texas" sweepstakes? Big Boy, the world's largest steam locomotive. The museum is open Wednesday through Sunday from 10am to 5pm; admission is $7 for adults, $3 for children 3 to 12, and free for children 2 and under.

The **African American Museum,** 3536 Grand Ave. (**©** 214/565-9026; www.aamdallas.org), is the only museum in the Southwest (and one of eight in the country) that focuses on the African-American experience and culture. The standout exhibit is the fine collection of African-American folk art, supplemented by a survey of African art objects and contemporary African-American art. Admission is free; it's open Tuesday through Friday from noon to 5pm, Saturday from 10am to 5pm, and Sunday from 1 to 5pm.

The newly renovated and renamed **Children's Aquarium at Fair Park,** 1462 First Ave. (📞 **479/554-7340;** www.childrensaquariumfairpark.com), contains a small but diverse collection of marine life. It highlights some of the weirder aquatic specimens in the marine and freshwater world, including walking fish, four-eyed fish, upside-down jellyfish, and desert fish. And who can resist watching the piranhas and sharks being fed? The newest and largest addition is the Amazon Flooded Forest, a 10,000-gallon tank with 30 species from the Amazon River. Normal hours are daily from 9am to 4:30pm; admission is $8 for adults, $6 for children ages 3 to 11.

The **Museum of Nature and Science,** 3535 Grand Ave. (📞 **214/428-5555;** www.natureandscience.org), is the former Dallas Museum of Natural History now merged with the Science Place and IMAX theater. Families can view the kind of wildlife that roamed Texas before steers and longhorns, namely dinosaurs, and explore permanent exhibits like "Paleontology Lab" and "Prehistoric Texas." You can also entertain the kids with more than 300 hands-on science exhibits—that include lifting a half-ton weight with one hand or playing with electricity—and the massive, domed IMAX theater. The Planetarium features stargazing shows from Monday through Saturday.

The museum is open Tuesday through Saturday from 10am to 5pm, Sunday from noon to 5pm; admission is $10 for adults, $9 for seniors, and $7 for children ages 2 to 11. Admission to the planetarium shows is $3.50 for all, while IMAX screenings are $7 for adults, $6 for seniors and children ages 3 to 12. Combo-pack tickets for all exhibits, including one IMAX screening, are $16 for adults, $14 for seniors, and $12 for children ages 2 to 11.

3809 Grand Ave. (bordered by S. Fitzhugh, Washington, and Parry aves., and Cullum Blvd.). 📞 **214/ 670-8400,** or 421-9600 for museum and event information. www.fairpark.org. Fair Park passport (combined admission): $24 adults and $14 children ages 3-12.

**Meadows Museum of Art** ★★ 👜 On the campus of Southern Methodist University is one of the city's best-kept secrets: the finest collection of Spanish art outside Spain (so significant, in fact, that it has been exhibited at the top-tier Thyssen-Bornemisza museums in Madrid and Barcelona). A Dallas oil magnate, Algur Meadows, went to Spain to search for oil, entertaining himself at the Prado Museum. He came up dry, but his sojourn into Spanish art history bore fruit: Meadows began to assemble a splendid collection of works from the 15th to the 20th century, including pieces by Spanish masters from the golden age of Spanish painting (such as Velázquez, Goya, Ribera, Murillo, and Zurbarán—just about the only big name missing is El Greco). Now in a building six times larger than the old site, Meadows Museum ranks among the best small museums with a singular focus in the U.S. Of special note among the nearly 700 items on display are Ribera's *Retrato de un Caballero de Santiago* and Goya's *El Corral de los Locos* (by many accounts, the finest Goya found in the U.S.), as well as a series of 200 works on paper by Goya. The 20th-century Spanish masters Picasso, Dalí, Miró, and Tàpies are also represented. Allow 1 or 2 hours for a visit.

Owens Fine Arts Center, SMU Campus, 5900 Bishop Blvd. (1 block north of Mockingbird Lane, west of I-75). 📞 **214/768-2516.** www.meadowsmuseumdallas.org. Admission $8 adults, $6 seniors, $4 students, free for children 11 and under; free for all Thurs after 5pm. Tues-Wed and Fri-Sat 10am-5pm; Thurs 10am-8pm; Sun noon-5pm. Free public tours Sept-May Sun 2pm and occasional Sun in summer. DART: Mockingbird.

**Swiss Avenue Historic District**   Toward the turn of the 20th century, the Dallas elite began to abandon the area that now comprises the Arts District and move east (near the modestly funky Lakewood neighborhood). Sprawling, grand homes from the early 1900s—English Tudor, Georgian, Spanish, you name it—line a broad avenue, about 4 blocks of which are listed on the National Register of Historic Places. The Wilson Blocks (2800 and 2900), named for Frederick Wilson, who built a number of the homes there, are especially attractive. Around the holidays, Swiss Avenue is a favorite for Christmas lights cruisers. A drive-by can be done in 15 minutes; allow a half-hour if you want to stroll.

Northeast of downtown, along Swiss Ave. btw. La Vista Dr. and Fitzhugh Ave. (take Fitzhugh east from I-75).

## MORE TO SEE & DO

**The Dallas World Aquarium** ☺   Housed in a former warehouse in the West End district, the Dallas aquarium *not* at Fair Park is a good place to hide out from the sun downtown. My niece and nephew enjoy communing with the stingrays, sea turtles, sharks, and reef fish. Their favorite, though, is "Orinoco—Secrets of the River," an immersion into the tropical rainforest of Venezuela, a cool area teeming with Peruvian squirrel monkeys, endangered Orinoco crocs, jaguars, and soft-billed toucans. "Mundo Maya" features a 400,000-gallon shark tank. Plan on about an hour's visit. A restaurant and a cafe are on the premises.

1801 N. Griffin (West End District). ✆ **214/720-2224.** www.dwazoo.com. Admission $21 adults, $17 seniors, $13 children 3–12, free for children 2 and under. Sept–Feb daily 10am–5pm; Mar–Aug daily 9am–5pm. DART: West End.

**Dallas Zoo** ☺   If you're headed west to Fort Worth and one zoo trip will do, you'd be better off waiting (the Fort Worth Zoo and the one in San Antonio are the best in Texas and two of the best in the country). Otherwise, if the kids are clamoring for some wild animals, the renovated Dallas Zoo—the oldest zoo in Texas, founded in 1888—isn't likely to disappoint (indeed, one exhibit, "Wilds of Africa," was named the top African zoo exhibit in the country by *The Zoobook: A Guide to America's Best*). The sprawling 95-acre park also features a habitat for rare Sumatran tigers, a chimpanzee forest, and a monorail safari ride. A couple of hours spent here should suffice for the kids.

650 S. R. L. Thornton Fwy. (in Oak Cliff, 3 miles south of downtown Dallas). ✆ **214/670-5656.** www.dallaszoo.com. Admission $15 adults, $12 seniors, $12 children 3–11, free for children 2 and under. Daily 9am–4pm. DART: Dallas Zoo.

## ESPECIALLY FOR KIDS

Older children who have studied the 1960s and Kennedy should appreciate the **Sixth Floor Museum.** Younger kids are likely to have a better time at the **Dallas Zoo,** or either the **Dallas Aquarium at Fair Park** or the **Dallas World Aquarium.**

**Fair Park** has plenty to offer families, especially if you happen to be in Dallas during the State Fair of Texas (Oct). Even if you miss the fair, Fair Park's **Museum of Nature and Science** is a great place to hide from the Texas sun. Girls of all ages (and open-minded boys) may find interactive inspiration at the new **Women's Museum.** Kids tend to like trains, so a whistle-stop at the **Age of Steam Railroad Museum** should be diverting.

The staging of life on the prairie at **Old City Park,** with actors re-creating the late–19th and early–20th centuries, is plenty of fun for both kids and adults. Check out family theater productions at the **Dallas Children's Theater,** Crescent Theater, 2215 Cedar Springs at Maple (✆ **214/978-0110**). The Dallas Museum of Art's

**Gateway Gallery** has cool interactive art displays for kids. Children who are into movies may want to check out Hollywood sets and memorabilia at the **Studios at Las Colinas.**

The **Plano Balloon Festival,** a 3-day event held in mid-September in Oak Point Park, 2801 E. Spring Creek Pkwy., is one of the country's largest. More than 100 hot-air balloons, many of them curious shapes and recognizable figures, launch each day at 7am and 6pm. It's worth the drive (and early rise), unless it's too windy to launch; call © **972/867-7566** or visit www.planoballoonfest.org for more information. **Sporting events,** such as games of the Cowboys, Rangers, Sidekicks, and Stars, draw huge family crowds. Finally, just getting around parts of Dallas can be fun for children; take the **DART light rail system** around downtown (especially direct to the Dallas Zoo) and be sure to hop aboard the historic **trolleys** that patrol McKinney Avenue.

Arlington, midway between Dallas and Fort Worth, is the big draw for families, with **Six Flags Over Texas** amusement park, **Texas Rangers baseball** (including the excellent Legends of the Game Baseball Museum), **Hurricane Harbor** water park, the **Palace of Wax & Ripley's Believe It or Not,** and more. If you're looking to combine shopping with entertainment for the kids, Texas malls are in themselves theme parks (with skating rinks and much more). See "Arlington," later in this chapter.

## ORGANIZED TOURS

**Gray Line/Coach USA** (© **800/256-4723;** www.grayline.com) is the big daddy of bus tours. It offers at least six themed sightseeing tours in the Dallas–Fort Worth area. A full complement of sightseeing tours of Dallas and Fort Worth is also handled by a local company, **All in One Tour Services** (© **214/698-0332;** www.allinone tourservices.com).

**Dallas Surrey Services,** 381 E. Greenbriar Lane (© **214/946-9911**), offers horse-drawn carriage tours of historic Dallas 7 nights a week, weather permitting. Standard tours originate in the West End and visit Dealey Plaza and the Texas School Book Depository, Pioneer Plaza, and the Arts District, lasting about 20 minutes ($30 for up to four people). Longer, custom tours can last up to an hour ($100, four people). **Belle Starre Carriages** (© **214/855-0410**) also offers horse-drawn tours of downtown Dallas, including Christmas Light Tours through Highland Park during the month of December, starting at $165 per carriage.

Hour-long, free **Walking Arts District Strolls** covering the zone's art and architecture are conducted the first Saturday of every month at 10:30am, departing in front of the Trammell & Margaret Crow Collection of Asian Art, 2010 Flora St. Call © **214/953-1977** for additional information and reservations.

## OUTDOOR ACTIVITIES

**BIKING, IN-LINE SKATING & JOGGING** White Rock Lake, 5 miles east of downtown Dallas (off Loop 12), is the most popular area for cycling, skating, and running (and, of course, walking). A 12-mile loop traces the banks of the lake. The park is open from 6am to midnight, though I wouldn't advise hanging about too long after dark falls. Nearby bike and skate shops offer rentals.

**GOLF** Golf legends such as Byron Nelson, Ben Hogan, and Lee Trevino hail from north Texas, which has a huge number of golf courses. These range from challenging championship courses to comfortable ones suited to players of all stripes. **TPC at the Four Seasons Resort and Club** (© **972/717-2400;** www.fourseasons.com/dallas/golf; greens fees $150), home of the PGA Byron Nelson Classic, is the best and most spectacular course in the area—but you'll have to stay at the Four Seasons (p. 70) to play. Another hotel golf course, rated among the top 50 resorts in the United States, is **Bear Creek Golf Club,** 3500 Bear Creek Court/DFW Airport (© **972/456-3200;** www.bearcreek-golf.com; greens fees and cart $25–$69, with twilight reduced rates available), featuring two nicely designed championship 18-hole courses on 355 acres of rolling hills.

The City of Dallas operates several courses open to the public. The newest addition is **Keeton Park Golf Course,** 2323 Jim Miller Rd., southeast of downtown Dallas off I-30 (© **214/670-8784;** www.keetonpark.com), which has pecan tree–lined fairways and numerous ponds. Greens fees are $16. **Tenison Golf Course,** 3501 Samuell Blvd. (© **214/670-1402;** www.tenisonpark.com), just 5 miles east of downtown, has two 18-hole courses divided by White Rock Creek. Greens fees are $14 to $34, and on weekends $17 to $42.

Local duffers (as well as football fans) rave about the **Cowboys Golf Club,** 1600 Fairway Dr., in Grapevine (© **817/481-7277;** www.cowboysgolfclub.com; greens fees all-inclusive VIP package $140, twilight play $75), which is certainly unique: Not only does it boast huge changes in elevation, but it claims to be the "world's first NFL-themed golf course." The clubhouse is packed with Dallas Cowboys memorabilia and Super Bowl trophies, and markers along the course pay tribute to key moments in Cowboys lore. Named among the "Best Places to Play" by *Golf Digest* (and rated one of the top five public courses in Texas) is **Buffalo Creek Golf Club,** 624 Country Club Dr., Rockwall (© **972/771-4003;** www.buffalocreek.americangolf.com), near Lake Ray Hubbard, a healthy drive from Dallas. Greens fees, including cart and range balls, are $69 Monday through Friday, $89 Saturday and Sunday. One of the most difficult courses is **Sleepy Hollow Country Club,** 4747 S. Loop 12 (© **214/371-3433**), just 10 minutes south of downtown, which is private but allows the public to play as guests. Greens fees with cart are $27 to $42. (It's $13 less to walk.)

Golf fanatics who like to imagine themselves winning the Masters or British Open may want to venture north of Dallas and Fort Worth, to Flower Mound, Texas, where the **Tour 18 Dallas** course reproduces 18 of the best-known holes in golf (from courses such as Winged Foot and Augusta National). The course, 8718 Amen Corner, Flower Mound (© **800/946-5310** or 817/430-2000; www.tour18-dallas.com), is west of I-35 E. and Hwy. 121. Greens fees are $65 to $140.

**TENNIS** Even though tennis in Dallas is mostly confined to swank (and off-limits) private tennis clubs, there are several public courts where visitors can play a few sets.

---

### Packin' Heat, Texas-Style

The right to own, use, and brag about firearms is a protected birthright in Texas. I'm not necessarily advocating this—I mean, personally I think it's a little odd that the local concealed-gun law allows Texans to take their pistols to church on Sunday, and museums have to post signs that warn "No Firearms"—but heaven knows I wouldn't dare offend gun owners. If you want to play Texan while in Big D, what better way than to fire off a few rounds? If that's your idea of R & R, the **DFW Gun Club & Training Center,** 1607 Mockingbird Lane (© **214/630-4866;** www.dfwgun.com), operates the DFW Gun Range for a little indoor shooting. Featured hilariously in the film *Borat* about the fictional reporter from Kazakhstan, the club offers shooting instruction and even concealed handgun license classes.

The following are city owned, but have privately run pro shops: **Fair Oaks,** 7501 Merriman Pkwy. (☎ **214/670-1495**), near White Rock Creek (4 miles north of White Rock Lake), has 16 lighted courts; **Fretz Park,** 14700 Hillcrest Ave. (☎ **214/ 670-6622**), where I took lessons as a kid, has 15 lighted courts.

## SPECTATOR SPORTS

Dallas, home to 2011's Super Bowl LXV, is sports mad, one of only six cities in the U.S. to support teams in all the major professional sports leagues. Tickets to pro sporting events are available from **Central Tickets** (☎ **817/335-9000**), **Star Tickets** (☎ **972/660-8300**), and **Ticketmaster** (☎ **214/373-8000**).

**AUTO RACING** For information on the Texas Motor Speedway, see "Auto Racing" in chapter 5, "Fort Worth."

**BASEBALL** The **Texas Rangers** (once owned by the former president George W. Bush) play from April to October at one of the finest stadiums in the country, **Rangers Ballpark in Arlington,** I-30 at Hwy. 157 (☎ **817/273-5100;** www.texas rangers.com), a home field that recalls the glory days of baseball. Of special interest is the fascinating **Legends of the Game Baseball Museum,** with rare pieces on loan from the Cooperstown Baseball Museum (the only stadium so fortunate). See p. 91 for additional information.

The **Frisco Rough Riders** (☎ **972/334-1909;** www.ridersbaseball.com), the Texas Rangers feeder team, play minor league at the new ballpark at Hwy. 121 S. between Dallas North Tollway and Parkwood Boulevard.

**BASKETBALL** The **Dallas Mavericks** (☎ **214/747-MAVS** [6287] or 665-4797; www.nba.com/mavericks), one of the top teams in the NBA, call the American Airlines Center home. The excellent arena, built by the same architect who created the critically acclaimed Rangers Ballpark in Arlington for the Texas Rangers, opened in 2001. Single-game tickets (available at Ticketmaster; ☎ **214/373-8000**) are $20 to $250 and can be a bit hard to come by, as popular as the Mavs are at home. Tours of the arena are available on nonevent days at 10:30am.

**FOOTBALL** The **Dallas Cowboys** (☎ **972/785-4800;** www.dallascowboys. com), five-time Super Bowl Champions and (at least formerly) "America's Team," played at **Texas Stadium** in Irving, the arena with the famous hole in the roof, for 38 years. The Cowboys' spectacular new stadium opened in 2009; it seats 80,000 and is the largest domed stadium in the country—and it still has a hole in the roof, albeit a retractable one. Individual game tickets, which cost $75 to $200, aren't easy to come by, so plan ahead if you want to avoid paying high broker's fees. The **Dallas Cowboys Cheerleaders,** who started a professional trend of scantily clad females bouncing around on the sidelines, still shimmy and cheer them on, big hairdos, cleavage, and all. Check with the Cowboys organization to find out whether and when tours of the new stadium are available. The **Dallas Desperados** play arena football (AFL) in the spring at American Airlines Stadium in Irving; for information, call ☎ **972/785-4900,** or visit www.dallasdesperados.com.

**GOLF** The PGA **Byron Nelson Championship,** named for a local legend, has been held in Dallas for the past 3 decades every May. Check out some of the top names in professional golf at the **Four Seasons Resort and Club** (call ☎ **972/717-1200** for tickets).

**HOCKEY** Dallas may not seem like the most logical place for a professional ice hockey team, but Big D has one of the best, the **Dallas Stars** (the 2000 Western Conference Champions), and Dallasites are wild about them. The Stars play at the

American Airlines Center; the season is September through April. The Stars sell out all their home games, so plan ahead if you want to see a game (✆ 214/GO-STARS [467-8277]; www.dallasstars.com). Tickets (available at Ticketmaster; ✆ 214/373-8000) range from $25 to $300, and family packs (tickets and food) are available.

**RODEO**    One of the top rodeos in Texas, and a huge draw for out-of-towners and travelers from abroad, is the **Mesquite Championship Rodeo,** about 20 miles northeast of downtown at Resistol Arena, 1818 Rodeo Dr. (✆ 800/833-9339 or 972/285-8777; www.mesquiterodeo.com). From April to September, you can check out some authentic professional rodeo action—bull riding, saddle and bareback riding, calf roping, and chuck-wagon races—on Friday and Saturday nights at 8pm (reserved grandstand seating $14; general admission $10 adults, $7 seniors, $4 children 11 and under). Animal-rights sympathizers might feel a bit squeamish watching some of the roping exercises, which violently snap calves' heads back. There's a petting zoo for kids and a gift shop selling Western duds just like the ones cowboys and their fans will be sporting. Rodeo season is April through October.

**SOCCER**    The newest professional team in the area, **FC Dallas,** plays outdoor soccer (MLS). Conference champions in 2006, FC Dallas moved from the Cotton Bowl to Pizza Hut Park in Frisco, 30 miles north of Dallas, and draws more than 1.5 million fans to its 20,000-capacity stadium. The season lasts from April to October. Tickets cost $9 to $60. For more information, call ✆ 888/FCD-GOAL (323-4625) or visit http://web.mlsnet.com/t104.

# SHOPPING

In Big D, shopping isn't merely a mundane chore necessary to outfit yourself, your kids, and your home. Shopping is a sport and pastime, a social activity and entertainment. Dallasites don't pull on sweats and go incognito to the mall; they get dolled up and strut their stuff. Having grown up in North Dallas, I know all too well that locals are world-class shoppers. Every time I return home, I initially have a hard time even finding my way around—retail outlets, mostly national chain stores, seem to continually reproduce like a computer virus, blanketing all four corners of every intersection in the bedroom communities that envelop Big D. The Dallas Convention and Visitors Bureau likes to tout that there are more shopping opportunities per capita in Dallas than in any other city in the United States. So if you're a shopper, and come from a place less rich in retail mania, you've got your work cut out.

If you need to focus your shopping attention, incline it toward Western duds (especially Texas-made cowboy boots) and upscale clothing and accessories (this is the home of world-famous Neiman Marcus, after all). Texans aren't generally fond of taxes (there's still no state income tax), but there is a state sales tax, and it's one of the highest in the country: 8.25%.

## GREAT SHOPPING AREAS

Downtown Dallas is largely eviscerated of shopping outlets as inhabitants have flocked to the suburbs. Only Neiman Marcus, the mother of all Dallas purveyors of luxury goods, has stayed put. The **West End MarketPlace** (www.dallaswestend. org) was carved out of an old candy and cracker warehouse to draw hungry tourists and get things going downtown. The real high-volume shopping is done north of downtown, in **Uptown** as well as **Highland Park, North Dallas** (north of LBJ Fwy.), and **suburbs** such as Plano and Frisco. The best spot in Plano is the chic **Shops at Legacy** (Legacy Dr. at the Tollway.

In the area that real estate agents have designated **Uptown,** a vintage trolley line travels along McKinney Avenue, allowing shoppers to jump off to duck into its many antiques shops, art galleries, furniture stores, restaurants, and specialty shops. **West Village** is an outdoor, European-style mall of chic shops, restaurants, bars, and a movie theater at the north end of McKinney Avenue. Knox and Henderson streets, bisected by Central Expressway, are lined with home-furnishing stores and antiques dealers, with an eclectic decoration shop or two mixed in. Routh and Fairmount streets have a large number of art galleries and antiques shops. **Greenville Avenue** is home to a dizzying array of funky shops, including antiques dealers and vintage clothing stores. The avenue gets a little funkier the farther south you travel, with Lower Greenville, in particular, home to plenty of bars and restaurants that make great pit stops. **Deep Ellum,** which rules the alternative night, is loaded by day with offbeat furnishings stores, art galleries, folk-art shops, and vintage resale shops. The newest and coolest district, with a smattering of indie-style small boutiques and vintage shops, is the **Bishop Arts District** in Oak Cliff. Of course, most locals tend to head straight for the malls, and if you're in Dallas doing some big-volume shopping, you might do the same; the best are listed below.

## NATIVE TO BIG D

**Neiman Marcus ★★★** (which my father-in-law never tires of calling "Needless Mark-ups"), established in 1907, is a local institution; its annual holiday catalog has become part of pop culture (a once-a-year opportunity to order "His & Her Mummies" or perhaps your own personal $20-million submarine). Beyond those attention-grabbing stunts, Neiman Marcus remains one of the classiest high-end retail stores around, and its downtown flagship store has a chic retro look that is suddenly very hip today. It's not to be missed, even if you can't fritter away your rent money on a pair of Manolo Blahniks. The downtown store, a beauty of retro 1960s style at 1618 Main St. at Ervay Street (✆ 214/741-6911; www.neimanmarcus.com), is open Monday through Saturday from 10am to 5:30pm; stores in the NorthPark and Prestonwood malls are open on Sunday.

Another department store where customers tend to be dripping in diamonds and have drivers waiting outside to gather the bags is the sophisticated **Stanley Korshak ★★,** a purveyor of sleek fashions for men and women in the Crescent Court hotel (Ste. 500) on McKinney Avenue between Maple and Pearl (✆ 214/871-3600; www.stanleykorshak.com). **Forty Five Ten ★★★,** 4510 McKinney Ave. (✆ 214/559-4510; www.fortyfiveten.com), is Dallas's most rarefied and chic emporium, with one-of-a-kind fashion (for both men and women), jewelry, and home decor items. Though it's plenty glitzy, the 8,000-square-foot shop almost qualifies as under-stated for Dallas; it's a terrific place if you're looking for something unique.

Dallas is an especially good place to pick up Western wear—boots, hats, shirts, and belts—whether you want to look the part of a real cowboy or prefer the more adorned "drugstore cowboy" look. Boots of all leathers and exotic skins, both machine- and handmade, from Texas boot companies (Justin, Tony Lama, and Nocona) are good deals in Dallas. You can even order custom-made boots if you've got a grand or so to burn. Compare pricing at any of the following, all of which have excellent selections, and be sure to ask about proper boot fit: **Boot Town,** 5909 Belt Line Rd. at Preston (✆ 972/385-3052; www.boottown.com), or 2821 LBJ Fwy. at Josey Lane (✆ 972/243-1151); **Wild Bill's,** West End MarketPlace, third floor (✆ 214/954-1050); **Cavender's Boot City,** 5539 LBJ Fwy. (✆ 972/239-1375); and **Western Warehouse,** 2475 Stemmons Fwy. (✆ 214/634-2668), or 10838 N. Central Expwy. at

Meadows (© 214/891-0888). Very fancy Western wear can be found at **Cowboy Cool ★★**, in the West Village at 3699 McKinney Ave. (© **214/521-4500;** www. cowboycool.com); it's the place to go if you want to drop $500 on a Western shirt or a grand on a unique pair of boots, all with a touch of rock 'n' roll to go with the country.

Vintage Western clothing can be a bit hard to come by. **Ahab Bowen ★★**, 2614 Boll St. (© **214/720-1874**), occasionally stocks vintage Western shirts, along with one of Dallas's best selection of other carefully chosen items for both men and women. Jam-packed **Gratitude Vintage Apparel & Nostalgia ★★**, 3613 Fairmount St. (© **214/522-2921;** www.gratitudevintage.com), moving into its third decade, has something for just about everyone at every price range, from costumes and cowboy boots to jewelry, lunch boxes, and funky hats. Another cool vintage shop is **Artfunkles Vintage Boutique,** in the West Village at 3699 McKinney Ave., Ste. C311 (© **214/526-5195**). (If you're looking for Western duds, though, and are headed to Fort Worth, there are several excellent Western wear stores clustered around the Stockyards; see "Shopping" in chapter 5.) Exclusive gift items for the upscale cowboy—sterling silver money clips, Michel Jordi wristwatches, belt buckles with longhorns and state-of-Texas and cowboy insignias—can be had for a price at **Bohlin Custom Shop ★**, 4230 Lyndon B. Johnson Fwy. (© **800/823-8340** or 972/960-0335; www.bohlinmade.com).

Dallas's coolest record store is **Good Records ★**, 1808 Lower Greenville Ave. (© **214/752-4663;** www.goodrecords.com), with in-store performances and a great selection of hard-to-find indie rock. **Dallas Farmers' Market ★**, 1010 S. Pearl Expwy. (© **214/939-2808;** www.dallasfarmersmarket.org), spread over 12 acres just south of downtown Dallas, is one of the nation's largest open-air produce markets. First opened in 1941, it looks across at the glittering Dallas skyline. Farmers from around the area sell directly to the consumer. The market is open daily from 7am to 6pm. For chocoholics, the must-visit destination is **Dude, Sweet ★★★**, 408 W. 8th St., in the Bishop Arts District in Oak Cliff (© **214/943-5943;** www.dudesweet chocolate.com), a funky little purveyor of imaginative, handmade chocolates and an amazing chocolate sauce in a retro medicine bottle. All their stuff makes great gifts.

## DEPARTMENT STORES & MALLS

It would be impossible to cover Dallas's dozens of major shopping malls here—and more difficult still to hit them all on your visit to Dallas. Following are a few of the best, both for the number and quality of stores and for their general ambience.

**NorthPark Center ★★**, Northwest Highway/Loop 12 at I-75 (© **214/363-7441**), is the most traditional mall and, to my mind, the most elegant. NorthPark has 160 shops and major anchor stores (including Neiman Marcus, Tiffany's, and Nordstrom), as well as natural lighting and, best of all, a rotating display of owner Ray Nasher's fabulous sculpture collection of modern masters throughout the mall (the majority of his collection can be seen at Nasher Sculpture Center). NorthPark had a makeover that doubled its size, making it the largest mall in the Metroplex, but respected the good taste of the original 1960s structure. Not a mall, but not far from NorthPark, is one of my favorite shopping stops in Dallas: the sprawling flagship store **Half Price Books Records & Magazines ★★** at 5915 E. Northwest Hwy., just east of Central Expressway (© **214/363-8374**). The massive selection of books—including art and architecture books, coffee-table books, books on tape, and language books—blows away almost any new bookstore, and everything is at half-price or less.

**Highland Park Village** ★★, Mockingbird Lane at Preston Road (☎ 214/559-2740), is as close as you'll get to Beverly Hills' Rodeo Drive in Dallas. This ultra-chic corner of high-end shopping in the midst of Dallas's most exclusive neighborhood was built in the 1930s—reportedly the first shopping mall in the U.S.—and sports an eclectic mix of today's most fashionable boutiques (such as Calvin Klein, Prada, Chanel, Bottega Veneta, and Hermès). Shops aren't enclosed like at a traditional suburban American mall; rather, they face inward for a more enjoyable (or shall we say, European) shopping experience.

The **Galleria,** LBJ Freeway and Dallas Parkway North (☎ 972/702-7100; www.dallasgalleria.com), is a huge mall with a light-filled atrium (said to mimic the original Galleria in Milan, Italy). It attracts some of Dallas's most sophisticated shoppers to Macy's, Nordstrom, Saks Fifth Avenue, Versace, Cartier, and Hugo Boss. You'll also find an ice-skating rink, a Westin Hotel, and a host of restaurants—but many people seem to come just to stroll.

# BIG D AFTER DARK

Dallas has a very lively nightlife scene, with enough in the way of performing arts and theater (now better than ever with the new AT&T Performing Arts Center) to entertain highbrows and more than enough bars and clubs of all stripes to satisfy the young and the restless. If you've come to north Texas to wrangle a mechanical bull, you may have to drop in on Fort Worth, but there are a couple of sturdy honky-tonks in Big D where you can strap on your boots and your best Stetson and do some two-steppin' and Western swing dancing.

## THE PERFORMING ARTS

In terms of culture, Dallas has had to play catch-up to Fort Worth and Houston, but the downtown Arts District has come a long way in a relatively short time, helped by the contributions of local arts patrons and an influx of buildings by world-renowned architects. The **Morton H. Meyerson Symphony Center** ★★, 2301 Flora St. at North Pearl (☎ 214/692-0203; www.dallassymphony.com), is home to the Dallas Symphony Orchestra, a very respectable outfit. The I. M. Pei–designed auditorium is equipped with excellent acoustics and a spectacular pipe organ. Tickets to events are as little as $12, and free concerts are occasionally held. (Free tours are available on selected days at 1pm; call in advance for schedule.)

But the big Arts District buzz belongs to the newest works by international architectural glitterati. The **Dallas Opera,** 2403 Flora St. (☎ 214/443-1000; www.dallasopera.org), performs at the stunning new **Winspear Opera House** ★★★, a gleaming red horseshoe within a glass box designed by Sir Norman Foster, part of the $340-million, 10-acre **AT&T Center for the Performing Arts** (☎ 214/880-0202;

 **Ticket Central**

For tickets to sporting events and performances, try **Central Tickets** (☎ 800/462-7979 or 817/335-9000; www.centralticketoffice.com), **Star Tickets** (☎ 888/597-STAR [7827]; www.startickets.com), or **Front Gate Tickets** (☎ 888/512-7469; www.frontgatetickets.com). For many events, there's little need to secure tickets in advance of your trip, but that's not the case with big sporting and musical performances.

www.attpac.org), which opened in 2009. Another star architect, Rem Koolhaas, along with Joshua Prince-Ramus, added an intimate but futuristic 600-seat theater cube to the complex: the **Wyly Theater** ★★★, 2400 Flora St. (© **214/526-8210;** www. dallastheatercenter.org). Other productions are held at Kalita Humphreys Theater, 3636 Turtle Creek Blvd., a gem and the only professional working theater built by the famed American architect Frank Lloyd Wright.

Traveling Broadway productions, such as *Stomp* and *West Side Story,* play at **Music Hall at Fair Park,** 909 First Ave. (© **214/565-1116;** www.liveatthemusichall. com). Less traditional theater is performed by the acclaimed **Kitchen Dog Theater Company,** 3120 McKinney Ave. (© **214/953-1055**). Of interest to families may be the shows put on by the **Dallas Children's Theater,** 2215 Cedar Springs (© **214/ 978-0110;** www.dct.org). A new venue hosting Latin-themed cultural events, including theater, dance, and music, as well as art exhibitions, is the colorful **Latino Cultural Center,** 2600 Live Oak (at Good Latimer) (© **214/670-3320**).

## LIVE POP, ROCK & JAZZ

**Deep Ellum,** the rowdy district east of downtown, continues to struggle after a quarter-century as the epicenter of live music and late-night dance clubs. It endured a near-death experience due to a sustained spate of unsettling gang violence, bar fights, robberies, occasional shootings, and mismanaged clubs, but recently it has experienced some signs of life. **Trees,** 2709 Elm St. (© **214/741-1122;** treesdallas. com), has been resurrected, and plays host to punk, rap, alternative and heavy metal, but other venerable stalwarts of the Dallas scene, including Club Clearview, Gypsy Tea Room, and Deep Ellum Blues, all have gone under in the past few years. Still hosting national touring acts of alternative and roots-based rock and country is the spacious **Sons of Hermann Hall** ★, 3414 Elm St. (© **214/747-4422;** www.sons ofhermann.com), a classic Texas dance hall that's equal parts pickup bar, live music venue, and honky-tonk, hosting indie rock, country, and occasional rockabilly acts. Like many classic Texas dance halls of its era, it's on the endangered list; to make ends meet, it hosts a lot of swing, blues, and "hot rhythm nights" dance lessons. **The Bone,** 2724 Elm St. (© **214/741-1993;** www.thebonedeepellum.com), in Deep Ellum, is ostensibly a blues club, but, much more than that, it's a crowded, sweaty, drinking spot for the young and rowdy. **Double Wide** ★★, 3510 Commerce St. (© **214/887-6510;** www.double-wide.com), is a down-and-dirty music club with a Southern twist; it's the place to go to get your trailer park on, with Lone Star beer, gimme caps, and live, loud rock and country music.

Christian music and culture is picking up some of the Deep Ellum void. For live, all-ages (really all ages—if you're 9 and under, you get in free!) rock and pop gigs, including emo (short for *emotional*) punk rock and Christian acts (sometimes a whole slew of bands in a single night), check out **the Door,** 2513 Elm St. (© **214/742- 3667;** www.thedoordallas.com), now in the old Gypsy Tea Room theater space.

**The Kessler** ★★, 1230 W. Davis St. (© **214/864-1748;** www.thekessler.org), a resurrected and recently renovated 1942 theater in Oak Cliff, hosts largely Texas acts (though many of national renown, such as Joe Ely, Centro-Matic, and the Gourds) playing indie rock, jazz, and alt-country. The **Palladium,** 1135 S. Lamar St. (© **972/ 854-5050;** www.thepalladiumballroom.com), is somewhere between a club and a large concert hall, with good lighting, sightlines, and sound for midsize rock, country, and alternative acts (such as the Black Crowes and Girl Talk). It contains a very intimate space (capacity 300) called **the Loft.** In Victory Park, just north of downtown, the slick new **House of Blues Dallas** ★★, 2200 N. Lamar St. (© **214/978-2583;**

www.houseofblues.com), is no ordinary juke joint; it's a 60,000-square-foot complex with a large concert hall, an outdoor patio, and a Southern restaurant. Live acts range from blues to soul and rock. In Uptown, **Renfield's Corner** ★, 2603 Routh St. (© 214/397-0300; www.renfieldscorner.com), is a nice little bar with a pair of patios, a great beer list, and good local bands playing free shows in the tiny back room. On weekends, it draws a big SMU/college crowd and can feel like a frat party.

Lower Greenville Avenue has been around forever, and is doing its best to fill the bill for bars and clubs in the wake of Deep Ellum's demise. The **Granada Theater** ★★★, 3524 Greenville Ave. (© 214/824-9933; www.granadatheater.com), is a converted old movie theater that now books such popular acts as Bob Dylan and Sigur Rós, which also appeal to a somewhat older but still hip crowd. **The Cavern** ★, 1914 Lower Greenville Ave. (© 214/828-1914; www.thecaverndallas. com), is a tiny but cool indie spot that books good alternative acts (such as Devendra Banhart) and has upstairs DJs for those who find the live space too claustrophobic.

Once a dark and atmospheric jazz cafe, **Sambuca** has gone upscale now that it's in Uptown, at 2120 McKinney Ave. (© 214/744-0820; www.sambucarestaurant. com). A spacious, thoroughly Dallas supper club, it draws a trendy crowd for cocktails, dinner, and live jazz (much of it jazz fusion to which you can dance) 7 nights a week. Perhaps Dallas's best club for live jazz is **Brooklyn** ★★, 1701 S. Lamar St. (© 214/428-0025; www.brooklynjazzcafe.com), which has a big space with an outdoor patio. **Balcony Club** ★, 1825 Abrams at La Vista (© 214/826-8104; www.thebalconyclub.net), upstairs from the Landmark (movie) Theater, is a cool, dark Art Deco spot with intimate booths, perfect for some relaxing beats and a drink. It has live jazz nightly. **Poor David's Pub** ★ (© 214/565-1295; www.poordavids pub.com), a venerable old club whose stage has been graced by many great Texas singer-songwriters (such as Guy Clark), is smoke-free and occupies decidedly not-poor digs (though it is cash only) at 1313 S. Lamar St. It aims to retain some of the old ambience, and provides a platform for live jazz and blues, albeit with slightly greater capacity.

**Dallas Alley,** in the West End, Munger Avenue at Marker Street (© 214/720-0170), is a touristy mix of bars and restaurants primarily aimed at businessmen entertaining clients and visitors staying in downtown hotels. From karaoke to country and oldies clubs, it's one-stop shopping for most groups looking for a night out on the town with a view of the skyline. Don't count on heaps of local flavor and authenticity, but the drinking and carousing seem contagious for most. The newest and best spot for big-name touring rock and pop acts is **Nokia Live Center** ★, 1001 NextStage Dr., Grand Prairie (© 972/854-5050).

## HONKY-TONK HEAVEN

**Gilley's Dallas,** a Big D branch of Houston's famous honky-tonk (which shot to fame with John Travolta on a bucking bronco in *Urban Cowboy*), finally opened at 1135 S. Lamar (© 888/GILLEYS [445-5397]; www.gilleysdallas.com). It is absolutely Texan in size, with more than 90,000 square feet to accommodate all those boots, hats, and hair. **Cowboys Red River Dancehall** ★★, 10310 Technology Blvd. (© 214/352-1796; www.cowboysdancehall.com/dallas), has live country music nightly, mechanical bull riding, a huge dance floor, and dance lessons. Worth the drive if you're a boot-scooter or country music fan is the must-see **Billy Bob's Texas** in Fort Worth (p. 134).

For a more intimate, down-and-dirty take on the honky-tonk scene, check out **Adair's Saloon** ★★, 2624 Commerce St., in Deep Ellum (© 214/939-9900;

www.adairssaloon.com), which the regulars call "Aayy-dares." It gets its share of clean-scrubbed SMU students, but mostly you'll find down-to-earth patrons and infectious country and redneck rock bands that go well with the cheap beer, shuffle-board, and tables and walls blanketed in graffiti. The perfectly greasy burgers with a whole jalapeño on top are surprisingly tasty; some say they're the best in Dallas. The only rule here is in plain English on the sign behind the bar: NO DANCIN' ON TABLES WITH SPURS.

## BARS & LOUNGES

Many of the Dallas spots for scenesters are in Uptown. **Crú,** 3699 McKinney Ave., Ste. 107 (© 214/526-9463), is a wine bar and restaurant that features an excellent wine list; most of its patrons treat it primarily as the former, sampling vintages from the many different wine flights. But the see-and-be-seen spot for wealthy Dallasites and visiting celebs (you'll know immediately if you fit in here) is the much-talked-about **Ghostbar ★** in the new W Hotel, 2440 Victory Park (© 214/871-1800). It's got a helipad tailor-made for scene-stealing arrivals. Before Ghostbar, the "it" nightlife spot was **Dragonfly,** 2332 Leonard St. (© 800/597-8399), at the restaurant of trendy Hotel ZaZa. On weekends, it is still stuffed to the rafters with guys and gals both busting out of their shirts, but otherwise it's a luxurious spot for a cocktail, such as predinner drinks poolside.

If you're looking for a quieter but still fashionable spot, venture inside Hotel Lumen, 6101 Hillcrest Ave. (© 214/219-8282), to **Social,** a swank lounge and restaurant that's a haunt of trendsetting nightlife types. In the Knox-Henderson district, the restaurant Park has a cool midcentury look and sidewalk garden terrace with superb cocktails; but its former garage space, **Bar Céline ★★**, 1921 Henderson Ave. (© 214/824-3343; www.barceline.com), tops the rest of the restaurant; with its speakeasy feel, chic brothel aesthetic and DJs, it's a great place for a late-night drink. The name sounds silly, but swanky **PM Nightlife Lounge,** 1530 Main St. (© 214/261-4501; www.pmnightlifelounge.com), downstairs at the Joule hotel, all chandeliers and red velvet, has become a downtown hot spot for the city's most stylish nightlife denizens. Among hotel bars, none is more chic than the gorgeous Art Deco space of **Bolla Bar ★**, 2927 Maple Ave. (© 800/921-8498), at the Stoneleigh Hotel in Uptown, where there's a good happy hour on weekdays.

**Bar Belmont ★★**, 901 Fort Worth Ave. (© 866/870-8010; www.belmont dallas.com), at the ultra-cool, retro Belmont Hotel in Oak Cliff, has a terrace with great views of the Dallas skyline and serves excellent cocktails. It's become a fashionable hangout for hip Bishop Arts types. Standing 560 feet aboveground in the Reunion Tower, **Five Sixty ★**, 300 Reunion Blvd. (© 214/741-5560; www.wolfgangpuck. com/restaurants/fine-dining/3917), is a sleek lounge and restaurant and terrific spot for viewing Dallas from on high and in slow, rotating motion. With a great happy hour and food by Wolfgang Puck, it's a particularly rewarding spot at sunset.

**The Old Monk ★**, 2847 N. Henderson Ave. (© 214/821-1880), is a dark, handsome bar 1 block east of Central Expressway with an excellent selection of Belgian beers, single malts, and great pub grub—go with the Belgian mussels with fries and spicy mayo. In Uptown, just off McKinney Avenue, **the Ginger Man,** 2718 Boll St. (© 214/754-8771), has a great beer garden and a beer selection to die for: about 200 beers from around the world, including 70 on tap.

A step up from karaoke is **Pete's Dueling Piano Bar,** 4980 Belt Line Rd., #200, Addison (© 972/726-7383; www.petesduelingpianobar.com), a rowdy piano bar where four accomplished players tickle the ivories on two baby grands and everybody sings along (enthusiastically) to crowd favorites by the Stones, Beatles, Johnny Cash, and even Eminem.

## DANCE CLUBS

**Lizard Lounge ★**, 2424 Swiss Ave. (at Good Latimer) (**℃ 214/826-4768;** www.thelizardlounge.com), is the city's edgiest dance club; slightly seedy but sexy, it trades in percolating dance beats and a hot crowd, with occasional live bands. Sunday night is Goth Night. The trendiest and slickest dance club is **Aura Lounge ★**, 2912 McKinney Ave. (**℃ 214/220-2872;** www.aurauptowndallas.com), with special events, go-go dancers, throngs of beautiful people, and guest DJs, Thursday through Saturday. For something out of the ordinary—Latinos dancing to Tejano and ranchero music—check out massive **Escapade 2009,** 10707 Finnell St. (**℃ 214/654-9950**).

## THE GAY & LESBIAN SCENE

The **Crew's Inn,** 3215 N. Fitzhugh Ave. (**℃** 214/526-9510), is cruise happy, but caters to the widest, rather than the wildest, common denominator of the gay community (it has angered some by reportedly banning drag queens and transgendered individuals). Another longtime favorite, with a consistently good vibe and a wall of video monitors, is **J. R.'s Bar and Grill ★**, 3923 Cedar Springs Rd. (**℃** 214/528-1004). **Village Station,** 3911 Cedar Springs Rd. (**℃** 214/559-0650), is a gay dance club that features nightly drag shows in the Rose Room and Trash Disco every Sunday. Although only nominally a gay bar, **Jack's Backyard ★★**, 2303 Pittman St. (**℃** 214/741-3131; www.jacksbackyarddallas.com), is very gay-friendly (both men and women) and features a cool lounge, laid-back gravel patio with live singer-songwriters and bands, and good bar food. **Sue Ellen's,** 3903 Cedar Springs Rd. (**℃** 214/559-0707), is a friendly gay and lesbian bar with live rock, a dance floor, and an outdoor patio. **Buddies II,** 4025 Maple Ave. (**℃** 214/526-0887), is tops for lesbians: hot music and SGWF looking for same. Gay country swing and line dancers should check out the **Texas Twisters** (www.texastwisters.org), a group that organizes two-stepping and the like for gays and lesbians around the Dallas area, frequently at the **Round-Up Saloon,** 3912 Cedar Springs Rd. (**℃** 214/522-9611), a gay country bar that has a Monday karaoke night.

# ARLINGTON

Sandwiched between Dallas and Fort Worth, the medium-size city of Arlington has become known as a pro-sports center and the family playground of the Metroplex. If you're a sports fan, or have kids in tow (or are a kid at heart), it makes a good day trip. If none of those apply, you're probably better off in Arlington's bigger and more important cousins. To get to Arlington, take I-30 from either Dallas or Fort Worth. If traffic is heavy, plan on the drive taking about an hour from either city. Having your own car is pretty much required to get around to any of the places below.

Arlington's **Visitor Information Center** is located at 1905 E. Randol Mill Rd. (**℃ 800/342-4305** or 817/461-3888; www.arlington.org).

### Coupon Discounts

In addition to the coupons available in the *Dallas/Fort Worth Area Visitors Guide* (available from tourist information offices), look for the brochure *The Dallas Metroplex: One Exciting Savings Place,* which has coupons worth $10 at Six Flags.

# The Top Attractions

**Rangers Ballpark in Arlington** ★ ☺  The home of the Texas Rangers professional baseball team is one of the finest ballparks in the country. The graceful, red-brick-and-granite 50,000-seat stadium was designed (by the architect David Schwarz, a favorite in Fort Worth) to echo classic American baseball parks. The flat, painted billboards in the outfield with retro graphics and the absence of glaring neon lend a yesteryear feel to the park. It's a terrific place to see a game, even for folks (like me) who aren't huge baseball fans.

1000 Ballpark Way, Arlington. ✆ **817/273-5220** or 273-5100 ticket office or 273-5099 tours. http://texas.rangers.mlb.com. Ballpark tours $10 adults, $8 seniors, $5 children 4-18. Mon-Sat 9am-4pm. Museum Apr-Sept Mon-Sat 9am-4pm, Sun 11am-4pm (game days 7:30pm); Oct-Mar Tues-Sat 10am-4pm. Take I-30 from either Dallas or Fort Worth and exit at Nolan Ryan Expwy./Ballpark Way.

**Ripley's Grand Prairie** ☺  Merged under one roof are now three oddballs of family fun. Louis Tussaud's Palace of Wax features wax dummies of movie stars and historical figures such as Mother Teresa, Tom Hanks as Forrest Gump, Jesus Christ, and Dorothy and her *Wizard of Oz* pals. Ripley's **Believe It or Not! Odditorium** is a collection of the hard-to-swallow and bizarre, such as the giraffe-necked woman of Burma and the double-eyed man of China. Really small kids may get freaked, but most children 6 and older are likely to find the exhibits pretty cool. The newest attraction is Ripley's Enchanted Mirror Maze. Check out the coupons available online. Allow 2 hours to enjoy this place.

601 E. Palace Pkwy., Grand Prairie. ✆ **972/263-2391.** www.grandprairie.ripleys.com. Admission to single attraction $17 adults, $9 children 4-12, free for children 3 and under. Combination visit to all 3 attractions $26 adults, $16 children 4-12, free for children 3 and under. Mon-Fri 10am-5pm; Sat-Sun 10am-6pm.

**Six Flags Hurricane Harbor** ☺  The biggest water park in north Texas is 3 million gallons of water and 50 acres of relief from the Texas sun. The kids will go nuts at such feature attractions as Hook's Lagoon (pirate ships and 12 levels of interactive features), Black Hole (a tentacle-like thrill ride that plunges through dark, wet tubes), and the Bubba Tub (an inner-tube ride that begins at the top of a 70-ft. tower). A couple of dozen more rides, slides, and pools, including a 1-million-gallon wave pool, will entertain and douse you and your family. Professional lifeguards are on duty.

1800 E. Lamar Blvd., Arlington. ✆ **817/640-8900.** www.sixflags.com/hurricaneharbortexas. $28 adults; $22 children 4 ft. tall or under, seniors, and visitors with disabilities; free for children 2 and under. Adult ticket deals available online. Mid-May to late Sept.; check website for days and hours.

**Six Flags Over Texas** ★ ☺  Now 40 years old, Six Flags is the place I used to dream about going as a kid. The 200-acre amusement park, one of the biggest and best in the country, is the top draw in Texas (and it can be a little crowded on summer weekends). It has Texas-size roller coasters, including the Texas Giant (once the world's tallest wooden coaster that hits speeds of more than 60 mph), Batman the Ride (a suspended looping coaster with six inversions and corkscrew spirals), and Mr. Freeze (one of the fastest and tallest roller coasters in the Southwest). There are also tons of shows, eateries, and nostalgic rides such as the Parachute Drop and the Log Ride, with its peculiar green water that thrilled my little girlfriends and me back in the '70s.

I-30 at Hwy. 360, Arlington. ✆ **817/640-8900.** www.sixflags.com/overtexas. $55 adults ($35 online), $35 children 4 ft. tall or under and seniors, free for children 2 and under. Mid-May to late Aug daily; Mar to mid-May and Sept-Oct weekends only; check website for hours and special deals.

**Trader's Village** A rollicking and locally famous flea market (spread out over 100 acres), Trader's Village has been trading everything under the sun since the early 1970s. It attracts a couple of thousand dealers each weekend and tens of thousands of shoppers search through the junk for the occasional find. There are also rides and games for the kids.

2602 Mayfield Rd., off Hwy. 360 in Grand Prairie, south of Arlington. © **972/647-2331.** www.traders village.com. Free admission. Sat–Sun 8am–dusk.

# FORT WORTH

by Neil Edward Schlecht

asygoing Fort Worth has lived for years in the shadow of Dallas, its brash cousin to the east. Yet the city exudes a quiet confidence, reserve, and sense of comfort that are often missing in Big D. Gradually, people are learning that Fort Worth has plenty that Dallasites might envy (including a 2011 Rose Bowl title for local football heroes, the TCU Horned Frogs).

Long nicknamed "Cowtown" (a sobriquet which the city has shied away from, given its newfound sophistication), Fort Worth still revels in its role as the gateway to the West; the mythic qualities of the American West—wide-open spaces and even grander dreams—are still palpable here. In the mid–19th century, on the heels of the war between Texas and Mexico, Fort Worth began as a frontier army town in the Republic of Texas, assigned with protecting settlers from Native American attacks. The outpost grew into the last major stop along the Chisholm Trail, the major thoroughfare of the great Texas cattle drives that took ranchers and their livestock 500 miles north to the railheads and more lucrative markets of Dodge City and Abilene, Kansas. The trail's importance transformed Fort Worth into a busy trading post. By 1881, more than five million head of cattle had been driven through town on their way to market. Saloons, bordellos, and gambling houses staked out the rough-hewn area of town called "Hell's Half Acre."

With the arrival of the railroad, the stampede of cattle north grew exponentially, and strategically positioned Fort Worth became a place for ranchers to keep their herds before moving them for sale. The Fort Worth Stockyards opened in 1890, followed by the arrival of major meatpacking plants, transforming Fort Worth into a major cattle shipping center and one of the country's top livestock markets. Fort Worth had become a wealthy city, a cow town to be reckoned with. The rise of the oil business in West Texas bolstered Fort Worth's commercial prospects, and oil fortunes replaced the cattle-ranching riches of the early–20th century.

If Fort Worth in frontier days was where the East fizzled out and the West began, today the city is a place where cowboy culture meets high culture. It is probably the most authentically Texan city in the state. Yet Fort Worth is as much a culture town as a cow town. The city is home not only to a tenacious pride in its Old West past, with plenty of modern-day cowboys and Western flavor, but also to one of the country's most celebrated highbrow art scenes. Cultural cognoscenti call it the "Museum Capital of the Southwest." Local oil-rich philanthropists have endowed the city with superlative collections of art and hired some of the world's most prestigious architects—Philip Johnson, Louis Kahn, and Tadao Ando—to build the esteemed Kimbell Art Museum (in the midst of an expansion by Rienzo Piano), enlarged Amon Carter Museum of Western Art, and spectacular Fort Worth Modern Art Museum. The city is also home to a symphony orchestra, an impressive botanical garden, several theater companies, and the Van Cliburn International Piano Competition. As it turns out, this cowboy town with a rough-and-tumble past has a remarkably sophisticated and arts-minded soul. Even if you come to the Dallas area with little time to spare, Fort Worth—laid-back, historic, friendly, and surprisingly progressive—is absolutely worth a visit. For me, it is the highlight of north Texas.

As if by well-devised plan, Fort Worth's downtown, a charming and dignified center of business and entertainment, is almost perfectly equidistant from the Stockyards National Historic District and the Cultural District. Fort Worth natives may like to keep the essential elements of their city separate, but they seem to recognize that they add up to a cohesive whole.

# ORIENTATION

## Arriving

See "Orientation" in chapter 4 for detailed information on getting to both Dallas and Fort Worth.

## Essentials

### VISITOR INFORMATION

Besides the DFW Airport Visitor Information (p. 53), the **Fort Worth Convention & Visitors Bureau** (© 800/433-5747 or 817/336-8791; www.fortworth.com) maintains tourist information centers downtown on Sundance Square at 508 Main St. (© **817/698-3300**); in the Stockyards National Historic District at 130 E. Exchange Ave. (© **817/624-4741**); and in the Cultural District at 3401 W. Lancaster Ave. (© **817/882-8588**). Of the three, only the one in the Stockyards is open Sundays (noon–4pm).

The city's events hot line is © **817/332-2000.**

### CITY LAYOUT

Fort Worth lies just west of I-35, which runs north-south. For most visitors, Fort Worth means three distinct districts, which the city calls the Western Triangle: the Stockyards National Historic District, 2 miles north of downtown; historic downtown, which includes Sundance Square, just north of I-30, running east-west; and the Cultural District, 2 miles west of downtown, just beyond the new West 7th Street development. See the Fort Worth map on p. 105 to help orient yourself.

## The Neighborhoods in Brief

**Stockyards National Historic District** This area was the focus of the old cattle-raising and livestock business of Fort Worth. Today, the district retains its Old West feel with rodeos and Wild West shows, as well as daily cattle drives down Exchange Avenue. A handful of hotels and restaurants aimed at visitors are located here, but it's not overly touristy.

**Downtown** Downtown is the center of the Fort Worth business community and includes **Sundance Square,** where much of the city's restaurant, bar, and theater nightlife and most business-oriented hotels are located. Staying in this area is best if you want to get around easily between the Cultural District, the Stockyards District, and downtown.

**Cultural District** Fort Worth's outstanding museums, including the Kimbell, Modern, and Amon Carter, are clustered in the Cultural District. Just south are parks and gardens, including the Fort Worth Zoo and Botanic Gardens. Art lovers will want to base themselves here, but the Stockyards District and downtown are better for families.

**Medical District** Immediately south of downtown, this is the site of major hospitals and several residential areas, and Fort Worth's major university, Texas Christian University (TCU). Many hotels and restaurants are located south of I-30 as well. There's no major benefit to basing yourself here, but it's where you'll find some of the cheaper hotels.

**West 7th Street Corridor** A neighborhood on the rise, this new development bridging downtown Fort Worth and the Cultural District has mushroomed in the last couple of years. Occasionally referred to as W7, it's home to a burgeoning number of chic shops, bars and restaurants, and condos.

## GETTING AROUND
### By Public Transportation

For information on getting to Fort Worth from **Dallas/Fort Worth International Airport (DFW),** see "Arriving/By Plane" in chapter 4.

Within the city, the only public transportation most visitors will need are city buses **(the T)** that run every 20 minutes among the three major districts, from the Fort Worth Zoo all the way to the Stockyards, making stops downtown on the way. Buses run daily from 6:15am to 10:15pm. The regular one-way fare is $1.50 for adults; 75¢ for seniors, travelers with disabilities, and students ages 6 to 16; and $3 ($1.50 students and seniors) for a day pass. Within the downtown area, service (on red, white, and blue buses) is free. Route 1 (brown) travels from North Main Street to the Stockyards; Route 2 (blue), from Camp Bowie to the Cultural District; and Route 7 (green), from University/Montgomery to the Cultural District. Pick up a schedule at any visitor information center or obtain information on schedules by calling ⓒ 817/215-8600 or by visiting www.the-t.com.

**Molly the Trolley,** a vintage-style trolley, operates three routes around Fort Worth: Downtown Get Around (daily 10am–10pm, free), Stockyards Shuttle (Sat only, $1.50 one-way), and Sundance Lunch Line (Mon–Fri, 11am–2pm, free). Call ⓒ 817/215-8600 or see www.mollythetrolley.com for route maps.

The **Trinity Railway Express (TRE)** is the most convenient and hassle-free way to travel to Dallas without having to worry about traffic. It's an express commuter train connecting the two cities, traveling to DFW Airport, Irving, Dallas's American Airlines Center (for Mavericks and Stars games), and Dallas Union Station ($5 one-way; $10 day pass). Pickup and drop-off points are the Texas & Pacific Station and the Intermodal Transportation Center downtown (at 9th and Jones sts.). Call ⓒ 877/215-8600 or 817/215-8600 or visit www.trinityrailwayexpress.org for route and schedule information.

### By Car

With the city's efficient bus and trolley services, you can quite easily manage to get around Fort Worth without a car. However, if you want to spend time in Dallas or Arlington, you'll be better off with an automobile. Car-rental agencies in Fort Worth include **Avis,** 801 W. Weatherford St. (ⓒ **800/230-4898;** www.avis.com); **Budget,** 1001 Henderson St. (ⓒ **800/527-0700;** www.budget.com); **Enterprise,** 2832 W. 7th St. (ⓒ **800/RENT A CAR** [736-8222]; www.enterprise.com); and **Hertz,** 917 Taylor St. (ⓒ **817/654-3131;** www.hertz.com).

# Fort Worth Stockyards National Historic District

**ACCOMMODATIONS** ■
Azalea Plantation Bed & Breakfast Inn **16**
Hyatt Place Fort Worth Historic Stockyards **11**
Miss Molly's Bed & Breakfast Hotel **6**
Stockyards Hotel **6**
Stonehouse Hotel **1**

**DINING** ◆
Cattlemen's Steakhouse **5**
Esperanza's Bakery **2**
Joe T. Garcia's Mexican Dishes **2**
Lonesome Dove Western Bistro **3**
Love Shack **4**

**ATTRACTIONS** ●
Billy Bob's Texas **7**
Cowtown Cattlepen Maze **10**
Cowtown Coliseum **8**
Grapevine Vintage Railroad **14**
Livestock Exchange Building/ Stockyards Museum **9**
Stockyards Station **15**
Texas Cowboy Hall of Fame **13**
White Elephant Saloon **12**

## By Taxi

You'll have to call a cab unless you're lucky enough to catch one outside a hotel. The major companies operating in Fort Worth are **Yellow Checker Taxi** (☏ 817/426-6262) and **Cowboy Cab** (☏ 817/428-0202). Fares are $2.25 (initial drop) and 20¢ for each additional ⅕ mile. Extras include $2 extra passenger charge, $3.60 airport exit fee, and $2.60 airport drop-off fee.

# [FastFACTS] FORT WORTH

**American Express**
There is an office at Gulliver's Travel, 2800 S. Hulen St., #110 (☏ 817/924-7766; Mon–Fri 9am–5pm).

**Babysitters** If your hotel doesn't offer baby-sitting services, contact **Baby Sitters of Dallas** (☏ 817/960-2174; www.babysittersofdallas.com) for child care; despite the name, they handle Fort Worth and Tarrant County.

**Dentists** Call ☏ 800/577-7320 for a dentist referral service.

**Doctors** Call the **Tarrant County Medical Society** (☏ 817/732-3997) for a doctor referral.

**Drugstores** Area locations for **CVS stores** include 4140 E. Lancaster Ave. (☏ 817/534-0261) and

8560 S. Hulen St. (☎ **817/292-0048).** . The CVS store at 3614 Camp Bowie Blvd. (☎ **817/870-1873** is open 24 hours.

**Hospitals**   The Medical District, south of downtown, has two large, full-service hospitals: **Columbia Plaza Medical Center,** 900 8th Ave. (☎ **817/336-2100**), and **Baylor All Saints Medical Center,** 1400 8th Ave. (☎ **817/926-2544**).

**Internet Access**   One centrally located cybercafe is **Cyber Rodeo,** 1309 Calhoun St., within the Rodeo Steakhouse (☎ **817/332-1288**). Free wireless hot spots include **8.0 Restaurant and Bar,** 111 E. 3rd St. (☎ **817/336-0880**), and **Flying Saucer Drought Emporium,** 111 E. 4th St. (☎ **817/336-7468**).

**Maps**   Any of the Fort Worth tourist information centers can provide you with free maps of all of Fort Worth or individual districts.

**Newspapers & Magazines**   Both the *Fort Worth Star-Telegram* and the *Dallas Morning News* "Weekend Guide" have plenty of arts, entertainment, and dining information for Fort Worth and the Metroplex, as does the free *Fort Worth Weekly.*

**Police**   For an emergency, dial ☎ **911.** For nonemergencies, call ☎ **817/871-6458.** The main police station in downtown Fort Worth is located at 350 W. Belknap St. (at Taylor St.).

**Post Office**   The main downtown post office, 251 W. Lancaster Ave. (☎ **817/348-0565**), is open Monday through Friday from 7:30am to 7pm.

**Safety**   For a city of more than 600,000 (and the 17th-largest city in the U.S.), Fort Worth is a relaxed and, from most appearances, very safe city.

Still, as in any large city, visitors should exercise caution and keep an eye on their handbags, especially at night, in major tourist destinations such as the Stockyards and the Cultural District, and downtown around Sundance Square. Beyond Sundance Square, which is very lively at night, much of downtown Fort Worth is virtually deserted after 9pm. Drive or take a taxi late at night.

**Taxes**   The general sales tax is 8.25%, hotel tax is 15%, and restaurant tax is 7%.

**Transit Info**   For general public transportation questions, call the **Fort Worth Transportation Authority** at ☎ **817/871-6200.** For "the T" bus schedule information, call ☎ **817/215-8600** or visit www.the-t.com.

**Weather**   For the latest weather information, call ☎ **817/787-1111.**

# WHERE TO STAY

Fort Worth may not be loaded with ultra-deluxe accommodations, but it does have a nice mix of affordable lodgings, including an attractive roster of Western-flavored small hotels and bed-and-breakfasts. They are spread fairly evenly among the major districts of interest, so you can stay on the main drag of the Stockyards, downtown on Sundance Square, or south of town near the Cultural District. Everything in Fort Worth is pretty close and easily accessible, though, so you needn't choose your hotel strictly according to your primary sightseeing interests.

At Stockyards District hotels, unlike in most places, weekend rates are higher than weekday rates. The rates quoted below do not include 15% hotel occupancy tax. Breakfast, either continental or buffet, is offered free at several hotels, as noted below. Do not assume that breakfast is included; if it is not, it can really add to your bill.

The rates cited below, it bears repeating, are high-season rack rates. At a minimum, request the lower corporate rate, and ask about special deals. Virtually all hotels offer some deals, especially on weekends when their business clientele dries up. This is not the case in the Stockyards, however, where prices rise on weekends. Check individual hotels' websites for special online offers.

0 1/8 mile
0 100 meters

↗ 2.5 miles to Stockyards

↗ 17.5 miles to DFW Airport

**1**

Trinity River

N Main St.

Bluff St.

E Belknap St.

E Weatherford St.

Grove St.

3rd St.

Heritage Park Plaza

**Tarrant County Courthouse**

Commerce St.

Main St.

**2**

Bluff St.

W. Belknap St.

W. Weatherford St.

Taylor St.

Cherry St.

1st St.

2nd St.

3rd St.

Florence St.

Henderson St.

Burnett St.

Lamar St.

5th St.

6th St.

**3**

**4**

**5**

**SUNDANCE SQUARE**

**6**

**7**

**8**

Jones St.

Calhoun St.

**9**

**9**

6th St.

7th St.

**10**

**11**

8th St.

8th St.

9th St.

**Greyhound Trailways Bus Depot**

5th St.

7th St.

Macon St.

Cherry St.

**Burnett Park**

Throckmorton St.

Houston St.

**Federal Building**

10th St.

10th St.

**U.S. Courthouse**

**City Hall**

**Fort Worth Convention Center**

12th St.

13th St.

**Train Station**

14th St.

15th St.

Texas St.

Burnett St.

Lamar St.

Taylor St.

Monroe St.

Jennings St.

**12**

**13**

13th St.

**14**

**Area of detail**

**FORT WORTH**

35W

**Dallas-Fort Worth Int'l Airport**

820

820

360

30

30

183

20

820

30

**15**

Lancaster Ave. West

5

**ATTRACTIONS** ●
Bass Performance Hall **8**
Fire Station No. 1/"150 Years of Fort Worth" exhibit **2**
Fort Worth Water Gardens **13**
Sid Richardson Museum **6**

**ACCOMMODATIONS** ■
The Ashton Hotel **9**
Etta's Place **5**

Hilton Fort Worth **10**
Omni Fort Worth Hotel **12**
TownePlace Suites Fort Worth Downtown **1**
The Worthington Renaissance Fort Worth Hotel **3**

**DINING** ◆
Brownstone **15**
Del Frisco's Double Eagle Steak House **11**
Ferré Ristorante e Bar **7**
Reata **4**
Six 10 Grille **9**
Tillman's Roadhouse **14**

# STOCKYARDS NATIONAL HISTORIC DISTRICT
## Expensive

**Stockyards Hotel** ★★   A true taste of the Old West, the Stockyards Hotel has, since 1907, been the heart of Fort Worth's illustrious cowboy and railroad past. It has hosted Bonnie and Clyde, Wild West poker games, gun-slinging fights, and country music stars. Behind the historic brick facade, each of the rooms works a different aspect of an Old West theme. You can stay in the Davy Crockett, Geronimo, or Victorian Parlor room, or sleep where Bonnie and Clyde hid out in the early '30s (that's cool enough to make it my favorite). The Stockyards Hotel gets the look and feel right: It's not a stretch to imagine cowboys riding up in a cloud of dust and tying up their horses to the posts out front, making it the ideal place to stay in Fort Worth for a real Western experience. The connected restaurant is the H3 Ranch Steakhouse, just a notch below the Cattlemen's Steakhouse (p. 114) around the corner, but a good place for wood-fired steaks, ribs, and spit-roasted pork and chicken. The bar, with horse-saddle bar stools, is called Booger Red's Saloon (where you can knock back a cold Buffalo Butt beer).

109 W. Exchange Ave., Fort Worth, TX 76106. ℂ **800/423-8471** or 817/625-6427. Fax 817/624-2571. www.stockyardshotel.com. 52 units. $189–$269 double; $269–$419 suite. Weekend and other packages available. AE, DC, DISC, MC, V. Valet parking $10. **Amenities:** Restaurant; concierge; room service. *In room:* A/C and fan, TV, hair dryer, Wi-Fi (free).

## Moderate

**Azalea Plantation Bed & Breakfast Inn** ★ 🍴   Near the Stockyards, but secluded on a couple of acres of oaks, magnolias, and azaleas, this peaceful 1948 plantation-style home invites relaxation: It has a gazebo and wooden yard swing, a fireplace in the parlor, crystal and china, and a Victorian dining room. There are two upstairs rooms and two cottages, all with comfortable beds. The Lily of the Valley Room has a whirlpool tub, king-size poster-bed, and veranda; the Bluebonnet Bungalow is a cottage with a cow-town theme; and the Rose of Sharon room has a king-size canopy bed and marble-floored bathroom, and opens onto a veranda. The Magnolia cottage features a private parlor and giant Jacuzzi. Although some guests might find the furnishings and decor to be a bit frilly for their tastes, others who love Victoriana and romantic touches will eat it up. Early-morning coffee and a "hearty plantation" breakfast will start you out on the right foot.

1400 Robinwood Dr., Fort Worth, TX 76111. ℂ **800/687-3529** or 817/838-5882. www.azaleaplantation. com. 4 units. $189 double; $209 cottage suite. Rates include breakfast. AE, DC, DISC, MC, V. Free parking. *In room:* A/C, TV/DVD/VCR, movie library, CD player, hair dryer, minibar, Wi-Fi (free).

**Hyatt Place Fort Worth Historic Stockyards** 😊 🍴   Although it seems out of place in this historic Western district, this revamped hotel is a welcome addition to Cowtown. Thankfully, it's set back from the main drag, so its large, generic facade doesn't disparage too greatly the look of the old cobblestone street lined with former stables and historic buildings. Its excellent location and good-value accommodations, which are clean and modern, if unexciting, are what recommend this hotel. It's not as Fort Worth cool as the Stockyards Hotel up the street, of course, but the convenience and cost will appeal especially to families—kids will appreciate the pool and cattlepen maze across the street, as well as the daily cattle run in front of the hotel.

132 E. Exchange Ave., Fort Worth, TX 76106. ℂ **817/626-6000.** Fax 817/626-6018. http://stockyards. place.hyatt.com. 102 units. $139–$279 double; $399 suite. Rates include continental breakfast. AE, DC, DISC, MC, V. Free parking. **Amenities:** Cafe; concierge; exercise room; outdoor heated pool; room service. *In room:* A/C, TV, hair dryer, minibar, Wi-Fi (free).

# Fort Worth Cultural District

**ACCOMMODATIONS** ■
Residence Inn Fort Worth Cultural District **3**
Residence Inn Fort Worth University **15**
The Texas White House Bed & Breakfast **20**

**DINING** ◆
Angelo's Barbecue **2**
Brix Pizza & Wine Bar **13**
Café Modern **4**
Kinkaid's Gro. Market Hamburgers **8**
Lanny's Alta Cocina Mexicana **6**
Nonna Tata **18**
Paris Coffee Shop **17**
Railhead Smokehouse **12**
Sardines Ristorante Italiano **1**
Spiral Diner & Bakery **19**

**ATTRACTIONS** ●
Amon Carter Museum of Western Art **7**
Fort Worth Botanic Garden **11**
Fort Worth Museum of Science and History **9**
Fort Worth Zoo **16**
Kimbell Art Museum **5**
Log Cabin Village **14**
Modern Art Museum of Fort Worth **4**
National Cowgirl Museum and Hall of Fame **10**
Thistle Hill House Museum **12**

**Miss Molly's Bed & Breakfast Hotel**   Above a raucous bar, Miss Molly's is a slightly bawdy little place (a former bordello, rumored to be haunted) that's seen all manner of folks come through, including cattle barons, outlaws, and railroaders. Today, it's much more likely to host couples looking to indulge in a little Old West romanticism and Stockyards partying. The landmark 1910 Victorian building, a second story wedged in among the saloons and Western shops on the main drag, is decorated with Western quilts, period pieces, and Victorian lamps. Rooms are named for their decorative theme; for example, the Cattlemen's room has a carved oak bed beneath mounted longhorns. Miss Josie's, the Victorian bedroom of the former madam and the closest thing to a den of iniquity, is twice as large as the other rooms. However, guests share three bathrooms (albeit with claw-foot tubs), the saloon downstairs and nearby bars can be noisy (often until 3am on weekends), and the "breakfast" part of B&B is a stretch.

109½ W. Exchange Ave., Fort Worth, TX 76106. © **817/626-1522.** Fax 817/625-2723. www.missmollys hotel.com. 7 units. $100–$175 double. Rates include breakfast. Special packages available. AE, MC, V. Free parking. *In room:* A/C.

### Inexpensive

**Stonehouse Hotel** 🗲   This funky stone house calls itself Fort Worth's "authentic cowboy hotel," and one look at the rooms, named Boot, Horse, Indian, and Wagon, and you'll know they ain't kidding. With rooms sporting simple wood paneling and tons of Texas touches, this literal stone house was originally a cowboy boardinghouse in the early 1920s. Although it borders on kitsch, if you've come to Cowtown for a Western experience, this may be your place. Rooms are comfortable, though with few amenities, and only the more expensive rooms have private bathrooms. Midweek, however, the place is a downright bargain (cheapest of all is Hayden's Hideout, with bunk beds for $25 per person).

2401 Ellis Ave. (at W. Exchange Ave.), Fort Worth, TX 76106. © **817/626-2589.** www.stonehousebed andbreakfast.com. 10 units. $100–$150 double (weekdays half-price). Special packages available. AE, DC, DISC, MC, V. Free parking. **Amenities:** Wi-Fi (free, in lobby).

## DOWNTOWN
### Expensive

**The Ashton Hotel** ★★★   Incorporating meticulously restored historic buildings on Main Street—the 1890 Winfree Building and the 1915 Fort Worth Club Building—this establishment fills an important niche in Fort Worth, proudly calling itself "the city's only small luxury hotel." With a superb location, just a few slow paces from Bass Performance Hall and Sundance Square, it features ample and impeccably decorated rooms, with custom-designed mahogany furnishings, inviting plush king-size beds and Italian linens, and attentive, professional service. Some rooms have romantic two-person claw-foot Jacuzzi tubs. The hotel is decorated with a collection of paintings from the Fort Worth Circle, a group of local artists active from the 1930s to the 1960s. The elegant and excellent restaurant, **Six 10 Grille,** serves breakfast, lunch, and dinner, as well as an elegant afternoon tea (p. 117).

610 Main St. (btw. 5th and 6th sts.), Fort Worth, TX 76102. © **866/327-4866** or 817/332-0100. Fax 817/332-0110. www.theashtonhotel.com. 39 units. $199–$349 double; $369 suite. Weekend, executive, and special promotional packages available. AE, DC, DISC, MC, V. Valet parking $15; self-parking $10 per day. Small pets accepted. **Amenities:** Restaurant; piano bar; babysitting; concierge; exercise room; room service. *In room:* A/C, TV, CD player, hair dryer, minibar, MP3 docking station, Wi-Fi (free).

**Omni Fort Worth Hotel** ★★★ ☺   A great addition to Fort Worth's high-end hotel market, this massive and sleek, high-rise hotel next to the Convention Center and across from the Fort Worth Water Garden—the city's top business hotel—opened in 2009. Shaped from local stone and sheathed in glass, it's a bit of Dallas on the exterior with Texas touches inside. The overall look is something like a luxury Western ski mountain hotel. It features a swank Mokara spa, Bob's Steak & Chop House restaurant, grand public rooms, and a lovely rooftop pool and cool terrace pool bar. Rooms, many with superb city and distant views, are warm, ample and elegant without being over the top, and they have excellent, roomy bathrooms. The courteous, attentive service is standout (they go to extra lengths for special occasions). While the hotel is about 12 blocks from Sundance Square, the convenient trolley does stop right in front of the hotel. Look for great packages and special deals online.

1300 Houston St., Fort Worth, TX 76102. © **888/444-OMNI** (6664) or 817/535-6664. Fax 817/882-8140. www.omnihotels.com/findahotel/fortworth.aspx. 614 units. $239–$299 double; from $349 suite. Weekend, executive, and special promotional packages available. AE, DC, DISC, MC, V. Valet parking $20; self-parking $15 per day. **Amenities:** 2 restaurants; 3 bars; children's programs; concierge; exercise room; outdoor pool; room service; spa. *In room:* A/C, TV, hair dryer, minibar, Wi-Fi (free).

**The Worthington Renaissance Fort Worth Hotel ★**    Until recently downtown's largest and swankiest hotel, the monolithic Worthington is the place where many modern-day cattle barons—oilmen and other execs—like to cool their boot heels in Fort Worth. It's a block from the courthouse and only steps away from Bass Performance Hall and the array of restaurants and bars clustered around Sundance Square. The hotel dominates one part of downtown like a huge, docked cruise ship. The large and elegant, surprisingly understated lobby hints at the spacious rooms, which are warm, sedate, and handsomely appointed. They have very comfortable beds, large writing desks, colorful accents, and large bathrooms. The Kalamatas Restaurant and Martini Bar serves Mediterranean cuisine and is open for breakfast, lunch, and dinner.

200 Main St., Fort Worth, TX 76102. © **817/870-1000.** Fax 817/338-9176. www.marriott.com/hotels/travel/dfwdt-the-worthington-renaissance-fort-worth-hotel. 474 units. $199–$289 double; from $359 suite. Romance, weekend, and other packages available. AE, DC, DISC, MC, V. Valet parking $22; self-parking $16 per day. Pets accepted with $200 deposit. **Amenities:** 2 restaurants; bar; babysitting; concierge; exercise room; Jacuzzi; indoor pool; room service; sauna; 2 outdoor tennis courts; Wi-Fi (free, in lobby). *In room:* A/C, TV, hair dryer, Internet ($13 per day), minibar.

## Moderate

**Etta's Place ✦**    In the heart of historic downtown, Etta's is more a cozy boutique hotel than a mom-and-pop B&B. Occupying the second floor of a landmark building, which once housed Fort Worth's venerable jazz club, Caravan of Dreams, on Sundance Square, the inn is within easy walking distance of downtown shops and restaurants, and just a short drive or trolley ride from the Cultural District and Stockyards. Named for Etta Place, the girlfriend of the Sundance Kid (said to be the most comely of Wild West women), the inn has spacious rooms with lots of light and Texas touches, including antique chairs, horseshoe lamps, and Americana quilts. The handsome library and music rooms, with clubby leather chairs, are great places to relax with a book or chat with other guests. There are six good-size rooms, three roomy luxury suites with king-size beds and kitchenettes, and Etta's Attic, a penthouse suite with a kitchenette. A full home-cooked breakfast is included.

200 W. 3rd St., Fort Worth, TX 76102. © **866/355-5760** or 817/255-5760. Fax 817/878-2560. www.ettas-place.com. 10 units. $150–$185 double; $200–$240 suite. Rates include breakfast. Special packages available. AE, DC, DISC, MC, V. *In room:* A/C, TV, hair dryer, Internet (free), kitchenette (in suites).

**Hilton Fort Worth ★ ✦**    This large, historic, and centrally located hotel opened in 1921 as the Texas Hotel and it's where JFK spent the night before—and was memorably photographed on—the day of his assassination in Dallas. A basement-to-penthouse makeover, which jettisoned an adjacent annex, has transformed this hotel from a dowdy also-ran to one of the top large business hotels in downtown Fort Worth. Behind a beautiful old brick facade is a soaring, impressive lobby; guest rooms are now swank and serene, with handsome (even masculine) color schemes, elegant furnishings, and plush bedding. Bathrooms have also been overhauled. Though the hotel has long been popular with groups, conventioneers, and other visiting business-people, it is now a superb place to stay for virtually anyone visiting Fort Worth (children stay free when occupying their parent's room), and it's a good value for this level of sophistication and style, and convenience to Sundance Square's lively restaurants and bars. The new in-house restaurant is a Ruth's Chris Steakhouse.

815 Main St., Fort Worth, TX 76102. ✆ 800/HILTONS (445-8667) or 817/870-2100. Fax 817/335-3408. www.hilton.com. 294 units. $169–$249 double. Special packages available. AE, DC, DISC, MC, V. Valet parking $18. Pets 75 lbs. and under accepted with $50 fee. **Amenities:** 2 restaurants; concierge; executive-level rooms; exercise room; room service. *In room:* A/C, TV, hair dryer, Internet ($10 per day).

**TownePlace Suites Fort Worth Downtown** ★ ☺ ✦  This brand-new (2010) hotel at the edge of downtown is a winner, hitting the sweet spot of affordability, comfort, and convenience. Although rooms aren't luxurious, they're spacious and very well equipped, and there's a great outdoor pool. This is an excellent option for anyone, including business travelers who need to be downtown, but especially great for families, with Sundance Square, the Cultural District, and the Stockyards within easy reach.

805 E. Belknap St., Fort Worth, TX 76102. ✆ 888/236-2427 or 817/332-6300. Fax 817/332-6301. www. marriott.com/hotels/travel/dfwtd-towneplace-suites-fort-worth-downtown. 140 units. $129–$189 double; rates include breakfast. AE, DC, DISC, MC, V. Free parking. Pets accepted with $100 fee. **Amenities:** Concierge; exercise room; outdoor pool. *In room:* A/C, TV, hair dryer, kitchen, minibar, Wi-Fi (free).

## CULTURAL DISTRICT
### Moderate

**Residence Inn Fort Worth Cultural District** ☺ ✦  An extended-stay hotel at the edge of the Cultural District (and perfectly convenient to downtown, which is less than a mile away), this large and very comfortable hotel is great for families and anyone staying awhile in Fort Worth. With an elegant stone exterior, a large outdoor pool, and nicely decorated rooms, it's a big step up from the standard Residence Inn. The spacious rooms, which include studios, one-bedroom suites, and two-bedroom suites, are essentially apartments, with full kitchens and large bathrooms. They're larger than just about any hotel room in town (save big-bucks presidential suites);

most have additional foldout sleeping couches and can easily accommodate a family of four.

2500 Museum Way, Fort Worth, TX 76107. ℂ **800/331-3131** or 817/885-8250. Fax 817/885-8252. www.marriott.com/hotels/travel/dfwrw-residence-inn-fort-worth-cultural-district. 149 units. $139–$229 double; $249–$259 suite. Rates include breakfast buffet and daily cocktail hour. AE, DC, DISC, MC, V. Free parking. Pets accepted with $100 fee. **Amenities:** Exercise room; Jacuzzi; heated outdoor pool; tennis courts (1 outdoor); Wi-Fi (free, in lobby). *In room:* A/C, TV, hair dryer, Internet (free), kitchen.

**The Texas White House Bed & Breakfast ★** 🗡  A big, handsome, and, yes, white house with a wraparound porch and backyard with gazebo, this elegant, immaculate country home is a fine place to kick up your boots. In the Medical District, near All Saints Episcopal Hospital, the house has hardwood floors, a spacious parlor, a living room with fireplace, a formal dining room, and well-maintained, warm accommodations with plush beds. There's no Lincoln Bedroom, but the Lone Star Room has nice antiques like a triple armoire, along with a parson's bench sitting area and claw-foot tub. The Land of Contrast Room is done in black and white and has a large bathroom and queen-size brass bed; it may be a little frilly for some cowboys. The Tejas Room has light-oak furniture, his-and-hers rocking chairs, and a large platform tub. The Mustang and Longhorn suites have special amenities such as a balcony porch and fireplace (the Mustang even has a two-person, in-room sauna). The friendly owners serve a full gourmet breakfast and are happy to make recommendations for all sorts of restaurants and activities.

1417 8th Ave., Fort Worth, TX 76104. ℂ **800/279-6491** or 817/923-3597. Fax 817/923-0410. www.texaswhitehouse.com. 5 units. $125–$145 double; $205–$235 suite. Rates include breakfast. Special honeymoon and anniversary packages available. AE, DC, DISC, MC, V. *In room:* A/C, TV, DVD/VCR/CD player (in suites), fridge (in suites), hair dryer.

### Inexpensive

**Residence Inn Fort Worth University** ☺ 🗡  A former apartment complex, Residence Inn still feels much more like a residence than a chain motel, and is ideal for extended stays. The spacious layouts, on two floors, include fully equipped kitchens and sitting areas. Most suites even have fireplaces. The penthouse suites are

## 😊 FAMILY-FRIENDLY hotels

**Hyatt Place Fort Worth Historic Stockyards** (p. 108)  Right on the cobblestoned, Old West street where there's a daily cattle run, and across from the fun Cowtown Cattlepen Maze, this is a great place for families who want to live it up in Cowtown—and there's an outdoor pool.

**Omni Fort Worth Hotel** (p. 110)  Though it's not for families on a budget, this elegant high-rise has a rooftop pool that kids will love.

**Residence Inn Fort Worth University** (p. 113)  Perfect for families, this friendly hotel has rooms that are more like apartments, with fully equipped kitchens

and comfortable sitting areas. When you tell the kids they can walk to the acclaimed Fort Worth Zoo, they're sure to think you've made the right choice.

**Residence Inn Fort Worth Cultural District** (p. 112)  The spacious rooms, full kitchens, outdoor pool, and foldout couches are just a few of the amenities that make this hotel, on the edge of the Cultural District, great for families.

**TownePlace Suites Forth Worth Downtown** (p. 112)  Very affordable, centrally located, and with an excellent outdoor pool, this new hotel is a winner for families.

lofts. Many visitors include relocating businesspeople and families, and the inn does its best to foster a community; every evening, there's a happy hour with free beer and wine and enough snacks to amount to a light evening meal. This place is great for families, as it's within walking distance of the Fort Worth Zoo and near the Cultural District, and it has a nice outdoor pool.

1701 S. University Dr., Fort Worth, TX 76107. © **800/331-3131** or 817/870-1011. Fax 817/732-2114. www.marriott.com. 120 units. $119–$159 double; $179–$199 suite. Rates include buffet breakfast. AE, DC, DISC, MC, V. Free parking. Pets accepted with $100 fee. **Amenities:** Exercise room; outdoor pool; room service; Wi-Fi (free, in lobby). *In room:* A/C, TV, Internet (free), kitchen.

# WHERE TO DINE

Fort Worth's dining scene may not be as lauded or as flashy as the one in Dallas, but it is increasingly sophisticated, with excellent steakhouses as well as innovative Southwestern and haute Mexican cuisine, alongside family-oriented Tex-Mex and barbecue joints. Two areas have emerged as new dining zones: the **West 7th Street** corridor, where there's been immense development in just the last couple of years; and **Magnolia Avenue,** in the Hospital District near TCU, Fort Worth's counterpart to Dallas's cutting-edge Bishops Arts District. In addition to the dining spots below, the Modern Art Museum of Fort Worth (p. 127) has a terrific fine-dining restaurant for lunch, Sunday brunch, and Friday dinner (and it has a kiddie menu, too): **Café Modern ★★** (© **817/840-2157**), headed by a Fort Worth native and CIA graduate, and overlooking the reflective pool (the restaurant was once named one of the best in the U.S. by *Gourmet* magazine). Another great lunch (and even breakfast spot) is the honey-tonk classic **Fred's Texas Café** (p. 134), known for its great chipotle-topped burgers, quail and eggs, and tacos.

## STOCKYARDS NATIONAL HISTORIC DISTRICT
### Expensive

**Cattlemen's Steakhouse ★ ☺** STEAK    Cattlemen's has been serving the good people of Fort Worth for more than 6 decades. It's a relaxed (if frequently boisterous), affordable, and nicely worn place for a thick steak in the heart of cattle country, just around the corner from the Stockyards' main drag. It's great for families: There are separate rooms, like pens, and the server provides place mats with barnyard animal stickers, a good kiddie menu, and a lollipop at the end of the meal. The thick, juicy, charcoal-broiled cuts of beef include a 13-ounce Kansas City sirloin, three cuts of rib-eye, a 16-ounce Texas T-bone, and a pretty good and juicy version of chicken-fried steak. The service is friendly and low key, and the crowd is a mix of families and, as my young nephew once observed, "lotsa men drinkin' wine and tellin' jokes." Those are the same guys who know that Cattlemen's is a good place to bust your aorta without breaking the bank.

2458 N. Main St. (at Exchange Ave.) © **817/624-3945.** www.cattlemenssteakhouse.com. Reservations recommended. Main courses $10–$18 lunch, $13–$44 dinner. AE, DC, DISC, MC, V. Mon–Thurs 11am–10:30pm; Fri–Sat 11am–11pm; Sun noon–9pm.

**Lonesome Dove Western Bistro ★★★** WESTERN    A wildly successful little restaurant, this cozy venture riding a wave of cowboy cool is decorated in the style of an old saloon, with a long bar, high-backed Mexican iron bar stools, copper-toned tin ceiling, bold paintings with Western themes, and a kitchen staff donning cowboy hats. The eclectic (and pricey) menu comes as a bit of a shock in the Old West Stockyards, but you'll be tested to have a finer meal in Fort Worth. Appetizers may include chile-rubbed foie gras brûlée (on Texas toast) and seared sweet lobster cakes with corn-and–black bean salsa and cilantro-orange butter sauce. The offbeat main courses opt for unique touches, such as the pancetta-wrapped Texas red fish or the grilled New Zealand deer chops with truffled mac-and-cheese and morels. Straight-up meat eaters will delight in the hand-cut prime steaks, priced by the ounce. For lunch, check out the fresh buffalo burger or quail quesadillas; the daily $9 "Stockyard Special" is always a great deal. Although Chef Tim Love, an *Iron Chef* winner, was not able to ride his celebrity to success in the hostile restaurant terrain of New York City (where an outpost of Lonesome Dove went belly up), he's doing just fine back home.

2406 N. Main St. (just south of Exchange Ave.) ℂ 817/740-8810. www.lonesomedovebistro.com. Reservations required. Main courses $9-$35 lunch, $25-$55 dinner. AE, MC, V. Tues–Sat 11am-2:30pm; Tues–Thurs 5-10pm; Fri–Sat 5-11pm.

### Inexpensive

**Joe T. Garcia's Mexican Dishes** ☺ 🍴 TEX-MEX   At this enduringly popular Cowtown Tex-Mex institution (opened in 1935) just south of the Stockyards, almost everyone knows that they don't have menus, do only two dinner dishes, and take only cash (or check). That's because they've been here many times before and will be back again and again. This restaurant, in a rambling home that looks like a pretty Mexican hacienda, has a lush outdoor patio sitting area (incredibly, large enough to seat 1,000 hungry eaters, though it never feels massified) set around a pool. Indoors is comfortably relaxed, but outdoors is the place to be—unless the Texas heat is suffocating. Ordering couldn't be simpler: Choose between a heaping plate of succulently grilled chicken or beef fajitas; a big family-style dinner with tacos and enchiladas; or chiles rellenos, tamales, and chicken *flautas* at lunch. Joe T.'s is a margarita factory, spitting out thousands of them—on the rocks and frozen (pitchers are a good deal at $15). Service can be a little erratic, though it's frequently lightning fast. A Mexican-style brunch is served on Saturday and Sunday from 11am to 2pm. A sister restaurant, **Esperanza's Bakery** (2122 North Main St), is especially good for breakfast.

2201 N. Commerce St. (at NW 22nd St.) ℂ 817/626-4356. www.joets.com. Reservations not accepted. Main courses $9.25-$15. No credit cards. Mon–Thurs 11am-2:30pm and 5-10pm; Fri–Sat 11am-11pm; Sun 11am-10pm.

**Love Shack** ★ ☺ 🍴 AMERICAN   Around the corner from his wildly successful Lonesome Dove restaurant, Tim Love created the ultimate burger shack. No more than a counter (with mostly outdoor seating) dispensing delicious burgers on store-bought buns and cardboard trays, and with nothing on the menu more than $8, it's the kind of place you'd wish for after a night at Billy Bob's, or when the kids are cranky. The burgers are a mix of prime tenderloin and prime brisket; if you're feeling indulgent, go for the Dirty Love burger, which piles on bacon curls, fried quail egg, and "love sauce." There are hot dogs, too; the standout is the Flying Texas Dog, a chicken-apple bratwurst combo with green chiles and onions. The Crazy Good Onion Rings speak for themselves. To top things off, there's beer and wine, fresh lemonade, root beer on tap, milkshakes (a different one each day), and live country music here, as well as next door at the White Saloon (now also part of Chef Love's burgeoning honky-tonk empire). There's now a second location, **So7 at Trinity Park,** 817 Matisse St. (ℂ 817/348-9655).

110 E. Exchange Ave. (just east of N. Main Ave.) ℂ 817/740-8812. www.shakeyourloveshack.com. Reservations not accepted. Main courses $3-$8. No credit cards. Mon–Wed 11am-7pm; Thurs and Sun 11am-9pm; Fri–Sat 11am-11pm.

**Brix Pizza & Wine Bar** (p. 119) Great inexpensive pies for the whole family, pure and simple, and a good selection of wines for the parents.

**Cattlemen's Steakhouse** (p. 114) No slick banker's steakhouse, this homey, well-worn place in the heart of the Stockyards has several separate rooms, and kids get place mats adorned with barnyard animal stickers, a kiddie menu, and a lollipop treat. The parents get what they come for: a good-value steak.

**Joe T. Garcia's Mexican Dishes** (p. 115) No menus? No problem. This Tex-Mex institution serves up two dishes daily, so you can spend less time deciding what to order and more time sipping margaritas. Parents and kids will both enjoy the delightful outdoor patio.

**Kincaid's Gro. Market Hamburgers** (p. 120) Burger heaven in Fort Worth is an old-time 1940s grocery store that makes some of the best burgers in Texas. Kids are sure to be entertained by the protocol: You place your order at the open kitchen in back, get a white paper bag with your name scrawled on it, pay at the register, and then pick out a spot at a communal table beneath a jungle of inflatable toys hanging from the ceiling.

**Love Shack** (p. 115) Gourmet burgers (and dogs, fries, and rings) by a celebrity chef, but the price is right, the meat is fresh-ground daily, there are different special milkshakes each day, and there's outdoor seating, all just a stone's throw from the daily cattle herd run in the Stockyards.

**Railhead Smokehouse** (p. 120) A Fort Worth barbecue fave that draws families every night of the week for its tasty barbecue and relaxed atmosphere. The place is noisy without rising to the levels of a Chuck E. Cheese's, and excellent-value children's plates will keep the kids happy.

**Spiral** (p. 119) Inexpensive and organic, this funky spot and its delectable desserts may have kids going vegan.

**Tillman's Roadhouse** (p. 118) This offbeat take on Southwestern cooking has a bit of Pee-Wee's Playhouse to go with the roadhouse, and the cook-at-your-own-table s'mores for dessert are family fun.

**5**

Where to Dine

FORT WORTH

# DOWNTOWN
## Expensive

**Brownstone** ★★ SOUTHERN Forth Worth's newest and hottest upscale restaurant, with Chef Casey Thompson, a finalist on TV's "Top Chef," in the kitchen, is another example of Cowtown's new sophistication. Sleek and modern, with handsome beige leather booths, a library bar, and open-air patio, it's an inviting space. Thompson is a big proponent of farm-to-table, sourcing the best local providers of meats, fish, and vegetables. Among the standouts are slow-cooked meats, including Kobe cheek pot roast and red wine–braised pork shoulder. Don't miss some of the spectacular sides, too, such as fried okra and winter squash succotash. Sunday brunch is one of the best bets in town, with tantalizing items such as bread pudding French toast served with a pair of farm-fresh eggs, and brisket and potato hash served with a spicy chile hollandaise.

840 Currie St. (south of W. 7th St.). © **817/332-1555.** www.brownstonerestaurants.com. Reservations recommended. Main courses $9–$48. AE, DC, MC, V. Tues–Thurs 5–10pm; Fri 11am–midnight; Sat 5pm–midnight; Sun 10:30am–10pm.

**Del Frisco's Double Eagle Steak House** ★★ STEAK Fort Worth's top steakhouse is a clubby two-level place for cattle barons, power brokers, jet-setters, and mere steak lovers. In a redbrick corner building (ca. 1890), huge top-notch steaks are the story. The filet mignon (in 8- and 12-oz. versions) is butter soft; other cuts of prime beef include marbled rib-eye, prime porterhouse, and Santa Fe peppercorn steaks. Pinstripe and new-economy types will love the cigar lounge, which has a nice selection of Robustos, and the deep wine cellar. Desserts, if you make it to them, are every bit as artery clogging and overwhelming as the main courses. For some Fort Worth natives, though, the high prices and Big D swagger are a bit much for their laid-back downtown. Cattlemen's Steakhouse is a bit more low key, though probably a step down in quality for beef lovers.

812 Main St. (at 8th St.) ✆ **817/877-3999.** www.delfriscos.com. Reservations recommended. Main courses $18–$48. AE, DC, DISC, MC, V. Mon–Thurs 5–10pm; Fri–Sat 5–11pm.

**Reata** ★ SOUTHWESTERN  Reata still proudly spearheads the Southwestern cuisine movement, which may have run its course elsewhere, but is perfectly at home in Cowtown. It moved to its current location after the great Fort Worth tornado of 2000 condemned its former home, the Bank One tower. Named for the ranch in the movie *Giant,* Reata now occupies the space formerly inhabited by Fort Worth's once-loved and sadly gone jazz club, Caravan of Dreams. It sports the great rooftop Grotto Bar and dining area inside the glass dome on the roof. The restaurant has basic fare, such as chicken-fried steak, chicken chiles rellenos, and marbled rib-eye, as well as more creative interpretations, such as *carne asada* (barbecued meat) with cacciota cheese enchiladas, which are consistently well prepared enough to keep more adventurous diners interested. Portions are still huge, and some dishes suffer from cheese, cream, and sauce overkill. Sunday brunch is a tried-and-true local favorite. The waitstaff are appropriately outfitted in jeans and cowboy vests; they efficiently herd the crowds of casual and big-night-out diners through this mainstay of Texas urban chic.

310 Houston St. (on Sundance Square) ✆ **817/336-1009.** www.reata.net. Reservations recommended. Main courses $16–$44. AE, MC, V. Daily 11am–2:30pm and 5–10:30pm.

**Six 10 Grille** ★★ NEW AMERICAN  Fort Worth natives aren't usually too impressed by anything too slick or haute, but this fine addition to the dining scene, in the elegant Ashton Hotel (p. 110), is one of the leaders in changing how diners think about this cow town. The New American menu, with Asian and Latin accents, is stellar at this sleek restaurant. Dine on dishes such as lamb tenderloin or Chilean sea bass with a shrimp-and-asparagus risotto. Lunch is more casual and inexpensive, with quesadillas, homemade chicken-fried steak, and buffalo burgers. The small but select wine list is, refreshingly, reasonably priced. Even if you're not staying at this fine hotel, make an effort to eat here, even if it's only for a rewarding breakfast.

610 Main St. (at E. 6th St.) ✆ **817/332-0100.** www.theashtonhotel.com/dining. Reservations recommended. Main courses $9–$13 lunch, $24–$38 dinner. AE, MC, V. Sun–Thurs 6:30am–9pm; Fri–Sat 6:30am–10pm.

## Moderate

**Ferré Ristorante e Bar** ★ TUSCAN  Occupying the coveted spot across the street from Bass Hall, this popular, upscale Italian restaurant caters to concertgoers as well as local business folk and couples heading to Sundance Square on date night. It's a smart-looking, spacious restaurant that's not overwhelming in size, with lots of windows that show off the huge angels of Bass Hall's illuminated facade. The menu doesn't aim for overly adventurous or showy dishes, though it does offer dependable Italian and Tuscan standards, including homemade pastas, such as sweet-potato gnocchi and orechietti with homemade fennel sausage, and gourmet, brick-oven pizzas. Among main courses, I especially like the Chilean sea bass with spinach-crimini risotto and clove-roasted pork loin.

215 E. 4th St. (across from Bass Hall, 1 block east of Sundance Square) ✆ **817/332-0033.** www.ferre restaurant.com. Reservations recommended. Main courses $14–$25. AE, MC, V. Tues-Thurs 4-10pm; Fri-Sat 4-11pm.

**Tillman's Roadhouse** ★★ ☺ SOUTHWESTERN  Imported from Dallas's supercool Bishops Arts dining district, where it's long served as the anchor, this recent arrival in the burgeoning West 7th Street nightlife zone hasn't lost a boot step expanding to Fort Worth. The funky and playful space, with pine-and-birch-tree walls, brocade wallpaper, twig sculptures, and rows of Murano chandeliers, is a combination of a Texas roadhouse with a Pacific Northwest "Twin Peaks" set piece. The menu is equally playful, but excellent: chipotle barbecue ribs, venison Frito pie, and chicken-fried hangar steak. For dessert, you can't miss the s'mores, with dark-chocolate bark and three flavors of marshmallows, brought to the table with your own little fire. The bar serves excellent cocktails, including the signature blood-orange margarita and ginger-lemon drop. If you're in Dallas, you might check out the original Tillman's, in the cool Bishop Arts District in Oak Cliff.

2933 Crockett St. (btw. Currie and Norwood sts., south of W. 7th St.) ✆ **817/850-9255.** www.tillmans roadhouse.com. Reservations recommended. Main courses $12–$29. AE, DC, MC, V. Tues-Sat 11am-2pm; Sun 10:30am-2pm; Tues-Thurs 5:30-10pm; Fri-Sat 5:30-11pm.

# CULTURAL (& HOSPITAL) DISTRICT
## Very Expensive

**Lanny's Alta Cocina Mexicana** ★★★ MEXICAN/MEDITERRANEAN  You'd never know by dining at this upscale, refined, small restaurant that the chef and owner is the great-grandson of the gentleman who opened the Stockyards' Joe T. Garcia's, a legendary slinger of crowd-pleasing fajitas, enchiladas, and margaritas. Lanny Lancarte takes an entirely different approach to Mexican dining, infusing it with Mediterranean flair (or perhaps it's the other way around—Mediterranean fare with Mexican accents). Whatever it is, it is stylishly presented, elegant, and delicious. It's also pricey (though lunch is a comparatively good deal). Kobe beef ceviche and tapas such as *mole*-braised pork tamales get one's taste buds in gear for prime *carne asada* with macaroni gratin or black sea bass in a poblano-and-asparagus sauce. The small house is warmly contemporary, with chocolate-brown leather chairs, terracotta–colored curtains, and modern track lighting. The five-course tasting menu ($60) is the best way to get a handle on Lancarte's cooking, and also a relatively good deal (with wine pairing, $100). The name Lanny's may sound casual, but the rest of it means "Mexican haute cuisine," a perfect description of its high aims.

3405 W. 7th St. (at Boland St., north of Camp Bowie Blvd.) ✆ **817/850-9996.** www.lannyskitchen.com. Reservations required. Main courses $12–$28 lunch, $28–$62 dinner. AE, DISC, MC, V. Tues-Fri 11:30am-2pm; Tues-Thurs 5:30-10pm; Sat 5:30-10:30pm.

### Expensive

**Nonna Tata** ★★ 🕯 ITALIAN  If you're tired of homogenous, bland Italian dining, venture over to this tiny and idiosyncratic hole in the wall tucked into Magnolia Avenue, where Donatella Trotti, Fort Worth's Italian grandma eminence, will make you a believer in perfectly prepared pastas and sauces. The very simple dining room has been redone, but the restaurant still doesn't ·take credit cards or reservations, doesn't have a liquor license (no matter, bring your own great bottle of Barolo; there's no corkage fee), and isn't open on weekends. Service can be erratic or painfully slow.

If you've got some patience and don't need much in the way of creature comforts or ambience (for me, the kitchen aromas are ambience enough), stick it out for excellent homemade puttanesca, great antipasti and fish dishes, and lovingly made desserts.

1400 W. Magnolia Ave. (btw. Fairmount and 6th aves.) ℰ **817/332-0250.** Reservations required. Main courses $13–$25. No credit cards. Tues–Fri 11:30am–2pm and 5:30–9pm.

## Moderate

**Brix Pizza & Wine Bar** ★ ☺ 🍴 PIZZA/ITALIAN  New York–style pizza has come to Fort Worth courtesy of a Sicilian, Daniele Puleo. This amiable and unpretentious pizzeria serves tasty and reasonably priced wood-fired pies, good homemade pastas, and fresh salads in a modern, relaxed setting. The Brooklyn pizza sports meatballs, and the Lezlie pizza has grilled chicken, jalapeños, and black olives. The wine list has a nice selection of American and Italian wines, including a couple of blowout bottles to dress up those pies.

2747 S. Hulen St. (at W. Vickery Blvd.). ℰ **817/924-2749.** www.brixpizzeria.com. Reservations recommended. Main courses $9–$12. AE, DISC, MC, V. Sun–Thurs 11am–10pm; Fri–Sat 11am–11pm.

**Sardines Ristorante Italiano** 🍴 ITALIAN  After a protracted, heated battle, this Fort Worth landmark, which forever had welcomed locals just across from the museums, finally succumbed to the big bad development monster (the old digs were flattened and transformed into a parking lot). The popular, quirky Italian restaurant moved to west Fort Worth and, amazingly, succeeded in transplanting its unique look and ambience—a cross between a smoky jazz dive and a neighborhood Italian joint in Brooklyn—to the new spot. All the antique pieces, metal signs, and photographs are relocated, and the dark and intimate feel is closely replicated. Sardines is perfect for dependable, generous helpings of Italian grub, inexpensive wine, and an abundance of good vibes and good nightly jazz starting at 7pm. Some veal dishes can be mediocre; your best bet is to stick to the list of good pastas such as linguine *alla rosa* (with artichokes, capers, and olive oil) and seafood.

509 University Dr. (at Rockwood Park Dr. N). ℰ **817/332-9937.** http://sardinesftworth.com. Reservations recommended. Main courses $11–$27. AE, DISC, MC, V. Mon–Thurs 4–11pm; Fri–Sat 4pm–midnight; Sun 3–11pm.

**Spiral Diner & Bakery** ★ ☺ 🍴 VEGETARIAN/VEGAN  Fort Worth doesn't skimp on barbecue and steak, so vegetarians will be delighted to find this hip, retro-styled 100% vegan cafe in the cool Magnolia Avenue district. Using organic and mostly locally sourced fresh ingredients, it serves casual and inexpensive, but creative and flavorful plates that will appeal to nonvegetarians, too—such as veggie pastas, burritos, sandwiches, and yummy salads. Sunday brunch features all-you-can-eat pancakes for just $5.95. Quite unexpected is the extensive, great beer list, focused on craft and organic brews from around the world (complementing great organic juices, smoothies, and coffees and teas). At a minimum, kids will like the homemade ice creams, milkshakes, chocolate chip cookies, and cupcakes. Check out the bakery's delightful, artful custom vegan cakes, too.

1314 W. Magnolia Ave. (btw. 6th Ave. and S. Lake St.). ℰ **817/332-8834.** www.spiraldiner.com. Reservations recommended. Main courses $7–$9. AE, DISC, MC, V. Tues–Sat 11am–10pm; Sun 11am–5pm.

## Inexpensive

**Angelo's Barbecue** ★ 🍴 BARBECUE  Fort Worth's classic Texas barbecue joint, in this spot since 1958, is the real deal, a Cowtown legend. A few blocks north of the Cultural District and west of downtown, it looks kind of like a large Texas Jaycees convention hall, with wood paneling, mounted deer and buffalo heads, metal ceiling fans, and Formica tables. It's nearly as full of flavor as the hickory-smoked barbecue. The sliced beef sandwich and beef brisket plates are the standard, though you can also detour toward salami, ham, turkey, and Polish sausage. The side dishes, such as coleslaw, pinto beans, and potato salad, are all excellent. Chicken and pork ribs are served all day "while they last," though hickory-smoked beef ribs don't make an appearance until after 3:30pm. Cold Bud comes in frosted steins. This place is so low key that there's not even "waitress service" until 3pm.

2533 White Settlement Rd. (at Vacek St., north of W. 7th St. and east of University Dr.). © **817/332-0357.** www.angelosbbq.com. Reservations not accepted. Main courses $3.50–$13. No credit cards. Mon–Sat 11am–10pm.

**Kincaid's Gro. Market Hamburgers** ☺ 🍴 AMERICAN  As down-home and folksy as could be, Kincaid's, a 1940s grocery store that one day started making burgers, is now a beloved institution in Fort Worth and the perennial winner of "Best Burger in Texas" polls. The standard order is a thick, juicy burger and fries or onion rings. There are a few other items, such as grilled chicken, hot dogs, and grilled-cheese sandwiches, but few people move beyond the time-tested basics. The large space, with pistachio-ice-cream-green cinder-block walls, has a few communal picnic tables in front, long rows of stand-up counters, and an open kitchen in back. Place your order at the kitchen, pick up a white paper bag with your name scrawled on it, pay at the register, and find a spot under the inflatable toys hanging from the ceiling.

4901 Camp Bowie Blvd. (at Eldridge St.). © **817/732-2881.** Reservations not accepted. Main courses $3.25–$8. No credit cards. Mon–Sat 11am–8pm; Sun 11am–3pm.

**Paris Coffee Shop** 🍴 DINER/BREAKFAST/BRUNCH  Around since the Great Depression, this big, wood-paneled dining room filled with hungry Texans for breakfast and lunch is a longtime down-home favorite. There's not an ounce of Paris in it, save the name. (Or maybe it's referring to Paris, Texas.) Service is classic Southern hospitality. Breakfast is the star: Choose from awesome pancakes, omelets, grits, and biscuits and gravy (on weekdays, you can get "red-eye gravy," made with coffee, cinnamon, and bacon grease). Lunch is such standard fare as sandwiches, plate lunches (with a choice of meats and vegetables for $7), and chili, though there are lunch specials such as enchiladas and ham steak—and that famous red-eye gravy. Try the pies; in a place like this, you know they're good.

700 W. Magnolia Ave. (at Hemphill St.). © **817/335-2041.** www.pariscoffeeshop.net. Reservations not accepted. Main courses $3.95–$7.25. AE, DISC, MC, V. Mon–Fri 6am–2:30pm; Sat 6–11am.

**Railhead Smokehouse** ★ ☺ BARBECUE  Neither the newest nor the oldest of Fort Worth's barbecue joints, Railhead is one of the best. It's slicker than Angelo's, but it still attracts the hats-and-boots crowd in their pickups, as well as soccer moms and families pulling up in Lexus SUVs for takeout. The smoky barbecued meat with tangy sauce gets rave reviews; the plates are heaping; and the ribs, sliced beef, fries, and cheddar peppers (cheese-stuffed jalapeños) are excellent. The chicken, though, gets universally panned. Come for absurdly cheap weekday plate specials and have a beer or margarita out on the patio, which is a happy-hour hot spot, or hang out at the lively bar, which often features live music. Cheap and filling children's plates are served, and you can also load up on barbecued meat by the pound, though I can't vouch for how well the stuff travels.

2900 Montgomery St. (at Vickery Blvd.). © **800/978-3211** or 817/738-9808. www.railheadonline.com. Reservations not accepted. Main courses $6.75–$17. AE, DISC, MC, V. Mon–Thurs 11am–9pm; Fri–Sat 11am–10pm.

# EXPLORING FORT WORTH

Despite its laid-back image and manageable size, Fort Worth abounds with sights, sounds, and things to do. Whether you're a cowboy, an aesthete, or a historian—or just plain folk—Fort Worth, an enjoyable, relaxed, and cultured city that's remarkably well organized for visitors, should prove entertaining. There are three distinct parts, each a couple of miles from one another: the **Stockyards National Historic District,** the focus of the city's cattle-raising and livestock auction legacy as the cow town of the cattle drives north in the 19th century; newly revitalized, historic **downtown,** a beautifully laid-out, clean, and renovated core built around Sundance Square; and the **Cultural District,** a world-class museum, arts, and architecture center with the superlative Kimbell Art Museum (perhaps Texas's finest art museum), the Amon Carter Museum of Western Art, and the fantastic new Modern Art Museum. We'll take them in that order, though where you start should match with your interest in either art or a living museum of the Old West.

**Coupon Discounts**

Visit the **Fort Worth Convention & Visitors Bureau website** for money-saving coupons at major attractions, including the Stockyards, Museum of Science and History, Cowgirl Museum, and Billy Bob's Texas, as well as the airport shuttle. Go to www.fortworth.com/visitors/special-offers and print out any of more than a dozen coupons.

Plenty of attractions in Fort Worth are free; pick up the flyer *Everything Free to Do in Fort Worth* at the visitor center to find out how much you can do for no money.

## THE TOP ATTRACTIONS
### The Stockyards National Historic District ★★

Just 2 miles north of downtown Fort Worth, off North Main Street, is the still-beating heart of Fort Worth's Old West heritage. The Stockyards National Historic District is part Western theme park and part living-history museum. The livestock industry's 1880s roots are in this district that became the biggest and busiest cattle, horse, mule, hog, and sheep marketing center in the Southwest (and quite a pocket of wealth). The 125-acre district encompasses the **Livestock Exchange Building,** the focus of old livestock business; **Cowtown Coliseum,** the world's first indoor rodeo arena; **Stockyards Station,** the former hog and sheep pens, now overrun with Western shops and restaurants; **Billy Bob's Texas,** known as the world's largest honky-tonk; **Western shops** and authentic **saloons,** such as the **White Elephant;** and the historic **Stockyards Hotel,** where bar stools are topped by saddles and Bonnie and Clyde once camped out while on the lam. Such Western heroes as Gene Autry, Dale

## CHRISTMAS IN THE stockyards

A fairly new tradition in the Stockyards, **Christmas in the Stockyards,** is held the first Saturday in December. Perfect for families, it features games, crafts, roping lessons, a parade, and Cowboy Ride for Toys, all of which is followed by the lighting of a 45-foot tree and Christmas carols. For more information, call ☏ **817/624-4741** or visit www.fortworthstockyards.org.

Amazingly, the Fort Worth Stockyards still retain the look and feel of the Old West. To enhance the atmosphere even more, a twice-daily "cattle drive" of the **Fort Worth Herd** takes place on the main drag, Exchange Avenue (at N. Main St.), at 11:30am and again at 4pm. About 15 head of 1-ton longhorn steers, led by cowhands dressed the part in 19th-century duds, rumble down the redbrick street past the Stockyards, on their way to grazing near the West Fork of the Trinity River and back again to the Stockyards. Claimed to be the world's only daily longhorn cattle drive, it's perfect for photo ops. The best places to view the longhorns are the on front lawn of the Livestock Exchange building and from the catwalk above the cattlepens. For more information, call © 817/336-HERD (4373).

Evans, Roy Rogers, and Bob Wills are honored in bronze along Exchange Avenue's **Trail of Fame.**

The **Fort Worth Stock Show & Rodeo** is held during the last 2 weeks of January and first week of February. Hands down, it's the time in Fort Worth to see a surfeit of rodeo performances, as well as the nation's oldest continuous livestock show. For information and tickets, call © **817/877-2420** or get tickets at Ticketmaster outlets or online at www.fwssr.com.

**Cowtown Cattlepen Maze** ☺ A "Texas-size human maze," constructed to resemble the cattlepens of the Old West, is a fun diversion for kids (and older folks eager to test their skills against the labyrinth). Parents can watch from the observation deck to track how the kids are doing.

E. Exchange Ave. (across from Stockyards Station). © **817/624-6666.** www.cowtowncattlepenmaze. com. Admission $5, free for children 4 and under. Special group rates and unlimited 45-min. runs for birthday parties. Daily 10am–dusk (5pm in winter, 8–9pm in summer). Closed Thanksgiving, Dec 25, and Jan 1.

**Stockyards Museum** This small museum, part of the North Fort Worth Historical Society, is located inside the historic Livestock Exchange building that dates from 1893. It displays artifacts—guns, barbed wire, furniture, and clothing—from Fort Worth's glory days. Have a look in the section on women at the exhibit of the 1920s Fort Worth Stock Show Queen's coronation and the 19th-century "bad luck" wedding dress, which "brought personal misery or disaster to everyone who wore it or planned to wear it." There's a livestock auction center inside the building, where you can see a few cowboys checking out the animals on the monitors. Allow a half-hour to visit the museum.

131 E. Exchange Ave. (just east of N. Main St.) © **817/625-5082.** Free admission (donation requested). Mon–Sat 10am–5pm.

**Texas Cowboy Hall of Fame** ☺ Fans of rodeo and the cowboy life will appreciate this small museum, in restored horse and mule barns, honoring the stalwarts of Texas rodeo, including such (Texas) household names as Larry Mahan and Ty Murray. On display are the honorees' saddles, chaps, belt buckles, and trophies collected over the course of their careers. Also of interest are the fully restored 60 Sterquell wagons dating from the 18th and 19th centuries. About an hour should be sufficient to take in the cowboys, though some visitors could do a run-through in half that time.

For those who want to broaden their knowledge of the Old West, the **National Cowboys of Color Museum & Hall of Fame,** east of the Stockyards at 3400 Mount Vernon Ave. (© **817/534-8801;** www.cowboysofcolor.org), pays much-needed tribute to a group of cowboys whose contributions were critical to opening the American West and are sadly often overlooked. The museum is open Wednesday through Saturday from 11am to 6pm; admission is $6 adults, $4 seniors, $3 students, free for children 5 and under.

128 E. Exchange Ave., Barn A (just east of N. Main St.) © **817/626-7131.** www.texascowboyhalloffame. com. Admission $5 adults, $4 seniors and students 13-17 with college ID, $3 children 3-12, $15 families. Discounts available online. Mon–Thurs 10am–6pm; Fri–Sat 10am–7pm; Sun 11am–5pm (open 1 hr. later June–July).

## Historic Downtown & Sundance Square ★

Charming, unassuming, and remarkably unhurried, downtown's centerpiece is Sundance Square (named for the Sundance Kid, who hid out here with the Hole-in-the-Wall Gang, and a prime stop along the Chisholm Trail during the cattle drives of the 1800s). It has 14 blocks of redbrick streets, late-19th-century buildings, and attractions that include the Bass Performance Hall, a couple of museums, and a pair of Art Deco movie theaters. It's a model of urban planning, and a real rarity in Texas: a place with sidewalks that invites nonmotored strolling. Downtown Fort Worth is lit up like a Christmas tree at night, and Sundance Square's bars and restaurants are the heart of downtown nightlife.

**Bass Performance Hall ★**   Fort Worth's magnificent music hall, inaugurated in 1998 and funded entirely by private donations, is a spectacular addition to the city's already thriving cultural life. Touted as one of the top 10 opera houses in the world, Bass Hall is a handsome showpiece, constructed in a tiered horseshoe shape with excellent acoustics and great sightlines. The work of the architect David Schwarz (who built the Rangers Ballpark in Arlington and the American Airlines arena), Bass Hall is a 10-story, 2,000-seat jewel. Gracing the exterior are two huge limestone angels, with trumpets to lips, heralding patrons to the evening's performance. Inside, the entrance hall is paved with cut Italian marble and the dome is painted with a

 **THE GRAPEVINE vintage RAILROAD**

To jump into the turn-of-the-20th-century Old West character of the Stockyards, don your best Western duds and hop aboard the **Grapevine Vintage Railroad.** The 100-year-old steam train of the Tarantula Railroad (purchased from Walt Disney and affectionately called "Puffy" by locals)—and its diesel brethren—makes the Trinity River Run, a 1-hour trip from Stockyards Station to 8th Avenue in Fort Worth, and another route travels along the Chisholm Trail to the Cotton Belt Depot in historic Grapevine, Texas. The trip to Grapevine is more involved and interesting (as well as more expensive) than the one that begins and ends in the Forth Worth Stockyards. The name Tarantula stems from a tale in the late–19th century, when a local newspaperman's plans for rail lines were derided as looking like "the legs of a hairy tarantula."

Call © **817/410-3123** or 410-8136 or visit www.gvrr.com for exact schedules and the running status of the steam train. The Trinity River Run round-trip fare is $10 adults, $9 seniors, and $6 children ages 3 to 12. The Grapevine to Fort Worth round-trip fare is $20 adults, $18 seniors, and $10 children ages 3 to 12.

Take a breather at the refreshing **Fort Worth Water Gardens,** designed by the famed architect Philip Johnson—4 acres of water (19,000 gal. per minute) cascading over cement and into five pools. It's at Commerce and 15th streets, downtown; call ☏ **817/871-7699** for more information.

Texas noonday sky, ringed by silvery laurel leaves. The bathrooms are charmingly decorated with notes from Dvorak's "Going Home." Guided tours—best for those with a keen interest in architecture—last about 45 minutes. Bass Hall hosts the Fort Worth opera, symphony, theater, and dance companies; see "Fort Worth After Dark," later in this chapter, for more details.

4th and Calhoun sts. (at Commerce St., just east of Sundance Square) ☏ **877/212-4280,** or 817/212-4325 information hot line. www.basshall.com. Free guided public tours Sat 10:30am (performance schedule permitting); meet in East Portal at corner of Calhoun and Commerce sts.

**Fire Station No. 1/150 Years of Fort Worth Exhibit**   Tucked away in historic Fire Station No. 1 (which dates from 1907), this annex of the Fort Worth Museum of Science and History tells the history of Cowtown from its frontier days and the Chisholm Trail cattle drives to the present day. It's good for a quick and painless overview of Old West history.

Corner of 2nd and Commerce sts. (just northeast of Sundance Square) ☏ **817/255-9300.** Free admission. Daily 9am–8pm.

**Sid Richardson Museum**   Admirers of art depicting the Old West should visit the Sid Richardson, open following a renovation by noted architect David Schwarz, and tack it onto a visit at the more important Amon Carter Museum (p. 125). This small but focused collection, which belonged to a Fort Worth oilman, comprises 60 paintings by Frederic Remington and Charles M. Russell, two late-19th- and early-20th-century biggies of Western art. The museum now has a new facade and galleries. If you're not a fan of colorful renderings of wagon trails and Native Americans on horseback, this may not be your glass of whiskey, but the museum does have a couple of great saddles with silver ornamentation. Allow about a half-hour for a visit.

309 Main St. (just north of Sundance Square) ☏ **817/332-6554.** www.sidrichardsonmuseum.org. Free admission. Mon–Thurs 9am–5pm; Fri–Sat 9am–8pm; Sun noon–5pm. Free tours; arrange in advance.

## The Cultural District ★★★

Fort Worth is the cultural capital of the Southwest, with the finest art museums in Texas and the most impressive small art museum in the country. The city essentially ropes off the Cultural District, making it an elite island by placing it safely apart from downtown business interests, a couple of miles west. Arts philanthropy has thrived in Fort Worth to a degree unmatched in Texas and many parts of the United States. Wealthy patrons and an enthusiastic city have welcomed some of the world's most celebrated architects, including Louis Kahn, Philip Johnson, Tadao Ando, and Rienzo Piano to create museums that make much larger and more cosmopolitan cities salivate with envy. The presence of the glorious Modern Art Museum, across the street from the Kimbell and down the block from Philip Johnson's expanded Amon Carter, has entrenched Fort Worth as perhaps the top art and architecture city between the two U.S. coasts. South of downtown is an area of parks, gardens, historic homes, and the Fort Worth Zoo, considered one of the top five zoos in the country.

**Amon Carter Museum of Western Art ★★**   Having undergone a major expansion by the original architect, Philip Johnson, tripling the size of its galleries, the Amon Carter is a splendid showcase for its wide-ranging collection of American art. The museum possesses the finest and most complete collection of works by Frederic Remington and Charles M. Russell, two giants of Western art, as well as a major photography collection (works by Ansel Adams, Man Ray, Elliot Porter, Robert Frank, Alfred Stieglitz, Walker Evans, and many others); early scenes of the West by John Mix Stanley and Albert Bierstadt; and important contemporary paintings by Marsden Hartley, Georgia O'Keeffe, Arthur Dove, and Stuart Davis. Amon G. Carter was the creator and publisher of the *Fort Worth Star-Telegram*. His original collection of 400 paintings, drawings, and works of sculpture by Remington and Russell has grown to more than 300,000 works. I suggest you allow about 2 hours here, though fans of Americana may need even more time.

3501 Camp Bowie Blvd. (at Montgomery St. and W. Lancaster Ave.). © **817/738-1933.** www.carter museum.org. Free admission (fee for special exhibits). Tues–Wed and Fri–Sat 10am–5pm; Thurs 10am–8pm; Sun noon–5pm. Free permanent collection public tours 2pm Thurs–Sun.

**Fort Worth Botanic Gardens ★ ☺**   Created during the Great Depression, this spacious showcase of more than 2,500 native and exotic species of plants in 109 acres of attractive gardens and natural settings is the oldest botanical garden in Texas. Its highlights include the Texas Rose Garden, 3,500 roses that bloom in late April and October; a serene, 7-acre Japanese Garden, which features waterfalls, a teahouse and meditation space, and colorful koi-stocked ponds; and a 10,000-square-foot conservatory of exotic plants and tropical trees from around the world. You can drive through roads in the gardens and park at several of the individual sites. Allow a couple of hours here, though it would be all too easy to while away an entire afternoon.

3220 Botanic Garden Blvd. (south of W. Lancaster Ave. and just west of University Dr.) © **817/871-7686.** www.fwbg.org. Free admission to gardens. Enclosed conservatory $1 adults, 50¢ seniors and children 4–12, free for children 3 and under. Japanese Garden $4 adults ($4.50 Sat–Sun and holidays), $3 children 4–12, free for children 3 and under. Botanic garden daily 9am–5pm. Conservatory Mon–Sat 10am–4pm; Sun 1–4pm. Grounds daily 8am–dusk. Facilities remain open 2 hr. later during daylight saving time.

**Fort Worth Museum of Science and History ★ ☺**   One of the largest of its kind in the country, with a domed Omni (IMAX) theater, a planetarium, eight exhibition galleries, and hands-on science displays, this museum offers tons of fun and adventure for families. Kids should eat up the life-size Lone Star dinosaurs (at "Dinodig," they can even hunt for fossils and dig for dinosaur bones), while younger ones can hang out at "Kidspace," which has a puppet theater and materials for building a house. When the tots and parents get hungry, a courtyard cafe on the premises makes for a good stop. The Cattle Raisers Museum, which closed its independent location in 2007, reopened here as a museum within a museum, in a 10,000-square-foot space dedicated to the history of the cattle industry. Allow a couple of hours here, unless the kids get cranky.

1501 Montgomery St. (south of intersection of Camp Bowie Blvd., W. Lancaster Ave., and Montgomery St.) © **888/255-9300.** www.fwmuseum.org. Exhibit $14 adults, $10 seniors and children 2–12. Omni Theater $7 adults, $6 seniors and children 2–12. Planetarium $5 adults, $4 seniors and children 3–12. Combination tickets available. Daily 10am–5pm. Closed Thanksgiving and Dec 24–25.

**Fort Worth Zoo ★★★ ☺**   One of the preeminent zoos in the country, the award-winning Fort Worth Zoo has a great layout of natural habitats and fantastic animals from around the world. I first took my nephew here for his fifth birthday, and we had a total blast (and he still remembers it a decade later). Among the 12 permanent exhibits: an "African Savannah" with endangered rhinos and giraffes; "Australian Outback and Great Barrier Reef" with kangaroos, wallabies, and lazy koalas; and "Asian Falls," with Komodo dragons, lots of apes, orangutans and rainforest monkeys, and Malayan and white tigers. "Texas Wild!" is an 8-acre expansion showcasing native Texas animals and a late-19th-century town, while the "Museum of Living Art" is a 30,000-square-foot herpetarium of 5,000 amphibians and reptiles, including North America's largest saltwater crocodile. Allow at least 2 or 3 hours here, though your kids probably won't want to leave.

1989 Colohial Pkwy. (east of University Dr. and just south of Trinity River). (℃ **817/759-7555.** www.fortworthzoo.org. Admission $12 adults, $9 seniors and children 3-12, free for children 2 and under; half-price tickets Wed. Mid-Feb to late Oct daily 10am–5pm; late Oct to mid-Feb daily 10am–4pm (open until 6pm Sat–Sun late Mar to mid-Sept).

**Kimbell Art Museum ★★★** One of the country's (if not the world's) top small museums, this remarkable and gracious place is the jewel in Cowtown's crown. In 1972, the great American architect Louis Kahn created perhaps his finest building to house the art collection of local philanthropist Kay Kimbell. His modern, natural concrete structure, a masterpiece of light, symmetry, and geometry, is a reference work in worldwide architectural studies. Its cycloid-shaped vaults are suffused with natural light entering discreetly through slatted skylights. The building is essentially a shell; it has no real interior walls, which allows curators total creativity through the use of movable walls to design exhibits. The TV art evangelist Sister Wendy Beckett calls the Kimbell "probably the nearest such an institution can come to perfection . . . one of the greatest achievements in the world." It is widely held to be the greatest museum building of the late–20th century. The museum is undergoing an audacious but respectful expansion (physically separate from the Kahn building, which will house the permanent collection) by the Pritzker Prize–winning architect Rienzo Piano, to be completed in 2013.

The permanent collection matches the grace and drama of the building. Though small, it contains several superlative works, ranging from prehistoric Asian and pre-Columbian pieces to European old masters (Velázquez, El Greco, Rubens, and Rembrandt) and the Impressionist and modern masters (Van Gogh, Monet, Cézanne, and Picasso). Outdoors is a Zen-like, sunken sculpture garden by Isamu Noguchi. With its reputation as such an outstanding place to display and view art, the Kimbell receives some of the finest national and international shows for which virtually every top-notch museum vies. Past major exhibits have included "Portraiture in the Age of Picasso" and "Gauguin and Impressionism." Depending upon your interest in, and the popularity of, the current traveling special exhibit, you might plan to spend a good 3 to 4 hours here.

3333 Camp Bowie Blvd. (btw. W. 7th St. and W. Lancaster Ave.). (℃ **817/332-8451.** www.kimbellart.org. Free admission to general collection; special exhibitions (including audioguide tour) $12 adults, $10 seniors and students, $8 children 6–11; half-price all day Tues and Fri 5–8pm. Tues–Thurs and Sat 10am–5pm; Fri noon–8pm; Sun noon–5pm. Closed July 4, Thanksgiving, Dec 25, and Jan 1.

**Log Cabin Village** ☺ Six mid-19th-century log cabins, presented as a living history museum, were transplanted to Forest Park southwest of downtown in the 1950s. The village includes a gristmill and actors decked out in pioneer costumes, who recreate the Old West of early Cowtown by posing as spinners, candle makers, and blacksmiths. Pay a visit primarily if you need an inexpensive way to entertain the kids.

If you're in Fort Worth at the end of January and first few days of February, you can't miss attending the Fort Worth Stock Show (officially known as the Southwestern Exposition and Livestock Show), which hearkens back to its earliest days at the end of the 19th century. At the Will Rogers Memorial Center near the art museums (on Amon Carter Square), you'll see horse shows and auctions, and be able to check out all sorts of livestock, from beef cattle to llamas and swine. There's plenty of entertainment during the show and also an all-Western parade on the first Saturday. The rodeo is especially lively during the Stock Show; tickets are $16 to $22. For more information and an exact schedule of events, call ☎ 817/877-2400 or visit www.fwssr.com.

2100 Log Cabin Village Lane (south of Trinity River and just west of University Dr.). ☎ **817/392-5881.** www.logcabinvillage.org. Admission $4.50 adults, $4 seniors and children 4-17, free for children 3 and under. Tues–Fri 9am–4pm; Sat–Sun 1–5pm.

**Modern Art Museum of Fort Worth** ★★★  The most noteworthy development in Fort Worth of the past decade—and one of the most important on the national culture scene—is the Modern, a landmark design by the celebrated modernist Japanese architect Tadao Ando and a true notch on the city's belt. It is my favorite museum—or work of architecture, period—since the debut of Frank Gehry's Guggenheim Bilbao in Spain. Opened in 2002, the museum, quickly hailed as a masterpiece, contains over 50,000 square feet of gallery space, making it second in size only to the Museum of Modern Art in New York among museums dedicated to contemporary and modern art. The galleries, with walls of warmly textured, poured concrete and 20-foot-high ceilings, are suffused with spectacular natural light and housed in three rectangular, flat-roofed pavilions built around a large pond. In fact the oldest art museum in Texas (chartered in 1892), the Modern possesses an impressive permanent collection of modern and contemporary paintings, sculpture, and works on paper by Picasso, Mark Rothko, Andy Warhol, Frank Stella, Robert Rauschenberg, David Smith, Gerhard Richter, Francis Bacon, and Jackson Pollock, as well as an impressive contemporary photography collection. A sculpture by Martin Puryear, *Ladder for Booker T. Washington,* proves very popular with kids; it's a two-story wooden ladder reaching to the ceiling, ever-so-narrow at the top. Another piece not to miss is Ron Mueck's stunningly lifelike and creepy *Seated Woman.* The outdoor sculpture collection includes large-scale works by Tony Cragg, George Segal, and Antony Gormley and a massive piece outside by Richard Serra. Plan to spend at least a couple of hours here. The restaurant overlooking the reflection pool, Café Modern, is an excellent spot for lunch—one of the better lunch restaurants in town, in fact.

3200 Darnell St. (across the street from the Kimbell Museum, btw. W. 7th St. and W. Lancaster Ave.). ☎ **866/824-5566** or 817/738-9215. www.themodern.org. Admission $10 adults, $4 students and seniors, free for children 12 and under; free for all Wed and 1st Sun of each month. Tues–Thurs and Sat–Sun 10am–5pm, Fri 10am–8pm; also Feb–Apr and Sept–Nov Tues until 7pm. Free public tours daily 2pm (no reservations). Call for information about artist-led tours (3rd Sun of the month) and lectures. Closed July 4, Thanksgiving, Dec 24-25, and Jan 1.

**National Cowgirl Museum and Hall of Fame** ★ ☺  Opened in 2002 in a beautiful, Texas-style Art Deco building, the latest addition to Fort Worth's Cultural District recognizes not just cowgirls, but the importance of an array of plucky women who shaped the American West. It's the only museum in the world honoring their pioneering spirit. A fun and educational visit for the entire family, the museum's interactive exhibits in three gallery spaces and a state-of-the-art theater depict cowgirls working their ranches, their role in the media and fashion (with displays of cowboy couture), and cutting-horse and barrel-racing displays. A rotunda with 12 cool, glass murals that slowly change as you walk through the hall honors more than 150 notable Western women (from Dale Evans and the first woman to cross the Rockies to Annie Oakley and the artist Georgia O'Keeffe). The interactive exhibits are terrific for little cowpokes of both sexes; kids can hop on a (simulated) bucking bronco and get filmed, have their pictures superimposed on old Western film posters, and listen to jukeboxes playing country tunes. Don't miss the gift shop, a great place to score such things as vintage suitcases, antique Western goodies, and rhinestone duds. Allow an hour or two.

1720 Gendy St. (east of intersection of Montgomery and Burnett-Tandy sts., next to Will Rogers Memorial Center). **② 800/476-FAME** (3263) or 817/336-4475. www.cowgirl.net. $10 adults, $8 seniors, $8 children 6–18, free for children 5 and under. Tues–Sun 10am–5pm. Closed Thanksgiving, Dec 24–25, and Jan 1.

**Thistle Hill House Museum**   This historic 1903 Georgian Revival mansion, the former residence of two prominent Fort Worth families, has been lovingly restored with period furnishings. The residence, rumored to be ghost ridden, has an elegant oak grand staircase and a wealth of interesting details, including eight fireplaces, five full bathrooms, and, unusual for the period, electric and gas lighting and built-in closets. The 45-minute guided tour, which has really jumped in price, relates the curious anecdotes of the mansion's history. The cattle baron W. T. Waggoner built the home for his eccentric daughter Electra (who took milk baths and is said to have been the first to spend $20,000 in a single day at Neiman Marcus); it then passed to Winfield Scott, who made many changes in the home, adding its limestone columns; and it finally became a girl's school, later abandoned. Included in the admission is a tour of the McFarland House, an 1899 Queen Anne-Victorian at 1110 Penn St.

1509 Pennsylvania Ave. (btw. 8th Ave. and Henderson St., south of I-30) **② 817/332-5875.** www.historicfortworth.org. Admission $15 adults, $7.50 seniors, $5 children 7–12. Tours on the hour Mon and Wed–Fri 11am–2pm, Sun 1–3pm.

## ESPECIALLY FOR KIDS

Fort Worth is loaded with activities for children. The top choice among the options is the **Fort Worth Zoo,** one of the very finest in the country, with a splendid array of exotic animals in natural habitats. Kids can play and learn at the **Fort Worth Museum of Science and History,** which has an Omni (IMAX) theater and hands-on science displays, including "Dinodig," where they can play amateur paleontologist. If the kids are restless and just need to get outside, take them to the **Fort Worth Botanic Garden,** with acres and acres of gardens, exotic plants, and tropical trees.

The **Stockyards National Historic District** has plenty to entertain little cowboys and cowgirls. Twice a day, a herd of longhorn cattle rumbles down brick-paved Exchange Avenue. **Texas Town** in Stockyards Station is a theme park of sorts: an Old West hotel, bar, outhouse, and jail, as well as a vintage ride park, with an antique merry-go-round. Actors in chaps and vests enact *High Noon* gun duels. Nearby, kids can try to find their way through the **Cowtown Cattlepen Maze,** designed to resemble the cattlepens of the Old West. An enjoyable excursion for families is the **Grapevine Vintage Train,** a steam locomotive (or its diesel substitute) that travels from Stockyards Station to 8th Avenue in Fort Worth and to historic Grapevine. Young cowboys and cowgirls will enjoy **horseback trail rides** at the Stockyard Station Livery (chuck-wagon dinners available for groups of 10 or more; call ✆ **817/624-3446** for more information), and, if you're here in January, the **Fort Worth Stock Show & Rodeo.** The gals may feel empowered by a visit to the **National Cowgirl Museum and Hall of Fame,** which has cool interactive exhibits (such as filming yourself on a bucking bronco). If the kids are hungry for more Old West adventures, trot them over to the **Cattle Raisers Museum,** now part of the Museum of Science and History, which depicts life on the range through talking ranchers and cattle and a theater presentation.

For additional family activities, such as Six Flags Amusement Park and professional spectator sports, see "Arlington" in chapter 4.

## ORGANIZED TOURS

Guided, Saturday-only **Walking Tours of the Stockyards,** with visits to the major sights, leave from the Visitor Information Center at 130 E. Exchange Ave. (✆ **817/625-9715;** www.stockyardsstation.com/walking-tours.html). Guided tours cost $6 to $7 for adults, $5 to $6 for seniors, and $4 to $5 for children ages 6 to 12, and they are given every 2 hours, Saturday from 10am to 4pm. The **Wrangler Walking Tour** takes in the Livestock Exchange, cattlepens on the Cattleman's Catwalk, Mule Alley, Cowtown Coliseum, Exchange Avenue, and the old Hog and Sheep Barns (Stockyards Station). The **Cowboy Walking Tour** adds a visit to Billy Bob's and a buck to the price.

Other walking tours of Fort Worth, as well as "step-on bus tours" and local author lunches, are offered by **Fort Worth Tours and Trails** (✆ **817/731-3875;** www.fwtoursntrails.com). Walking tours of historic downtown and the Stockyards are $10 each.

## OUTDOOR ACTIVITIES

**BIKING, IN-LINE SKATING & JOGGING** Excellent for all outdoor activities are **Trinity Park** (near the Cultural District just north of I-30) and **Forest Park** (south of I-30). Depression-era Trinity Park encompasses the Botanic Garden and 8 miles of cycling and jogging trails. Forest Park is the site of another well-known Fort Worth landmark, the Fort Worth Zoo. The scenic **Trinity River Trails,** which run 35 miles along the Trinity River, are my choice for biking, hiking, and in-line skating. Pick up a map at a tourist information center.

Serious runners may want to come prepared to participate in (or watch) the **Cowtown Marathon** (including a half-marathon, 10K, 5K, and three-person marathon relay), which for 27 years has drawn runners from around the world to the Stockyards National Historic District in late February. Call ✆ **817/735-2033** for specific dates and other information. You can also obtain a monthly runners' calendar at ✆ **800/433-5747.**

**GOLF** Fort Worth has five inexpensive public courses. **Meadowbrooks Golf Course,** 1815 Jenson Rd. (✆ **817/457-4616**), just east of downtown, is one of the top 25 municipal golf courses in Texas. The popular par-71 course is set amid rolling terrain. Also at the top of the list is **Pecan Valley Golf Course,** 6400 Pecan Dr. (✆ **817/249-1845**); it has two 18-hole golf courses: the "River" and the "Hills." **Rockwood Golf Course,** 1851 Jacksboro Hwy. (✆ **817/624-1771**), has a short 18-hole course and an additional, fairly difficult 9 holes called the Blue Nine. **Sycamore Creek Golf Course,** Martin Luther King, Jr., Freeway (✆ **817/535-7241**), is a 9-hole layout with narrow tree-lined fairways. The **Z. Boaz Golf Course,** 3200

Lackland Rd. (☏ 817/738-6287), west of downtown, is a pretty straightforward, 18-hole course. Greens fees for all five public courses range from $11 to $26, depending on the day and time. For general information, visit www.fortworthgolf.org.

**HORSEBACK RIDING** **Stockyards Station Livery,** 130 E. Exchange Ave. (☏ 817/624-3446), offers horseback trail riding for riders of all skill levels (as well as wagon rides and chuck-wagon dinners). Trail riding costs $22 for the first hour and $15 for each additional hour.

**TENNIS** The swank **Worthington Renaissance** hotel (p. 111) has two rooftop courts available for $10 per day to nonguests; call to reserve (☏ 817/882-1000). The public can get on an indoor or outdoor court at the **Don McLeland Tennis Center,** 1600 W. Seminary Dr. (☏ 817/921-3134), or the **TCU Tennis Center,** 3609 Bellaire Dr. N. on the campus south of downtown (☏ 817/921-7960), which has two dozen lit outdoor courts and five indoor courts. There are **public clay courts** at 7100 S. Hulen St. (☏ 817/292-9787).

## SPECTATOR SPORTS

See "Spectator Sports" in chapter 4 for professional football, baseball, soccer, basketball, and more hockey and golf.

**AUTO RACING** The **Texas Motor Speedway,** I-35 W. at Hwy. 114, north of Fort Worth (☏ 817/215-8500; www.texasmotorspeedway.com), is said to be the third-largest sporting complex in the world. It's the place to see NASCAR, Indy, and motorcycle racing. Plan on joining a crowd; more than 150,000 people can attend the races here.

**GOLF** Fort Worth's stop on the PGA tour is the **Colonial Invitational,** which takes place every May at Fort Worth's prestigious Colonial Country Club (☏ 817/927-4278 or 927-4280; www.colonialfw.com).

**HOCKEY** The **Texas Brahmas** of the Central Hockey League (CHL) play from January to March at the NYTEX Sports Centre in Rockland Hills. Call ☏ 817/336-3342 or visit www.brahmas.com for news and ticket information.

**RODEO/LIVESTOCK SHOWS** Fort Worth's famous **Cowtown Coliseum,** 121 E. Exchange Ave. (☏ 817/625-1025), is the top place to see professional rodeo. Rodeos are usually every Friday and Saturday night (tickets $7.50–$15). Popping up frequently on the Coliseum schedule is **Pawnee Bill's Wild West Show,** a reenactment of the original, which was once the largest Wild West show anywhere. Events range from trick roping to trick shooting and are accompanied by Western music and an arena full of buffaloes, longhorns, and horses. For information and tickets, call ☏ 888/COWTOWN (269-8696) or 817/625-1025, or visit www.stockyardsrodeo.com. Look for coupons in the *Fort Worth Key Magazine,* available at tourist information offices.

The **Kowbell Rodeo,** about 15 minutes from downtown, has rodeos year-round on Saturday and Sunday nights, as well as bull riding Monday, Wednesday, and Friday evenings. Call ☏ 817/477-3092 for more information.

The big event in Fort Worth is the annual **Southwestern Exposition and Livestock Show & Rodeo,** which is staged from the end of January to early February (www.fwssr.com). The nation's oldest livestock show features a Western parade, auctions, and cowboys and cowgirls at the nightly rodeo at **Will Rogers Memorial Center,** located in the Cultural District at 3301 W. Lancaster Ave. (☏ 817/877-2400).

# SHOPPING

## Great Shopping Areas

Fort Worth can't compare to Dallas as a shopping mecca (nor, I suspect, would it want to), but, especially if you're looking for Western clothing and souvenirs of cow-town history, you're in luck. The top tourist area, the **Stockyards National Historic District** (and particularly **Stockyards Station,** a mall of pure Texan shops converted from the old sheep and hog pens) has plenty of authentic Western fashions, antiques, art, and souvenirs, many found in shops inhabiting historic quarters. **Sundance Square** in the downtown historic district is gushing with art galleries, museum gift shops, and fashionable clothing and furnishing stores, most in turn-of-the-20th-century buildings. The **Downtown Fort Worth Rail Market,** a European-style market that bills itself as "Texas's First True Public Market," is located in the historic Santa Fe Warehouse, 1401 Jones St. (© 817/335-6758). It has a good farmers' market and a couple of dozen permanent merchants. Along Camp Bowie Boulevard in the **Cultural District,** there are a number of art galleries and design-oriented shops, and the burgeoning **West 7th Street** corridor (known to some as W7) has a number of cool boutiques to complement its restaurants, bars, and condos.

If you're in town during the period from late November through mid-December, don't miss the **Western Mercantile show** (© 817/244-6188; www.nchacutting.com) in the Amon G. Carter Exhibit Hall in the Cultural District. Besides demonstrations of cutting horses, there are booths selling custom saddles, boots, and every kind of Western paraphernalia you can imagine (as well as luxe custom horse trailers).

## Western Gear

Two of the best Western shops—for real ropers, urban cowboys, and rodeo queens—are on the Stockyards' classic Exchange Avenue. Family-owned **M. L. Leddy's ★**, 2455 N. Main at Exchange (© 817/624-3149; www.leddys.com), with the big neon boot sign out front, is one of the city's oldest Western wear shops. Originally a boot maker and saddlery, it has fine cowboy duds such as handmade belts, formalwear, custom-made boots, and saddles, and the best-selling top-of-the-line cowboy hat, the pure Beaver. (It has another, slightly slicker and "uptown" shop, called **Leddy's Ranch at Sundance,** 410 Houston St., © 817/336-0800, with a full range of boots and Western clothing.) Across the street from the Stockyards Hotel, **Maverick ★★**, 100 E. Exchange Ave. (© 817/626-1129; www.maverickwesternwear.com), has such high-end Western wear as hand-embroidered shirts, saloon-ready 19th-century-style suits, and other swank cowboy duds. It also has a long bar, so you can grab a longneck (plenty of bejeweled shoppers do) and look the part of the cowboy or cowgirl you are (or hope to become).

Also in the Stockyards, **Ponder Boot Company ★★**, 2358 N. Main St. (© 817/626-3523; www.ponderboot.com), is the place to go for custom boots. Step inside and choose your leather and get your own brand or initial on a boot that will last you a lifetime and cost not much more than a top-of-the-line factory-made boot (most will run $600–$850). Georgia, the owner, will demonstrate the superior quality of one of her handmade, custom boots using a pair of dissected boots (if you ask nicely).

Downtown near Sundance Square, **Peters Brothers Hats ★**, 909 Houston St., at 9th Street (© 800/TXS-HATS [897-4287]; www.petersbros.com), has been around since 1911, stocking Stetsons and hats of all kinds, including Western fedoras and custom-made cowboy hats. Also check out **Retro Cowboy,** 406 Houston St. in Sundance Square (© 817/338-1194), for women's Western apparel, sterling silver jewelry, and men's vintage shirts. **Teskey's Uptown,** 2913 W. Crockett St. (© 817/332-2525;

http://teskeys.com), has some swank, pricey Western duds for men and women, as well as very trendy shirts and jeans. If the duds at these upscale Western stores are a bit too dear for your cowboy wallet, check out **Western Wear Exchange,** 2809 Alta Mere, 183S at I-30 (© **817/738-4048**), a rare resale shop dealing exclusively in Western wear. If it's already broken in, you'll be closer to looking and feeling the part of a real roper.

Once you've got the duds, you need the tunes. **Ernest Tubb's Record Shop,** 140 E. Exchange Ave., in Stockyards Station (© **800/229-4288** or 817/624-8449; www. etrecordshop.com), has a great stock of honky-tonk, cowboy, and country-and-western recordings, including old vinyl and hard-to-find stuff.

### Antiques & Furnishings

**Bum Steer,** 2400 N. Main St. (© **817/626-4565**), just a block from the Stockyards' main drag, sells Western antiques, vintage clothing, chaps and saddles, mounts and hides, and those lovable antler chandeliers. Just up the street is **Cross-Eyed Moose,** 2340 N. Main St. (© **817/624-4311**), run by the same folks and stocking slightly more affordable Western goods, some used clothing and antiques, as well as custom furnishings, game mounts, and Western decorative stuff. I picked up a great used pair of $10 boots here for my nephew. The **Antique Colony,** 7200 Camp Bowie Blvd. (© **817/731-7252**), has some 120 dealers of antiques and collectibles.

### Department Stores & Malls

**Stockyards Station,** 140 E. Exchange Ave. (© **817/625-9715**), once the Southwest's largest hog and sheep marketing center, has been converted into a cute center with several dozen restaurants and shops featuring Western apparel, Lone Star wines, country-and-western music, leather goods, Texas products, and arts and crafts. There's even a **Stockyards Wedding Chapel** (© **817/624-1570**) for cowboys and girls dying for a true Old West ceremony.

**University Park Village,** 2 blocks south of I-30 on South University Drive near Texas Christian University (© **817/654-0521**), is an upscale shopping center with Talbot's, Williams-Sonoma, Ann Taylor, Voyagers the Travel Store, and Wolf Camera.

# FORT WORTH AFTER DARK

Despite its decent size, Fort Worth still feels like a small town, and some young people looking for a bigger scene continue to split for Big D on weekends. Still, Fort Worth has a few good nightlife options, especially at the two extremes of the scale: high culture and cowboy culture. Whether you're inclined toward opera, symphony, and theater, or up for some boot-scootin', Fort Worth has some fine venues. **Exchange Avenue** in the Stockyards is where you want to be on weekends for some hot Western swing, Texas shuffle, and honky-tonk tunes. The street becomes a cruising strip of souped-up trucks, guys and dolls in cowboy and cowgirl finery strutting their stuff, and dancers ducking into honky-tonks and cowboy discos. Meanwhile, **Sundance Square** is full of bars, restaurants, cafes, and movie theaters, and is mobbed on weekend nights (luckily, there's plenty of free parking after 5pm and on weekends right in and around the square). **City Streets,** 425 Commerce St. (© **817/335-5400**), is a one-stop-shopping entertainment complex, generic and mild-mannered but popular with visitors for its range of bars, lounges, and pool halls—and, of course, happy hours. W7, the new development along West 7th Street between the Cultural District and downtown, is the newest place to hang out, dine, and drink.

For listings, check out the "Entertainment" section of the *Fort Worth Star-Telegram* or check the weekly listings posted on its website, www.dfw.com. For tickets, try Arts Line at **Ticketmaster** (📞 817/467-ARTS [2787] or 214/631-ARTS [2787]; www. ticketmaster.com) or **Texas Tickets** (📞 817/277-3333).

## THE PERFORMING ARTS

Elegant **Bass Performance Hall** ★★, located at 4th and Calhoun streets (btw. Commerce and Calhoun sts.) (📞 877/212-4280 or 817/212-4280; www.basshall. com) is one of the top places in the country to see a musical or theater performance. Home to the distinguished Fort Worth Symphony Orchestra, its stage has welcomed an eclectic range of productions including *The Nutcracker,* Handel's *Messiah, Madame Butterfly,* Broadway shows (such as *Bring in 'Da Noise, Bring in 'Da Funk*), and pop, jazz, and country concerts by the likes of Tony Bennett, k.d. lang, Nanci Griffith, and Pink Martini, as well as dance/theater performances such as *Stomp.*

**Casa Mañana Theater** ★, 3101 W. Lancaster Ave., at University Drive (📞 817/ 332-2272; www.casamanana.org), is the country's first permanent theater designed for the musicals-in-the-round. The aluminum geodesic dome with an oval stage underwent a $3-million renovation a few years ago. Casa, as it's known locally, has been around for more than 50 years, and it puts on a wide range of dramas, comedies, and musicals, and is home to one of the top children's theater operations in the United States, mounting productions such as *Aladdin.*

The **Jubilee Theatre,** 506 Main St. (📞 817/338-4411; www.jubileetheatre. org), is home to intimate African-American theater, staging such dramas as *Brother Mac* (adapted from Shakespeare's *Macbeth*) and *A Raisin in the Sun,* as well as musicals such as *Lysistrata Please* (a rock version of the Aristophanes classic) and *Road Show,* an original production.

The **Rose Marine Theater,** 1440 Main St. (📞 817/624-8333; www.rosemarine theater.com), a movie theater dating from the 1920s just south of the Stockyards, has been restored and converted by the Latin Arts Association; here, you'll find plays in Spanish, Latin films, and other arts targeting the Latino population.

For film, probably the best place to catch a current mainstream movie is **Movie Tavern at West 7th Street,** 2872 Crockett St. (📞 682/503-8101), where you can also have a movie-themed cocktail (Casablanca Cosmo, anyone?) and some cinema grub while you watch.

## THE BAR SCENE

The oldest bar in Fort Worth and the site of the city's most famous gunfight in 1897, **White Elephant Saloon** ★, 106 E. Exchange Ave. (📞 817/624-1887), is an authentic Cowtown saloon, a great place to knock back a Lone Star longneck in the afternoon or check out some live Western music nightly on the small stage. The atmospheric bar is decorated with donated hats (from the likes of Ray Wylie Hubbard and Jimmie Dale Gilmore) and cases of porcelain and ceramic white elephants. There's also a nice beer garden, with live bands under the trees. **Booger Red's Saloon**, 109 W. Exchange Ave. (📞 817/625-6427), the bar in the Stockyards Hotel, has horse-saddle bar stools and makes a great place to start off the evening with a couple of beers.

On Sundance Square, **Flying Saucer Draught Emporium** ★★, 111 E. 4th St. (📞 817/336-7470; www.beerknurd.com/stores/fortworth), is a beer snob's dream, boasting 75 beers on tap and 125 bottles, including a slew of American microbrews and exotics such as Belgian *guerze* and German seasonals. For the novice or anyone looking for something new, there are "flights," sampler trays from around the world. With an outdoor patio and rooftop terrace, the place can get rowdy on weekends with cigar-smoking types and Texas Christian University students, but it's still one of the best places in Fort Worth to wet your whistle. Food tends toward such beer-complementary items as bratwurst and beer cheese soup. It also features an eclectic roster of live music on weekends. A swank bar with an outdoor patio, a good happy hour, and live music in warm months, **8.0**, 111 E. 3rd St. (© **817/336-0880;** www.eightobar. com), on Sundance Square, is frequented by Fort Worth's young and beautiful.

Remaining true to its grungy roots, despite the slick high-rise condo and restaurant development of West 7th Street going up literally all around it, **Fred's Texas Café ★★**, 915 Currie St. (© **817/332-0083;** www.fredstexascafe.com), remains a classic. Its outdoor covered patio is a great place for a cold beer (and a great Diablo Burger) as well as live bands on most nights of the week. It's vintage Fort Worth, with—my apologies to locals—a dose of "Keep Austin Weird" thrown in. Part of the burgeoning restaurant-and-bar scene on Magnolia Avenue, in the Hospital District, **The Usual,** 1408 W. Magnolia Ave. (© **817/810-0114**), is a sleekly modern, smoke-free, minimalist space with a midcentury vibe and excellent (if pricey) Prohibition-era cocktails; check out happy hour from 4 to 6pm and all night Sundays and Mondays.

## HONKY-TONK HEAVEN

The one place that's practically a required stop in Fort Worth is **Billy Bob's Texas ★★★**, 2520 Rodeo Plaza (© **817/624-7117;** www.billybobstexas.com). A cavernous barn for prize cattle in a former life, this absurdly large honky-tonk (according to the proprietors, the world's largest) is a symbol of Texas for many people and pretty much a Western theme park. With 40 bar stations, a monster dance floor for hard-core boot-scootin', a rodeo arena, video games, pool tables, mechanical bulls, and pro bull riding, it's 125,000 square feet (er, 7 acres) of country-and-western heaven. Open more than 20 years now, Billy Bob's continues to draw the biggest names in country music, including George Jones, LeAnn Rimes, Willie Nelson, and Jerry Jeff Walker. Its fame is such that you'll see real ropers in their best hats and tight jeans, along with drugstore cowboys and a lot of German and Japanese tourists, all soakin' up the flavor. Located in the heart of the Stockyards, Billy Bob's does business Monday through Saturday from 11am to 2am, and Sunday from noon to 2am. The cover charge varies according to the musical act; day visits cost $1. Don't miss the pro live bull riding on Friday and Saturday at 9 and 10pm; admission is $2.

Another time-tested "Texas-size" honky-tonk is the family-owned and -operated **Stagecoach Ballroom ★**, 2516 E. Belknap St. at the corner of Sylvania Avenue, off Airport Freeway (© **817/831-2261;** www.stagecoachballroom.com), a real

### Everybody, Get in Line

If you want to learn to line dance, shuffle, and two-step like a Texan, why not do it in one of the most famous honky-tonks in the world, **Billy Bob's Texas?** Wendell Nelson, who's been at Billy Bob's for 2 decades, is the dance man who will lead you through the basics.

Free classes are Thursdays at 7pm. Call © **817/923-9215** for additional information. For a more intimate experience, waltz and swing classes are also offered every Wednesday at 6:30pm at **Pearl's Dancehall & Saloon** (© 817/624-2800).

# grapevine

One of the oldest settlements in north Texas, Grapevine—north of DFW Airport, about 25 miles from Fort Worth—is known for its handsomely restored historic Main Street, the Grapevine Opry, several Texas wineries, and a number of art galleries housed in turn-of-the-20th-century buildings. Downtown there are some 75 historic buildings, including the **Torian Log Cabin,** Liberty Park, 201 S. Main St., and the **1901 Cotton Belt Train Depot.** The **Grapevine Opry,** which inhabits the 1940 Palace Theatre at 308 S. Main St. (© **817/481-8733**), holds foot-stomping hootenannies on Saturday nights and features concerts by top-name country stars throughout the year.

The **Grapevine Visitor Information Center** is located at 701 S. Main St. (© **800/457-6338** or 817/410-8136; www.ci.grapevine.tx.us). You can pick up information about **wine tours** and tastings at La Buena Vida Vineyards, La Bodega Winery, and North Star Winery.

The best way to visit old Grapevine is by train. The Tarantula Steam Train travels from Stockyards Station in Fort Worth to historic Grapevine; see p. 123 for additional information on this nostalgic locomotive. Otherwise, take Hwy. 114 NW from Dallas or Hwy. 121 NE from Fort Worth.

contender for most authentic old-time dance hall in Texas. It sports traditional country music and dance, and is a good spot to pick up some moves if you're not exactly a smooth-footed kicker. Wednesday is Ladies Night, and cover charges for live music guests range from $6 to $15. (There is live music on Wed and Fri–Sun, beginning at 7pm. Thurs nights are newly dedicated to "smoke-free" C&W, Big Band, and Back to the '50s dancing, 6–10pm; $5 cover. Also, look for Lone Star Talent Night contests on Tues.)

I'll always lament the demise of the poetically named Western dance hall **Big Balls of Cowtown,** once a bordello called Pearl's Hotel. However, the space is now inhabited by **Pearl's Dancehall & Saloon ★**, 302 W. Exchange Ave. (© **817/624-2800;** www.pearlsdancehallandsaloon.com), featuring live traditional, Western swing and honky-tonk music Wednesday to Saturday. Although it's a bit spiffier in its new incarnation, it's still the coolest spot in the Stockyards for nontouristy C&W music (featuring name acts such as Dale Watson) and dancing. Free dance lessons are given every Wednesday at 6:30pm.

Also in the Stockyards District, there's often live country music at **Rodeo Exchange,** 221 W. Exchange Ave. (© 817/626-0181), and **Ernest Tubb's Record Shop,** 140 E. Exchange Ave. (© 817/624-8449), the latter only on Saturday afternoons.

## OTHER LIVE MUSIC

Sadly, Fort Worth's legendary jazz venue, **Caravan of Dreams,** bit the dust several years ago. While nothing has sprung up to fill its big shoes, there is a handful of other live music venues in town that don't go the country route. The top rock venue in town is the **Ridglea Theater ★**, 6025 Camp Bowie Blvd. (© 817/738-9500; www.ridgleatheater.com), a restored 1940s Art Deco theater that plays host to touring alternative rock and (mostly) metal bands. **Aardvark ★**, 2905 W. Berry St. (© 817/926-7814; www.the-aardvark.com), is a cool small space that hosts a wide-ranging roster of pop, alternative rock, and neo-folk acts, such as Son Volt and the Gourds, with small cover charges Tuesday through Saturday. For good local and regional acts of mostly indie rock and alt-country, including Texas stalwarts such as Junior Brown and Heartless Bastards, throughout the week, **Lola's Sixth Street ★★**, 2736 W. 6th St. (© **817/877-0666;** www.lolasfortworth.com), is an intimate venue with three bars (including two cool outdoor patios) and daily happy hours.

For traditional live C&W, also check out the bands scheduled at two of the most famous spots in Fort Worth, **Billy Bob's Texas** and **White Elephant Saloon**, as well as **Pearl's Dancehall and Saloon** and **Stagecoach Ballroom** (see above).

A sister of the clubs of the same name in Austin and Dallas, **Pete's Dueling Piano Bar,** 621 Houston St. (© **817/335-PETE** [7383]; www.petesduelingpiano bar.com), has shows Wednesday through Saturday at 8pm; four expert pianists play pop and rock standards and encourage loud audience singalongs. Calling Pete's a "piano bar" probably doesn't do it justice; you won't hear Bach, but you will hear Johnny Cash.

## RODEO

The **Stockyards Championship Rodeo** is held most weekends on Friday and Saturday nights at Cowtown Coliseum in the Stockyards, 121 E. Exchange Ave. (© **817/888-COWTOWN** [269-8696]; www.stockyardsrodeo.com). Tickets range from $4.50 for children to $15 for adults in reserved box seats. **Pawnee Bill's Wild West Show** (p. 130) runs during summer months and holiday weekends.

# HOUSTON & EAST TEXAS

by David Baird

Situated on a flat, nearly featureless Gulf Coast plain, Houston sprawls out from its center in vast tracts of subdivisions, freeways, office parks, and shopping malls. In undisturbed areas, you'll find marshy grasslands in the south and woods in the north. Meandering across this plain are several bayous on whose banks cypress and southern magnolia trees sometimes grow. Many visitors, imagining the Texas landscape as it is usually drawn—barren and treeless—are surprised by such green surroundings. However, the city is at the tail end of a large belt of natural forest coming down through east Texas, and the climate is much the same as coastal Louisiana and Mississippi—warm and humid, with ample rainfall.

---

Houston is the fourth-most-populated city in the United States. If we compare the populations of greater metro areas rather than cities, then it ranks only 10th. Yet in geographical expanse, Houston ranks second. The city is more than half as large as the state of Rhode Island and continues to expand outward. But in the past several years, there has been a shift in residential construction toward downtown and the inner city.

Houston is not usually considered a tourist destination; most visitors come for business or family reasons and are lured into playing tourist only after arriving. It's a business town, and the oil and gas industry remains the big enchilada, but other sectors have added so much to the local economy that the contribution of oil and gas is now only about 50%. The Texas Medical Center is the largest concentration of medical institutions in the world. It's virtually a city within a city, with 14 hospitals and many clinics, medical schools, and research facilities. Construction and engineering companies also contribute much to the economy, and the newest big player is high-tech.

Houston's society is socially and economically wide open. Houstonians inherently dislike being told what to do, and this dislike cuts across the political spectrum: Opinion surveys show that gun control is highly unpopular, but so is government control over reproductive rights. Among urban planners, Houston is famous (or infamous) as the only major U.S. city that doesn't have zoning, allowing the market to determine land use instead. On the plus side, this love for individual freedoms gives Houston a dynamism that is palpable and has brought a flood of newcomers from around the world, who have found here a welcoming city. Houston seems to be growing more cosmopolitan every day, as ethnic restaurants and specialty shops spring up throughout the city along with exotic temples and churches—Taoist, Buddhist, Hindu, Islamic, Russian Orthodox—built much as they would be back in the mother country.

On the minus side, this is the land of Enron, the go-go company that preached the gospel of deregulation to state and federal governments and then abused its new freedoms. Also, Houston struggles with an air-pollution problem that has the local government painfully considering unpopular regulations to keep the city in compliance with the Clean Air Act.

In the field of the arts, one can find proof of the city's vigor. Houston has an excellent symphony orchestra, highly respected ballet and opera companies, and an energetic theater scene that few cities can equal in quantity or quality. There are some excellent museums, too, and, if art isn't your bag, there's the world-famous NASA Space Center, which is like nothing else on this planet. While you're enjoying the attractions, keep your eyes open and you can appreciate another thing for which Houston is known: its architecture, which stands out for its bold, even brash character. This is, after all, home to the first dome stadium—the Astrodome—which was billed at the time as "the eighth wonder of the world." Several buildings are striking for their dramatic appearance as well as for their irreverence—one skyscraper is crowned with a Mayan pyramid, another wryly uses the architectural features of Gothic churches for a bank building, and a pair of towers in the Medical Center unmistakably represent two giant syringes. There is little that is staid about this city, and the more time you spend here, the more you appreciate this fact.

# ORIENTATION

## Arriving

### BY PLANE

Houston has two major airports: the **George Bush Intercontinental Airport (IAH),** 22 miles north of downtown, and the smaller **William P. Hobby Airport (HOU),** 9 miles southeast of downtown. Both shuttle companies listed below offer service between the airports.

### George Bush Intercontinental Airport (IAH)

Houston's primary airport (www.fly2houston.com/iahhome) functions as a hub for Continental Airlines, though it's serviced by all major national and international carriers. The airport has all the facilities of major international airports, including ATMs and currency exchange desks.

**GETTING TO & FROM THE AIRPORT**   Taxi service from IAH to downtown costs $45 to $55 and the ride takes about 30 minutes; getting to the Galleria area costs a few dollars more. **Super Shuttle** (© 800/258-3826; www.supershuttle. com) ferries passengers to and from this airport to almost all hotels. Prices vary according to the hotel's location. A ride to or from downtown costs $25, and $7 for each person traveling with you. Shuttle ticket counters are at all airport terminals. **Houston Metro** (© 713/635-4000; www.ridemetro.org), Houston's mass transit system, has begun running nonstop buses between downtown and the airport's Terminal C. In the baggage claim area, you'll find a ticket counter labeled "Metro Airport Direct." The fare is $4.50. Buses run every 30 minutes from 5am to 8pm. They drop off (and pick up) passengers downtown at 815 Pierce St., across the street from the Metro Transit Center. Metro also has regular bus service to and from the airport,

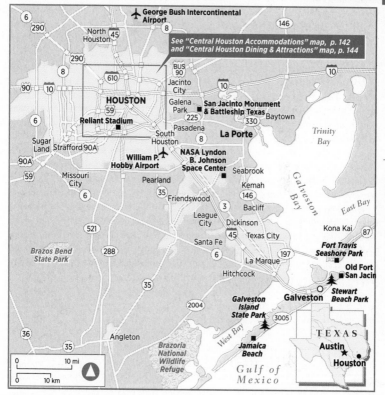

See "Central Houston Accommodations" map, p. 142
and "Central Houston Dining & Attractions" map, p. 144

which runs until midnight (route 102). The fare is $1.25. Exact change is required, but dollar bills are accepted. Buses run about every 40 minutes, and travel time to downtown is 1 hour, a little longer during rush hour.

The major car-rental companies have counters at each terminal. John F. Kennedy Boulevard is the main artery into and out of the airport. When leaving the airport, you'll see signs pointing toward either the North Freeway (I-45) or the Eastex Freeway (Tex. 59). Both take you downtown, but the Eastex is shorter and usually quicker.

## William P. Hobby Airport (HOU)

Hobby Airport (www.fly2houston.com/hobbyhome) is used mostly by Southwest Airlines. All major car-rental agencies have counters here with either staff or a service phone. Taxis from Hobby to the downtown area cost about $30, and to the Galleria area, $40. For airport shuttle service, see above.

## BY CAR

Houston is connected to Dallas and Fort Worth by I-45, and to San Antonio, New Orleans, and Beaumont by I-10. From Austin, you can take either Tex. 71 through Bastrop to Columbus, where it joins I-10, or Tex. 290 east through Brenham.

## BY TRAIN

**Amtrak** (© **800/872-7245;** www.amtrak.com) trains from New Orleans, Chicago, and Los Angeles (and points in between) arrive and depart from the **Southern Pacific Station** at 902 Washington Ave. (© **713/224-1577**), close to downtown.

## Visitor Information

The **Greater Houston Convention and Visitors Bureau (GHCVB)** has an elaborate visitor center located in the city hall building at 901 Bagby St. between Walker and McKinney (© **713/437-5556;** www.visithoustontexas.com). Enter through the door on Walker. Here, you can get lots of brochures, a range of city maps, architectural and historical guides, and answers from the center's staff. Pick up a copy of the *Official Guide to Houston* magazine; it has a helpful calendar of events. You can also play with the interactive computer stations and see a short introductory film of the city. The center is open Monday to Saturday from 9am to 4pm. There are a few designated parking spots on Walker for visitors; these are free and have a 1-hour limit. If they are full, park your car at the underground lot that is 1 block north of city hall.

For advance information, try © **800/4-HOUSTON** (446-8786) or 713/437-5200, or www.visithoustontexas.com. You can request a copy of their *Visitors Guide*. Other websites you might find helpful are operated by the local newspapers. The *Houston Chronicle* (**www.chron.com**) is the daily newspaper, and the *Houston Press* (**www.houstonpress.com**) is the free weekly tabloid, which has a large entertainment section.

## City Layout

Houston is a difficult city in which to find your way around; it was built with no master plan, and most of its streets are jumbled together with little continuity. The suburban areas look alike and have indistinctive street names, usually ending in "crest," "wood," and "dale." To make matters worse, the terrain is so flat that the only visible points of reference are tall buildings. However, for the visitor, things aren't so bad. Most of the main attractions are not far off the freeways or other main arteries. With a basic knowledge of these, you can keep your bearings and get from one place to another.

To understand the layout of Houston's freeways, it's best to picture a spider web with several lines radiating out from the center, which are connected to each other by two concentric circles. The lines that radiate outward are in the following clockwise order: At 1 o'clock is the Eastex Freeway (Tex. 59 north), which usually has signs saying CLEVELAND, a town in east Texas; at 3 o'clock is the East Freeway (I-10 E. to Beaumont and New Orleans); between 4 and 5 o'clock is the Gulf Freeway (I-45 S. to Galveston); at 6 o'clock is the South Freeway (Tex. 228 to Lake Jackson, Freeport, and Surfside); between 7 and 8 o'clock is the Southwest Freeway (Tex. 59 to Laredo; look for signs that read VICTORIA); at 9 o'clock is the Katy Freeway (I-10 W. to San Antonio); at 10 o'clock is the Northwest Freeway (Tex. 290 to Austin); and at 11 o'clock is the North Freeway (I-45 N. to Dallas). The first circular freeway is Loop 610 (known as "the Loop"), which has a 4- to 5-mile radius from downtown. The second is known alternately as Sam Houston Parkway or Beltway 8. It has a 10- to 15-mile radius and is mostly a toll road except for the section in the area of the Bush Intercontinental Airport.

In addition to the freeways, there are certain arteries that most newcomers would do well to know. Here are brief descriptions of each.

**Main Street** bisects downtown and then heads south-southwest, changing its name to South Main. It passes through the Museum District, then along Hermann

Park and Rice University before reaching the Texas Medical Center. This stretch of South Main has lots of green space and is lined with oak trees. Beyond the Medical Center, the street passes by the Reliant Park football stadium, an exhibition center, and the old Astrodome.

In the middle of the Museum District is a traffic circle called **Mecom Fountain,** where South Main intersects **Montrose Boulevard.** Montrose runs due north from the Mecom Fountain, crossing Westheimer Road and Buffalo Bayou. It gives its name to the Montrose area and is lined by several bistros around the Museum District. After it crosses the bayou, Montrose becomes Studemont and then Studewood when it enters a historic neighborhood known as the Heights.

**Westheimer Road** is the east-west axis around which most of western Houston turns. It begins in the Montrose area and continues for many miles through various urban and suburban landscapes without ever seeming to come to an end. Past the Montrose area, Westheimer crosses Kirby Drive and then passes by River Oaks, a neighborhood for Houston's rich folk. Farther along is Highland Village Shopping Center, then Loop 610, where it enters the popular commercial district known as the Galleria area or Uptown. Farther west, Westheimer passes an endless series of fast-food restaurants, strip malls, and chain retail stores as it runs through suburbia.

**Kirby Drive** is an important north-south artery. It intersects Westheimer Road by River Oaks and runs due south, skirting the Greenway Plaza and passing under the Southwest Freeway. Once south of the freeway, Kirby enters University Place, a neighborhood that curls around the western borders of the Rice University campus and is the favorite residential area for Houston's doctors, lawyers, and other professionals. Kirby eventually intersects South Main Street in the vicinity of Reliant Stadium.

## The Neighborhoods in Brief

**Downtown** Once a ghost town in the evenings and on weekends, downtown Houston is now quite popular. Restaurants and bars are opening (and in some cases closing) in quick succession. Hotels have multiplied, too. In the northwest side of downtown is Old Market Square and the theater district, where Houston's symphony orchestra, ballet, opera, and principal theater company all reside. East of Main Street, within walking distance, is the George Brown Convention Center; the baseball park, Minute Maid Field (formerly Enron Field); and the Toyota Center basketball arena. Also fueling downtown's revitalization is a light rail that runs up and down Main Street and connects to the Museum District and the Medical Center. Beneath downtown is a network of pedestrian tunnels lined by shops and restaurants, forming an underground city. As is typical of Houston, almost all of these tunnels are private, not public, developments. South of downtown is **Midtown,** an area in transition, with town houses and shops gradually

replacing vacant lots and small office buildings. Vietnamese shopkeepers and restaurateurs have settled into the western side, especially along Milam Street, where you can find an array of excellent Vietnamese restaurants with reasonable prices.

**East End** Before Houston was established on the banks of Buffalo Bayou, the town of Harrisburg already existed 2 miles downstream. As Houston grew eastward, it incorporated Harrisburg, leaving behind little of the old town. A small commercial Chinatown lies a couple of blocks east of the convention center; beyond that, the area is residential. The inner East End is an up-and-coming neighborhood of mixed ethnicity. As you move farther east, the residences mix with small-scale manufacturing, auto mechanic and body shops, and service industries for the ship channel. In the far southern part is NASA's Space Center Houston; Kemah, Houston's version of Fisherman's Wharf; and Galveston Island. Most hotels located in this area are along

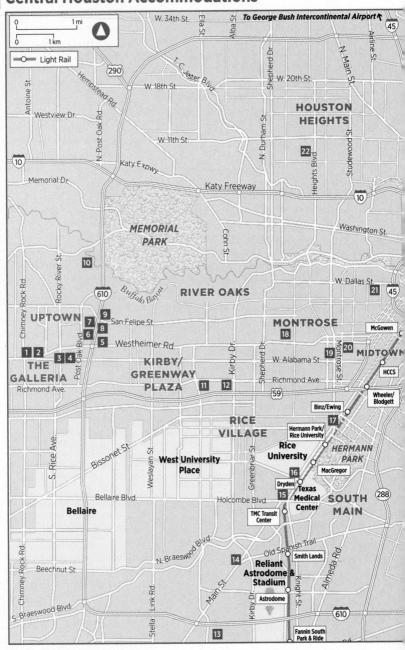

To George Bush Intercontinental Airport ↑

**HOUSTON HEIGHTS**

**MEMORIAL PARK**

Buffalo Bayou

**RIVER OAKS**

**UPTOWN**

**THE GALLERIA**

**MONTROSE**

**MIDTOWN**

**KIRBY/ GREENWAY PLAZA**

**RICE VILLAGE**

**West University Place**

**Rice University**

**HERMANN PARK**

**Bellaire**

**Texas Medical Center**

**SOUTH MAIN**

**Reliant Astrodome & Stadium**

○— Light Rail

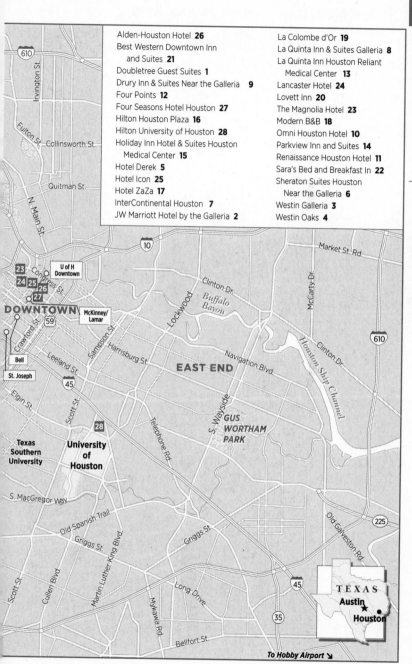

Alden-Houston Hotel **26**
Best Western Downtown Inn
  and Suites **21**
Doubletree Guest Suites **1**
Drury Inn & Suites Near the Galleria **9**
Four Points **12**
Four Seasons Hotel Houston **27**
Hilton Houston Plaza **16**
Hilton University of Houston **28**
Holiday Inn Hotel & Suites Houston
  Medical Center **15**
Hotel Derek **5**
Hotel Icon **25**
Hotel ZaZa **17**
InterContinental Houston **7**
JW Marriott Hotel by the Galleria **2**

La Colombe d'Or **19**
La Quinta Inn & Suites Galleria **8**
La Quinta Inn Houston Reliant
  Medical Center **13**
Lancaster Hotel **24**
Lovett Inn **20**
The Magnolia Hotel **23**
Modern B&B **18**
Omni Houston Hotel **10**
Parkview Inn and Suites **14**
Renaissance Houston Hotel **11**
Sara's Bed and Breakfast In **22**
Sheraton Suites Houston
  Near the Galleria **6**
Westin Galleria **3**
Westin Oaks **4**

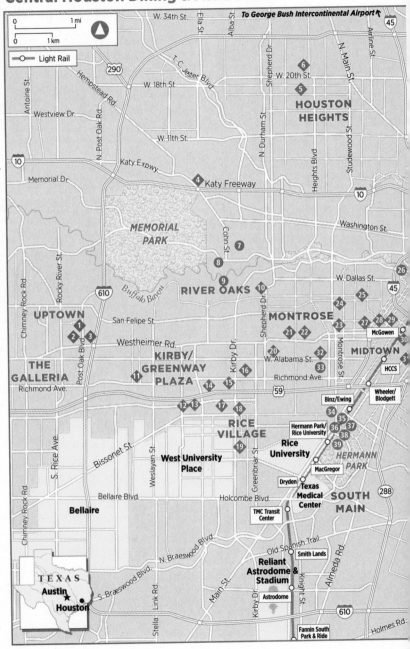

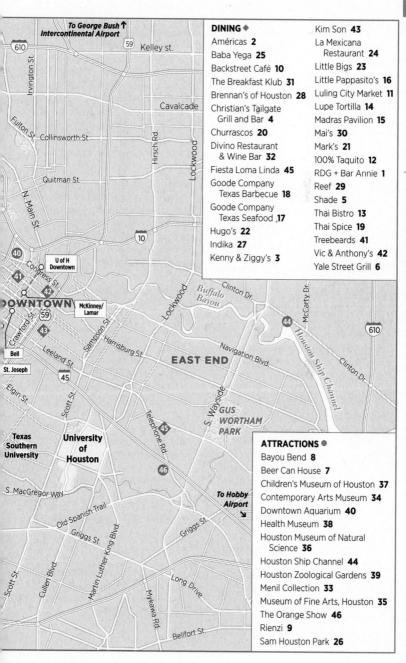

**DINING** ◆

Américas **2**

Baba Yega **25**

Backstreet Café **10**

The Breakfast Klub **31**

Brennan's of Houston **28**

Christian's Tailgate Grill and Bar **4**

Churrascos **20**

Divino Restaurant & Wine Bar **32**

Fiesta Loma Linda **45**

Goode Company Texas Barbecue **18**

Goode Company Texas Seafood **17**

Hugo's **22**

Indika **27**

Kenny & Ziggy's **3**

Kim Son **43**

La Mexicana Restaurant **24**

Little Bigs **23**

Little Pappasito's **16**

Luling City Market **11**

Lupe Tortilla **14**

Madras Pavilion **15**

Mai's **30**

Mark's **21**

100% Taquito **12**

RDG + Bar Annie **1**

Reef **29**

Shade **5**

Thai Bistro **13**

Thai Spice **19**

Treebeards **41**

Vic & Anthony's **42**

Yale Street Grill **6**

**ATTRACTIONS** ●

Bayou Bend **8**

Beer Can House **7**

Children's Museum of Houston **37**

Contemporary Arts Museum **34**

Downtown Aquarium **40**

Health Museum **38**

Houston Museum of Natural Science **36**

Houston Ship Channel **44**

Houston Zoological Gardens **39**

Menil Collection **33**

Museum of Fine Arts, Houston **35**

The Orange Show **46**

Rienzi **9**

Sam Houston Park **26**

the Gulf Freeway. The main reason for staying here is that hotel rates, for the most part, are economical, and the location between downtown, Hobby Airport, and the above-mentioned attractions makes the East End convenient.

**South Main** South of downtown and midtown is the **Museum District** and Hermann Park. This lovely part of town has lots of green space. Most of the museums are within a few blocks of one another. Here also are the Houston Zoological Gardens and the Rice University campus. On the south side of the park begins the Texas Medical Center. A bit farther south is a complex of buildings holding Reliant Stadium and the old Astrodome. This part of town has many hotels to suit all budgets. The location is convenient, and the city's light rail connects this area with downtown.

**Montrose & the Heights** Directly west of downtown is the Montrose area, a hip, artsy, and colorful part of town known for its clubs, galleries, and shops. The Museum District extends into this neighborhood to include the famous Menil Collection and its satellite galleries, a must-see for any visitor interested in the arts. Upscale in certain sections, downscale in others, the Montrose contains a broad cross-section of Houston society. It's also the de facto center of Houston's large and active gay community. North of the Montrose area, across Buffalo Bayou, is the Heights. It was conceived and built as an independent, planned residential community in the 1890s and remained so until 1918, when it was annexed by Houston. One curious fact about the Heights is that the original articles of incorporation required it to be "dry" (no sale of alcohol)— and this has stood in place ever since. Consequently, only a few good restaurants are here. But there's great shopping, especially for antiques and folk art. With downtown to the east, the Museum District to the south, and Kirby to the west, the Montrose area and the Heights are well located.

**Kirby District & Greenway Plaza** The area bordering Kirby Drive from River Oaks to University Place has the most restaurants of any district in Houston. Near Kirby Drive's midway point, where it crosses the Southwest Freeway, is the Greenway Plaza, an integrated development of office buildings, movie theaters, shops, and a sports arena, which has been made over into a well-known megachurch called Lakewood. Farther south is Rice Village, a retail development consisting of 16 square blocks of smart shops and restaurants. It is phenomenally popular with Houstonians and visitors and attracts all kinds of shoppers and diners.

**Uptown** Farther west, all the way to Loop 610, is where Uptown begins. It is still informally called the **Galleria area,** after the large indoor shopping mall, entertainment, and hotel complex. But the district's business owners had to devise another name for it because the developer of the Galleria protected its name so jealously that it became problematic to use the word in any commercial context. Thus, we have "Uptown." Shops, restaurants, and other businesses front Westheimer Road and Post Oak Boulevard.

**North Houston** All the neighborhoods described above, except for the Heights, are south of I-10, which bisects Houston into northern and southern halves. North Houston is largely a mix of working- and middle-class neighborhoods and commercial centers and, with the exception of the Heights, has little to offer visitors. Over the years, developers tried to establish upscale communities here, but an inherent quality of suburbanism is that you can always build farther out, and with each successive subdivision, the inner suburbs lose a little more of their luster. Ultimately, the developers took this to its logical extreme, skipping over vast tracts of land to build so far north that the city will never touch them. Thus, Woodlands and Kingwood, two upscale residential developments, are so far out that one can't consider them part of Houston.

# GETTING AROUND

## By Car

Houston is organized around the automobile. Having a car is almost a necessity unless you confine your explorations to the downtown area and the South Main corridor (including the Museum District), which are connected by the light rail. This makes it possible to stay in a downtown or South Main hotel and go up and down this corridor with ease. For trips to other parts of the city, you can use the hotel's shuttle, if available, or the occasional taxi.

Houston's freeways are no place for the meek: Many drivers don't obey speed limits, bob and weave through the lanes, and make their turnoffs at the last possible moment. You should have a clear idea of where you're headed and what exit you need to take before getting on a freeway. All this said, I actually enjoy driving Houston's freeways. It's a good way to grasp what it's like to be a Houstonian. My own practice is not to bother looking down at the speedometer; for all practical purposes, it's irrelevant. It's more important to stay in the flow of traffic at the same speed as most of the cars around you. As freeway systems go, Houston's is logical and has good directional signs. Traffic can be slow during rush hour or anywhere there's construction. You can use the **Texas Department of Transportation Info Hot Line** (© 713/802-5074) to check for lane closures on local freeways. The *Houston Chronicle* provides this information, too, as well as info on street closures. Don't be surprised to encounter construction during your visit.

**RENTALS** The prices for rental cars in Houston are lower than those for many tourist destinations, but tacked onto the final cost are several taxes that raise the price by as much as 27%. Keep this in mind when the salesperson tries to upgrade you to a higher-priced model. As is the case when renting cars elsewhere, you probably don't need to buy extra insurance if you're already covered by personal auto insurance. The major car-rental companies with locations around the city include **Alamo** (© 800/462-5266; www.alamo.com), **Avis** (© 800/230-4898; www.avis.com), **Budget** (© 800/527-0700; www.budget.com), **Dollar** (© 800/800-3665; www.dollar.com), **Enterprise** (© 800/736-8222; www.enterprise.com), **Hertz** (© 800/654-3131; www.hertz.com), **National** (© 800/227-7368; www.nationalcar.com), and **Thrifty** (© 800/847-4389; www.thrifty.com).

## By Public Transportation

**LIGHT RAIL** The **Metropolitan Transportation Authority (Metro;** © 713/635-4000; www.ridemetro.org) inaugurated its first light rail line in 2004. So far, it's been a big success with locals and is quite helpful for visitors, as it ties together some of the main areas of interest—downtown, the Museum District, the Medical Center, and Reliant Park. Train tickets cost $1.25 and are valid as bus transfers if the ticket holder is not traveling in the return direction. Train tickets can be purchased at each station from vending machines that accept cash, debit cards, and credit cards. The other option is to buy a "Q fare card" for multiple trips and load it with as much money as you think you'll need. The trains run as frequently as every 6 minutes and in slow times are not more than 18 minutes apart.

*Note:* In the past few years, there have been numerous collisions involving the light rail train and private vehicles. The train usually wins. Almost all of these accidents occurred because the drivers of the cars were distracted. Pay attention to directional signs and signals when crossing the rail line. There are a few confusing intersections: at the end of the line, where Main Street reaches Buffalo Bayou, in the Medical Center, and where the tracks shift from Main Street to San Jacinto. Otherwise, it's all straightforward.

**BUS SERVICE**   The citywide bus service operated by Metro can get you to most places in the city. To find out what bus to catch and where and when to catch it, your best option is to call the customer service number listed above. The staff can tell you over the phone how to get from point A to point B. If you're planning in advance, you can use the website and click on "Trip Planners." Once you know the bus routes you're going to use, you can download schedules from the same website. The standard bus fare is $1.25 for travel inside Loop 610 (seniors pay 60¢ and children 3 and under ride free); exact change is required, and the machines accept dollar bills. If needed, ask for a transfer, which will be good for 3 hours for other buses or the train. Metro no longer operates downtown trolleys.

## By Taxi

Taxis are plentiful in the city, but trying to hail one on the street can be an exercise in frustration. Call ahead or use hotel taxi stands. The principal companies are **Yellow Cab** (✆ 713/236-1111), **Fiesta Cab** (✆ 713/225-2666), **Liberty Cab** (✆ 800/TAXICAB [829-4222]), and **United Cab** (✆ 713/699-0000). Rates are set by the city: $4 for the first mile and $1.85 for each additional mile, plus a fuel charge, depending on the current price of gas.

# [FastFACTS] HOUSTON

**Area Codes**   Houston has 10-digit dialing for local calls. Local numbers begin with one of three area codes: 713, 281, or 832.

**Dentists**   For a referral, call ✆ 800/922-6588.

**Doctors**   For minor emergencies or to see a doctor without an appointment, call **Texas Urgent Care** at ✆ 281/477-7490.

**Drugstores**   **Walgreens,** 3317 Montrose Blvd., at Hawthorne Street (✆ 713/520-7777), is open 24 hours a day. In the vicinity of the Medical Center, there is a 24-hour **CVS Pharmacy** at 7900 S. Main St. (✆ 713/660-8934).

**Hospitals**   The **Ben Taub General Hospital,** 1502 Taub Loop, at the Texas Medical Center (✆ 713/873-2600),

has a fully equipped emergency room.

**Internet Access**   If you're not traveling with a computer and your hotel doesn't have a business center, Houston's main library and all its branches have computers for public use; go to **www.houstonlibrary.org** to find locations. Faster connections can be had for a price at **Copy.com,** 1201-F Westheimer Rd., in the Montrose area (✆ 713/528-1201); it has several computers and is open from 7am to midnight on weekdays, 11am to 7pm on Saturdays, and noon to 9pm Sundays. If you have a computer and would prefer not to use your hotel's computer connections, check out the usual Internet haunts—coffee bars and

restaurants and the public areas of certain hotels.

**Maps**   Salespeople, repairmen, and others who must travel about rely on something called a "Key Map," a binder of detailed maps that divides Houston into a grid system. This homegrown creation became so popular here that it has been copied by map companies in other cities. It may offer more information than most visitors want. You can buy standard street maps at any drugstore and at many convenience stores, and you'll find some helpful maps of downtown, the Museum District, and other parts of the city at the visitor center in city hall.

**Newspapers & Magazines**   The local daily is

the *Houston Chronicle.* The *Houston Press,* a free weekly that covers local politics and culture, can be found around town at restaurants, stores, and just about anywhere people congregate.

**Police**   Dial ℂ **911** in an emergency; for nonemergencies, dial ℂ **311.**

**Post Office**   The downtown branch, 401 Franklin St. (ℂ **713/226-3066**), is open Monday through Friday from 9am to 7pm and Saturday from 9am to noon.

**Safety**   Houston is a safe town for visitors. Exercise caution at night in the downtown areas that lie outside the theater district.

**Taxes**   The local hotel tax is 17%, while the local sales tax is 8.25%.

**Transit Information** Call the Texas Dept. of Transportation's hot line at ℂ **713/802-5074.**

**Weather**   Call ℂ **713/ 228-8703.**

# WHERE TO STAY

Downtown and the Uptown/Galleria area have most of the city's comfortable hotels. Both are generally good locations for getting to know the city. In choosing a hotel, don't forget to give some thought about where you'll be spending your time in Houston. See "The Neighborhoods in Brief" section, earlier in this chapter. East side hotels along the Gulf Freeway work well for those wanting to visit NASA, Kemah, and Galveston. The Montrose Area is great for those wanting to combine shopping with museum visits. And keep in mind Houston's light rail. It increases the utility of all the hotels located along its corridor, including the Medical Center and South Main.

*Tip:* So many hotels have been built downtown that there is an oversupply of rooms. Rates have fallen, and deals and packages are available. Houston is a business-driven city, so discounted weekend rates are quite common. The discounts work to shrink the price difference between a merely acceptable hotel room, and a great hotel room, so if you're coming on a weekend, consider upgrading to a luxury hotel; for just a few extra dollars, you can get a much better room and location.

The hotel listings that follow include the prevailing rates for double occupancy and do not include Houston's 17% hotel tax. Rates will go higher for the rodeo in February and during large conventions, and they can go lower in the summer. Always ask about promotional rates. Most hotels have only nonsmoking rooms, but when they do offer smoking rooms, it's noted in the review.

## Downtown
### VERY EXPENSIVE

**Four Seasons Hotel Houston** ★★★   This member of the luxury hotel chain does everything right. It stands out especially in the areas of service (reliable concierge, attentive staff, and a luxury spa) and spaciousness (everything about the hotel is large—guest rooms, suites, and common areas). Most impressive is the ease with which services are provided. Need a fridge, a fax machine, or a VCR delivered to your room? No problem. Need your suit dry-cleaned at 2 am for use later that day? No problem. A large, well-trained staff makes it all possible.

The hotel's location is convenient, by the city's convention center, baseball park, and basketball arena. Connected to the hotel is a small shopping center and the Houston Center Athletic Club, whose facilities are available to guests free of charge. (The hotel has a large, well-equipped health club of its own and offers guests access to a nearby racquet club, too.) The pool/patio area has been enlarged and now looks like that of a resort hotel in size and style, with views of the surrounding skyline. It has no equal in downtown or central Houston. The recently remodeled guest rooms display a contemporary look with clean lines and sharply contrasting wood tones. Beds are dressed with a top sheet over the comforter. Rooms bordering the pool are popular, and some corner rooms come as standards and have good views. Smoking rooms are available.

1300 Lamar St., Houston, TX 77010. © **800/819-5053** or 713/650-1300. Fax 713/652-6220. www. fourseasons.com/houston. 404 units. $295–$345 double; $395–$545 executive suite; $850 and up specialty suites. Weekend rates available. AE, DC, DISC, MC, V. Valet parking $30. Pets 15 lb. and under accepted. **Amenities:** Restaurant; 2 bars; babysitting; concierge; health club; large outdoor pool; room service; sauna; spa. In room: A/C, TV/DVD, hair dryer, minibar, Wi-Fi ($13 per day).

## EXPENSIVE

### Alden-Houston Hotel ★★★
This hotel, originally called the Sam Houston, is under new management, which is working hard to add service and comfort. The decor is modern—sleek, uncluttered interiors that aim for simplicity but avoid the "lab" look. The guest rooms exert a comforting, quieting influence—a respite from bustling downtown Houston. They also rack up lots of style points with unexpected touches, such as nicely chosen fixtures and luxuriously dressed beds. The standard rooms are good size and have ample, very attractive bathrooms. The two kinds of suites are larger. All the rooms have good electronics, with power strips and MP3 docking stations. The original Sam Houston Hotel was opened in the '20s and closed in the '70s. At that time, its location wasn't in the best part of downtown; now the location is great, just 2 blocks from the ballpark and Main Street. Some smoking rooms are available. The hotel's corner bar is a great place to wind down, either inside or outside.

1117 Prairie St., Houston, TX 77002. © **877/813-1888** or 832/200-8800. Fax 832/200-8811. www.alden hotels.com. 97 units. $199–$299 double; from $274 suite. Weekend rates and packages available. AE, DC, DISC, MC, V. Valet parking $28. Pets 20 lb. and under accepted with $150 deposit and $25 per day fee. **Amenities:** Restaurant; bar; exercise room; room service. In room: A/C, TV/DVD, CD player, hair dryer, minibar, MP3 docking station, Wi-Fi (free).

### Hotel Icon ★★★
Unlike many traditional hotels with conservative American Colonial furniture or neoclassical elements—what I call the "George Washington slept here" look—Hotel Icon goes more for the "Lola Montez slept here" look: lots of texture and ornament, a boudoir feel to the rooms, and a touch of refined decadence, all of which makes the Icon a fun place to stay. In renovating the Union National Bank Building (built in 1912), the designers sought to capture something of the feel of that golden age of excess. The most fun is to be had in the suites on the top floor, each named after a glorious old hotel. These rooms are extralarge and plush and touched by a bit of idiosyncrasy. The standard rooms also have plenty of atmosphere. The higher rate is for rooms with extralarge bathrooms with an opening in the wall, which allows a view of the bedroom and TV from the bathtub.

220 Main St., Houston, TX 77002. © **800/323-7500** or 713/224-4266. Fax 713/223-3223. www.hotel icon.com. 144 units. $150–$250 double; from $349 suite. AE, DC, DISC, MC, V. Valet parking $28. Pets 35 lbs. and under accepted with $250 deposit. **Amenities:** Restaurant; bar; concierge; health club and spa; room service. In room: A/C, TV, hair dryer, minibar, Wi-Fi (free).

### Lancaster Hotel ★★★
For those who enjoy the performing arts and nightlife, there is no better place to stay in Houston, given the hotel's close proximity to the downtown action. The Lancaster occupies a small 12-story building that dates from the 1920s and looks all the smaller for being near the Chase Tower (the tallest skyscraper in the western U.S.). Rooms are a little smaller than their counterparts at other downtown hotels, but furnished with the character of an old hotel. Bathrooms

are ample with lots of counter space. Service is excellent and includes many personal touches. Within 1 block of the Lancaster is the symphony, ballet, opera, and Alley Theatre; the concierge will reserve your tickets at these and other venues in the Theater District. Also a block away is Bayou Place, where you can catch a live blues or rock act, and within a few blocks are many restaurants and clubs.

701 Texas Ave., Houston, TX 77002. ℰ **800/231-0336** or 713/228-9500. Fax 713/223-4528. www.the lancaster.com. 93 units. $100–$200 double; $200–$350 suite. AE, DC, DISC, MC, V. Valet parking $30. Pets 50 lbs. and under accepted with $50 deposit and $50 fee per visit. **Amenities:** Restaurant; bar; concierge; exercise room; room service. *In room:* A/C, TV, CD player, hair dryer, minibar, Wi-Fi (free).

**The Magnolia Hotel ★★**   Opened in 2003 in what was the Houston Post-Dispatch Building (ca. 1926), the Magnolia goes for an anachronistic blend of new and old. The guest rooms mix gold scalloped trim and traditional patterned fabrics with the clean lines of modern furniture. The overall effect is interesting and comfortable, and the rooms are large. The bathrooms have quality amenities and fixtures. Suites are very large and have a full kitchen and dining area. The studio suites are especially attractive and come with a kitchenette. The mezzanine club provides a free continental breakfast in the morning, along with cocktails and snacks in the afternoon and evening (the hotel doesn't have a restaurant, but does have a kitchen for room service). This club is designed to be a comfortable place where guests can relax outside the four walls of their hotel room, socialize, perhaps play a little billiards in the game room, read the paper in the library, or surf the Web over a drink.

1100 Texas Ave., Houston, TX 77002. ℰ **888/915-1110** or 713/221-0011. Fax 713/221-0022. www.magnolia hotels.com. 314 units. $149–$199 double; $209–$269 studio suite; $349 1-bedroom suite. Rates include continental breakfast and evening cocktails. AE, DC, DISC, MC, V. Valet parking $28. **Amenities:** Bar; concierge; executive-level rooms; exercise room; Jacuzzi; heated rooftop pool; room service. *In room:* A/C, TV, hair dryer, minibar, Wi-Fi (free).

## MODERATE

**Best Western Downtown Inn and Suites**   Located in the shadow of downtown's skyline, this hotel has a convenient location and extralarge rooms with one king-size bed or two queen-size beds, as well as microwaves. On the downside, style takes a back seat to comfort and convenience, and there's no restaurant or room service. The greatest savings are enjoyed during the week; for weekends, check rates at the nicer downtown hotels, which give better discounts.

915 W. Dallas St., Houston, TX 77019. ℰ **800/528-1234** or 713/571-7733. Fax 713/571-6680. www.best western.com. 76 units. $159 double; $169 suite. Rates include continental breakfast. AE, DC, DISC, MC, V. Free parking. **Amenities:** Exercise room; Jacuzzi; outdoor pool. *In room:* A/C, TV, fridge, hair dryer, Wi-Fi (free).

# East End

## EXPENSIVE

**Hilton University of Houston**   This is unlike any other Hilton Hotel in that it is part of the Conrad Hilton College of Hotel and Restaurant Management and is staffed by not only professional full-timers, but also students performing their lab work. It deserves consideration because of its location on the university campus between downtown and Houston's southeast side attractions, and its service, which is usually quite good. Rooms throughout the hotel's eight floors have large, L-shaped layouts with modern furnishings that include a sleeper sofa. Eric's, the hotel's restaurant, is far better than most hotel restaurants and its menu has a Latin flair. The University Center next door has a health club, large pool, game room, and beauty salon, and guests have access to all of them. There's a parking garage with a low ceiling and it cannot accommodate vehicles such as large SUVs and pickup trucks. Smoking rooms are available.

4800 Calhoun Rd., Houston, TX 77004. © **800/HOTELUH** (468-3584) or 713/741-2447. Fax 713/743-2472. www.hilton.com. 86 units. $169–$239 double. AE, DC, DISC, MC, V. Parking $15. **Amenities:** Restaurant; bar; access to nearby health club and spa; room service. *In room:* A/C, TV, hair dryer, Wi-Fi (free).

## MODERATE

### Drury Inn & Suites Houston Hobby 🦡
This hotel, in the vicinity of the Hobby Airport, is virtually identical to the Drury Inn & Suites Near the Galleria (p. 158). The rooms and amenities are competitively priced and discounted a lot on weekends, and the property is well managed. Suites are large with a fridge and microwave. Complimentary snacks are served in the afternoon from Monday to Thursday. Guests also receive an hour of free long-distance calls within the U.S.

7902 Mosley Rd., Houston, TX 77061. © **800/378-7946** or ©/fax 713/941-4300. www.druryhotels.com. 134 units. $89–$170 double; $149–$210 suite. Rates include breakfast buffet. AE, DC, DISC, MC, V. Free parking. Pets accepted with restrictions. **Amenities:** Exercise room; Jacuzzi; heated indoor/outdoor pool. *In room:* A/C, TV, hair dryer, Wi-Fi (free).

## South Main

### EXPENSIVE

**Hilton Houston Plaza ★★**   In terms of amenities, service, and location, this is one of the best hotels around the Medical Center. Consequently, it enjoys a high occupancy rate, especially with people attending medical conferences. As the occupancy rate increases, so do the prices. Weekend rates can be a bargain here. Try to book early, and, if you have any flexibility, get rates for different dates. Most of the rooms are suites, which, for the money, are a better value than their standard king room.

The hotel's facilities set this hotel apart from neighboring hotels. The large rooms are comfortable and well furnished. The building is 19 stories tall. Ask for a room facing out over Rice University. The hotel's location on the rim of the Medical Center can actually be an advantage over its principal Medical Center rivals (a Marriott and a Crowne Plaza) because it makes getting to and from the hotel easier, avoiding the Medical Center traffic jams and the tight parking garages.

6833 Travis St., Houston, TX 77030. © **800/HILTONS** (445-8667) or 713/313-4000. Fax 713/313-4660. www.houstonplaza.hilton.com. 181 units. $129–$220 double; $149–$260 suite. AE, DC, DISC, MC, V. Valet parking $22; self-parking $15. **Amenities:** Restaurant; bar; health club; Jacuzzi; large outdoor heated pool; room service; sauna. *In room:* A/C, fridge, hair dryer, minibar, Wi-Fi ($12 per day).

**Hotel ZaZa ★★★**   This place may be the perfect marriage of old property and new owners. The former Warwick Hotel enjoys a great location in the center of the Museum District, which is close by Hermann Park and Rice University—the greenest part of the city. Rooms are done up with flair, and the more expensive the room, the more flair. The hotel is 12 stories tall. At the top of both the building and the room rate chart are the expensive "concept suites," which are definitely for the party set and put you right into vacation mode. Style elements across the range of rooms include lots of texture, such as silk and leather. There's also better lighting than at other hotels, adding a touch more drama. About 100 rooms have balconies, and most are balcony king or double rooms that are a little smaller than the suites, but with good views from almost any direction. There is an attractive pool and terrace on the second floor, overlooking Mecom Fountain. Bordering the terrace are guest rooms that are popular with sun worshipers.

5701 Main St., Houston, TX 77005. © **888/880-3244** or 713/526-1991. Fax 713/526-0359. www.hotel
zazahouston.com. 315 units. $199–$224 double; from $229 suites. AE, DISC, MC, V. Valet parking $24.
Pets accepted with $50 fee. **Amenities:** Restaurant; bar; concierge; exercise room; heated outdoor
pool; room service; spa. *In room:* A/C, TV, fridge, hair dryer, minibar, MP3 docking station, Wi-Fi (free).

## MODERATE

### Holiday Inn Hotel & Suites Houston Medical Center
This hotel has a good
location across from the Medical Center, at the intersection with Holcombe Boulevard. It often offers big discounts on weekend rates. Rooms are a good size and are
comfortable. They've recently been freshened up with better bed linens. Some suites
have full kitchens. Unfortunately, there's a shortage of staff at the front desk and at
guest services, so getting your needs met is an exercise in patience. The same is true
for the hotel restaurant.

6800 S. Main St., Houston, TX 77035. © **800/HOLIDAY** (465-4329) or 713/528-7744. Fax 713/528-
6983. www.holiday-inn.com. 285 units. $90–$145 double; $165–$190 suite; from $300 apt. Special rates
available for hospital outpatients. AE, DC, DISC, MC, V. Free parking. **Amenities:** Restaurant; bar; exercise room; small pool; room service. *In room:* A/C, TV, hair dryer, Wi-Fi ($10 per day).

## INEXPENSIVE

### La Quinta Inn Houston Reliant Medical Center 🔥
This two-story motel is
just down the road from the Astrodome and Reliant Stadium. The guest rooms are
comfortable and attractive, albeit unmistakably motel-like. More important is the fact
that they shield out the noise from the freeway; this place is remarkably quiet. Guests
enjoy extras such as free local calls, as well as large TVs and spacious, well-lit bathrooms. The location, next to Loop 610 South, is good for getting around to the most
popular parts of the city. It's a straight shot to the Galleria/Uptown area on the freeway, and to the Rice Village, via Buffalo Speedway.

9911 Buffalo Speedway (at Loop 610), Houston, TX 77054. © **800/531-5900** or 713/668-8082. Fax
713/668-0821. www.lq.com. 114 units. $89–$109 double. Rates include continental breakfast. Children 17
and under stay free in parent's room. AE, DISC, MC, V. Free parking. **Amenities:** Outdoor pool. *In room:*
A/C, TV, Wi-Fi (free).

### Parkview Inn and Suites
This is a basic motel with two stories of rooms lining
a large parking lot. The quietest rooms are the ones at the back of the property; the
front ones can be noisy. All rooms have simple painted-wood furniture and two full-
size beds or a king-size bed; suites come with a small fridge and microwave. Suites
are twice the size of the standard rooms and come with kitchenettes, a dining table
and chairs, and a sleeper sofa. Bathrooms are small. For this part of Houston, it
doesn't get much more economical than this place.

9000 S. Main St., Houston, TX 77025. © **713/666-4151.** Fax 713/666-3393. 98 units. $49–$79 double;
$100 suite. AE, DISC, MC, V. Free parking. **Amenities:** Outdoor pool. *In room:* A/C, TV.

# Montrose/The Heights

## EXPENSIVE

### La Colombe d'Or ★
If you enjoy the small scale of a B&B and rooms that don't
look like hotel rooms, but want more space, privacy, and in-room dining, this is the
hotel for you. The five suites are extremely large, with hardwood floors, area rugs,
antiques, king-size beds, and sizable bathrooms. Some suites come with separate
dining rooms, and the in-room service, from either the bar or the restaurant, is one of
the things for which this hotel is known. The hotel occupies a mansion that was built
in the 1920s for oilman Walter Fondren. The interior has some beautiful architectural

features, and its location puts you close to museums, restaurants, and the downtown area. The top floor of the original house is now an art gallery.

3410 Montrose Blvd., Houston, TX 77006. ℂ **713/524-7999.** Fax 713/524-8923. www.lacolombedor. com. 5 units. $199–$275 suite. AE, DC, DISC, MC, V. Free valet parking. Pets accepted with $150 deposit. **Amenities:** Restaurant; bar; room service. *In room:* A/C, TV, hair dryer, Wi-Fi (free).

## MODERATE

**Lovett Inn ★ 🍴** Located a block off Westheimer and 3 blocks from Montrose Boulevard, this B&B is on a quiet street right in the middle of the busy restaurant and club district of the Montrose area. The house dates from the early 1900s and was built by one of Houston's mayors. Most rooms are large (well above the usual size for B&Bs). The four rooms in the main house and two in the carriage house are attractive and well furnished with period pieces, wood floors, and area rugs, yet eschew the cutesy quality of many B&Bs. Almost all have private balconies and MP3 docking stations. There are also four town-house units around the corner (two units per house), which have separate entrances and greater privacy. These are comfortable yet modern. Guests can also rent both units of a town house, which includes use of a full kitchen and living area.

501 Lovett Blvd., Houston, TX 77006. ℂ **800/779-5224** or 713/522-5224. Fax 713/528-6708. www. lovettinn.com. 12 units. $115–$160 double; $99–$130 town-house unit; $220 town-house double unit. Rates include continental breakfast. AE, DC, DISC, MC, V. Free parking. **Amenities:** Outdoor pool; Wi-Fi (free, in lobby). *In room:* A/C, TV, fridge (in some), hair dryer.

**Modern B&B ★** There is no law that says a bed-and-breakfast must be in a period house. This one actually occupies two modern town houses in the heart of the Montrose district, and it exists because the original project fell through when Enron tanked. It's great for those who like modern architecture (exposed beams, airy spaces). It's also good for those who like baked goods, espresso coffee, and an honor bar. Rooms vary but are grouped in three categories: "Mod" rooms, which are on the ground floor (with the bathroom up a flight of stairs), "Standard" (one of which comes with a Jacuzzi), and "Top Shelf," which are much larger than the others and have the use of a large porch. The owner, Lisa Collins, lives on the premises, is a gracious host, and keeps lots of information on things to do in town. All of these factors make this B&B a great alternative to a hotel. Ms. Collins also rents out a few apartments as guesthouses. These vary in price, but a couple are a real bargain for a big family.

4003 Hazard, Houston, TX 77098. ℂ **800/462-4014** or 832/279-6367. www.modernbb.com. 8 units. $100–$200 double; $150–$300 guesthouse. Rates include full breakfast. 3-night minimum for holidays. AE, DC, DISC, MC, V. Children accepted with guesthouse rentals. Pets accepted with $30 per day fee. **Amenities:** Exercise room. *In room:* A/C, TV (DVD upon request), hair dryer, MP3 docking station, Wi-Fi (free).

**Sara's Bed and Breakfast Inn ★** For the traditional B&B experience—period decor, themed rooms, beautifully furnished common rooms—this is the place to stay. Sara's occupies a large Texas Victorian house in the Heights. From here, it's easy to get to all of central Houston. The house is immaculately kept and brightly decorated. Guest rooms come with a queen-size or king-size bed and plenty of modern amenities, including flatscreen TVs. The rooms are furnished with character, but aren't fussy. Some are inspired by other Texas cities, including Fort Worth, San Antonio, and Galveston. The carriage house suite is extralarge and has king-size and double beds.

941 Heights Blvd., Houston, TX 77008. ℂ **800/593-1130** or 713/868-1130. Fax 713/868-3284. www. saras.com. 11 units. $115–$155 double; $125–$175 suite. Rates include full breakfast. AE, DC, DISC, MC, V. Free parking. Children 11 and under not permitted. *In room:* A/C, TV/VCR, hair dryer, Wi-Fi (free).

# Kirby District

## VERY EXPENSIVE

**Renaissance Houston Hotel** ★★ The only hotel in the Greenway Plaza (though there are several nearby), this 20-story hotel enjoys access to Greenway's office buildings through its concourse level of shops, including a food court, post office, and movie theater. It's also connected to the Houston City Club by another walkway, and hotel guests can enjoy the use of its facilities, including indoor tennis and racquetball courts, and a jogging track. The hotel's location off the Southwest Freeway means quick access to either downtown or Uptown. All standard rooms are spacious and decorated in an eclectic style that makes them a bit more interesting than your standard hotel room. They are slated for a thorough refurbishing in 2011 (all the common areas were remodeled in 2010).

6 Greenway Plaza E., Houston, TX 77046. ✆ **800/HOTELS-1** (468-3571) or 713/629-1200. www. renaissancehotels.com. 388 units. $249–$299 double; $350–$1,200 suite. Weekend rates available. AE, DC, DISC, MC, V. Valet parking $18; self-parking $14. Pets 25 lbs. and under accepted free. **Amenities:** 2 restaurants; bar; babysitting; concierge; executive-level rooms; health club; outdoor heated pool; room service; sauna. In room: A/C, TV, fridge, hair dryer, Internet ($13 per day).

## MODERATE

**Four Points** This is a businessperson's hotel that's comfortable and well situated. It has easy access to the freeway, and you can get in and out quickly without having to negotiate a parking garage. The location is convenient—between downtown, the Rice University/Village area, and the Galleria. After being remodeled in 2010, rooms now have plenty of light. The furnishings are modern and functional without looking cheap; some rooms have sleeper sofas. Improvements include plush mattresses—for one king-size bed or two full-size beds—and nicely finished, medium-size bathrooms.

2828 Southwest Fwy., Houston, TX 77098. ✆ **800/368-7764** or 713/942-2111. Fax 713/526-8709. www. fourpoints.com. 216 units. $129–$189 double. Weekend rates available. AE, DC, DISC, MC, V. Free parking. **Amenities:** Restaurant; bar; exercise room; outdoor pool (open in season); room service. In room: A/C, TV, hair dryer, Internet (free).

# Uptown

## VERY EXPENSIVE

**Hotel Derek** ★★★ The creators of this hotel have gone to great lengths to separate it from the pack. They've even given it a persona—its namesake, Derek, a fictitious aging rock star/hotel owner. Given the premise, it would have been easy to lapse into cliché, but not so. Yes, there are some nods to the 1960s, but these are cleverly mixed with unexpected touches and the playful use of materials new and old to express a lighthearted vision of the counterculture. With the guest rooms, the designers have succeeded in creating a space that is functional for the business traveler while having the feel of a "pad" with all the accompanying informality. The decor is modern: The desk, side tables, and bathroom counter are thick glass with metal supports; the mattresses are mostly king size. The sitting area is a wonderful mohair-and-velvet built-in stretching the width of the room. Thoughtful details include the use of baskets instead of drawers, and safes that are big enough to accommodate a briefcase. Spa treatments are also available.

2525 W. Loop South, Houston, TX 77027. ✆ **866/292-4100** or 713/961-3000. Fax 713/297-4393. www. hotelderek.com. 314 units. $290–$350 double; $350–$400 studio; from $550 suite. Weekend and promotional rates available. AE, DC, DISC, MC, V. Valet parking $23. Pets 50 lb. and under accepted with $50 fee. **Amenities:** Restaurant; bar; concierge; exercise room; outdoor pool; room service. In room: A/C, TV, CD player, hair dryer, Internet ($12 per day), minibar.

**JW Marriott Hotel by the Galleria** ★★ On Westheimer, facing the Galleria, this high-rise hotel has lots of amenities and a central location. Standard rooms are a little smaller than at the Westin hotels, while the executive rooms are larger. Both are better designed and furnished than their counterparts. The service and amenities are better, too. Bathrooms are well lit, with makeup mirrors and terry-cloth robes provided. The room decor is a good-looking mix of modern and traditional. Much emphasis is placed on the beds, which are plush and comfortable; you have a choice of two double beds or one king-size bed with a pullout sofa. Avoid guest rooms on the fifth floor, where the health club is located—a smell of chlorine sometimes infiltrates the air-conditioning. However, the health club is first rate and well staffed. A racquetball court is open to guests.

5150 Westheimer Rd., Houston, TX 77056. ℂ **800/228-9290** or 713/961-1500. Fax 713/961-5045. www.jwmarriotthouston.com. 514 units. $279–$339 double; from $745 suite. AE, DC, DISC, MC, V. Valet parking $27; self-parking $17; limited free parking. **Amenities:** Three restaurants; bar; concierge; concierge-level rooms; health club; Jacuzzi; heated indoor/outdoor pool; room service. *In room:* A/C, TV, fridge, hair dryer, MP3 docking station, Wi-Fi ($13 per day).

**Omni Houston Hotel** ★★ ☺ This hotel is an island of tranquillity in Uptown's sea of commotion. Flanking it on one side is a broad expanse of lawn with a decorative pool fed by cascading water and adorned with a couple of black swans; on the other side is the heavily wooded Memorial Park. Though it feels as if you're miles from the busy Uptown malls, you're not. The modern exterior of this 11-story building—angular lines, bold colors, stark surfaces—is set to advantage by the verdant surroundings. The guest rooms have a view of Memorial Park with downtown in the background or a view of the pools, lawn, and black swans. The rooms are large and decorated in a mix of modern and traditional. The Omni Kids Program, with special games and goodies for children, makes this a great choice for families.

4 Riverway, Houston, TX 77056. ℂ **888/444-6664** or 713/871-8181. Fax 713/871-8116. www.omnihouston.com. 378 units. $269–$299 double; from $440 suite. Promotional rates available. AE, DC, DISC, MC, V. Valet parking $28; free self-parking. Pets 25 lb. and under accepted with $50 fee. **Amenities:** Restaurant; 2 bars; babysitting; children's programs; concierge; health club and spa; Jacuzzi; 2 large outdoor pools (1 heated); room service; sauna. *In room:* A/C, TV, CD player, hair dryer, minibar, Wi-Fi (free).

**Sheraton Suites Houston Near the Galleria** The rooms at this all-suite hotel are attractive, with more character than most hotel rooms in the Galleria area. The headboards and accents are postmodern, and the granite countertops are snazzy. These suites aren't as big as those at the Doubletree Guest Suites (see below), but they are more attractive. An easy-to-use retractable door makes the living room and bedroom usable as one large space or as two separate rooms, with the large bathroom accessible from either room. Bed options include two doubles or a king. Some rooms have sleeper sofas. On weekends, the hotel gets mainly families. The best rooms face westward away from Loop 610. There are 18 business suites with features such as fax machines and copiers. This hotel is 2 blocks from the Galleria.

2400 W. Loop South, Houston, TX 77027. ℂ **800/325-3535** or 713/586-2444. Fax 713/586-2445. www.sheratonsuiteshouston.com. 281 suites. $309–$329 suite. AE, DC, DISC, MC, V. Valet parking $18; self-parking $12. Pets 80 lb. and under accepted free. **Amenities:** Restaurant; bar; babysitting; concierge; state-of-the-art exercise room; Jacuzzi; small heated outdoor pool; room service. *In room:* A/C, TV, fridge, hair dryer, Wi-Fi (free).

**Westin Galleria and Westin Oaks** ✋ Similar in size, name, and appearance, these two hotels are often confused by travelers who arrive believing their destination has been reached, only to find they must renegotiate the mall parking lot. The Westin

**Doubletree Guest Suites** (p. 157)
The two-bedroom suites here are a good value, and the full kitchens and dining areas allow flexibility with such things as breakfast, snacks, and takeout meals.

**Omni Houston Hotel** (p. 156)  With its Omni Kids Program, this hotel makes a

special effort to keep younger children amused. Kids receive a packet of goodies at check-in, and parents can even request a small, pretend suitcase that holds more games. As part of the program, the concierge can organize activities and trips for children to such places as the zoo.

Oaks is on the east side of the Galleria mall (the side closest to Loop 610) and faces Westheimer Road. It's a family hotel, with no alcohol in the minibars. The Westin Galleria is attached to the west side of the Galleria and faces West Alabama Street. It targets business travelers, with a business center and dining that's more formal than at the Westin Oaks.

In other aspects, the hotels are much alike, a mix of good and bad. On the good side, their location allows you to walk from your hotel room into the shopping mall without ever having to leave the great indoors. The rooms are extralarge, the beds are comfortable, and the balconies—an uncommon feature in urban hotels—allow you to enjoy the view of perpetual motion below and the serene skyline above (get a north-facing room at the Westin Oaks, a south-facing room at the Westin Galleria). On the bad side, the rooms are awkwardly designed and plainly furnished. Another problem is the service: There wasn't enough staff present during my visits, and the concierge, once located, didn't inspire confidence. This might be acceptable for a hotel in a lower price range, however, and fortunately, the discounting of rates is quite common at both hotels.

**Galleria:** 5060 W. Alabama St., Houston, TX 77056. ✆ **800/WESTIN-1** (937-8461) or 713/960-8100. Fax 713/960-6553. www.westingalleriahoustonhotel.com. 487 units. **Oaks:** 5011 Westheimer Rd., Houston, TX 77056. ✆ **800/WESTIN-1** (937-8461) or 713/960-8100. Fax: 713/960-6554 (Westin Oaks). www.westinoakshouston.com. 406 units. Both hotels: $299 double; $545 suite. AE, DC, DISC, MC, V. Valet parking $27; free self-parking. **Amenities:** Restaurant; bar; concierge; access to nearby health club ($12 per day); heated outdoor pool; room service. *In room:* A/C, TV, hair dryer, minibar, Wi-Fi ($12 per day).

## EXPENSIVE

**Doubletree Guest Suites** ★ ☺   This 26-story hotel, located a block west of the Galleria shopping complex, has extralarge suites, each with a fully equipped kitchen (including microwave and dishwasher) and a dining area for four people. (A grocery store is 4 blocks away, and Kenny & Ziggy's, a deli with takeout, is even closer.) The bedroom includes two full-size beds or a king bed; the sitting room has a sofa or two, armchairs, and a large TV. The furniture and decor are plain but comfortable and ideal for families with small children. Bathrooms are large with plenty of counter space. There's also a coin-op laundry facility. The hotel is well priced, gets a lot of repeat business, and is a favorite for extended stays. The service is good. Smoking rooms are available.

5353 Westheimer Rd., Houston, TX 77056. ✆ **800/222-TREE** (8733) or 713/961-9000. Fax 713/877-8835. http://doubletree1.hilton.com. 335 suites. $169 1-bedroom suite; $289 2-bedroom suite. AE, DC, DISC, MC, V. Valet parking $22; self-parking $12. Pets 45 lbs. and under accepted with $50 fee. **Amenities:** Restaurant; bar; concierge; exercise room; Jacuzzi; outdoor pool; room service. *In room:* A/C, TV, hair dryer; Wi-Fi ($10 per day).

**InterContinental Houston** ★ This hotel offers upscale lodgings in a prime location only a block from the Galleria. The rooms are comfortable, with insulated windows that keep them remarkably quiet. Outfitted with high-tech amenities, the rooms are furnished with expensive materials, including marble, granite, and leather. Highlights include oversize safes with outlets for recharging cellphones or computers, comfortable pillow-top beds, and desks with lots of workspace and multiple connection options.

2222 W. Loop South, Houston, TX 77027. ✆ **800/327-0200** or 713/627-7600. Fax 713/961-3327. www. houston.intercontinental.com. 485 units. $179–$289 double; from $575 suite. Promotional rates and packages available. AE, DC, DISC, MC, V. Valet parking $27; self parking $16. **Amenities:** Restaurant; bar; concierge; health club; Jacuzzi; heated outdoor pool; room service. *In room:* A/C, TV, CD player, fridge, hair dryer, minibar, Wi-Fi ($11 per day).

## MODERATE

**Drury Inn & Suites Near the Galleria** 🥄 This inn is one of the best lodging values in this area. Rooms are midsize and comfortable, with extralong double beds for tall guests. Instead of the usual easy chair and ottoman, there's a recliner; the TV is larger than usual. King rooms are slightly larger than standard rooms and have a microwave and fridge. While the bathrooms are good size, but with limited counter space. The hotel doesn't have a restaurant, but it provides free evening snacks from Monday through Thursday and a breakfast buffet every morning. The pool area, with indoor and outdoor sections, is great for this price range. Guests also receive an hour of free long-distance calls within the U.S.

Post Oak Park at W. Loop South, Houston, TX 77027. ✆ **800/378-7946** or ✆/fax 713/963-0700. www. druryhotels.com. 134 units. $99–$159 double or king room; $124–$179 suite. Rates include breakfast buffet. AE, DC, DISC, MC, V. Free parking. Pets accepted with restrictions. **Amenities:** Exercise room; Jacuzzi; indoor/outdoor heated pool. *In room:* A/C, TV, fridge, hair dryer, Wi-Fi (free).

**La Quinta Inn & Suites Galleria** You can tell at first glance that this inn is a new breed of La Quinta, with a gurgling fountain in the lobby, a fitness room, and a fairly large, outdoor heated pool with a separate hot tub. Proximity to the shopping along Post Oak and in the Galleria seals the deal. Standard rooms are medium to large and come with two double beds; the "King Plus" room comes with a king-size bed and a recliner.

1625 W. Loop South, Houston, TX 77027. ✆ **800/687-6667** or 713/355-3440. Fax 713/355-2990. www. lq.com. 173 units. $115–$155 double; $135–$185 king plus; $199 suite. Rates include breakfast. AE, DC, DISC, MC, V. Free parking. **Amenities:** Jacuzzi; heated outdoor pool. *In room:* A/C, TV, hair dryer, Wi-Fi (free).

# Near Bush Intercontinental Airport

## EXPENSIVE

**Houston Airport Marriott** ★ This hotel is right in the middle of the airport itself between terminals B and C, and it's on the airport tram line, which means no messing with taxis, shuttle buses, or rental cars. With this enviable location, the hotel hosts many guests attending business conferences. The revolving rooftop restaurant adds to the hotel's popularity—you'll see planes landing and taking off with a view that is pretty much the same as that of the airport's control tower. Guest rooms at the hotel are large and attractively furnished. The bathrooms are not especially large, but the beds are comfortable, and everything else about the rooms is great. The restaurant is a lovely place for dinner, which is served from 5:30 to 10pm (open for lunch to groups only).

18700 JFK Blvd., Houston, TX 77032. ✆ **800/228-9290** or 281/443-2310. Fax 281/443-5294. www. marriott.com. 566 units. $249–$289 double; $425 suite. Weekend rates available. AE, DC, DISC, MC, V.

Free self-parking. **Amenities:** 2 restaurants; 2 bars; executive-level rooms; exercise room; Jacuzzi; heated outdoor pool; room service. *In room:* A/C, TV, hair dryer, Wi-Fi ($10 per day).

## MODERATE

### Clarion Inn Bush Intercontinental Airport ⬥

As far as airport hotels go, this one has the most extras for the buck. Rooms are large, comfortable, and well equipped, with two phone lines (including a cordless phone), free local calls, microwaves, and in-room safes. Most have two full beds. Services include a free airport shuttle and breakfast (but no restaurant).

15615 JFK Blvd., Houston, TX 77032. © **877/424-6423** or 281/987-8777. Fax 281/987-9317. www.clarion hotel.com/hotel-houston-texas-TXB26. 101 units. $120–$140 double. Weekend rates available. Rates include breakfast. Children 17 and under stay free in parent's room. AE, DC, DISC, MC, V. Free parking. **Amenities:** Free airport transfers, exercise room; Jacuzzi; outdoor pool. *In room:* A/C, TV, fridge, hair dryer, Wi-Fi (free).

# WHERE TO DINE

The Houston restaurant scene, like the city itself, is cosmopolitan. The primary influences come from Louisiana, Mexico, and Southeast Asia, but you can find restaurants serving just about any other cuisine. Houston's native cooking consists of steaks, chili, barbecue, soul food, and Tex-Mex. For locals, the proper accompaniment for any of these would be beer or iced tea. The extralarge glass of iced tea is a cultural fixture in this town, just as in the rest of the state. It's the perfect palate cleanser after a bite of something dense and spicy, such as enchiladas in chili gravy.

## Downtown/Midtown

### VERY EXPENSIVE

**Brennan's ★★** SOUTHERN/CREOLE   Fine dining à la New Orleans: Brennan's opened in 1967 as a sister restaurant to the famous New Orleans original, and it's a perennial favorite on most local "Top Restaurant" lists. It's now independent and serves some great dishes that the original doesn't. The various dining rooms are strikingly elegant and some of the most lovely in all of Houston. The service is superb, and the menu will be new territory to most diners, except those coming from Louisiana. The selection of dishes varies daily, but usually has a few classic Creole specialties such as rouxless seafood gumbo and turtle soup. Brennan's is also known for its chef's table, located in the kitchen with some clear partitions to keep away most of the kitchen clatter. The chef's table must be reserved far in advance and can accommodate between 4 and 10 people at $80 per person. For that price, guests are treated to several of the chef's special creations right as they come off the stove.

3300 Smith St. (at Stuart St.). © **713/522-9711.** www.brennanshouston.com. Reservations recommended. Main courses $27–$35. AE, DC, DISC, MC, V. Mon–Sat 11am–2pm; Sun 10am–2pm; daily 5:45–10pm. Take Smith St. (one-way headed south from downtown); when it crosses Elgin St./Westheimer Rd., look for the restaurant on your right. Be careful not to pass it, or you'll enter the Southwest Fwy.

**Vic & Anthony's ★** STEAK   This is a steakhouse of the posh sort, with lots of wood, stone, and leather. These kinds of places are supposed to look substantial, and Vic & Anthony's doesn't disappoint. The rooms have an establishment feel, with a touch of drama. Once seated, you'll be tempted by the long list of appetizers. But remember that you've come here mainly to eat steak, so ignore other menu distractions (and perhaps the protestations of your dining companion) and go right for the 40-ounce USDA Prime porterhouse steak for two (your fellow diner will thank you later). This and the individual steaks are what this place is all about. To loosely translate Sancho Panza: "Hunger is the best condiment." And steak is always enjoyed best when you're ravenous. It's one of those deep Paleolithic pleasures.

1510 Texas Ave. © **713/228-1111.** www.vicandanthonys.com. Reservations recommended. Main courses $27–$48. AE, DISC, MC, V. Sun–Thurs 5–10pm; Fri 11am–11pm; Sat 5–11pm.

## EXPENSIVE

**Reef** ★★★ SEAFOOD   I first met Bryan Caswell, the chef/owner of Reef, when he was the chef de cuisine for Bank, Jean Georges's local restaurant, until it closed. He's a friendly, no-nonsense sort of guy, and his present restaurant reflects these personal traits. Almost all the seafood, except for something such as a salmon dish, is locally fished from the Gulf of Mexico. Freshness is absolute, and the careful cooking brings it out without complicating things or making too much of a production. Examples of this would be the popular "crispy-skin snapper," delicately sautéed with the skin intact until the flesh is just right and the skin is crispy. It's served with tomato brown butter, which compliments it nicely. The redfish on the half shell is another example, grilled in a way that retains the juices. The menu includes beef and chicken dishes, but the standout is the pecan-smoked pork chop. The restaurant occupies a former auto dealership, with the dining room in the old showroom with big plate glass windows. At night, it's a very attractive dining spot. Lunch is a good deal.

2600 Travis St. (at McGowan). © **713/526-8282.** www.reefhouston.com. Reservations recommended. Main courses $19–$29. AE, MC, V. Mon–Thurs 11am–10pm; Fri 11am–11pm; Sat 5–11pm.

## MODERATE

**Mai's** ★ VIETNAMESE   Occupying a two-story brick building with green awnings on Milam Street in the midtown area, Mai's is the last of a half-dozen Vietnamese restaurants you'll pass in the preceding 6 blocks. In several ways, it's the best choice, but it doesn't necessarily have a lock on good Vietnamese food. I do appreciate, however, its dependability and the long hours it keeps, because you never know when you'll have a yen for a bowl of Vietnamese noodles (and they're all good). This would be a good place to try *pho*, the national dish, a soup to which you add vegetables and aromatic herbs and lime juice. Sample the ever-popular spring and summer rolls served with *nam pla* and/or peanut sauce, and try a chicken stir-fry with chile and lemon grass. Favorites include the *nam noung* (ground pork and shrimp with thin vermicelli) and the Mekong sweet-and-sour soup (try the catfish version).

3403 Milam St. © **713/520-7684.** Reservations recommended on weekends. Main courses $7–$16. AE, DC, DISC, MC, V. Mon–Thurs 10am–3am; Fri–Sat 10am–4am.

## INEXPENSIVE

**The Breakfast Klub** 🍴 BREAKFAST/BRUNCH   In midtown, this is the hip place for a late breakfast or casual lunch. On the menu are such down-home items as biscuits and gravy; pork chops and eggs; and catfish and grits. Standard breakfasts are available, too. You place the order at the counter and then take a seat. On Saturday mornings, the line goes out the door. The choice of coffees is good. The surroundings are simple, with the works of local artists on the walls and a mix of soft jazz and gospel on the stereo. For lunch, the Klub serves sandwiches and salads and an occasional special, such as crawfish fettuccine.

3711 Travis St. © **713/528-8561.** www.thebreakfastklub.com Breakfast $6–$9; sandwiches $5–$8. AE, DISC, MC, V. Mon–Fri 7am–2pm; Sat 8am–2pm.

# fast food À LA HOUSTON

When you need to find a meal that can be had quickly and cheaply, you don't have to suffer at the hands of the national fast-food chains, where the fare tastes the same whether you're in Houston or Honolulu. A number of local chains do a good job of cooking up fast food with character. Here are four worth considering:

In 1962, the Antone family, originally from Lebanon, opened an exotic import grocery store on Taft Street near Allen Parkway called **Antone's.** There, they introduced Houston to their now-famous po' boy (sub) sandwiches, which caught on in a big way. For lunch, you can't go wrong with one of these, which come already prepared. Get the original green label or the super red label, both of which are a combination of ham, salami, cheese, pickles, and special chow chow on fresh baked bread. Antone's locations include 2424 Dunstan Rd. (in the Village), 8110 Kirby Dr. (near Reliant Stadium), and 3823 Bellaire Blvd. (at Stella Link Blvd., just west of the Medical Center). You can also find these po' boys for sale at some of the small grocery stores in town.

**Beck's Prime** is a local chain of upscale burger joints that are known for big juicy burgers and great shakes. Locations include 2902 Kirby Dr. (near Westheimer Rd.), 1001 E. Memorial Loop (in Memorial Park by the golf course), and 910 Travis St. (in the downtown tunnel system below Bank One Center).

**Café Express** operates under the guiding principle that fast food can be nutritious, fresh, and cooked with at least some artistry. The owner of the chain is the chef at RDG + Bar Annie. Specialties at Café Express include a variety of salads, lively pasta dishes, juicy roast chicken, and various sandwiches. There are several items for children, including small burgers, which are sure to please. One location is in the basement of the Fine Arts Museum (the new building); other locations include 3200 Kirby Dr. (near the Village), 1422 W. Gray St. (in the River Oaks Shopping Center), 650 Main St. (downtown), and 1101 Uptown Park (just off Post Oak Blvd. in the Galleria area).

**James Coney Island Hot Dogs** started up in Houston in the 1930s. It's famous for its Texas-style chili dogs. (Most Houstonians consider hot dogs without chili as either unfulfilled potential or foreign novelty.) You can also order the chili with or without beans or as a chili pie. For hot dogs, I recommend the Texas chili dog. There are 20 locations around Houston, in the Kirby District (3607 Shepherd Dr. at the corner of Richmond Ave.), in the Galleria area (1600 S. Post Oak Blvd.), and out along the Gulf Freeway (6955 Gulf Fwy. and 10600 Gulf Fwy.).

**Treebeards** ★ 🍴 CREOLE   This place gets my vote for best food for your money. Others see it the same way, and this is why Treebeards restaurant on Old Market Square gets such a crowd of office workers for lunch. Beat the crowd by going late or early, and you won't have to wait in line. The chicken-and-shrimp gumbo, the étouffée, and the jambalaya are all good, but I somehow always return for the red beans and rice. Food is served cafeteria-style. Look for three more downtown locations: 1117 Texas Ave. (next to Christ Church Cathedral), 1100 Louisiana St. (in the tunnel), and 700 Rusk St., at the corner of Louisiana Street.

315 Travis St. (btw. Preston and Congress sts.). © **713/228-2622.** www.treebeards.com. Reservations not accepted. Main courses $7–$10. AE, DC, MC, V. Mon–Fri 11am–2pm; Fri 5–9pm.

# East End

## MODERATE

**Kim Son** VIETNAMESE/CHINESE   The menu is the most imposing part of this casual, highly regarded Vietnamese restaurant. Don't worry, though, because there are no poor choices among the 100 or so options. Enjoy finely prepared delicacies as well as the expected fare, such as terrific spring rolls and lovely noodle dishes. (The pan-seared shrimp with jalapeños and onions proves a delightful combination.) The menu includes several vegetarian dishes. Look for the exotic fish pool at the entrance.

2001 Jefferson St. ℂ **713/222-2461.** www.kimson.com Reservations accepted only for parties of 8 or more. Main courses $8–$22. AE, DC, DISC, MC, V. Daily 11am–midnight. Located in the small Chinese commercial center 1 block east of the Brown Convention Center and the elevated Tex. 59 Fwy.

## INEXPENSIVE

**Fiesta Loma Linda** ★★ TEX-MEX   I like my Tex-Mex restaurants to be homey, unpretentious places where you're not likely to run into the see-and-be-seen crowd. Of course, that was true of all Tex-Mex restaurants before the rise of the fajita, which eventually pulled Tex-Mex into the orbit of the truly trendy. Loma Linda brings to mind those simpler times with its un-self-conscious decorations and furniture and its utter lack of anything approaching trendiness. It also has an old-time 1930s tortilla maker specially designed to make the old-fashioned puffy tortillas that you always used to get when ordering chili con queso. The things to order here are, of course, the puffy chili con queso for an appetizer and the puffy beef tacos, the Texas-style enchiladas with chili gravy, and the combination dinners.

2111 Telephone Rd. ℂ **713/924-6074.** www.fiestalomalinda.com. Reservations not accepted. Main courses $6–$10; lunch specials $7–$8. AE, DC, DISC, MC, V. Sun–Thurs 10am–10pm; Fri–Sat 10am–11pm. Located 6 blocks off the Gulf Fwy. (I-45). Exit Telephone Rd. and turn north; it will be on your right.

# Montrose/The Heights

## VERY EXPENSIVE

**Mark's** ★★★ NEW AMERICAN   Mark Cox has a good idea of the direction in which American cooking should be headed—fresh ingredients prepared in a manner that's new and creative while being hearty and satisfying. Mark's has a set menu that changes seasonally and a menu of daily specials. A representative sampling of dishes might include grilled shrimp on a bed of fennel, basil, and tomato with a crab risotto; bourbon-glazed pork with yams and an apple compote; roasted breast of chicken with Mississippi-style grits scented with white truffles; or lamb in a basil sauce with white-cheddar potatoes. The restaurant occupies an abandoned church on Westheimer; the main dining room is in the nave and the choir loft. Alongside the nave, the owners have built an eye-catching, smaller dining room with Gothic rib vaulting.

1658 Westheimer Rd. ℂ **713/523-3800.** www.marks1658.com. Reservations recommended. Main courses $20–$40. AE, DC, DISC, MC, V. Mon–Fri 11am–2pm; Mon–Thurs 6–11pm; Fri–Sat 5:30pm–midnight; Sun 5–10pm.

## EXPENSIVE

**Backstreet Café** ★★ NEW AMERICAN   Wonderful cooking, a good selection of wines, and excellent service make this place perennially popular, especially in good weather when diners flock to the tree-shaded patio. The starters are delicious creations, especially the lobster potpie and the smoked corn crab cakes. Among the main courses, the meatloaf tower with mushroom gravy and garlic mashed potatoes warms my heart like nothing else and is a work of architectural splendor. A delicious lighter option would be the pecan-crusted chicken. Side dishes can be anything from corn pudding to fried green tomatoes. Dining areas include two upstairs rooms, one downstairs, and the patio. For dessert, try the bread pudding, with macadamia nut brittle and vanilla ice cream (if you dare). Don't even try to park your car; let the valet do it.

1103 S. Shepherd Dr. © **713/521-2239.** www.backstreetcafe.net. Reservations recommended. Main courses $15–$28. AE, DC, DISC, MC, V. Sun–Thurs 11am–10pm; Fri–Sat 11am–11pm. Despite the address, the restaurant is located 1 block east of Shepherd Dr. and 2 blocks north of W. Gray St. and the River Oaks Shopping Center, off McDuffie St.

## Divino Restaurant & Wine Bar ★★ ITALIAN/WINE BAR

Only 15 years ago, such a place couldn't have existed in Houston—a neighborhood restaurant serving northern Italian food and showcasing an elaborate wine list. That it has thrived is a testament not only to the cooking, but also to the changing palates of Houstonians. Divino's owner is a native who has lived in Italy for years and is passionate about the cooking. Listed on the menu are classic Italian dishes and items that blend tradition with personal inspiration, as well as southern Italian dishes. Wine is a big deal here; the restaurant has its own wine newsletter and even sells by the case at good prices. (*Tip:* If, after your meal, you feel like having something sweet and fattening, walk across the street to the Chocolate Bar and get some ice cream. This sweet shop makes some of the best ice cream—several varieties of chocolate and a white-chocolate lemon that is irresistible.)

1830 W. Alabama St. © **713/807-1123.** www.divinohouston.com. Reservations recommended. Main courses $14–$28. AE, DISC, MC, V. Mon–Thurs 5:30–10pm; Fri–Sat 5:30–10:30pm.

## Hugo's ★★★ MEXICAN

Chef Hugo Ortega offers up excellent cuisine originating from the interior region of Mexico, often with a wonderful contemporary twist. For an appetizer, try the tostadas or the *sopecitos* (small, thick handmade tortillas with toppings) or the lobster tacos. Main courses include duck in a *mole poblano* (the classic dark red, bittersweet sauce of the Mexican highlands) and a chile relleno with roasted chicken smothered in a *pipián* (a spicy sauce in a base of ground roasted pumpkin seeds). In addition, there's a seasonal menu. Chef Ortega has local sources for hard-to-get fresh ingredients, which, when available, become part of the food. For dessert, the specialty is the homemade Mexican hot chocolate, accompanied by small *churros* (the Spanish equivalent of doughnuts). These are delicious, but so are the margaritas, which, for me, also make an excellent dessert. The dining room is large and airy with comfortable furniture. There is a high ceiling made of pressed tin, part of the original building (1935), which was once a drugstore. Sometimes the noise reverberates a bit.

1602 Westheimer Rd. (at Mandell St.). © **713/524-7744.** www.hugosrestaurant.net. Reservations recommended. Main courses $15–$25. AE, DC, DISC, MC, V. Sun–Thurs 11am–10pm; Fri–Sat 11am–midnight.

## Indika ★★ CONTEMPORARY INDIAN

The best thing about this restaurant is that the owners, who are Indian, have no interest in being "authentic," which can only hamstring an imaginative chef. The seasonal menus glory in the variety of ingredients at the disposal of the modern Western cook and offer dishes that are combinations of these, and yet are expressions of thoroughly Indian sensibilities. A simple example would be the salmon tikka, which is offered as a special. Cooked tandoori-style, it is slightly blackened and crispy around the edges while perfectly moist inside. I can't think of a better way to prepare it. Quail, portobello mushrooms, and poblano chiles also appear on the menu. Among the appetizers is a warmed Camembert topped with mango chutney and pistachios and served with an Indian flatbread, as well as very light crabmeat samosas. Among the desserts is a chocolate and cardamom bread pudding. Everything is delicious. Consider this place for a Sunday brunch if you're in a festive mood. The restaurant is in a modern building with an airy, medium-size dining room and an outdoor patio area. The bar is known for its inventive cocktails.

516 Westheimer Rd. ✆ **713/524-2170.** www.indikausa.com. Reservations recommended. Main courses $18–$28. AE, DISC, MC, V. Tues–Fri 11:30am–2:30pm and 6–10:30pm; Sat 6–10:30pm; Sun 11am–3pm.

**Shade** ★★ NEW AMERICAN  Although some in the cuisine world feel that American cooking is less about tradition than about innovation and borrowing from other cultures, local celebrity chef Claire Smith is immune to such opinions. Her cooking is purposeful and shows a distinctly American sensibility, not some bowdlerized version of foreign cooking for local tastes. It is often new and inventive, and when not inventive, it's just plain good. The salads are fresh and well dressed, the soups are soul satisfying, and the main courses show flash. The restaurant's decor also shows some flash—unabashedly modern, simple, and with a couple of playful references to 1960s Dada. Shade is in the Heights and is a pioneer of another sort in being the first to circumvent the neighborhood's 100-year-old code prohibiting the sale of drinks. Cheers!

250 W. 19th St. ✆ **713/863-7500.** www.shadeheights.com. Reservations recommended. Main courses $14–$30. AE, DISC, MC, V. Mon–Fri 11am–2:30pm and 5–10pm; Sat 9am–3pm and 5–10:30pm; Sun 9am–3pm and 5–9pm.

## MODERATE

**Baba Yega** 🏠 LIGHT FARE/VEGETARIAN  Set in a small bungalow on a side street off Westheimer, Baba Yega is one of the hippest places in the Montrose. The restaurant has several small dining areas, all agreeable, particularly the garden veranda in back. Next door is an herb shop that belongs to the owner, and, whenever possible, he cooks with his own herbs. The most popular lunch items are the sandwiches, including several vegetarian choices. For dinner, the daily specials are what most people order, which usually include at least one chicken and one fish dish. Tuesday is the Italian Special, a plate of pasta and a glass of wine.

2607 Grant St. ✆ **713/522-0042.** www.babayega.com. Reservations not accepted. Main courses $10–$16; sandwiches $7–$9. AE, DC, DISC, MC, V. Sun–Thurs 11am–10pm; Fri–Sat 11am–11pm.

## INEXPENSIVE

**Christian's Tailgate Grill and Bar** 🏠 BAR/GRILL  I include this place not only because the burgers are really good, but also because it's a very Texas sort of place—a combination neighborhood bar and burger joint. Just west of the Heights, at the northeast corner of the intersection of Washington and I-10, Christian's is set in a large shack with a cement floor and cheap furniture. Catfish po' boys and Cajun fried chicken are also on the board. Happy hour runs all day Saturday, 5 to 8pm weekdays. It has a pool table and a couple of electronic games.

7340 Washington Ave. ✆ **713/864-9744.** www.christianstailgate.com. Burgers $5–$8. AE, DISC, MC, V. Mon–Fri 10am–9pm; Sat 11am–9pm.

**La Mexicana Restaurant** ★★ MEXICAN  Once a little Mexican grocery store, La Mexicana started serving tacos and gradually turned exclusively to the restaurant business. It's well known for delicious Mexican breakfasts such as *huevos a la mexicana* (eggs scrambled with onions, tomatoes, and serrano chiles) or *migas* (eggs cooked with fried tortilla strips)—both particularly good, as are their *frijoles* (black beans) and the green *salsa de mesa*—and classic enchilada plates (red and green are good choices). Some dishes are quite authentic, such as the *nopalitos en salsa chipotle* (cactus leaves cooked in chipotle chile sauce) or the tacos *de guisado de puerco* (pork stewed in dried chile sauce) or *de chicharrón en salsa verde* (pork cracklings in tomatillo sauce—one of my favorites, but not for everyone). Other dishes are Tex-Mex standbys, such as the fajitas and the combination plates. There's a choice of dining outside or inside.

1018 Fairview St. ✆ **713/521-0963.** www.lamexicanarestaurant.com. Reservations not accepted. Main courses $7–$14. AE, DC, DISC, MC, V. Daily 7am–11pm.

**Little Bigs** 🎁 AMERICAN    It's no secret that burgers and wine go really well together, so it's surprising there aren't more places like this little spot where you can enjoy two of your favorite things together. Actually, the menu consists of sliders (meat or bean patties), three to an order and in four varieties: burger, with or without caramelized onion; pulled pork; breaded chicken; and black bean. The bread for these sliders is baked on the premises; likewise, the meat is ground fresh, and the potatoes are cut into fries here, too. The wine list is not extensive, but it's priced right and has something to please just about everyone. The time to go is when the weather is pleasant, so that you can sit outdoors under the trees. Inside, it's tight and a little loud.

2703 Montrose Blvd. (just north of Westheimer). ✆ **713/521-2447.** www.littlebigshouston.com. Reservations not accepted. Main courses $6–$8. AE, MC, V. Sun–Wed 11am–10pm; Thurs 11am–11pm; Fri–Sat 11am–3am.

**Yale Street Grill** AMERICAN    This old lunch counter in the Heights is as quirky as they come. The grill shares space with a gift store, so you'll see plenty of the "decorative arts" on display, as well as framed photos of iconic stars who haven't eaten here, mixed with a few minor celebrities who have. For breakfast, the chocolate chip pancakes are the big sellers, and for lunch, the patty melt on rye and the specials (Monday's is chicken-fried steak, and Friday's is meatloaf). On weekends, breakfast is served all day. In addition to the seats at the counter, there's a single row of tables and a row of old-style booths that date back to 1951, when the Grill moved to its present location.

2100 Yale St. ✆ **713/861-3113.** Breakfast $4–$7.50; sandwiches $5–$7.50; lunch specials $7.50. AE, DISC, MC, V. Daily 7am–4:30pm.

## Kirby District

### EXPENSIVE

**Churrascos** ★★ SOUTH AMERICAN/STEAK    When this restaurant first opened, it caught on like a house afire. The owners have since opened another restaurant, Américas (p. 168), so the crowds have thinned somewhat, but fans of this place couldn't be happier. Churrascos is simpler than Américas. The main draw is the beef tenderloin butterflied, grilled, and served with chimichurri sauce, the garlicky Argentine condiment that always accompanies steak. Also very different for the Houston dining scene are the fried plantain chips served at every table, the Argentine empanadas, the Cuban-style black-bean soup, and the Peruvian-style ceviche. Grilled vegetables come "family style" with every entree. For dessert, the restaurant is justifiably famous for its *tres leches* cake.

2055 Westheimer Rd. ✆ **713/527-8300.** www.cordua.com. Reservations recommended. Main courses $8–$10 lunch, $15–$28 dinner. AE, DC, DISC, MC, V. Mon–Thurs 11am–10pm; Fri 11am–11pm; Sat 5–11pm.

### MODERATE

**Goode Company Texas Seafood** SEAFOOD    Jim Goode, a local restaurateur, operates a few places on or just off Kirby Drive. He does a great job with local cooking, which is why I like to steer visitors here. This restaurant is my favorite place to

**FAMILY-FRIENDLY** restaurants

**Café Express** (see "Fast Food à la Houston," earlier in this chapter)   These restaurants serve miniature burgers that kids just love, while the parents can enjoy salads, roast chicken, or pasta.

**James Coney Island Hot Dogs** (see "Fast Food à la Houston," earlier in this chapter)   What hot dog place isn't popular with kids? Most of these restaurants are decorated in bright colors that make them especially attractive to the young, and they offer kid specials.

**Lupe Tortilla** (p. 166)   This is a great place to go when the kids don't feel like sitting still, and the parents want something more in the way of real food than what kiddie places offer. The fajitas are excellent. When the weather is cooperating, the patio is perfect for a relaxing meal.

get catfish fried in cornmeal, executed here to a Texas T. Lighter choices include the mesquite-grilled flounder or red snapper. Texas-style seafood is a lot like Southern seafood, but with some Mexican and Southwestern influences, such as grilling with mesquite wood, and using fresh chiles, such as in the Mexican seafood cocktail known as a *campechana*. Here, it's usually made with shrimp and crawfish tails (depending on what's fresh). A *campechana* sauce is tomato based, like the American version of cocktail sauce, but gently spiked with green chile instead of horseradish, providing a nice, fresh piquancy, to which a little chopped avocado and some cilantro and onion are added. Gumbo and oyster po' boys are also on the menu.

2621 Westpark Dr. ℃ **713/523-7154.** www.goodecompany.com. Reservations not accepted. Main courses $12–$23. AE, DC, DISC, MC, V. Sun–Thurs 10am–10pm; Fri–Sat 10am–11pm.

**Little Pappasito's** TEX-MEX   This member of the Pappas family's restaurant empire serves a quality version of Tex-Mex at slightly higher prices than the norm, with higher quality ingredients. It's well known for beef and chicken fajitas, which are grilled over a fire as they should be, and not fried on a griddle. You really can't go wrong with any of the dishes here, from the guacamole to the cheese enchiladas. The main problem here is that the restaurant is very popular and the parking lot is too small. Waiting a half-hour for a table is not uncommon. But if you go between the standard mealtimes, the place is a delight.

2536 Richmond Ave. ℃ **713/522-5066.** www.pappasitos.com. Reservations not accepted. Main courses $12–$24. AE, MC, V. Sun–Thurs 11am–10pm; Fri–Sat 11am–11pm.

**Lupe Tortilla** ☺ TEX-MEX   Don't let the silly name draw your attention away from the important fact that this kid-friendly establishment offers the family a perfect respite from shopping or sightseeing. While the kids burn off some excess energy on the restaurant's playscape, the parents can relax at a table, sipping one of the restaurant's excellent margaritas, and choose from the menu's Tex-Mex dishes. Featured are superb fajitas and other grilled specialties, such as the Three-Pepper Cheese Steak or the milder Steak Lupe. There are nachos and *chalupas* and the like for kids, and, for the adults . . . uh, did I mention the margaritas?

2414 Southwest Fwy. ℃ **713/522-4420.** www.lupetortilla.com. Reservations not accepted. Main courses $10–$15. AE, MC, V. Sun–Thurs 11am–9pm; Fri–Sat 11am–10pm.

**Madras Pavilion** ★★ INDIAN/VEGETARIAN   The way I see it, no one does vegetarian as well as the Indians, especially those of the south. They've had centuries of practice and know what they're doing. As evidence, I would offer this restaurant—an unassuming establishment tucked into a strip center on Kirby. It's a good choice as a respite from steaks, fajitas, barbecue, and other Texas specialties. The food is mouthwatering, and there's plenty to choose from: curries, different flavored rices, delicacies such as *masala dosai* (rice flour crepes filled with a deliciously spiced mixture of potatoes and onion) with or without chutney, *paneer* (cottage cheese curds usually cooked in spinach), a full range of Indian bread, including the puffy *channa batura,* served with chickpea curry, and a spicy pizzalike dish, *uthappam.* Most of these are spicy, but there is also much to choose that is mild. With such variety, you would do well to go midday, when you can try a bit of everything from the lunch buffet ($8 on weekdays, $10 on weekends). Service can be slow.

3910 Kirby (1 block north of the Southwest Fwy., facing a parking lot on the north side of the building). © **713/521-2617.** Reservations not accepted. Main courses $9–$15. MC, V. Mon–Fri 11:30am–3pm; Mon–Thurs 5:30–9:30pm; Fri 5:30–10pm; Sat–Sun 11:30am–10pm.

**Thai Bistro ★★** THAI   Houston is particularly rich in Thai restaurants. This one is in a strip center along the Southwest Freeway, practically next door to a taco joint, 100% Taquito, that I recommend below. You, the reader, might suspect that I'm being lazy for listing two restaurants practically next door to each other, but if you go and taste the food, you'll see that I only have your best interests at heart. If you have an appetite, do yourself a favor and order the assorted appetizer platter. From there, you can go in any number of directions: healthy (barbecued lemon grass tofu or lettuce wraps), spicy (blazing noodles), classic (pad Thai), or curry (Panang). These are all favorites. Also on the menu are some Vietnamese-style vermicelli dishes, which are there through historical accident. The restaurant used to be Vietnamese, and when the present owner bought the place, the neighborhood regulars wouldn't allow him to drop these dishes from the menu.

3241 Southwest Fwy. © **713/669-9375.** www.txthaibistro.com. Main courses $7–$10 lunch, $10–$16 dinner. AE, DC, DISC, MC, V. Mon–Fri 11am–3pm and 5–10pm; Sat 11am–10:30pm; Sun 11am–9pm.

**Thai Spice ★ 🍴** THAI   In Rice Village, the popular retail area, there are three commendable Thai restaurants, each with its own loyal following. Of these, Thai Spice gets the nod, mostly because the service is friendlier and the dining area is roomier, more attractive, and better furnished, but also because the food is a particularly appealing interpretation of Thai that doesn't burn out your taste buds. The lunch buffet is noteworthy for being more complete than in most other places. The dinner menu is well laid out and doesn't confuse you with options by listing the same basic dish four times. The spicy shrimp soup is good, and the Summer Palace is a great spicy option for a stir-fry. There are also several mild dishes, including a wonderfully simple, grilled lemon grass chicken breast. All of the curries are worth ordering, and the pad Thai is excellent. This restaurant has another location in the Heights at 420 W. 19th St. (© **713/880-9992**).

5117 Kelvin Dr. (at Dunstan St.). © **713/522-5100.** www.thaispice.com. Main courses $8.50–$13; lunch buffet $9. AE, DC, DISC, MC, V. Mon–Sat 11am–2:30pm (lunch buffet) and 5–10pm; Sun 11:30am–3pm and 5–9pm.

## INEXPENSIVE

**Goode Company Texas Barbecue** BARBECUE   Mr. Goode cooks up some great barbecue at this rickety joint on Kirby, 4 blocks south of the Southwest Freeway. Especially tasty are the pork ribs and the brisket, but you can also get duck, chicken, and links. Order by the pound, the plate, or the sandwich. For dessert, the pecan pie is a must. Beer signs and country music on the jukebox set the scene.

5109 Kirby Dr. ⓒ **713/522-2530.** www.goodecompany.com. Barbecue plates $8–$14. AE, DC, DISC, MC, V. Daily 11am–10pm.

**Luling City Market** BARBECUE   This is great barbecue served in a traditional setting, which for Texas barbecue joints means that any effort spent decorating appears, at least, as purely an afterthought and, at most, as the owner's misguided attempt to find a place for all the objets d'art that have been cluttering up his attic. This place follows the minimalist approach. Service is lunch-counter style. I recommend the ribs and the sausage. At night, the quiet little bar fills up with regulars with whom you can chew the fat, mostly about sports. **Note:** This place has no official connection to the famous City Market barbecue in the town of Luling, but you can tell that someone may have learned to cook there.

4726 Richmond Ave. ⓒ **713/871-1903.** www.lulingcitymarket.com. Reservations not accepted. Barbecue plates $10–$14. AE, DC, DISC, MC, V. Mon–Sat 11am–9pm; Sun noon–7pm.

**100% Taquito** MEXICAN   The owner hails from Mexico City, where, more than anywhere else in Mexico, good *taquerías* (taco joints) are enshrined right up there with all that Mexicans hold dear. Tacos in Mexico are usually served on small, soft tortillas and sprinkled with a little fresh cilantro and onion. The traditional fillings might be prepared on a grill, on a griddle, or in a stew pot. To explain a few terms: *al pastor* is pork that has been marinated in *ancho chile, guajillo chile,* annatto, and sour orange and served with a little grilled pineapple; *tinga* is pork or beef stewed in a chipotle sauce; and *barbacoa* is a simple style of Mexican barbecue. All are delicious, as are the *banderillas:* fried *taquitos* done up like the Mexican flag. Tacos are served in small orders of three. One order would be enough if you're just feeling peckish, two if you're hungry.

3245 Southwest Fwy. ⓒ **713/665-2900.** www.100taquito.com. Orders of 3 tacos $4–$6. AE, DISC, MC, V. Daily 11am–10pm.

## Uptown
### VERY EXPENSIVE

**Américas** ★★ SOUTH AMERICAN   This is a different sort of place to dine. From the over-the-top decor to the menu of dishes loosely inspired by the national cuisines of the New World, there is nothing ho-hum about dining here. On my first visit, I was a bit overwhelmed, but on subsequent visits I've gotten quite comfortable with the place. When crowded, it's noisy, but the furniture is comfortable, and there are several large round booths that are fun. As with its sister restaurant, Churrascos, one of the favorites is the grilled tenderloin—always a good choice. But for something more inventive, try the relleno, a boneless pork loin stuffed with the *masa* of a tamal, topped with a grilled shrimp, and bathed in a butter sauce with a *hint* of habanero chile. Or perhaps the *chileno,* a broiled Chilean sea bass with sweet corn and poblano spoon bread.

1800 Post Oak Blvd. ⓒ **713/961-1492.** www.cordua.com. Reservations recommended. Main courses $18–$45. AE, DC, DISC, MC, V. Mon–Thurs 11am–10pm; Fri 11am–11pm; Sat 5–11pm.

**RDG + Bar Annie** ★★★ SOUTHWESTERN   Singing the praises of this restaurant makes me feel like nothing more than a member of the choir. Over the past 20 years, no restaurant in Houston has received more coverage, more acclaim, and more awards than RDG + Bar Annie. If you're looking for *the* restaurant in Houston, and especially if you're on a fat expense account, this should be your choice. Those of us who aren't so fortunate can save money by going for lunch or ordering from the bar menu. One of the restaurant's signature dishes is crabmeat tostadas, available on the dinner, lunch, and bar menus. These are wonderful compositions of fresh lump crabmeat, avocado, a little finely shredded cabbage, and a touch of piquancy. Delicious main courses include the cinnamon-roasted pheasant, the beef with *chile pasilla* sauce, or the red fish with pumpkinseed sauce. The tortilla soup is one of the perennial favorites on the menu. Everything I sampled has been delicious and different. The dining room is perfectly in character with the restaurant—nice and quiet, softly lit, with lots of dark woodwork.

1800 Post Oak Blvd. (just south of San Felipe). ✆ **713/840-1111.** www.rdgbarannie.com. Reservations recommended. Main courses $28–$45. AE, DC, DISC, MC, V. Mon 6:30–10pm; Tues–Fri 11:30am–2pm and 6:30–10pm; Sat 6:30–10:30pm.

## MODERATE

**Kenny & Ziggy's ★** DELI   This is a good place to know about if you're staying in the Uptown/Galleria area. Delis aren't common in Houston, and good ones are especially rare. This one is the real deal. It's smack-dab in the middle of Uptown (in a strip center on the northeast corner of the intersection of Westheimer and Post Oak), and it offers the convenience of takeout that you can call in, and a full-service restaurant. So, if you have an urge for an honest pastrami on rye, you won't be disappointed. There are many sandwiches and a variety of dinners, from corned beef and cabbage to Hungarian goulash to grilled snapper. Bulk deli items (meats, cheeses, and lox) are sold by the pound.

2327 Post Oak Blvd. ✆ **713/871-8883.** www.kennyandziggys.com. Sandwiches (served with 2 sides) $9–$16; dinners $15–$18. MC, V. Mon–Fri 7am–9pm; Sat–Sun 9am–9pm.

# SEEING THE SIGHTS

Because Houston isn't a major tourist destination, there isn't much in the way of tourism infrastructure except for the downtown visitor center. Most of the available resources are geared toward conventions and large groups, not independent travelers. From the visitor center, there is often a visitors' tour of downtown that looks at architecture, public sculpture, the tunnel system, and the view from the observation deck of the JP Morgan Chase Tower, the tallest building in Houston.

## The Top Attractions
### DOWNTOWN

**Downtown Aquarium** ☺   In the northwest corner of downtown, a few blocks from the visitor center, is this aquarium/restaurant/amusement park complex. The major exhibit consists of several tanks in the main building, which display different aquatic ecosystems. These are nicely done, and lots of little tanks hold highly specialized species from places like the Amazon. There are also touch tanks and an exhibit of rare white tigers. Upstairs is a seafood restaurant where you can enjoy another large aquarium while you have a bite to eat. Outside the building, the main attraction is a large shark tank, which you view from a glass tunnel while seated in a miniature train. There's a Ferris wheel and a carousel, which, along with the train ride through the shark tank, require separate tickets. The main exhibit takes about an hour; the train ride takes 10 minutes, with 2 to 3 minutes inside the glass tunnel.

410 Bagby St. ✆ **713/223-3474.** www.downtownaquarium.com. Admission $9.25 adults; $8.25 seniors; $6.25 children 2–12. Shark voyage $5. Sun–Thurs 10am–9pm; Fri–Sat 10am–11pm.

**Downtown Tunnel System**   There are 6 miles of tunnels below Houston's downtown, comprising an interconnected series of restaurants, shops, and businesses of all varieties. You can get a map of the tunnels from the city's visitor center. It's good to have the map because it's easy to get turned around if you don't know the city's downtown.

Accessible from the visitor center in city hall and all neighboring buildings, as well as most downtown hotels. Free admission. Mon–Fri 7am–6pm.

**Heritage Society at Sam Houston Park**   A couple of blocks from Houston's visitor center is this park, which serves as a repository for eight of Houston's oldest houses and buildings, moved here from their original locations. The oldest one dates from before Texas's independence; it's a small, simple cabin originally built close to where NASA is today. Another house was built by a freed slave in 1870. There's a church dating from 1892. The Heritage Society restored them to their original state and furnished them with pieces from the appropriate eras. The only way to see these buildings is by guided tour, which leaves every hour on the hour from the tour office at 1100 Bagby St.; it takes about 45 minutes. The guides are well informed and add a lot to a visit here. You can do a cellphone tour, but you won't get answers to the questions inspired by seeing these houses. The Heritage Museum can be visited without taking the tour. It's free and features permanent exhibits on Texas history.

1100 Bagby St. ✆ **713/655-1912.** www.heritagesociety.org. Tours $10 adults, $8 seniors, free for children 18 and under. Tues–Sat 10am–4pm; Sun 1–4pm. Closed major holidays.

## EAST END & BEYOND

**Battleship *Texas* and San Jacinto Monument & Museum** ★ ☺   On the San Jacinto Battleground in 1836, Texas won its independence from Mexico with a crushing surprise attack by the Texan forces, whose battle cry was "Remember the Alamo!" To commemorate that victory, civic leaders in 1936 built a towering obelisk as tall as the Washington Monument, but topped with a Texas Lone Star. In the base of the monument is a small museum of Texas history with some interesting exhibits, such as one about the relatively unsung Texas hero "Deaf" Smith, and a collection of watercolors of the Mexican War painted by Sam Chamberlain. There is also a small auditorium where you can watch a 35-minute documentary of the battle. If you would like to view some of the Port of Houston as well as the rest of the land for miles around, you can take the elevator up to the observation room in the top floor of the tower, which is more than 500 feet aboveground.

Across from the monument, in roughly the same place where the Texans began their advance, is the USS *Texas*. Built in 1914, before improvements in warplane technology made these large dreadnought battleships vulnerable, it is the last of its kind. Between the wars, the navy modernized the ship with anti-aircraft and torpedo defenses, but it's still surprising that it survived World War II, having fought in both the Atlantic and the Pacific theaters. When you visit, you can clamber up to its small-caliber guns or onto the navigation bridge, inspect the crew's quarters, and check out the engine room. Life onboard was no picnic—the quarters were cramped and facilities were minimal—so it's interesting to learn that this ship was considered a lucky assignment. Plan on at least an hour to see the *Texas*, and another hour for the monument.

3523 Battleground Rd. ✆ **281/479-2431.** www.tpwd.state.tx.us/park/sanjac. Park admission $1 adults and children 13 and over; free for children 12 and under. Battleship admission $10 adults and children 13 and over, $5 seniors, free for children 12 and under; free admission to the monument and museum; observation room $4 adults, $3.50 seniors, $3 children; movie $4.50 adults, $4 seniors, $3.50 children.

Daily 9am–6pm. Take the La Porte Fwy. (Tex. 225) east from Loop 610 E. Exit Battleground Rd. (Tex. 134) and turn left.

**Houston Ship Channel** ★  For those fortunate enough not to live among the industrial areas of the Texas Gulf Coast, the landscape of refineries and their intricate tangle of pipes, their forests of cooling towers and stacks, and their fields of tanks are as exotic as the Zanzibar coast. If you find this sort of thing intriguing, you can take a free boat ride on the M/V *Sam Houston,* which tours the upper 7 miles of the deep water channel. The boat dates from the 1950s and has a lovely cabin trimmed in mahogany as well as fore and aft observation decks. I hail from Houston, but rarely have the opportunity to see the ship channel up close, and I enjoyed this trip. You should probably make reservations well in advance during the summer months, when it is quite popular, though I'm told that the ship channel is best seen in cooler weather, when there is no risk of bad smells. The trip takes a total of 90 minutes, during which you will most likely see large container ships, tall grain elevators, tugs, and barges. If, after the trip, you want to see more of the channel, you can drive to the San Jacinto Battlefield, where the Battleship *Texas* is on display (see review above).

7300 Clinton Dr. at Gate 8. ℂ **713/670-2416.** www.portofhouston.com. See website for security regulations, including the prohibition of cameras. Call or visit website to make reservations, which are required. Free admission. Tues–Wed and Fri–Sat 10am and 2:30pm; Sun and Thurs 2:30pm. Closed Sept and holidays. Take the Gulf Fwy. S.; get on Loop 610 E., which takes you over the ship channel; exit Clinton Dr. Turn right on Clinton (look for small green signs pointing the way); after a mile, you'll come to a traffic light and a sign reading PORT GATE 8. Turn left.

**Kemah Boardwalk** ☺  Many visitors to Space Center Houston (see review below) will go out for seafood afterward at nearby Kemah, which is as touristy as the Houston area gets. It used to be a rustic shrimping port on Galveston Bay where you could buy some shrimp and a beer and sit by the dock on an afternoon to watch the shrimp boats come in. Most of the pier was washed away in 1984 by a hurricane, and in the 1990s it was bought by a developer who built the boardwalk, several amusement rides, restaurants, a hotel, and some touristy stores and attractions. The restaurants overlook the water; if you stroll down the boardwalk, you'll pass all of them. Pick the one that most appeals to you. Among the attractions is a 50,000-gallon, floor-to-ceiling aquarium housing more than 100 species of tropical fish in the Aquarium Restaurant.

Tex. 146, Kemah. ℂ **877/285-3624.** www.kemahboardwalk.com.

**The Orange Show** ★★ ☺ 📧  This may not be the "greatest show on earth," but it must be the quirkiest. In truth, it's not a show at all, at least not as we commonly understand the word. Rather, it's the life work of one man, former postman Jeff McKissack, who spent his last 25 years assembling a collection of found objects and building materials into an architectural collage that students of folk art call a "folk art environment." It stands in a quiet working-class neighborhood just off the Gulf Freeway, where it dares to be different. With the many flagpoles, spindles, wagon wheels, and wrought-iron birds rising up from behind its walls, it seems like an outpost for spontaneity in a wilderness of cookie-cutter ranch-style houses.

Inside, the viewer is presented with all kinds of curiosities: two small arenas, observation decks, a small museum, and lots of cheerful wrought-iron decoration and tile work. Inscriptions adorn the walls; many of these honor that best of all fruits, "The orange: a great gift to mankind." Seeing the whole thing takes less than an hour. Upon the death of Mr. McKissack, the Orange Show fell into decay until it was rescued by the Orange Show Foundation, located in the house across the street. The foundation is a center for Houston's folk-art world and the organizer of the Art Car Parade and the Art Car Ball (see "Texas Calendar of Events," in chapter 2). It is also the organizer of Eyeopener Tours (see "Organized Tours," later in this section). If you like folk art, consider purchasing their driving-tour audiocassette of Houston's other folk-art treasures. (The tape comes with a map.)

2401 Munger St. © **713/926-6368.** www.orangeshow.org. Admission $1 adults, free for children 11 and under. Summer Wed–Fri 9am–1pm, Sat–Sun noon–5pm; spring and fall Sat–Sun noon–5pm. From downtown, take Gulf Fwy. Exit Telephone Rd. and make the 3rd right off the feeder road onto Munger (before you get to the Telephone Rd. intersection).

**Space Center Houston ★★★ ☺**  Space Center Houston is the visitor center for NASA's Johnson Space Center. It's the product of the joint efforts of NASA and Disney Imagineering. Located about 25 miles from downtown Houston, it's easily the most popular attraction in the area and there's nothing like it anywhere else in the world. You'll find plenty of exhibits and activities to interest both adults and children, and they do a great job of introducing the visitor to different aspects of space exploration.

The center banks heavily on interactive displays and simulations on the one hand and actual access to the real thing on the other. For instance, the "Feel of Space" gallery simulates working in the frictionless environment of space by using an air-bearing floor (something like a giant air-hockey table). Another simulator shows what it's like to land the lunar orbiter. For a direct experience of NASA, you can take the 1½-hour tram tour that takes you to, among other places, the International Space Station Assembly Building and NASA control center. You get to see things as they happen, especially interesting if there's a shuttle mission in progress. You might also see astronauts in training.

But if you're really fascinated by the history and present status of space exploration, consider taking a Level 9 tour. There's only one tour per day, Monday through Friday, and each tour is limited to 12 people. To take the tours, you should call ahead and make a reservation. Included in the tour is an extended visit to both the historic and the new mission control centers, a visit to the astronauts' training facility, the space simulation lab, and lunch in the astronauts' cafeteria. The guide is an experienced NASA employee, who can answer almost any question you have about space exploration. The Level 9 tour lasts 5 hours and costs $90.

1601 NASA Rd. 1, Clear Lake. © **281/244-2100.** www.spacecenter.org. Admission (including tours and IMAX theater) $20 adults, $19 seniors, $16 children 4–11. June–July daily 10am–7pm; Aug–May Mon–Fri 10am–5pm, Sat–Sun 10am–6pm. Closed Christmas. Take the Gulf Fwy. to NASA Rd. 1, turn left, and go 3 miles.

## SOUTH MAIN/MUSEUM DISTRICT

**Children's Museum of Houston ★★ ☺**  The goal behind the Children's Museum is to have a place where children can engage the world around them on their own terms, a place that will spark their imaginations, and where they will learn the joy of discovery. It's for children up to 12 years old, but even if you're without kids in tow, you might like to take a glance at the museum's fun exterior. It's a playful send-up of the classical museum facade and is well suited for this institution that blurs the distinction between museum and playhouse. This is bigger and better than any children's museum I have seen, and it recently finished an expansion that doubled its size.

Exhibits include "Kidtropolis," a re-creation of the adult world for children, which includes a TV station, a police station, an ambulance, a bank, and a grocery store, and children jump in to play different roles in a make-believe society. "Powerplay" is obviously for burning energy—among other things, it includes a descending set of inclined steps that require quite a bit of effort to get through. "Invention Convention" challenges kids to design objects fit to do specific tasks. And, of course, there has to be something with water, in this case, "Flow Works," where children can play with an artificial stream and control jets of water without getting too wet. Specifically for the smaller ones is "Tot Spot," focusing on the 6-month- to 3-year-old crowd, helping build motor skills through ingenious forms of play.

1500 Binz St. ☎ **713/522-1138.** www.cmhouston.org. Admission $8 adults and children, $7 seniors, free for children under 1; free family night Thurs 5–8pm. Tues–Wed and Fri–Sat 9am–6pm; Thurs 9am–8pm; Sun noon–6pm. Closed major holidays. On the same street as the Museum of Fine Arts, Houston (the street name changes from Bissonnet to Binz), 4 blocks to the east.

**Contemporary Arts Museum**   This silver-aluminum parallelogram, set on the corner of Montrose and Bissonnet diagonally to the Fine Arts Museum, presents temporary exhibitions of modern art and design. It has no permanent collection; what you might find here is purely the luck of the draw. When I go to the Museum of Fine Arts (see below), I always stick my head into the CAM to see what's going on because it's right across the street and it's free.

5216 Montrose Blvd. ☎ **713/284-8250.** www.camh.org. Free admission. Wed 11am–7pm; Thurs 11am–9pm; Fri 11am–7pm; Sat–Sun 11am–6pm. Closed Thanksgiving, Christmas, and New Year's Day.

**The Health Museum** ★★★ ☺   We've all heard about what an amazing thing the human body is, but how much do we really know about its workings? This family museum will surprise most visitors with its extensive use of audio, video, holograms, and medical technology to provide a graphic view of human physiology.

Because of the Texas Medical Center, Houston has a large medical community, which has been the driving force behind the creation of this museum. With additional contributions from corporations and individual doctors, it has constructed an eye-catching interactive exhibition called the **Amazing Body Pavilion.** The exhibit is itself a metaphor for the body. Visitors enter through the mouth and proceed down the digestive tract, learning about all the organs that process our food. (Children seem to think this is pretty cool.) The exhibit covers the major organs in ways that provide lots of interaction for children, and explanatory text and monologues by little holographic figures are well written and provide info that most adults will find interesting.

The museum has added a small, high-tech movie theater, which at present is included in the general admission price. It presents a short movie exploring the bizarre world of the microbes that inhabit our epidermis. This movie (and presumably others to follow) was produced by the Health Museum in conjunction with a museum in Boston. The rest of the museum space is dedicated to temporary exhibits.

Of course, with its name, and the fact that so many doctors were involved in its creation, you can be sure there will be some preaching about the need for a good diet and to avoid smoking, and don't expect the museum's snack bar to offer any junk food. But do check out the gift shop with its intriguing assortment of items. Seeing the exhibit takes a little more than an hour. *One other note:* You might want to ask at the front desk about the next scheduled organ dissection. When I was there, the organ of the month was the sheep brain; I opted to forgo the performance.

1515 Hermann Dr. ☎ **713/521-1515.** www.mhms.org. Admission $8 adults, $6 seniors and children 3–12, free for all Thurs 2–5pm. Tues–Sat 9am–5pm (also Mon in summer); Sun noon–5pm. Closed Thanksgiving and Christmas. 1 block south of the Children's Museum (parking entrance is on Hermann Dr., and the door is on Crawford St.).

**Hermann Park** This park has 545 acres of land and lies just beyond the Museum District, on the east side of South Main Street. It recently underwent an extensive makeover to its large pond, miniature train, and the various foot trails, picnic areas, and playscapes. The parkland has wooded areas and an 18-hole public golf course. On the north side of the park, across from the Health Museum, is the garden center with beautiful rose gardens, which are well worth a visit in the spring and fall when they have the most blooms. In the same area is a garden of aromatic herbs, which is fun to explore, as well as a Japanese garden and the Miller Outdoor Theater, which often holds free plays and musical performances.

Fannin St. at Hermann Park Dr. Open year-round.

**Houston Museum of Natural Science** ★★ ☺ This is one of the best natural history/natural science museums you'll ever find. Yes, it has everything you'd expect (and some things you might not): dinosaur skeletons, displays of Texas wildlife, a stunning gem and mineral collection, and exhibits on early cultures of the Americas, climatology, chemistry, and oil and gas exploration. But what gets most of the buzz is the miniature rainforest environment created in the Butterfly Center. You can walk among hundreds of living butterflies as they fly about in the steamy air near a small waterfall. As you enter, you pass through the insect zoo, which holds some fascinating and bizarre living specimens of beetles, spiders, and other bugs that you wouldn't want running around.

Also in the museum is an IMAX theater and a planetarium. The museum equipped the planetarium with computer-animation projectors that enhance the quality of its programs about stars, galaxies, nebulae, and other astral bodies. Check the website for its shows, which are heavy on cosmology and astrophysics, but also include laser shows. In years past, the directors have assembled some great temporary exhibits, so ask about any that might be open during your visit. By the end of 2012, the museum's large expansion project—a vast exhibition hall to house the museum's large collection of dinosaurs—should be completed. Located in the northwest corner of Hermann Park, the museum is about 3 blocks from the Museum of Fine Arts.

5555 Hermann Park Dr. ✆ **713/639-4629.** www.hmns.org. Museum $15 adults, $10 seniors and children 3–11 (free after 2pm Tues); Butterfly Center $8 adults, $7 seniors and children; IMAX tickets $11 adults, $9 seniors and children. Wed–Mon 9am–5pm; Tues 9am–8pm; hours for Butterfly Center and IMAX can differ.

**Houston Zoological Gardens** ☺ Located within Hermann Park is this 50-acre zoo featuring a gorilla habitat, rare albino reptiles, a cat facility, a large aquarium, and vampire bats. Every few years, the zoo builds a new facility for a portion of its residents. The Brown Education Center, open daily from 10am to 6pm, allows visitors to interact with the animals.

1513 N. MacGregor Dr. ✆ **713/533-6500.** www.houstonzoo.org. Admission $12 adults 12–64, $8 children 2–11, $6.50 seniors. Mid-Mar to early Nov daily 9am–7pm; early Nov to mid-Mar daily 9am–6pm.

**Museum of Fine Arts, Houston (MFAH)** ★★★ This is by far the best and biggest public art museum in Texas. It's a wonderful testament to what a lot of oil money can do, and the manner in which it evolved tells something about the development of the city's sense of aesthetics. The original museum, built in the 1920s, was pure neoclassical—the attitude was that if Houston were to have a museum, it should look like a museum. In the '50s, Mies van der Rohe, grand architect of the International Style, was hired to build an addition. In the '70s, it received yet another addition, also designed by Mies. Both of these were bold statements of modern architecture—

Hot and humid, Houston has earned the unofficial title of "Air-Conditioning Capital of the World." If you're unaccustomed to high humidity and its consequences (profuse sweating, bad-hair days), you might want to take it easy at first and work on acquiring some degree of philosophical acceptance.

One more thing: Bopping around Houston in summertime means jumping from the frying pan into the freezer. You'll be repeatedly going from steamy outdoors into superchilled shops, restaurants, and so on. The natives are used to it, but many visitors complain—to deaf ears, I might add.

lots of glass and steel forming a light and airy space—but, unfortunately, not the kind of space that lends itself well for much of the museum's collection.

In the '90s, the museum's directors hired Spanish architect Rafael Moneo to design a building that would be a return to traditional galleries—the Audrey Jones Beck Building, across South Main Street from the main building. (A tunnel connects the two; make a point of visiting it.) The new building aims at reconciling the boldness of modernism with the staid character of traditional design. Constructed with rich materials and designed on grand proportions, the building feels monumental. All the galleries on the second floor take advantage of interesting "roof lanterns," which allow Houston's plentiful natural light to enter in regulated amounts. The Beck building doubles MFAH's gallery space and allows the directors to attract first-rate traveling exhibitions. The museum's collection of more than 40,000 pieces is varied, but it is perhaps strongest in the area of Impressionist and post-Impressionist works, baroque and Renaissance art, and 19th- and 20th-century American art. There is also a fine collection of African tribal art, as well as ancient artwork from several civilizations.

Aside from the two gallery buildings, the Cullen Sculpture Garden designed by Isamu Noguchi is located across Bissonnet from the main building, and the Glassell School of Art can be seen just to the north of the sculpture garden. Look for a building made of a strangely reflective glass brick (another architectural pun). The museum also owns two collections of the decorative arts, which are displayed in two mansions in the River Oaks area; see Bayou Bend (p. 176) and Rienzi (p. 177).

1001 Bissonnet St. ✆ **713/639-7300.** www.mfah.org. Admission $7 adults, $3.50 seniors and children 6–18, free for all Thurs. Tues–Wed 10am–5pm; Thurs 10am–9pm; Fri–Sat 10am–7pm; Sun 12:15–7pm.

## MONTROSE

**Menil Collection** ★★★ ◈ Here, on display in an unremarkable neighborhood near the University of St. Thomas, is one of the world's great private collections. Jean and Dominique de Menil arrived in Houston in the 1940s, fleeing the war in Europe. For more than 4 decades, they purchased and commissioned works of art; brought artists, architects, and academics to the city; organized groundbreaking exhibitions; and did much for Houston's art museums and for the art departments of Rice University and St. Thomas University. Their collection, especially the modern art, is vast, so much so that only a fifth of it can be exhibited in the museum at one time. The structure housing the collection was designed by Renzo Piano, who worked closely with Mrs. de Menil. It's graceful and personable and doesn't seek to impress the visitor or impose itself on the collection. In these qualities, it's the physical embodiment of Mrs. de Menil's ideas about experiencing art. From the moment you walk into the museum, there is nothing between you and the art—no grand lobby with marble stairway, no large banners or gift shop vying for attention, no tickets to buy, no tape-recorded tours. Viewing the art becomes a direct and personal experience.

The Menil Collection is concentrated in four areas: antiquity, Byzantine and medieval, tribal, and 20th century. This may seem an incongruous mix, but, strangely enough, it holds together. The collectors never intended to gather up the most artworks representative of a period; they simply followed their own tastes, which were modern. And one interesting consequence of this fact (intended or not) is that, in walking through these galleries one right after another, the viewer gradually discerns a universality in some modern art that connects it all the way back to antiquity and across the boundaries of Western culture to the tribal peoples of other continents.

In addition to the main museum, four satellite buildings form a museum campus. One of these satellite buildings is the much-talked-about **Rothko Chapel,** with its 14 brooding paintings by Mark Rothko, created specifically for this installation and the last works before the artist's death. In front of the chapel stands Barnett Newman's *Broken Obelisk.* A block south of the Rothko Chapel is the **Byzantine Fresco Chapel Museum,** which is worth seeing as much for the building that houses them (designed by François de Menil, son of Jean and Dominique) as for the frescoes themselves, which were ransomed from international art thieves. Across the street from the main museum, in a building also designed by Renzo Piano, is a permanent exhibition of the works of Cy Twombly, which are easy to view because of the gallery's exquisite light. It lends a luminous quality to the large artworks, and just being in the place somehow livens one's spirits. Finally, **Richmond Hall,** 2 blocks south of the campus, holds an installation by minimalist neon-light artist Don Flavin.

1515 Sul Ross St. ℰ **713/525-9400.** www.menil.org. Free admission. Wed–Sun 11am–7pm.

## KIRBY DISTRICT

**Bayou Bend** ★★    Ima Hogg was the daughter of Gov. Jim Hogg, a man who obviously had a cruel sense of humor. Miss Hogg, however, did not grow up shy and self-effacing. Long after the governor was dead, she was a power to be reckoned with in local affairs and did much to keep the chicanery in city hall to a minimum. Her mansion, Bayou Bend, was built in the 1920s by Houston's most prominent architect, John F. Staub. It holds in its 28 rooms a treasure-trove of American furniture, paintings, and decorative objects dating from Colonial times to about 1870, and is set amid 14 acres of beautifully tended gardens in a variety of styles. This is a must-see for antiques collectors and gardeners.

Part of the Museum of Fine Arts, the house can be seen by self-guided audio tour or by guided tour, which is preferable. Reservations are recommended for the 60-minute guided tour, which leaves every 15 minutes. Bayou Bend is on the backside of River Oaks, but is unapproachable from the main entrance to the neighborhood. The only way to get there is to go down Memorial Drive, which follows the north shore of Buffalo Bayou, and then turn left onto Westcott to enter the grounds.

1 Westcott St. ℰ **713/639-7750.** www.mfah.org/bayoubend. Admission (includes audio tour) $10 adults, $8.50 seniors, $5 youths 10–17, free for children 9 and under. Gardens only $3. Guided house tours (except Aug): Tues–Thurs 10–11:30am and 1–2:45pm; Fri–Sat 10–11:15am. Self-guided house tours: Fri–Sun 1–5pm (except Aug: Tues–Sat 10am–5pm; Sun 1–5pm). Self-guided gardens tours: Tues–Sat 10am–5pm; Sun 1–5pm.

**Beer Can House**    This bungalow house in a modest neighborhood west of the Heights belonged to John Milkovisch, who began decorating it in 1968. His material of choice was beer cans, which was fortunate because he liked drinking beer. Over the years and with the helpful drinking of his wife and neighbors, Milkovisch was able to transform his little bungalow into an eye-catching structure that became famous throughout the city as the Beer Can House. After he died, his widow came to an arrangement with the Orange Show Foundation, which purchased the house and helped to maintain it until her death. After a period of restoration and structural repair, the house is open for public viewing. It's an amazing sight, with practically every surface covered with aluminum or glass (from beer bottles).

222 Malone St. ⓒ **713/926-6368.** www.beercanhouse.org. Admission $2; guided tour $5. Sat–Sun noon–5pm.

**Rienzi**   In a 1950s River Oaks mansion designed by John F. Staub, the Museum of Fine Arts displays its collection of European decorative arts. Most of the collection predates 1800. Both the house and the collection were donated by the family that lived here. This museum will be of most interest to collectors of English porcelain and of no interest to children. On Sundays you can take a self-guided tour, from 1 to 4pm.

1406 Kirby Dr. ⓒ **713/639-7800.** www.mfah.org/rienzi. Admission $6 adults, $4 seniors. Wed–Fri 10am–3pm; Sat 10am–4pm; Sun 1–4pm. Reservations required.

## FARTHER AFIELD

**George Ranch Historical Park** ☺   Experience the life of four generations of a Texas family on this 400-acre outdoor museum, a working cattle ranch. Wander through a restored 1820s pioneer farm, an 1880s Victorian mansion, an 1890s cowboy encampment, and a 1930s ranch house. Savor Victorian-style tea on a mansion porch or sit around the campfire with cowboys during a roundup and watch crafts demonstrations such as rope twisting. Picnic areas are provided. Plan to spend a half-day here.

10215 FM 762, Richmond. ⓒ **281/343-0218.** www.georgeranch.org. Admission $9 adults, $8 seniors 62 and older, $5 children 5–15. Tues–Sat 9am–5pm. Take the Southwest Fwy. (Tex. 59 S.); before getting to the town of Richmond, exit FM Hwy. 762 and go 6 miles south.

**National Museum of Funeral History**   Do you give much thought to how you would like to be remembered once you've shuffled off this mortal coil? Or perhaps your thoughts just naturally drift toward things funereal? If so, then this private museum is the thing for you. Its owner, Service Corporation International, is the largest funeral company in the United States, and it has obviously taken pains to assemble the nation's largest collection of funeral memorabilia. The exhibits include a restored horse-drawn hearse, antique automobile hearses, and a 1916 Packard funeral bus. You can see memorabilia and trivia from the funerals of many famous people, including Martin Luther King, Jr., John Wayne, Elvis, Abraham Lincoln, JFK, Nixon, and many more. Other attractions include a full-size replica of King Tut's sarcophagus and exhibits on how other cultures remember the departed, including Day of the Dead celebrations in Mexico.

415 Barren Springs Dr. (north Houston, near airport). ⓒ **281/876-3063.** www.nmfh.org. Admission $10 adults, $9 seniors and veterans, $7 children 3–11, free for children 2 and under. Mon–Fri 10am–4pm; Sat 10am–5pm; Sun noon–4pm.

**SplashTown** ☺   Located in Spring, Texas, about 45 minutes from downtown Houston, SplashTown is a highly popular water park with a variety of fast and slow amusements and plenty of water slides. It holds special events and live entertainment throughout the season, which is generally from midspring to early fall.

21300 I-45 at Louetts Rd., Spring, TX. © **281/355-3300.** www.splashtownpark.com. $35 admission, $30 children under 48 in. Daily 11am–9pm during summer months. Hours vary; call or check website. Follow I-45 N. toward Dallas; take exit 69-A.

## Especially for Kids

Houston is kid-friendly. Easily half of the above-mentioned attractions are geared toward kids or have a large component especially suitable for them.

A tour of southeast Houston will take you to the **Orange Show,** with which young kids display an almost instinctual connection; the boat trip on the **Ship Channel;** a visit to the **Battleship *Texas;*** and the wonders of **Space Center Houston.** After that, there's a visit to the boardwalk in **Kemah** or a trip to the **beach** or to **Moody Gardens** in Galveston (see "Galveston" in chapter 7).

South of downtown, you have the Museum District, which includes the **Children's Museum,** the **Houston Museum of Natural Science,** and **the Health Museum.** And, of course, there's **Houston Zoological Gardens,** which has a special children's zoo that explores the different ecological zones of Texas. To the north is **SplashTown,** a water park, and to the southwest is the **George Ranch Historical Park** for kids interested in cowboys and the Old West.

## Organized Tours

If you'd like a bus tour of the city to help you get your bearings, you're out of luck. Companies such as Gray Line offer tours only to conventions and visiting groups, not the general public. There is, however, a different kind of tour that can introduce you to what makes Houston unique. If you're planning to be in Houston during the second weekend of the month, you might be able to sign up for one of the offbeat tours offered by **Eyeopener Tours.** Part of the Orange Show Foundation, in some months they put together a tour that focuses on a particularly interesting aspect of the city. Transportation by charter bus, snacks, and drinks are included in the price (usually around $70). Past tours have included folk-art sites of the city, places of worship, architectural highlights and lowlights, blues centers, and ethnic markets. Most of those who participate are resident Houstonians who want to learn about an unknown part of the city. Eyeopener Tours also sells an audiocassette and map for a self-guided tour of Houston's folk-art environments. This is helpful if you're pretty good at following directions and working with a map. For information, call © **713/926-6368** or check www.orangeshow.org/tours.

The other option is to hire a guide. You can find one through the Web page of Houston's **tour guide association** (www.ptgah.com). One of the founding members, Sandra Lord, operates a tour agency called **Discover Houston Tours** (© **713/222-9255;** www.discoverhoustontours.com). In addition to individual guide services, it hosts some regularly scheduled walking tours of downtown and other places, along with the occasional special-interest tour.

# SPORTS & OUTDOOR ACTIVITIES

## Outdoor Fun

**BIKING, JOGGING & WALKING**   By far the most popular jogging and walking track is in **Memorial Park.** This is a large and beautiful park clothed in pine trees along Buffalo Bayou west of downtown. It's easy to reach; take Memorial Drive, which follows the north bank of Buffalo Bayou, from downtown to the park. It can be very crowded. There is a lovely hike-and-bike trail along the banks of **Buffalo Bayou** from North Shepherd to downtown. It runs along both banks of the bayou for 1.5 miles, so you can run a 3-mile loop. It has lovely vistas of the downtown skyline and is decorated with numerous sculptures that can be both fun and interesting (and it takes you right into the Theater District). During the day it's fine, but I wouldn't advise venturing along the bayou at night. To rent a bike in this area, see **West End Bicycles** at 5427 Blossom St. (© **713/861-2271;** www.westendbikes.com). They can set you up and give you information about good rides.

A 10-mile hike-and-bike trail runs along the banks of **Brays Bayou** from Hermann Park through the Medical Center, where it goes under South Main Street and then heads southwest almost all the way to Beltway 8.

**GOLF**   Houston proper has public golf courses at most of the city's biggest parks, but with the exception of the Memorial Park Golf Course, the best public courses are outside the city. Probably the best public course (and one of the most difficult) in the area is the **Tournament Players Course at the Woodlands,** located 25 miles north of Houston in the Woodlands (© **281/364-6440**). Greens fees range from $95 to $125; tee times must be made at least 3 days in advance. One of the loveliest and best-regarded courses in the area is the **Longwood Golf Club,** 13300 Longwood Trace in Cypress (© **281/373-4100;** www.longwoodgc.com), at the northwest edge of Houston; to get there, take Tex. 290 (45 min. from downtown). Fees are $42 to $85 and include cart; tee times should be reserved 7 days in advance. Another course that a lot of people like is **Tour 18 Houston** (© **281/540-1818;** www.tour18golf.com), which copies 18 of the greatest holes in golf. The course is at 3102 FM 1960 East in Humble, about 12 miles north of Houston and about 35 minutes from downtown. Greens fees are $45 to $80; reservations can be made 30 days in advance.

In town are some municipal courses that are cheap, but it can be somewhat tricky to get tee times for them. The **Memorial Park Golf Course** (© **713/862-4033** or www.memorialparkgolf.com to reserve a tee time) is the most enjoyable. Greens fees are $28 to $55. **Hermann Park's golf course** (© **713/526-0077**) is centrally located, with greens fees ranging from $28 to $55. At both the Memorial Park and Hermann Park courses, there is an extra $15 fee for reservations made more than 3 days in advance.

**TENNIS**   Of course, the best strategy for getting in some tennis is to stay at a hotel with courts. **Memorial Park** has some of the best of the public courses; make reservations well in advance by calling © **713/867-0440.**

## Spectator Sports

If you're in Houston and decide on the spur of the moment to get tickets to a game, you can call **Ticket Stop,** 5925 Kirby Dr., Ste. D (© **713/526-8889**), a private ticket agency. They charge extra for the tickets, so it's best to buy direct or in advance if possible.

**BASEBALL**   **Houston Astros** fans enjoy the indoor/outdoor downtown stadium, Minute Maid Field. Its retractable roof is open mostly in the early part of the season before the weather gets too hot. With a little planning, tickets aren't hard to come by; call © **877/9-ASTROS** (927-8767) or visit www.astros.com.

**BASKETBALL**   The **Houston Rockets** (www.nba.com/rockets) play at the Toyota Center. It's downtown at 1510 Polk St., just south of the convention center and baseball park. The Rockets are a popular team, and tickets must be purchased well in advance. You can do so online or by calling © 866/446-8849.

**FOOTBALL**   The **Houston Texans** play host to opponents at high-tech Reliant Stadium. It's located off South Main, not far from the Medical Center. For information and/or tickets, call © 832/667-2390, or check out www.houstontexans.com.

**GOLF TOURNAMENTS**   The **Shell Houston Open** is held in late March or early April. For information and tickets, call © 281/454-7000 or go to www.shell houstonopen.com.

**RODEO**   Houstonians go all-out "Western" for a couple of weeks in early March, when the **Houston Livestock Show and Rodeo** is held. Billed as the largest of all rodeos, it includes the usual events such as bull riding and calf roping, as well as performances by famous country artists. It is now held in Reliant Stadium. Call © 832/667-1000, or go to www.hlsr.com for more information. For tickets, call **Ticketmaster** at © 713/629-3700.

**SOCCER**   The **Houston Dynamo** competes in America's MLS league. They play home games at Robertson Stadium on the University of Houston campus, but the team has completed an agreement with the city to build a new stadium downtown. This wouldn't be ready until the 2013 season. For more information or to buy tickets, call © 713/276-7500, or go to www.houstondynamo.com.

# SHOPPING

If you're anywhere in Houston, you probably aren't far from a mall, and there are many more than can be mentioned here. They're usually located at or near an intersection of a freeway with the Loop or Beltway 8 or other major artery. These are good for general shopping, but hold little of interest for most visitors. A different story is the outlet malls, the principal one being **Katy Mills** out at the far western boundary of Houston, in the town of Katy. Take the Katy Freeway (I-10 W.) until you spot the signs; the drive is about 25 miles. This mall is a mammoth collection of about 200 factory outlet stores with a large selection of merchandise at discount prices. The size of the discounts varies; some are good deals. There are also restaurants and a large movie theater.

## Great Shopping Areas

Whether you're a purposeful shopper or a last-minute accidental one, you'll need to know something about the shopping terrain of Houston. Of course, the main shopping area in Houston is Galleria/Uptown, but other areas have a diversity of stores that might be just what you're looking for.

### DOWNTOWN

**Foley's,** the oldest of Houston's department stores, is now a **Macy's.** The original store on Main Street at Lamar, a five-story building that occupies an entire block, is still a popular shopping destination (© 713/405-7035). It carries several lines of expensive clothing and perfumes as well as some moderately priced ones. The other happy shopping ground downtown is the **Shops at Houston Center,** 1200 McKinney St., across from the Four Seasons (© 713/759-1442; www.shopsathc.com). It's a group of about 40 small stores, mostly boutiques and specialty shops.

## EAST END

Just the other side of the freeway from the George Brown Convention Center is a commercial **Chinatown,** where you can find all kinds of goods imported from across Asia. Furniture, foods, curios—you can browse your way through a number of little import stores, all within a 4-block area, between Dowling on the east, Chartreuse on the west, Rusk on the north, and Dallas on the south.

## MONTROSE/THE HEIGHTS

Along Westheimer from Woodhead to Mandell, you'll find several antiques and junk shops that are perfect for the leisurely shopper who's out to find a diamond in the rough. If after browsing through these, you haven't had your fill, a grouping of similar stores can be found on 19th Street in the Heights. In these dozen or so stores, merchandise is set down just about anywhere the owners can find a place for it, and dusting is a once-in-a-while practice. This is for bargain hunters. Don't ever accept the first price you're offered at these places—they almost always will lower the price. (For the more discriminating antiques stores, go to the Kirby District.)

Among the antiques stores on 19th Street, a Latin American folk-art shop called **Casa Ramírez,** 241 W. 19th St. (© 713/880-2420), displays a panoramic collection of Mexican folk art from across the country. And in another part of the Heights is a store selling clothing and housewares designed by local artists: **Hello-Lucky,** 1025 Studewood St. (© 713/864-3556).

Also along Westheimer are some vintage clothing stores. North of Westheimer, on West Gray where it intersects with Shepherd, is the **River Oaks Shopping Center,** which is Houston's oldest shopping center. It's 2 blocks long and extends down both sides of West Gray in white-and-black Art Deco style. It's a chic collection of galleries, boutiques, antiques shops, and specialty stores, as well as some fine restaurants and an art cinema.

## KIRBY DISTRICT

Kirby is more uniformly upscale than the Montrose. Where it begins by Westheimer, there are a couple of strip malls, the largest of which is **Highland Village,** 4000 Westheimer (© 713/850-3100). Highland Village, like so much of the retail business in this part of town, is aimed at the upper-middle-class shopper with such stores as Williams-Sonoma and Pottery Barn and a few one-of-a-kind boutiques. From this part of Kirby Drive to where it passes the Rice Village is a section known informally as Gallery Row, with a mix of galleries, designer showrooms, and shops of antiques and special furnishings. Finally, the **Village** is a 16-block neighborhood of small shops mixed with outlets from high-dollar national retailers. A few of the small shops are survivors from simpler times and they're now a bit at odds in the environment of day spas, expensive shoe stores, and famous designer boutiques. There is also a wide variety of restaurants in the Village when it's time to take a break from browsing.

## UPTOWN

The **Galleria,** 5075 Westheimer Rd. (© 713/622-0663), occupies a long stretch of land along Westheimer and Post Oak. It has 320 stores that include big department stores such as Saks Fifth Avenue, Lord & Taylor, Neiman Marcus, and Nordstrom, and small designer retailers such as Gucci, Emporio Armani, and Dolce & Gabbana. Across Westheimer from the Galleria is another shopping center called **Centre at Post Oak.** If you're looking for the finest in Western wear, go to **Pinto Ranch,** 1717 Post Oak Blvd. (© 713/333-7900; www.pintoranch.com). This store sells high-end Western clothing, boots, belt buckles, hats, and saddles.

## SOUTHWEST

In southwest Houston just beyond the Loop is where the Asian bazaar meets American suburb. This fascinating area is simultaneously adventure shopping and an exploration into the brave new world of postmodern America. First, drive down **Harwin Drive** between Fondren and Gessner. You will see stores and strip malls selling jewelry, designer clothes, sunglasses, perfumes, furniture, luggage, and handbags. Most stores are run by Indian, Pakistani, Chinese, and Thai shopkeepers, but other cultures are represented, too. Occasionally one will get raided for selling designer knockoffs. Everything is said to be at bargain-basement rates, but buyer beware. What I like the best are the import stores where you never know what you'll find. Farther out, on **Bellaire Boulevard** in the middle of a large commercial Chinatown, is an all-Chinese mall, where you can get just about anything Chinese, including tapes and CDs, books, food and cooking items, of course, and wonderful knickknacks.

# HOUSTON AFTER DARK
## The Performing Arts

For fans of the performing arts, Houston is fertile ground. Few cities in the country can equal it for the quality of its resident orchestra, opera, ballet, and theater companies. In addition, there are several organizations that bring talented artists and companies here from around the country and the world, presenting everything from Broadway shows to Argentine tango groups to string quartets. Tickets aren't usually discounted for the opera, ballet, or symphony, but you should ask anyway. For information about performances, visit **www.houston-guide.com** or the websites of the various organizations listed below.

The symphony, the ballet, the opera, and the Alley Theatre (the city's largest and oldest theater company) all hold their performances in the theater district downtown. The opera and the ballet share the **Wortham Center,** 500 Texas Ave. (© **713/237-1439**); the symphony plays a block away at **Jones Hall,** 615 Louisiana St. (© **713/227-3974**); and the **Alley Theatre** is one of those rare companies that actually owns its own theater, located at 615 Texas Ave. (© **713/228-8421**), adjacent to the symphony. Also in the theater district is **Hobby Center for the Performing Arts,** 800 Bagby St. (© **713/315-2400**), which is shared by the Society for Performing Arts and Theater Under the Stars.

The **Society for the Performing Arts (SPA),** 615 Louisiana St. (box office © **713/227-4772;** www.spahouston.org), is a nonprofit organization that brings to Houston distinguished dance companies, jazz bands, theater productions, and soloists. Within SPA, there's a program called the Broadway Series, which brings popular productions from Broadway and London's West End for performances in Jones Hall, the Wortham Center, and the Hobby Center.

Following are brief descriptions of the principal organizations; there are many more, especially independent theater companies that present several plays a year.

## CLASSICAL MUSIC, OPERA & BALLET

The **Houston Symphony** (© 713/224-7575; www.houstonsymphony.org) is the city's oldest performing arts organization. Its season is from September to May, during which it holds about 100 concerts in Jones Hall. The classical series usually contains a number of newer compositions with visits by several guest conductors and soloists from around the world. There is also a pops series and a chamber music series, which often holds its performances at Rice University.

**Da Camera of Houston** (© 713/524-5050; www.dacamera.com) brings classical and jazz chamber music orchestras to the city and holds concerts either at the Wortham or in the lobby of the Menil Collection. You can buy tickets from the box office at 1427 Branard St. in the Montrose area.

The nationally acclaimed **Houston Grand Opera** is the fifth-largest opera company in the United States. Known for being innovative and premiering new operas such as *Nixon in China,* its productions of classical works are brilliant visual affairs. The opera season is from October to May. For tickets and information, go to the Wortham Center box office at 550 Prairie St. during regular business hours, or buy online at www.houstongrandopera.org.

The **Houston Ballet** (© 713/227-2787; www.houstonballet.org) has garnered enormous critical acclaim from across the country. A lot of the credit belongs to director Ben Stevenson, who came to Houston more than 25 years ago under the condition that the company create its own school of dance. Called the Houston Ballet Academy, it now supplies the company with 90% of its dancers, and other graduates dance in many top ballet companies. The company tours a great deal, but manages around 80 performances a year at the Wortham Center in Houston. You can buy tickets over the phone or at their website.

## THEATER

The **Alley Theatre,** 615 Texas Ave. (© 713/228-8421; www.alleytheatre.org), has won many awards for its productions. It has a large theater and an arena theater, and during the year the company uses both to stage about 10 different productions, ranging from Shakespeare to Stoppard and even a musical or two. Ask about half-price tickets sold on the day of the show for weekday and Sunday performances. You can also take advantage of pay-what-you-can days, but you must show up in person to buy the tickets. Box office hours are Monday through Saturday from 10am to 6:30pm and Sunday from noon to 6:30pm.

**Theatre Under the Stars,** 800 Bagby St. (© 713/558-8887; www.tuts.org), specializes in musicals that it either brings to town or produces itself, averaging 200 performances annually. The organization got its name from having first worked at Miller Outdoor Theater in Hermann Park. It uses the Hobby Center for the Performing Arts.

The **Ensemble Theatre,** 3335 Main St. (© 713/520-0055; www.ensemble houston.com), is the city's largest black theater company. Founded in 1976, the Ensemble has grown from a band of strolling players into a resident professional company of 40 actors and eight directors. Their specialty is African-American and experimental theater.

## The Club & Music Scene

Having a night on the town in Houston doesn't require a lot of planning, but pick up a copy of the *Houston Press,* the free weekly that you can find at many restaurants and shops. It provides a good rundown of the musical and comedy acts in town, and it includes a lot of advertising from the clubs. There's also the daily paper, the *Chronicle,* which has a well-organized entertainment section, and a pullout published on Thursdays. If you want to know what's going on in the clubs before you get to Houston, try their websites, **www.houstonpress.com** and **www.chron.com**.

In general, the most popular locations for nightspots are downtown, around the theater district and Old Market Square; and in the Montrose area, along Westheimer, and along Washington streets. There are a lot of clubs in these places and you can move around quickly until you find something you like.

## MEGACLUBS

In the theater district in downtown Houston, a developer has converted the old convention center into a complex of restaurants, clubs, bars, and a concert hall. It's called **Bayou Place** (© 713/227-0957) and is located at 500 Texas Ave. It houses the **Verizon Wireless Theater,** which usually has live rock or jazz acts or comedy (© 713/230-1666; www.verizonwirelesstheatre.com); the **Hard Rock Cafe** (© 713/227-1392), with some live acts on the weekends; and **Slick Willie's** (© 713/225-1277), a billiards club. Also, there are a few video and dance bars with canned music that are very popular with a younger crowd.

Also downtown is the **House of Blues** (© 888/402-5837) at 1207 Caroline St. This is one of several clubs belonging to a national chain. Its size, and the fact that it is also a booking agency, enables it to bring in many name acts, as well as some hot up-and-coming ones. The name is a bit misleading. It works with bands that play every genre of popular music, and shows no preference for any particular style, including the blues. The Houston venue has two restaurants and three stages of varying size. To see who's performing, go to the website www.hob.com.

## ROCK

One of the best venues for catching live rock acts is the old Houston institution known as **Fitzgerald's,** 2706 White Oak Dr. (© 713/862-3838). It occupies an old Polish dance hall near the Heights neighborhood and gets talented local and touring bands. Look for their advertisement in the *Houston Press* to see who's playing while you're in town and to check ticket prices.

One of the most popular clubs for live rock acts in Houston is the **Continental Club** at 3700 Main St. (at Alabama St.) (© 713/529-9899). It's an offshoot of the famous Austin club and gets many of the same touring acts. Inside the club, you'll find a funky bar area with lots of old rock concert posters. The crowd can include folks of just about any age, depending on who's playing. For the calendar, go to www.continentalclub.com/houston.html.

## JAZZ

To hear some jazz, your best bet is one of two club/restaurants downtown that are fairly similar and close by each other. If you're not wild about the band at one, you can walk over to the other. The more formal and expensive place is in the old Rice Hotel and is called **Sambuca Jazz Café,** 909 Texas Ave. (© 713/224-5299). It gets a dressed-up crowd and lines up some talented bands. The **Red Cat Jazz Café** is at 924 Congress St. (© 713/226-7870), 3 blocks away. I heard a great band here playing interesting arrangements of bebop standards. Both cafes require a drink minimum depending on the night of the week and which band is playing.

## BLUES

Try the **Big Easy Social and Pleasure Club,** 5731 Kirby Dr. (© 713/523-9999), in the Rice Village. This club lines up a lot of local blues talent that is uncommonly good, as well as touring zydeco acts. The clientele is a real mix of everything from yuppies to bikers. Admission can be anywhere between $5 and $15, depending upon the act.

## FOLK & ACOUSTIC

A folk and bluegrass institution in Houston is **McGonigel's Mucky Duck** (© 713/528-5999). It serves pub grub and burgers, wine and beer, and live music every night (except Sun, when it's closed). Wednesday Irish jam sessions are free, as are Mondays. The club is at 2425 Norfolk St., near Kirby Drive where it intersects the Southwest Freeway.

**Anderson Fair,** 2007 Grant St. (© **832/212-4057**), is a survivor from the 1960s, and looks every bit the product of its age. In its many years, it has nurtured several folk artists who went on to become big names in folk, including Nanci Griffith. It's open only on Fridays and Saturdays. People of all ages hang out here, though there are a lot of former hippies. It's located a block off Montrose, behind the Montrose Art Supply building.

## COUNTRY & WESTERN

**Blanco's** (© **713/439-0072**) is a Texas-style honky-tonk that packs 'em in Mondays through Fridays, attracting all sorts, from River Oaks types to tool pushers. Lots of good Texas bands like to play here, so it's a good opportunity to see a well-known band in a small venue. There's a midsize dance floor. Monday through Wednesday is open-mic night, usually with one or another local band. Thursday and Friday have live music, and the club is closed on Saturdays for private parties. It's located at 3406 W. Alabama St., between Kirby Drive and Buffalo Speedway. When there's live music, the cover ranges from $5 to $15.

## The Bar Scene

**La Carafe,** 813 Congress St. (© **713/229-9399**), has been around for ages, and the small two-story brick building it occupies, even longer. In fact, it is the oldest commercial building in the city and sits slightly askew on a tiny lot facing Old Market Square. Its jukebox is something of a relic, too, with the most eclectic mix possible and some obscure choices. The clientele consists of mostly older downtowners who were here before the resurgence, as well as office types, in-line skaters, and reporters from the *Chronicle*. For sheer character, no place can beat it.

Another bar with a unique flavor is **Marfreless,** 2006 Peden St. (© **713/528-0083**). This is the darkest bar I've ever been in. The background music is always classical, and the ambience is understated. Little alcoves here and there are considered romantic. The only trouble is finding the bar itself. It's in the River Oaks Shopping Center on West Gray. If you stand facing the River Oaks Theater, walk left and then make a right into the parking lot. Look for an unmarked door under a metal stairway.

## Gay & Lesbian Nightlife

Most of Houston's gay nightlife centers on the Montrose area, where you'll find more than a dozen gay bars and clubs, mostly along lower Westheimer Road and Pacific Street. For current news, pick up a copy of *Houston Voice*.

For a large and popular dance club, go to **Rich's,** 2401 San Jacinto St. (© **713/759-9606**), in the downtown area. Rich's gets a mixed crowd that's mostly gay men and women. It's noted for its lights and decorations and a large dance floor with a mezzanine level. It's very popular on Saturdays. For something more low key, try **EJ's,** 2517 Ralph St. (© **713/527-9071**), in the Montrose area. It's just north of the 2500 block of Westheimer. Gay men of all ages come for drinks and perhaps a game of pool. There's also a dance floor, and a small stage for the occasional drag show.

# SIDE TRIPS TO EAST TEXAS

## Piney Woods & Big Thicket National Preserve

From **Beaumont** (from Houston, take I-10 E. toward New Orleans, and you'll arrive in Beaumont in 1½ hr.), if you drive north on Tex. 69, you'll immediately enter the forestland known in Texas as the **Piney Woods.** This is a lovely part of the state that stretches all the way north to Arkansas. Tex. 69 runs through the heart of it and is one of the most enjoyable drives in the state, especially in the fall or the early spring, which are my favorite times for visiting east Texas. Several of the attractions described below can be reached by this road. The first of these is the **Big Thicket National Preserve.** The information station for the preserve (© **409/246-2337;** www.nps.gov/bith) is 30 miles from Beaumont, 8 miles past the town of Kountze. It will be on the right, just off the highway at the intersection of Hwy. 69 and Farm Road 420. The station is open daily from 9am to 5pm, except for Christmas and New Year's Day.

The Big Thicket is a lowland forest that occupies a region of swamps, bayous, and creeks. It's dotted with the occasional meadow, but for the most part grows so dense as to become impassable. In earlier times, it extended over 3 million acres and was an impenetrable and hostile place for early settlers. Stories abound of people getting lost in these woods and of outlaws using the place for their hideouts. With lumbering, oil exploration, roads, and settlement, the Big Thicket has been reduced to a tenth of its original size. Of what's left, almost 100,000 acres have been preserved by acts of Congress. The preserved area is not one large expanse of land, but 12 separate units, most of which follow the courses of rivers, creeks, and bayous.

The most remarkable thing about the Big Thicket is its diversity of life: The land is checkered with different ecological niches that bring together species coexisting nowhere else. It has been called the American Ark. Hickory trees and bluebirds from the Eastern forests dwell close by cactuses and roadrunners from the American Southwest, and southern cypress trees and alligators from the Southern coastal marshes. The variety is astonishing. Of the five species of North American insect-eating plants, four live inside the Big Thicket.

For the visitor, the area provides opportunities for hiking, canoeing, and primitive camping. Some of the units are closed during hunting season (mid-Sept to mid-Jan) and some might be closed by flooding. You can get maps and detailed information about the hiking trails, free permits for primitive camping, and books about this fascinating area at the information station. The trails here range from .5 to 20 miles. Although leaving the designated hiking trails is permitted, you must be careful not to get lost; trailblazing in this dense brush can be slow going and painful. Canoeing in some ways has an advantage over hiking, though it limits your travel to waterways with easy access for dropping off and picking up the canoes. At the station, you can get information about canoe outfitters who operate from the towns of Kountze and Silsbee, mostly just from late spring to early fall. For lodging and food, you'll have to rely on the establishments in one of the nearby towns; there are no such facilities in the preserve. If you're in Kountze during lunchtime on any weekday, the most interesting place to eat is at the county courthouse, where most of the locals show up.

## National Forests

North and west of the Big Thicket, the ecological complexity gives way to pine forest habitat. Inside this large belt of pine forest are four national forests that provide opportunities for hiking, camping, boating, and fishing. These areas are a nice

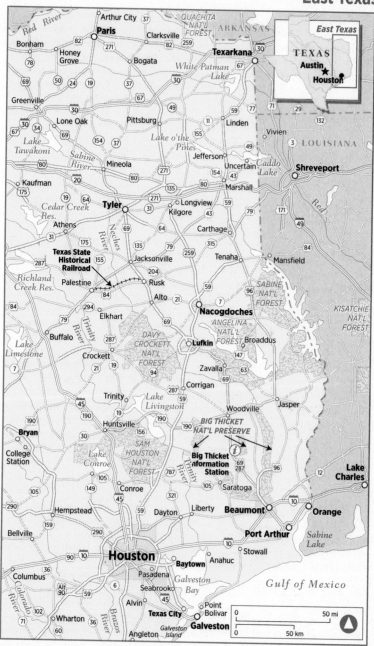

# race relations IN EAST TEXAS

Travelers to east Texas might well wonder about visiting here. In past years, there have been several news stories about racially motivated hate crimes. These stories provoke—but leave unanswered—questions like "Will visitors feel safe here? Will they feel welcome?" And because the news coverage focuses on the crime first and the community second, it can invoke in the reader's mind the prevailing image of the old Southern town—closed, repressive, and ready to explode, where outsiders are viewed as either meddlers or provocateurs. This isn't the case, but one can't deny that racial prejudice exists in east Texas, that there are groups of the Klan here, and that hate crimes have occurred. Given these facts, you might be surprised by what I say next—that race relations in east Texas, as they play out day to day, are far from seething; rather, they are actually open, respectful, and even cordial. I've spent time in these places and I've looked into this issue. The Klansmen may be out there, but they are isolated and marginalized. Their rallies are usually better attended by the press than by their own members. In short, civil society in east Texas is not broken and divided.

A case in point is the town of Jasper (pop. 9,000), where James Byrd, an African-American man, was brutally murdered by three whites in 1998. I was there some years ago on an assignment to interview people from all sectors of society. I went expecting to find a polarized community, but what I heard and saw convinced me that Jasper was no powder keg. Roughly half of the town's population is black, and blacks occupy several of the most powerful positions in

the community, including the office of mayor. Their personal safety was a non-issue for them. Yes, some people were thought to be prejudiced, but they didn't consider these people dangerous, even though one of the killers did, in fact, come from the community. The black and white communities in Jasper do tend to congregate among themselves, but they also interact and share a sense of community.

In other east Texas towns, I've encountered a greater or lesser degree of separation, but always with an easy interaction. The exception to this is the all-white town of Vidor (pop. 11,000), which lies about 10 miles east of Beaumont. Vidor is infamous as a stronghold of the Klan. It has been labeled by *Texas Monthly* magazine as the most hate-filled town in Texas. In 1994, the Department of Housing and Urban Development persuaded four black families to integrate Vidor's public housing, but after being harassed, snubbed, and threatened, these families chose to move.

Integration still hasn't made it to Vidor, but it has to the rest of east Texas. Its progress, to be sure, has been uneven. Vestiges of segregation remain, especially with housing: A recent study found Beaumont and Port Arthur to have the most segregated neighborhoods of any large city in Texas. Progress has been quicker in fields such as education, employment opportunities, and access to services. Nowadays racial discrimination has retreated to more subtle manifestations (the same sort of thing you'll find elsewhere) and the infrequent but chilling acts of a small throwback group filled with hate.

getaway, especially in the nonsummer months when the weather is more agreeable. They are much less visited than national parks and forests elsewhere. You can easily get to them from either Beaumont or Houston. Hwy. 69 leads directly into **Angelina National Forest**, about 50 miles north of Kountze. And the **Sam Houston**

**National Forest** is only 55 miles north of Houston (take I-45). The other two are **Davy Crockett National Forest,** north of Sam Houston National Forest, and the **Sabine National Forest,** east of Angelina National Forest, on the Louisiana border. Each of these forests is roughly 150,000 acres, and each has more or less the same activities: hiking, camping, boating, and fishing, with such facilities as boat ramps, camping grounds, and hiking trails. For canoeing, there are a few interesting places in these forests, but they're mostly large expanses of open water and not as fun as what you'll find in the Big Thicket or Caddo Lake (described below).

When the weather is agreeable, the forests are lovely places for hiking, especially in Sam Houston National Forest or Davy Crockett, which have the majority of trails. One hiking trail in Sam Houston is 126 miles long and crosses private property in three or four places; this is a real standout for Texas, which despite its image isn't such a wide-open state. Landowners here are firm believers in barbed-wire fences and the rights of private property, but this trail makes use of the goodwill of local landowners. Fishing draws many visitors, and a lot of places rent boats and equipment and can sell a temporary fishing license ($20) in the towns that lie in or next to these national forests. Your best bets for fishing are the Angelina or Sabine forests.

For general information about a specific national forest, visit **www.southern region.fs.fed.us/texas** or call one of the following numbers. The **Sam Houston National Forest** ranger offices are in the town of New Waverly (© **936/344-6205**); **Davy Crockett National Forest** ranger offices are in Crockett (© **936/655-2299**); **Angelina National Forest** ranger offices are in Zavalla (© **936/897-1068**); and the **Sabine National Forest** ranger offices are in Hemphill (© **409/787-3870**).

## Caddo Lake & Jefferson

**Caddo Lake** and the town of **Jefferson** (pop. 2,600) share a curious history. The former owes its origin, and the latter its glory days, to an immense, naturally occurring logjam on the Red River, which was known as the "Great Raft." This logjam existed for centuries and stretched from 80 to 150 miles along the river, raising the water level upstream enough to form Caddo Lake and to make Big Cypress Bayou navigable by steamboat as far as Jefferson. The town became the biggest river port in Texas and the sixth-largest city. In fact, commerce was so good in Jefferson during the mid–19th century that, of the Texas ports, only Galveston shipped more tonnage. But this prosperity came to an abrupt end when the Army Corps of Engineers dynamited the raft in 1873, shrinking the lake and isolating the town. The lake is back, owing to an earthen dam built by the Corps in 1914.

The town is back, too, but now its livelihood depends in large part on B&Bs and antiques stores. The return of good times to Jefferson dates from about 1961, with the restoration of the old Excelsior Hotel (now called Excelsior House) by the town's garden club. This sparked a restoration frenzy that has made Jefferson the best-restored town in east Texas. The entire central part of town is listed in the National Register of Historic Places, with a number of antebellum houses (several turned into B&Bs), churches, and commercial buildings listed. It is a pleasant place to visit and stroll about. Weekends are when the town is most lively, with several tours offered; weekdays are when you get the best lodging rates. One of the best attractions is robber baron Jay Gould's personal railroad car, the **Atalanta** ($2 guided tour). It is in great condition, has a fascinating history, and gives the visitor a wonderful idea of luxury travel in the late–19th century.

# TEXAS STATE railroad

After passing through the Angelina National Forest, Hwy. 69 continues through Lufkin before reaching the town of Rusk, a drive of about 60 miles. Here, you can ride an old steam locomotive train 25 miles through pine forest to the town of Palestine and back again. Many railroad enthusiasts consider this to be one of the best steam train rides in the country. Passengers travel in vintage railway cars, in either first class (which has air-conditioning in summer only) or coach class. The train runs on a limited schedule (usually weekends) from March to May and August, and Thursday to Sunday from June to July. The round-trip journey through pine forest takes 4 hours and costs $37 adults and $19 children ages 3 to 11 for general seating, and $40 adults and $21 children for an air-conditioned car seat. These rates are for the diesel train. Rates for the steam train run $4 higher. For general information and reservations, check out the website www.texasstaterr.com, or call ☎ **903/683-2561** or 888/987-2461.

Jefferson provides better lodging than what you'll find at Caddo Lake, and when in Jefferson, the place to stay is the **Excelsior House** (☎ **903/665-2513;** www.the excelsiorhouse.com) at 211 W. Austin St. It has been in continuous operation, more or less, since 1850. The 15 rooms are all furnished with antiques, many here before the hotel was purchased by the garden club. Guests are invited to take a fun little tour of the hotel (nonguests $4). Room rates run from $119 to $149. You can also stay at one of the many B&Bs in town. For a list of these as well as information on tours, contact the **Marion County Chamber of Commerce** at ☎ **888/GO-RELAX** (467-3529) or 903/665-2672, or visit www.jefferson-texas.com. There are several dining options, including **Matt's,** 109 N. Polk St. (☎ **903/665-9237**), a Tex-Mex joint, and the **Bakery Restaurant,** 201 W. Austin St. (☎ **903/665-2253**), for home cooking, both of which I recommend.

Jefferson is situated between two lakes. To the west is Lake o' the Pines, which is good for swimming and general recreation, but the real point of interest is Caddo Lake, some 10 miles to the east. It is a large lake of 26,800 acres, half of which is in Louisiana; the more interesting half is in Texas, where the lake breaks up into smaller channels removed from most of the boat traffic. The small town of **Uncertain** (pop. 300) is on the western shore of the lake. Here you can take a tour and find lodging. Near Uncertain is **Caddo Lake State Park** (☎ **903/679-3351**). Like several state parks, it has cabins for rent, which are popular and must be reserved well in advance by calling the central reservation number at ☎ **512/389-8900.** It also has campsites, which you can reserve by calling the park.

Caddo Lake is for boating or canoeing, not swimming. Instead of being an open expanse of water, it's more like a watery forest broken up into several smaller areas. Cypress trees draped in Spanish moss crowd the lake's broken shore, their roots rising from the murky water in deformed shapes. The lake also harbors abundant wildlife, including alligators, otters, water snakes, and many types of waterfowl.

For a tour, you have several options. You can get a seat on an old-fashioned steamboat that runs from spring to fall. **Caddo Lake Steamboat Co.** (☎ **877/894-4678**) offers a 1-hour trip along the main water channels, which costs $15 per person. It's fun, especially for kids, but for a closer look at the lake and its wildlife, try a tour on a pontoon boat (1½ hr.) that takes you beyond the main channel of the lake; contact **Caddo Grocery** in Uncertain (© **903/789-3495**). For a still closer look, contact **Mystique Tours** (© **903/679-3690**), run by David J. Applebaum, a highly recommended guide. The tour takes 2 to 3 hours on a 14-foot pontoon boat. Your final option is to rent a canoe and paddle into the quiet parts of the lake. These areas have few motorboats because they're too shallow and have too many roots below the surface. A couple of places to explore are Carter's Lake and Clinton Lake. Talk to the state park rangers, who can point out canoe routes on a map, and also put you in touch with the concessionaire.

# THE TEXAS GULF COAST

by David Baird

**7**

The Texas coast stretches for more than 350 miles between Louisiana and Mexico. It's predominantly flat and sandy, with large bays and skinny barrier islands tripling the amount of shoreline. The sand varies in color from white to light brown, and the water is warm and calm and usually a dull green. It can be cloudy on some days and quite clear on others, especially the farther south you go.

Though the natural features along this coast are fairly uniform, there is one notable difference: rainfall. The eastern and central parts of Texas are much wetter than south Texas. Rivers, bayous, and creeks pour into estuaries and marshy wetlands, creating a fertile habitat that supports a broad range of wildlife. Along this coast are several national wildlife refuges, the most famous being the one at Aransas, which is the winter home of the endangered whooping crane. South of Corpus Christi, the land is arid, which makes the water clearer, especially on the protected side of the barrier islands. South Padre Island has more sand dunes than the barrier islands to the north, and water on its sheltered side is extrasalty because evaporation removes water faster than it is added.

There are plenty of activities for visitors on the Texas Gulf Coast, including all manner of watersports. Birding and eco-tourism are also major draws. Thanks to its short and mild winters, the Gulf Coast attracts a lot of "winter Texans," retired residents of the northern United States and Canada who spend at least part of the winter in the south Texas warmth.

The largest cities on this coast are Corpus Christi and Galveston. Both offer the visitor a choice of recreation, lodging, and dining options. Farther south, at the very tip of the state, is the town of South Padre Island, the best-known purely tourist resort in the state. This chapter covers everything from Galveston to South Padre Island, but not the bit of coast between Galveston and Port Arthur, at the Louisiana border (and believe me, nobody considers the Port Arthur coast for its recreational activities).

## GALVESTON

50 miles E of Houston

Galveston is a port city on a barrier island opposite the mainland coast from Houston. Its main attraction is the downtown historic district with its Victorian commercial buildings and houses. Parts of the town are

# The Texas Gulf Coast

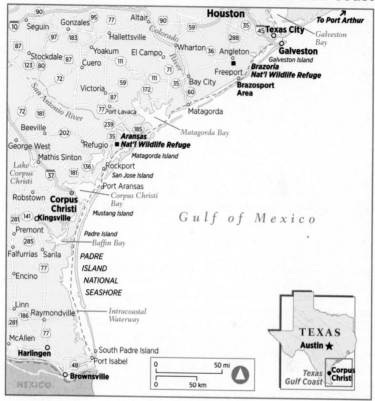

beautifully restored and ideal for just strolling around. The beaches are another attraction. They draw crowds of Houstonians and other Texans during the summer. The city is only an hour's drive from Houston and is a good destination for families; it's a quiet town with many points of interest, including Moody Gardens and the tall ship *Elissa*, and it's not far from NASA and Kemah. Galveston is not a boomtown like Houston. Its population of 60,000 remains fairly stable.

## Essentials

**GETTING THERE**  The nearest commercial airports are in Houston (see chapter 6). Take the Gulf Freeway (I-45 S.) from Houston. After crossing over to Galveston Island, the highway becomes a wide boulevard called Broadway.

**ORIENTATION**  Broadway, Galveston's main street, doesn't cut directly across the island to the seashore; instead, it slants eastward and arrives at the seashore on the east end of the island, in front of Stewart Beach. Streets crossing Broadway are numbered; those parallel to Broadway have letters or names.

The **East End Historic District** and the old **Strand District** are north of Broadway. The Historic District is the old silk-stocking neighborhood that runs from 9th to 19th streets between Broadway and Church Street. It has many lovely old houses.

# HURRICANE IKE & aftermath

To the casual observer, Galveston seems to have made a full recovery from Hurricane Ike, which hit on September 12, 2008. You can still find some boarded-up housing and a few business locales for lease, but by and large the city is back. In fact, the Strand, the grand old commercial part of town, has never been prettier. All the buildings have been restored, and most of the stores have returned or been replaced by new businesses. It's quite pleasant to walk down the streets past the old iron storefronts and admire their architecture.

A good number of the old oak trees that shaded the island were killed by the seawater, and many of the trunks of these dead trees were left in place and carved into sculptures. This profusion of new public art just might be the most visible evidence of Ike. (You can get a brochure from the visitor center with a map indicating where these new public sculptures are located.)

All the major museums are open again. The beaches look good. And for the visitor, Galveston is back and just as much fun as ever.

Three large mansions-turned-museums have regular tours (pending post-hurricane renovations; see "What to See & Do," below), and the city's historical preservation society holds tours of several private houses in May (inquire at the visitor center). The Strand District is the restored commercial district that runs between 19th and 25th streets between Church Street and the harbor piers. When cotton was king, Galveston was a booming port and commercial center, and the Strand was dubbed the "Wall Street of the Southwest." What you see now are three- and four-story buildings along 6 blocks of the Strand and along the side streets; many of these are Victorian ironfronts, so called because the facades included structural and decorative ironwork. This was a common building practice before the turn of the 20th century. Nowadays, the Strand is a shopping and dining area with a wide variety of stores.

**VISITOR INFORMATION** If you're planning a trip, check the **Galveston Convention & Visitors Bureau** website at www.galvestoncvb.com or call ✆ **888/GAL-ISLE** (425-4753). If you're in town already, visit their information center at 2328 Broadway, the carriage house of the Ashton Villa (✆ **409/763-4311**). It's open daily from 9am to 5pm.

**GETTING AROUND** Most of Galveston's hotels, motels, and restaurants are located along the sea wall from where Broadway meets the shore all the way west past 60th Street.

## What to See & Do

The beaches are the most popular attraction for Houstonians and other Texans who come for a day or a weekend. They are not quite as nice as those at more popular beach resorts; the sand is closer to brown than white and the water isn't transparent. But, on the other hand, they are pure sand without rocks, and the water has the nice, warm temperature of the Gulf of Mexico. **East Beach** and **Stewart Beach,** operated by the city, have pavilions with dressing rooms, showers, and restrooms, ideal for day-trippers. Stewart Beach is located at the end of Broadway, and East Beach is about a mile east of Stewart Beach. There's a $5-per-vehicle entrance fee. These beaches suffered less from Hurricane Ike than other beaches in the area. Beaches at

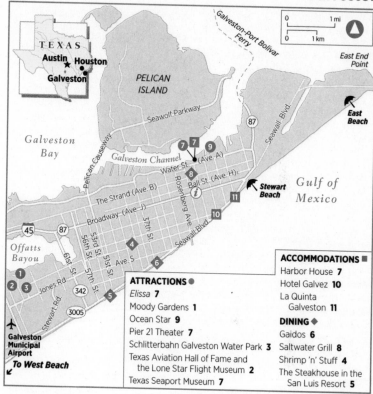

**ATTRACTIONS** ●

*Elissa* **7**
Moody Gardens **1**
Ocean Star **9**
Pier 21 Theater **7**
Schlitterbahn Galveston Water Park **3**
Texas Aviation Hall of Fame and
   the Lone Star Flight Museum **2**
Texas Seaport Museum **7**

**ACCOMMODATIONS** ■

Harbor House **7**
Hotel Galvez **10**
La Quinta
   Galveston **11**

**DINING** ◆

Gaidos **6**
Saltwater Grill **8**
Shrimp 'n' Stuff **4**
The Steakhouse in the
   San Luis Resort **5**

other parts of the island are free. Those along the western shore suffered extensive erosion but have been coming back.

Another activity popular with visitors and locals alike is to walk, skate, or ride a bike atop the sea wall, which extends 10 miles along the shoreline.

There are several tours in Galveston, but you should call for availability: **Galveston Harbour Tours** (© **409/763-1877**) is part of the Texas Seaport Museum, located on Pier 22. It offers four 1-hour tours per day, which depart from the same pier. These are entertaining tours, and you'll most likely see dolphins, drilling rigs, and massive cargo ships. The tour costs $10 for adults, $8 for children 3 to 14. **Duck Tours** (© **409/621-4771;** www.galvestonducks.com) offers its trademark amphibious bus tour. Tours start at the seawall and 25th Street. The scheduling is irregular, so call ahead for departure times. Tours cost $15 for adults and $10 for children.

On Broadway, a few massive 19th-century mansions are open for tours: **Ashton Villa,** 2328 Broadway (© **409/762-3933**); **Moody Mansion,** 2618 Broadway (© **409/762-7668**); and the **Bishop's Palace,** 1402 Broadway (© **409/762-2475**).

## MUSEUMS

Except for Moody Gardens and its neighbor, the Lone Star Flight Museum (see below), most of Galveston's museums are in and around the Strand, the old commercial center.

# THE great STORM

At the end of the 19th century, Galveston was a thriving port and a fast-growing city with a bright future. In fact, it was the largest city in Texas and had the third-busiest port in the country. Of course, being on the Gulf meant the risk of a hurricane, but the prevailing thought held that the shallow bottom on the western shore of the Gulf of Mexico would prevent the formation of large waves and blunt the force of any approaching storm. This assumption held sway even though a storm in 1886 completely wiped out the Texas port town of Indianola. But more evidence to the contrary came in the form of a massive storm that hit Galveston in September 1900.

It came ashore at night with a 20-foot surge that washed completely over the island. Houses were smashed into matchwood and their dwellers spilled out into the dark waters. By morning, more than 6,000 islanders—one out of every six—were drowned. The city's population dropped even further when many of the survivors moved elsewhere to rebuild their lives on safer shores. Those who remained went to work to prevent a recurrence of the disaster. Galveston erected a stout sea wall that now stretches out along 10 miles of shoreline with several jetties of large granite blocks projecting out into the sea. It also filled in land under the entire city, raising it 17 feet in some places and jacking up all the surviving houses to the new level. Despite all the effort, Galveston would never regain its momentum. The memory of "the storm" proved too compelling for many of Galveston's merchants, who preferred the safety of an inland port and provided impetus for the dredging of the Houston Ship Channel, which was completed in 1914. Houston then became a boomtown, taking Galveston's place as the commercial center for the area.

**Pier 21 Theater** (☎ 409/763-8808) shows a short documentary about the 1900 storm that devastated the town, and another about a one-time Galveston resident, the pirate Jean Laffite. Tickets are $4 or $5, depending on the show. On the same pier is the **Texas Seaport Museum** (☎ 409/763-1877; www.tsm-elissa.org) and the *Elissa,* a restored tall ship. Admission for both is $8 for adults, $5 for children 6 to 18, and free for children 5 and under. The museum also offers a boat tour of the harbor (see above).

Next door, at Pier 19, is a one-of-a-kind museum about offshore drilling rigs. You already may have noticed in the harbor the massive rigs that are often parked on the opposite shore. These rigs are tremendous feats of engineering and are some of the largest free-standing constructions ever built. They are often in the Port of Galveston being reconditioned. Most visitors have never seen one up close, but here you have an opportunity to scamper around on one: the **Ocean Star** (☎ 409/766-STAR [7827]; www.oceanstaroec.com), which is an old rig that's been converted into a museum. Through a short film, scale models, actual drilling equipment, and interactive displays, every aspect of the drilling process is explored, including the many rather daunting engineering challenges. The film, the exhibits, and the rig itself will be fascinating to those with a grasp of technical and engineering issues. Others might find this boring, but anyone will appreciate the broader aspects and the sheer size of these constructions. Admission is $8 for adults, $5 for seniors and students 7 to 18, and free for kids 6 and under. Hours for this and the other museums around the Strand are roughly the same, daily from 10am to 4pm (until 5pm in summer).

**Moody Gardens** ☺    Moody Gardens, an education/entertainment museum, is easily recognizable for its three large glass pyramids. It suffered relatively little damage from Ike. The first pyramid built was the rainforest pyramid, which holds trees, plants, birds, fish, and butterflies from several different rainforest habitats. A stroll through the building will fascinate anyone who has never been in a rainforest environment. The unusual species of Amazonian fish, birds, and butterflies are not often seen in zoos. The aquarium pyramid displays life from four of the world's oceans: penguins from Antarctica, harbor seals from the northern Pacific, and reef dwellers from the Caribbean and South Pacific. There is also a petting aquarium for those who feel compelled to touch the little darlings. The discovery pyramid displays space exploration, but doesn't come close to the nearby Space Center Houston. Also of note are the two IMAX theaters: One is 3-D and the other is a Ridefilm. On top of all this, there is a pool and white-sand beach for children and parents and an old paddle-wheel boat that journeys out into the bay. Allow 5 hours to cover the major attractions at Moody Gardens, or 2 hours for only the rainforest habitat. A large hotel and spa are also on the grounds.

Just down the road at 2002 Terminal Dr. is the **Texas Aviation Hall of Fame and the Lone Star Flight Museum** (✆ **409/740-7106;** www.lsfm.org). It has two hangars filled with aircraft in varying states of reconstruction. Many of its planes are from World War II, and for a good sum of money, the folks here will take you up in one of their classic planes. Admission to the museum is $8 for adults, and $5 for seniors and kids 5 to 17. Allow 1½ hours for a visit.

1 Hope Blvd. ✆ **800/582-4673.** www.moodygardens.org. Admission prices for individual exhibits and IMAX vary depending on the season. Full-day pass for all exhibits and theaters $40 (sometimes cheaper off season). Summer daily 10am–9pm; rest of year Sun–Thurs 10am–6pm, Fri–Sat 10am–8pm.

**Schlitterbahn Galveston Water Park ★ ☺**    This addition to Galveston's attractions comes from the central Texas town of New Braunfels, where, for the past 25 years, the Schlitterbahn water amusement park has pioneered different water rides and has been voted best water park by the Travel Channel. It has now established sister parks here in Galveston and in South Padre Island, the two biggest family destinations on the coast. This one is close by Moody Gardens. It has a wealth of tube chutes, wave tanks, and other rides. And, unlike the other two parks, this one has a large section that can be enclosed and heated for the winter season, keeping the park open throughout December.

2026 Lockheed Dr. ✆ **409/770-9283.** www.schlitterbahn.com. Summer rates $38 adults (12 and older), $32 children 3–11 and seniors. Daily 10am–8pm in summer (closes earlier fall and winter).

## FESTIVALS

The three most popular festivals on the island are **Mardi Gras** (Feb or Mar), the **American Institute of Architects (AIA) Sandcastle Competition** (June), and **Dickens on the Strand** (first weekend in Dec). For Mardi Gras, book a hotel room well in advance; it is a tremendously popular celebration with parades, masked balls, and a live-entertainment district around the Strand. Mardi Gras here has some advantages over New Orleans—there are fewer tourists, and it's very lively without all the public displays of drunkenness. For info, call ✆ 888/425-4753 or visit www.mardigrasgalveston.com.

The most unusual event is the annual **AIA Sandcastle Competition.** Workers from more than 70 architectural and engineering firms around the state show up on East Beach and get serious about the building of sand castles and sand sculptures, taking this pastime to new heights, literally. It all happens in 1 day, and the results are phenomenal. Call ✆ **713/520-0155** or check www.aiasandcastle.com for more information.

For its Christmas celebration, Galveston hosts Dickens on the Strand, a street party for which revelers dress up in Victorian costumes. The entire affair is a testament to just how much we associate traditional Christmas with the Victorian era (perhaps largely due to Dickens himself). The Strand—with its Victorian architecture and the association with its namesake—is a natural venue for such a celebration. The party includes performers, street vendors, readings of Dickens, and music. Admission is $10 in advance or $12 the day of the event for adults; $4 in advance for children ages 7 to 12, or $6 same day; and free for children 6 and under. Those dressed in full Victorian costume are admitted free. Though Houstonians often come down for it, I'm not convinced it's worth the trip, but rather something you might enjoy if you're already in the area. Call ✆ **409/765-7834** for more information.

## Where to Stay

All the economical hotel/motel chains have properties in Galveston, with higher prices for lodgings along the sea wall. Of the big chains, **La Quinta Galveston,** 1402 Seawall Blvd. (✆ **800/531-5900**), ranks highly. Galveston also has eight B&Bs, most of which are in Victorian-era houses. You can make inquiries through the association website: www.galvestonbedandbreakfast.com.

**Harbor House ★ 🏨**   A very different kind of hotel for Galveston, the Harbor House is built on a pier and overlooks the harbor instead of a beach. This hotel has an excellent location, near the Strand District and next to a few restaurants and museums that have taken over the neighboring piers. The architecture and exterior design are different as well. The newly restored, nautical-style guest rooms and one-bedroom suites are large and well appointed in a contemporary style without a lot of clutter. Bleached wood floors, Berber carpets, and exposed wood and steel super-structure give it a feel unlike other hotels. There are nine marina slips should you come with your boat. All rooms come with a fridge and microwave. Guests here can enjoy the amenities of the nearby sister property on the Strand, the Tremont House.

No. 28, Pier 21, Galveston, TX 77550. ✆ **800/874-3721** or 409/763-3321. Fax 409/765-6421. www.harborhousepier21.com. 42 units. $89–$170 double; $189–$270 suite. Rates include continental breakfast. AE, DC, DISC, MC, V. Parking $10. **Amenities:** Room service. *In room:* A/C, TV, fridge, hair dryer, MP3 docking station, Wi-Fi (free).

**Hotel Galvez ★★**   This is the original grand hotel in Galveston, which is celebrating its 100-year anniversary in 2011. All the common areas retain the feel of an old resort hotel, including the landscaped approach and grand, airy lobby. If you enjoy this sort of ambience and are looking for a place to relax, the Galvez is an excellent choice. The hotel has recently installed a full-service spa to make a stay here even more luxurious. The guest rooms are spacious and have been entirely renovated since the hurricane in 2008. They have all the comforts, but don't share the feel of the rest of the hotel. The hotel fronts the seawall in the central part of town, which, at the time of its construction, was the outskirts. This is no longer the case, and the best beaches are not within walking distance. However, it is only a short drive to these beaches or to the historic part of Galveston.

2024 Seawall Blvd., Galveston, TX 77550. ✆ **800/WYNDHAM** (996-3426) or 409/765-7721. Fax 409/765-5780. www.wyndham.com. 231 units. $129–$245 double; from $349 1-bedroom suite; from $449 2-bedroom suite. Extra person $20. Special packages available. AE, DC, DISC, MC, V. Valet parking

$12; free self-parking. **Amenities:** Restaurant; 2 bars; babysitting; bikes; exercise room; nearby golf course; Jacuzzi; large, heated outdoor pool; room service; sauna; spa. *In room:* A/C, TV, hair dryer, minibar, MP3 docking station, Wi-Fi (free).

## Where to Dine

People come to Galveston for seafood, and with all the variety, they won't be disappointed. There are local representatives of chain restaurants such as Landry's and Joe's Crab Shack, but for the best of Galveston's seafood, try one of the places listed below. If you're craving steak, the best in town is **the Steakhouse in the San Luis Resort,** 5222 Seawall Blvd. (© 409/744-1500).

**Gaidos** ★★ SEAFOOD   Owned and operated by the Gaido family for four generations, this restaurant is a Galveston tradition. The Gaidos have maintained quality by staying personally involved in all aspects of the restaurant—thus the seafood is fresh and the service attentive. The soups and side dishes are mostly traditional Southern and Gulf Coast recipes that are comfort food for the longtime customers. Main dishes are mainly seafood, but include a few chicken, pork, and beef items. The stuffed snapper is the best I've had. If pompano is on the menu, it's worth considering. Steaks and pork chops are high quality and well prepared. The menu varies seasonally. The large dining room is inviting, and a sizable bar area is a nice place to wait for a table.

3800 Seawall Blvd. © **409/762-9625.** Reservations accepted for large parties. Main courses $15–$33; complete dinners $19–$29. AE, DISC, MC, V. Daily 11:45am–10:30pm (closes 1–2 hr. earlier in low season).

**Saltwater Grill** ★★ SEAFOOD   This restaurant takes pains to serve the freshest seafood and prints up daily menus, which usually include original seafood pasta dishes, traditional entrees, and Pacific Fusion recipes. You might try the Gulf redfish pan-sautéed and topped with lump crabmeat, a fish dish with an Asian bent, or gumbo and/or bouillabaisse. A few nonseafood options are available as well. The preparation shows a light touch, and the starters are excellent. The asparagus spears are fried in a tempura-style batter so thin as to be translucent—and cooked perfectly. Situated in an old building near the Strand, the dining room is a pleasant mix of past and present, formal and informal.

2017 Post Office St. © **409/762-FISH** (3474). Reservations recommended. Main courses $14–$29. AE, MC, V. Mon–Fri 11am–2pm and 5–10pm; Sat 5–11pm.

**Shrimp 'n' Stuff** 🍤 SEAFOOD   This small, unassuming restaurant where you order at the counter is thought by many locals to serve the best seafood for the money. The seafood is mostly fried Southern style and served with hush puppies. I love the fried fish and the oysters most of all. Especially popular are the oyster and the shrimp po' boys, the fried shrimp, and the seafood platter.

3901 Ave. O. © **409/763-2805.** Reservations not accepted. Main courses $8–$14. AE, DC, MC, V. Sun–Thurs 10:30am–8pm; Fri–Sat 10:30am–9pm.

# BRAZOSPORT

65 miles SE of Galveston; 50 miles S of Houston; 185 miles NW of Corpus Christi

There's no town or city called Brazosport; rather, it describes southern Brazoria County and its communities. These towns, which have a combined population of about 90,000, include Clute, Freeport, Surfside Beach, Lake Jackson, Angleton, Quintana Beach, and Brazoria. They are directly south of Houston, about a 1½-hour drive from downtown. This is where the Brazos River flows into the Gulf. The area is a contrasting mix of elements. The towns that aren't on the beach have a pleasant small-town atmosphere. In the fishing towns, you'll find shrimp and fishing boats docked by the water. The beach towns (like Surfside) are vacation communities with lots of beach houses owned by Houstonians. In other parts, giant petrochemical plants dominate the landscape (an especially large Dow Chemical plant lies btw. Surfside and Freeport). But the coast also has large areas of protected wetlands and a rich variety of bird species—the annual Christmas bird count in Freeport often reports more species of birds seen in a single day than at any other location in the United States.

## Essentials

**GETTING THERE**   The nearest commercial airports are in Houston (see chapter 6). From Houston, take Tex. 288 south about 45 miles to Angleton, the Brazoria County seat. Lake Jackson is another 10 miles south on Tex. 288, and Bus. 288 leads from Angleton to Clute (10 miles south). Texas highways 332 and 288 intersect in Lake Jackson, heading southeast around it and Clute, and then divide, 332 continuing southeast to Surfside Beach and 288 heading south to Freeport and Quintana. Brazoria is just west of Lake Jackson on Tex. 332.

**GETTING AROUND**   The only practical way to explore this area is by car; the attractions are all within a 45-minute drive. Traffic and parking are seldom an issue. The major roads are Texas highways 288, 332, 35, and 36. Tex. 288/332 wraps around the west and south sides of Lake Jackson and Clute, where many motels are located.

**VISITOR INFORMATION**   Although most of the towns in the Brazosport area have their own chambers of commerce, and some have visitor centers, you can get areawide information from the **Clute Visitors Bureau,** 1014-B Lazy Lane, Clute, TX 77531 (© **888/GO-CLUTE** [462-5883] or 979/265-2508; www.goclute.com); and the **Brazosport Convention & Visitors Council,** 300 Abner Jackson Pkwy., Lake Jackson, TX 77566 (© **888/477-2505** or 979/285-2501; www.visitbrazosport.com). Both organizations operate visitor centers.

**FAST FACTS**   The **Brazosport Regional Health System,** 100 Medical Dr. (just off Tex. 288), Lake Jackson (© **979/297-4411**), has a 24-hour emergency room. **Clute's post office,** located at 530 E. Main St., is open Monday through Friday from 8:30am to 4:30pm, Saturday from 10am to noon. The **Lake Jackson post office,** 210 Oak Dr. S., is open Monday through Friday from 8:30am to 5pm, Saturday from 10am to 2pm.

## What to See & Do
### THE TOP ATTRACTIONS

**Brazoria County Historical Museum**   This museum, located in the 1897 Brazoria County Courthouse, will be of most interest to those curious about Texas history. A major part of the museum is dedicated to the first Anglo colony established in Texas, under the supervision of Stephen F. Austin. In the 1820s, he brought 297 families into the area by way of the Brazos River and established the colony's center upstream. These original settlers became known as "the old 300." The large exhibit, which contains 68 panels, replicas of the era's weapons and tools, and a variety of artifacts and documents, is located in the historic courtroom on the second floor (access for visitors with disabilities is available). Most of the rest of the museum is

# BIRDING along THE TEXAS COAST

The coastal plains of Texas are a haven for birds. The area is rich in resident species and is the winter home to many more. It has a variety of habitats—freshwater and saltwater marshes, tidal zones, prairies, and woodlands—and abundant food sources. It's also smack in the middle of the great flyway for birds migrating from the northern parts of the U.S. and Canada to Central and South America. On their southward journey, this is the last chance for R & R before they fly over the Gulf of Mexico, and on the return, it's their first landfall.

For these reasons, the Texas Gulf Coast attracts lots of birders and sponsors several birding events. Throughout the regions noted in this chapter, there are plenty of birding opportunities, even when none is specifically mentioned. The best times to visit are during the migration seasons and in winter. Most of the annual events are held in the Brazosport and Corpus Christi areas. Here are

a few highlights: The towns of Lake Jackson and Rockport hold festivals for viewing hummingbirds (lots of them) when they fly through here in September. Also in late September or early October, local birders in Corpus Christi hold the annual hawk count at Hazel Bazemore County Park, where tens of thousands of raptors of various species fly through here following the Nueces River. In April, Brazosport holds its annual Migration Celebration, when local birders serve as guides on birding walks. For specific information, contact local visitor centers listed in this chapter. The state publishes three helpful maps called **"The Great Texas Coastal Birding Trail,"** one for each section of the Texas coast. These list 300 viewing sites and give driving directions and descriptions for each. Call (C) **888/900-2577** or check out the maps at the following website: www.tpwd.state.tx.us/huntwild/wild/wildlife_trails/coastal.

devoted to changing exhibits that include historic subjects such as the courthouses of Texas and the Civil War's impact on the area. Allow at least 1 hour for a visit.

100 E. Cedar St., just off Bus. 288, Angleton. (C) **979/864-1208.** www.bchm.org. Free admission (donations welcome). Mon–Fri 9am–5pm; Sat 9am–3pm. Closed major holidays.

**The Center for the Arts & Sciences ★ ii** This facility includes a fine natural history museum, a small planetarium, an attractive art gallery, two theaters for a variety of performing arts events, and a nature trail. You'll need at least 2 hours to see it. The **Museum of Natural Science** has a collection of more than 14,000 seashells, and is credited with instigating the movement to make the lightning whelk the official state shell of Texas. Also in its 12,000-square-foot floor space are exhibits on archaeology, fossils, dinosaurs, rocks, and minerals (including a fluorescent mineral room), and a collection of jade and ivory carvings. The **planetarium** has a 30-foot dome and lots of high-tech projection equipment to produce a variety of night-sky experiences. A .75-mile self-guided **nature trail** meanders through bottomland along Oyster Creek adjacent to the center. The center's **art gallery** presents nine exhibits each year, ranging from local artists to national shows.

400 College Blvd., Clute. (C) **979/265-7831.** www.bcfas.org. Free admission to the museum, art gallery, and nature trail; planetarium $4 adults, $3 students. Museum and art gallery Tues–Sat 10am–4pm; Sun 2–5pm; closed major holidays. Planetarium shows Tues 7pm. Nature trail daily dawn–dusk. From the intersection of Tex. 332 and 288 in Lake Jackson, head east on Oyster Creek Dr., through Lake Jackson and into Clute; Oyster Creek Dr. becomes College Dr. after it crosses the railroad tracks in Clute. The center is just ahead on the left, adjoining the campus of Brazosport College.

**Sea Center Texas**   Sea Center Texas began through the concerted effort of several individual employees of Dow Chemical who formed the Coastal Conservation Association. Their goal was to bring back the redfish or red drum, whose numbers had fallen dramatically in the 1980s through a confluence of events: two particularly bad freezes, an increase in popularity with sports fishermen, and chef Paul Prudhomme's recipe for blackened redfish, which put the dish on restaurant menus all over the country. The employees persuaded Dow to allow them to create a hatchery using one of the ponds on its property. The effort, begun in 1996, was successful and has grown over the years to become an elaborate, high-tech hatchery that releases close to 15 million young fish every year, primarily red drum, but also speckled trout and flounder. You can visit the hatchery and see some beautiful aquariums as well, which represent many of the fish species and marine life found at different depths of the Gulf. A shallow touch pool contains blue crabs, hermit crabs, snails, urchins, and other marine creatures that can be handled, and just outside the visitor center is a 5-acre wetland with elevated boardwalks and signs discussing the numerous birds and other wildlife you might encounter. The facility is a joint project of Dow Chemical and Texas Parks and Wildlife. Allow 1 hour for a visit.

300 Medical Dr., Lake Jackson. ☏ **979/299-1808.** Free admission (donations welcome). Tues–Sat 9am–4pm; Sun 1–4pm. For hatchery tours, call ☏ 979/292-0100 for reservations. Closed major holidays. From Tex. 332/288, turn west onto Plantation Dr. to Medical Dr. and turn north (right), then follow the signs.

## OUTDOOR ACTIVITIES

Birding, fishing, and hanging out on the beach are the top outdoor pursuits here.

**BIRDING/WILDLIFE VIEWING**   The Brazosport area has three national wildlife refuges and many more publicly and privately held nature preserves. Of the national refuges, the most developed is the **Brazoria National Wildlife Refuge,** which covers 43,388 acres and was established to protect coastal wetlands for migratory birds and other wildlife. The Information Center, located near the entrance to the refuge, has interpretive panels, and a boardwalk outside the Information Center leads across wetlands, where you may spot an alligator. The boardwalk provides access to the .6-mile Big Slough Birding Trail. The refuge also has a 2-mile hiking and biking trail that follows an abandoned railway line and provides views across a terrain of prairie, where you might see more than a dozen species of sparrows, white-tailed hawks, and white-tailed kites. In addition, there's a 7-mile driving tour with access to several observation decks. The refuge, which also allows fishing and hunting, is open September through May daily from 8am to 4pm, and during the summer, it's open the same hours the first weekend of each month and intermittently during the week. Admission is free. To get to the refuge, take FM 523 north from Freeport or south from Angleton to C.R. 227, which you follow 1¾ miles northeast to the refuge entrance. For additional information, contact the refuge at ☏ **409/849-7771** or visit http://southwest.fws.gov.

In the community of Quintana Beach, the **Neotropical Bird Sanctuary** is located on Lamar Street across from the Quintana Beach Town Hall (☏ **979/233-0848**), where you can get a bird checklist and other information. This small, wooded preserve is open 24 hours a day with free admission. It's a hot spot for viewing migrant birds that follow the Brazos River to the coast.

**FISHING**   This area offers excellent fishing for grouper, ling, amberjack, and red snapper—the state record 36.1-pound red snapper was caught in 1995 off the Freeport coast. Anglers can choose from about a dozen charter fishing boats, most based in Freeport Harbor, such as **Underwater Expeditions,** 1010 S. 2nd St. (© **979/233-1811;** www.underwaterexpeditions.com), which takes 12-hour deep-sea fishing trips at $150 per adult on weekends, $125 weekdays. Longer trips and exclusive charters are available. There are numerous places for shore, beach, pier, and jetty fishing, including Quintana and Surfside beaches, and a number of public boat ramps—check with one of the visitor bureaus (see "Visitor Information," above) for locations.

**FUN ON THE BEACH**   The beaches here are far from pristine; they tend to be rocky, and the sand is more brown than white. Even so, it's still fun to dig your toes into the cool sand, walk along the shore, build a sand castle, watch the freighters and shorebirds, and look for seashells among the stones. Driving is permitted on most beaches here, except for the pedestrian-only beach at **Quintana Beach County Park,** 5th Street, in the community of Quintana (© **800/872-7578** or 979/233-1461; www.brazoria-county.com/parks/quintana). The park has a campground (see "Camping," below), good bird-watching, a playground, horseshoe pits, and a picnic area, and charges a $6 per vehicle day-use fee.

## Where to Stay

Among the national chain motels in the Brazosport area is **La Quinta Inn,** 1126 Tex. 332 W., Clute (© **800/531-5900** or 979/265-7461), with spacious, attractive rooms. Other reliable chains include the **Days Inn,** 805 Tex. 332 W., Clute (© **800/329-7466** or 979/265-3301); **Ramada Inn,** 925 Tex. 332, Lake Jackson (© **800/272-6232** or 979/297-1161); and **Super 8,** 915 Tex. 332, Lake Jackson (© **800/800-8000** or 979/297-3031). Also see the information on **Quintana Beach County Park** under "Camping," below. Tax adds about 13% to lodging bills unless otherwise noted.

**Roses & the River**   A Texas farmhouse–style B&B sitting on almost 3½ wooded acres is a relaxing place to stay. The Sam Bernard River flows by the back of the house, and along its banks, oak trees grow, draped in Spanish moss. The entryway is lined with rose bushes that bloom year-round, although they really burst out in October and November. There are plenty of places to sit and gaze at the river, including a long veranda, which stretches along the entire back of the house. The three guest rooms, all upstairs, are each named for a specific kind of rose and are cheerful and inviting. Each of the spacious rooms comes with a very large bathroom (one with a fantastic claw-foot spa tub), and one queen-size bed. Guest rooms have a few antiques, but furnishings are mostly contemporary. Two rooms have views of the river; the third overlooks the rose garden. The owners are rose cultivators. They are easygoing folks who make people feel very much at home. The full breakfasts are delicious—the B&B is a popular spot for group dinners and weddings, for the food as much as the setting.

2434 C.R. 506, Brazoria, TX 77422. © **800/610-1070** or 979/798-1070. Fax 979/798-1070. www.roses andtheriver.com. 3 units. $150 double (tax included). Rates include full breakfast. AE, DISC, MC, V. Children 11 and under not permitted. From Brazoria, go southwest on Tex. 521, cross the San Bernard River, and take the first right turn, onto C.R. 506. After about 1½ miles, lodging is on the right. *In room:* A/C, TV/DVD/VCR, hair dryer, no phone.

## CAMPING

**Quintana Beach County Park** (on 5th St., in Quintana; © **800/872-7578** or 979/233-1461) is practically on the water. The campsites are fairly close together, but it's a short walk to the beach. There are 56 sites (including 19 pull-through RV sites) and a small group of grassy "tent-only" sites. The campground has paved roads, showers, a self-serve laundry, an RV dump station, picnic tables, grills, a playground, and horseshoe pits. Boardwalks lead from the campground to the beach. Camping rates

## TEXAS'S most DESERTED BEACH

Heading down the coast toward Corpus Christi, you come to Matagorda Bay, one of the least developed areas of the coast, with lots of small fishing towns and farming communities. This region has its charm, and life here is really laid-back. Protecting the coast is Matagorda Island, a 38-mile-long strip of land covering almost 44,000 acres. It's mostly federal and state land set aside as a wildlife refuge. Aside from a small state park with camping areas and a historic lighthouse, there is little development. But there are plenty of beaches, pristine and deserted, on which you will not see motorized vehicles; they are prohibited. You can swim, hike, hunt for seashells, do some bird-watching (more than 300 species of birds have been spotted here, including the whooping crane), or comb the beaches. Fishing is also popular. Many locals fish in the surf here.

But if you decide to visit the island, you'll need to bring your own water and food, since they cannot be purchased there. Primitive campsites at the state park cost $8 per night (up to four

people). An outdoor cold-water rinse is available near the boat docks. The state used to operate a passenger ferry to the island from the town of Port O'Connor, but it was damaged in a fire and never repaired. The lack of a ferry makes the island even more remote. You can hire a boat to pick you up and drop you off from Port O'Connor for between $75 and $125. For more information, contact **Matagorda Island State Park and Wildlife Management Area** (✆ **979/244-6804;** www.tpwd.state.tx.us/park/matagisl/matagisl.htm).

Port O'Connor is a sleepy little town that serves as a weekend residence for city dwellers. Activities include fishing and kayaking. A good place to stay is the **Poco Loco Lodge,** 305 Adams St. (✆ **361/983-0300;** www.thepocoloco lodge.com). The owners can hook you up with a boat captain or a kayak outfitter. The six rooms are large, comfortable, and beautifully maintained. They come with full kitchens, snacks, and beer, and cost $99 to $119. There's a nice little beach a couple of blocks away.

from May to September are $19 for primitive tent sites and $25 to $27 for RV sites with full hookups. From October to April, rates are $20 for tent sites and $22 to $24 for full hookups. Day use costs $8 per vehicle. There are several cabins with sleeping areas, bathrooms, and kitchens (but no linens or kitchen utensils), which rent for $135 to $160 from May to September and $120 to $145 from October to April. From Tex. 36/288 in Freeport, turn right onto FM 1495, and after crossing the Intercoastal Waterway on a swing bridge, turn left onto Quintana Road, which becomes Lamar Street in Quintana. Turn right on 8th Street, then left on Burnett Street to 5th Street.

## Where to Dine

**Café Annice** ★ REGIONAL AMERICAN    This casual, modern restaurant has a decidedly uptown feel and is a favorite of local businesspeople. Lunch choices include a variety of sandwiches, such as the Caesar wrap—chicken breast, romaine lettuce, carrots, red onions, plum tomatoes, and a homemade Caesar spread, all wrapped in a roasted garlic and herb tortilla. Dinner entrees feature tempting selections of seafood, Angus beef, and chicken, including the excellent chicken Annice—breaded chicken topped with mushrooms, artichokes, tomatoes, and capers, sautéed with Marsala wine and served with grilled vegetable ragout and garlic mashed potatoes.

24 Circle Way, Lake Jackson. ✆ **979/292-0060.** Reservations accepted only for large parties. Main courses $8–$11 lunch, $10–$23 dinner. AE, DISC, MC, V. Mon–Fri 11am–2pm; Sat 11am–2:30pm; Mon–Thurs 5–9pm; Fri–Sat 5–10pm. Closed major holidays. From Tex. 332/288, turn northeast onto This Way; take the first left onto Circle Way and follow it around to downtown.

**Red Snapper Inn** SEAFOOD  The menu is primarily classic seafood such as shrimp sautéed with garlic and mushrooms, or grilled boneless flounder stuffed with crabmeat dressing. You'll also find some Greek touches such as baked shrimp with feta cheese and fresh tomatoes, and the sautéed filet of snapper in a sauce of pulverized onions, oregano, lemon juice, and olive oil. Also a good bet: the oysters *en brochette*, grilled bacon-wrapped oysters (not breaded) with meunière butter and served on rice pilaf. Nonseafood items include a charbroiled choice 14-ounce rib-eye steak, the very popular charbroiled Greek meatballs with spaghetti, and that Texas standard, chicken-fried steak with cream gravy.

402 Bluewater Hwy., Surfside Beach. ✆ **979/239-3226.** Reservations accepted only for large parties. Main courses $13–$19. No credit cards. Mon–Fri 11am–2pm and 5–9pm; Sat–Sun 11am–9pm. As you enter Surfside Beach on Tex. 332, you come to a traffic light; turn northeast (left) onto Bluewater Hwy. The restaurant will be on your right a few blocks down.

# CORPUS CHRISTI

207 miles SW of Houston; 377 miles S of Dallas; 143 miles S of San Antonio; 691 miles SE of El Paso

The bay area around Corpus Christi offers visitors the greatest variety of activities of any place along the Texas Gulf Coast. This and the following three sections (Rockport, Port Aransas, and Padre Island National Seashore) cover the major destinations in the bay area. These destinations are only about 45 minutes from one another at most, so you can hop around pretty easily. Whether you stay in Corpus Christi, Port Aransas, or Rockport, you'll find great lodging, good food, and lots to do.

Corpus Christi is a major deepwater seaport with a big, beautiful bay. It has fewer than 300,000 inhabitants, but it feels much less populated. The downtown is easy to enjoy, and probably the best place to stay when visiting. It's relatively calm because most of the locals live on the south side of the bay, along the S.P.I.D. freeway. That's where you'll find most of the traffic, too. The two biggest attractions are the State Aquarium and the USS *Lexington* aircraft carrier, which are next to each other on the bay just north of downtown, across Harbor Bridge. High season for Corpus Christi is from May to September. But the weather is so mild that most of the activities can still be enjoyed during the off season, when you can move around without the crowds.

## Essentials

### GETTING THERE

**BY PLANE**  The **Corpus Christi International Airport (CRP)** is located within the city limits on the south side of Tex. 44, west of Padre Island Drive/Tex. 358 (✆ **361/289-0171;** www.cctexas.com/airport). It's served by **American Eagle** (✆ **800/433-7300**); **Atlantic Southeast/Delta** (✆ **800/221-1212**); **Continental/Continental Express** (✆ **800/523-3273**); and **Southwest** (✆ **800/435-9792**). All the major car-rental agencies can be found here.

**BY CAR**  Tex. 35 follows the Gulf Coast—albeit slightly inland—from the Houston and Galveston area to Corpus Christi. From San Antonio, follow I-37 southeast to Corpus Christi. Before you see the town, you'll pass the city's oil refining complex.

## GETTING AROUND

Most visitors to Corpus Christi will use a car to get around. This is an easy city to navigate. Traffic isn't bad except during rush hour.

In the downtown area, highways I-37 and Tex. 286 (known as the Crosstown Expwy.) intersect. Connected to both is Corpus Christi's busiest freeway, known as South Padre Island Drive, or S.P.I.D., as it appears on signs. It does, in fact, lead to Padre Island. For a nice drive around the bay from the downtown area, take Ocean Drive, which skirts the south shore.

## VISITOR INFORMATION

Contact the **Corpus Christi Convention & Visitors Bureau,** 1201 N. Shoreline Blvd. (© **800/678-6232;** www.visitcorpuschristi.org). If you're already in Corpus, go to the visitor center located at 1823 N. Chaparral St. (© **800/766-2322**). It's open from 9am to 5pm Tuesday through Saturday for most of the year, but in the summer, its schedule changes and it's open Thursday to Tuesday.

**FAST FACTS** The **Corpus Christi Medical Center** (www.ccmedicalcenter. com) has three locations: Doctors Regional, 3315 S. Alameda St. (© **361/761-1400**); Bay Area, 7101 S. Padre Island Dr. (© **361/761-1200**); and the Heart Hospital, 7002 Williams Dr. (© **361/761-6800**). The main **post office,** 809 Nueces Bay Blvd., is open Monday through Friday from 8am to 5pm.

# What to See & Do

## THE TOP ATTRACTIONS

**Texas State Aquarium** ☺  Several tanks display a variety of ecosystems found in the Gulf of Mexico and coastal Texas, from coral reefs with sharks and barracuda swimming about, to jetty systems populated by crabs and flounders, to east Texas swamps and their alligators. Specialty tanks are dedicated to some of the most curious forms of sea life, such as octopuses, turtles, and sea horses. In the touch pools, you can touch a stingray or bamboo shark—if that's what you really want to do. A wonderful addition to the aquarium is "Dolphin Bay," a protected environment for Atlantic bottle-nosed dolphins that are unable to survive in the wild. Children enjoy the "Kids' Port Playground," and there's also a gift shop and food court. Allow 2 hours for a visit.

2710 N. Shoreline Blvd. © **800/477-4853** or 361/881-1200. www.texasstateaquarium.org. Admission $16 adults, $14 seniors 60 and older, $11 children 3–12, free for children 2 and under. Daily 9am–5pm; until 6pm Memorial Day to Labor Day. Closed Thanksgiving and Christmas.

**USS *Lexington* Museum on the Bay** ★★  This World War II–era aircraft carrier is a floating naval museum. During the war, the *Lexington* was in almost every major operation in the Pacific theater, and planes from its decks destroyed 372 enemy aircraft in flight and an additional 475 on the ground. It was dubbed "The Blue Ghost" because of the ship's blue-gray color, and because Japanese propaganda radio broadcaster Tokyo Rose repeatedly and mistakenly announced that the *Lexington* had been sunk. The *Lexington* was modernized in the 1950s and served in the U.S. 7th Fleet, including duty during the Vietnam War.

Tours of the "Lady Lex" are self-guided. A big-screen theater shows IMAX movies, and a video details the history of the ship with historic film footage. There are several exhibits, such as a Navy Seal submarine and interpretive displays of ship engines, plus a flight simulator that, for $4 per person, provides a wild 5-minute ride simulating the experience of flying. But a more concrete sense of what life was like on this

# Corpus Christi

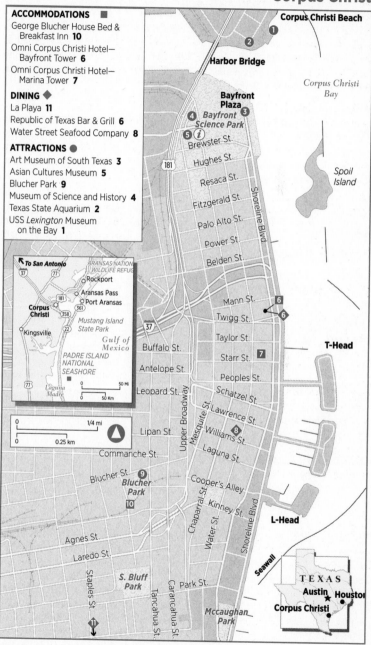

**ACCOMMODATIONS** ■

George Blucher House Bed & Breakfast Inn **10**

Omni Corpus Christi Hotel—Bayfront Tower **6**

Omni Corpus Christi Hotel—Marina Tower **7**

**DINING** ◆

La Playa **11**

Republic of Texas Bar & Grill **6**

Water Street Seafood Company **8**

**ATTRACTIONS** ●

Art Museum of South Texas **3**

Asian Cultures Museum **5**

Blucher Park **9**

Museum of Science and History **4**

Texas State Aquarium **2**

USS *Lexington* Museum on the Bay **1**

Corpus Christi Beach

Harbor Bridge

*Corpus Christi Bay*

Bayfront Plaza

*Bayfront Science Park*

Brewster St.

Hughes St.

Resaca St.

Fitzgerald St.

Palo Alto St.

Power St.

Belden St.

Shoreline Blvd

*Spoil Island*

To San Antonio

ARANSAS NATION[AL] WILDLIFE REFU[GE]

Rockport

Aransas Pass

Port Aransas

Corpus Christi

Kingsville

*Mustang Island State Park*

*Gulf of Mexico*

PADRE ISLAND NATIONAL SEASHORE

*Laguna Madre*

Mann St.

Twigg St.

Taylor St.

Starr St.

Peoples St.

Schatzel St.

Lawrence St.

Williams St.

Laguna St.

Buffalo St.

Antelope St.

Leopard St.

Lipan St.

Commanche St.

Upper Broadway

Mesquite St.

T-Head

Blucher St.

*Blucher Park*

Cooper's Alley

Kinney St.

Chaparral St.

Water St.

Shoreline Blvd

L-Head

Agnes St.

Laredo St.

*S. Bluff Park*

Park St.

Staples St.

Carancahua St.

Tancahua St.

*Mccaughan Park*

Seawall

**TEXAS**

Austin ★  Houston

Corpus Christi

0 — 1/4 mi
0 — 0.25 km

carrier is gained by boarding the actual ship, climbing up and down ladders between decks, seeing the ship's hospital and mess hall, and exploring its narrow passages. Not many museums can do this sort of thing. On the flight deck are more than a dozen aircraft from the 1930s to the 1960s, including an F-14A Tomcat and a Cobra helicopter. You can also get a close-up look at the ship's 40-millimeter anti-aircraft guns. The *Lexington* has a large gift shop and a snack bar. Allow at least 2 hours for a tour.

*Note:* Although some parts of the USS *Lexington* are easily accessible by anyone, seeing many of the best parts, such as the flight deck, bridge, and engine room, involves climbing a lot of steep, old metal stairs and ladders, stepping over metal barricades, and maneuvering through tight passageways. Those with mobility problems probably won't be able to get to everything.

2914 N. Shoreline Blvd., in Corpus Christi Bay. ℂ **800/523-9539** or 361/888-4873. www.usslexington. com. Admission $13 adults, $8 children 4–12, $11 seniors 60 and older and active military. Free admission to the Hangar Deck for those with disabilities. Daily 9am–5pm; until 6pm Memorial Day to Labor Day.

## OTHER ATTRACTIONS

Just north of downtown is the city's striking convention center. Nearby are several small to medium-size museums, including the **Art Museum of South Texas,** the **Asian Cultures Museum,** and the **Museum of Science and History.** Before going to any of them, first step into the Corpus Christi visitor center to see if any coupons are available. Visiting these museums is a nice way to spend a rainy afternoon. I like the Museum of Science and History best of all. For the 500th anniversary of Columbus's first voyage to the New World, Spain built three replicas of ships he used, the *Nina,* the *Pinta,* and the *Santa Maria,* and sailed them to the Americas; somehow the Museum of Science and History acquired these replicas. You can even get on board one of them, and the experience gives you a new estimation of Columbus's daring and courage.

Adding to Corpus Christi's small-town amusements is a minor-league baseball team in the Texas league called the **Corpus Christi Hooks** (ℂ **361/561-4665;** www. cchooks.com). Home games are played at Whataburger Field, which is a delightful ballpark at the water's edge, near the foot of the Harbor Bridge. (Whataburger is a successful chain of burger joints with restaurants all across the South and Southwest. It began in Corpus Christi in 1950. During your stay here, you'll see lots of these restaurants with their trademark orange-and-white roofs.)

## OUTDOOR ACTIVITIES

Watersports, birding, and fishing are the most popular activities. Certain parts of this area lend themselves to different kinds of watersports. Birding is good throughout; it just depends on the species for which you're looking. Here is a rundown of activities and where best to enjoy them.

**FISHING/BOATING**   For deep-sea fishing, you might be better off going to Port Aransas, which is on Mustang Island facing the open water. You'll save fuel costs that way. For bay fishing, you can find guides and charter boats in Corpus Christi, Rockport, or Port Aransas. Shoreline fishing is popular in these parts, with numerous piers, jetties, and beaches, depending on your tastes. In Corpus Christi, a charter boat usually costs from $300 to $400 for a full-day trip for one or two people. For a good fishing guide, contact the visitor center, or check its website for certified guides. There are various cruises around the bay. **Captain Clark's Flagship** (ℂ **361/884-8306;** www.captclarksflagship.com) has a large boat that offers tours. It's moored at the marina in downtown Corpus Christi, on the People's Street T-Head (pier). If you prefer a smaller boat, look on the same T-Head for **Harrison's Landing** (© 361/881-8503; www.harrisonslanding.net). This company operates the *Japonica*, an open 50-foot boat, which is well suited for cruising the bay and used for a variety of tours.

**SAILING**    Corpus Christi has a wonderful bay for sailing and a lively sailing community. Every Wednesday evening, there's a friendly sailboat race that you can watch from the downtown marina. If you want to do some sailing, you have a few options: renting a boat (if you're a certified captain) or going sailing with a captain (where you would perform the role of crew), either by yourself or as part of a group. The outfit with the most flexibility is Harrison's Landing (see above). It has a sailing academy and regularly does introductory sailing cruises. Corpus Christi also has a nonprofit organization that works with people with disabilities who want to sail. **Corpus Christi Sail Away** (© 361/881-3325; www.ccsailaway.org) is located on the Coopers Alley L-Head, also at the downtown marina.

**SEA KAYAKING**    This sport can be combined with fishing or nature photography. Most of the interesting sites are near the Rockport/Fulton area—see the "Rockport" section, below—but you can rent kayaks in several places in Corpus Christi.

**WINDSURFING**    Corpus Christi's reputation for good breezes also draws a lot of windsurfers. Annual windsurfing regattas are held here. An ideal place to windsurf or take lessons is at Bird Basin in the Padre Island National Seashore, which is described later in this chapter.

**WHOOPING CRANE TOURS**    The world-famous whooping cranes inhabit the Aransas National Wildlife Preserve from mid-November to mid-April. The best place to buy a ticket for a tour boat is Rockport, which lies closest to the preserve. You can also rent kayaks there and paddle around the shore of the preserve, but under no circumstances are you allowed to set foot on land. For more info, see the "Rockport" section below.

## Where to Stay

Most of the chain motels are along S.P.I.D. south of downtown. I prefer staying downtown, either in the B&B mentioned below or around the marina. Both locations put you close to most of the visitor activities in Corpus Christi, as well as several dining spots. If you're on a budget, try the **Super 8 Motel-Bayfront,** 411 N. Shoreline Blvd. (© 361/884-4815). It's clean and well maintained. Rooms facing the water don't have a balcony, but share an open walkway. Prices range from $65 to $95 for a double, depending on the season and view. Another well-located economical choice is on the bay north of downtown, by the USS *Lexington* and the Radisson hotel: the **Sea Shell Inn,** 202 Kleberg Place (© 361/888-5291), with rates of $50 to $100 double. Room tax adds 15% to rates, and the highest rates in the Corpus Christi area are in summer.

**George Blucher House Bed & Breakfast Inn** ★★★    This wonderful B&B combines the ambience of an elegant historic home with modern amenities, including private bathrooms and plush robes. Built in 1904 for George and Alice Von Blucher, this 5,000-square-foot inn was purchased in 1999 by history buff Tracey Smith, who thoroughly researched the home's past before beginning restoration. After about a year of work, the B&B opened with six rooms, each named after one of the Blucher children. The ultra-feminine Pearl's Room is pink, with American and French antiques, a queen-size bed, and a private balcony with views of downtown; Nellie's Room is decorated in a floral motif, with American and French country furnishings and two twin beds. Most rooms are upstairs, but one ground-level unit, Jasper's Room, is wheelchair accessible.

The attention to detail that Ms. Smith showed in restoring the house also shows in her management of the B&B. The bed linens are first rate and coffee is readily available. Breakfasts here are a splendid event, and might include entrees such as chicken-pecan quiche, or eggs Benedict with artichokes, spinach, and cream cheese; and a fruit dish such as baked apple with maple syrup and pecans, all wrapped in a puff pastry. A library has a comfortable sitting area and chess, dominos, backgammon, and other games. In addition, the inn is across the street from **Blucher Park,** a prime bird-watching area. Ms. Smith is an informative and gracious innkeeper.

211 N. Carrizo St., Corpus Christi, TX 78401. © **866/884-4884** or 361/884-4884. Fax 361/884-4885. www.georgebluicherhouse.com. 6 units. $119–$189 double. Rates include full breakfast. Holiday and special event weekends minimum 2-night stay. AE, DISC, MC, V. Children 12 and under not permitted. *In room:* A/C, TV/VCR, fax, hair dryer, Wi-Fi (free).

**Omni Corpus Christi Hotel ★★**   This is the best choice in Corpus Christi for those seeking a full-service hotel. It consists of two towers, Bayfront and Marina. I prefer the 20-story Bayfront tower for its private balconies (the balconies of the Marina tower are not accessible). The guest rooms are comfortably furnished in a modern style, and standard rooms have two double beds or one king-size bed, large working desks, plush chairs, large closets, and several telephones. Floor-to-ceiling windows afford spectacular views of the Gulf, particularly from the upper floors. One of the three on-site restaurants is the highly rated **Republic of Texas Bar & Grill** (see below). Because this hotel gets a lot of weekday business travelers, you're likely to find good rates on weekends.

900 and 707 N. Shoreline Blvd., Corpus Christi, TX 78401. © **800/843-6664** or 361/887-1600. Fax 361/887-6715. www.omnihotels.com. 821 units. $129–$159 double; from $300 suite. AE, DC, DISC, MC, V. Valet parking $14; self-parking $9. Pets 25 lbs. and under accepted with $50 fee. **Amenities:** 3 restaurants; 2 bars; free airport transfers; bikes; children's programs; concierge; state-of-the-art health club and spa; indoor/outdoor heated pool; room service. *In room:* A/C, TV, hair dryer, Wi-Fi (free).

## CAMPING

RVers have plenty of camping choices in the Corpus Christi area, and although many of the RV parks will accept tents, the rates are often the same as for sites with RV hookups; those in tents will be surrounded by RVs. Visitors in tents should camp at nearby Padre Island National Seashore (see that section later in this chapter) or one of the other public parks in the area.

Among RV parks here, the best is **Colonia del Rey,** 1717 Waldron Rd., near the entrance to Padre Island (© **800/580-2435** for reservations, or 361/937-2435; www.campingfriend.com/coloniadelrey), which has a swimming pool, a Jacuzzi, and all the other usual amenities, and can accommodate rigs up to 85 feet long. Some sites have telephones, and rates are $28 to $37 for full hookups, including cable TV.

## Where to Dine

For a quick bite, you can try a burger from the chain that began here in Corpus Christi—**Whataburger.** At least you won't have trouble finding one here; they're everywhere, and they're generally open late. In addition to the places listed below, you might consider dining at **Tavern on the Bay** (© 361/881-8503) if the weather is nice. It's an outdoor restaurant on the water, located on the Peoples Street T-Head. It serves American food and is particularly known for its lobster bisque.

**La Playa** ★★ 🏠 TEX-MEX   Part of the enjoyment of hanging out in south Texas is the excellent Tex-Mex cuisine. This place has some great food and a menu large enough to meet everyone's tastes. The fajitas garner most of the attention here, but the restaurant's forte might be the enchiladas, of which there are several kinds. Especially good are the Tex-Mex ones with traditional chili gravy or the green enchiladas with a tangy sauce. Something that's different on the menu (and very popular) is the deep-fried stuffed avocado. Order it if you dare. For dessert, try the sopapillas or the flan. A second location is at 7118 S.P.I.D.

4201 S.P.I.D. ⓒ **361/980-3909.** Main courses $8–$16. AE, MC, V. Mon–Sat 11am–10pm; Sun 11am–9pm.

**Republic of Texas Bar & Grill** ★★★ 📷 STEAK/SEAFOOD   This is the spot to celebrate a special occasion. Located on the 20th floor of the Bayfront Tower at the Omni Corpus Christi Hotel, this restaurant is expensive and special. It has a terraced dining room, which, from every table, affords breathtaking views of the bay and city through extra-tall plate-glass windows. Appetizers include a giant portobello mushroom, stuffed with sweet sausage and garlic-herb cheese. This is primarily a steakhouse, and all beef is USDA Prime, hand-cut and grilled over a fire of oak and mesquite. The menu usually lists several game dishes, such as mesquite-grilled quail, and seafood. Sides include huge baked Idaho potatoes and garlic mashed potatoes, which are good, but the house specialty hash browns are exquisite. Service is excellent.

At the Omni Corpus Christi Hotel, 900 N. Shoreline Blvd. ⓒ **361/886-3515.** www.omnihotels.com/republic. Reservations recommended. Main courses $19–$50. AE, DISC, MC, V. Mon–Sat 5:30–10:30pm; Sun 5:30–9pm.

**Water Street Seafood Company** ★★ SEAFOOD   Great seafood and good prices are the reasons to come here or to the sister property in the same building—the Water Street Oyster Bar. Menus are the same in both places. The cooking combines Southern and Mexican influences, such as the Gulf crab cakes served with a spicy rémoulade-and-mango salsa. You can order several seafood standards (especially grilled and fried dishes), but you might want to try one of their originals, such as the pecan-crusted oysters (which are something special) or, if it's listed, the bacon-wrapped shrimp stuffed with crabmeat. Nonseafood dishes include salads, steaks, chicken, and soups (including a delicious Mexican-style chicken vegetable soup with large chunks of avocado). Service is friendly and helpful. I have a slight preference for the Water Street Oyster Bar, as it is smaller and less noisy, with somewhat better service.

309 N. Water St. ⓒ **361/882-8683.** Reservations not accepted. Main courses $12–$20. AE, DISC, MC, V. Sun–Thurs 11am–10pm; Fri–Sat 11am–11pm.

# ROCKPORT ★★

35 miles NE of Corpus Christi; 182 miles SW of Houston; 161 miles SE of San Antonio

Rockport and its sister town, Fulton, are on a neighboring bay north of Corpus Christi. The bay is sheltered by San Jose Island. The two towns have a combined population of 9,000. Rockport has more character than its neighbor and has become an art town, with resident artists, galleries, and the Rockport Art Center. The old downtown area is small and colorful, with shops, galleries, and restaurants. But Rockport isn't in danger of becoming a fancy place; it's comfortable and feels lived in. Old-style motel courts, still the most common lodging options here, are testaments to a time not so long ago, when Rockport was a summer retreat for Texans looking for a quiet, economical place to enjoy the water. That's changing. A modern subdivision

# WHOOPING CRANES: BACK FROM THE brink OF EXTINCTION

By and large, there are two kinds of tourists who come to the Rockport area in winter: winter Texans fleeing the harsh cold of their northern homes and nature enthusiasts who come to visit another sort of winter Texan, the magnificent whooping cranes. The largest birds in America, these cranes fly in from northwest Canada in October/November and leave again in the spring. An adult male stands 5 feet high and can have a wingspan of 8 feet. They are elegant, too: Elongated legs and throat give them dramatic lines, and the plumage has a classic appeal that never goes out of fashion—solid white with black wing tips, black eyeliner, and just a touch of red accent on the top of the head. It would be a tremendous blow to lose these creatures to oblivion, but that is almost what happened—and their comeback story is probably the most famous of all the cases of wildlife conservation.

Before the arrival of the Europeans, these birds inhabited the Gulf and Atlantic shores in winter and northern Midwest and Canada in summer. But hunting and loss of habitat dwindled the population until, by 1941, only 15 birds survived. All were members of the flock that winters here on the central Texas coast. A concerted effort requiring the contributions of many dedicated biologists and field workers was launched to save them. The team first pushed for laws preserving the summer and winter nesting grounds and all the major stopover points along the 2,400 miles of the migration route. The cranes were slow to come back, but through protection and public education, their mortality rates decreased and the population began to grow. This was difficult and took time because these cranes are slow to mature and don't reproduce until their fourth year. And even then, the female lays only two eggs and raises only one chick. Worried that, with only one flock, the species was vulnerable, biologists began stealing the second eggs and hatching them elsewhere. They have established a nonmigrating population in south-central Florida and another population that they've been "teaching" to migrate between Wisconsin and western Florida. So far it's working, but the Aransas flock is still the largest and only natural population of "whoopers" in the world, with more than 200 birds.

The best way to view the birds is from the deck of a boat. Several boats specialize in birding and whooping crane tours. They skirt along the coast of the refuge, which is the favorite feeding grounds for the cranes. A few are listed below.

marina community has developed between the two towns, and a Wal-Mart and a Holiday Inn Express have arrived.

This part of the coast is particularly lovely. Notable are the many windswept oak trees, a favorite subject for artists and emblematic of the area. Of course, water is everywhere. A large protected wetlands area to the north, the Aransas National Wildlife Refuge, is the winter home to the only natural colony of whooping cranes in the world. But this is only one of several natural areas in the region. Birding and fishing are two of the major draws. If a beach is what you're looking for, the best ones are out on the barrier islands described in the next two sections on Port Aransas and Padre Island National Seashore.

# Essentials

**GETTING THERE**   Rockport is 40 minutes from Corpus Christi. Take Tex. 35 over the Harbor Bridge toward Portland. Well after the Aransas Pass turnoff, take the exit labeled MARKET ST. (FM 1069). Both Rockport and Fulton are on Bus. 35, which continues north over the Copano Bay Causeway to the Aransas National Wildlife Refuge.

**VISITOR INFORMATION**   For maps or info, contact the **Rockport–Fulton Area Chamber of Commerce,** 404 Broadway, Rockport, TX 78382 (© **800/242-0071** or 361/729-6445; www.rockport-fulton.org). The office is open Monday to Friday from 9am to 5pm and Saturday from 9am to 2pm.

**FAST FACTS**   The nearest full-service hospital, with a 24-hour emergency room, is **North Bay Hospital,** 11 miles south of Rockport at 1711 W. Wheeler Ave., Aransas Pass (© 361/758-8585). The **post office,** located at 1550 FM 2165 in Rockport, is open Monday through Friday from 9am to 4:30pm, Saturday from 9am to noon.

## What to See & Do
### THE TOP ATTRACTION

This region is among the nation's premier bird-watching destinations, and the best spot for birding here is the **Aransas National Wildlife Refuge ★★** (© **361/286-3559;** http://southwest.fws.gov). More than 300 species of birds have been spotted here, but the whooping crane, which winters here from November to April, is the big draw.

In addition to birds, the refuge is home to about 30 species of snakes (only four are poisonous), turtles, lizards, and the refuge's largest reptile, the American alligator. Mammals commonly seen include white-tailed deer, javelina, wild boars, raccoons, eastern cottontail rabbits, and nine-banded armadillos. Also present, but only occasionally seen, are bobcats and opossums.

A 16-mile paved auto tour loop meanders through a variety of habitats, offering access to a 40-foot observation tower, a boardwalk that leads through a salt marsh to the coastline, and other viewing areas. The refuge has nine walking trails, ranging from .1 to 1.4 miles, a picnic area, and an impressive Wildlife Interpretive Center with information, exhibits, a bookstore, and administration offices. There are also seasons for hunting and saltwater fishing access. Camping is not permitted.

The refuge is located about 36 road miles northeast of Rockport via Tex. 35, FM 774, and FM 2040. It's open daily from just before sunrise to just after sunset; the Wildlife Interpretive Center is open daily from 8:30am to 4:30pm. Admission to the refuge costs $5 per vehicle ($3 if there's only one person). Binoculars are available to borrow at the Wildlife Interpretive Center. Insect repellent is recommended year-round.

### OUTDOOR ACTIVITIES

**FISHING**   There are public fishing piers in Fulton Harbor and at Rockport Beach Park, as well as numerous other areas. Fishing guides offer bay and deep-sea fishing trips, and rates vary considerably. Contact **Gold Spoon Charters** (© **361/727-9178;** www.goldspooncharters.com), **Green Hornet Fishing Guide Service** (© **361/749-5904**), and **Hook Line & Sinker** (© **866/993-3131** or 361/727-0910).

**KAYAKING**   All the different bays around Rockport are well sheltered by the barrier islands. In some places, the water gets quite shallow and is broken into narrow channels by mangroves. One such place is called Lighthouse Lakes. This is perfect territory for kayaking, which you can combine with birding, fishing, or nature photography. You can rent kayaks from **Rockport Adventures** (© 877/892-4737; www. rockportadventures.com). This outfit also has pick-up and drop-off services.

**PARKS**   Anglers and birders especially like **Goose Island State Park** (© 361/729-2858; www.tpwd.state.tx.us/park/goose), which is home to the Big Tree, a giant live oak with seemingly countless twisting branches, which is estimated to be more than 1,000 years old. It's more than 35 feet in circumference, 44 feet high, and has a crown spread of 90 feet. The park has a short paved hiking and biking path, two playgrounds, picnic tables and grills, a boat ramp, and a lighted fishing pier. Fish caught here include speckled trout, redfish, flounder, and sheepshead. Crabbing and oystering are also popular. There are 102 campsites with water and electrical hookups and 25 sites with water only, and the park also has restrooms with showers and an RV dump station. Entrance to the park costs $5 per person per day (free for children 12 and under), and camping costs an additional $10 to $15 per night, with reservations available (© 512/389-8900). The park is about 12 miles from Rockport. Follow Tex. 35 north 10 miles to Park Road 13, which you follow 2 miles east to the park entrance. There are several preserves and wildlife sanctuaries in and around the area, which make for good birding.

**WHOOPING CRANE TOURS/DOLPHIN TOURS**   From November to March, a number of companies offer 3- to 4-hour whooping crane and birding tours on shallow-draft boats. Most of these boats leave out of Fulton harbor, so you might want to go down and check them out for yourself and find one with a convenient departure time. Several boats do dolphin tours, as well, in summer when the whooping cranes have left. **Capt. Tommy Moore** (© 877/892-4737 or 361/727-0643; www.whoopingcranetours.com) is a good choice for a whooping crane tour. He has a good boat with an elevated observation deck, and he works regularly as a guide for serious birders. Check with the Rockport–Fulton Area Chamber of Commerce (see "Visitor Information," above) for information on land-based birding tours.

## INDOOR ATTRACTIONS

**Fulton Mansion ★**   Constructed between 1874 and 1877 by cattle baron George Fulton, this mansion is a local architectural landmark. The site is managed by the Texas Parks and Wildlife Department, which offers hourly tours (except at noon) from 9am to 3pm Wednesday to Saturday. Built in French Empire style, it was notable in its day for having indoor plumbing and other modern conveniences. The materials used are rich and varied, and the interiors are impressive.

316 S. Fulton Beach Rd. © **361/729-0386.** www.visitfultonmansion.com. Admission $6. By tour only. Call ahead to verify. Wed-Sat 10am-3pm; Sun. 1-3pm. Closed major holidays.

**Rockport Center for the Arts ★**   Part of the charm of Rockport is that its small downtown area is such an inviting place to hang about and relax, and this center is a good place to begin. The Main Gallery presents about 10 changing exhibits each year, ranging from local to international artists. There are often displays of students' work, and sometimes hands-on exhibits in the Garden Gallery. The Members Gallery presents an eclectic selection of works by members of the Rockport Art Association, which manages the center. The association sponsors the Rockport Art Festival each summer, in late June and/or early July, and also sponsors a series of art classes, workshops, and concerts (call for the current schedule).

902 Navigation Circle, Rockport. © **361/729-5519.** www.rockportartcenter.com. Free admission. Tues-Sat 10am-4pm; Sun 1-4pm.

**Texas Maritime Museum**   From pirates to shipbuilding to offshore oil drilling, this excellent small museum brings to life the story of the Texas Gulf Coast, with lots of hands-on exhibits, historic fishing gear, and strange-looking, old outboard motors. Among its changing and permanent exhibits, you'll see artwork, such as the *Lighthouses of Texas* watercolors by Harold Phenix, and a life-size ship's bridge where you can imagine yourself on the high seas. On the museum grounds is a survival capsule (used to escape offshore oil rigs in emergencies), a 26-foot-long lifeboat, and a replica of a scow sloop fishing boat. Allow at least 1 hour to visit.

1202 Navigation Circle, Rockport. ℂ **361/729-1271.** www.texasmaritimemuseum.org. Admission $6 adults, $5 seniors 60 and older, $3 children 6–12, free for children 5 and under. Tues–Sat 10am–4pm; Sun 1–4pm. Closed major holidays.

# Where to Stay

Among the national chain motels in the Rockport and Fulton areas are the **Best Western Inn by the Bay,** 3902 N. Tex. 35, Fulton (ℂ **800/235-6076** or 361/729-8351); **Days Inn,** 1212 E. Laurel St. (at Tex. 35), Rockport (ℂ **800/329-7466** or 361/729-6379); and **Holiday Inn Express,** 901 Hwy. 35 N., Rockport (ℂ **888/727-2566** or 361/727-0283).

**Crane House ★★★** 📷   This is truly an unforgettable, one-of-a-kind lodging. It consists of one attractive, comfortable bungalow with two bedrooms (one king bed and two twin beds), two bathrooms, a fully equipped kitchen, a living area, and a large screened porch with rocking chairs. But it could be a shack with bunk beds and an outhouse and still be special, because it offers those rare commodities of privacy, solitude, and natural beauty, all in abundance. It sits alone on 824 acres bordering the Aransas National Wildlife Refuge, with a mile of coastline on St. Charles Bay (use of kayak included). The owners are in partnership with the Texas Nature Conservancy to protect more than 200 acres of wetlands that are part of the property. As if that weren't enough, a pair of whooping cranes are daily visitors to the backyard, along with deer and various bird species, and to view or photograph them you have to go no farther than the porch. You must book well in advance. Crane House is located just across the Capano Causeway in Lamar.

911 S. Water St., Rockport, TX 78382 (for reservations). ℂ **361/729-7239.** www.cranehouseretreat.com. 1 unit. $225–$275. No credit cards. Pets accepted. *In room:* A/C and fans, TV/DVD.

**Hoopes' House ★★**   With some B&Bs, like this one, you know the second you walk in that you're looking at a labor of love. The owners have taken great pains in restoring the historic 1890s house and furnishing the rooms. The main house has four garden rooms and a new wing houses four additional guest rooms. The garden rooms are larger and offer more privacy (like the San Jose and the Aransas), but the rooms in the house have more character and are absolutely charming (the Live Oak and the Black Jack). The pool is great, the grounds are immaculate, and the innkeeper is an easygoing, down-to-earth type.

417 N. Broadway, Rockport, TX 78382. ℂ **800/924-1008** or 361/729-8424. Fax 361/790-9288. www.hoopeshouse.com. 8 units. $175 double. Rates include full breakfast. AE, MC, V. Children 11 and under not permitted. **Amenities:** Bikes; Jacuzzi; outdoor pool. *In room:* A/C, TV, fridge (in some), hair dryer, Wi-Fi (free, in new wing rooms).

**The Lighthouse Inn ★★**   For a full-service hotel, this independently owned lodging right on the water is your best choice. All rooms and suites have balconies with a view of the bay and a couple of rocking chairs from which to enjoy it. Pelicans like to fish right off the shore. Standard rooms are medium size, immaculate, and comfortably furnished. They come with two queen-size beds. The suites have a full kitchen, a completely separate sitting area, and two TVs.

200 S. Fulton Beach Rd., Rockport, TX 78382. ☎ **866/790-8439** or 361/790-8439. Fax 361/790-7393. www.lighthousetexas.com. 78 units. $99–$199 double; $149–$209 captain's suite; $299–$399 2-bedroom suite. Rates include full breakfast. AE, DC, DISC, MC, V. **Amenities:** Restaurant; bar; exercise room; Jacuzzi; outdoor pool; room service. *In room:* A/C and fan, TV/DVD, hair dryer, Wi-Fi (free).

## Where to Dine

Most of the independent restaurants in the area are clustered on Fulton Beach Road by the Fulton harbor.

**Latitude 28°02′** ★★ SEAFOOD    It's always great to eat at a restaurant that serves locally caught seafood, and the folks who own this restaurant, Craig and Ramona Day, make sure to get the freshest catch from local suppliers. In addition to the seafood, that goes for other local products, including meats and vegetables. For this reason, they characterize their cooking as coastal cuisine. Some of the favorite dishes here include the stuffed shrimp and the fish Gilroy (encrusted with garlic breadcrumbs). Pay close attention to the nightly featured dishes. Nonseafood dishes include beef, chicken, and vegetarian options. The dining room is simple, comfortable, and attractive, and tables are well spaced. The walls serve as gallery space for works by local artists.

105 N. Austin St., Rockport ☎ **361/727-9009.** www.latitude2802.com. Reservations recommended. Main courses $15–$35. AE, DISC, MC, V. Tues–Sun 5–10pm.

**Los Comales** ★ MEXICAN/TEX-MEX    An unpretentious Mexican food joint just a few blocks from Rockport's downtown area, Los Comales serves up some excellent dishes from a fairly large menu. All of the standards, such as fajitas, and the sides, such as *borracho* beans, are prepared well. One of the dishes for which this place is known is the stuffed, deep-fried avocado. Also terrific are the enchiladas, especially the *enchiladas verdes*, which come with a generous amount of tomatillo sauce. You can also ask for some uncommon vegetarian dishes such as spinach and mushroom enchiladas.

431 Hwy. 35. ☎ **361/729-3952.** Main courses $8–$17. AE, DISC, MC, V. Mon–Sat 11am–10pm; Sun 11am–9pm.

# PORT ARANSAS ★★

30 miles NE of Corpus Christi; 155 miles S of San Antonio

Port Aransas is a funky, Texas-style beach town located on the north end of Mustang Island. It has nearly 4,000 permanent residents, but at any given time, at least 2,000 island condo dwellers descend on the town for groceries, a beer, and such. Unlike Corpus Christi and Rockport, Port Aransas is situated on open water. (Actually, it's open water in one direction, and the bay in the other.) Hence, you get big, broad, sandy beaches, and some watersports not offered at the other destinations. Rockport also has other economic activities besides tourism, which is not really true for Port A (as the locals call it), which depends on winter Texans, fishing enthusiasts, surfers, and sun worshipers for its existence. This is why the town has a bit more of a party spirit, which you can easily discern if you go barhopping here. That said, the perfect time *not* to come here is during spring break, when college students fill the town and disrupt the calm, small-town feel of the place.

## Essentials

**GETTING THERE & GETTING AROUND**    Port Aransas is just over 30 minutes from Corpus Christi. The quickest way to get here is to take South Padre Island

Drive (S.P.I.D.) out to Mustang Island and then drive north. But you can also get here by taking Tex. 35 north, as you would go to Rockport, but take the exit for Aransas Pass (Hwy. 361) and keep going until you see signs for the ferry. The ferry is free, a very short ride, and it drops you off in the middle of town. Port Aransas is compact, and most of the watersports activities can be found by just walking around the town's harbor.

**VISITOR INFORMATION**   Just after you get off the ferry, you'll see the visitor center on your right at 421 W. Cotter Ave. (© **800/452-6278** or 361/749-5919; www.portaransas.org). The staff is very helpful.

**FAST FACTS**   The nearest full-service hospital, with a 24-hour emergency room, is **North Bay Hospital** at 1711 W. Wheeler Ave., Aransas Pass (© **361/758-8585**).

## What to See & Do

**BEACHCOMBING**   Okay, so maybe you want a beach that's completely free of cars and all signs of human settlement, where you can walk along in perfect communion with nature. If so, the obvious choice is San Jose Island, right across from Port Aransas. It's privately owned by a Texas oil family and kept pristine. Transporting people to the island is the Jetty Boat ($10 per adult, $5 per child round-trip), which makes 10 trips daily. Purchase tickets at **Fisherman's Wharf** at 900 N. Tarpon St. (© **800/605-5448** or 361/749-5760). *Note:* Whatever you might need on the island, you'll have to bring with you. This island is also a good place to collect seashells.

**BEACH CRUISING**   Texas beaches tend to be broad and flat and extend for miles. Driving is permitted on most beaches, and cruising is one of the favorite pastimes of the vacationing Texan. The idea is to pack a cooler in the car filled with picnic supplies; take along other essentials such as towels, beach chairs, and perhaps a beach umbrella; and then drive to the beach and slowly cruise along until you find your spot. Always go very slow (it's a matter of courtesy) and stay on the packed sand; don't get into the loose stuff. The beach on the Gulf side of Mustang Island is miles long, but isn't continuous; there are places where you have to get back on the road. But somewhere along there, you'll find your spot. One possibility is at **Mustang Island State Park ★★** (© **361/749-5246**; www.tpwd.state.tx.us/park/mustang), which has more than 5 miles of wide, sandy beach, with fine sand, few rocks and broken shells, and almost enough waves for surfing.

**BIKE RENTAL**   Port A is a nice town to explore on a bike. You can rent one with **Nautical Wheelers,** located at 428 S. Alister St. (© **361/749-3003**).

**DOLPHIN TOURS**   **Dolphin Watch** runs dolphin and nature tours on its boat, the *Mustang.* Call (© **361/749-6969**) or just inquire at Woody's Sports Center, listed below.

**FISHING**   A lot of fishermen complain that the bay around Port A is overfished. Still, I've run into a few boats that have had good luck. The town has more than 200 fishing guides. If you want to try deep-sea fishing from a party boat (rather than chartering your own boat), see the guys at Fisherman's Wharf, listed above. They have two large boats that go out regularly. If you want to charter, try **Woody's Sports Center** at 136 W. Cotter (© **361/749-5271** or 749-5252; www.gulfcoastfishing.com).

**GOLFING**   Port Aransas has a new golf course called **Newport Dunes** (© **361/749-4653**). Designed by Arnold Palmer, it makes use of conservation techniques to minimize environmental impact.

**SURFING**   Port A is known in Texas as a favored spot by the local surfers. There are a couple of places on the island to rent boards. I recommend Ted Nicholson at

**Board House Surf & Skate Shop** (© 361/765-0222; www.boardhousesurfshop. com), located at 509 N. Alister St. He rents and sells boards and surfing gear, gives lessons, and is full of pointers on the local surfing.

## Where to Stay

There are a number of motels in town, but only one belongs to a national chain, **Best Western Ocean Villa** at 400 E. Ave. G (© **800/WESTERN** [937-8376]). Two local motels I like are **Alister Square Inn** at 122 S. Alister St. (© **888/749-3003**), and **Captain's Quarters Inn** at 235 W. Cotter (© **888/272-6727**).

Condos are the most popular form of lodging on the island. The beach condos in the town area are smaller buildings, but as you drive south, you pass large condo properties on the beach, which are scattered along several miles of shore. Condo owners will contract with agencies to rent these out by the week, and these agencies advertise a lot in town and on the Web. I had dealings with one agency, **Starkey Properties** (© **888/951-6381**; www.starkeyproperties.com), which proved to be very professional.

For RVs as well as campsites, try Mustang Island State Park. Call for reservations (© **512/389-8900**). For a nice location closer to town, try **On the Beach RV Park** at 907 Beach Access Rd. (© **361/749-4909**).

**Balinese Flats and Piers** 🍴 This stylish little establishment in the middle of town blends rustic elements with modern comforts. All of the units are comfortable and beautifully decorated with Mexican tiles, furniture, and accents. The Flats section has two-bedroom units with full kitchens and roomy living and dining areas, with ground-level access. The Piers consists of studios and one-bedroom apartments with private decks, and it has views of the water from the protected side of the island. Rooms have one or two queen-size beds, or two twin beds. An upstairs veranda is a great place to enjoy a drink.

121 Cutoff Rd., Port Aransas, TX 78373. © **888/951-6381** or 361/749-1880. www.balineseflats.com. 14 units. $165–$185 2-bedroom; $125–$145 studio/1-bedroom. MC, V. *In room:* A/C, TV/DVD, hair dryer, kitchen (in some), Wi-Fi (free).

**The Tarpon Inn** ★★ This is a lovely, old two-story hotel that dates from 1886. It's well conserved and has plenty of character. Standard rooms are pretty small; go for one of the premium rooms, or better still, one of the two suites, which are extralarge and comfortable. The FDR suite (no, FDR didn't sleep here; he just fished here) has a large sitting room, a kitchen, a dining room, and a private porch. More romantic is the upstairs corner suite with a marvelous queen-size bed and a large tub in the bedroom. If these are over your budget, go for room no. 21, a premium unit with a queen-size bed, spacious and with a large bathroom. This is a relaxing property. There are no TVs and no phones in the guest rooms.

200 E. Cotter, Port Aransas, TX 78373. © **800/365-6784** or 361/749-5555. Fax 361/749-4305. www. thetarponinn.com. 24 units. $99–$110 double; $135–$145 premium; $195–$250 suite. 2-night minimum stay on weekends. Pets 35 lbs. and under accepted with $25 fee per night. AE, MC, V. **Amenities:** Restaurant; outdoor pool. *In room:* A/C and fans, no phone, Wi-Fi ($5 per day).

## Where to Dine

Port Aransas has a surprising number of good restaurants for a town of its size. Following are the three most interesting ones.

**La Playa** ★★ MEXICAN/SEAFOOD This establishment has no connection with the restaurant in Corpus Christi that shares its name. It's run by a Houston man who has been in the restaurant business for years. The food is extremely fresh and nicely prepared. Try the excellent fish tacos, a tangy *campechana* (Mexican-style seafood cocktail), or rich seafood enchiladas. Popular with the locals are the guacamole, which is prepared at the table, and the margaritas. Other dishes that deserve mention are the Tex-Mex enchiladas and the chicken al chipotle. Vegetarian specials are available. The setting is casual, the service excellent, and the furniture comfortable. You can't reserve a table, but you can call ahead to get your name on the waiting list.

222 Beach St. © **361/749-0022.** Reservations not accepted. Main courses $8–$15; nightly specials $18–$24. No credit cards. Tues–Thurs 5–9pm; Fri–Sat 5–10pm (half-hour later in summer).

**Shells** ★★ STEAK/SEAFOOD/LIGHT FARE  The owner of this restaurant, Heber Stone, had a hand in creating and running several of Austin's most highly acclaimed restaurants. He and his family have settled into Port A to take it easy and cook only enough to keep active. A chalkboard lists all dishes for that particular day. Lunch items are mostly sandwiches and salads and pasta. Dinner entrees are much more elaborate affairs. On my visits, the restaurant was serving, among other tempting items, prime center-cut sirloin with a balsamic caramelized garlic glaze, sirloin medallions on top of grilled focaccia with a Gorgonzola sauce, and seared amberjack with a chile-lime sauce. The appetizers include Chinese dumplings, Thai spring rolls, and sushi. *Note:* This restaurant is very small, and it's common to have to wait for a table. Hours are not strictly kept, so don't show up at the last minute, or you might find they've stopped serving.

522 E. Ave. G. © **361/749-7621.** Reservations not accepted. Main courses $7–$12 lunch, $13–$23 dinner. DISC, MC, V. Daily 11:30am–2:30pm and 5–9pm.

**Venetian Hot Plate** ★★ ITALIAN  This restaurant's curious name owes its existence to an error in translation, and by the time the Italian owners were made aware of their mistake, it was too late to change it. The food, however, doesn't suffer from any problem in translation. Wonderful pasta dishes and a grilled polenta with bits of crumbled Gorgonzola are things to consider. There are nightly specials, and the set menu changes seasonally. The owner cares a lot about wine and prices it reasonably. The dining room is comfortable and peaceful.

232 Beach St. © **361/749-7617.** Reservations recommended. Main courses $13–$20; specials $20–$30. AE, DISC, MC, V. Tues–Sat 5–9 or 10pm; Sun on holiday weekends.

# PADRE ISLAND NATIONAL SEASHORE ★

37 miles SE of Corpus Christi; 180 miles S of San Antonio; 414 miles S of Dallas

Some 70 miles of delightful white-sand beach, picturesque sand dunes, and warm ocean waters make Padre Island National Seashore a favorite year-round playground along the Texas Gulf Coast. One of the longest stretches of undeveloped coastline in America, this is an ideal spot for swimming, sunbathing, fishing, beachcombing, windsurfing, and camping. It also provides excellent opportunities for bird-watching and a chance to see several species of rare sea turtles. The island was named for Padre José Nicolás Balli, a Mexican priest who, in 1804, founded a mission, settlement, and ranch about 26 miles north of the island's southernmost tip.

Padre Island is a barrier island, essentially a sandbar that helps protect the mainland from the full force of ocean storms. As with other barrier islands, one of the constants of Padre Island is change; wind and waves relentlessly shape and re-create the island, as grasses and other hardy plants strive to get a foothold in the shifting sands. Padre Island's Gulf side, with miles of beach accessible only to those with four-wheel-drive vehicles, has wonderful surf fishing, while the channel between the island and mainland—the Laguna Madre—has excellent windsurfing and a protected area for small powerboats and sailboats.

## Essentials

**GETTING THERE**    From Corpus Christi, take Tex. 358 (South Padre Island Dr.) southeast across the JFK Causeway to Padre Island, and follow Park Road 22 south to the national seashore. The drive takes 45 minutes to an hour.

**VISITOR INFORMATION**    For information, contact **Padre Island National Seashore,** P.O. Box 181300, Corpus Christi, TX 78480-1300 (© **361/949-8068;** www.nps.gov/pais). The Park Service also maintains a recorded beach- and road-condition information line (© **361/949-8175**). The park is open 24 hours a day.

The **visitor center complex,** along Park Road 22 at Malaquite Beach, has an observation deck, a bookstore, and a variety of exhibits, including one on the endangered Kemp's ridley sea turtle. In the same complex, **Padre Island Park Company** (© **361/949-9368**) sells camping and fishing supplies and gift items, and rents chairs, umbrellas, body boards, and other beach toys. The visitor center is open from 8:30am to 6pm Memorial Day through Labor Day, and from 8:30am to 4:30pm the rest of the year (closed Dec 25), and the store is usually open similar hours.

**FEES & REGULATIONS**    Entry costs $10 per vehicle (good for 7 days) or $5 per individual on foot or a bike. In addition, there is a $5 user fee at Bird Island Basin. Regulations here are much like those at other National Park Service properties, which essentially require that visitors not disturb wildlife or damage the site's natural features and facilities. Pets must be leashed and are not permitted on the swimming beach in front of the visitor center. Although driving off road is permitted on some sections of beach, the dunes, grasslands, and tidal flats are closed to all vehicles.

**WHEN TO GO**    Summer is the busiest time here, although it is generally hot, with highs in the 90s (30s Celsius) and very humid. Sea breezes in late afternoon and evening help moderate the heat. Winters are mild, with highs from the 50s to the 70s (teens to the 20s Celsius), and lows in the 40s and 50s (single digits to the teens Celsius). Only occasionally does the temperature drop below 40°F (4°C), and a freeze is extremely rare. Hurricane season (June–Oct) is the rainiest time of the year and also has the highest surf. September to November is a good time to visit, usually still warm enough for swimming, but not nearly as hot or crowded as in summer.

**SAFETY**    Swimmers and those walking barefoot on the beach should watch out for the Portuguese man-of-war, a blue jellyfish that can cause an extremely painful sting. There are also poisonous rattlesnakes in the dunes, grasslands, and mud flats.

**RANGER PROGRAMS**    Various **interpretive programs** are held year-round, ranging from guided beach or birding walks to talks outside the visitor center and evening campground campfire programs. These programs usually last from 30 to 45 minutes and cover subjects such as migrating or resident birds, seashells, the island's plant life or animals, or things that wash up on the beach. There's also a **Junior Ranger Program** for kids 5 to 13, who answer questions in a free booklet and talk with rangers about the national seashore to earn certificates, badges, and sea-turtle stickers.

## What to See & Do

### EXPLORING THE HIGHLIGHTS BY CAR

Padre Island National Seashore has an 8½-mile paved road, with good views of the Gulf and dunes, that leads to the visitor center complex. In addition, most of the beaches are open to licensed street-legal motor vehicles; some sections have hard-packed sand that makes an adequate roadbed for two-wheel-drive vehicles, while most of the beach requires four-wheel-drive. See "Four-Wheeling," below.

### OUTDOOR ADVENTURES

**BEACHCOMBING** The best times for beachcombing are usually early mornings and immediately after a storm, when you're apt to find a variety of seashells, seaweed, driftwood, and the like. These items can be collected, but live animals and historical or archaeological objects should be left. Among shells sometimes found at Padre Island are lightning whelks, moon snails, Scotch bonnets, Atlantic cockles, bay scallops, and sand dollars. The best shell hunting is often in winter, when storms disturb the water and thrust shells ashore; and many of the best shells are often found on

## THE RACE TO save THE SEA TURTLES

The Gulf of Mexico is home to five species of sea turtles, all of which are either endangered or threatened, including the Kemp's ridley, considered to be the most endangered sea turtle in the world with only about 3,000 in existence. Kemp's ridleys have almost circular shells, grow to about 2 feet long, and weigh about 100 pounds. Adults are olive green on top and yellow below, and their main food source is crabs. Their main nesting area historically is along a 16-mile stretch of beach at Playa de Rancho Nuevo in Tamaulipas, Mexico, and although females lay about 100 eggs at a time, only about 1% of the hatchlings survive to adulthood.

In the 1970s, an international effort was begun to establish a second nesting area at Padre Island National Seashore, using the theory that sea turtles always return to the beach where they were hatched to lay their eggs. More than 22,000 eggs were gathered from Playa de Rancho Nuevo between 1978 and 1988, placed in boxes containing Padre Island sand, and shipped to Texas, where they were placed in incubators. After hatching, about 13,500 baby turtles were released on the beach at

Padre Island National Seashore and allowed to crawl into the water for a quick swim. Fearing that the young turtles would become lunch for predators, National Park Service biologists captured them and sent them to a marine fisheries lab in Galveston, where they spent up to a year growing big enough to have a better chance of survival in the wild. They were then tagged and released into the Gulf of Mexico.

Since then, some of the turtles have returned to Padre Island and other sections of the Texas Gulf Coast to nest, and Park Service workers have collected a number of eggs for incubation and eventual release. The eggs are collected in late spring and summer, and anyone seeing a nesting sea turtle is asked not to disturb it, but to report its location to National Seashore personnel. The public can attend releases of the hatchlings, which usually occur in June and August and at other times with less frequency. For information on release dates, go to the park website and click on "Sea Turtle Science and Recovery." Though it's difficult to estimate the total turtle population in the wild, most observers believe it's growing.

Little Shell and Big Shell beaches, accessible only to those with four-wheel-drive vehicles. Metal detectors are not permitted on the beach.

**BIRDING & WILDLIFE VIEWING**   More than 350 species of birds frequent Padre Island, and every visitor is bound to see and hear at least some of them. The island is a key stopping point for a variety of migratory species traveling between North and Central America, making spring and fall the best time for bird-watching. Since a number of species winter at Padre Island, there's good birding almost year-round except for the summer. Additionally, this is the northern boundary of some Central American species, such as green jays and jaçanas.

Birding here is very easy, especially with a four-wheel-drive vehicle, which can move down the coast to the more remote stretches of beach. Experienced bird-watchers say it is best to remain in your vehicle, because humans on foot scare off birds sooner than approaching vehicles. As would be expected by its name, Bird Island Basin is also a good choice for birders as long as the marshes have water. The most commonly observed bird is the laughing gull, which is a year-round resident. Other species to watch for include rare brown pelicans, plus the more common American white pelicans, long-billed curlews, great blue herons, sandhill cranes, ruddy turnstones, Caspian and Royal terns, willets, Harris's hawks, reddish egrets, northern bobwhites, mourning doves, horned larks, great-tailed grackles, and red-winged blackbirds.

In addition to birds, the island is home to the spotted ground squirrel, which is often seen in the dunes near the visitor center, as well as white-tailed deer, coyotes, black-tailed jack rabbits, lizards, and a number of poisonous and nonpoisonous snakes.

**BOATING**   A boat ramp is located at Bird Island Basin, which provides access to Laguna Madre, a protected bay that is ideal for small powerboats and sailboats. Boat launching is not permitted on the Gulf side of the island, except for sailboats and soft-sided inflatables. To rent a sailboard, contact **Worldwinds Windsurfing** (© 361/949-7472; www.worldwinds.net). Personal watercraft are not permitted in Laguna Madre (except to get from the boat ramp to open water outside the park boundaries), but are allowed on the Gulf side beyond the 5-mile marker.

**FISHING**   Fishing is great year-round. Surf fishing is permitted everywhere along the Gulf side, except at Malaquite Beach, and yields whiting, redfish, black drum, and speckled sea trout; anglers in Laguna Madre catch flounder, sheepshead, and croaker. A Texas fishing license with a saltwater stamp is required. Licenses, along with current fishing regulations and some fishing supplies, are available at **Padre Island Park Company** (© 361/949-9368). For current license information, contact the Texas Parks and Wildlife Department (© 800/792-1112; www.tpwd.state.tx.us).

**FOUR-WHEELING**   Licensed and street-legal motor vehicles (but not ATVs) are permitted on most of the beach at Padre Island National Seashore (but not Malaquite Beach or the fragile dunes, grasslands, and tidal flats). Most standard passenger vehicles can make it down the first 5 miles of South Beach, but those planning to drive farther south down the island (another 55 miles are open to motor vehicles) will need four-wheel-drive vehicles. Markers are located every 5 miles, and those driving down the beach are advised to watch for soft sand and high water, and to carry a shovel, jack, boards, and other emergency equipment. Unless otherwise posted, the speed limit on the beach is 15 mph. Northbound vehicles have the right of way.

### For Travelers with Disabilities

Specially designed fat-tire wheelchairs for use in the sand, and even in the water, are available at no charge at the visitor center. They do require someone to push.

**HIKING**  The national seashore has miles of beach that are ideal for walking and hiking. There's also the paved and fairly easy **Grasslands Nature Trail,** a .8-mile self-guided loop trail that meanders through grass-covered areas of sand dunes. Numbered posts correspond with descriptions of plants and other aspects of the natural landscape in a free brochure available at the trail head or the visitor center. You'll need insect repellent to combat mosquitoes, and because western diamondback rattlesnakes also inhabit the area, stay on the trail and watch where you put your feet and hands.

**SWIMMING & SURFING**  Warm air and water temperatures make swimming practically a year-round activity here—January through March is really the only time it's too chilly—and swimming is permitted along the entire beach. The most popular swimming area is 4½-mile-long Malaquite Beach, also called Closed Beach, which is closed to motor vehicles. You have to jostle for a spot only at spring break and on summer weekends. *Note:* There are no lifeguards on duty here. Although waves are not of the Hawaii or California size, they're often sufficient for surfing, which is permitted in most areas, but not at Malaquite Beach.

**WINDSURFING**  The Bird Island Basin area on Laguna Madre is considered one of America's best spots for windsurfing because of its warm water, shallow depth, and consistent, steady winds. **Worldwinds Windsurfing** (© **361/949-7472;** www. worldwinds.net) sells and rents windsurfing equipment and wet suits here, and offers windsurfing lessons during the summer. Call for current fees and a schedule.

## Where to Stay & Dine

The closest hotels and restaurants are in Corpus Christi; see that section earlier in this chapter. If you want to stay in the park, you'll have to camp.

   **Malaquite Campground** ★, a developed campsite at Padre Island National Seashore about a half-mile north of the visitor center, is a great spot to bed down, with 50 sites ($8 per night) that are available on a first-come, first-served year-round. Sites, within 100 feet of the beach, have good views of the Gulf, and the campground has cold showers, restrooms, and picnic tables. There are no RV hookups, but there is a dump station. For those who don't mind its limitations, it's definitely the best place to camp; it gets crowded only during spring break and on summer weekends.

# SOUTH PADRE ISLAND

286 miles S of San Antonio; 366 miles SW of Houston; 531 miles S of Dallas; 815 miles SE of El Paso

South Padre Island is a long, long barrier island that shares its name with the resort town at its southern tip. Any farther south and you would be in Mexico. The beach is much like that on the northern portion of the island, but the water here often seems clearer. Padre Island is a great place to stretch out on the beach, feel the Gulf breeze blowing, and hear nothing but the wash of the surf. If you get bored, you can busy yourself with boat rides, watersports, or taking the kids to the popular local water park.

This part of the island is narrow—2 or 3 blocks wide—and the town starts at the southern tip and extends north for about 5 miles, with a good bit of vacant land the farther north you go. It's a small town. Most of it consists of stores, hotels, a small convention center, restaurants, condos, and vacation houses. Regular housing is in short supply because storm insurance and other costs make it prohibitive. Most of the locals commute from the mainland, from either Port Isabel or Brownsville.

South Padre Island gets a lot of families who make the trip by car or RV. Many come from northern Mexico, driving up from cities such as Monterrey and Saltillo. It also gets winter Texans, along with some convention business. Conventioneers and weekenders will often come by plane, via the airports at Harlingen or Brownsville. You'll find reasonably priced flights from major cities in Texas, mostly on Southwest Airlines or Continental Express. South Padre Island is famous for being a spring-break destination. Hotels will fill up with college kids, often several to a room. It's a good time to be somewhere else.

## Essentials

### GETTING THERE

**BY PLANE**    The closest airports are the **Brownsville/South Padre Island International Airport** (BRO) (© 956/542-4373; www.flybrownsville.com) in Brownsville (about 28 miles southwest) and the **Valley International Airport** (HRL) (© 956/430-8600; www.flythevalley.com) in Harlingen (about 40 miles west). All of the major car-rental companies have desks at these airports.

**BY CAR**    From U.S. 77/83, which connects to Harlingen, McAllen, and Corpus Christi, take Tex. 100 east to Port Isabel and then across the Queen Isabella Causeway to the south end of South Padre Island. From Brownsville, take Tex. 48 northeast to Tex. 100.

### GETTING AROUND

A car is handy on South Padre Island, and parking and traffic congestion are not usually a problem, except during spring break and on summer weekends. The town's main street is Padre Boulevard. It runs north-south down the middle of the island. Running parallel 1 block on either side are Laguna Boulevard (west) and Gulf Boulevard (east). You don't have to drive much once you're here, since many of the major hotels, restaurants, and beaches are within walking distance of each other. Also, there is a free year-round bus service called **the Wave** (© 956/761-1025), which operates daily from 7am to 7pm. There are two different buses. Both run the length of the town, and one goes into Port Isabel (each is clearly marked). They pass every 30 minutes along Padre Boulevard.

### VISITOR INFORMATION

Contact the **South Padre Island Convention and Visitors Bureau,** 600 Padre Blvd., South Padre Island, TX 78597 (© 800/767-2373 or 956/761-6433; www.sopadre.com), which operates a visitor center. The center is just a few blocks north of the entry point on the east side of the boulevard beside a Wells Fargo branch office. Hours are Monday to Friday 8am to 5pm and Saturday and Sunday from 9am to 5pm. On weekdays in the summer, the office stays open an extra hour later. You can pick up maps or talk to the staff for suggestions and advice.

**FAST FACTS**    Health services are available at **Valley Regional Island Clinic,** 3000 Padre Blvd. (© 956/761-4524). The **post office** is at 4701 Padre Blvd. and is open Monday through Friday from 8am to 4pm, Saturday from 10am to noon.

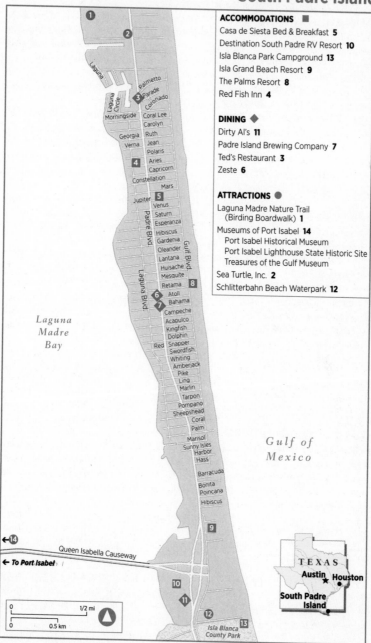

# South Padre Island

**ACCOMMODATIONS** ■

Casa de Siesta Bed & Breakfast **5**
Destination South Padre RV Resort **10**
Isla Blanca Park Campground **13**
Isla Grand Beach Resort **9**
The Palms Resort **8**
Red Fish Inn **4**

**DINING** ◆

Dirty Al's **11**
Padre Island Brewing Company **7**
Ted's Restaurant **3**
Zeste **6**

**ATTRACTIONS** ●

Laguna Madre Nature Trail
(Birding Boardwalk) **1**
Museums of Port Isabel **14**
  Port Isabel Historical Museum
  Port Isabel Lighthouse State Historic Site
  Treasures of the Gulf Museum
Sea Turtle, Inc. **2**
Schlitterbahn Beach Waterpark **12**

Laguna

Palmetto
Parade
Coronado
Morningside    Coral Lee
Carolyn
Georgia    Ruth
Verna    Jean
Polaris
Aries
Capricorn
Constellation
Mars
Jupiter
Venus
Saturn
Esperanza
Hibiscus
Gardenia
Oleander
Lantana
Huisache
Mesquite
Retama
Atoll
Bahama
Campeche
Acapulco
Kingfish
Dolphin
Red  Snapper
Swordfish
Whiting
Amberjack
Pike
Ling
Marlin
Tarpon
Pompano
Sheepshead
Coral
Palm
Marisol
Sunny Isles
Harbor
Hass
Barracuda
Bonita
Poincana
Hibiscus

Laguna
Circle

Padre Blvd.

Gulf Blvd.

Laguna Blvd.

*Laguna
Madre
Bay*

*Gulf of
Mexico*

Queen Isabella Causeway

← To Port Isabel

0        1/2 mi
0    0.5 km

Isla Blanca
County Park

T E X A S
Austin ★  ● Houston
**South Padre
Island**  ●

## What to See & Do

### DISCOVERING THE AREA'S PAST

Shipwrecks, tempests, and war, as well as some of the happier aspects of life along the southern Texas coast, are the focus of the **Museums of Port Isabel.** Museum headquarters are in the Port Isabel Historical Museum, 317 E. Railroad Ave., Port Isabel (© 956/943-7602; www.portisabelmuseums.com), and there's also the Treasures of the Gulf Museum and a historic lighthouse. These are in downtown Port Isabel, are within easy walking distance of each other, and make for a good activity on a rainy day. Allow a half-hour to 1 hour to visit each one.

The **Port Isabel Historical Museum ★**, located in a restored 1899 Victorian commercial building, houses exhibits that describe the history of the area from the time it was a supply depot during the Mexican-American War, through the Civil War and the area's development as a shrimping and fishing port. There are interactive exhibits, a large display of Mexican-American War artifacts, and a fascinating 1906 Victor Morales "Fish Mural." The displays about shipwrecks will interest kids and adults alike. Nearby, the **Treasures of the Gulf Museum** focuses on three Spanish shipwrecks that occurred in 1554 just off the coast. Exhibits include murals, artifacts, and various hands-on activities, such as a children's discovery lab. There is also a theater and gift shop.

The **Port Isabel Lighthouse State Historic Site,** at the west end of the Queen Isabella Causeway, is hard to miss. This 72-foot-high lighthouse, which helped guide ships through Brazos Santiago Pass to Point Isabel from 1852 until 1905, now affords panoramic views of Port Isabel and South Padre Island, and as far as the eye can see over the Gulf of Mexico. Also on the property is a replica of the lighthouse keeper's cottage made from the 1850 blueprints for the original. The cottage contains exhibits on the history of the lighthouse, and there's a picnic area.

Both museums are open Tuesday through Saturday from 10am to 4pm (last entry at 3:30pm), and the lighthouse and cottage are open daily from 9am to 5pm (last entry at 4pm). Admission to each site is $3 adults, $2 for seniors 55 and older, $1 for students with ID, and free for children 4 and under. Combination tickets for all three sites cost $7 for adults, $5 for seniors, and $2 for students.

### OUTDOOR ACTIVITIES

**BIRD-WATCHING**    More than 300 species of birds can be found during different times of the year. The **Laguna Madre Nature Trail,** adjacent to the South Padre Island Convention Centre at the north end of town, is a boardwalk that meanders out over the wetlands of the Laguna Madre and around a freshwater pond. There are a few blinds where you can set up a scope and sit for hours unseen by the birds. The boardwalk is wheelchair accessible and open 24 hours, free of charge. For birding tours in the bay, contact George and Scarlet Colley of **Fins to Feathers Photo Safaris** (© 956/739-2473; www.fin2feather.com). They take small groups out into the Laguna Madre for 3-hour trips.

**DOLPHIN-WATCHING**    Dolphin tours are a big activity on this island. For a great tour limited to small groups, contact **Fins to Feathers,** listed above. Scarlet Colley is a dolphin researcher and has filmed many hours of dolphin activity. The tour lasts 1½ hours. Another option is to take a large-boat tour, for which you can sign up at the marina, at the southern end of the island. A couple of companies offer tours. The preferred one is the **Original Dolphin Watch** (© 956/761-4243).

## FACE TO FACE WITH A sea TURTLE

Each of the seven worldwide species of sea turtles is either threatened or endangered, and five species are found in the Gulf of Mexico. Ila Loetscher, affectionately dubbed the "Turtle Lady," founded Sea Turtle, Inc., in 1977 to help protect the most endangered species of sea turtles, Kemp's ridley. The organization supports conservation and rehabilitation of all marine turtles, and operates a rehabilitation center where you can see four of the five Gulf of Mexico sea turtle species. Volunteers give presentations with live sea turtles Tuesday through Sunday at 10am, which help you identify the different species and explain how we can help protect them. Self-guided and guided tours of the facility, including the turtle tanks, are available at other times. **Sea Turtle, Inc.,** is located at 6617 Padre Blvd. (📞 **956/ 761-4511;** www.seaturtleinc.com). The suggested donation is $3 for adults and $1 for children. It's open Tuesday through Sunday from 10am to 4pm. Allow at least 45 minutes, and please buy something in the gift shop—all proceeds go to saving the sea turtles!

**FISHING**   There have been record-setting catches made in the waters around South Padre Island: The state-record blue marlin, at 876½ pounds, was taken offshore.

The beach and jetties are easily accessible and very popular with "winter Texans." There are numerous local charter captains specializing in offshore big-game fishing, where anglers try for blue marlin, white marlin, sailfish, swordfish, wahoo, tuna, and mako shark. Offshore fishing also includes red drum, spotted sea trout, snapper, grouper, tarpon, and king mackerel.

The Laguna Madre, on average only 2 feet deep, is perfect for world-class light-tackle sport fishing. The lush carpet of sea grasses on its bottom provides good habitat and food for red drum, spotted sea trout, flounder, black drum, and snook, and locals brag that there are more of these fish per acre than in any other bay on the Texas Gulf.

The **Texas International Fishing Tournament (TIFT)** has been going strong for more than 60 years and attracts more than 1,000 participants each July. The 5-day event includes bay, offshore, and tarpon fishing divisions, and is open to anglers of all ages. Visit www.tift.org or contact the **South Padre Island CVB** (📞 **800/767-2373** or 956/761-6433; www.sopadre.com) for details.

**SCHLITTERBAHN BEACH WATERPARK**   This is operated by the same corporation that owns the highly popular water park in the German Hill Country town of New Braunfels—hence the German name. It's not nearly as large as the original, but it has a wave pool and several water rides that require sturdy bathing suits. It also has calmer facilities such as wading and floating pools that work well for those just trying to relax. My favorite feature is the river that connects the rides so that you don't have to spend all your time out of the water waiting in line. Admission prices are $48 adults and $40 children 3 to 11 years old. The park closes during the winter (mid-Sept to mid-Apr). It's located at 33261 State Park Rd. 100. For information, call 📞 956/772-7873 or visit www.schlitterbahn.com.

**SUNBATHING & SWIMMING**   The beaches of South Padre Island are some of the best on the Gulf: The sand is fine and white, and the water is warm and shallow. In town, there are 23 access points with free parking, plus the county has a park at each end of town, each with a $4 all-day parking fee. My favorite stretch of beach is in the county park north of town. Incidentally, although lined with hotels and condos, the shoreline and adjacent beaches are public and open to everyone.

**WINDSURFING**   With winds about 15 mph year-round, these waters are ideal for windsurfing. Spring and fall are best, usually with beautiful weather. Hurricane season runs from August to early November, but is not often a serious problem.

# Where to Stay

Room rates vary widely in South Padre Island over the course of the year, with the lowest rates usually in winter. There are more condo units on this island than there are regular hotel rooms. These will work if you plan to stay here more than a few days. Most, but not all, rent by the week. Often, there's a one-time cleaning fee when you lease a condo, so it's a better deal the longer you stay. A complete list of condos is on the South Padre Island website: **www.sopadre.com**. Among the national chain motels in South Padre Island are **Days Inn,** 3913 Padre Blvd. (© **800/329-7466** or 956/761-7831); **Comfort Suites,** 912 Padre Blvd. (© **800/424-6423** or 956/ 772-9020); and **Super 8,** 4205 Padre Blvd. (© **800/800-8000** or 956/761-6300). Room tax adds about 13%. Most hotels are nonsmoking; if they have smoking rooms, it's mentioned in the review.

### Casa de Siesta Bed & Breakfast ★
Attractive rooms connected by a broad, shaded breezeway encircle a leafy garden and patio. The design makes for privacy and relaxation. On an island known as a family destination, it's nice to find an oasis for grown-ups. A small swimming pool completes the picture. The rooms are very large and decorated in a Mexican and Southwestern style: Saltillo tile floors, wrought-iron work, and folk art. You have a choice of two double beds or one king-size bed; three rooms come with four-poster beds. All have showers with attractive tile work. Smoking is allowed outside only.

4610 Padre Blvd., South Padre Island, TX 78597. © **956/761-5656.** Fax 956/761-1313. www.casade siesta.com. 12 units. $99–$150 double. Extra person $20. Rates include full breakfast. AE, MC, V. Pets accepted with $15 per day fee. Children 11 and under not permitted. **Amenities:** Pool. *In room:* A/C, TV, fridge.

### Isla Grand Beach Resort ★
This hotel used to be the Radisson, and it remains the nicest full-service hotel in town. The popular beach in front of the hotel is completely refurbished. The cabanas—the "standard" rooms—are attractive and comfortable. Those with beach views are the best, and those with ocean views are the most expensive. The rooms in the tower, which are actually two-bedroom condos, are large, handsomely appointed units that sleep up to six, and have two full bathrooms, a full kitchen, and a spacious living/dining room. Reserve one above the third floor for the sake of quiet.

500 Padre Blvd., South Padre Island, TX 78597. © **800/292-7704** or 956/761-6511. Fax 956/761-1602. www.islagrand.com. 193 units. $279–$319 double; $499 condo. AE, DC, DISC, MC, V. **Amenities:** Restaurant; bar; children's programs; exercise room, 2 Jacuzzis; 2 outdoor pools (1 heated); room service; 4 outdoor lit tennis courts. *In room:* A/C, TV, fridge, hair dryer, kitchen (in condos), Wi-Fi (free).

### The Palms Resort 👫
Of the three traditional beach motels that still exist, this is the nicest. The property is well maintained and well managed. If you want to be on the beach, this is a great option. Rooms are attractive and spacious and have kitchenettes. Most have a small dining area and such extras as marble countertops and

flatscreen TVs. Rooms on the southern side of the building are best. Bathrooms are attractive, some with tub/shower combinations.

3616 Gulf Blvd., South Padre Island, TX 78597. ✆ **800/466-1316** or 956/761-1316. Fax 956/761-1310. www.palmsresortcafe.com. 29 units. $80–$230 queen suite; $100–$275 palms or king suite. AE, MC, V. **Amenities:** Restaurant; heated outdoor pool. *In room:* A/C and fan, TV, fridge, Wi-Fi (free).

**Red Fish Inn ★**    This peaceful two-story house on the bay side of the island has wraparound porches on both floors and is a relaxing place to stay. Rooms have queen-size beds and a tropical feel, with a nod toward our neighbors south of the border. Two face the bay, affording views of stunning sunsets over the Laguna Madre. Most rooms have showers only; one has a tub/shower combo. There are rocking chairs on the porches to entice you to sit back and relax. The inn has a boardwalk along the water and a new pier for the use of the fishing boat. The owner provides guided fly-fishing trips and instruction. The homemade breakfast includes fresh fruit and juices, eggs, and tamales.

207 W. Aries Dr., South Padre Island, TX 78597. ✆ **956/761-2722.** Fax 956/761-8683. www.redfishinn. com. 7 units. $135–$175 double; $195 suite. Rates include full breakfast. Fishing packages available. AE, DISC, MC, V. *In room:* A/C, Wi-Fi (free).

## CAMPING

**Isla Blanca Park ★★** (✆ **956/761-5493**), on the southern tip of South Padre Island, is our choice for a developed campground on the island, with easy beach access. Part of the Cameron County Park System (P.O. Box 2106, South Padre Island, TX 78597), this well-maintained facility has 600 paved sites, many of which are pull-through, and more than half have full RV hookups. The park also has restrooms with showers, a dump station, a sandy beach, a fishing jetty, a boat ramp and marina, a playground, a bike trail, and beach pavilions with concessions. There is a primitive tent area right on the Laguna Madre. Rates are $29 to $35.

Those looking for a developed resort should head to **Destination South Padre RV Resort** (✆ **800/867-2373** or 956/761-5665; www.destinationsouthpadre.com), just south of the Queen Isabella Causeway on Padre Boulevard. It offers 190 gravel sites with full hookups, restrooms with showers, a guest laundromat, and security. There's a large heated pool, spa, boat dock, rec hall and game room, and numerous planned activities. Rates are $35 to $45. There are pet restrictions, and tents are not allowed.

## Where to Dine

If you're staying in a condo with a kitchen, and you have many mouths to feed, you'll be going to the grocery store in Port Isabel. Also, you'll find that Zeste, listed below, is a great resource for packaged foods not found anywhere else nearby.

**Dirty Al's ★** 🐟 SEAFOOD    Al has been a fixture here for 20 years. Most of that time, he was running a bait shop and serving tacos on the side just to fishermen. Now, his restaurant is what keeps him busy. The main attractions are the fried shrimp baskets, the stuffed crabs, the blackened fish, and the fried oyster baskets. Al fries up the best shrimp on the island here, and his prices are rock bottom. The restaurant/bait shop is beside the marina (which is south of the bridge). Picnic tables are scattered out in front where diners can wait for their name to be called (this place is crowded for dinner). Al has opened a second-story dining room. It helps with the wait for a table, but not for the crowded parking lot.

1 Padre Blvd. ✆ **956/761-4901.** Reservations accepted only for parties of 6 or more. Main courses $9–$15. AE, MC, V. Daily 11am–8pm.

**Padre Island Brewing Company** BREW PUB/REGIONAL AMERICAN   The food here (and some pretty decent beer, too) makes Padre Island Brewing Company a popular place. The cooked-to-order burgers and sandwiches, such as the chicken fajita served on a French roll, are the surest things. Entrees include steaks, baby back ribs, Texas quail, stuffed chicken breast, crab-stuffed flounder, and breaded beer-batter shrimp. Eat outside on the second-story deck for terrific views, or inside, with a view of the brewing vats.

3400 Padre Blvd., at Bahama St. ℂ **956/761-9585.** Main courses $8–$18. AE, DISC, MC, V. Tues–Sun 11:30am–10:30pm; Mon 5–10:30pm.

**Ted's Restaurant** 🐟 AMERICAN   For breakfast or lunch, this homey establishment in a converted house serves decent food for a good price. The food is the usual stuff for Texas. Breakfast dishes include eggs, pancakes, waffles, and *migas* (scrambled eggs with onions, tomatoes, chiles, cheese, and tortilla strips). The #4 breakfast (fajitas and eggs) is the local favorite. For lunch, you can choose from fajitas, burgers, sandwiches, and salads. The staff takes pride in their fajitas. The tuna-and-avocado sandwich isn't bad either.

5717 Padre Blvd. ℂ **956/761-5327.** Main courses $5–$8. MC, V. Daily 7am–2:30pm.

**Zeste** ★★ 🍴 DELI   This specialty market is an ideal addition to South Padre Island's dining options, and is positively heaven sent for the condo renter in need of gourmet takeout options. Walking through the door, you're immediately in the mood for food when your nose catches a whiff of herbs and fresh-baked bread from the kitchen. Go to the food case and pick your entree and two sides, uncork a bottle, and dine at leisure in the market's pleasant but small dining area, or take it all to go. The daily menu varies, but usually includes Italian and Mediterranean entrees, as well as something like an herb-roasted chicken or tenderloin, and vegetarian options (excellent appetizers, sides, soups, and desserts, too). You can order an entire picnic. The market section sells specialty foods, olives, wines, imported beers, coffees, and gourmet packaged foods. On Friday nights, Zeste serves tapas, and occasionally on Thursday nights, there are wine tastings.

3508 Padre Blvd. ℂ **956/761-5555.** Plates $9–$15. AE, DISC, MC, V. Wed–Mon 11am–8pm. Extended summer and weekend hours.

# After Dark (or Perhaps After Noon)

Not far away are two places with ample deck space above the water. **Louie's Backyard,** 2305 Laguna Blvd. (ℂ **956/716-6406**), is a large and popular establishment serving American food and operating a full bar. During high season, there is live music nightly. **Wahoo Saloon,** 201 W. Pike St. (ℂ **956/761-5344**), is smaller and simpler. On Fridays during the summer, the city puts on a small fireworks show after dark, which can be enjoyed from any of these places.

When in need of a proper beach bar where you can work your toes into the sand while enjoying a cold beer, cross to the ocean side of the island and head to **Wanna-Wanna,** at the Island Inn motel, 5100 Gulf Blvd. (ℂ **956/761-7677**).

# SAN ANTONIO

by David Baird

S an Antonio, home to the Alamo and the River Walk, is more colorful than any other big city in Texas. It's often compared with New Orleans, Boston, and San Francisco as one of America's most distinctive cities. In short, it's one of a kind. If you're looking for a destination for the whole family, you can't go wrong with San Antonio. It has a downtown area that is comfortable, fun, and safe, and on its outskirts are two large theme parks—SeaWorld and Six Flags Fiesta Texas.

---

For most of its history, San Antonio was the largest city in Texas, the "cosmopolitan" center, where multiple cultures—Native American, Mexican, Anglo, and German, among others—came together and coexisted. In 1718, the native Coahuiltecan Indians sought protection from Apache raids and invited the Spaniards to establish a mission here. A few years later, by order of the king of Spain, 15 families came from the Canary Islands to settle here. (The oldest families in San Antonio can trace their family trees back to these colonists.) The settlement grew and prospered. The church eventually built five missions along the San Antonio River. But during the fight for Mexican Independence and then Texan Independence (1821 and 1836, respectively), San Antonio was the site of several hard-fought battles, including the famous siege of the Alamo. This greatly reduced the population for more than a decade until the city began to attract thousands of German settlers fleeing the revolutions in Europe. So many came that by 1860, German speakers in the city outnumbered both Spanish and English speakers. Throughout the following decades, these different immigrant groups would accommodate each other and forge a unique local culture.

The city continued to grow. In the early 1900s, it showcased the first skyscraper in Texas. But San Antonio wasn't growing fast enough to keep up with Houston or Dallas. By the 1920s, it had become Texas's third-largest city and had arrived at a crossroads. Would it follow Houston and Dallas in their bull rush toward growth and modernism? Or would it go its own way, preserving what it thought most valuable?

This dilemma took the form of a political dispute over the meandering San Antonio River. A city commission recommended draining the riverbed and channeling the water through underground culverts to free up space for more downtown buildings. This outraged many locals. A group of women's clubs formed to save the river and create an urban green space along its banks (and this was decades before anyone in Texas had ever heard of urban planning). The women's campaign was multipronged and even included a puppet-show dramatization. They were victorious. The river was saved, as was San Antonio's heritage. Plans were laid for the Paseo del Rio or River Walk, which would eventually became the city's crowning feature and a point of local pride.

Of course, there are many other aspects to life here that foster pride and a sense of identity. They may not be so photogenic as the River Walk, but they add a richness to the culture that a visitor to San Antonio can easily notice and enjoy.

# ORIENTATION

## Arriving

### BY PLANE

The **San Antonio International Airport (SAT)** (C) 210/207-3411; www.ci.sat. tx.us/aviation) is 7 miles north of downtown. It is compact, easy to navigate, and has two terminals.

**GETTING TO & FROM THE AIRPORT**   Loop 410 and U.S. 281 S. intersect just outside the airport. If you're renting a car here, it should take about 15 to 20 minutes to drive downtown via U.S. 281 S.

Most of the hotels within a radius of a mile or two provide **free shuttle service** to and from the airport (be sure to check when you make your reservation). If you're staying downtown, you'll most likely have to pay your own way.

**VIA Metropolitan Transit's bus no. 5** is the cheapest ($1.10) way to get downtown, but also the slowest; it'll take from 40 to 45 minutes.

**SATRANS** (C) 800/868-7707 or 210/281-9900; www.saairportshuttle.com), with a booth outside each of the terminals, offers shared van service from the airport to downtown hotels for $18 per person one-way, $32 round-trip. Vans run from about 7am until 1am; phone 24 hours in advance for van pickup from your hotel.

There's a **taxi** queue in front of each terminal. Airport taxis charge about $25 to get downtown.

### BY TRAIN

San Antonio's train station is located at 350 Hoefgen St., in St. Paul's Square, on the east side of downtown near the Alamodome and adjacent to the Sunset Station entertainment complex. Cabs are readily available from here. Lockers are not available, but Amtrak will hold passengers' bags in a secure location for $2 per bag. Information about the city is available at the main counter.

### BY BUS

San Antonio's bustling **Greyhound** station, 500 N. St. Mary's St. (C) 210/270-5834), is located downtown about 2 blocks from the River Walk. The station, open 24 hours, is within walking distance of a number of hotels, and many public streetcar and bus lines run nearby.

## Visitor Information

The main office of the **City of San Antonio Visitor Information Center** is across the street from the Alamo, at 317 Alamo Plaza (C) 800/252-6609 or 210/207-6748). Hours are daily 9am to 5pm, except Thanksgiving, Christmas, and New Year's, when the center is closed. Its website can be helpful, too: www.visitsanantonio.com.

The center gives visitors a free copy of the magazine *San Antonio Travel and Leisure Guide,* published semiannually by the **San Antonio Convention and Visitors**

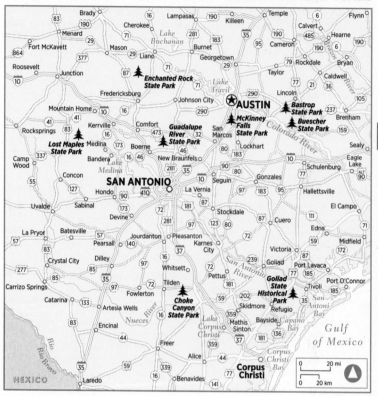

**Bureau (SACVB).** It has maps and listings and is something you can pore over during an idle moment. Also at the center are racks and racks of brochures and some free magazines heavy on advertisements, such as *Fiesta,* with interesting articles about the city, and *Rio,* a tabloid focusing on the River Walk. You can find these last two publications at many of the downtown hotels and shops. Both list sights, restaurants, shops, cultural events, and some nightlife.

Also free—but more objective—is San Antonio's alternative paper, the **Current.** Though skimpy, it is a good source for nightlife listings. The **San Antonio Express-News** is the local newspaper. It's got a good arts/entertainment section called "The Weekender," which comes out on Friday and is available around town.

## City Layout

San Antonio lies at the southern edge of the Texas Hill Country and is mostly flat. Streets are jumbled, especially in the old parts of town, while a number of the thoroughfares leading in and out of town follow old Spanish trails or 19th-century wagon trails.

**MAIN ARTERIES & STREETS**  Most of the major roads in Texas meet in San Antonio, where they form a rough wheel-and-spoke pattern. There are two loops:

I-410 circles around the city, coming to within 6 to 7 miles of downtown in the north and east, and as far out as 10 miles in the west and south; and Hwy. 1604 forms an even larger circle with a 13-mile radius. The spokes of the wheel are formed by highways I-35, I-10, I-37, U.S. 281, U.S. 90, and U.S. 87. Occasionally, two or three highways will merge onto the same freeway. For example, U.S. 90, U.S. 87, and I-10 converge for a while in an east-west direction just south of downtown, while U.S. 281, I-35, and I-37 run together on a north-south route to the east; I-10, I-35, and U.S. 87 bond for a bit going north-south to the west of downtown.

Among the most major of the minor spokes are Broadway, McCullough, San Pedro, and Blanco, all of which lead north from the city center into the most popular shopping and restaurant areas of town. Fredericksburg Road goes out to the Medical Center from just northwest of downtown. You may hear locals referring to something as being "in the loop." That doesn't mean it's privy to insider information, but rather, that it lies within the circumference of I-410, and is therefore in central San Antonio.

Downtown is bounded by I-37 to the east, I-35 to the north and west, and U.S. 90 (which merges with I-10) to the south. Within this area, Durango, Commerce, Market, and Houston are the important east-west streets. Alamo on the east side and Santa Rosa (which turns into South Laredo) on the west side are the major north-south streets.

## The Neighborhoods in Brief

The older areas described here, from downtown through Alamo Heights, are all "in the loop" (410). The Medical Center area in the Northwest lies just outside it, but the rest of the Northwest, as well as North Central and the West, are expanding beyond even Loop 1604.

**Downtown**  Site of San Antonio's original Spanish settlements, this area includes the Alamo and other historic sites, along with the River Walk, the Alamodome, the convention center, the Rivercenter Mall, and many high-rise hotels, restaurants, and shops. It's also the center of commerce and government, so many banks and offices, as well as most city buildings, are located here. Downtown is fun and vibrant. The River Walk is the centerpiece, but there's a lot more that can be seen and appreciated that takes a bit of exploring.

**King William**  The city's first suburb, this historic district directly south of downtown was settled in the mid- to late 1800s by wealthy German merchants who built some of the most beautiful mansions in town. It began to be yuppified in the 1970s, and, at this point, you'd never guess it had ever been allowed to deteriorate. Only three of the area's many impeccably restored homes are open to the public, but a number have become bed-and-breakfasts. As you can imagine, the location is ideal for those who want to explore the central city.

**Southtown**  Alamo Street marks the border between King William and Southtown, an adjoining neighborhood. Long a depressed area, it's become trendy thanks to a Main Street refurbishing project and the opening of the Blue Star arts complex. You'll find a nice mix of Hispanic neighborhood shops and funky coffeehouses and galleries here, but few hotels worth staying in.

**South Side**  The old, largely Hispanic southeast section of town that begins where Southtown ends (there's no agreed-upon boundary, but I'd say it lies a few blocks beyond the Blue Star arts complex) is home to four of the city's five historic missions. Thus far, it's been left alone and remains a group of quiet working-class neighborhoods with pockets of small businesses.

**Monte Vista Area**  Immediately north of downtown, Monte Vista was established soon after King William by a conglomeration of wealthy cattlemen, politicos, and generals who moved "on to the hill" at the turn of the 20th century. A number of the area's large houses have been split into apartments for students of nearby Trinity

University and San Antonio Community College, but many lovely old houses have been restored in the past 30 years. This is a highly desirable place to live, and a great place to stay during a visit. There are several bed-and-breakfasts and most are located on quiet streets that are within easy reach of downtown. In addition, there are several good dining spots nearby.

**Fort Sam Houston** Built in 1876 to the northeast of downtown, Fort Sam Houston boasts a number of stunning officers' homes. Much of the working-class neighborhood surrounding Fort Sam is run-down, but renewed interest in restoring San Antonio's older areas is beginning to have some impact here, too.

**Alamo Heights Area** In the 1890s, when construction in the area began, Alamo Heights was at the far northern reaches of San Antonio. This is now home to San Antonio's well-heeled residents and holds most of the fashionable shops and restaurants. **Terrell Hills** to the east, **Olmos Park** to the west, and **Lincoln Heights** to the north are all offshoots of this area. It is home to the Quarry, once just that, but now a ritzy golf course and popular shopping mall. Shops and restaurants are concentrated along two main drags: Broadway and, to a lesser degree, New Braunfels. Most of these neighborhoods share a single zip code ending in the numbers "09"—thus the local term "09ers," referring to the area's affluent residents. The Witte Museum, San Antonio Botanical Gardens, and Brackenridge Park are all here.

**Northwest** These mostly characterless neighborhoods surround the south Texas Medical Center (a large grouping of health-care facilities referred to as the **Medical Center**). The area includes lots of condominiums and apartments, and much of the shopping and dining is in strip malls (the trendy, still-expanding Huebner Oaks retail center is an exception). The farther north you go, the nicer the housing complexes get. The high-end Westin La Cantera resort, the exclusive La Cantera and Dominion residential enclave, several tony golf courses, and the Shops at La Cantera, San Antonio's fanciest new retail center, mark the direction that development is taking in the far northwest part of town, just beyond Six Flags Fiesta Texas and near the public Friedrich Park. It's becoming one of San Antonio's prime growth areas.

**North Central** San Antonio is inching toward Bulverde and other Hill Country towns via this major corridor of development clustered from Loop 410 north to Loop 1604, east of I-10 and west of I-35, and bisected by U.S. 281. The airport and many developed industrial strips line U.S. 281 in the southern section, but the farther north you go, the more you see the natural beauty of this area, hilly and dotted with small canyons. Recent city codes have motivated developers to retain trees and native plants in their residential communities.

**West** Although SeaWorld has been out here since the late 1980s, and the Hyatt Regency Hill Country Resort settled here in the early 1990s, other development was comparatively slow in coming. Now the West is booming with new midprice housing developments, strip malls, schools, and businesses. Road building hasn't kept pace with growth, however, so traffic can be a bear.

# GETTING AROUND

If you're staying downtown, a car is more of a hindrance than an asset: Traffic can be a pain, and public transportation is good. If you're staying in King William or Monte Vista, you can get by without a car, but it would come in handy to see the attractions outside the downtown area. If you're bunking anywhere else in San Antonio, however, you'll definitely want wheels—and you might as well rent them at the airport, where all the major car-rental companies are represented at each of the terminals.

# By Public Transportation

**BY BUS**  **VIA Metropolitan Transit Service** offers regular bus service for $1.10, with an additional 15¢ charge for transfers. Express buses cost $2. You'll need exact change. Call ✆ **210/362-2020** for transit information, check the website at **www.viainfo.net**, or stop in one of VIA's many service centers. The most convenient for visitors is the downtown center, 260 E. Houston St., open Monday to Friday 7am to 6pm, Saturday 9am to 2pm. A helpful bus route is the no. 7, which travels from downtown to the San Antonio Museum of Art, Japanese Tea Garden, San Antonio Zoo, Witte Museum, Brackenridge Park, and the Botanical Garden. *Tip:* During large festivals such as Fiesta and the Texas Folklife Festival, VIA offers many Park & Ride lots that allow you to leave your car and take a bus downtown.

**BY STREETCAR**  In addition to its normal bus lines, VIA offers four convenient downtown bus routes that cover all the most popular tourist stops. The buses look like trolleys, cost $1.10 (exact change required; drivers carry none), and are color coded by route. It's a good idea to pick up a route map for all four at the visitor center.

# By Car

If you can avoid driving downtown, by all means do so. The pattern of one-way streets is confusing and parking is limited. It's not that the streets in downtown San Antonio are narrower or more crowded than those in most old city centers, but there's no need to bother with driving when public transportation is so convenient.

Rush hour lasts from about 7:30 to 9am and 4:30 to 6pm Monday through Friday. The crush may not be bad compared to that of Houston or Dallas, but it's getting worse. Because of San Antonio's rapid growth, you can also expect to find major highway construction or repairs going on somewhere in the city at any given time. For updates, log on to the Texas Department of Transportation's website at **www.dot.state.tx.us**.

**PARKING**  There are plenty of parking lots scattered around the north and east sides of downtown, within a few blocks of the main attractions. These run about $5 to $7 per day. Parking meters are not plentiful in the heart of downtown, but you can find some on the streets near the River Walk and on Broadway. The cost is $1 per hour (which is also the time limit) near the courthouse, 75¢ in other locations. There are some inexpensive (2 hr. for $1) meters at the outskirts of downtown. *Note:* Although very few signs inform you of this fact, parking at meters is free after 6pm Monday through Saturday and all day Sunday, except during special events.

# By River Taxi

**Rio Taxi Service** (✆ **800/417-4139** or 210/244-5700; www.riosanantonio.com) operates daily from 9am to 9pm. Its 12 pickup locations are marked by Rio Taxi signs with black-and-yellow checker flags. You buy your tickets once you board. At $4 one-way, $10 for an all-day pass, or $25 for a 3-day pass, it's more expensive than ground transport, but it's a treat.

# By Taxi

Cabs are available outside the airport, near the Greyhound and Amtrak terminals (only when a train is due, however), and at most major downtown hotels, but they're next to impossible to hail on the street; most of the time, you'll need to phone for one in advance. The best of the taxi companies in town (and also the largest, because it represents the consolidation of two of the majors) is **Yellow Checker**

**Cab** (☎ **210/222-2222**), which has an excellent record of turning up when promised. The base charge on a taxi is $2; add $2.15 for each mile.

# [FastFACTS] SAN ANTONIO

**Dentist** To find a dentist near you in town, contact the San Antonio District Dental Society, 3355 Cherry Ridge, Ste. 214 (☎ **210/732-1264**).

**Doctor** For a referral, contact the Bexar County Medical Society at 6243 W. IH-10, Ste. 600 (☎ **210/301-4368;** www.bcms.org), Monday through Friday from 8am to 5pm.

**Drugstores** Most branches of CVS (formerly Eckerd) and Walgreens, the major chain pharmacies in San Antonio, are open late Monday through Saturday. There's a CVS downtown at 211 Losoya/River Walk (☎ **210/224-9293**). Call ☎ **800/925-4733** to find the Walgreens nearest you; punch in the area code and the first three digits of the number you're phoning from and you'll be directed to the closest branch.

**Hospitals** The main downtown hospital is Baptist Medical Center, 111 Dallas St. (☎ **210/297-7000**). Christus Santa Rosa Health Care Corp., 333 N. Santa Rosa St. (☎ **210/704-2011**), is also downtown. Contact the San Antonio Medical Foundation (☎ **210/614-3724**) for information about other medical facilities in the city.

**Hot Lines** Contact the National Youth Crisis Hot Line at ☎ **800/448-4663;** Rape Crisis Hot Line at ☎ **210/349-7273;** Child Abuse Hot Line at ☎ **800/252-5400;** Mental Illness Crisis Hot Line at ☎ **210/227-4357;** Bexar County Adult Abuse Hot Line at ☎ **800/252-5400;** and Poison Control Center at ☎ **800/764-7661.**

**Newspapers & Magazines** The *San Antonio Express-News* is the only mainstream source of news in town. See "Visitor Information," earlier in this chapter, for magazine recommendations.

**Police** Call ☎ **911** in an emergency. The nonemergency number is ☎ **311.** The Texas Highway Patrol can be reached at ☎ **210/531-2220.**

**Safety** The crime rate in San Antonio has gone down in recent years, and there's a strong police presence downtown (in fact, both the transit authority and the police department have bicycle patrols); as a result, muggings, pickpockets, and purse snatchings in the area are rare. Still, use common sense as you would anywhere else: Walk only on well-lit, well-populated streets. Also, it's generally not a good idea to stroll south of Durango Avenue after dark.

**Taxes** The sales tax here is 8.25%, and the city surcharge on hotel rooms increases to a whopping 16.75%.

# WHERE TO STAY

Most visitors to San Antonio want to stay downtown so they can be close to the River Walk and many of the major attractions. Staying downtown is a lot of fun, but to get a feel for San Antonio that you won't get downtown, consider the King William neighborhood or Monte Vista. Both are interesting places in their own right, both are close to downtown, and both have dining and entertainment spots nearby.

Of course, there are other parts of the city where you can stay, but I don't see any point in doing so if you're coming to explore San Antonio. On the other hand, if the main objective is a relaxing vacation, then another option would be to stay at one of the resorts or hotels on the west/northwest side of San Antonio, near the two big

# Greater San Antonio Accommodations, Dining & Attractions

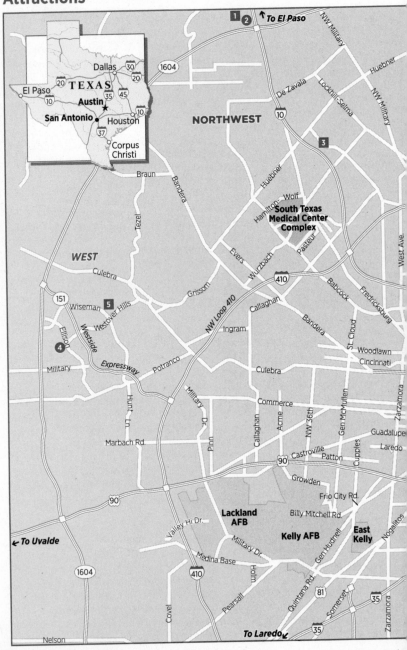

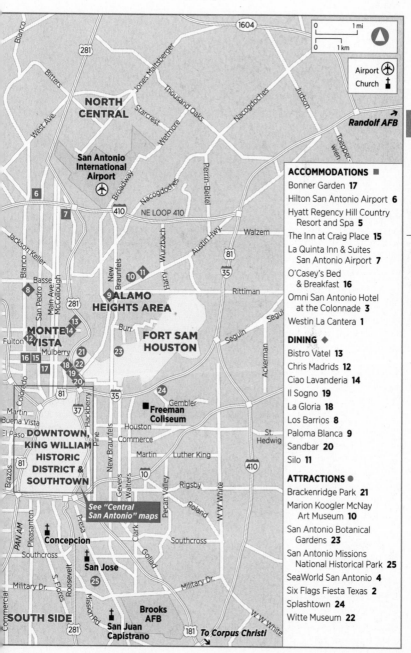

**ACCOMMODATIONS** ■

Bonner Garden **17**

Hilton San Antonio Airport **6**

Hyatt Regency Hill Country
Resort and Spa **5**

The Inn at Craig Place **15**

La Quinta Inn & Suites
San Antonio Airport **7**

O'Casey's Bed
& Breakfast **16**

Omni San Antonio Hotel
at the Colonnade **3**

Westin La Cantera **1**

**DINING** ◆

Bistro Vatel **13**

Chris Madrids **12**

Ciao Lavanderia **14**

Il Sogno **19**

La Gloria **18**

Los Barrios **8**

Paloma Blanca **9**

Sandbar **20**

Silo **11**

**ATTRACTIONS** ●

Brackenridge Park **21**

Marion Koogler McNay
Art Museum **10**

San Antonio Botanical
Gardens **23**

San Antonio Missions
National Historical Park **25**

SeaWorld San Antonio **4**

Six Flags Fiesta Texas **2**

Splashtown **24**

Witte Museum **22**

theme parks: SeaWorld and Six Flags Fiesta Texas. Then you can combine swimming, golfing, and shopping with spa treatments and amusement parks and make the drive into San Antonio when you're up for a change of pace.

**DOWNTOWN**   It's important to shop around. Rates float up and down depending upon occupancy, and occupancy is driven by conventions and smaller conferences. These have their quirks—convention people will tend to group in certain hotels, and many conferences are based at a particular property. Since hotels do not fill up evenly, you should check rates at different properties and, if you have flexibility, inquire about different dates. If you want to see the big picture, check out this website, where you can find what meetings are taking place during your travel dates: http://meetings. visitsanantonio.com/meeting-calendar. The high season for conventions in San Antonio is both fall and spring.

**KING WILLIAM**   There's no doubt that this neighborhood and the larger South-town area are happening places these days—more about the arts and leisure than business, and a perfect choice for grown-ups wanting to spend a relaxing weekend, or longer if possible. The monthly street fair on South Alamo (First Fridays) is quite popular with visitors. The best option is to lodge in one of the grand old houses in King William. Downtown is only a 15-minute walk away, via the River Walk or South Alamo Street. Prices don't fluctuate the way they do at large hotels. For a larger selection of properties, check out the website of the **San Antonio Bed & Breakfast Association:** www.sanantoniobb.org.

**MONTE VISTA**   B&Bs in this neighborhood are an especially good value. The houses are beautiful; the neighborhood is quiet, despite its central location; and some interesting neighborhoods are on all sides. It's either a 30-minute walk or a short and easy bus ride to downtown. There are several new things happening nearby, including the redevelopment of the old Pearl Brewery. You can also expect B&Bs to provide fax and other business services, and these days most provide Wi-Fi.

With a few exceptions, the vast majority of the other lodgings around town are low-priced chains. The most convenient are clustered in the northwest, near the Medical Center, and in the north central area, around the airport. For a full alphabetical listing of the accommodations in the city, mapped by area and including rate ranges as well as basic amenities, phone the **San Antonio Convention and Visitors Bureau** (© **800/447-3372**) and request a lodging guide. The "Accommodations" section of **www.sanantoniovisit.com** is also a good resource.

Wherever you decide to stay, try to book as far in advance as possible—especially if the property is located downtown. And don't even think about coming to town during Fiesta (the third week in Apr) if you haven't reserved a room 6 months in advance.

Now a few words about the listing info: The rates noted here are prevalent for most of the year, before taxes (16.75%). They can go both higher and lower, again, depending on occupancy. Almost all the large hotels are nonsmoking properties; when smoking rooms are available, it's noted in the review. Parking fees are always per day and pet fees are per visit, unless specified otherwise.

## Downtown

### VERY EXPENSIVE

**Hotel Contessa ★★**   This is one of the newest hotels built on the river, and its location makes you wonder why it took so long to build here. Fronting the property is a massive cypress tree crowning a small bit of land that creates a slight bend in the

# Central San Antonio Accommodations

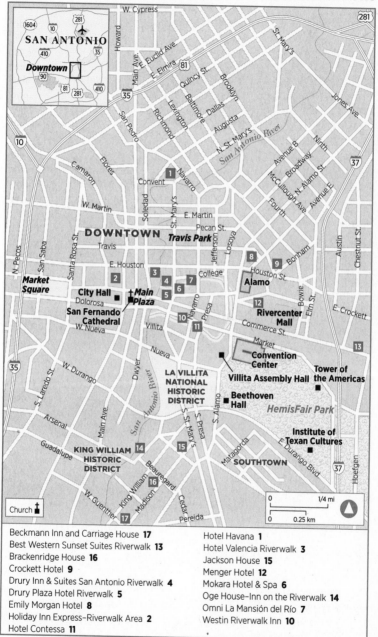

Beckmann Inn and Carriage House **17**
Best Western Sunset Suites Riverwalk **13**
Brackenridge House **16**
Crockett Hotel **9**
Drury Inn & Suites San Antonio Riverwalk **4**
Drury Plaza Hotel Riverwalk **5**
Emily Morgan Hotel **8**
Holiday Inn Express–Riverwalk Area **2**
Hotel Contessa **11**

Hotel Havana **1**
Hotel Valencia Riverwalk **3**
Jackson House **15**
Menger Hotel **12**
Mokara Hotel & Spa **6**
Oge House–Inn on the Riverwalk **14**
Omni La Mansión del Río **7**
Westin Riverwalk Inn **10**

river—a popular wedding spot, and, consequently, the hotel gets lots of weddings. The architecture and decor are less traditional than that of the neighboring Westin. Guest rooms surround a soaring atrium with lots of light and bold colors. All rooms are suites with either a king-size bed or two double beds, a large bathroom, and a sizable living area. Both the furniture and lighting are more comfortable than many hotels in this category. The bedrooms have either a river or city view. The best river views are down low, level with the cypress trees, and the best city views are up high.

Hotel operations are handled by Benchmark, which, in my experience, does a commendable job at providing services and running properties. Whether you stay here or at the Westin next door would depend largely on the rates, the availability of "riverview" rooms, and the importance of having a balcony (Westin).

306 W. Market St. (at Navarro), San Antonio, TX 78205. ℰ **866/435-0900** or 210/229-9222. Fax 210/229-9228. www.thehotelcontessa.com. 265 units. $219–$289 suite; from $260 executive suite. AE, DC, DISC, MC, V. Valet parking $28. Pets 50 lbs. and under accepted for $50 per night. **Amenities:** Restaurant; bar; babysitting; concierge; exercise room; Jacuzzi; outdoor heated pool; room service; spa. *In room:* A/C, TV, hair dryer, minibar, Wi-Fi (free).

**Hotel Valencia Riverwalk**   The Valencia is the hippest hotel on the River Walk. It's a good choice for the design-conscious traveler or anyone who feels in a rut. The hotel's design counteracts the effect of the bright sunlight and busy street scene by easing the sensory load. It avoids the grandiose and has subdued lighting and a sonic background of falling water. The hotel makes a modern statement with primitive materials and lots of texture (stone, clay, and bamboo). The drama is provided in subtle ways, such as the play of light and shadow. Guest rooms work equally well for business or leisure travelers. They are large and comfortable and made to feel larger by the lack of clutter and the use of solid colors over patterns (in tones of gray, black, and cream). Gone are the ubiquitous draperies and in their place are shutters. A heavy built-in counter running the length of the room provides ample desk and counter space. Bathrooms are standard size, but well appointed. The priciest rooms have river views from narrow balconies. In addition to the hotel's own restaurant, Citrus, there is the popular Acenar (not associated with the hotel) on the bottom floor (p. 253).

150 E. Houston St. (at St. Mary's), San Antonio, TX 78205. ℰ **866/842-0100** or 210/227-9700. Fax 210/227-9701. www.hotelvalencia.com. 213 units. $199–$239 double; from $350 suite. AE, DC, DISC, MC, V. Valet parking $29. **Amenities:** Restaurant; bar; concierge; exercise room; room service; spa. *In room:* A/C, TV, hair dryer, minibar, Wi-Fi (free).

**Mokara Hotel & Spa** ★★★   This hotel is the best choice for anyone wishing to add pampering and relaxation to the San Antonio experience. Everything about this hotel is relaxing, and the spa is large, elaborate, and highly rated. Guestrooms and suites have high ceilings, walls painted in cool shades of elemental colors, and lots of soft natural light. Many have balconies overlooking the river, large enough to accommodate a couple of chairs. The decor is modern and polished with accents reflecting the rustic San Antonio of old. Marble bathrooms are oversize and have jetted tubs and separate showers. The rooftop cafe and pool area provides yet another way to take in San Antonio in a relaxing way. To all this, add the easy, personal, and unobtrusive attention of the staff, and you have the total experience. The location is on one of my favorite stretches of the River Walk—quiet, yet close to the main restaurant section, as well as the restaurants along East Houston Street. If you'll be making much use of the spa, consider booking one of the spa-level rooms, which have hardwood floors and allow direct access to the facilities. A full-service salon is also on the premises.

212 W. Crockett St. (at St. Mary's), San Antonio, TX 78205. ☎ **866/605-1212** or 210/396-5800. www.mokarahotelsandspas.com. 99 units. $259–$289 double; $359-$389 river-view double; from $800 suite. AE, DC, DISC, MC, V. Valet parking $32. **Amenities:** Restaurant; cafe; babysitting; concierge; gym; Jacuzzi; heated outdoor pool; room service; sauna; spa. *In room:* A/C, TV, hair dryer, minibar, MP3 docking station, Wi-Fi (free).

**Omni La Mansión del Río ★★★**   This hotel is pure San Antonio and is the favorite choice of Texan out-of-towners. The core of the building was constructed in 1852 for a seminary, which later became old St. Mary's College. The Southwestern look of the hotel is a reflection of this heritage and not some phony affectation. Architectural elements such as old-style Mexican tile floors, wrought-iron work, and beamed ceilings lend the hotel a sense of place that's not just a corporate concept. Moreover, La Mansión makes being on the river more enjoyable than does its high-rise neighbors. The balconies of the river-view rooms are level with the tall cypress and palm trees that line the river bank and look out over a particularly attractive stretch of the River Walk. I could idle away many hours on one of those balconies. Other rooms have courtyard views and, though not quite as much fun, are preferable to many of the standard rooms of other hotels. Rooms are, for the most part, large, comfortably furnished, and don't go overboard with the decor. The Omni chain took over the property in 2006 and provides attentive, personal service. Guests have signing privileges at the Mokara (another Omni property on the opposite bank) for that hotel's restaurant, fitness room, spa, and salon.

112 College St. (between St. Mary's and Navarro), San Antonio, TX 78205. ☎ **800/292-7300** or 210/518-1000. Fax 210/226-0389. www.omnilamansion.com. 338 units. $169–$229 double; $219–$279 ambassador room; from $750. suite AE, DC, DISC, MC, V. Valet parking $32. Pets 25 lb. and under accepted for $50. **Amenities:** Restaurant; bar; babysitting; children's programs; concierge, outdoor heated pool; room service. *In room:* A/C, TV, hair dryer, minibar, Wi-Fi (free).

**Westin Riverwalk ★★ ☺**   This property was designed to blend in architecturally with the older structures that flank it on this (relatively) quiet section of the river bend, while its clean lines reflect a more modern aesthetic. Rooms, however, are furnished in a traditional style and are large and comfortable. All the "river-view" rooms have balconies. My favorites are on the fourth floor, where the balconies are a tad larger and you're a little closer to the river. "City-view" rooms are the same, except for the balcony, and have interesting views. There are nice details for the business traveler, such as an ample desk with stone countertop and convenient connections. Of course, the property includes Westin's signature "Heavenly Beds," which are exactly that. Perhaps in a nod to its many high-end Latin American business visitors, the hotel has a traditional *merienda* (light meal) on Wednesday to Friday evenings, which includes Mexican hot chocolate, sweet bread, cookies, and refreshments (it's free to hotel guests). This Westin has also nicely incorporated several kid-friendly features (see "Family-Friendly Hotels" on p. 247). Service at the hotel is very attentive.

420 W. Market St. (at Navarro), San Antonio, TX 78205. ☎ **800/WESTIN-1** (937-8461) or 210/224-6500. Fax 210/444-6000. www.westin.com/riverwalk. 539 units. $339–$429 double; from $419 suite. AE, DC, DISC, MC, V. Valet parking $30. Pets 40 lbs. and under accepted free. **Amenities:** Restaurant; cafe; bar; babysitting; children's programs; concierge; exercise room; outdoor heated pool; room service; spa. *In room:* A/C, TV, hair dryer, minibar, Wi-Fi ($12–$20 per day).

## EXPENSIVE

**Emily Morgan Hotel ★★ ✦**   This hotel next to the Alamo is in a 1920s Gothic skyscraper that for a while was the tallest building in the western U.S. It rises high above the Alamo and has many rooms overlooking the grounds of the old mission. The location is ideal for visitors: close by the attractions, shops, restaurants, and River Walk. The guest rooms are contemporary, plush, and streamlined. Black lacquer finishes, flatscreen TVs, and sliding doors to the bathroom add to the sleek appearance. The Emily Morgan is considerably less expensive than many comparable hotels on the river, and the combination of style, comfort, and history is hard to beat. The hotel is popular with repeat visitors and has been voted one of the top hotels by a couple of travel magazines. This is a fun place to stay—the lobby bar during happy hour can be a lively scene.

705 E. Houston St. (at Ave. E), San Antonio, TX 78205. © **800/824-6674** or 210/225-5100. Fax 210/225-7227. www.emilymorganhotel.com. 177 units. $169–$269 double; $229–$279 suite. Special rates available. AE, DC, DISC, MC, V. Valet parking $26. Pets accepted with $75 fee. **Amenities:** Restaurant; bar; concierge; exercise room; Jacuzzi; outdoor heated pool; room service; sauna. *In room:* A/C, TV, CD player, hair dryer, Wi-Fi ($9.95).

**Menger Hotel** ★  In the late–19th century, anyone who was someone stayed only at the Menger, which opened its doors in 1859 and has never closed them. Ulysses S. Grant, Sarah Bernhardt, and Oscar Wilde were among those who walked—or, rumor has it, in the case of Robert E. Lee, rode a horse—through the halls, ballrooms, and gardens. Successfully combining the original, restored building with myriad additions, the Menger now takes up an entire city block. The hotel's location is terrific—between the Alamo and the Rivercenter Mall, a block from the River Walk. Its public areas, particularly the Victorian lobby, are gorgeous. The **Menger Bar** (p. 273) is one of San Antonio's historic taverns, and while nearly every historic hotel in town promotes a ghost, this one claims to have no fewer than 32. Rooms in the modern sections tend to be a bit plain, so request one of the refurbished rooms on the fourth and fifth floors. Decor ranges from ornate 19th-century to modern. If you want one of the antiques-filled Victorian rooms, be sure to request it when you book.

204 Alamo Plaza (at Crockett St.), San Antonio, TX 78205. © **800/345-9285** or 210/223-4361. Fax 210/228-0022. www.mengerhotel.com. 316 units. $169–$229 double; $250–$495 suite. Internet specials available. AE, DC, DISC, MC, V. Valet parking $25. Pets accepted with $50 fee. **Amenities:** Restaurant; bar; exercise room; Jacuzzi; outdoor pool; room service; spa; Wi-Fi (free, in lobby). *In room:* A/C, TV, hair dryer, Internet.

## MODERATE

**Crockett Hotel** ★ 🍴  This hotel is a bit of a hybrid, consisting of the original historical landmark building (expanded in 1927) and several low-slung, motel-style units surrounding what may be downtown's nicest swimming pool and a tropical landscaped courtyard. Rooms in both sections of the hotel are attractive; all were remodeled in 2007 and have a clean, uncluttered look. Check for deals; rooms here are discounted for every imaginable reason. The location is excellent, by the Alamo and the Rivercenter Mall and close by the river.

320 Bonham St. (at Crockett St.), San Antonio, TX 78205. © **800/292-1050** or 210/225-6500. Fax 210/225-7418. www.crocketthotel.com. 138 units. $139–$157 double; from $345 suite. Special packages available. Rates include continental breakfast. AE, DC, DISC, MC, V. Valet parking $20. **Amenities:** Restaurant; bar; outdoor pool; room service. *In room:* A/C, TV, hair dryer, Wi-Fi (free).

**Drury Inn & Suites San Antonio Riverwalk/Drury Plaza Hotel Riverwalk** 🍴  Both of these properties occupy old San Antonio skyscrapers. Rooms at the Inn & Suites can have river views (for which you pay a little extra) and are a little smaller than their counterparts at the Plaza Hotel Riverwalk, where rooms run about

$10 more. Some have good views of San Fernando cathedral, especially lovely at night. I'm not a fan of the way guest rooms are decorated at Drury Inns, but this chain does a good job of offering comfort and location at a good price. The suites are worth the extra money. Both properties have direct access to the River Walk and have preserved the original lobbies. Make a point of entering the Plaza Hotel Riverwalk. It was built in 1929, the heyday of exuberance right before the big stock market crash—50-foot ceilings, travertine marble, gold accents—it's a magnificent vision.

201 N. St. Mary's St. (at Commerce St.), San Antonio, TX 78205. *©* **800/DRURY-INN** (378-7946) or 210/212-5200. Fax 210/352-9939. www.druryhotels.com. 150 units. $129–$164 double; $164–$199 suite. Special packages available. Rates include full breakfast. AE, DC, DISC, MC, V. Valet parking $18; self-parking $14. Small pets accepted. **Amenities:** Restaurant; exercise room; 2 Jacuzzis; 2 outdoor/indoor pools. *In room:* A/C, TV, fridge, hair dryer, Wi-Fi (free).

### Holiday Inn Express San Antonio—River Walk *🏊*   This hotel occupies the 1878 Bexar (pronounced *bear*) County Jail building, which explains its stout, fortress-like appearance. The interior was gutted, so you won't see vestiges of the jail; only the bars on the front windows remain. Rooms are a good size and well maintained. The bathrooms are a bit larger than what you usually see in this price range and have uncommon touches such as polished granite countertops. The largest rooms come with two queen beds and are quite comfortable. Other options include a king bed and the studio king. Service here is attentive if minimal, in keeping with the "express" concept of the hotel. The location is in the western part of downtown San Antonio. It's a safe area, only 3 blocks from the River Walk and several more to the Alamo and the main restaurant area.

120 Camaron St. (btw. Houston and Commerce), San Antonio, TX 78205. *©* **800/HOLIDAY** (465-4329) or 210/281-1400. Fax 210/228-0007. www.hiexpress.com. 82 units. $109–$129 double. Rates include continental breakfast. AE, DC, DISC, MC, V. Off-site parking $16. **Amenities:** Exercise room; Jacuzzi; outdoor heated pool. *In room:* A/C, TV, fridge, hair dryer, Wi-Fi (free).

### Hotel Havana ★   Liz Lambert, the owner of Hotel Santa Cecilia and Hotel San Jose in Austin, recently purchased this classic, three-story hotel by the River Walk in the northern part of downtown. She has removed the clutter and decorated the rooms in a spare manner that lets the cool white walls, dark-wood trim, and handsome wood floors take center stage. Rooms and suites are furnished with a mix of new and old pieces. As with the owner's other properties, there is a careful eye toward design. Though these rooms have never had closets, they are now equipped with large retro fridges. You can request a continental breakfast served in your room.

1015 Navarro St. (btw. St. Mary's and Martin sts.), San Antonio, TX 78205. *©* **210/222-2008.** Fax 210/222-2217. www.havanasanantonio.com. 27 units. $149–$199 double; $209–$599 suite. Rates include continental breakfast. AE, DC, DISC, MC, V. Self-parking $10. Pets accepted for $25 fee. **Amenities:** Bar; concierge; room service. *In room:* A/C and fan, TV, fridge, hair dryer, minibar, Wi-Fi (free).

## INEXPENSIVE

### Best Western Sunset Suites—Riverwalk ★ *🏊*   This hotel is a rare combination of economy and location. The reception and lobby area are in a two-story brick building from 1896. The suites are in a new building next door and are large, comfortable, and equipped with sleeper sofas and microwaves. The hotel is located next to the freeway, but the rooms are quiet. The Rivercenter Mall, River Walk, and convention center are 2 blocks away. This part of downtown near the old train station is known as Sunset Station and has been redeveloped to include several restaurants and entertainment venues.

1103 E. Commerce St. (at Hwy. 281), San Antonio, TX 78205. © **866/560-6000** or 210/223-4400. Fax 210/223-4402. www.bestwesternsunsetsuites.com. 64 units. $109–$165 suite. Special rates available. AE, DC, DISC, MC, V. Free parking. **Amenities:** Exercise room. *In room:* A/C, TV, fridge, hair dryer, mini-bar, Wi-Fi (free).

## King William Historic District

### EXPENSIVE

**Jackson House ★★**  Built in a restrained Victorian style, the Jackson House (1894) is to my mind one of the most beautiful and distinctive properties in the area. It has been restored with great care and imagination by Liesl and Donald Noble, both from families who have lived in the King William neighborhood and San Antonio for generations. The common rooms exhibit original fixtures and rare Texas long-leaf pine flooring, with wallpaper in elegant William Morris designs. The furniture reflects the Victorian age and is selected with a careful eye to detail. This is a comfortable place to stay, too. There is a large, enclosed Jacuzzi behind the house, and afternoon snacks and refreshments are served. The rooms are uncluttered and have all the modern conveniences. The three downstairs rooms feature high ceilings that make them feel a bit larger and allow for a little more fun in the design. All come with gas fireplaces and mantelpieces. Four are furnished with a queen-size bed, two with a king-size bed.

107 Madison St. (off St. Mary's St.), San Antonio, TX 78204. © **800/242-2770** or 210/223-2353. www.nobleinns.com. 6 units. $159–$225 double; $199–$295 suite. Rates include full breakfast, afternoon snacks, and beverages. Corporate rates available. AE, DC, DISC, MC, V. Free parking. Children 13 and older accepted. **Amenities:** Jacuzzi. *In room:* A/C and fan, TV, hair dryer, Wi-Fi. (free).

**Oge House—Inn on the Riverwalk ★★**  The Oge House is a massive structure built in 1857 in antebellum neoclassical style. It's furnished with European antiques of similar or complementary style and sits on a large landscaped property that backs up to the river. The common areas, the yard, and the 10 guest rooms are spacious. The bathrooms are much more than what you would expect at a B&B—large, with showers and tubs, and some with oversize spa showers and/or Jacuzzi tubs. Many rooms also have fireplaces and views of the grounds, and one looks out on the river from its own balcony. The units downstairs don't have as much light as those on the upper two floors, but they're larger and more private, with separate entrances. A couple have sofa beds to accommodate a third guest. An ample breakfast is served at individual tables, either in the stately dining room or out on the veranda; in-room breakfast service can be arranged for the suites.

209 Washington St. (at Turner St.), San Antonio, TX 78204. © **800/242-2770** or 210/223-2353. www.nobleinns.com. 10 units. $179–$269 double; $259–$349 suite. Rates include full breakfast. Corporate traveler rates available. AE, DC, DISC, MC, V. Free parking. Children 16 and older accepted. *In room:* A/C, TV/DVD, fridge, hair dryer, Wi-Fi (free).

### MODERATE

**Beckmann Inn and Carriage House**  This 1886 Queen Anne house has a beautiful wraparound porch, which is perfect for enjoying the serenity of the King William area. The house is located at the southern end of the neighborhood, right by the river, which at this level is unpopulated by tourists. You couldn't find a more relaxing spot so close to downtown. The common rooms are trimmed in elegant woodwork and furnished with antiques of the period, evoking a feeling for times past. Guest rooms are also furnished in antique period pieces, including queen-size carved wooden beds. Two of them, as well as the carriage house, have private entrances. A full breakfast—perhaps cranberry French toast topped with orange twist—is served in the formal dining room, but you can also enjoy your coffee in a cheerful sun room.

**FAMILY-FRIENDLY** hotels

**Hyatt Regency Hill Country Resort and Spa** (p. 248) In addition to its many great play areas (including a beach with a shallow swimming area) and proximity to SeaWorld, this hotel offers Camp Hyatt—a program of excursions, sports, and social activities for children 3 to 12. The program fills up fast during school breaks and other holidays, when reservations are mandatory.

**O'Casey's Bed & Breakfast** (p. 248) Usually B&Bs and family vacations are a contradiction in terms, but O'Casey's is happy to host well-behaved kids. *Best bet:* Stay in the separate guesthouse with the foldout bed, and then join the main-house guests for breakfast in the morning.

**Omni San Antonio Hotel at the Colonnade** (p. 249) This hotel's proximity to the theme parks, as well as in-room Nintendo and various other Omni Kids features, makes it appealing to families.

**Westin La Cantera** (p. 249) It's close to Six Flags Fiesta Texas and has two pools just for children, along with the Enchanted Rock Kids Club—an activities program for ages 5 through 12—May through Labor Day.

**Westin Riverwalk** (p. 243) Though not as family-friendly as the Westin La Cantera, this hotel still offers such amenities as free in-room movies, a kids' treat pack upon check-in, and bedtime stories told over the phone.

222 E. Guenther St. (at Madison St.), San Antonio, TX 78204. ✆ **800/945-1449** or 210/229-1449. Fax 210/229-1061. www.beckmanninn.com. 5 units. $110–$155 double. Rates include full breakfast. AE, DC, DISC, MC, V. Free parking. *In room:* A/C and fan, TV, fridge, hair dryer, Wi-Fi (free).

**Brackenridge House** 🎒 These days, many B&Bs are beginning to resemble boutique hotels, with an almost hands-off approach on the part of the hosts. If you seek out B&Bs because you prefer warmer, more traditional treatment, this King William abode is likely to suit you. It's not just that the house is homey rather than fancy—although it has its fair share of antiques—but that owners Sue and Bennie (also known as the King of King William) Blansett instantly make you feel welcome. They provide little extras and are quick to help you find whatever you need. The common areas are comfortable, especially the upstairs deck attached to the back of the house. Guest rooms and suites are located in the main house and carriage house, the latter a two-bedroom apartment with a full kitchen and living area. It affords more privacy and works well for those traveling with kids and/or a pet.

230 Madison St. (btw. Beauregard and Turner sts.), San Antonio, TX 78204. ✆ **800/221-1412** or 210/271-3442. www.brackenridgehouse.com. 6 units. $120–$200 double; $145–$275 suite; $150–$275 carriage house. Rates include full breakfast (except carriage house). Monthly rates available for carriage house. 2-night minimum. Sat–Sun. AE, DC, DISC, MC, V. Free parking. Small pets accepted in carriage house. **Amenities:** Outdoor heated pool; Jacuzzi. *In room:* A/C and fan, TV/DVD, fridge, hair dryer, Wi-Fi (free).

## Monte Vista Historic District
### MODERATE

**Bonner Garden** ★ 🍸 This is a fascinating house built in 1910 for Louisiana artist Mary Bonner. She had suffered two house fires before moving to San Antonio, so she had this one built of solid cement and plaster. There is wood inside, in the form of beautiful trim work, including the staircase, the moldings, and door and window jambs, but no framing. Rooms are large, well furnished, and uncluttered. The downstairs

Portico Room has a painted blue sky with billowing clouds on the ceiling and it's fun to gaze at it from the bed. This room has a private poolside entrance. The two upstairs corner rooms are quite large and comfy, and one room has a large Jacuzzi tub. Mary Bonner's former studio, separate from the main house, is large, too. A rooftop deck affords a sparkling nighttime view of downtown. All in all, this is a very comfortable place to stay. It also has something not commonly found at B&Bs: a large, 45-foot swimming pool. Margi, one of the owners, bakes her own pastries for breakfast.

145 E. Agarita Ave. (at McCullough Ave.), San Antonio, TX 78212. © **800/396-4222** or 210/733-4222. Fax 210/733-6129. www.bonnergarden.com. 6 units. $115–$155 double; $165 suite; $130 studio. Rates include full breakfast. Special and corporate rates available. 2-night minimum Sat–Sun. AE, DISC, MC, V. Free parking. **Amenities:** Outdoor pool. *In room:* A/C, TV/VCR, hair dryer, Internet (free).

### The Inn at Craig Place ★

This 1891 mansion-turned-B&B appeals to history, art, and architecture buffs alike. It was built by one of Texas's most noted architects, Alfred Giles, for H. E. Hildebrand, a major public figure at the time. The living room holds a mural by Julian Onderdonk, an influential Texas landscape artist, who grew up in Monte Vista in the 1880s. But that's all academic. More to the point, this place is gorgeous, with forests of gleaming wood and clean Arts and Crafts lines, as well as cushy couches and a wraparound porch. Rooms are equipped for modern needs and are very luxurious; all have working fireplaces and hardwood floors, and provide robes, slippers, feather pillows, and down comforters.

117 W. Craig Place (off N. Main Ave.), San Antonio, TX 78212. © **877/427-2447** or 210/736-1017. Fax 210/737-1562. www.craigplace.com. 5 units. $140–$185 double. Corporate rates and special packages available. Rates include full breakfast. AE, DC, DISC, MC, V. Free parking. Children 12 and older accepted. **Amenities:** Concierge; access to nearby fitness club. *In room:* AC and fan, TV/DVD, CD player, hair dryer, no phone, Wi-Fi (free).

## INEXPENSIVE

### O'Casey's Bed & Breakfast ☺ 🎷

If there's a twinkle in John Casey's eye when he puts on a brogue, it's because he was born on U.S. soil, not the *auld sod*. But he and his wife, Linda Fay, exhibit a down-home friendliness that's no blarney. This Irish-themed B&B is one of the few around that welcomes families and is well equipped to handle them. One suite in the main house has a sitting area with a futon large enough for a couple of youngsters; another has a trundle bed for two kids in a separate bedroom. The two studio apartments in the carriage house have full kitchens. All of this is not to suggest that accommodations are utilitarian—far from it. Rooms in the main house, a gracious structure built in 1904, feature hardwood floors and antiques, and many bathrooms display claw-foot tubs. There's a wraparound balcony upstairs, too. For a treat, ask Linda (a professional pianist) and John (a choir director and singer) to perform a few numbers for you.

225 W. Craig Place (btw. San Pedro Ave. and Main St.), San Antonio, TX 78212. © **800/738-1378** or 210/738-1378. www.ocaseybnb.com. 7 units. $89–$110 double; $110 apt. Rates include full breakfast. Special packages available. DISC, MC, V. Free parking. Pets accepted in apts. only for $10 per week. *In room:* A/C, TV, Wi-Fi (free).

## West/Northwest

### VERY EXPENSIVE

### Hyatt Regency Hill Country Resort and Spa ★★★ ☺

This resort and the Westin La Canterra target the exact same public—families (and when school is in session, groups and conferences). They offer a lot of the same things: easy access to theme parks (the Hyatt is built by SeaWorld, the Westin by Six Flags Fiesta, Texas), lots of swimming pools and tennis courts, plenty of organized activities for kids and teens, and plenty of activities for grown-ups. The Hyatt puts in a little more effort with kid and family activities than the Westin. It has a more homey feel and one feature that seems to delight everybody—the 950-foot-long Ramblin' River (entirely man-made), where you can relax in the water while letting the current pull you along. The setting, on 200 acres of former ranch land on the far-west side of San Antonio, is idyllic, including a 27-hole golf course.

The resort's interiors are contemporary, use a good bit of the native limestone, and with something of a country look. Rooms are large and comfortable. Some ground-floor rooms have direct access to the grounds so you don't have to go through the lobby. New to the Hyatt are 16 "Respire Rooms" built for people who have a difficult time with the pollen of the Texas Hill Country. These are equipped with enhanced air scrubbers, special coatings on all the surfaces to repel pollen, and hypoallergenic everything. There are also seven rooms for smokers, which come with the same air filtering. The spa is low key and relaxing and has a full range of treatments.

9800 Hyatt Resort Dr. (off Hwy. 151, between Westover Hills Blvd. and Potranco Rd.), San Antonio, TX 78251. © 800/55-HYATT (554-9288) or 210/647-1234. Fax 210/520-4075. http://hillcountry.hyatt.com. 500 units. $249–$400 double; $450–$2,550 suite. Special packages available. AE, DC, DISC, MC, V. Valet parking $15; self-parking free. **Amenities:** 6 restaurants; 2 bars; bikes; children's programs; concierge; concierge-level rooms; golf course; health club; 5 Jacuzzis; 4 outdoor pools; room service; sauna; spa; 3 outdoor tennis courts (1 lit). *In room:* A/C, TV, fridge, hair dryer, MP3 docking station (in suites), Wi-Fi ($10 per day).

**Westin La Cantera** ★★★ ☺    This resort is grander and less homey than the Hyatt. It will find more favor with golfers for its two championship courses (in addition to the much-praised La Cantera, there's a newer Arnold Palmer–designed course) plus a golf academy. In addition to being next to Fiesta Texas, the Westin is also next to the newest and best shopping mall in San Antonio—the Shops at La Cantera. This resort is more romantic than the Hyatt, too, with rocky outcroppings and gorgeous views from its perch on one of the highest points in the San Antonio area. Remnants of the limestone quarry on which the resort was built are incorporated into the four swimming pools interconnected with bridges, channels, and a dramatic waterfall.

Rooms are large and decorated in mix of modern and traditional furnishings. As with other Westin hotels, the beds are quite comfortable. Bathrooms are large, and there's plenty of closet space. If you want to go larger, the junior suites offer quite a bit more for the extra cost. Many rooms have balconies with views of the neighboring hills. The "casitas" are in a section set apart from the main building and have their own pool. These are larger, quieter, and more private. Each has its own patio.

16641 La Cantera Pkwy. (take the La Cantera Pkwy. exit off I-10 and turn left; resort entrance is ¾ mile ahead, on the right), San Antonio, TX 78256. © 800/WESTIN-1 (937-8461) or 210/558-6500. Fax 210/641-0721. www.westinlacantera.com. 508 units. $259–$369 double; from $380 suite; from $350 casita. AE, DC, DISC, MC, V. Valet parking $14; self-parking free. **Amenities:** 5 restaurants; 2 bars; children's programs; concierge; concierge-level rooms; 2 golf courses; health club and spa; Jacuzzi; 5 outdoor pools; room service; 2 tennis courts; Wi-Fi (free, in lobby). *In room:* A/C, TV, hair dryer, Internet (free or $5–$10 per day high-speed), minibar.

# EXPENSIVE

**Omni San Antonio Hotel at the Colonnade** ★ ☺    This polished granite high-rise off I-10 W. is convenient to SeaWorld, Six Flags Fiesta Texas, the airport, and the Hill Country, and the shops and restaurants of the 66-acre Colonnade complex are within easy walking distance. Guest rooms are furnished comfortably in traditional style. The hotel gets a lot of business travelers, but the proximity to the theme parks, the various Omni Kids features at the hotel, and the large pool make it a good choice for families. The exercise facilities are quite good, and guests can get treadmills brought into their rooms as part of the Omni "Get Fit" program. Even at the busiest of times, service here seems prompt and courteous.

9821 Colonnade Blvd. (at Wurzbach), San Antonio, TX 78230. © **800/843-6664** or 210/691-8888. Fax 210/691-1128. www.omnihotels.com. 326 units. $169–$249 double; from $289 suite. Special packages available. AE, DC, DISC, MC, V. Valet parking $12 per day; self-parking free. Pets 25 lb. or under accepted for $50 fee. **Amenities:** Restaurant; bar; free airport transfers; concierge; state-of-the-art health club and spa; indoor/outdoor pools; room service. *In room:* A/C, TV, hair dryer, minibar, Wi-Fi (free).

## North Central (Near the Airport)

### EXPENSIVE

**Hilton San Antonio Airport ★**   The rooms at this airport Hilton offer a bit of local character, with a few Southwestern decorative touches. They're attractive and spacious. The hotel is straight west of the airport, on the north side of Loop 410, making it easy to access. Of course, it's predominantly a business traveler's hotel, but it doesn't have that ambience, thanks to the cheerful lobby with a colorful Texas mural, the large outdoor pool, and the family-oriented **Tex's Grill,** which serves some mean Texas barbecue. Such nongeneric features as an outdoor putting green also help make your stay enjoyable. But while this hotel may be playful, it also knows how to get down to business with its service and amenities.

611 NW Loop 410 (San Pedro exit), San Antonio, TX 78216. © **800/HILTONS** (445-8667). Fax 210/377-4674. www.hilton.com. 384 units. $139–$199 double; from $175 suite. AE, DC, DISC, MC, V. Valet parking $15; self-parking $10. **Amenities:** Restaurant; bar; free airport transfers; nearby golf course; exercise room; Jacuzzi; outdoor heated pool; room service. *In room:* A/C, TV, hair dryer, Wi-Fi ($11 per day).

### MODERATE

**La Quinta Inn & Suites San Antonio Airport**   Bunched up around the intersection of Hwy. 281 and Loop 410 are various airport hotels. Among them is this property, which is nicely located so that it doesn't front either freeway. It's still easy to find, has an airport shuttle that can also take you to any restaurant in a 2-mile radius, and has easy access to Hwy. 281 S., which leads to downtown. The property was recently built and is well maintained. Guest rooms are plain, but comfortable and functional. The bathrooms are a cut above the competition in this category—they have a little more room and better lighting.

850 Halm Blvd., San Antonio, TX 78216. © **800/753-3757** or 210/342-3738. Fax 210/348-9666. www.lq.com. 276 units. $95–$150 double. Rates include free breakfast buffet. AE, DC, DISC, MC, V. Free parking. Pets accepted for free. **Amenities:** Free airport transfers; exercise room; outdoor pool; spa. *In room:* A/C, TV, fridge, hair dryer, Internet (free).

# WHERE TO DINE

Visitors to San Antonio usually have Tex-Mex food on their minds, and for good reason. There is a wealth of variety here and lots of tradition. But the restaurant scene in San Antonio is a lot more sophisticated and cosmopolitan than many people realize. Good French, Italian, and New American cuisine abounds, and some one-of-a-kind restaurants will make any stay here memorable. Many of the best-known restaurants are downtown, but keep in mind the many excellent restaurants in other parts of town that can add to your range of dining choices. There are two areas within walking distance of downtown that merit special mention.

# Central San Antonio Dining & Attractions

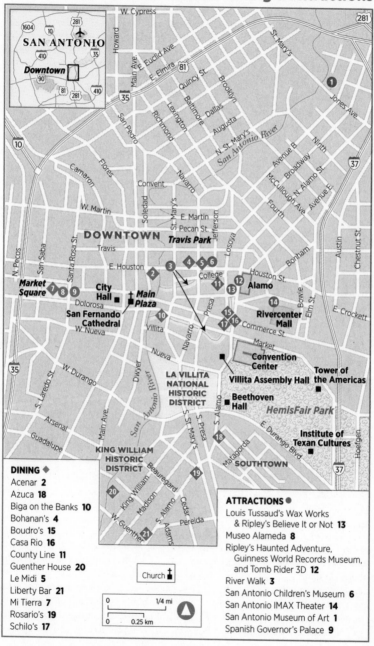

**DINING** ◆
Acenar **2**
Azuca **18**
Biga on the Banks **10**
Bohanan's **4**
Boudro's **15**
Casa Rio **16**
County Line **11**
Guenther House **20**
Le Midi **5**
Liberty Bar **21**
Mi Tierra **7**
Rosario's **19**
Schilo's **17**

Church ✝

0        1/4 mi
0   0.25 km

**ATTRACTIONS** ●
Louis Tussaud's Wax Works
  & Ripley's Believe It or Not **13**
Museo Alameda **8**
Ripley's Haunted Adventure,
  Guinness World Records Museum,
  and Tomb Rider 3D **12**
River Walk **3**
San Antonio Children's Museum **6**
San Antonio IMAX Theater **14**
San Antonio Museum of Art **1**
Spanish Governor's Palace **9**

One is the area with the ongoing redevelopment of the old Pearl Brewery. The developers are making this a major gourmet focal point for the city. First, they persuaded the Culinary Institute of America to open a school here, which was recently inaugurated in October 2010. Then they lured San Antonio's most famous chef, Andrew Weissman, from downtown. He moved his seafood restaurant, Sandbar, here and opened a new Italian restaurant once he closed his famous Le Rêve. In addition to other restaurants, there's a farmers market and plans are in the works for a microbrewery.

The other place that merits special mention is Southtown, the eclectic, vivacious area just downstream from the city center. This area includes the King William neighborhood, but is predominantly a Mexican-American area with neighborhood eateries and *taquerías* (taco shops), which has become a popular place for artists, gallery owners, and innovative restaurateurs. One well-known fixture on the San Antonio scene, the Liberty Bar, which used to occupy the iconic "leaning saloon" north of downtown, has moved here and set up business in a former convent.

## Downtown

### VERY EXPENSIVE

**Biga on the Banks** ★★★ NEW AMERICAN    You can eat well on the River Walk, but there are only a few fine dining spots worth visiting. This is one of them. Biga on the Banks serves international cuisine with a nod to local flavors. Fittingly, it's located on the ground floor of the International Center building. The entrance is from St. Mary's, not the river. You'll enter a dining room that is modern and airy with high ceilings, clean lines, and large windows looking out over the river. The chef/owner is Bruce Auden, a Brit who found his way to San Antonio, where he has won much acclaim from the national press for his cooking.

The menu changes daily, but you're certain to find his popular Angus beef rib-eye served with Shiner Bock–battered onion rings and habanero catsup. You'll also find a number of Asian-inspired dishes, including lettuce wraps of minced venison, buffalo, ostrich, and pheasant accompanied by two spicy dipping sauces, or duck confit *bao* buns (those unearthly doughy balls filled with seasoned meat that can be slightly salty, spicy, and sweet). Also worth ordering is the mustard-crusted Australian lamb. For dessert, the signature offering is the sticky toffee pudding from Mr. Auden's homeland. If you're willing to eat before 6:30pm or after 9pm, you can enjoy a three-course prix fixe for $37 per person or four-course prix fixe for $43.

International Center, 203 S. St. Mary's St./River Walk. ✆ **210/225-0722.** www.biga.com. Reservations recommended. Main courses $27–$40. AE, DC, DISC, MC, V. Sun–Thurs 5:30–10pm; Fri–Sat 5:30–11pm.

**Bohanan's** ★★★ STEAK/SEAFOOD    Considered by many to be the best steakhouse in the state, Bohanan's has everything a proper Texas steakhouse should: comfortable chairs, white tablecloths, lots of dark woodwork, and a good bar. The upstairs dining room has an air of establishment, soft lighting, and a hint of nostalgia for the good old days. The cuts of prime beef come from Allen Bros. of Chicago, the pork is Kurobuta, and if you want Akaushi beef, they have that, too. Steaks are beautifully grilled over mesquite. Seafood is flown in fresh from various suppliers, and the way they grill a red snapper topped with crabmeat makes me nostalgic for the good old days, when quality seafood prepared this way was more common. Service is provided by an experienced waitstaff. As with many steakhouses in this class, all sides are a la carte. The restaurant is located in the central downtown area just a block or two from the River Walk.

219 E. Houston St. ✆ **210/472-2600.** www.bohanans.com. Reservations recommended. Main courses $17-$46; steaks $34-$125. AE, DC, DISC, MC, V. Mon-Fri 11am-2pm; Mon-Thurs 5-10pm; Fri-Sat 5-11pm; Sun 5-9pm.

## EXPENSIVE

**Boudro's** ★ AMERICAN   Everybody loves this old standby on the River Walk. The kitchen uses fresh local ingredients—Gulf Coast seafood, Texas beef, Hill Country produce—and the preparations and presentations do them justice. The setting is also out of the ordinary, in a turn-of-the-century limestone building with hardwood floors and a handmade mesquite-wood bar. You might start with the guacamole, prepared tableside and served with tostadas, or the "seacakes" (pan-fried Texas crab cakes). Both dishes are well prepared. The prime rib, blackened on a pecan-wood grill, is deservedly popular, as is the black Angus rib-eye served with roasted rosemary potatoes. Portions are hearty. Lighter alternatives include the tortilla soup, the coconut shrimp with orange horseradish, and the rosemary-grilled yellowfin tuna. For dessert, the whisky-soaked bread pudding is a good choice, and the lime chess pie with a butter pastry crust is divine. Service is attentive, but if you can, I suggest going for a late lunch to avoid the crowd.

421 E. Commerce St./River Walk. ✆ **210/224-8484.** www.boudros.com. Reservations recommended. Main courses $20-$33. AE, DC, DISC, MC, V. Sun-Thurs 11am-11pm; Fri-Sat 11am-midnight.

**Le Midi** ★★★ FRENCH   This new restaurant is part of the burgeoning dining scene on Houston Street, a couple of blocks off the River Walk. It serves classic country French food from the south of France. Chef-owner Nicolas Lebas is adept at layering contrasting tastes and textures, but knows when to let simplicity speak for the food. I enjoyed a delicious green salad that was simplicity itself, followed by a plate of the house pâté that combined sweet, salty, and acidic flavors on a background rich in what is often called *umami* (savoriness). The small menu changes often, but you will always find well-known classics, such as lemon sole or *coq au vin* (chicken with wine). This being Texas, the menu lists a couple of steaks as well. The small dining room has glass windows on two sides and feels airy. Across the street, you can see the old Majestic theater. On show nights, Le Midi offers a $29 three-course prix fixe from 5 to 7pm. Make a reservation, then go early and allow lots of time for the meal. Le Midi has a small cocktail bar that is classic.

301 E. Houston St. (at Navarro) ✆ **210/858-7388.** www.lemidirestaurant.com. Reservations recommended. Main courses $20-$34. AE, DISC, MC, V. Tues-Fri 11:30am-2:30pm; Tues-Thurs 5-10pm; Fri-Sat 5-11pm.

## MODERATE

**Acenar** ★ MEXICAN   This restaurant on the River Walk below the Hotel Valencia is a collaboration between Lisa Wong of Rosario's (see below) and Bruce Auden of Biga. It's a large, casual restaurant decorated in bold, modern Mexican colors. You can dine indoors or outdoors on a couple of terraces above the river. The "updated" Mexican fare includes such standards as ceviche (fish "cooked" in lime juice marinade) or guacamole made at the table, as well as some original dishes, such as crepes with duck in a tamarind-cherry–grilled onion sauce or the ever-popular *camarones al Diablo* (shrimp in butter with a hint of chipotle served over cilantro-flavored rice). I also wouldn't hesitate to order the fish tacos served with a sweet and spicy mayo and shredded cabbage. For steak lovers, Acenar serves *arrachera* (fajitas) on a sizzling skillet with tortillas and all the sides.

146 E. Houston St. (next to the Hotel Valencia). ☎ **210/222-CENA** (2362). www.acenar.com. Reservations not accepted (priority seating for large parties). Main courses $7–$13 lunch, $15–$25 dinner. AE, DC, MC, V. Sun–Thurs 11am–10pm; Fri–Sat 11am–11pm.

**County Line** ★ BARBECUE  This place serves the best barbecue on the River Walk. It's a well-known outfit from Austin that doesn't take shortcuts, cooks everything slowly with indirect heat, and does a good job with side dishes. The kitchen also bakes its own bread, an uncommon occurrence with barbecue joints. I believe the cooks do their best work with the pork ribs and the brisket, which come with sauce on top (you can always ask for sauce on the side). If you're feeling like something with less of a smoke flavor, they serve grilled steaks, too. You have the option to dine outside by the river or inside; I would opt for outside.

111 W. Crockett St., Ste. 104. ☎ **210/229-1941.** Reservations not accepted. AE, DISC, MC, V. Main courses $10–$17 lunch, $13–$28 dinner. Daily 11:30am–10:30pm.

## INEXPENSIVE

**Casa Rio** TEX-MEX  I often hear the question, "Where's the best place to eat Tex-Mex at a good table by the river?" The answer is that your options are many and few; many bad options and a few passable ones. Of these, my choice would be Casa Rio. When the weather is glorious, few things are more enjoyable than getting a table at the water's edge; ordering a big platter of something spicy, meaty, and crispy; and sipping a frozen margarita. This place has an excellent location, not as crowded as most, and, so long as you stick to the Tex-Mex classics, you'll do fine. Steer clear of the tortilla soup and the tamales (which aren't really a Tex-Mex forte) and go with something like *flautas* (deep-fried filled tortillas), enchiladas, tacos, or fajitas. Enjoy. This is San Antonio, after all, and you're supposed to eat these things.

430 E. Commerce St./River Walk. ☎ **210/225-6718.** www.casa-rio.com. Reservations not accepted. AE, MC, V. Main courses $7–$17. Daily 11am–11pm (weather permitting).

**Mi Tierra** 📷 TEX-MEX  If you've come to San Antonio with the idea of tasting traditional Tex-Mex as it is cooked day in and day out, this is a great place. Sure, you see out-of-towners finding their way here because the restaurant is so famous, but you see a lot more locals who know their city and their restaurants. The atmosphere is unselfconsciously *so* San Antonio. I love it. Past the bar are three dining rooms. I like the first one the best, but walk around and have a look. In the last room is a big mural of famous San Antonians. Order the Tex-Mex and bring your appetite. You can start with the *botanas* (appetizer) platter, which has a good smattering of such dishes as *flautas* and mini-tostadas. The top-shelf margarita makes a nice accompaniment. Then move on to the classic Tex-Mex enchiladas bathed in chili gravy.

218 Produce Row (Market Square). ☎ **210/225-1262.** www.mitierracafe.com. Reservations accepted for large groups only. Breakfast $7–$10; lunch and dinner $8–$19. AE, DISC, MC, V. Open 24 hrs.

**Schilo's** ☺ 🍴 GERMAN/DELI  This place looks like it's been here since they built the Alamo. The large, open room with its worn wooden booths is classic. It makes for a good place to stop, rest your feet, and enjoy a hearty bowl of split-pea soup or a piece of the signature cherry cheesecake. They also make a mean Reuben sandwich. German live bands play on Saturday from 5 to 8pm. The menu has a large kid-friendly selection and retro low prices. Come Friday or Saturday evening if you want to be serenaded by accordion music.

424 E. Commerce St. ☎ **210/223-6692.** Reservations for large groups at breakfast and dinner only. Sandwiches $5–$7; hot or cold plates $5–$7; main dishes (served after 5pm) $7–$8.95. AE, DC, DISC, MC, V. Mon–Sat 7am–8:30pm.

# King William/Southtown

## MODERATE

**Azuca** ★ NUEVO LATINO   "Azuca!" (short for *azucar*, or sugar) was the trademark rallying cry of the late, great Cuban diva Celia Cruz. And this Southtown restaurant strives to bring the same kind of verve to the table that she brought to the stage. The menu incorporates dishes from all over Latin America, which is known for, among other things, dishes highlighting fresh tropical ingredients, bright colors, and bold flavors. There's a large sampling of Caribbean dishes, several of which include characteristic ingredients of the region, such as brightly colored *achiote* (spices) and fried plantains. From South America, you have the grilled meats of southern Brazil and Argentina, as well as some delicious Bolivian empanadas (stuffed pastries). Mexico is, of course, heavily featured, too. The menu is large and has several original dishes inspired by traditional Latin American cooking and adapted to Texan tastes.

The setting is colorful, with contrasting bold tones and modern lines. On weekends, live salsa and merengue gets cranking, and a lot of people show up to drink *mojitos*. On Thursday evenings, Azuca has a slightly milder entertainment: flamenco dancing.

713 S. Alamo St. ✆ **210/225-5550.** www.azuca.net. Reservations recommended. Main courses $7–$11 lunch, $14–$27 dinner. AE, DC, DISC, MC, V. Restaurant Mon–Thurs 11am–9:30pm; Fri–Sat 11am–10:30pm. Bar Mon–Thurs 4–11pm; Fri–Sat 4pm–2am.

**Liberty Bar** ★★ NEW AMERICAN   The Liberty Bar has just completed the move from the old, leaning saloon building on Josephine Street to its new location on South Alamo. The new home makes for a completely different atmosphere, but how could it be otherwise after moving from a former brothel to a former convent? The new location is actually more comfortable and less cramped, with dining areas on the ground floor and upstairs by the bar. The rustic, hewn chairs are actually solid and comfortable, and the tables well separated. The cooking remains about the same, making an innovative use of many ingredients. Prices are reasonable and portions are generous. On my last visit, I sampled a goat-cheese appetizer in a sauce made with *chile cascabel* and *piloncillo* (Mexican raw brown sugar), served with griddle-cooked bread; a perfectly dressed green salad with roasted hazelnuts, apples, and bits of pecorino cheese and prosciutto; and a grilled chicken breast wrapped in *hoja santa* (Mexican herb). Pay attention to the daily specials—I've had good luck with them. For something lighter, try one of the innovative sandwiches, such as the portobello with smoked gouda and saffron aioli. Bread is made in-house and is used for a classic bread pudding with hard sauce. The Liberty Bar is a great option for vegetarians.

1111 S. Alamo St. ✆ **210/227-1187.** www.liberty-bar.com. Reservations accepted. Main courses $10–$16; sandwiches $9–$14. AE, DISC, MC, V. Restaurant: Sun–Thurs 11am–10:30pm; Fri–Sat 11am–midnight. Bar: Sun–Thurs noon–11pm; Fri–Sat noon–midnight.

**Rosario's** ★★ TEX-MEX   This colorful restaurant is a favorite meeting place for happy hour and dinner. Owner Lisa Wong succeeded in pulling Tex-Mex out of its traditional setting—the typical Mexican food restaurant, decorated with bullfight posters, Mexican calendars, and mariachi sombreros. Rosario's is modern and fun. The dining rooms have lots of natural light, cheerful colors, a splash of neon light, and polished cement floors. The contemporary Tex-Mex fare, prepared with fresh ingredients, lures locals and visitors alike. The ceviche (white fish, onions, and jalapeños marinated in lime juice) tastes fresh, and the fish tacos make for a good light meal. For something more substantial, you have several options, including the chicken chipotle or the chile relleno. The large size of the rooms means that you generally don't have to wait long for a table, but it also means that the noise level can make conversation difficult. I like to go at midafternoon on a weekday, when the place is uncrowded and happy hour is about to begin (4pm). On Friday and Saturday nights, there's live music starting at 8 or 9pm.

910 S. Alamo St. © **210/223-1806.** www.rosariossa.com. Reservations not accepted. Main dishes $6–$9 lunch, $8–$23 dinner. AE, DC, DISC, MC, V. Mon–Sat 11am–11pm; Sun 11am–9pm.

## INEXPENSIVE

**Guenther House** ★ ☺AMERICAN   If you're not staying in a King William B&B, this is the easiest way to visit one of the neighborhood's historic homes and have a good meal at the same time. Hearty breakfasts and light lunches are served both indoors—in a bright, cheerful old-style dining room added on to the Guenther family residence (1860)—and outdoors on a trellised patio. The Guenther family owns the old Pioneer Flour Mill, which is in plain sight right across the river, its old-fashioned crenellated tower adding charm to the view. It's fairly natural that the restaurant would emphasize baked goods. If you're looking for the maximum old Southern experience, order the biscuits and gravy, but if you're not in the mood for something different, the waffles and pancakes are quite good. For something less filling, try the breakfast tacos.

Breakfast is served till closing at 3pm. The lunch menu is on the light side and includes an excellent chicken salad (made with black olives) and mild chicken enchiladas made with flour tortillas. From the baked treats to the BLT sandwiches served here, this place is a hit with the kids. Adjoining the restaurant is a small museum, a Victorian parlor, and a mill store with baking items, including mixes, cookbooks, and kitchen gear. The house fronts a lovely stretch of the San Antonio River.

205 E. Guenther St. © **210/227-1061.** www.guentherhouse.com. Reservations not accepted. Breakfast $4–$8; lunch $6–$8. AE, DC, DISC, MC, V. Daily 7am–3pm. House and mill store Mon–Sat 8am–4pm; Sun 8am–3pm.

# Monte Vista Area

## EXPENSIVE

**Il Sogno** ★★★ ITALIAN   When Andrew Weissman made the move from downtown to the old Pearl Brewery, he decided to close his highly acclaimed Le Rêve and open a simpler Italian restaurant instead. This probably has something to do with his change in position from executive chef to restaurateur. So, despite the name being an Italian translation of Le Rêve, do not expect this restaurant to be the Italian equivalent of the old one. It has a simpler concept and more straightforward menu. Still, it's quite good. The daily menu includes pastas, pizzas, and main courses, and there are always some specials. The ingredients are fresh and of the highest quality and the wine list is an extensive exploration of Italy's winemaking culture. Il Sogno has only 19 tables indoors and doesn't take reservations, but you can call ahead to be put on the waiting list.

200 E. Grayson St., Pearl Brewery. © **210/223-3900.** Reservations not accepted. Main courses $20–$30. AE, DC, MC, V. Tues–Fri 7:30–10am; Sat 8:30–10am; Tues–Sat 11:30am–2pm and 6–9:30pm; Sun 6–9pm.

**Sandbar** ★★★ SEAFOOD   Also at the Pearl Brewery is Andrew Weissman's new Sandbar, a modern, minimally decorated affair with white-tile wainscoting and commercial light fixtures, which remind me of old fish markets. In contrast to the casual surroundings is the food, in its variety, freshness, and preparation. Using various suppliers, the restaurant receives 10 to 15 kinds of oysters flown in from the East and

West coasts. Lobster, caviar, diver scallops—the sea's bounty is rarely so well represented. The top half of the daily menu celebrates the enjoyment of this bounty in something closest to its purest state: oysters on the half shell, sashimi, boiled shrimp, and ceviche. There's a nod to a few traditional dishes, too: chowder, lobster rolls, fish and chips, and whole fried fish. In the lower half of the menu, you'll see the day's prepared dishes, which strive to complement, not supplement, the freshness of the seafood. Chef Chris Carlson believes in keeping preparation to a minimum. Though reservations aren't accepted, you can call ahead and get on the waiting list.

200 E. Grayson St., Pearl Brewery, Ste. 117. © **210/222-2426.** Reservations not accepted. Main courses $20-$36. AE, DC, DISC, MC, V. Tues–Sat 11:30am–10pm.

## MODERATE

**La Gloria ★** MEXICAN   If you're not going to Mexico, you can still enjoy that country's delicious street food at this attractive, playfully decorated eatery at the Pearl Brewery. You're not going to see yellow cheddar or American cheese here; this place does it up Mexican-style by finishing several dishes with a light crumbling of a fresh farmer's cheese or a dried *cotija* and perhaps a light drizzle of Mexican cream. Get in line to place your order from a wide-ranging menu that includes dishes from across the country. On the back of the menu is an explanation of the different items, and the staff is happy to explain further. It's clear that chef-owner Johnny Hernandez and his staff put a lot of thinking into how to bring these Mexican delicacies to America. Not everything is exactly how you would get it in its native land, but who can resist the temptation to improve dishes according to their own tastes? Mr. Hernandez does a good job of it. The only thing I would avoid are the *tlayudas* (tortilla snack), which are near impossible to reproduce outside of Oaxaca.

100 E. Grayson St., Pearl Brewery. © **210/267-9094.** www.lagloriaicehouse.com. Reservations not accepted. Main courses $5-$14. AE, DISC, MC, V. Sun–Mon and Wed–Thurs 11am–10pm; Fri–Sat 11am–midnight.

**Los Barrios** TEX-MEX   This very popular Tex-Mex joint has been around since the '70s, when it first opened in a former Dairy Queen. The excellent Tex-Mex enchiladas are made of red tortillas and cheese bathed in a hearty chili gravy. Or you could go for the five-enchilada plate, with one of every variety served here. Departures from Tex-Mex include *cabrito* (goat) in salsa and the *milanesa con papas,* described on the menu (accurately) as a Mexican-style chicken-fried steak. Portions are large. If you're watching what you eat, you can easily satisfy hunger pangs with a *chalupa Vallarta* a la carte ($4), and you'll get a large red tortilla stacked with chicken, lettuce, tomato, guacamole, carrot strips, jalapeños, cheese, and sour cream. Nothing at Los Barrios is too spicy.

Mondays and Tuesdays are popular for "Fajita Nights," when you can get a pound of fajitas with all the sides for $14 ($18 regular price). Wednesdays are "Margarita Nights," and on Thursdays, there's a special on longnecks.

4223 Blanco Rd. © **210/732-6017.** Reservations accepted only for large groups. Dinners $9-$14. AE, DISC, MC, V. Mon–Thurs 10am–10pm; Fri–Sat 10am–11pm; Sun 9am–10pm.

## INEXPENSIVE

**Chris Madrids** ☺ AMERICAN/TEX-MEX   This is a fun, down-home hamburger joint where Tex-Mex meets Americana. It's been around forever and is known for its extralarge "macho" burger, which is a supersize version of any of their standard burgers. Two burgers merit special mention: the ever-popular "tostada burger," which comes with crushed tortilla chips, refried beans, and real cheddar; and the "cheddar cheesy" burger, which in its "macho" state is intimidating (and I've never been intimidated by

**Chris Madrids** (p. 257)  The kid-friendly menu includes burgers, nachos, fries, and various combinations thereof, and the casual atmosphere and down-home cooking make it popular with families.

**Guenther House** (p. 256)  With its menu of waffles, pancakes, and other breakfast goodies, this inexpensive

restaurant is a perennial favorite with the little ones.

**Schilo's** (p. 254)  A high noise level, a convenient location near the River Walk (but with prices far lower than anything else you'll find there), and a wide selection of familiar food make this German deli a good choice for the family.

a burger before). The cheddar oozes out over the large burger, engulfing even the platter. The french fries are made in-house and are well worth ordering. The kid-friendly menu also includes chicken sandwiches, nachos, and *chalupas* (tostadas). The main dining area is a large room with a cement floor and high framed ceiling. There is also an outdoor patio in back.

1900 Blanco Rd. (just south of Hildebrand). ✆ **210/735-3552**. www.chrismadrids.com. Reservations not accepted. Burgers $5–$8. AE, DC, DISC, MC, V. Mon–Sat 11am–10pm.

## Alamo Heights Area
### EXPENSIVE

**Bistro Vatel** ★★ ✇ FRENCH  In 1671, the great French chef Vatel killed himself out of shame because the fish for a banquet he was preparing for Louis XIV wasn't delivered on time. Fortunately, his descendant, Damian Watel, has less stress to contend with in San Antonio, where diners are very appreciative of the chef's efforts to bring them classic French cooking at reasonable prices. Comfortable furniture, ample space, white tablecloths, and excellent service make for a satisfying dining experience. You can't go wrong with the rich escallop of veal with foie gras and mushrooms, and fans of sweetbreads will be pleased to find them beautifully prepared in truffle crème fraîche sauce. Your best bet is the prix-fixe dinner; choose from four appetizers (perhaps shrimp *vol au vent*) and entrees such as roasted quail, then enjoy the dessert of the day.

218 E. Olmos Dr. at McCullough. ✆ **210/828-3141**. www.bistrovatel.com. Reservations recommended Fri–Sun. Main courses $15–$27; prix-fixe dinner $35. AE, MC, V. Tues–Sat 11am–9pm; Sun 5–9pm.

**Silo** ★★ NEW AMERICAN  For my money, this is one of the best places for fine dining when you want something other than French food. Compared to many chic restaurants that try to get attention by creating fanciful-sounding dishes with a "cutting-edge" use of ingredients, Silo quietly goes about its business, focusing on creating satisfying dishes that deliver something new without gimmickry. The menu changes often, but some representative examples of the cuisine include the chipotle-marinated pork tenderloin with white-cheddar andouille grits and peach chutney, the crab spring rolls with shitake mushrooms and tantalizing dipping sauces, some pan-seared scallops treated very simply, and some wonderful mango-wasabi crab cakes.

1133 Austin Hwy. ✆ **210/824-8686**. www.siloelevatedcuisine.com. Reservations recommended. Main courses $20–$40; prix fixe (salad, entree, dessert) $25–$35 (5:30–6:30pm nightly). AE, DC, DISC, MC, V. Daily 11am–2:30pm; Sun–Thurs 5:30–10pm; Fri–Sat 5:30–10:30pm.

## MODERATE

**Ciao Lavanderia** ★ ITALIAN   In an open, cheery storefront with postmodern tributes to the business that used to reside here (exposed ductwork, an old washing machine), you can savor the expert renditions of some of the classic dishes of Italy: pastas, thin-crust pizzas (baked in a wood-burning brick oven), and risotto. The calzone or the panini makes for a satisfying lunch, as does one of the wide variety of salads. The dinner options include a mouth-watering pork tenderloin wrapped in prosciutto and served with creamy polenta. Everything is fresh and delicious, and the portions are geared toward a normal human appetite. This restaurant is an excellent choice for vegetarians, and the kitchen can make gluten-free versions of all but a few of the pastas. A good selection of wines enhances an already optimal experience.

226 E. Olmos Dr. ✆ **210/822-3990.** www.ciaofoodandwine.com. Reservations accepted only for large parties. Pastas and pizzas $8–$18; main courses $15–$23. AE, DC, DISC, MC, V. Mon–Fri 11am–2pm; Mon–Thurs 5–9:30pm; Fri–Sat 5–10pm.

**Paloma Blanca** ★ MEXICAN   Something about this place reminds me of a certain class of restaurant you find in the fashionable neighborhoods of Mexico City. Perhaps it's the large windows facing a walled patio area graced with a fountain and decorative plants, or it's the modern leather furniture and decor in the bar area. On the menu are some great soups, such as the cream soup flavored with the mild poblano chile (if you like that combination of cream and poblano, but want to forgo a soup course, try the *pollo en crema poblana*). Several mainstays of Mexican cooking are offered: enchiladas in a dark, earthy *mole* sauce, or in a tangy *salsa verde*; steak *a la tampiqueña* (perhaps the most common menu item in Mexico); and a red snapper cooked in the style of Veracruz. Of course, Tex-Mex standards are on the menu, too, and you can find some hearty vegetarian dishes such as a great vegetable chile relleno. A separate gluten-free menu is available for anyone who requests it. The bar is comfortable and has a full margarita menu, which I'm pretty sure is gluten-free as well. Keep this place in mind if you just want to enjoy some savory finger food with drinks in attractive surroundings. The bar area is comfortable and the menu has plenty of appetizers and finger foods.

5600 Broadway. ✆ **210/822-6151.** www.palomablanca.net. Reservations recommended only for large groups. Main courses $10–$25. AE, MC, V. Mon–Wed 11am–9pm; Thurs–Fri 11am–10pm; Sat 10am–10pm; Sun 10am–9pm.

# SEEING THE SIGHTS

San Antonio has a wide selection of attractions that can satisfy a variety of interests. You can easily fill your time hitting each one on your list, but I suggest you set aside a little time for aimlessly strolling about the city's downtown.

Before you visit any of the paid attractions, stop in at the **San Antonio Visitor Information Center,** 317 Alamo Plaza (✆ **210/207-6748**), across the street from the Alamo, and ask for their *SAVE San Antonio* discount book; it includes coupons for everything from the large theme parks to some city tours and museums. Many hotels also have a stash of discount coupons for their guests.

## The Top Attractions
### DOWNTOWN AREA

**The Alamo** ★★   Upon seeing the Alamo for the first time, most visitors react with surprise at how small it is. Though the shape of the facade of the Alamo is widely recognized, most Americans think of it as a large fortress. This only underscores how heroic and desperate were the actions of the Alamo's defenders, who in 1836 barricaded themselves in this former mission and held off a siege by a large Mexican army for 13 days. Also, it should be noted, the defenses for the battle were much larger than what you see today on the mission grounds. Missions often had large enclosed areas in front of the church, known as *atrios*. The wall enclosed all of what is now Alamo Plaza and extended even a bit farther in the direction of the river.

The Alamo today is more a shrine than a museum. It's main purpose is to honor the fallen. The siege played an important role in Texas independence, both strategic and iconic. The actions of its defenders, whether real or imagined, went a long way toward creating the larger-than-life mystique that Texas eventually acquired. Among the defenders were famous men of their day, such as Davy Crockett and Jim Bowie, and the idea of their sacrifice for Texas independence gave added meaning to the struggle almost immediately. "Remember the Alamo!" became the battle cry at San Jacinto, when the Texans finally defeated the Mexican army and captured its general, López de Santa Anna.

The outlying buildings of the original mission are gone. Only the **Long Barrack** (formerly the *convento,* or living quarters for the missionaries) and the much-photographed **mission church** are still here. The exhibits don't do a great job of explaining how the battle developed. If you want to understand more, see the IMAX show in the nearby Rivercenter Mall. A larger **museum** and gift shop are at the back of the complex. A peaceful **garden** and an excellent **research library** (closed Sun) are also on the grounds. Interesting historical presentations are given every half-hour by Alamo staffers; for private, after-hour tours, call ℂ **210/225-1391**, ext. 34. Allow about 1½ hours for a visit to the Alamo.

300 Alamo Plaza. ℂ **210/225-1391.** www.thealamo.org. Free admission (donations welcome). Mon-Sat 9am-5:30pm; Sun 10am-5:30pm. Closed Dec 24-25. Streetcar: Red or Blue lines.

**King William Historic District** ★    San Antonio's first suburb, King William was settled in the late–19th century by prosperous German merchants who displayed their wealth through extravagant homes and named the 25-block area after Kaiser Wilhelm of Prussia. The area has gotten so popular that tour buses have been restricted after certain hours. But it's much more pleasant to be on foot here than in a tour bus (and you can now walk from downtown to King William by taking the River Walk's southern extension). You can stroll down tree-shaded King William Street and admire the old houses and their beautifully landscaped yards. Stop at the headquarters of the **San Antonio Conservation Society,** 107 King William St. (ℂ **210/224-6163;** www.saconservation.org), and pick up a self-guided walking-tour booklet outside the gate. If you go at a leisurely pace, the stroll should take about an hour. The **Steves Homestead Museum** at 509 King William St. (ℂ **210/225-5924**), built in 1876 for a lumber magnate; and **Villa Finale** (also 1876) at 401 King William St. (ℂ **210/223-9800**), the former home of preservationist Walter Mathis, are open for tours. Both tours are great, but you need to make reservations. If you have lunch at the Guenther House (p. 256), you can see a good bit of that mansion at no charge, but there's not as much to see as in either of the museums.

East bank of the river just south of downtown. Streetcar: Blue line.

**La Villita National Historic District** ★    Developed by European settlers along the east bank of the San Antonio River in the late–18th and early–19th centuries, La Villita was revitalized in the late 1930s by artists and craftspeople and the San Antonio

Conservation Society. Today, the boutiques, crafts shops, and restaurants occupy this historic district, which resembles a Spanish/Mexican village, replete with shaded patios, plazas, brick-and-tile streets, and some of the settlement's original adobe structures, including the house of General Cós, the Mexican military leader who surrendered to the Texas revolutionary army in 1835. It'll take you only about 20 minutes to do a quick walk-through, unless you're an inveterate shopper—in which case, all bets are off.

Bounded by Durango, Navarro, and Alamo sts. and River Walk. © **210/207-8610.** www.lavillita.com. Free admission. Shops daily 10am–6pm. Closed Thanksgiving, Dec 25, and Jan 1. Streetcar: Red, Purple, or Blue lines.

**Market Square** ★ It may not be quite as colorful as it was when live chickens squawked around overflowing, makeshift vegetable stands, but Market Square still transports you south of the border. Stalls in the indoor El Mercado sell everything from onyx paperweights and manufactured serapes to high-quality crafts from the interior of Mexico. Across the street, the Farmers' Market, which formerly housed the produce market, has carts with more modern goods.

Bring your appetite along with your wallet: In addition to two Mexican restaurants, almost every weekend sees the emergence of food stalls selling specialties such as *gorditas* (chubby corn cakes topped with a variety of goodies) or funnel cakes (fried dough sprinkled with powdered sugar). Most of the city's Hispanic festivals are held here, and mariachis usually stroll the square. The Museo Alameda (see "More Attractions," below) provides a historic context to an area that can seem pretty touristy—though no more so than any Mexican border town.

Bounded by Commerce, Santa Rosa, Dolorosa, and I-35. © **210/207-8600.** http://tavernini.com/mercado. Free admission. El Mercado and Farmers' Market Plaza summer daily 10am–8pm; winter daily 10am–6pm; restaurants and some shops open later. Closed Thanksgiving, Dec 25, Jan 1, and Easter. Streetcar: Red, Purple, or Yellow lines.

**The River Walk (Paseo del Río)** ★★★ Below the streets of downtown San Antonio lies another world, alternately soothing and exhilarating, depending on where you venture. The quieter areas of the 5 miles of winding riverbank, shaded by cypresses, oaks, and willows, exude a tropical, exotic aura. The River Square and South Bank sections, chockablock with sidewalk cafes, tony restaurants, bustling bars, high-rise hotels, and even a huge shopping mall, have a festive, sometimes frenetic feel. Tour boats, water taxis, and floating picnic barges regularly ply the river, and local parades and festivals fill its banks with revelers.

Although plans to cement over the river after a disastrous flood in 1921 were stymied, it wasn't until the late 1930s that the federal Work Projects Administration (WPA) carried out architect Robert Hugman's designs for the waterway, installing cobblestone walks, arched bridges, and entrance steps from various street-level locations. And it wasn't until the late 1960s, when the River Walk proved to be one of the most popular attractions of the HemisFair exposition, that its commercial development began in earnest. There's a real danger of the River Walk becoming overdeveloped, but plenty of quieter spots still exist. If you're caught up in the sparkling lights reflected on the water on a breezy night, you might forget there is anyone else around.

**San Antonio Museum of Art** ★★ This attraction may not be top-listed by everyone, but I enjoy doable (read: not overwhelmingly large) museums with interesting architecture and collections related to the cities in which they're located—and this one definitely fits the bill. Several castlelike buildings of the 1904 Lone Star

Brewery were gutted, connected, and transformed into a visually exciting exhibition space in 1981. Although holdings range from early Egyptian, Greek, Oceanic, and Asian collections to 19th- and 20th-century American artwork, it's the Nelson A. Rockefeller Center for Latin American Art, opened in 1998, that is the jewel of the collection. This 30,000-square-foot wing hosts the most comprehensive collection of Latin American art in the United States, with pre-Columbian, folk, Spanish colonial, and contemporary works. You'll see everything here from magnificently ornate altarpieces to a whimsical Day of the Dead tableau. The Lenora and Walter F. Brown Asian Art Wing represents another major collection, the largest Asian art collection in Texas and one of the largest in the Southwest. Allow 3 hours for a visit to the museum.

200 W. Jones Ave. © **210/978-8100.** www.samuseum.org. Admission $8 adults, $7 seniors, $5 students with ID, $3 children 4–11, free for children 3 and under. Free general admission Tues 4–9pm (fee for some special exhibits). Tues 10am–9pm; Wed–Sat 10am–5pm; Sun noon–6pm. Closed Thanksgiving, Dec 25, Jan 1, Easter, and Fiesta Friday. Bus: 7, 8, 9, or 14.

## ALAMO HEIGHTS AREA

**Marion Koogler McNay Art Museum** ★★★   Well worth a detour from downtown, this museum is one of my favorite spots. With a knockout setting on a hill north of Brackenridge Park and a panoramic view of the city, this sprawling Spanish Mediterranean–style mansion (built in 1929) is so picturesque that it's often used as a backdrop for weddings and photo shoots. The art collection, though not the equivalent of collections in bigger cities, is quite good if you enjoy modern art. It has at least one work by each of the American and European masters of the past 2 centuries, including Van Gogh, Manet, Gauguin, Degas, O'Keeffe, Hopper, Matisse, Modigliani, Cézanne, and Picasso, to name just a few of the artists. The McNay occasionally hosts major traveling shows and, with the new addition, will probably host more of these exhibits. It'll take you 2 hours to go through this place at a leisurely pace, longer if it's cool enough for you to stroll the beautifully landscaped, 23-acre grounds dotted with sculptures.

6000 N. New Braunfels Ave. © **210/824-5368.** www.mcnayart.org. Admission $8 adults, $5 seniors, $5 students w/ID, free for children 12 and under. Tues–Wed and Fri 10am–4pm; Thurs 10am–9pm; Sat 10am–5pm; Sun noon–5pm. Closed Jan 1, July 4th, Thanksgiving, and Dec 25. Bus: 14.

**Witte Museum** ★ ☺   A family museum that adults will enjoy almost as much as kids, the Witte focuses on Texas history, natural science, and anthropology, with occasional forays as far afield as the Berlin Wall. Your senses will be engaged along with your intellect: You might hear birdcalls as you stroll through the Texas Wild exhibits, or feel rough-hewn stone carved with Native American pictographs beneath your feet. Children especially like exhibits devoted to mummies and dinosaurs, as well as the "EcoLab," with live Texas critters ranging from tarantulas to tortoises. But the biggest draw for kids is the terrific HEB Science Treehouse, a four-level, 15,000-square-foot science center that sits behind the museum on the banks of the San Antonio River; its hands-on activities are geared to all ages. Also on the grounds is a butterfly and hummingbird garden, as well as three restored historic homes. Allow 2 hours for a visit to the museum. *Note:* Several years ago, the museum acquired the wonderful Herzberg Circus Collection, parts of which are regularly incorporated into the museum's exhibits.

3801 Broadway (adjacent to Brackenridge Park). © **210/357-1900.** www.wittemuseum.org. Admission $7 adults, $6 seniors, $5 children 4–11, free for children 3 and under, free for all Tues 3–8pm. Mon and

Wed–Sat 10am–5pm; Tues 10am–8pm; Sun noon–5pm. Closed 3rd Mon in Oct, Thanksgiving, and Dec 24–25. Bus: 7, 9, or 14.

## SOUTH SIDE

**San Antonio Missions National Historical Park** ★★  The Alamo was just the first of five missions established by the Franciscans along the San Antonio River to Christianize the native population. The four other missions, which now fall under the aegis of the National Park Service, are still active parishes, run in cooperation with the Archdiocese of San Antonio. But the missions were more than churches: They were whole communities. The Park Service has assigned each mission an interpretive theme so visitors learn about the roles missions played in early San Antonio society. You can visit them separately, but if you have the time, see them all; they were built uncharacteristically close together and—now that you don't have to walk there or ride a horse—it shouldn't take you more than 2 or 3 hours to see them. If your time is limited, definitely visit San José and try to make it to San Francisco, even though it's the farthest from downtown.

**Concepción,** 807 Mission Rd. at Felisa, built in 1731, is the oldest unrestored Texas mission—it looks much as it did 280 years ago. **San José** ★★, 6701 San José Dr. at Mission Road, established in 1720, was the largest, best known, and most beautiful of the Texas missions. It was reconstructed to give visitors a complete picture of life in a mission community. Popular mariachi Masses are held here every Sunday at noon (come early if you want a seat). Moved from an earlier site in east Texas to its present location in 1731, **San Juan Capistrano,** 9101 Graf at Ashley, doesn't have the grandeur of the missions to the north, but the original simple chapel and the wilder setting give it a peaceful, spiritual aura. The southernmost mission in the San Antonio chain, **San Francisco de la Espada** ★, 10040 Espada Rd., also has an ancient, isolated feel, although the beautifully maintained church shows just how vital it still is to the local community.

Headquarters: 2202 Roosevelt Ave. Visitor Center: 6701 San José Dr. at Mission Rd. ℰ **210/932-1001.** www.nps.gov/saan. Free admission (donations accepted). All missions daily 9am–5pm. National Park Ranger tours daily. Closed Thanksgiving, Dec 25, and Jan 1. Bus: 42 stops at Mission San José (and near Concepción).

## FAR WEST/NORTHWEST

**SeaWorld San Antonio** ★ ☺  Leave it to Texas to provide Shamu, the performing killer whale, with its most spacious digs: At 250 acres, this SeaWorld is the largest marine life adventure park in the world. If you're a theme park fan, you're likely to be fascinated by the walk-through habitats where you can watch penguins, sea lions, sharks, tropical fish, and flamingos do their thing. But the aquatic acrobatics at such stadium shows as "Shamu Adventure," combining live action and video close-ups, and "Viva," where divers and synchronized swimmers frolic with whales and dolphins, might be even more fun.

You needn't get frustrated just looking at all that water, because there are loads of places here to get wet. The Lost Lagoon has a huge wave pool and water slides aplenty, and the Texas Splashdown flume ride and the Rio Loco river-rapids ride also are splashy fun; younger children can cavort in Shamu's Happy Harbor and the L'il Gators section of the Lost Lagoon. Nonaquatic activities include the Steel Eel, a huge "hypercoaster," and the Great White, the Southwest's first inverted coaster—which involves going head over heels during 2,500 feet of loops (don't eat before either of them).

10500 SeaWorld Dr., 16 miles northwest of downtown San Antonio at Ellison Dr. and Westover Hills Blvd. ℗ **800/700-7786.** www.seaworld.com. 1-day pass $59 adults, $54 seniors (55 and older), $50 children ages 3–9, free for children 2 and under. Special discounts available. Early Mar to late Nov; days of operation vary; open 10am, closing times vary. Call ahead or check website for current information. Bus: 64. From Loop 410 or from Hwy. 90W, exit Hwy. 151 W. to the park.

**Six Flags Fiesta Texas ★ ☺**  Kids of all ages can thrill to the Tornado, an extremely wet-and-wild tunnel and funnel-tubing experience; the Superman Krypton Coaster, nearly a mile of twisted steel with six inversions; the Rattler, one of the world's highest and fastest wooden roller coasters; the 60-mph-plus Poltergeist roller coaster; and Scream!, a 20-story space shot and turbo drop, to name just a few. Laser games and virtual reality simulators complete the technophile picture. Feeling more primal? Wet-'n'-wild attractions include the Lone Star Lagoon, the state's largest wave pool; the Texas Treehouse, a five-story drenchfest whose surprises include a 1,000-gallon cowboy hat that tips over periodically to soak the unsuspecting; and Bugs' White Water Rapids. If you want to avoid both sogginess and adrenaline over-load, there is a vast variety of food booths, shops, crafts demonstrations, and live shows. This theme park still has some local character, dating back to the days when it was plain old Fiesta Texas: Themed areas include a Hispanic village, a Western town, and a German town.

17000 I-10 W. (corner of I-10 W. and Loop 1604). ℗ **800/473-4378** or 210/697-5050. www.sixflags.com/parks/fiestatexas. Admission $55, $40 children 48 in. and under, free for children 2 and under. Special discounts available. Daily late May to mid-Aug; Sat–Sun Mar to lateMay and mid-Aug to Oct; open 10am, closing times vary depending on season, as late as 10pm in summer. Call ahead or visit website for current information. Bus: 94 (summer only). Exit 555 (La Cantera Pkwy.) on I-10 W.

# More Attractions

## DOWNTOWN AREA

**Museo Alameda**  Inaugurated in 2007, the Museo Alameda is the nation's largest museum celebrating Hispanic-American culture. Its 20,000-square-foot exhibition space is divided into 11 galleries. Though the museum doesn't have a permanent collection, it has many resources to lean on, including a close association with the Smithsonian Institution. The exhibits each last about 4 months and seek to illuminate some aspect of the Latino experience in America; to explore through art and artifact what America represents for Hispanic-Americans, and what the old home-land—be it Mexico or another country—comes to signify, as well. Such a broad purpose embraces art and history to piece together its narrative on Latino culture, leaning heavily on the expertise of curators of these exhibitions. The building proper is an attractive addition to the area around Market Square. It injects color and bold modern lines. The main decorative feature is some elaborate stainless-steel panels that variously bring to mind the wrought-iron work of colonial Latin America and the humble decorative practice of cutting designs into folded paper (*papel picado*). Allow 2 hours for a visit here.

101 S. Santa Rosa Blvd. (at Commerce, in Market Square). ℗ **210/299-4300.** www.thealameda.org. Admission $4 adults, $2 seniors and students, free for all Tues. Tues–Sat noon–6pm. Streetcar: Red, Purple, or Yellow lines.

**San Fernando Cathedral ★**  Construction of a church on this site, overlooking what was once the town's central plaza, was begun in 1738 by San Antonio's original Canary Island settlers and completed in 1749. Part of the early structure—the oldest cathedral sanctuary in the United States and the oldest parish church in Texas—is incorporated into the cathedral built in 1868. Jim Bowie got married here, and General Santa Anna raised the flag of "no quarter" from its roof during the siege of the Alamo in 1836. The cathedral has undergone major interior and exterior renovations and its most impressive addition is a 24-foot-high gilded *retablo* (altarpiece). Allow a half-hour for a visit.

115 Main Plaza. ✆ **210/227-1297.** www.sfcathedral.org. Free admission. Daily 6am–7pm. Gift shop Mon–Fri 9am–4:30pm, Sat 9am–5pm. Streetcar: Purple or Yellow lines.

**Spanish Governor's Palace ★ 🎁** This is the oldest, best-preserved structure in San Antonio. It began as a one-room house built in 1722. Three other rooms were added in 1749 (the date is shown on one of the doorways, along with the insignia of Spanish King Ferdinand VI). It served as the residence and headquarters for the captain of the Spanish garrison and became the seat of Texas government in 1772, when San Antonio was made capital of the Spanish province of Texas. It remained as such until 1821 when Mexico gained its independence. The last captain of San Antonio de Béxar, Juan Ignacio Pérez, and his descendants remained in the house until the 1860s. By 1928, when the city purchased the house, it had served as the residence for several businesses, including a tailor's shop, barroom, and schoolhouse. The five rooms are furnished as they might have been in the 18th century. There's a shaded garden and patio in back with a stone fountain and mosaic flooring, a 19th-century addition that remains quite attractive. If your visit elicits questions, talk to the staff who are very helpful and know a great deal about the house's history. Allow a half-hour for a visit here.

105 Plaza de Armas. ✆ **210/224-0601.** www.spanishgovernorspalace.org. Admission $4 adults, $3 seniors, $2 children 7–13, free for children 6 and under. Tues–Sat 9am–5pm; Sun 10am–5pm. Closed Jan 1, San Jacinto Day (Apr 21), Thanksgiving, and Dec 25. Streetcar: Purple line.

## Parks & Gardens

**HemisFair Park ☺** Built for the 1968 HemisFair, an exposition celebrating the 250th anniversary of the founding of San Antonio, this urban oasis boasts **water gardens** and a **wood-and-sand playground** constructed by children (near the Alamo St. entrance). Among its indoor diversions are the **Institute of Texan Cultures** and the **Tower of the Americas.** The **Schultze House Cottage Garden ★**, 514 HemisFair Park (✆ **210/229-9161**), created and maintained by Master Gardeners of Bexar County, is also worth checking out for its heirloom plants, varietals, tropicals, and Xeriscape area. Look for it behind the Federal Building.

Bounded by Alamo, Bowie, Market, and Durango sts. No phone. www.sanantonio.gov/sapar/hemisfair. asp. Streetcar: Blue, Yellow, or Purple lines.

**San Antonio Botanical Gardens ★** Take a horticultural tour of Texas at this gracious 38-acre garden, comprising everything from south Texas scrub to Hill Country wildflowers. Fountains, pools, paved paths, and examples of Texas architecture provide visual contrast to the flora. The formal gardens include one for the blind, along with Japanese, herb, biblical, and children's gardens. Perhaps most outstanding is the $6.9-million Lucile Halsell Conservatory complex, a series of greenhouses replicating a variety of tropical and desert environments. The 1896 Sullivan Carriage House, built by Alfred Giles and moved stone by stone from its original downtown site, serves as the entryway to the gardens.

555 Funston Place (at N. New Braunfels Ave.). ✆ **210/207-3250.** www.sabot.org. Admission $8 adults; $6 seniors, students, and military; $5 children 3–13; free for children 2 and under. Daily 9am–5pm. Closed Dec 25 and Jan 1. Bus: 7, 9, or 14.

## Especially for Kids

The prime spots for kids in San Antonio are SeaWorld and Six Flags Fiesta Texas. In addition to these sights, detailed in "The Top Attractions" and "More Attractions," above, there's the **San Antonio IMAX Theater Rivercenter** ★, 849 E. Commerce St., in the Rivercenter Mall (© **800/354-4629** for recorded schedule information, or 210/247-4629; www.imax-sa.com). Kids can view *Alamo: The Price of Freedom* on a six-story-high screen with a stereo sound system, a surefire way to get them psyched for the historical battle site just across the street.

Adults may get a bigger charge out of the waxy stars and some of the oddities collected by the globetrotting Mr. Ripley at the nearby **Louis Tussaud's Wax Works & Ripley's Believe It or Not,** 301 Alamo Plaza (© **210/224-9299;** www.plaza waxmuseum.com), just down the block, but there's plenty for kids to enjoy at this twofer attraction. The walk-through wax Theater of Horrors usually elicits some shudders, and at Believe It or Not, youngsters get a kick out of learning about people around the world whose habits are even weirder than their own. Just down the block are the combined attractions: **Ripley's Haunted Adventure, Guinness World Records Museum,** and **Tomb Rider 3D,** 329 Alamo Plaza (© **210/226-2828**). There's something for everyone at this multimillion-dollar entertainment complex, whether you like getting spooked by high-tech haunts, marveling at the odd things people will do to break records, or hearing about the world according to Davy Crockett—as reported by his friend, the bear.

Also downtown, the **San Antonio Children's Museum** ★★, 305 E. Houston St. (© **210/21-CHILD** [212-4453]; www.sakids.org), provides a wonderful introduction to the city for pint-size folks and grown-ups alike. San Antonio's history, population, and geography are all explored through such features as a miniature River Walk, a multicultural grocery store—and even a miniature dentist's office. See also "San Antonio After Dark," below, for the **Magik Theatre.**

If the family gets overheated, head to **Splashtown,** 3600 N. I-35 (© **210/227-1100;** www.splashtownsa.com), which includes a huge wave pool, hydro tubes nearly 300 feet long, a Texas-size water bobsled ride, more than a dozen water slides, and a two-story playhouse for smaller children.

## Organized Tours

San Antonio's organized tours basically provide you with an efficient way to get around and pick up some local lore. **Alamo Sightseeing Tours,** 122 Losoya St. (© **210/492-4144;** www.alamosightseeingtours.com), has a variety of full and half-day tours. **Grand Trolley Tours,** 321 Alamo Plaza (© **210/492-4144;** www.grand trolleytours.com), touches on all the downtown highlights, plus two of the missions in the south. If you want to get off at any of these sights, you can pick up another trolley (they run every 45 min.) after you're finished. To get up close and personal with the River Walk, try a **Rio San Antonio River Cruise.** This amusing, informative tour, lasting from 35 to 40 minutes, will take you more than 2 miles down the most built-up sections of the Paseo del Río, with interesting sights pointed out along the way. Ticket offices are at the Rivercenter Mall and River Walk, under the Market Street Bridge (© **210/244-5700;** www.riosanantonio.com).

# SPORTS & OUTDOOR ACTIVITIES

Most San Antonians head for the hills—that is, nearby Hill Country—for outdoor recreation. Some suggestions follow for sports in or around town; also see "Hill Country Side Trips from San Antonio," later in this chapter.

**BIKING** With the creation and continuing improvements of the biking paths along the San Antonio River, part of the larger **Mission Trails** project (see the San Antonio Missions National Historical Park listing, earlier in this chapter), local and visiting cyclists will finally have a good place within the city to spin their wheels (it's not quite there yet, but soon . . .). Other options within San Antonio itself: **Brackenridge Park; McAllister Park** on the city's north side, 13102 Jones Maltsberger Rd. (© 210/207-PARK [7275] or 207-3120); and around the area near **SeaWorld of Texas.** If you didn't bring your own bike, **Blue Star Bike Shop,** in Southtown at 1414 S. Alamo St. (© 210/212-5506; www.bluestarbrewing.com), will rent cruisers and other bikes ($20 for 6 hr.). Another bike rental place is **Brackenride** (© 210/826-7433), at 3619 Broadway.

**GOLF** Golf has become a big deal in San Antonio, with more and more visitors coming to town expressly to tee off. Of the city's six municipal golf courses, two of the most notable are **Brackenridge,** 2315 Ave. B (© 210/226-5612), the oldest (1916) public course in Texas, featuring oak- and pecan-shaded fairways; and northwest San Antonio's $4.3-million **Cedar Creek,** 8250 Vista Colina (© 210/695-5050), repeatedly ranked as south Texas's best municipal course in golfing surveys. For details on these and other municipal courses, log on to www.sanantonio.gov/sapar/golf.asp. Other options for unaffiliated golfers include the 200-acre **Pecan Valley,** 4700 Pecan Valley Dr. (© 210/333-9018), which crosses the Salado Creek seven times and has an 800-year-old oak near its 13th hole; the high-end **Quarry,** 444 E. Basse Rd. (© 800/347-7759 or 210/824-4500; www.quarrygolf.com), on the site of a former quarry and one of San Antonio's newest public courses; and **Canyon Springs,** 24405 Wilderness Oak Rd. (© 888/800-1511 or 210/497-1770; www.canyonspringsgc.com), at the north edge of town in the Texas Hill Country, lush with live oaks and dotted with historic rock formations.

There aren't too many resort courses in San Antonio because there aren't too many resorts, but the two at the **Westin La Cantera,** 16401 La Cantera Pkwy. (© 800/446-5387 or 210/558-4653; www.lacanteragolfclub.com)—one designed by Jay Morish and Tom Weiskopf, the other by Arnold Palmer—have knockout designs and dramatic hill-and-rock outcroppings to recommend them. Expect to pay $55 to $60 per person for an 18-hole round at a municipal course with a cart, from $70 up to $130 (Sat–Sun) per person at a private resort's course. Twilight (afternoon) rates are often cheaper. To get a copy of the free *San Antonio Golfing Guide,* call © 800/447-3372.

**HIKING** The 240-acre **Friedrich Wilderness Park,** 21480 Milsa St. (© 210/698-1057; www.wildtexas.com/parks/fwp.php), operated by the city of San Antonio as its only nature preserve, is crisscrossed by 5.5 miles of trails that attract birdwatchers as well as hikers; a 2-mile stretch is accessible to people with disabilities.

**RIVER SPORTS**   For tubing, rafting, or canoeing along a cypress-lined river, San Antonio river rats head 35 miles northwest of downtown to the 2,000-acre **Guadalupe River State Park,** 3350 Park Rd. 31 (© **830/438-2656;** www.tpwd.state.tx. us/park/guadalup), near Boerne. About 5 miles north of Hwy. 46, just outside the park, you can rent tubes, rafts, and canoes at the **Bergheim Campground,** FM 3351 in Bergheim (© **830/336-2235**).

**TENNIS**   With a reservation, you can play at the 22 lighted hard courts at the **McFarlin Tennis Center,** 1503 San Pedro Ave. (© **210/732-1223**), for the very reasonable fee of $3 per adult per hour ($1 for students and seniors), or $3.50 per adult ($2 students/seniors) after 5pm.

## Spectator Sports

**BASKETBALL**   Spurs madness hits San Antonio every year from mid-October through May, when the city's only major-league franchise, the **San Antonio Spurs,** shoots hoops. The Spurs are now based at the AT&T Center. Ticket prices range from $20 for nosebleed-level seats to $100 for seats on the corners of the court. Tickets are available at the Spurs Ticket Office in the AT&T Center, which is at One AT&T Center Pkwy. (© **210/444-5819**), or via Ticketmaster San Antonio (© **210/224-9600;** www. ticketmaster.com). Get schedules, players' stats, and promotional news—everything you might want to know or buy relating to the team—online at www.nba.com/spurs.

**GOLF**   The **AT&T Championship,** an Official Senior PGA Tour Event, is held each October at the Oak Hills Country Club, 5403 Fredericksburg Rd. (© **210/698-3582**). One of the oldest professional golf tournaments, now known as the **Valero Texas Open,** showcases the sport in May. Visit www.pgatour.com/r/schedule for information about both.

**RODEO**   If you're in town in early February, don't miss the chance to see 2 weeks of Wild West events such as calf roping, steer wrestling, and bull riding at the annual **San Antonio Stock Show and Rodeo.** You can also hear major live country-and-western talent. Call © **210/225-5851,** or visit www.sarodeo.com for information on schedules.

# SHOPPING IN SAN ANTONIO

San Antonio provides the shopper with a variety of large malls and little enclaves of specialized shops. You'll find everything here, from the utilitarian to the unusual: a huge Sears department store, a Saks Fifth Avenue fronted by a 40-foot pair of cowboy boots, a mall with a river running through it, and some lively Mexican markets.

You can count on most shops around town being open from 9 or 10am to 5:30 or 6pm Monday through Saturday, with shorter hours on Sunday. Malls are generally open Monday through Saturday 10am to 9pm and on Sunday noon to 6pm. Sales tax in San Antonio is 8.25%.

## Shopping Areas

Most out-of-town shoppers will find all they need **downtown,** between the large Rivercenter Mall, the boutiques and crafts shops of La Villita, the colorful Mexican wares of Market Square, the Southwest School of Art and Craft, and assorted retailers and galleries on and around Alamo Plaza. More avant-garde boutiques and galleries, including Blue Star, can be found in the adjacent area known as Southtown.

Most San Antonians prefer to shop in the malls along Loop 410, especially North Star, Huebner Oaks, and Alamo Quarry Market. The city's large-scale mall, **Shops at La Cantera,** is out along the outer loop (Loop 1604). It's an outdoor mall with a blue-ribbon collection of stores, including the city's only Neiman Marcus and only Nordstrom, and it has plenty of smaller retail stores and boutiques that cater to a well-heeled customer base. More upmarket retail outlets can be found closer to downtown in the fancy strip centers that line Broadway, where it passes through Alamo Heights (the posh Collection and Lincoln Heights are particularly noteworthy).

## Art

**ArtPace,** in the northern part of downtown, and the **Blue Star Arts Complex,** in Southtown, are the best venues for cutting-edge art, but **Finesilver Gallery,** 816 Camaron St., Ste. 1 and 2, just north of downtown (℗ **210/354-3333;** www.fine silver.com), is a good alternative. Downtown is home to several galleries that show more established artists. Two of the top ones are **Galería Ortiz,** 102 Concho St., in Market Square (℗ **210/225-0731**), San Antonio's premier place to buy Southwestern art; and **Nanette Richardson Fine Art,** 555 E. Basse Rd. (℗ **210/930-1343;** www.nanetterichardsonfineart.com), with a wide array of oils, watercolors, bronzes, ceramics, and handcrafted wood furnishings.

For more information on other galleries and the art scene in general, visit the Office of Cultural Affairs' website (www.sahearts.com), with listings of several local galleries, and schedules for events held during Contemporary Art Month in March.

## Crafts/Folk Art

Mexican folk art and handicrafts make wonderful take-homes from San Antonio, and several of the best places to find them are in Southtown. The best collection is at **San Angel Folk Art,** 1404 S. Alamo St., Ste. 110, in the Blue Star Arts Complex (℗ **210/226-6688;** www.sanangelfolkart.com), chockablock with colorful, whimsical, and well-made wares. Also located in Southtown is **Garcia Art Glass, Inc.,** 715 S. Alamo St. (℗ **210/354-4681;** www.garciaartglass.com), where you can find beautiful glass bowls, wall sconces, and mobiles. Often, glass blowers are at work behind the store, manipulating molten glass while they listen to Chicano music blaring from the radio. Downtown, next to the ticket office for the Metropolitan Theatre, is a colorful store filled with Mexican handwork called **Casa Salazar,** 216 E. Houston St. (℗ **210/472-2272**). Just north of downtown, near Monte Vista, the two-level **Alamo Fiesta,** 2025 N. Main St. at Ashby (℗ **210/738-1188;** www.alamofiesta. com), catering to local Hispanic families, has a huge selection of crafts at extremely reasonable prices. Not everything is very portable, but the bracelets and other pretty baubles made out of glass beads definitely are.

## Malls & Shopping Centers

Although it's officially **Alamo Quarry Market,** 255 E. Basse Rd. (℗ **210/824-8885;** www.quarrymarket.com), no one ever calls this relative newcomer to the mall scene anything but "the Quarry"—in large part because from the early 1900s until 1985 the property was in fact a cement quarry. This unenclosed mall has a series of large emporiums (such as Borders and Old Navy) and smaller upscale boutiques (Laura Ashley and Aveda). Starring Saks Fifth Avenue–the one fronted by the huge pair of cowboy boots—and upscale shops such as Abercrombie & Fitch and Williams-Sonoma, **North Star Mall,** Loop 410, between McCullough and San Pedro

(© **210/340-6627;** www.northstarmall.com), is the crème de la crème of the San Antonio indoor malls. But there are many sensible shops here, too, including a Mervyn's department store. Both the Quarry and North Star Mall are about 15 minutes from downtown.

At the light-filled, bustling **Rivercenter Mall,** 849 E. Commerce St. (© **210/225-0000;** www.shoprivercenter.com), you can pick up a ferry from a downstairs dock, listen to bands play on a stage surrounded by water, or visit the IMAX theater and a comedy club. The 130-plus shops, anchored by Dillard's and Foleys, run the price gamut, but tend toward upscale casual. Upscale shoppers migrate to the far northwest part of town, to the **Shops at La Cantera,** 16401 La Cantera Pkwy. Check **www.shoplacantera.com** for details.

## Western Wear

A one-stop shopping center for all duds Western, **Boot Hill** at Rivercenter Mall, 849 E. Commerce St., Ste. 213 (© **210/223-6634**), is one of the few left in town that's locally owned. At **Lucchese Gallery,** 255 E. Basse, Ste. 800 (© **210/828-9419;** www.lucchese.com), footwear is raised to the level of art. If it ever crawled, ran, hopped, or swam, these folks can probably put it on your feet. Lucchese is far better known than **Little's Boots,** 110 Division Ave. (© **210/923-2221;** www.davelittle boots.com), but this place—established in 1915—uses as many esoteric leathers and creates fancier footwear designs. If you're willing to wait awhile, you can have hand-customed leather boots made. The late Pope John Paul II, Prince Charles, and Dwight Yoakam all had headgear made for them by **Paris Hatters,** 119 Broadway (© **210/223-3453;** www.parishatters.com), in business since 1917 and still owned by the same family. About half of the sales are special order, but the shelves are stocked with high-quality ready-to-wear hats.

## Markets

Two large indoor markets, **El Mercado** and the **Farmers' Market**—often just called, collectively, the Mexican market—occupy adjacent blocks on Market Square at 514 W. Commerce St., near Dolorosa (© **210/207-8600**). Competing for your attention are more than 100 shops and pushcarts and an abundance of food stalls. The majority of the shopping booths are of the border-town sort, filled with onyx chess sets, cheap sombreros, and the like, but you can also find a few higher quality boutiques. Come here for a bit of local color, good people-watching, and food.

# SAN ANTONIO AFTER DARK

San Antonio has its symphony and its Broadway shows, and you can see both at one of the most beautiful old movie palaces in the country. But much of what the city has to offer is not quite so mainstream. Latin influences lend spice to some of the best local nightlife. Don't forget, San Antonio is the birthplace of Tejano music, a unique blend of German polka and northern Mexico ranchero sounds (with a dose of pop added for good measure). It also celebrates its Mexican heritage with colorful dance troupes, known as *ballet folklórico,* who perform to more traditional Mexican music. And Southtown, with its many Hispanic-oriented shops and galleries, celebrates its art scene with the monthly First Friday, a kind of extended block party.

For the most complete listings of what's on while you're visiting, pick up a free copy of the weekly alternative newspaper, the *Current,* or the Friday "Weekender" section of the *San Antonio Express-News.* You can also check out the website of **San Antonio Arts & Cultural Affairs:** www.sanantonio.gov/art. There's no central office in town for tickets, discounted or otherwise. You'll need to reserve seats directly through the theaters or clubs, or, for large events, through **Ticketmaster** (*©* **210/224-9600;** www.ticketmaster.com). Generally, box office hours are Monday to Friday 10am to 5pm, and 1 to 2 hours before performance time. The **Majestic** and **Empire** (see "Major Arts Venues," below) also have hours on Saturday 10am to 3pm.

## The Performing Arts

The San Antonio Symphony is the city's only resident performing arts company of national stature, but smaller, less professional groups keep the local arts scene lively, and cultural organizations draw world-renowned artists. The city provides them with some unique venues—everything from standout historic structures such as the Majestic, Empire, Arneson, and Sunken Garden theaters to the state-of-the-art AT&T Center.

### MAJOR ARTS VENUES

If you're visiting San Antonio from May to August, you might want to catch a performance at the **Arneson River Theatre,** La Villita (*©* **210/207-8610;** www.lavillita.com/arneson). Built by the Work Projects Administration (WPA) in 1939 as part of architect Robert Hugman's design for the River Walk, this unique theater has a stage on one side of the river, where it narrows considerably, and the seating on the opposite side. Most performances are *ballet folklórico.*

The baroque Moorish/Spanish revival–style **Majestic Theatre,** 230 E. Houston St. (*©* **210/226-3333;** www.majesticempire.com), hosts some of the best entertainment in town—the symphony, major Broadway productions, big-name solo performers.

There's always something happening at the **Guadalupe Cultural Arts Center,** 1300 Guadalupe St. (*©* **210/271-3151;** www.guadalupeculturalarts.org), the main locus for Latino cultural activity in San Antonio. Visiting or local directors put on six or seven plays a year; the Xicano Music Program celebrates the popular local conjunto and Tejano sounds; and the CineFestival, running since 1977, is one of the town's major film events.

Smaller than its former rival the Majestic (see above), just down the block, the **Empire Theatre,** 226 N. St. Mary's St. (*©* **210/226-5700;** www.majesticempire.com), hosts a similarly eclectic array of acts, including musical performance, lectures, and literary events.

### CLASSICAL MUSIC

The **San Antonio Symphony,** 222 E. Houston St. (*©* **210/554-1000** or 554-1010 box office; www.sasymphony.org), was founded in 1939. It celebrated its 50th anniversary by moving into the Majestic Theatre, the reopening of which was planned to coincide with the event. The symphony still plays there, but it may move to the Municipal Auditorium in 2011 or 2012. The city is in talks with several parties, but nothing definite has been agreed upon. The symphony's season runs from September to May and usually has two concert series, one classical and the other pops. The music director is Sebastian Lang-Lessing. Tickets range from $19 to $90, and $19 to $62 for pops.

### THEATER

Most of San Antonio's major road shows turn up at the Majestic or Empire theaters (see "Major Art Venues," above), but several smaller theaters are of interest, too. The

**Actors Theater of San Antonio,** 1920 Fredericksburg Rd. (© **210/738-2872**), uses local talent for its productions, which tend to be in the off-Broadway tradition. Their venue is the Woodlawn Theatre, opened as a movie house in 1945. The community-based **Josephine Theatre,** 339 W. Josephine St. (© **210/734-4646**; www. josephinetheatre.org), puts on an average of five productions a year—mostly musicals—at the Art Deco–style theater, only 5 minutes from downtown.

**Magik Theatre,** Beethoven Hall, 420 S. Alamo St., in HemisFair Park (© **210/227-2751**; www.magiktheatre.org), performs shows for children and families. It's one of very few organizations that perform for children to have its own professional company and venue. The theater, Beethoven Hall, used to belong to an old German singing society and has 600 seats. Shows are popular, so you need to reserve in advance, especially on weekends. Magik Theatre performs a full season of plays, mostly adaptations from children's books.

Whether it's an original piece by a member of the company or a work by a guest artist, anything you see at the **Jump-Start Performance Company,** 108 Blue Star Arts Complex, 1400 S. Alamo St. (© **210/227-JUMP** [5867]; www.jump-start.org), is likely to push the social and political envelope.

## The Club & Music Scene

The closest San Antonio comes to having a club district is the stretch of North St. Mary's Street between Josephine and Magnolia—just north of downtown and south of Brackenridge Park—known as the **Strip.** This area was hotter about 15 years ago, but it still draws a young crowd to its restaurants and lounges on the weekend. The River Walk clubs tend to be touristy, and many of them close early because of noise restrictions.

In addition to the **Alamodome,** 100 Montana St. (© **210/207-3663**; www.san antonio.gov/dome), the major concert venues in town include **Verizon Wireless Amphitheater,** 16765 Lookout Rd., north of San Antonio just beyond Loop 1604 (© **210/657-8300**; www.vwatx.com); and, when the Spurs aren't playing there, downtown's **AT&T Center,** One AT&T Center Pkwy. (© **210/444-5000**; www. nba.com/spurs).

### COUNTRY & WESTERN

John T. Floore, the first manager of the Majestic Theatre, opened up **Floore's Country Store,** 14664 Old Bandera Rd., 2 miles north of Loop 1604 (© **210/695-8827**; www.liveatfloores.com), in 1942. A couple of years later, he added a cafe and a dance floor—at a half-acre, the largest in south Texas—and since then, the establishment has hosted country greats such as Willie Nelson, Hank Williams, Sr., Lyle Lovett, and Dwight Yoakam. The lively 1880s-style **Leon Springs Dancehall,** 24135 I-10, Boerne Stage Road exit (© **210/698-7072**; www.leonspringsdancehall.com), can pack some 1,200 people into its 18,000 square feet. Lots of folks come with their kids when the place opens at 7pm. Some of the best local country-and-western talent is showcased here on Friday and Saturday nights, the only 2 nights the dance hall is open.

### JAZZ & BLUES

If you like big bands and Dixieland, there's no better place to listen to music downtown than the **Landing,** Hyatt Regency Hotel, River Walk (© **210/325-2495**; www.landing.com), one of the best traditional jazz clubs in the country. You might have heard cornetist Jim Cullum on the airwaves: His American Public Radio

## CONJUNTO: AN american CLASSIC

Although conjunto is one of our country's original contributions to world music, for a long time few Americans outside Texas knew much about it.

It evolved at the end of the 19th century, when south Texas was swept by a wave of German immigrants who brought with them popular polkas and waltzes. These sounds were easily incorporated into—and transformed by—Mexican folk music. The newcomer accordion, cheap and able to mimic several instruments, was happily adopted, too. With the addition at the turn of the 20th century of the *bajo sexto,* a 12-string guitarlike instrument used for rhythmic bass accompaniment, conjunto was born.

San Antonio is to conjunto music what Nashville is to country. The most famous *bajo sextos,* used nationally by everyone who is anyone in conjunto/Tejano music, were created in San Antonio by the Macías family—the late Martín and now his son, Alberto. The undisputed king of conjunto, **Flaco Jiménez**— a mild-mannered triple-Grammy winner

who has recorded with the Rolling Stones, Bob Dylan, and Willie Nelson, among others—lives in the city. And San Antonio's **Tejano Conjunto Festival,** held each May, is the largest of its kind, drawing aficionados from around the world—there's even a conjunto band from Japan.

Most of the places to hear conjunto and Tejano are off the beaten tourist path, and they come and go fairly quickly. Those that have been around for a while—and are visitor-friendly— include **Arturo's Sports Bar & Grill,** 3310 S. Zarzamora St. (© 210/923-0177), and **Cool Arrows,** 1025 Nogalitos St. (© **210/227-5130**). For live music schedules, check the Tejano/Conjunto section under "Entertainment" and "Music" of www.mysanantonio.com, the website of the *San Antonio-Express News.* You can also call **Salute!** (see above) to find out which night of the week they're featuring a Tejano or conjunto band. Best yet, just attend one of San Antonio's many festivals—you're bound to hear these rousing sounds.

program, *Riverwalk, Live from the Landing,* is now broadcast on more than 160 stations nationwide. The live jazz at tiny **Salute!,** 2801 N. St. Mary's St. (© **210/732-5307;** www.saluteinternationalbar.com), tends to have a Latin base, but you never know what you're going to find here—anything from synthesized '70s sounds to conjunto.

## The Bar Scene

**A MICROBREWERY**   Preppie and gallery types don't often mingle, but the popularity with college kids of the **Blue Star Brewing Company,** 1414 S. Alamo, no. 105 (© 210/212-5506), in the Blue Star Arts Complex, demonstrates the transcendent power of good beer (the pale ale is especially fine).

**A HISTORIC BAR**   More than 100 years ago, Teddy Roosevelt recruited men for his Rough Riders unit at the dark, wooded **Menger Bar,** Menger Hotel, 204 Alamo Plaza (© 210/223-4361); they were outfitted for the Spanish-American War at nearby Fort Sam Houston. Constructed in 1859 on the site of William Menger's earlier successful brewery and saloon, the bar was moved from its original location in the Victorian hotel lobby in 1956, but 90% of its historic furnishings remain intact.

You can still see an "X" on the bar put there by prohibitionist Carrie Nation, and Spanish Civil War uniforms hang on the walls.

**LOCAL FAVORITE**   During the week, lawyers and judges come to unwind at the **Cadillac Bar & Restaurant,** 212 S. Flores St. (✆ **210/223-5533**), in a historic stucco building near the Bexar County Courthouse and City Hall; on weekends, singles take the stand.

**A COCKTAIL BAR**   The bar at Le Midi, 301 E. Houston St. (✆ **210/858-7388**), is one of the new breed of cocktail bars that exercises good judgment and painstaking care to serve the best possible cocktails without the flash or the ubiquitous maraschino cherry.

**A WINE BAR**   Zinc (✆ **210/224-2900**), at 209 N. Presa St., in the downtown area, is enjoyed for its cozy, laid-back feel. Hardwood floors, exposed brick walls, and shelves of books give it an intimate, relaxing feel.

**A MARTINI BAR**   The River Walk's nod to retro chic, **Swig** (✆ **210/476-0005;** www.swigmartini.com), at 111 W. Crockett St., is so popular it spurred a national chain. Single-barrel bourbon, single-malt scotch, and a wide selection of beer and wines fill out the drink menu, but martinis are always the top seller. Nightly live jazz and cigar smoke are part of the scene.

**A SPORTS BAR**   If you want to hang with the Spurs, come to **Tex's Grill,** San Antonio Airport Hilton and Conference Center, 611 NW Loop 410 (✆ **210/340-6060**), regularly voted San Antonio's best sports bar. A second locale, Tex's on the River, is at the Hilton Palacio del Rio on the River Walk.

## The Gay & Lesbian Scene

Tina Turner, Deborah Harry, and La Toya Jackson—the real ones—have all played the **Bonham Exchange,** 411 Bonham St. (✆ **210/271-3811;** www.bonham exchange.com), a high-tech dance club near the Alamo. While you may find an occasional cross-dressing show here, the mixed crowd of gays and straights, young and old, come mainly to move to the beat under wildly flashing lights. Main Street just north of downtown has three gay men's clubs in close proximity (it's been nicknamed the "gay bar mall"). **Pegasus,** 1402 N. Main St. (✆ **210/299-4222**), is your basic cruise bar. The **Silver Dollar,** 1418 N. Main St. (✆ **210/227-2623**), does the country-and-western thing. **The Saint,** 1430 N. Main St. (✆ **210/225-7330**), caters to dancing fools. Covers are low to nonexistent at all three. Popular lesbian bars include **Bermuda Triangle,** 119 El Mio Dr. (✆ **210/342-2276**), and **Petticoat Junction,** 1812 N. Main St. (✆ **210/737-2344**).

# SMALL-TOWN TEXAS

If you want to get out of San Antonio and away from the crowds, and see a less touristy part of Texas, then consider this day trip to a few of the old towns to the east of San Antonio. The trip includes a smattering of things: a little history, an old county jail, some antiques shopping, a tour of Texas's last independent brewery, and some award-winning barbecue, plus plenty of local color. It's best to go on a weekday, when the brewery is open for tours. This is a relaxing trip—the roads are good, the traffic is light, and the driving is easy. There won't be any crowds, which is especially important during wildflower season in the spring. Visitors show a strong preference for the Hill Country, but the wildflowers do not.

# Gonzales

Start by heading out of San Antonio east on I-10 to Hwy. 183 (60 miles), then south to the town of **Gonzales** (12 miles). One of the original Anglo settlements made under agreement with the Mexican government, Gonzales was a hotbed for Texas independence and saw the first hostilities of the war. While driving around the town, you're sure to see signs and banners with the words "Come and take it" below an image of a canon. This was the battle cry of the local settlers when, in October 1835, a regiment of Mexican cavalry came to collect a small cannon that had been lent to the settlement to fend off the Comanche. What followed was more of a skirmish than a battle, but it set Texas on the road to independence. A few months later, the town was burned to the ground by orders of Gen. Sam Houston when the Texan army retreated eastward, during the so-called Runaway Scrape.

In the oldest part of Gonzales (pop. 7,000), the streets are still named after saints, following the original layout proposed by the Mexican government. There's a relatively large business sector with old brick storefronts, which tells of past prosperity. Occupying a few of these (and a couple of warehouses, too) is **Discovery Architectural Antiques** (✆ **830/672-2428;** www.discoverys.com) at 409 St. Francis St. It sells all manner of old building materials, including original lumber, doors, windows, hardware, stained glass, and small details, such as doorknobs.

The **town courthouse** is one of the prettiest in Texas. It was built in 1898 in Richardsonian Romanesque (a style named after the architect who built Trinity Church in Boston). It was designed by J. Riely Gordon, who also designed Bexar County Courthouse in San Antonio and the Comal County Courthouse in New Braunfels. This is the best of the three and is one of the best-preserved courthouses in the state, having retained its clock tower and original roof. The interior is well preserved, too. It contains a few paintings, one of which depicts the town around 1925. The **old jailhouse,** which sits at the opposite corner of the square (facing St. Lawrence St.), is home of the chamber of commerce and visitor center. It dates from 1887 and is open to visitors. It must have been a grim sight for prisoners, to judge by the way the cells were built and by the gallows room, which was used for executions until the 1920s, when capital punishment was brought under state control. Gonzalez did have a criminal element, and its most famous member was John Wesley Harden (son of a Methodist preacher). He killed several men in the Sutton-Taylor feud, which raged throughout several counties in this part of Texas during the 1870s. For a while, he was jailed in Gonzales (in an earlier jailhouse) but managed to escape.

Gonzales has several large houses in the old part of town, as well as a **Pioneer Village** (✆ **830/672-2157;** www.gonzalespioneervillage.com), which is at the north end of town, on 2122 N. St. Joseph St. It holds a collection of 19th-century buildings brought here from different parts of the county and restored, including a ranch house, a cabin, and a saloon. It's open from 10am to 2pm Tuesday to Saturday. Admission is $5 per adult, $3 for children 4 to 13, free for children 3 and under. It's probably a good idea to call ahead to make sure someone is there. You also need to be mindful of the time because you'll want to get to the next town, Shiner, before either 11:30am or 1pm, when the brewery tours start. It's 20 minutes away.

# Shiner

Shiner (pop. 2,000) is home to the **Spoetzl brewery,** the makers of Shiner beer. This is the last independent brewery in Texas, and in 2009 celebrated its 100th anniversary.

Take Hwy. 90 east for 18 miles. When you drive into Shiner, the brewery will be on your left. It's the highest structure in town.

Shiner Bock beer, sold in brown longnecks, is now available in various parts of the country, but, as late as the 1970s it was available only seasonally and only in central and southeast Texas. But it soon shot up in popularity until it's now the default beer in Austin, San Antonio, and most other parts of central Texas.

Free tours are offered Monday to Friday, at 11:30am and 1pm, and take about 30 minutes, with beer tastings before and after in the hospitality room. It's an impressive tour—especially the bottling plant. You can see the bottles move along a conveyor that looks like a long amusement ride. It loops around the entire brewery, guiding bottles in and out of several machines, until capped, labeled, and filled with beer; then they are deposited in boxes ready for shipping.

All the Shiner beer sold is made at this small brewery; no production is contracted out to other plants.

## Flatonia

After your immersion in German/Czech beer culture, it's time to move on. From the brewery, take a left on Hwy. 95 N. and drive 18 miles to **Flatonia** (pop. 1,000). This is a small agricultural town and railroad depot. Really, the main reason to come here is because it's on the way to the next destination, and also because you can tell your friends back home that you were in Flatonia, Texas. (The name doesn't actually refer to its lack of topography, but you don't have to mention that.) If you want to know more about the town, you will pass right by the **town archives and museum** (on your right). It's occasionally open, and you can stretch your legs while examining a few antiques.

## Luling

From Flatonia, head back west on I-10. Your destination is **Tiny Texas Houses** (© 830/875-2500; www.tinytexashouses.com). The owner builds small, fully functional, energy-efficient houses, using recycled lumber and hardware. Examples of his houses are on view for anyone who stops by. They're beautiful and distinctive, and are small enough to transport by truck. The business is on the southeast corner of the intersection of I-10 and Hwy. 80 (exit 628).

**Luling** (pop. 5,000) has some of the best barbecue in the state. The town is divided down the middle by the railroad tracks. Where the highway crosses the tracks, look for **City Market** (© 830/875-9019) on the left, a few doors down at 633 E. Davis St. It's open Monday through Saturday until 6pm. Luling is also known for watermelon, and it has a festival during the last week of June called the **Watermelon Thump.** If you arrive during the festival, you will have a hard time scoring some barbecue, as the town gets crowded.

In the 1920s and 1930s, Luling was at the center of a central Texas oil boom. After you finish your barbecue, you can stroll down Davis Street to no. 421, where you'll find the **Central Texas Oil Patch Museum** (© 830/875-1922; www.oilmuseum. org). This very large space is filled with artifacts of the early days of oil extraction and of the city of Luling. It's an interesting exhibit, and the building itself, with its old-time tin ceiling, is a pleasure to see. While you are there, you can pick up a brochure and map for the **Pumpjack Tour.** Within the city are several pumpjacks (those rocking-horse-like machines that bob up and down in oil fields). Denizens of Luling started dressing up the pumpjacks for fun, and then the local chamber of commerce commissioned Texas sign artist George Kalesik to decorate some. The pumpjacks are located close enough together that you can see the majority on foot.

After your visit to Luling, you can return to San Antonio or head to San Marcos or New Braunfels.

# HILL COUNTRY SIDE TRIPS FROM SAN ANTONIO

San Antonio lies at the southern edge of the Hill Country, Austin at its eastern edge. The interstate highway I-35 that runs between these two cities parallels a geological feature called the Balcones Escarpment, a fault zone created when the Edwards Plateau, a thick shelf of limestone, was gently pushed up about 1,000 feet above the coastal plains. This plateau extends for hundreds of miles north and west of San Antonio and Austin; the part closest to these cities is called the Hill Country. The extra elevation makes the climate a little milder, and the water pouring through the limestone creates an abundance of natural springs (and lots of caverns and caves, too).

In the 19th century, these features attracted many German and Czech settlers who were fleeing the social upheavals in Europe. They established small towns that now dot the area and add a little contrast to the prevailing cowboy culture. The mild climate, rolling hills, and abundant springs continue to attract visitors to this part of the state, with summer camps, guest ranches, and resorts serving a public that comes here to enjoy the outdoors.

## Boerne

Boerne is the seat of Kendall County and has over 6,000 residents. It was founded in 1849 by German settlers who earlier had come to Texas to form a utopian community in an area northwest of Austin. That community disintegrated, partly owing to poor location. This wasn't a problem for Boerne, located on the banks of Cibolo Creek. In fact, it actually got a reputation for having a healthful environment and, by the 1880s, became a popular health resort. Boerne was named for German political writer, Ludwig Börne (1786–1837), whose ideas resonated with many Germans in the turbulent 1840s, including those who settled here.

Despite being so close to San Antonio, Boerne has retained its small-town atmosphere. It's known for the Boerne Village Band, an old-time brass band, of which there are several in central Texas but few as good. It occasionally holds concerts in the gazebo on the main plaza and bills itself as the oldest continuously operating German band in the world outside Germany (it first tuned up in 1860). Boerne is also known for its collection of 19th-century limestone buildings in the old downtown area. These buildings include a small historical museum, boutiques, and restaurants. Most are along the *Hauptstrasse,* or main street, which is also decorated with old-fashioned lampposts and German street signs. Here, you'll find lots of crafts and antiques shops.

One of the most popular sights around Boerne is the **Cave Without a Name,** 325 Kreutzberg Rd., 12 miles northeast of Boerne (© **830/537-4212;** www.cavewithout aname.com). Hour-long tours of six large chambers are offered throughout the day. The chambers are well lit and display plenty of features and living rock. The cave is open Memorial Day through Labor Day daily 9am to 6pm, and off season daily 10am to 5pm. Admission is $14 adults and $7 children.

# A taste OF ALSACE IN TEXAS

Just 20 miles west of San Antonio (via U.S. 90 W.), Castroville has become something of a bedroom community for San Antonio, but the center of town retains its heritage as an old Alsatian community. Henri Castro, a Portuguese-born Jewish Frenchman, received a 1.25-million-acre land grant from the Republic of Texas in exchange for his commitment to colonize the land. He founded it on a scenic bend of the Medina River in 1842. Second only to Stephen F. Austin in the number of settlers he brought over, Castro recruited most of his 2,134 immigrants from the Rhine Valley, especially from the French province of Alsace. A few of the oldest citizens still can speak Alsatian, a dialect of German, though the language is likely to die out in the area when they do.

Get some insight into the town's history at the **Landmark Inn State Historic Site,** 402 E. Florence St., Castroville, TX 78009 (✆ **830/931-2133;** www.visit landmarkinn.com, which also counts a nature trail, an old gristmill, and a stone dam among its attractions. The park's centerpiece, the **Landmark Inn,** offers

eight simple rooms decorated with early Texas pieces dating up until the 1940s.

For a delicious taste of the past, visit **Haby's Alsatian Bakery,** 207 U.S. 90 E. (✆ **830/931-2118**), owned by the Tschirhart family since 1974 and featuring apple fritters, strudels, stollens, breads, and coffeecakes. It's open Monday to Saturday 5am to 7pm.

For additional information, contact the **Castroville Chamber of Commerce,** 802 London St., P.O. Box 572, Castroville, TX 78009 (✆ **800/778-6775** or 830/538-3142; www.castroville.com), where you can pick up a walking-tour booklet of the town's historic buildings, as well as a map that details the local boutiques and antiques shops (they're not concentrated in a single area). It's open 9am to noon and 1 to 3pm Monday through Friday.

**Note:** Downtown Castroville tends to close down on Monday and Tuesday, and some places are shuttered on Wednesday and Sunday as well. If you want to find everything open, come on Thursday, Friday, or Saturday.

## WHERE TO STAY

Now an appealing B&B in the heart of town, **Ye Kendall Inn,** 128 W. Blanco Rd., Boerne, TX 78006 (✆ **800/364-2138** or 830/249-2138; www.yekendallinn.com), opened as a stagecoach lodge in 1859. The rooms ($110–$130) and suites ($140–$200) are attractively decorated, some with Victorian antiques, others with American rustic pieces. Historic cabins ($160–$180) transported to the grounds are available, too.

## WHERE TO DINE

**The Limestone Grille,** in Ye Kendall Inn (see above), 128 W. Blanco Rd. (✆ **830/ 249-9954**), has an atmospheric dining room and serves New American cuisine. It's open for lunch Monday through Saturday, dinner Tuesday to Saturday, brunch only on Sunday; entrees are moderate to expensive. The more casual **Bear Moon Bakery,** 401 S. Main St. (✆ **830/816-BEAR** [2327]), is ideal for a hearty breakfast or light lunch. Organic ingredients and locally grown produce enhance the flavor of the inventive soups, salads, sandwiches, and wonderful desserts. It's open Tuesday to Saturday 6am to 5pm, Sunday 8am to 4pm, and is inexpensively priced. A fun place for lunch or dinner is the **Dodging Duck Brewhaus** (✆ **830/248-DUCK** [3825]), at 402 River Rd. It's on Cibolo Creek and has a welcoming outdoor dining area in front. The food is mainly sandwiches, soups, steaks, and a bit of seafood. There are normally four different local brews to choose from, or you can order a sampler. Prices are moderate.

## Bandera

Bandera is a small town of 1,000 inhabitants 30 miles west of Boerne. It began as a lumber camp and is now a popular getaway for city folk to come and enjoy rodeos and other cowboy activities. It's the seat of Bandera County, and a commercial center for all the surrounding guest ranches and working ranches. At first glance, it doesn't look like much, but if you walk around and eat at the restaurants, and stick your head in some shops, it still feels like you're miles from anywhere. People are open and friendly, and most have that unhurried way about them, which denotes a life unfettered by schedulers and smart phones.

### WHAT TO SEE & DO

Interested in delving into the town's roots? Pick up a self-guided tour brochure of historic sites—including **St. Stanislaus** (1855), the country's second-oldest Polish parish—at the **Bandera County Convention and Visitors Bureau,** 1206 Hackberry St., Bandera, TX 78003 (© **800/364-3833** or 830/796-3045; www.bandera cowboycapital.com), open Monday to Friday 9am to 5pm and Saturday 9am to 2pm. Or explore the town's living traditions by strolling along Main Street, where a variety of craftsmen work in the careful, hand-hewn style of yesteryear. Shops include **Kline Saddlery** (© **830/522-0335**), featuring belts, purses, briefcases, and flask covers, as well as horse wear; the **Stampede** (© **830/796-7650**), a good spot for Western collectibles; and the huge **Love's Antique Mall** (© **830/796-3838**), a one-stop shopping center for current local crafts as well as things retro. Off the main drag, buy beautiful customized belt buckles, spurs, and jewelry at **Hy O Silver,** 715 13th St. (© **830/796-7961**). Naturally, plenty of places in town, such as the **Cowboy Store,** 302 Main St. (© **830/796-8176**), can outfit you in Western duds.

### THE GREAT OUTDOORS

Most people come to Bandera to do some horseback riding. This is easy to arrange. Most of the guest ranches offer horseback rides for day-trippers, and the going rate is about $35 to $40 an hour. But it's even easier and more cost effective if you elect to stay at a guest ranch (see below). This is one of the best ways to experience some of the beautiful country out there.

You can also enjoy the pretty little Medina River, which runs right by the town. There are a couple of outfitters who rent tubes and kayaks. One is the **Bandera Beach Club Kayak & Tube Rental,** 1106 Cherry St. (© **830/796-7555**). Another is the **Medina River Company** (no phone), at 1307 N. Main St., next to the Longhorn Saloon at the north end of town. You'll see a big sign. Swimming is another option, with a couple of good swimming spots just upstream from the town. In that part of the river, the current is usually slow, but check it before you decide to go swimming.

### STAYING AT A GUEST RANCH

At the **Dixie Dude Ranch,** P.O. Box 548, Bandera, TX 78003 (© **800/375-YALL** [9255] or 830/796-7771; www.dixieduderanch.com), a longtime favorite retreat, you're likely to see white-tailed deer or wild turkeys as you trot on horseback through a 725-acre spread. The down-home, friendly atmosphere keeps folks coming back year after year. Rates are $135 per adult per night.

# THE HILL COUNTRY wine trail

Wine-tasting jaunts through the Hill Country are becoming more and more popular. Though most people don't know it, Texas has an old connection to wine-making and viticulture. Domesticated grapes first came to Texas in the late–16th century when Franciscan friars brought them from Mexico for cultivation at the Spanish missions. From the missions, the cultivation of grapes spread to the general populace and continued to be practiced long after Texas separated itself from Mexico. In fact, during the 1870s, a Texan grape grower, Thomas Munson, saved the French winemaking industry by shipping to France a number of root stocks that were resistant to the disease phylloxera, which had ravaged the vineyards of France and central Europe. The French were able to graft their own varietals to these root stocks and save their vineyards from ruin.

Viticulture in Texas would surely have kept developing had it not been for Prohibition. Not until the 1970s was grape growing able to reestablish itself. At first it grew in fits and starts, but then took off in the 1990s. In the Hill Country, it has taken the form of small wineries. These now number more than 30. They can be visited at any time of year, but spring and fall are perhaps best. There are several wineries in and around Fredericksburg that are open to the public throughout the week, but the rest open their tasting rooms only on weekends. For more information about Hill Country wineries, see www.texaswinetrail.com.

Between New Braunfels and Boerne, you will find:

○ **Dry Comal Creek Vineyards** ((℗ 830/855-4076; www.dry comalcreek.com), at 1471 Herbelin Rd., is just off Hwy. 46 between New Braunfels and Bulverde. It's known for being one of the first wineries to highlight a local varietal called Black Spanish and make it the predominant grape in wines. This grape is a descendant of the cuttings brought from Mexico long ago by Franciscan friars. Available are red and white wines made with this grape and a wonderful port. Also of note is the bone-dry French colombard.

Between Boerne and Fredericksburg:

○ **Sister Creek Vineyards** ((℗ 830/324-6704; www.sister creekvineyards.com), in Sisterdale, close to the intersection of R.R. 473 and FM 1376, is in a gloriously rough-hewn old cotton gin that dates from 1885. You can stroll through some of the fermentation rooms and see the large vats and oak barrels used in the production of the wine.

○ **Comfort Cellars Winery** ((℗ 830/995-3274; www.comfort cellars.com), at 723 Front St., in the town of Comfort, has a full range of wines from dry to sweet, but the latter are what sell the most, including an intriguing orange chardonnay and what the owner calls sweet *rojo* (red).

○ **Singing Water Vineyards** ((℗ 830/995-2246; www.singing watervineyards.com) is located 2 miles east of Comfort at 316 Mill Dam Rd. The winery is best known for its sauvignon blanc and a merlot/cabernet blend.

In the Fredericksburg area:

○ **Fredericksburg Winery** ((℗ 830/990-8747; www.fbg winery.com) is on Fredericksburg's Main Street. It's run by three brothers who are rebels in the winemaking business. They flout traditions and challenge conventional wisdom in winemaking, from using clear rather than green glass bottles to actually making a decent gewürztraminer in the Texas heat. Visitors will always find something out of the ordinary, and the wines available for tasting are always changing.

- **Bell Mountain Vineyards** (☎ 830/685-3297; www.bell mountainwine.com) is located 14 miles north of Fredericksburg off Hwy. 16. The tasting room at the vineyard is open only on Saturday. But the vineyard has opened a tasting room on Fredericksburg's Main Street, above the Rathskeller Restaurant.
- **Grape Creek Vineyard** (☎ 820/644-2710; www.grapecreek.com). Just 10 miles east of town on Hwy. 290, in the direction of Stonewall, are four beautiful vineyards loosely bunched together. Grape Creek is one of them—situated on a hilltop with a panoramic vista that you can enjoy from beneath a copse of old oak trees. Try the cabernets and the fumé blanc.
- **Torre di Pietra** (☎ 830/744-2829; www.texashillcountrywine.com) is another impressive winery with an inviting terrace. Most people go for the cabernet/syrah/Sangiovese blends.
- **Becker Vineyards** (☎ 830/644-2681; www.beckervineyards.com) in the spring offers a field of blooming lavender for the enjoyment of the visitor. The tasting room is within an old-style stone barn, and the old bar was taken from a saloon in San Antonio. This is probably the Hill Country's most famous vineyard. It grows classic French varietals with which it makes some skillfully produced cabernet and Viognier, among many others.
- **Woodrose Winery** (☎ 830/644-2539; www.woodrosewinery.com) has another beautiful outdoor

setting for sampling the wines. The cabernet sauvignon is popular.

In the Northern Hill Country and Lakes:

- **Flat Creek Vineyards** (☎ 512/267-6310; www.flatcreekestate.com) is on the north side of upper Lake Travis. From Austin, take Hwy. 183 to Cedar Park and go west on RM 1431 for 14 miles, then left on Singleton Bend Road (there's a sign). This is one of the grandest of Hill Country vineyards, with a large tasting room affording wide vistas of rolling terrain. Only a few of the wines here use locally grown grapes.
- **Pillar Bluff Vineyards** (☎ 512/556-4078; www.pillarbluff.com) is the treasure for those who stay on Hwy. 183 all the way to Lampasas (66 miles from Austin), and then take FM 1478 west, to these two small wineries owned by twin brothers Gill and Bill Bledsoe. Gill Bledsoe produces an interesting white merlot, a full-flavored cabernet, and a medium dry port, among other wines.
- **Texas Legato** (☎ 512/556-9600; www.texaslegato.com), is within sight of Pillar Bluff; this winery, owned by Bill Bledsoe, produces merlot and Malbec wines.
- **Alamosa Wine Cellars** (☎ 325/628-3313; www.alamosawinecellars.com) is 25 miles west of Lampasas, near the tiny town of Bend. The owners have been careful to select varietals that they believe have the best chance of producing outstanding wines when grown in Texas. Try the Tempranillo, which is bottled under the label "El Guapo," the Viognier, and a fruity Grenache.

Tubing on the Medina River and soaking in a hot tub are among the many activities at the **Mayan Ranch,** P.O. Box 577, Bandera, TX 78003 (② **830/796-3312** or 460-3036; www.mayanranch.com), another well-established family-run operation ($150 per adult). The ranch provides plenty of additional Western fun for its guests during high season—things like two-step lessons, cookouts, hayrides, singing cowboys, or trick-roping exhibitions.

The owner of **Silver Spur Guest Ranch,** 9266 Bandera Creek Rd., Bandera, TX 78003 (② **830/796-3037** or 460-3639; www.ssranch.com), used to be a bull rider, so the equestrian expertise of the staff is especially high. So is the comfort level. The rooms in the main ranch house and the separate cabins are individually decorated, with styles ranging from Victorian pretty to country rustic ($135 per adult). The ranch, which abuts the Hill Country State Natural Area, also boasts the region's largest swimming pool, some roaming buffalo, and a great kids' play area.

## WHERE TO DINE

Dining in Bandera is downright cheap. You should stick to country cooking and Tex-Mex. One place is **O.S.T.** (② **830/796-3836**), named for the Old Spanish Trail that used to run through Bandera. It's been open since 1921 and has the feel of an old place with wooden paneling, framing, and furniture. Along one side of the main dining room is a bar with saddles for barstools. It opens at 6am every day for breakfast and closes around 9pm. It serves burgers, Tex-Mex, and is known for the chicken-fried steak platter. One thing to check out is the John Wayne room, which is covered in photos and old movie posters of "the Duke." There is a corner dedicated to other Western stars, too.

**Brick's River Cafe,** 1105 Main St. (② **830/460-3200**), is behind the River Oak Inn at the north end of town. It serves up down-home country standards such as chicken-fried steak, fried catfish, and liver and onions. The menu includes green salads, too, and plenty of vegetable side dishes. There's a deck perched in back (half enclosed, half open-air) from which you can look out over the Medina River. It's open daily for lunch and dinner.

**Mi Pueblo,** 706 Main St. (② **830/796-8040**), offers a large variety of Tex-Mex cooking, including fajitas and some good green enchiladas. It's open for all three meals.

## SOME LOCAL HONKY-TONKS

Don't miss **Arkey Blue & the Silver Dollar Bar** ★★ (② **830/796-8826**), a genuine spit-and-sawdust cowboy honky-tonk on Main Street, which is usually called Arkey's. At the **Bandera Saloon,** 401 Main St. (② **830/796-3699**), the deck is out front and overlooks the town's main drag, but the boot-scootin' to live rockabilly and country music takes place inside the large, barnlike structure.

# AUSTIN

by David Baird

I n almost anything you read or hear about Austin, you will be told that it is a laid-back city. "Laid-back" has become Austin's defining trait. First-time visitors get here and expect to find a city whose denizens all move about and express themselves in the unhurried manner of Willie Nelson. They must feel a little put upon when they drive into town, only to find bearish traffic, pushy drivers, and a downtown that looks uncomfortably similar to Houston or Dallas.

Over the years, Austin has gotten bigger and busier, but it hasn't lost its essential nature. Stay here for a couple of days and the laid-back quality will sink in. Austinites are personable, gracious, and open, and for them, the simple pleasures of life hold a great deal more attraction than the rat race. At times, it seems that everyone you meet is either a musician or a massage therapist, or has some sort of alternative career.

Austinites of all walks of life enjoy the outdoors. Barton Springs is the preferred spot for a swim; the popular hike-and-bike trail that encircles Town Lake is a favorite place for either a leisurely walk or a serious run. The city streets and bike lanes are filled with Austin's many cyclists. Just outside of town are several parks, nature preserves, rivers, and lakes. Hand in hand with this love of the outdoors is a strong environmental consciousness, which is reflected in the local government. Austin leads the nation in green energy production, has the most aggressive recycling and energy conservation programs in the state, and, though starting late, has instituted programs to reduce traffic and urban sprawl.

Finally, one can't talk about Austin for very long without mentioning the rather large university at its center. The University of Texas (UT) has brought thousands of bright, young students here who, once they get their degrees, decide they don't want to leave. They stay and add to a large pool of educated people looking for a livelihood. This has attracted large, high-tech companies that seek an educated workforce. Austin has also been fertile grounds for many local start-up companies in all kinds of fields.

Austin is now big enough to be many things to many people. To me, it's the creative center and the social and environmental conscience of Texas.

# ORIENTATION

## Arriving

**BY PLANE** The **Austin-Bergstrom International Airport (AUS)** (© 512/530-ABIA [2242]; www.ci.austin.tx.us/austinairport) is on the site of the former Bergstrom Air Force Base, just off Hwy. 71 (Ben White Blvd.) and only 8 miles southwest of the capitol. There's a visitor information booth on the lower level of the terminal, open daily from 7am to 11pm.

Taxis usually form a line outside the terminal, though occasionally you won't find any waiting. To ensure off-hour pickup in advance, phone **American Yellow Checker Cab** (℗ **512/452-9999**) before you leave home. The ride between the airport and downtown costs around $25, including tip.

If you're not in a huge rush to get to your hotel, **SuperShuttle** (℗ **800/BLUE VAN** [258-3826] or 512/258-3826; www.supershuttle.com) is a less expensive alternative to cabs, offering comfortable minivan service to hotels and residences. Prices range from $14 one-way ($24 round-trip) to a downtown hotel to $20 ($32 round-trip) to a hotel in the northwestern part of town. The drawback is that you often must share your ride with several others, who may be dropped off first. You don't have to book in advance for pickups at the airport, but you must phone 24 hours ahead of time to arrange for a pickup when departing.

For $1, you can go from the airport to downtown or the university area on a city bus called the **Airport Flyer** (no. 100). It runs until about midnight. The passenger pickup is outside the arrival gates, close to the end of the concourse. Buses depart about every 40 minutes. You can grab a route schedule from the city's visitor information office, by the baggage carousels. Or you can download it from the **Capital Metro Transit** website (www.capmetro.org). Most of the major car-rental companies have outlets at the airport. The trip from the airport to downtown by car or taxi can take anywhere from 20 to 45 minutes, much more if you're headed to north Austin. During rush hour, there are often backups along Hwy. 71.

**BY TRAIN** The **Amtrak** station (℗ **512/476-5684**) is at Lamar and West First Street, in the southwest part of downtown. There are generally a few cabs waiting to meet the trains, but if you don't see one, you'll find a list of phone numbers for taxi companies posted near the pay phones. Some of the downtown hotels provide courtesy pickup from the train station. A cab ride shouldn't run more than $5 or $6 (there's a $3 minimum charge).

**BY BUS** The **bus terminal** is near Highland Mall, about 10 minutes north of downtown and close to the I-35 motel zone. There are some hotels within walking distance, and many others a short cab ride away; a few taxis usually wait outside the station. If you want to go downtown, you can catch either bus no. 7 (Duval) or bus no. 15 (Red River) from the bus stop across the street. A cab ride downtown—about 10 minutes away on the freeway—should cost around $10.

## Visitor Information

The **Austin Visitor Center** is downtown at 209 E. Sixth St. (℗ **866/GO-AUSTIN** [462-8784]; www.austintexas.org) and is open Monday through Friday from 9am to 5pm, and Saturday and Sunday from 9am to 6pm (closed Thanksgiving, Christmas, and Easter). You can pick up tourist information pamphlets downtown at the **Old Bakery and Emporium,** 1006 Congress Ave. (℗ **512/477-5961**), open Monday to Friday 9am to 4pm, and the first two Saturdays in December from 10am to 3pm. The **Capitol Visitors Center,** 112 E. 11th St. (℗ **512/305-8400;** www.texascapitol visitorscenter.com), a Texas Department of Transportation travel center, dispenses information on the entire state; it's open Monday through Saturday 9am to 5pm, Sunday noon to 5pm, and it's closed on major holidays.

For entertainment listings, pick up the free alternative newspaper, the **Austin Chronicle,** distributed to stores, hotels, and restaurants around town every Thursday. It's got a close rival in **XLent,** the free weekend entertainment guide put out by the city's daily newspaper, *Austin-American Statesman,* which also comes out on Thursday.

## City Layout

In 1839, Austin was laid out in a grid on the northern shore of the Colorado River, bounded by Shoal Creek to the west and Waller Creek to the east. The section of the river abutting the original settlement is now known as Lady Bird Lake, and the city has spread far beyond its original borders in all directions. The land to the east is flat Texas prairie; the rolling Hill Country begins on the west side of town.

**MAIN ARTERIES & STREETS**   I-35, forming the border between central and east Austin, is the main north-south thoroughfare; Loop 1, usually called Mo-Pac (it follows the course of the Missouri-Pacific railroad, although some people like to say it got its name because it's "mo' packed"), is the west-side equivalent. Hwy. 290, running east and west, merges with I-35 where it comes in on the north side of town, briefly reestablishing its separate identity on the south side of town before merging with Hwy. 71 (which is called Ben White Blvd. btw. Hwy. 183 and Lamar Blvd.). Hwy. 290 and Hwy. 71 split up again in Oak Hill, on the west side of town. Not confused enough yet? Hwy. 2222 changes its name from Koenig to Northland and, west of Loop 360, to Bullcreek, while, in the north, Hwy. 183 is called Research Boulevard. (Looking at a map should make all this clear as mud.) Important north-south city streets include Lamar, Guadalupe, and Burnet. If you want to get across town north of the river, use Cesar Chavez Street (once known as First St.), 15th Street (which turns into Enfield west of Lamar), Martin Luther King, Jr., Boulevard (the equivalent of 19th St., and often just called MLK), 38th Street, or 45th Street.

## The Neighborhoods in Brief

Although Austin, designed to be the capital of the independent Republic of Texas, has a planned, grand city center similar to that of Washington, D.C., the city has spread out far beyond those original boundaries. These days, with a few exceptions detailed below, locals tend to speak in terms of landmarks (the University of Texas) or geographical areas (east Austin) rather than neighborhoods.

**Downtown**   The original city, laid out by Edwin Waller in 1839, runs roughly north from the Colorado River. The river has been dammed in several places, forming a series of lakes. By downtown, it is called Lady Bird Lake. The first street on the north shore of Town Lake used to be called First Street; now it's called **Cesar Chavez Street.** Downtown extends north up to 11th Street, where the capitol building is. The main north-south street is **Congress Avenue.** It runs from the river to the capitol. Downtown's eastward limit is the I-35 freeway, and its westward limit is Lamar Boulevard. This is a prime sightseeing (it includes the capitol and several historic districts) and hotel area, with music clubs, restaurants, shops, and galleries. There are a lot of clubs on and around **Sixth Street,** just east of Congress, in the **Warehouse District,** centered on Third and Fourth streets just west of Congress, and in the **Red River District,** on (where else?) Red River, between Sixth and 10th streets.

**South Austin**   For a long time, not a lot was happening south of Town Lake. This was largely a residential area—a mix of working-class folks and bohemians lived here. **South Congress** (also known as SoCo and the Avenue), the sleepy stretch of Congress Avenue running through the middle of south Austin, was lined with cheap motels. Then, in the 1980s, it started taking off. The area became attractive to store and restaurant owners who liked the proximity to downtown without the high rents. Trendy shops moved into the old storefronts. Yuppies started buying houses in the adjoining neighborhoods. Today, south Austin is one of the preferred places to live. **Fairview Park** and **Travis Heights,** adjoining neighborhoods between Congress and I-35, are perhaps the most popular.

**Central Austin** This is a larger area that includes downtown and the university campus. It's not a precisely defined area. If you were to travel north from Town Lake through the downtown area and past the capitol, you would come across a complex of state government office buildings (btw. 15th and 19th sts.). Past that would be the University of Texas campus (19th to 26th sts.). Farther north, you get to the **Hyde Park** neighborhood (35th to 51st sts.). Hyde Park got its start in 1891 as one of Austin's first planned suburbs; renovation of its Victorian and early Craftsman houses began in the 1970s, and now there's a real neighborhood feel to this pretty, tree-lined area. Beyond Hyde Park, numbered streets disappear. You pass through a couple of neighborhoods, and eventually you come to Research Boulevard. For a lot of Austinites, this is where central Austin ends and north Austin begins.

**West Austin** West of Lamar is **Clarksville,** formerly a black community founded in the 1870s by freed slaves. It's now a neighborhood of small, old houses that command high prices. To the west of Clarksville, on the other side of the Mo-Pac Freeway, is a more tony neighborhood called **Tarrytown,** which extends as far as Lake Austin (upstream from downtown, the Colorado river bends around in a more northerly direction, where another dam creates this long, narrow lake).

**East Side** East of I-35 are several neighborhoods, which are predominantly Hispanic and African American. Because it has a central location, this area is gentrifying at a quick pace.

**West Lake** The name denotes the townships that are on the opposite side of Lake Austin from west Austin. This is an affluent suburban area that includes the communities of **Rollingwood** and **Westlake Hills.** If you head upstream to the next dam, you come to Lake Travis, a large lake with lots of marinas and lakeside communities, such as **Lakeway.** But you don't have to live here to play here: This is also where those who live in central Austin come to splash around and kick back on nice weekends.

**Northwest** This is where most of the high-tech industry is located. It is largely suburban. It includes the Arboretum, a large mall and surrounding shopping area, and a new mall called the Domain. Farther north are the bedroom communities of Round Rock and Cedar Park.

# GETTING AROUND

## By Public Transportation

Austin's public transportation system, **Capital Metropolitan Transportation Authority** (www.capmetro.org), operates more than 50 bus routes. A day pass on Metro costs $2; express service from various Park & Ride lots costs $3. You'll need exact change or fare tickets (see below) to board the bus. Call ✆ **800/474-1201** or 512/474-1200 (TTY 512/385-5872) from local pay phones for point-to-point routing information.

Cap Metro now has light-rail service between downtown and the bedroom communities in the north. This service is of little use to visitors as it runs only during commuting times Monday to Friday. There is discussion about expanding service times.

## By Car

With its lack of traffic planning, driving in Austin is a bit of a challenge. Don't fall into a driver's daze anywhere in town; you need to be as vigilant on the city streets as you are on highways. The former are rife with signs that suddenly insist LEFT LANE MUST TURN LEFT or RIGHT LANE MUST TURN RIGHT—generally positioned so they're noticeable only when it's too late to switch.

The highways offer their own challenges. I-35—nicknamed "the NAFTA highway" because of the big rigs speeding up from Mexico—is mined with tricky on-and-off ramps and, around downtown, a confusing complex of upper and lower levels; it's easy to miss your exit or find yourself exiting when you don't want to. The rapidly developing area to the northwest, where Hwy. 183 connects I-35 with Mo-Pac and the Capital of Texas Highway, requires particular vigilance, as the connections occur abruptly.

**PARKING**  Unless you have congressional plates, you're likely to find the selection of parking spots downtown extremely limited during the week; as a result, lots of downtown restaurants offer valet parking (with hourly rates in the range of $4–$6). There are a number of lots around the area, costing anywhere from $5 to $7 per hour, but the most convenient ones tend to fill up quickly. If you're lucky enough to find a metered spot, it'll run you 75¢ per hour, with a 2-hour limit, so bring change. Although there's virtually no street parking available near the capitol before 5pm during the week, there is a free visitor garage at 15th and San Jacinto streets (2-hr. time limit).

In the university area, trying to find a spot near the shopping strip known as the Drag can be just that. However, cruise the side streets and you'll find a pay lot that's not filled. The two most convenient on-campus parking garages are located near San Jacinto and East 26th streets and off 25th Street between San Antonio and Nueces. There's also a (free!) parking lot near the LBJ Library, but it's a good walk from the central campus. Log on to **www.utexas.edu/business/parking/resources** for additional places to drop off your car.

## By Taxi

The major cab companies in Austin are **Austin Cab** (② **512/478-2222**) and **American Yellow Checker Cab** (② **512/452-9999**). The flag-drop charge is $2.05, and it's $2.05 for each mile after that. When gas is expensive, taxis will add a fuel surcharge.

# [FastFACTS] AUSTIN

**Doctor**  The Medical Exchange (② **512/458-1121**) and Seton Hospital (② **512/324-4450**) both have physician referral services.

**Drugstores**  You'll find many Walgreens, CVS, and Randalls drugstores around the city; most HEB grocery stores also have pharmacies. Several Walgreens are open 24 hours. Have your zip code ready and call ② **800/925-4733** to find the Walgreens branch nearest you.

**Emergencies**  Call ② **911** if you need the police, the fire department, or an ambulance.

**Hospitals**  **Brackenridge,** 601 E. 15th St. (② **512/324-7000**); **St. David's,** 919 E. 32nd St. at I-35 (② **512/397-4240**); and **Seton Medical Center,** 1201 W. 38th St. (② **512/324-1000**), have good and convenient emergency-care facilities.

**Internet Access** If you're traveling with your own computer, go to the following website for a list of hot spots: **www.austin wirelesscity.org/hotspot-list.php**. If you don't have a machine, and your hotel can't help you out, you can go to a public library (see the above website for locations) or a local FedEx Office.

**Newspapers & Magazines** The daily *Austin American-Statesman* (www.austin360.com) is the only large-circulation mainstream newspaper in town. The *Austin Chronicle* (www.auschron.com), a free alternative weekly, focuses on the arts, entertainment, and politics. Monday through Friday, the University of Texas publishes the surprisingly sophisticated *Daily Texan* (www.dailytexanonline.com) newspaper, covering everything from on-campus news to international events.

**Police** The nonemergency number for the Austin Police Department is ✆ **311.**

**Post Office** The city's main post office is located at 8225 Cross Park Dr. (✆ **512/342-1252**); more convenient to tourist sights are the Capitol Station, 111 E. 17th St., in the LBJ Building, and the Downtown Station, 510 Guadalupe St. For information on other locations, call ✆ **800/275-8777.**

**Safety** Austin has been ranked one of the five safest cities in the United States, but that doesn't mean you can throw common sense to the wind. It's never a good idea to walk down dark streets alone at night, and major tourist areas always attract pickpockets, so keep your purse or wallet in a safe place. Although Sixth Street itself tends to be busy, use caution on the side streets in the area.

**Taxes** The tax on hotel rooms is 15%. Sales tax, added to restaurant bills as well as to other purchases, is 8.25%.

**Transit Information** Call Capital Metro Transit (✆ **800/474-1201** or 512/474-1200 from local pay phones; TTY 512/385-5872).

**Weather** Check the weather at ✆ **512/451-2424** or www.news8austin.com/content/weather.

# WHERE TO STAY

Austin's downtown hotels don't discount their rates as much as those in other Texas cities. There are just not enough rooms to make discounting necessary. Demand is greater than supply. Obviously, the free market is supposed to correct such an imbalance and, in 2007, there were eight hotel projects lined up for the downtown area. But then came the financial crisis when banks stopped loaning money, even to large hotel chains. This stopped all but one of the projects. And even that project, the W Hotel, had financing problems, which slowed construction and eventually required refinancing. The rest of the new construction remains on hold.

In looking for discounts, keep in mind the calendars of the state legislature and the University of Texas. Lawmakers and lobbyists converge on the capital from January through May of odd-numbered years, so you can expect tighter bookings. The beginning of fall term, graduation week, and football weekends—UT's football stadium now seats 100,000—will also fill lots of hotel rooms.

The busiest season, however, is the month of March, when the South by Southwest (SXSW) music festival fills entire hotels. It is designed to coincide with UT's spring break, usually the third week of the month. SXSW is the largest gathering of the year for the music industry. It attracts thousands of music fans, and lots of producers and music company execs. Now there's also a film and media festival held the week before the music begins. So, try to avoid coming in March. Another time when the hotels are busy is in September for the Austin City Limits Music Festival. This festival has become immensely popular and attracts lots of out-of-towners.

If you're coming here to see what Austin's all about, consider staying somewhere in the central part of town. You'll enjoy your stay more because traffic in Austin can be bad, and making your way around an unfamiliar city can be hard. You don't have to stay downtown. Consider the hotels in south Austin, in and around South Congress or close to Lady Bird Lake. This is a comfortable area to stay, with lively foot traffic, and most of the places of interest are close. Also, consider the areas near the University of Texas, such as Hyde Park, West Campus, and a even a little farther to the north. Here, too, it's easy to get around, and you get a good feel for Austin.

*Tip:* If you're on a tight budget and looking for bargain discounts, you should know that there are two major clusters of hotels in Austin. One surrounds the intersection of I-35 and Ben White Blvd. (Hwy. 71), and the other is north of there, where I-35 intersects Hwy. 290 E. The latter cluster is a better location for three reasons: one, it's closer to downtown; two, it has better dining options; and three, you're not limited to using I-35—there are alternative routes for getting around. This cluster includes some economical lodgings, such as **Studio 6,** at 6603 IH-35 (℃ **512/458-5453;** www.staystudio6.com), and **Hawthorn Suites,** at 935 La Posada Dr. (℃ **512/459-3335;** www.hawthorn.com).

Please note that rates listed below do not include the city's 15% hotel sales tax, and they are the prevailing rates during normal times of the year. During festival times and other occasions when hotels will fill up, the rates will rise.

## Downtown

### VERY EXPENSIVE

**The Driskill** ★★★   Opened in 1886, the Driskill is Austin's original grand hotel and national historic landmark. It has seen its share of history. Lyndon Johnson wrapped up his presidential campaign and received the election results here. The Daughters of the Republic of Texas, the saviors of the Alamo, met here to agree on their plan of action. It was here, too, that the Texas Rangers plotted their ambush on Bonnie and Clyde. Indeed, all kinds of plots have been hatched here.

The Driskill offers guests a choice between rooms in the original 1886 building (labeled Historic) or in the 1928 addition (Traditional); the latter are the better deal, especially those on the 12th floor, which have higher ceilings. Rooms are well lit, distinctively decorated, and furnished with period pieces. Bathrooms in many rooms are on the small side, but are sleek and attractive and come with several amenities, including plush bathrobes. This hotel is on Austin's lively Sixth Street, and some of the Historic rooms with balconies can catch street noise. Also, some of the Traditional king rooms are small. The hotel refurnished all the rooms in 2008, which included replacing all mattresses and installing flatscreen televisions. It has been awarded the Five Dog Bone Award for pet-friendliness by the readers of *Animal Fair* magazine. The Driskill has a handful of smoking rooms.

604 Brazos St. (at E. Sixth St.), Austin, TX 78701. ℃ **800/252-9367** or 512/474-5911. Fax 512/474-2214. www.driskillhotel.com. 189 units. $250–$340 double; from $345 suite. AE, DC, DISC, MC, V. Valet parking $26. Pets 25 lb. and under accepted with $50 fee. **Amenities:** 2 restaurants; bar; concierge; health club; room service. *In room:* A/C and fan, TV, hair dryer, Wi-Fi (free).

**Four Seasons Austin** ★★★ ☺   This member of the well-known luxury chain has an ideal location on the north shore of Town Lake, with great views and close proximity to all the downtown hot spots. Large, comfortable rooms, an excellent spa, beautifully manicured grounds, and direct access to Austin's Hike and Bike Trail are just a

# Greater Austin Accommodations, Dining & Attractions

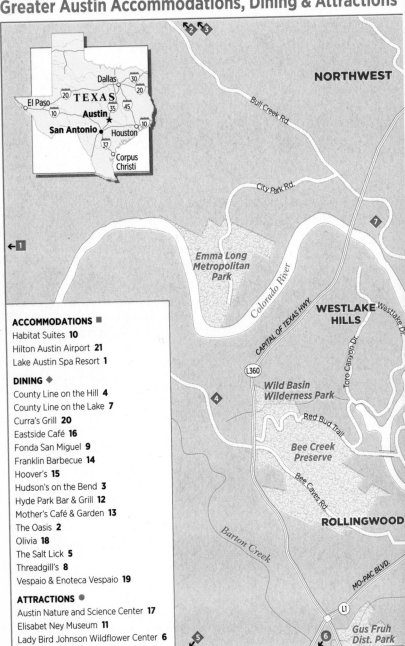

**ACCOMMODATIONS** ■
Habitat Suites **10**
Hilton Austin Airport **21**
Lake Austin Spa Resort **1**

**DINING** ◆
County Line on the Hill **4**
County Line on the Lake **7**
Curra's Grill **20**
Eastside Café **16**
Fonda San Miguel **9**
Franklin Barbecue **14**
Hoover's **15**
Hudson's on the Bend **3**
Hyde Park Bar & Grill **12**
Mother's Café & Garden **13**
The Oasis **2**
Olivia **18**
The Salt Lick **5**
Threadgill's **8**
Vespaio & Enoteca Vespaio **19**

**ATTRACTIONS** ●
Austin Nature and Science Center **17**
Elisabet Ney Museum **11**
Lady Bird Johnson Wildflower Center **6**

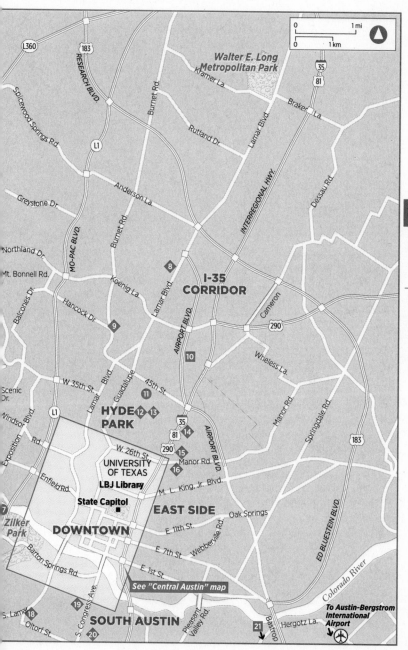

Walter E. Long
Metropolitan Park

RESEARCH BLVD.

Spicewood Springs Rd.

Greystone Dr.

Northland Dr.

Mt. Bonnell Rd.

Balcones Dr.

MO-PAC BLVD.

Scenic
Dr.

Windsor
Rd.

Exposition
Rd.

Zilker
Park

Anderson La.

Burnet Rd.

Koenig La.

Hancock Dr.

W. 35th St.

Lamar
Blvd.

Guadalupe

45th St.

Lamar Blvd.

AIRPORT BLVD.

Kramer La.

Rutland Dr.

Lamar Blvd.

Dessau Rd.

INTERREGIONAL HWY.

Braker La.

Cameron

290

Wheless La.

Manor Rd.

Springdale Rd.

183

I-35
CORRIDOR

8

9

10

11

HYDE
PARK

12  13

35

81

14

290

15

AIRPORT BLVD.

W. 26th St

UNIVERSITY
OF TEXAS

LBJ Library

State Capitol

DOWNTOWN

Enfield Rd.

Barton Springs Rd

7

Manor Rd.

16

M. L. King, Jr. Blvd.

EAST SIDE

Oak Springs

E. 11th St.

Webberville Rd.

E. 7th St.

E. 1st St.

ED BLUESTEIN BLVD.

Colorado River

See "Central Austin" map

S. Lamar

Oltorf St.

18

S. Congress Ave.

19

20

SOUTH AUSTIN

Pleasant
Valley Rd.

Bastrop

21

Hergotz La.

To Austin-Bergstrom
International
Airport

0          1 mi
0          1 km

few reasons for staying here. Of course, there's the famous Four Seasons service, which sets this hotel apart from others. Few places in Austin can make life easier.

The look of the hotel is part modern, part traditional, and part Texas: polished stone floors, with plush area rugs, deep easy chairs and sofas, and a smattering of Western art. It's a seamless blend of muted tones, without calling attention to itself. It's a look common to many other luxury hotels and can be described as contemporary design on Valium. The guest rooms have the same feel, plush and conservative. The city views are fine, but the ones of the lake are finer still. You can choose a room with or without a balcony.

If you're traveling with toddlers, the staff can provide necessary gear like strollers and baby seats, and there are plenty of weekend activities. For older kids, there are complimentary things such as popcorn and soda or milk and cookies, so notify the hotel when you make reservations.

98 San Jacinto Blvd. (at First/Cesar Chavez St.), Austin, TX 78701. © **800/332-3442** or 512/478-4500. Fax 512/478-3117. www.fourseasons.com/austin. 291 units. $320–$480 double; from $570 suite. Special packages available. AE, DC, DISC, MC, V. Valet parking $25. Pets 15 inches or under accepted with advance notice. **Amenities:** Restaurant; bar; babysitting; bikes; concierge; exercise room; outdoor heated saltwater pool; room service; spa. *In room:* A/C, TV/DVD, CD player, hair dryer, minibar, MP3 docking station, Wi-Fi ($10–$15 per day).

**Hyatt Regency Austin ★★★**   Austin's Hyatt Regency may have the best location of any hotel in town. It sits on Lady Bird Lake's south shore (strictly speaking, this is south Austin, but its size and feel are downtown traits). This gives the north-facing rooms not only lake vistas, but the downtown skyline as a backdrop. The most popular of these have balconies. Also, right below the hotel is the dock for boat tours to see the bats (under Congress Ave. bridge) and other Lady Bird Lake excursions. You can rent paddle boats and canoes from this dock, as well, or take advantage of the Hike and Bike Trail. The Hyatt rents bikes to guests who prefer riding to walking. Rooms have good beds and a comfortable, modern-functional look and are, for the most part, of average size. Hyatt has just completed installing "Respire Rooms" at this hotel for the benefit of allergy suffers (central Texas is the promised land for allergists). These come with beefed-up air scrubbers, special coatings on all surfaces, and hypoallergenic everything. For smokers, the hotel still offers a few rooms, which come with enhanced air-filtering technology.

208 Barton Springs Rd. (at S. Congress), Austin, TX 78704. © **800/233-1234** or 512/477-1234. Fax 512/480-2069. http://austin.hyatt.com. 446 units. $199–$314 double; $450–$650 suite. Special rates available. AE, DC, DISC, MC, V. Valet parking $18; self-parking $12. **Amenities:** 2 restaurants; bar; bikes; concierge; executive-level rooms; exercise room; Jacuzzi; outdoor pool; room service. *In room:* A/C, TV, hair dryer, MP3 docking station, Wi-Fi ($9.95 per day).

## EXPENSIVE

**Doubletree Guest Suites Austin** ☺ ☀   If you're not going to be near the lake, you might as well be near the capitol. This hotel is one of the most comfortable places to stay in the downtown area and a favorite with lobbyists and state contractors. Standard one-bedroom suites are oversize and a bargain for the price. Many come with balconies. The two-bedroom suites all have balconies and are only slightly more expensive. Many rooms have a view of the capitol. A full range of appliances with all the requisite cookware allow guests to prepare meals in comfort. Unlike kitchens in many all-suite hotels, the ones here are separate—you don't have to stare at dirty dishes after you eat—and dishwashers are in all kitchens. (The housekeepers wash up every day, regardless.) These suites appeal to families, with practical considerations for those

# Central Austin Hotels, Dining & Attractions

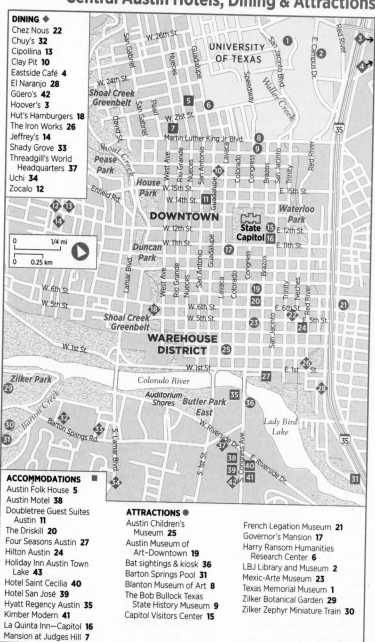

**DINING ◆**
Chez Nous **22**
Chuy's **32**
Cipollina **13**
Clay Pit **10**
Eastside Café **4**
El Naranjo **28**
Güero's **42**
Hoover's **3**
Hut's Hamburgers **18**
The Iron Works **26**
Jeffrey's **14**
Shady Grove **33**
Threadgill's World
  Headquarters **37**
Uchi **34**
Zocalo **12**

**ACCOMMODATIONS ■**
Austin Folk House **5**
Austin Motel **38**
Doubletree Guest Suites
  Austin **11**
The Driskill **20**
Four Seasons Austin **27**
Hilton Austin **24**
Holiday Inn Austin Town
  Lake **43**
Hotel Saint Cecilia **40**
Hotel San José **39**
Hyatt Regency Austin **35**
Kimber Modern **41**
La Quinta Inn—Capitol **16**
Mansion at Judges Hill **7**

**ATTRACTIONS ●**
Austin Children's
  Museum **25**
Austin Museum of
  Art–Downtown **19**
Bat sightings & kiosk **36**
Barton Springs Pool **31**
Blanton Museum of Art **8**
The Bob Bullock Texas
  State History Museum **9**
Capitol Visitors Center **15**

French Legation Museum **21**
Governor's Mansion **17**
Harry Ransom Humanities
  Research Center **6**
LBJ Library and Museum **2**
Mexic-Arte Museum **23**
Texas Memorial Museum **1**
Zilker Botanical Garden **29**
Zilker Zephyr Miniature Train **30**

with small kids, such as cribs and high chairs. For the most part, they are attractively furnished and in good shape; however, the hotel plans to start renovating all the rooms in summer 2011.

303 W. 15th St. (at Guadalupe), Austin, TX 78701. ℂ **800/222-TREE** (8733) or 512/478-7000. Fax 512/478-3562. www.doubletree.com. 189 units. $179–$269 1-bedroom suite; $239–$319 2-bedroom suite. Special discounts available. AE, DC, DISC, MC, V. Valet parking $21; self-parking $17. Pets 50 lb. and under accepted for $40 fee. **Amenities:** Restaurant; bar; concierge; golf course nearby; exercise room; Jacuzzi; outdoor heated pool; room service; sauna. *In room:* A/C, TV, hair dryer, kitchen, Wi-Fi ($11 per day).

**Hilton Austin**   This hotel directly across from the convention center discounts rooms when there's no convention in town. The best rooms are the odd-numbered ones, which face west and have views of downtown. Regular rooms are average size and attractively furnished. Bathrooms are well appointed for the price category and normal size. The service here is attentive, and there seems to be plenty of staff on hand to help. There is a full health club on the property, which costs an extra $10 for the first day and $5 for each day thereafter.

500 E. 4th St., Austin, TX 78701 ℂ **800/HILTONS** (445-8667) or 512/482-8000. Fax 512/486-0078. www.hilton.com. 800 units. $189–$384 double; from $550 suite. Special packages available. AE, DC, DISC, MC, V. Valet parking $27; self-parking $20. Pets 75 lb. and under accepted for $50 fee. **Amenities:** 2 restaurants; bar; executive-level rooms; health club and spa; heated outdoor pool; room service. *In room:* A/C, TV, hair dryer, minibar, Wi-Fi ($14 per day).

## MODERATE

**Holiday Inn Austin Town Lake** ☺   The most upscale Holiday Inn in Austin, this high-rise hotel is situated on the north shore of Lady Bird Lake, at the edge of downtown, and just off I-35. Rooms are in two towers: one round, one square. Many of the units have sofa beds, which works for families, especially because kids stay free (and if they're 11 and under, they eat for free at the hotel restaurant, too). Other amenities include a rooftop pool large enough for swimming laps, happy-hour specials, and a big-screen TV in the lounge. Following a thorough hotel renovation in 2007, furniture and appliances were replaced in the guestrooms, and the fitness center was newly equipped. Rooms in both towers are about the same size, if not the same shape. All provide views of the lake.

20 N. I-35 (exit 233, Riverside Dr./Lady Bird Lake), Austin, TX 78701. ℂ **800/HOLIDAY** (465-4329) or 512/472-8211. Fax 512/472-4636. www.holiday-inn.com/austintownlake. 320 units. $129–$199 double. Special discounts available. AE, DC, DISC, MC, V. Free self-parking. **Amenities:** Restaurant; bar; executive-level rooms; exercise room; outdoor pool; room service. *In room:* AC, TV, fridge, hair dryer, Wi-Fi (free).

**La Quinta Inn—Capitol** 🏷   Practically on the grounds of the state capitol, this is a great bargain for both business and leisure travelers. Rooms are more attractive than those in your typical motel: TVs are larger, the furnishings are far from cheesy, and perks such as free local phone calls, free high-speed Internet access, and free continental breakfasts keep annoying extra charges off your bill. The sole drawback is the lack of restaurants on the premises, though several are just a few blocks away. If you don't want to leave the hotel, there's always pizza delivery. Smoking is permitted in five rooms.

300 E. 11th St. (at San Jacinto), Austin, TX 78701. ℂ **800/NU-ROOMS** (687-6667) or 512/476-1166. Fax 512/476-6044. www.lq.com. 159 units. $129–$175 double; $185–$210 suite. Rates include continental breakfast. AE, DC, DISC, MC, V. Valet parking $13. Pets accepted free. **Amenities:** Exercise room; outdoor pool. *In room:* A/C, TV, hair dryer, Wi-Fi (free).

# South Austin

## VERY EXPENSIVE

**Hotel Saint Cecilia ★★★**   The Saint Cecilia sits on a large, secluded estate just off South Congress, and takes its inspiration from the patron saint of music and poetry. The original house (1888) holds five suites, and there are six poolside bungalows and three studios on a private wooded property. All guestrooms except one are oversize (though it has a view of the Austin skyline). They're designed with clean lines and attractive spaces, and each has its own outdoor area. Large bathrooms are stocked with lotions and bath salts. In each room, you'll find a turntable connected to a Geneva sound system. A vintage vinyl-record collection is at the hotel reception area, as well as a library with films and books on poetry and writing. But the capper in each room is the exclusive Swedish Hastens handcrafted bed, not found in other hotels in North America.

112 Academy Dr.(1 block east of S. Congress Ave.), Austin, TX 78704. © **512/852-2400.** Fax 512/852-2401. www.hotelsaintcecilia.com. 14 units. $290–$610 double. Rates include full breakfast. AE, DC, DISC, MC, V. Free parking. Pets under 25 lb. accepted with $25 fee per day. **Amenities:** Bar; bikes; concierge; outdoor pool; room service. *In room:* A/C, TV/DVD, fridge, hair dryer, minibar, Wi-Fi (free).

**Kimber Modern ★★★**   This boutique hotel should be the choice of design-conscious travelers who can't bear to be lodged in the standard cubical room off the standard long and dreary corridor. The hotel is strictly modern, not the usual cookie-cutter kind of modern, but an architectural work of art, tailored toward the independent urban traveler. Obviously, a great deal of thought and effort went into its construction, especially because of how it fits into the space of the property—a wedge-shaped lot on an incline. Five rooms and one suite surround a courtyard with a broad deck shaded by oak trees. This setting is a great place to relax and enjoy a little leisure time, which the hotel encourages with a free happy hour. The rooms are lovely, with sophisticated touches and sleek layouts and fixtures. A continental breakfast is provided in the lounge in the mornings. The staff is very accommodating.

110 The Circle (1 block east of S. Congress Ave.), Austin, TX 78704. © **512/912-1046.** www.kimbermodern.com. 6 units. $250–$295 double; $295–$330 suite. Rates include continental breakfast and afternoon drinks. AE, MC, V. Free parking. Children 15 and under not permitted. **Amenities:** Concierge; access to nearby health club; Internet (free, in lobby). *In room:* A/C, fans, TV, fridge, hair dryer, MP3 docking station, no phone, Wi-Fi (free).

**Hotel San José ★★**   This bungalow-style hotel, a revamped 1930s motor court, gets a lot of attention from the national press for a design that weds beauty to simplicity. The San Jose is a good choice for design enthusiasts and hipsters, who enjoy both the nonconformist vibe and the social scene in south Austin. Other travelers may think that the minimalist rooms are overpriced. Even if you don't stay here, you might enjoy the hotel's wine bar in the late afternoon/early evening. The rooms are indeed spare and furnished with beds and chairs made from Texas pine, but they also have amenities such as CD players. Most rooms have pleasant small outdoor sitting areas. The design achieves a certain serenity that evaporates the moment you step out into South Congress Avenue's lively street scene. Right across the way is the famous Continental Club, a great place for happy hour. Book a room in back to avoid the Congress Avenue traffic noise.

1316 S. Congress Ave. (south of Nelly), Austin, TX 78704. © **800/574-8897** or 512/444-7322. Fax 512/444-7362. www.sanjosehotel.com. 40 units. $95–$105 double with shared bathroom; $160–$260 double with private bathroom; $280–$375 suite. AE, DISC, MC, V. Free parking. Pets accepted for $10

## IT pays TO STAY

Two downtown accommodations at prime locations will save you money. **Extended Stay America Downtown,** 600 Guadalupe St. (at Sixth St.), Austin, TX 78701 (☏ **800/EXT-STAY** [398-7829] or 512/457-9994; www.extstay.com), and **Homestead Studio Suites Austin—Downtown/Town Lake,** 507 S. 1st St. (at Barton Springs), Austin, TX 78704 (☏ **888/782-9473** or 512/476-1818; www.homesteadhotels.com), will run you from $400 to $500 per week for a room. Full kitchens and coin-op laundries at both bring your costs down even more.

per day. **Amenities:** Bar/lounge; coffee shop; bikes; outdoor pool; room service. *In room:* AC, TV/DVD player, CD player, hair dryer, Wi-Fi (free).

### INEXPENSIVE

**Austin Motel ★ ✦** This establishment, the best lodging bargain on South Congress, is one of the old motels built when this was the main road to San Antonio. Built in 1938, it has been in the hands of the same family since the 1950s. A convenient (but not quiet) location in the heart of SoCo and great rates make this place very popular. It has a classic kidney-shaped pool, a great neon sign, free HBO, and a certain quirkiness that's part of the local charm. It also has one of those rarities: real single rooms, so those traveling on their own don't have to pay for a bed they're not sleeping in. All rooms are different, many decorated with murals, such as room no. 257 with a cactus mural. You can check out pictures of the rooms before you make a reservation by going to the website.

1220 S. Congress St., Austin, TX 78704. ☏ **512/441-1157.** Fax 512/441-1157. www.austinmotel.com. 41 units. $70–$96 single; $87–$96 double; $119–$127 poolside and deluxe; $178 suite. AE, DC, DISC, MC, V. Free parking. Pets accepted with $15 fee. **Amenities:** Outdoor pool. *In room:* A/C, TV, fridge (in some), hair dryer, Wi-Fi (free).

## Central

### EXPENSIVE

**Mansion at Judges Hill ★★** All the rooms in this elegant boutique hotel are furnished and decorated with more character than you'll find at any of the local chain hotels. This is true of the rooms in the modern building at the rear of the property and especially for the ones in the original mansion. In the historic Mansion rooms, the second-story signature units are the most fun; they all open onto a sweeping upstairs porch and have tall ceilings and large bathrooms with special amenities (including L'Occitane toiletries and bathrobes). Beds have particularly good mattresses and linens. The third-floor rooms are a little smaller, but lovely and with a real feel of the old house. The ground floor holds the bar and the restaurant.

The modern building is called the North Wing. Built in 1983 in the rear of the property, it offers rooms far from the traffic sounds coming from Martin Luther King, Jr., Boulevard. The rooms vary quite a bit. Most come without tubs. The deluxe king rooms are the nicest (particularly no. 212). The West Campus location is convenient to the university and to downtown.

1900 Rio Grande (at MLK, Jr., Blvd./19th St.), Austin, TX 78705. ☏ **800/311-1619** or 512/495-1800. www.judgeshill.com. 48 units. $169–$229 North Wing; $189–$299 Mansion. Special packages available. AE,

DC, DISC, MC, V. Free parking. Pets accepted with restrictions and $50 fee. **Amenities:** Restaurant; bar; nearby exercise room, room service. *In room:* A/C, TV, CD player, hair dryer, minibar, Wi-Fi (free).

## MODERATE

**Austin Folk House** ★★ 🎖   You get the best of both worlds at this appealing B&B that combines old-time charm with new plumbing. When it was transformed from a tired apartment complex at the beginning of the new millennium, this 1880s house near the University of Texas got a complete interior overhaul, but it maintained such integral traditional assets as the comfy front porch. The sunny rooms have cheerfully painted walls and wiring to accommodate megachannel cable TVs, private phone lines, broadband cable access, and radio/alarms with white noise machines. At the same time, nice antiques and such amenities as fancy bedding and towels, candles, robes, expensive lotions, and soaps make you feel like you're in a small luxury inn. The lavish breakfast buffet is served in a dining room decorated with the folk art for which the B&B is named. Prices are reasonable for all this, while the free off-street parking, near the heart of UT, puts this place at a premium all by itself.

506 W. 22nd St. (at Nueces), Austin, TX 78705. ✆ **866/472-6700** or 512/472-6700. www.austinfolk house.com. 9 units. $95–$225 double. Special discounts available. Rates include full breakfast. AE, DISC, MC, V. Free parking. Children 5 and under not permitted. *In room:* A/C and fan, TV/VCR, hair dryer, Wi-Fi.

**Habitat Suites** ★★ ☺ 🎒   This hotel, located in one of the satellite buildings of Highland Mall, is an island of ecological awareness in a sea of mainstream commercialism. It was converted into a green hotel in 1991, committed to using natural materials and cleaning products over synthetics and chemicals, saving—and even generating—electricity, recycling materials, conserving water, growing organic foods, and acting in a socially conscious manner. For the guests, it means never running the risk of getting a room that reeks of chemicals, and lodgings are ideal for anyone with chemical sensitivities. It also means friendly service—the hotel staff has bought into the green concept and even enjoys a profit-sharing arrangement; consequently, the staff-retention rate is way above the industry average. There are healthful food choices for breakfast (but not to the exclusion of regular fare), and if you decide to cook for yourself, you can make use of some of the organically grown vegetables, when available. All of these green activities are performed without fanfare, though the hotel quietly piles up awards for its eco-consciousness. Rooms are oversize and have complete kitchens. Sheets and towels are of natural materials. Paints are water-based. The furniture, though not of the latest style, is comfortable (pieces are refinished or reupholstered to avoid adding to the waste stream). Each room has a small separate outdoor area with chairs. The location is central, just 2 miles north of the university campus. It's not noisy, and the hotel institutes quiet hours between 9pm and 9am.

500 E. Highland Mall Blvd. (take exit 222 off I-35 to Airport Blvd., take a right to Highland Mall Blvd.), Austin, TX 78752. ✆ **800/535-4663** or 512/467-6000. Fax 512/467-6000. www.habitatsuites.com. 96 units. $137 1-bedroom suite; $207 2-bedroom suite. Special packages available. Rates include full breakfast and afternoon wine and snacks (except Sun). AE, DC, DISC, MC, V. Free parking. **Amenities:** Jacuzzi; outdoor pool. *In room:* A/C, TV, fridge, hair dryer, kitchen, Wi-Fi (free).

# Westlake/Lake Travis

## VERY EXPENSIVE

**Lake Austin Spa Resort** ★★★   If you had to create the quintessential Austin spa, it would be laid-back, located on a serene body of water, offer lots of outdoor activities, and serve superhealthy food that lives up to high culinary standards. You can check off every item of that wish list here. The spa takes advantage of its proximity to

## FAMILY-FRIENDLY hotels

**Doubletree Guest Suites** (p. 292) and **Habitat Suites** (p. 297) The word "suites" in the name of these properties says it all. These accommodations offer spacious, not-in-your-face quarters, plus the convenience (and economy) of kitchen facilities, so you don't have to eat out all the time.

**Four Seasons Austin** (p. 289) Tell the reservations clerk that you're traveling with kids, and you'll be automatically enrolled in the free amenities program, which provides age-appropriate snacks—cookies and milk for children 9 and under, popcorn and

soda for those older—along with various toys and games waiting when you arrive. You don't have to travel with all your gear, because the hotel will provide such items as a car seat, stroller, playpen, bedrails, disposable pacifiers, a baby bathtub, shampoo, powder and lotions, bib, bottle warmers, and disposable diapers.

**Holiday Inn Austin Town Lake** (p. 294) You're near lots of the outdoor play areas at Town Lake, and kids stay for free and those 11 and under eat for free. It's hard to beat that!

the Highland Lakes and the Hill Country with such activities as combination canoe/hiking trips and excursions to view wildflowers. The aromatic ingredients for soothing spa treatments, such as a honey-mango scrub, are grown in the resort's garden, also the source for the herbs used at mealtimes. Guest rooms, many in cottages with private gardens, fireplaces, and hot tubs, are casually elegant, with all-natural fabrics and locally crafted furniture.

This resort is a destination spa that has piled up awards and been included on virtually all top-10 lists for spas (ranked as top destination spa in North America by Condé Nast *Traveler* for 2010). If you go, you'll see why. It's simply an incredibly relaxing experience, with a winning combination of beauty; a welcoming, knowledgeable staff; and delicious cuisine. There are 3- to 7-night packages available.

1705 S. Quinlan Park Rd. (5 miles south of Hwy. 620), Austin, TX 78732. © **800/847-5637** or 512/372-7300. Fax 512/266-1572. www.lakeaustin.com. 40 units. 3-night package $1,635–$2,585 (per person) double; 7-night package $4,045–$7,125 (per person) double. Rates include all meals, classes, and activities. Spa treatments/personal trainers cost extra. Special packages available. AE, DC, DISC, MC, V. Free parking. Dogs accepted in Garden Cottage rooms for $250 fee. Children 13 and under not permitted. **Amenities:** Restaurant; health club and spa; 1 indoor/2 outdoor pools; room service. *In room:* A/C, TV/DVD, CD player, hair dryer, Wi-Fi (free).

## At the Airport

### MODERATE

**Hilton Austin Airport** ★ This Hilton's circular shape gives Austin's only full-service airport hotel, formerly the headquarters of Bergstrom Air Force Base, a distinctively modern look. Although the hotel retains few of the features that once made it one of three Cold War bunkers in the U.S. where the president could be flown for safety in the event of a nuclear attack, the building remains rock solid—and blissfully soundproof. (If you stay here, ask for a sheet that details the fascinating history of "the Donut," which also served as a strategic air command center during the Vietnam War, the Persian Gulf War, and Desert Storm.) These days, the dome serves as a skylight for a bright and airy lobby. The theme throughout is Texas Hill Country, with lots of limestone and wood, and plenty of live plants for good measure. Large, comfortable rooms are equipped with all the amenities.

9515 New Airport Dr. (½ mile from the airport, 2 miles east of the intersection of Hwy. 183 and Hwy. 71), Austin, TX 78719. © **800/445-8667** or 512/385-6767. Fax 512/385-6763. www.hilton.com. 273 units. $159–$199 double; from $190 suite. Special discounts available. AE, DC, DISC, MC, V. Valet parking $15; self-parking $11. Pets accepted. **Amenities:** Restaurant; lounge; free airport transfers; concierge; executive-level rooms; exercise room; outdoor pool; room service, Wi-Fi (free, in lobby). *In room:* A/C, TV, hair dryer, minibar, MP3 docking station.

# WHERE TO DINE

The Austin dining scene has a preponderance of barbecue and Tex-Mex joints, but other types of cuisine are well represented. Many restaurants are concentrated in and around downtown and the area immediately south of Lady Bird Lake. In other parts of the city, they tend to be set along major commercial corridors. But in some old neighborhoods, a few will be tucked away in small clusters on fairly quiet streets, and these are some of the most interesting local restaurants.

## Downtown
### EXPENSIVE

**Chez Nous** ★★ ♠ FRENCH   This small bistro is a great choice for a quiet lunch or dinner. The setting is attractive and casual—small tables decorated with a few fresh flowers sticking out from old anisette bottles, Folies Bergère posters on the wall. The French owners have prospered by consistently providing high-quality service and food at reasonable prices. The most popular choice here is the prix-fixe dinner with a choice of soup, salad, or pâté; one of three designated entrees; and crème caramel, chocolate mousse, or brie for dessert. The main courses might include a *poisson poivre vert* (fresh fish of the day with a green-peppercorn sauce) or a simple but delicious roast chicken. Everything from the pâtés to the profiteroles is made on the premises. Of the main courses, one of my favorites is the lamb chops crusted in fine herbs and grilled.

510 Neches St. © **512/473-2413.** www.cheznousaustin.com. Reservations accepted only for parties of 6 or more. Main courses $20–$30; prix fixe $27. AE, DC, DISC, MC, V. Tues–Fri 11:45am–2pm; Tues–Sun 6–10:30pm.

### MODERATE

**Clay Pit** ★ ♠ INDIAN   The old building that houses this restaurant had been a saloon for many years, as far back as the 1870s. The thick limestone walls and rough wood floors show their age, and the proportions of the large room still bring to mind the old saloon. But oh, how the custom and wares have changed! The Clay Pit is known for Indian cooking with a bit of a twist. A good example is the starter of perfectly cooked coriander calamari served with a piquant cilantro aioli. For an entree, consider *Khuroos-E-Tursh,* baked chicken breast stuffed with nuts, mushrooms, and onions, and smothered in a cashew-almond cream sauce; or one of the many dazzling vegetarian dishes.

At night, the dining room is softly lit, creating an attractive and romantic setting for dates or special occasions. During the day, it's something quite different—a place to grab a quick, economical lunch from the buffet of typical Indian standards. The restaurant is located near the courthouse and state office buildings just north of the capitol, so it gets a fair number of office workers. Keep this in mind should you get hungry while touring either the capitol or the university campus.

1601 Guadalupe St. © **512/322-5131.** www.claypit.com. Reservations recommended. Lunch buffet $7.50; main courses $10–$20. AE, DC, DISC, MC, V. Mon–Fri 11am–2pm; Sat noon–3pm; Mon–Thurs 5–10pm; Fri–Sat 5–11pm.

## INEXPENSIVE

**El Naranjo** ★★ MEXICAN   I first met the owners Iliana de la Vega and her husband, Ernesto Torrealba, many years ago in Oaxaca City. They had just opened a restaurant, which would eventually win acclaim from major publications both in Mexico and abroad and become a hot spot on the travel circuit through interior Mexico. But troubled times came to Oaxaca. They moved to a couple of different places in the U.S. before settling into Austin and have now opened another eatery, decidedly more modest—a food trailer parked in the Rainey Street District, just south of Cesar Chavez and east of Red River Street. Here, you can get a reduced sampling of her cooking while sitting on picnic benches in front of a closed house that they eventually want to turn into a full-service restaurant. If you're there on a weekend night, you can get the best tacos *al pastor* in Austin, with or without cheese. Any day of the week, you can get light and delicious fish or shrimp tacos. For something more substantial, try the *mole* (which varies depending on the day and the week), and for appetizers, I like the mushroom *empanadas*.

85 Rainey St. ✆ **512/474-2776.** Plates $5–$11. AE, MC, V. Mon–Thurs 5–10pm; Fri–Sat 5–11pm.

**Hut's Hamburgers** 🍴 AMERICAN   This classic burger shack is very Austin. In 1939, it opened its doors as Sammie's Drive-In, serving the traditional-style Texas burger with lettuce and onions. Today, it serves 19 types of burgers, including a vegetarian garden burger (which is very Austin, too). As you might expect, you can also get fries and shakes, the usual burger complements, but, for those who enjoy onion rings, this place is a special treat. Also on the menu are blue-plate specials of meatloaf, chicken-fried steak, and fried catfish. The decor consists of sports pennants and '50s memorabilia.

807 W. 6th St. ✆ **512/472-0693.** Sandwiches and burgers $5–$8; plates $8–$9. AE, DISC, MC, V. Daily 11am–10pm.

**The Iron Works** ★ BARBECUE   Some of the best barbecue dishes in Austin are served in one of the most unusual settings. Until 1977, this building housed the ironworks of the Weigl family, who came over from Germany in 1913. You can see their ornamental crafts all around town, including at the state capitol. Cattle brands created for Jack Benny ("Lasting 39"), Lucille Ball, and Bob Hope are displayed in front of the restaurant. The beef ribs are the most popular order, with the brisket running a close second. Lean turkey breast and juicy chicken are also smoked to perfection.

100 Red River St. (at E. First St.). ✆ **800/669-3602** or 512/478-4855. www.ironworksbbq.com. Reservations accepted only for large parties. Lunch $3–$5; main courses $6–$13. AE, DC, MC, V. Mon–Sat 11am–9pm.

## South Austin

### EXPENSIVE

**Olivia** ★★★ NEW AMERICAN   If you are in search of creative cooking that extends your gastronomical horizons, are fond of light and angular modern architecture, and want to sample some of the best food from local farmers, this is the right choice. Olivia is far and away the brightest newcomer to Austin's fine dining scene. The entire dining experience—food, setting, and service—rivals any restaurant in Austin. The chef/owner, James Holmes, is intent on getting it all correct, from the new building, to the staff, to the suppliers. His cooking has a good bit of Mediterranean influence, but with Austin sensibilities. More than any other restaurant in

Austin, Olivia emphasizes local produce. The menu varies a bit each day and has sufficient variety to satisfy just about any taste without sacrificing focus or quality. The building, with lots of glass and a soaring roof, has an open feel and many architectural details that can be admired during a meal; the same perspective is enjoyed on an outside patio.

2043 S. Lamar Blvd. © 512/804-2700. www.olivia-austin.com. Reservations recommended. Main courses $20–$30. AE, MC, V. Fri–Sat 11am–2pm; Sun 10:30am–2:30pm; Sun–Thurs 5:30–10pm; Fri–Sat 5:30–11pm.

**Uchi** ★★★ ASIAN/JAPANESE    Chef/owner Tyson Cole has garnered all kinds of acclaim from the local and national press. He loves to play with ingredients familiar to Texans to create Asian dishes that are beautifully presented and exciting to Austin's tastes. His *Uchiviche*—citrus-marinated whitefish and salmon mixed with tomato, peppers, cilantro, and chiles—will make a believer out of you. It's not only the seafood that gets the culinary crossover treatment: Brie, pumpkin, shiitake mushrooms, and asparagus are among the food items that you can order tempura-style. The skewered kobe beef should satisfy those who eschew vegetables and fish. Choose from a long list of cold sakes—especially the rare upmarket brands—for the perfect complement. Uchi has legions of fans among the public, which means that you need to make reservations pretty far in advance or you'll have to wait for a table at the bar. The space, a converted 1930s bungalow done up in Asian reds and blacks, is at once dramatic and spare.

801 S. Lamar Blvd. © 512/916-4808. www.uchiaustin.com. Reservations recommended. Main courses $18–$30. AE, DISC, MC, V. Mon–Thurs 5–10pm; Fri–Sat 5–11pm.

**Vespaio & Enoteca Vespaio** ★ ITALIAN    Austin isn't really known for its Italian food, but when Austinites want Italian, this is their preferred destination. Vespaio's swanky old storefront with lots of exposed brick and glass is an elegant setting, and the food is worth waiting for, but you can drop quite a bit of dough on expensive wines while you're doing so. Your best bet is to get an order of the crispy calamari (they're huge) while waiting for a table. The spaghetti alla carbonara is super, as is the veal scallopini with mushrooms. Many come for the pizza. Try the *boscaiola*, topped with wild boar sausage and Cambozola cheese. Among the 10 chalkboard nightly specials, the mixed meat and seafood grills are usually top-notch. *Note:* Reservations are limited to off-peak hours and days.

Next door is the Enoteca, which is more informal, a bit less expensive, and serves lighter fare. It's open for lunch and dinner. The dining room is a little more cramped, but is a very attractive space, perfect for an afternoon coffee, a panini, or a glass of wine. There's a small outdoor patio, too. One of the starters served here is a plate of crispy fried risotto balls filled with fontina. There's a small cold case filled with Italian delicacies for those interested in taking something back to their hotel room.

**Vespaio:** 1610 S. Congress Ave. © 512/441-6100. www.austinvespaio.com. Reservations accepted. Pizzas $17–$18; pastas and main courses $21–$28. AE, DISC, MC, V. Tues–Fri 5:30–10:30pm; Sat 5–10:30pm; Sun–Mon 5:30–10pm. Bar daily 5pm–midnight. **Enoteca Vespaio:** © 512/441-7672. Reservations not accepted. Pizzas and pastas $12–$16. AE, DISC, MC, V. Mon–Sat 11am–10pm; Sun 10am–3pm.

## MODERATE

**Curra's Grill** ★★ ☺ MEXICAN    This plain, unassuming restaurant has a strong local following for its large menu of interior Mexican dishes and moderate prices. The tortillas are handmade. The Mexican tamales (not the kind usually served in Texas) come in several flavors and are quite good, with moist, spongy *masa* (dough). You can build your own enchiladas from a selection of sauces and fillings—I like the *mole* and the *chile pasilla*. The Yucatecan *cochinita pibil* (pork baked in a marinade of achiote, sour orange, and herbs and spices) is tender and complex. The *pescado veracruzano* is fish baked in a sauce of tomatoes, onions, olives, and capers. It's a bit different from the dish as served in its home of Veracruz, but great nonetheless. There are also a lot of Tex-Mex options as well, such as the tostadas, piled high with lettuce and crumbled fresh cheese. For dessert, the flan can't be beat.

614 E. Oltorf St. ✆ **512/444-0012.** www.currasgrill.com. Reservations accepted only for large parties. Main courses $8–$17. AE, DISC, MC, V. Sun–Thurs 7am–10pm; Fri–Sat 7am–11pm.

**Güero's** ★ ☺ TEX-MEX    This is one of the main hangouts on south Congress. It occupies an old feed store that dates from the time when south Austin was a low-rent area at the margins of the city. The restaurant has retained as much of the old feed store as it could, capturing the homey informality that Austinites love. Floors of worn wood and stained cement; brick walls coated in old, faded paint; tall ceilings; a tin roof; cheap tables and chairs—it's welcoming and friendly. It's also popular, and noisy when crowded. I like it best during off hours. The restaurant makes its own tortillas by hand for dishes such as tacos (and the tacos *al pastor,* served Mexican-style on small tortillas, folded around deliciously seasoned, grilled pork with pineapple, onion, and cilantro, is one of the dishes for which this place is known). Lots of people come for the *queso* (cheese). I like the chicken breast marinated in achiote and Mexican oregano, which can be served on a salad, in enchiladas, or in tacos. If you're trying to get your vegetables, the spinach enchiladas will work. Otherwise, go with some of the Tex-Mex combo plates. None of the food is particularly spicy.

1412 S. Congress Ave. ✆ **512/447-7688.** www.guerostacobar.com. Reservations not accepted. Main courses $7–$19. AE, DC, DISC, MC, V. Mon–Fri 11am–11pm; Sat–Sun 8am–11pm.

**The Salt Lick** ★ ☺ BARBECUE    It's 12 miles from the junction of U.S. 290 W. and FM 1826 to the Salt Lick, but you'll start smelling the smoke during the last 5 miles of your trip. Moist chicken, beef, and pork, as well as terrific homemade pickles—not to mention the pretty, verdant setting—more than justify the drive. If you indulge in the all-you-can-eat family-style platter of beef, sausage, and pork ribs, you might have to pass on the fresh-baked peach cobbler, which would be a pity. In warm weather, seating is outside at picnic tables under oak trees; in winter, fireplaces blaze in a series of large, rustic rooms. The Salt Lick prides itself on its sauce, which has a sweet-and-sour tang. If you like your barbecue with a brew, you'll need to tote your own in a cooler, because Hays County is dry. Kids 3 and under eat for free. But you don't have to drive all the way out to the country for a smoked-meat fix: The Salt Lick's airport branch is convenient and quick.

18300 FM 1826, Driftwood. ✆ **512/858-4959** or 888/SALT-LICK (725-8542) mail order. www.saltlick bbq.com. Reservations accepted only for large parties. Main courses $6–$20. No credit cards. Daily 11am–10pm.

## INEXPENSIVE

**Chuy's** ☺ TEX-MEX    In the row of low-priced, friendly restaurants that line Barton Springs Road just east of Zilker Park, Chuy's stands out for its determinedly wacky decor—hubcaps lining the ceiling, Elvis memorabilia galore—and its sauce-smothered Tex-Mex food. You're not likely to leave hungry after specials such as Chuy's enchiladas, piled high with smoked chicken and cheese and topped with sour cream, or one of the "big as yo' face" burritos, stuffed with ground sirloin, cheese, and beans.

## GROCERY STORE dining

Austinites have a fondness for dining in grocery stores, and I'm not talking about grazing the produce aisle. Indeed, the city's two grocery palaces, **Central Market** and **Whole Foods,** have large dining areas. Austinites like the casual feel of a grocery store and the convenience of mixing dining with the opportunity to pick up a couple of things forgotten on the last shopping trip. But for visitors, it's a good choice, too. Both of these stores are popular destinations, so you can grab a bite and explore Austin's utopian vision of fine grocery shopping. The food is good, quick, and wholesome, and you control the portions. The prices are moderate and compare favorably to sitting down in a full-service restaurant. In both stores, indoor and outdoor seating is available, sometimes with live music. Whole Foods probably has more variety, though it's more self-serve and can be a little confusing. Food at both places is available during regular store hours.

Chuy's is popular and doesn't take reservations; most people wait for a table by grabbing a seat in the bar area and ordering appetizers and "Mexican martinis" (like margaritas, but bigger and with olives). Try to stay away from the free nacho bar, if you can. Other locations have sprouted up: in the north on 10520 N. Lamar Blvd. (© 512/836-3218), in the northwest at 11680 N. Research Blvd. (© 512/342-0011), and far south at 4301 W. William Cannon Dr. (© 512/899-2489).

1728 Barton Springs Rd. © 512/474-4452. www.chuys.com. Reservations not accepted. Main courses $8–$12. AE, DISC, MC, V. Sun–Thurs 11am–10pm; Fri–Sat 11am–11pm.

**Shady Grove** ★ AMERICAN    Also on Barton Springs Road is this ironic salute to Americana. The restaurant captures a bit of the feel of David Lynch's vision of small town "Twin Peaks," including the corny touches. Stonework and yellow-pine planks make up a good bit of the dining room's interior. Deep booths lining the walls and windows covered by old-fashioned Venetian blinds complete the picture. The menu adds to the ambience with such classics as Freddie's Airstream Chili, meatloaf, and fried catfish. Shady Grove is known for its burgers made with ground sirloin. A popular choice is the green chile cheeseburger. Also, the Hippie Sandwich (grilled eggplant, veggies, and cheese with pesto mayonnaise) is a good bet.

When the weather is agreeable, most patrons sit out on the large patio shaded by trees. On Thursdays during spring and summer, this is the site of a free concert series called Shady Grove Unplugged. It features popular local artists and runs from 7 to 10pm.

1624 Barton Springs Rd. © 512/474-9991. www.theshadygrove.com. Reservations not accepted. Main courses $8–$13. AE, DC, DISC, MC, V. Sun–Thurs 11am–10pm; Fri–Sat 11am–11pm.

## West Austin

### VERY EXPENSIVE

**Jeffrey's** ★★★ NEW AMERICAN    This little bistro in the old Clarksville neighborhood west of downtown has been a destination for food lovers for over 25 years. Some locals feel that its arrival marked the first steps of the city's march toward a food and dining culture. In keeping with the tone set by the surrounding neighborhood, the restaurant and bar area are cozy, comfortable, and informal. The furniture and lighting are handled nicely, and you relax from the moment you ease into a dining chair.

Most of the appetizers rotate with seasons, but one in particular, a signature dish of Jeffrey's, will be there year-round: the crispy oysters on yucca chips topped with habanero honey aioli. There's also an updated version ("Octavia") created by the new chef, Deegan McClung. He likes to layer rich flavors together for the main courses, and he's good at it. The seasonally changing menu normally includes several dishes that are new terrain to most diners. Of course, the popular Jeffrey's Burger is no different. For those wanting to save money and still sample the cuisine, Jeffrey's has a bar menu with several appetizers (and the Jeffrey's Burger). You can save even more during happy hour, from 5 to 7 pm.

1204 W. Lynn St. © **512/477-5584** or 477-5587. www.jeffreysofaustin.com. Reservations recommended. Main courses $19–$44; tasting menu $75, $107 with wine. AE, DC, DISC, MC, V. Mon–Thurs 6–10pm; Fri–Sat 5:30–11pm; Sun 6–9:30pm.

## MODERATE

**Cipollina** ★★ 🛍 ITALIAN/NEW AMERICAN   This neighborhood bistro has a past that it's never managed to shake, and it involved pizza and sandwiches. This is what happens when you're a neighborhood business. People don't forget. But Cipollina changed. It kept the pizzas on the menu, but it made them new and out of the ordinary (such as bacon with Gorgonzola, apples, and arugula, or prosciutto with truffle oil, Gruyère, and oregano). This brings them more in line with the rest of the cooking, which is also original, but not overboard. The new chef, Daniel Hunt, believes that quality ingredients shouldn't be overworked. The restaurant does its best to use local suppliers, but won't sacrifice quality. The oyster-mushroom risotto and the duck-confit tortellini exemplify both this quality and restraint. The menu changes seasonally, and there's usually a reasonably priced prix fixe. Sandwiches have been relegated to the lunch menu, but they are out of the ordinary, too. Simple elegance is the prevailing character of the dining room, with comfortable furniture, lots of room, and a light touch with the decoration. To finish off your meal, walk a block south to Caffe Medici for some of the best espresso in Austin.

1213 W. Lynn St. © **512/477-5211.** www.cipollina-austin.com. Reservations not accepted. Main courses $7–$16 lunch, $11–$19 dinner; 3-course prix fixe $25, $35 with wine. AE, MC, V. Sun–Thurs 11am–10pm; Fri–Sat 11am–10:30pm.

## INEXPENSIVE

**Zocalo** 🍴 MEXICAN/FAST FOOD   This fast-food Mexican cafe in the Clarksville neighborhood has light, healthful fare for reasonable prices. The ingredients are fresh, and the tortillas are handmade. The soft tacos, which come three to the order, accompanied by rice and beans, are just the right amount to satisfy an appetite, but not too much. The fillings vary between vegetables, fish, fowl, and fajitas. Unlike Tex-Mex, they don't come topped with cheese. Specialties include the "Zocalo Plate" (a version of *chilaquiles con pollo*), which is made of tortilla pieces cooked with chicken in a green sauce and topped with crumbled fresh cheese and sour cream. The tostada salad comes with black beans, avocado, cilantro, roasted jalapeños, and a lime dressing. The list of soups is also good, and look for the daily specials every weekday. The dining area is flooded by natural light from tall windows, and an outdoor area is open when the weather is agreeable.

1110 W. Lynn St. © **512/472-8226.** www.zocalocafe.com. Plates $7–$10. AE, DISC, MC, V. Mon–Fri 11am–10pm; Sat–Sun 10am–10pm.

**FAMILY-FRIENDLY restaurants**

**Curra's Grill** (p. 301), **Güero's** (p. 302), **Hoover's** (p. 307), and **Threadgill's** (p. 306) all have special menus for kids 12 and under, as well as casual, kid-friendly atmospheres and food inexpensive enough to feed everyone without taking out a second mortgage. **Chuy's** (p. 302) is great for teens and aspiring teens, who'll love the cool T-shirts, Elvis Presley kitsch, and green iguanas crawling up the walls. **The Salt Lick** (p. 302) serves all-you-can-eat family-style platters, and kids 3 and under eat for free. **County Line on the Hill** (p. 307) has a kids' menu, and kids can make their own barbecue sandwiches. They also enjoy the large outdoor area.

## Central

### EXPENSIVE

**Fonda San Miguel** ★ MEXICAN   This was one of the first restaurants to introduce fine dining a la Mexicana to Texas. It's a local landmark, but in the last couple of years, it has been in a holding pattern, keeping the quality up, but not showing much life. The swinging door to the kitchen has seen plenty of action as several chefs have come and gone since Miguel Rávago retired. Still, there's much to be said for a well-made *mole poblano* or *cochinita pibil*. Though the dinner menu doesn't have much that's new, many like it that way. Fonda enjoys a faithful clientele that is locked in. These customers seek the dishes they know, and the dining experience, when taken as a whole, is thoroughly enjoyable. There's something about the graceful rooms, rich colors, and attractive lighting that makes for a charming evening. Sunday brunch is a big deal at Fonda, with a more interesting selection of dishes (such as fruit gazpacho and *chilaquiles*). Now, if money were no object . . .

2330 W. North Loop. © **512/459-4121** or 459-3401. www.fondasanmiguel.com. Reservations recommended. Main courses $18–$31; Sunday brunch $50. AE, DC, DISC, MC, V. Restaurant Mon–Thurs 5:30–9:30pm; Fri–Sat 5:30–10:30pm; Sun brunch 11am–2pm. Bar Mon–Sat 5pm–closing.

### MODERATE

**Hyde Park Bar and Grill** ◢ AMERICAN   In the Hyde Park neighborhood's little enclave of restaurants along Duval Street, this place is easy to spot due to the landmark giant fork out front. Not only is it easy to find, but it's easy to get to and park your car, and, at least during off-hours, it's easy to get a table here. If you do have to wait, then it's easy to have a drink at the bar. On weekends, this place is popular, especially when there are events at the university. In addition to the chicken-fried steak and more healthful options, such as the roast chicken or any of the various salads, people come here for the battered french fries, which are perennially voted best fries in Austin. The atmosphere at Hyde Park—a one-story former home now divided into different dining rooms—is cozy, and the service is quick and unobtrusive.

4206 Duval St. © **512/458-3168.** www.hydeparkbarandgrill.com. Reservations not accepted. Lunch $5–$10; main courses $10–$16. AE, DC, DISC, MC, V. Daily 11am–midnight.

### INEXPENSIVE

**Mother's Café & Garden** ◢ VEGETARIAN/VEGAN   This neighborhood vegetarian restaurant is attractive, spacious, and softly lit. The dining rooms are understated and modern with touches of hominess. They conjure up Austin's laid-back mood in much the same way as the old place did before it was gutted by fire in 2007 (caused, in an ironic twist, by a homeless man who was cooking some meat behind the restaurant late one night). Vegetarians are among the mellowest denizens of Austin's latent hippie culture, making this place welcome relief from some of the more frenetic eateries in town. If there's a signature dish, it might be the artichoke enchiladas with mushrooms and black olives. Many prefer the zingier barbecued tofu. Aside from these and other regionally inspired dishes, there are vegetarian standards such as spinach lasagna, a vegetable stir-fry, and a popular veggie burger. If you order a salad, check out the cashew-tamari dressing, which is quite good. Desserts are made in-house, and their only fault is that they're too healthful. There's a popular Sunday brunch from 10am to 3pm.

4215 Duval St. ② **512/451-3994.** www.motherscafeaustin.com. Reservations not accepted. Main courses $8–$10. DISC, MC, V. Mon–Fri 11:15am–10pm; Sat–Sun 10am–10pm.

**Threadgill's** ★ ☺ AMERICAN/SOUTHERN   If you want a side of music history along with heaping plates of down-home food at good prices, this Austin institution is for you. When Kenneth Threadgill obtained Travis County's first legal liquor license after the repeal of prohibition in 1933, he turned his Gulf gas station into a club. His Wednesday-night shows were legendary in the 1960s, with performers such as Janis Joplin turning up regularly. In turn, the Southern-style diner that was added in 1980 became renowned for its huge chicken-fried steaks, as well as its vegetables. You can get fried okra, broccoli-rice casserole, garlic-cheese grits, black-eyed peas, and the like in combination plates or as sides.

Eddie Wilson, the current owner of Threadgill's, was the founder of the now-defunct Armadillo World Headquarters, Austin's most famous music venue. (The south Austin branch, 301 W. Riverside Dr., ② **512/472-9304,** is called Threadgill's World Headquarters.) Across the street from the old Armadillo, it's filled with music memorabilia from the club and a state-of-the-art sound system. Unlike the original location, it lays on a Sunday brunch buffet and a "howdy" hour during the week. Both branches still double as live-music venues.

6416 N. Lamar Blvd. ② **512/451-5440.** www.threadgills.com. Reservations not accepted. Lunch $8–$9; main courses $10–$17. DISC, MC, V. Mon–Sat 11am–10pm; Sun 11am–9pm.

## East Side

### MODERATE

**Eastside Cafe** ★★ AMERICAN   This was one of the earliest eateries to open in this rapidly changing area just east of the university, on the other side of the I-35 freeway. Eastside Cafe remains popular with student herbivores and congressional carnivores alike. Diners enjoy eating on a tree-shaded patio or in one of a series of small, homey rooms in a classic turn-of-the-century bungalow.

This restaurant gears its menu to all appetites. You can get half-orders of such pasta dishes as the smoked salmon ravioli, the mixed field green salad topped with warm goat cheese, and entrees like the sesame-breaded catfish. There's also a daily blue-plate special, which is usually a good deal. Each morning, the gardener informs the head chef about the vegetables ready for harvesting from the restaurant's organic garden (and from the farm, about 2 miles out of town). An adjoining store carries gardening tools, cookware, and the cafe's salad dressings.

2113 Manor Rd. ② **512/476-5858.** www.eastsidecafeaustin.com. Reservations recommended. Pastas $14–$18; main courses $10–$22. AE, DISC, MC, V. Mon–Thurs 11:15am–9:30pm; Fri 11:15am–10pm; Sat 10am–10pm; Sun 10am–9:30pm (Sun brunch 10am–3pm).

## INEXPENSIVE

**Franklin Barbecue** ★★ 🍴 BARBECUE    Look for a blue-and-white trailer parked at the back of a fenced vacant lot on the north-bound feeder road of I-35. Aaron and Stacy Franklin have been serving food out of this trailer for only a year of so, and word of their old-style barbecue has spread like wildfire. Aaron cooks it for 18 hours, using a low-temperature oak fire. The problem is that until he finds a bigger smoker (the current smoker is in a second trailer standing behind the first), he sells out of meat by 1pm or so. The popularity is well founded. The ribs, brisket, and sausage taste very much like the small-town barbecue outside of Austin. If you don't want to drive that far, but want to sample traditional barbecue, you should schedule a trip here. Franklin also has a couple of twists: pulled pork, which is uncommon in central Texas, and an espresso-flavored barbecue sauce in addition to a traditional one. The lot has a few picnic tables where you can enjoy the food, and you can also get takeout. Also, check the website for changes, since Aaron says he's looking to move out of the trailer and into a full kitchen.

3421 N. I-35 (at Concordia St.) ✆ **512/653-1187.** www.franklinbarbecue.com. Lunch $7.75–$8.75. AE, DISC, MC, V. Wed–Sun 11am–1pm.

**Hoover's** ★ ☺ AMERICAN/SOUTHERN    This is down-home comfort food at its best. When native Austinite Alexander Hoover, long a presence on the local restaurant scene, opened up his own place near the neighborhood where he grew up, he looked to his mother's recipes and added a bit of Cajun and Tex-Mex food for inspiration. Fried catfish, meatloaf, and gravy-smothered pork chops, with sides of macaroni-and-cheese or jalapeño-creamed spinach, come to the table in generous portions. For a sandwich, try the muffaletta. If you haven't yet tried that Texas standard, the chicken-fried steak, this is a great place to do so. Check the chalkboard for daily specials, seasonal side dishes, and available desserts. If coconut cream pie is on the list, making a decision is much easier. The crowd is a mix of the East Side African-American community, UT students, and food lovers from all around town.

2002 Manor Rd. ✆ **512/479-5006.** www.hooverscooking.com. Reservations not accepted. Main courses $8–$9 lunch, $10–$15 dinner. DC, DISC, MC, V. Mon–Fri 11am–10pm; Sat–Sun 8am–10pm.

# Westlake/Lake Travis

## VERY EXPENSIVE

**Hudson's on the Bend** ★★ NEW AMERICAN    If you're game for game, served in a civilized setting, come to Hudson's. Soft candlelight, fresh flowers, and attentive service combine with out-of-the-ordinary cuisine to make this worth a special-occasion splurge. Set in an old house some 1½ miles southwest of the Mansfield Dam, near Lake Travis, Hudson's has several softly lit, romantic dining rooms. The restaurant is famous for serving game, including diamondback rattlesnake cakes, but most diners come for the mixed grill of venison, rabbit, quail, and buffalo. It's quite expensive, but where else will you be able to buy a plate of food like this? There's also a superb trout served with tangy mango-habanero butter and a memorable pecan-smoked duck breast. Hudson's indoor dining rooms can be noisy on weekends. Opt for the terrace if the weather permits.

3509 Hwy. 620 N. ✆ **512/266-1369.** www.hudsonsonthebend.com. Reservations required on weekends. Main courses $25–$50. AE, DC, DISC, MC, V. Sun–Thurs 6–9pm; Fri–Sat 5:30–10pm.

## MODERATE

**County Line on the Hill** ★ ☺ BARBECUE    Opened in 1975, this scenic hillside barbecue restaurant is the original of the County Line chain. The original business

# food trucks PARK IN AUSTIN

Food concession trailers are all the rage across the U.S. these days, especially in late-night entertainment areas like SoCo. Here, "meals-on-wheels" has taken on a whole new meaning with a centrally located strip of Airstream and RV eateries on the Avenue. In laid-back Austin, no one is in a hurry to eat on the run, so here tables are set up and little lights hang above the gravel parking lot, making this food trailer court a place to gather with friends, grab good food, and stay awhile. The *Wall Street Journal* called SoCo's Mighty Cone one of "The Top-10 Trailers in America." Currently located in the gravel parking lot next to Congress Avenue Baptist Church (1511 S. Congress Ave.), the trailers may soon find a new location on South Congress when a new boutique hotel is built on this spot. For more info, visit www.austinfoodcarts.com.

Here's a list of a few fun trailers to try:

○ **The Mighty Cone:** Known for hot and crunchy fried wraps (or "cones") made with chicken, shrimp, or avocado and served with mango aioli and slaw. It's no wonder this place gets such raves—its haute cuisine counterpart is the elegant, highly acclaimed Hudson's on the Bend restaurant on Lake Travis, whose chefs helped launch this hot trailer stop.

○ **Flip Happy Crepes:** Featuring tasty tarragon-mushroom crepes with goat cheese, caramelized onions, spinach, and tomatoes.

○ **Love Puppies Brownies:** Homemade brownies made by people who love puppies. Voted Austin's Best Kept Secret in the 2009 Best of Austin readers' poll in *The Austin Chronicle.*

○ **Torchy's Tacos:** Go for the green chile pork tacos topped with *queso fresco,* cilantro, onions, and lime.

○ **Hey Cupcake!:** Among their quirky cupcakes is "the Michael Jackson"—chocolate on the inside with cream cheese icing.

○ **Vaquero Cocina:** Yummy smoked brisket and sweet plantain chips.

○ **The Holy Cacao:** Ooooh, I love their sweet S'mores on a Stick and chocolate mint grasshopper cake-balls.

—*Janis Turk*

on this site, dating from the 1920s, was a speakeasy, positioned strategically on the "county line." But these days people come for the barbecue. Some critics deride these restaurants as "suburban" barbecue, but that doesn't stop crowds from packing in here nightly. This restaurant is now a little less packed since it started opening for lunch; but if you don't get here before 6pm for dinner, you can wait as long as an hour to eat. Should this happen, sit out on the deck and soak in the views of the Hill Country. County Line is known for its big beef ribs, but I like the pork ribs better. The brisket is lean unless you specify "moist," which I also recommend. Sausage and chicken are also good bets. The slow-cooking method employed here makes for consistently good barbecue. The sides, beans, slaw, and potato salad aren't just afterthoughts, and the bread is baked in-house. The atmosphere is rustic country house with such nostalgic accents as old signs and photos. County Line on the Lake (northwest), 5204 FM 2222 (© **512/346-3664**), offers the same menu, and is also open for lunch and dinner.

6500 W. Bee Cave Rd. ☏ **512/327-1742.** Reservations not accepted. Main courses $11–$27 ($6–$8 for children 11 and under). AE, MC, V. Mon–Fri 11:30am–2pm; Mon–Thurs 5–9pm; Fri 5–10pm; Sat 11:30am–10pm; Sun 11:30am–9:30pm (closes daily half-hour earlier in winter).

**The Oasis** AMERICAN/TEX-MEX   This is the required spot for Austinites to take out-of-town guests at sunset. From the multilevel decks nestled into the hillside hundreds of feet above Lake Travis, visitors and locals alike cheer—with toasts and applause—as the fiery orb descends behind the hills on the opposite shores. No one ever leaves unimpressed. The food is another matter entirely: It can be erratic. Keep it simple—nachos, burgers—and you'll be okay. Then add a margarita and kick back. It doesn't get much mellower than this.

6550 Comanche Trail, near Lake Travis. ☏ **512/266-2442.** www.oasis-austin.com. Reservations not accepted. Main courses $12–$20. AE, DC, DISC, MC, V. Mon–Fri 11:30am–10pm; Sat–Sun 11am–10pm (closes 1 hr. earlier in fall/winter).

# SEEING THE SIGHTS

I have two pieces of advice for visitors to Austin. First, don't hesitate to ask Austinites for directions or advice, since they're friendly and approachable. It's common practice here for complete strangers to engage in conversation. Indeed, one of the great things about Austin is how welcoming the city is. Second, take full advantage of the city's Visitor Information Center at 209 E. 6th St. It offers free walking tours and pamphlets for self-guided tours, and is the point of departure for motorized city tours (and the center will know if a tour is cancelled).

What sets Austin apart from other Texas cities, and what puts it on all those "most livable" lists, is the amount of green space and outdoor activities available to its citizens, whose attitude toward the outdoors borders on nature worship. From bats and birds to Barton Springs, from the Highland Lakes to the hike-and-bike trails, Austin lays out the green carpet for its visitors. You'd be hard-pressed to find a city that has more to offer fresh-air enthusiasts.

## The Top Attractions

### DOWNTOWN

**State Capitol** ★★ ♦   The history of Texas's legislative center is as turbulent and dramatic as that of the state itself. The current capitol, erected in 1888, replaced a limestone statehouse that burned down in 1881. A land-rich but otherwise impecunious Texas government traded 3 million acres of public lands to finance its construction. Gleaming pink granite was donated to the cause, but a railroad had to be built to transport the material some 75 miles from Granite Mountain, near the present-day town of Marble Falls. Texas convicts labored on the project alongside 62 stonecutters brought in from Scotland.

It is the largest state capitol in the country, covering 3 acres, and is second in size only to the U.S. Capitol—but still, in typical Texas style, measuring 7 feet taller (though still not the tallest state capitol building). The cornerstone alone weighs 12,000 pounds, and the total length of the wooden wainscoting runs approximately 7 miles. A splendid rotunda and dome lie at the intersection of the main corridors. The House and Senate chambers are located at opposite ends of the second level. Go up to the third-floor visitors' gallery during the legislative sessions if you want see how politics are conducted Texas-style.

# GOING batty

Austin has the largest urban bat population in North America. Some visitors are dubious at first, but it's difficult to be unimpressed by the sight of 1.5 million of the creatures, who emerge from under the Congress Avenue Bridge shortly before dusk and flitter through the air in a long winding ribbon above the river on the east side of the bridge.

Each March, free-tailed bats migrate from central Mexico to various roost sites in the Southwest. In 1980, when a deck reconstruction of Austin's bridge created an ideal environment for raising bat pups, some 750,000 pregnant females began settling in every year. Each bat gives birth to a single pup, and by August, these offspring take part in nightly forays for bugs, usually around dusk. Depending on the size of the group, they might consume anywhere from 10,000 to 30,000 pounds of insects a night—one of the things that makes them so popular with Austinites. By November, these youngsters are old enough to fly back south with their group on the winds of an early cold front.

While the bats are in town, an educational kiosk designed to dispel some of the more prevalent myths about them is set up each evening on the south bank of the river, just east of the bridge. You'll learn, for example, that bats are not rodents, they're not blind, and they're not in the least interested in getting in your hair. **Bat Conservation International** (🕾 512/327-9721; www.batcon. org), based in Austin, has lots of information, as well as bat-related items for sale. Log on to the website or phone 🕾 800/538-BATS (2287) for a catalog. To find out what time the bats are going to emerge from the bridge, call the *Austin American-Statesman* **Bat Hot Line** (🕾 512/416-5700, category 3636). A lot of people don't know this, but sometimes the bats don't leave all at once. If you can still hear bats chattering from beneath the bridge, sit tight; you may have an encore presentation.

The expansion project of the 1990s doubled the amount of office space, all of it underground. Almost 700,000 tons of rock were chiseled out to create an underground annex (often called the "inside-out, upside-down capitol"). It's connected to the capitol and four other state buildings by tunnels. To prevent the expansion from seeming too much like a cave, extensive skylights were installed and the main corridors designed as atriums. Opt for a 30- to 45-minute free guided tour (and afterwards, you're free to explore the building on your own). Include the Capitol Visitors Center (see "More Attractions," below), and figure on spending about 2 hours here. Wear comfortable shoes; you'll be doing a lot of walking.

11th and Congress sts. 🕾 **512/463-0063.** www.tspb.state.tx.us. Free admission. Mon–Fri 7am–10pm; Sat–Sun 9am–8pm; hours extended during legislative sessions (held in odd years, starting in Jan, for 140 straight calendar days). Closed all major holidays. Free guided tours Mon–Fri 8:30am–4:30pm; Sat 9:30am–3:30pm; Sun noon–3:30. Bus: Multiple bus lines.

## SOUTH AUSTIN

**Barton Springs Pool** ★★ ☺ The Native Americans who settled near here believed these waters had spiritual powers, and today's residents still place their faith in the abilities of the spring-fed pool to soothe and cool. Each day, approximately 32 million gallons of water from the underground Edwards Aquifer comes bubbling to the surface here, and at one time, this force powered several Austin mills. Although the original limestone bottom remains, concrete was added to the banks to form uniform sides for what is now a swimming pool of about 1,000×125 feet. Maintaining a constant 68°F (20°C) temperature, the amazingly clear water is bracing in summer and warming in winter, when many hearty souls brave the cold for a dip. Lifeguards are on duty for most of the day, and a large bathhouse operated by the Parks and Recreation Department provides changing facilities and a gift shop.

Zilker Park, 2201 Barton Springs Rd. (℗ **512/476-9044.** www.ci.austin.tx.us/parks/bartonsprings.htm. Admission $3 adults, $2 ages 12–17, $1 seniors and children 11 and under (admission charged only after 8am mid-Mar to Oct; free for early birds). Daily 5am–10pm except during pool maintenance (Thurs 9am–7pm). Bus: 30 (Barton Creek Square).

**Lady Bird Johnson Wildflower Center ★★★** Mrs. Johnson founded the Wildflower Center to research native species and habitat and educate the public on the benefits of gardening with these plants and wildflowers. The center has a large staff and scores of volunteers, 279 acres of land, large greenhouses, and an elaborate rainwater collection system. The facility's research library is the largest in the United States for the study of native plants. For visitors, the main attractions are the 12 acres of beautiful gardens displaying 650 species of native plants (most of which are labeled) in varying habitats, 2 miles of trails, and an observation tower. There is also a large and colorful gift shop and a cafe serving soups and sandwiches. Free lectures and guided walks are usually offered on the weekends—it's best to phone or check the website for current programs. General interest travelers should allow about 2 hours for a visit here.

4801 La Crosse Ave. (℗ **512/292-4200.** www.wildflower.org. Admission $8 adults, $7 students and seniors 60 and older, $3 children 5–12, free for children 4 and under (rates sometimes increase during height of wildflower season Mar–Apr). Tues–Sat 9am–5:30pm; Sun noon–5:30pm. Take Loop 1 (Mo-Pac) south to La Crosse Ave. and turn left.

# CENTRAL AUSTIN

**Blanton Museum of Art ★** Located on the University of Texas campus (across the street from the Bob Bullock Museum), the Blanton houses the university's art collection, which is ranked among the top university collections in the United States. Most notable is the Suida-Manning Collection, a gathering of Renaissance works by such masters as Veronese, Rubens, and Tiepolo, which was sought after by many other museums. Other permanent holdings include the Mari and James Michener collection of 20th-century American masters, a large collection of Latin American art, and a collection of 19th-century plaster casts of monumental Greek and Roman sculpture.

The museum has been a big success in its first few years, attracting large crowds. The directors are working hard to increase public involvement through a variety of events. On the first Friday of every other month, it hosts a little happening called "B scene," which mixes art with live music, wine, finger foods, and socializing. It costs $12 and runs from 6 to 11pm. On the third Thursday of every month, the museum holds events that mix different activities with the arts, such as yoga or literature, starting at 6:30pm. Check the website for other events. Across a small plaza from the museum's main door are the museum's store and cafe. The store provides entertaining shopping with a good variety of uncommon merchandise (including some good gift items), and the cafe is an attractive place to recharge with coffee or a bite to eat. You should allow about 1½ hours for a museum visit.

Martin Luther King, at Congress. (℗ **512/471-7324.** www.blantonmuseum.org. $9 adults, $7 seniors (65 and over), $5 youths 13–25, free for children 12 and under, free for all Thurs. Tues–Fri 10:30am–5pm; Sat 11am–5pm; Sun 1–5pm. Closed university holidays. Bus: UT Shuttle.

**The Bob Bullock Texas State History Museum** ★ ☺  This museum offers a view of Texas history that's different from the most common treatments. There's more emphasis on the many contributions from unheralded groups, with many exhibits presenting some surprising and uncommonly known facets of life in Texas. The building that houses the museum is impressive. Three floors of exhibits are arrayed around a rotunda set off by a 50-foot, polished granite map of Texas. The permanent displays—everything from Stephen F. Austin's diary to Neil Armstrong's spacesuit—and rotating exhibits are interesting. Still, for all the interactive video clips and engaging designs (lots of different rooms to duck into), the presentations don't strike me as dramatically different from those in other history museums. The real treat is the multimedia, special-effects Spirit Theater, the only one of its kind in Texas, where you can experience the high-speed whoosh of the great Galveston hurricane and feel your seat rattle as an east Texas oil well hits a gusher. Austin's only IMAX Theater with 3-D capabilities is pretty dazzling, too, though the films don't necessarily have a direct relation to Texas history. If you do everything, plan to spend at least 2½ to 3 hours here.

1800 N. Congress Ave. ✆ **512/936-8746.** www.thestoryoftexas.com. Exhibit areas: $7 adults, $6 seniors 65 and over, $4 youths 5–18, free for children 4 and under. IMAX Theater: $7 adults, $6 seniors, $5 youths. Texas Spirit Theater: $5 adults, $4 seniors, $4 youths. Combination tickets available. Mon–Sat 9am–6pm; Sun noon–6pm. Phone or check website for additional IMAX evening hours. Closed Jan 1, Easter, Thanksgiving, and Dec 24–25. Bus: UT Shuttle.

**LBJ Library and Museum** ★ 🖋  A presidential library may sound like a big yawn, but this one's almost as interesting as the 36th president to whom it's devoted. Lyndon Baines Johnson's popularity in Texas and his many successes in Washington are often forgotten in the wake of his actions regarding the Vietnam War. The story of Johnson's long political career, starting with his early days as a state representative and continuing through to the Kennedy assassination and the groundbreaking Great Society legislation, is told through a variety of documents, mementos, and photographs. You can take the elevator up to the top floor to view a replica of the Oval Office decorated in the same manner as during Johnson's presidency. The room is a bit smaller than the actual Oval Office. Other exhibits might include anything from photographs of the American Civil Rights era to a display of gifts to LBJ from various other world leaders. You'll also see an animatronic version of LBJ. Dressed in his clothes and speaking with the same folksy delivery that he used when talking to reporters, the life-size, gesticulating figure is either amusing or creepy, depending upon your perspective. From 1971, when the library was dedicated, until his death in 1973, Johnson himself kept an office in this building, which commands an impressive campus view. A large, free parking lot next to the library makes it one of the few UT campus sights that's easy to drive up to. Allow 2 hours for a visit here.

University of Texas, 2313 Red River St. ✆ **512/721-0200.** www.lbjlibrary.org. Free admission. Daily 9am–5pm. Closed Dec 25. Bus: 15; UT shuttle.

## More Attractions

### DOWNTOWN

**Austin Museum of Art—Downtown**  This has become the main gallery space for Austin's local art association. It represents a sizable expansion from the association's other location in the Laguna Gloria mansion in west Austin. The downtown gallery hosts some interesting, often highly original, exhibits. It's not formal at all and can be visited in an hour, or as an afterthought if you're downtown with some time on your hands. You can always check what's currently on display by going to their website.

823 Congress Ave. (at 9th St.). ℗ **512/495-9224.** www.amoa.org. Admission $5 adults, $4 seniors 55 and over and students, $1 for all Tues, free for children 11 and under. Tues–Wed 10am–5pm; Thurs 10am–8pm; Fri 10am–5pm; Sat 10am–6pm; Sun noon–5pm.

**Capitol Visitors Center** ★   At the southeast corner of the capitol grounds is Texas's oldest state office building, the 1857 General Land Office. At present, the building houses the visitor center for the capitol. It's a curious structure and looks a bit out of place with its Romanesque-medieval style and mock crenellated towers. Also uncommon is the surfacing of the exterior walls—scored stucco to imitate stone blocks. The short story writer O. Henry worked in this building as a draftsman for the General Land Office (1887–1891), and you'll find an exhibit on the first floor remembering him. He based two stories on his experiences here. Also on the first floor is a gift shop selling all kinds of books, decorative items, and merchandise commemorating aspects of the Texas capitol, and an information desk that is somewhat redundant. The second floor hosts rotating exhibits about some aspects of the Texas capitol.

*Tip:* The Texas Department of Transportation staffs an information desk on the first floor of the visitor center. If you'll be driving around Texas at all, you can pick up a state map and a helpful travel guide here for free. The guide lists almost all the towns in Texas and describes what's of interest in each one.

112 E. 11th St. (southeast corner of capitol grounds). ℗ **512/305-8400.** www.texascapitolvisitorscenter.com. Free admission. Mon–Sat 9am–5pm; Sun noon–5pm.

**The Driskill**   Col. Jesse Driskill was not a modest man. When he opened a hotel in 1886, he named it after himself, put busts of himself and his two sons over the entrances, and installed bas-relief sculptures of longhorn steers to remind folks how he had made his fortune. Nor did he build a modest property. The ornate four-story structure, which originally boasted a sky-lit rotunda, has the largest arched doorway in Texas over its east entrance. It was so posh that the state legislature met here while the 1888 capitol was being built. The hotel has had its ups and downs over the years, but was restored to its former glory in the late 1990s. You'll enjoy the magnificent retro lobby where you can get coffee or food, sit at a table, and take it all in at leisure. At the front desk, you can get some historical information on the hotel. For a full hotel review, see p. 289.

604 Brazos St. ℗ **512/474-5911.** www.driskillhotel.com. Free admission. Open year-round.

**Governor's Mansion** ★   This venerable public building suffered serious damage when it was targeted by arsonists on the night of June 8, 2008. At the time, the mansion was closed for renovation. Officers of the Department of Public Safety, charged with guarding the building and grounds, did not detect the intruders, and apparently some of the closed-circuit cameras were not working. All of this has made it difficult to catch the vandals. Workers managed to stabilize the structure and protect it from the elements, but extensive restoration is necessary. With all the budget problems faced by the state, there has been difficulty allocating funds. However, restoration work has begun and the projected completion date is February 2012.

The house was built by Abner Cook in 1856. Originally, it had no indoor toilets (there are now seven). The nation's first female governor, Miriam "Ma" Ferguson, entertained her friend Will Rogers in the mansion, and Gov. John Connally recuperated here from gunshot wounds received when he accompanied John F. Kennedy on his fatal motorcade through Dallas. Among the many historical artifacts on display is a desk belonging to Stephen F. Austin and portraits of Davy Crockett and Sam Houston.

*Tip:* Projected completion dates can be iffy, so if you'll be in Austin after February 2012, check the website. If the mansion is open, only a limited number of visitors will be allowed in for 1-hour tours, so make your required reservations as far in advance as possible.

1010 Colorado St. ⓒ **512/463-5516** (recorded information) or 512/463-5518 (tour reservations). www.txfgm.org. Free admission. Tours generally offered every 20 min. Mon–Thurs 10am–noon (last tour starts 11:40am). Closed some holidays and at the discretion of the governor; call the 24-hr. information line to see if tours are offered the day you want to visit.

**Mexic-Arte Museum**   Though it has a small permanent collection of 20th-century Mexican art, photographs from the Mexican revolution, and a fascinating array of masks from the state of Guerrero, this museum is best known for the yearly "Young Latino Artists" show. This show isn't held at the same time every year, but it's usually a summer event. You'll have to check the website for dates. The show's curators choose different artists each year, and usually arrange an eye-catching exhibit. The other time of year when Mexic-Arte is especially entertaining is during and around *Día de Muertos* (end of Oct/beginning of Nov) when the curators construct an altar to some recently deceased celebrity, and the museum store supplements its usual merchandise with some fun and traditional *calavera* (skull) artwork. Allow a half-hour for a visit here.

419 Congress Ave. ⓒ **512/480-9373.** www.mexic-artemuseum.org. Admission $5 adults, $4 seniors and students, $1 children 11 and under. Mon–Thurs 10am–6pm; Fri–Sat 10am–5pm; Sun noon–5pm.

# CENTRAL

**Elisabet Ney Museum** ★   Elisabet Ney was a celebrated German sculptor who carved the likenesses of philosophers, statesmen, and kings (Schopenhauer, Garibaldi, Bismarck, Ludwig II, among others). She was also a woman of ideas and was part of a circle of intellectuals in Munich. With the rise of the anti-intellectual Prussians in Germany, she and her scientist husband decided to flee Europe just before the war of 1870, first to Georgia, then to Texas. Strong willed and independent, she moved to Austin by herself in 1891 because she was bored with life on the family farm near Hempstead, Texas. She constructed the studio that is now part of the museum and got busy creating sculptures of Texas leaders, including Stephen F. Austin and Sam Houston. She also had an immediate impact on Austin society, entertaining all the local intelligentsia, politicians, and visiting celebrities, such as William Jennings Bryan and Enrico Caruso. After her death in 1907, her friends claimed the studio-residence for a museum. It's a great way to spend an hour or two, if you have the chance. You can see many full-size plaster studies, many of which she had shipped from Germany, some that she created in Texas, including the ones for Austin and Houston. You can also see some miniatures, photos, and personal effects. The building itself is worth a visit, too.

304 E. 44th St. ⓒ **512/458-2255.** www.elisabetney.org. Free admission. Wed–Sat 10am–5pm; Sun noon–5pm. Bus: 1 or 5.

**Harry Ransom Humanities Research Center** ★ 🖋   The special collections of the Harry Ransom Center (HRC) contain approximately one million rare books (including a Gutenberg Bible, one of only five complete copies in the U.S.); 30 million literary manuscripts (including those by James Joyce, Ernest Hemingway, and Tennessee Williams); five million photographs, including the world's first; and more than 100,000 works of art, with several pieces by Diego Rivera and Frida Kahlo. Most of this wealth remains the domain of scholars (although anyone can request a look at it), but parts of the collection are regularly exhibited in the gallery on the ground floor. I've seen some fascinating exhibits here, covering everything from the beat generation to the American '20s, to the technology of the written word. Check the website for the various lectures, plays, and poetry readings held here, too, and for displays at the affiliated Leeds Gallery.

University of Texas, Harry Ransom Center, 21st and Guadalupe sts. © **512/471-8944.** www.hrc.utexas. edu. Free admission. Galleries Tues–Wed and Fri 10am–5pm; Thurs 10am–7pm; Sat–Sun noon–5pm; call for reading-room hours. Closed university holidays. Bus: UT shuttle.

**Texas Memorial Museum** ★ ☺ 🖗     The two biggest attractions at this museum are both in the lobby. One is the skeleton of the largest flying creature on record—the Texas pterosaur. It's suspended from the ceiling and, with its 40-foot wingspan, looks very threatening (something similar to how a hawk must appear to a mouse). The other is a blue cut topaz almost the size of a fist. After you've seen those two objects, and since you're at the museum already, you might want to explore a little further. On the floor below the lobby is the main paleontology exhibit, with several more impressive skeletons. It's well designed for getting you to conceptualize the vastness of time. The great thing about this museum is that just about any staff person you run into will have a Ph.D. and can provide an intelligent answer to just about any question you have. The floor above the lobby is dedicated to Texas natural history, and has some dioramas and other exhibits. The fourth floor is an exhibition on evolution and biodiversity. It's well assembled and has several interactive displays, including a model of the HIV virus. In Texas, such an exhibit could be considered controversial, so it's interesting to read the comments left by visitors, which are collected in a binder. The gift shop has lots of science toys. Allow 1½ hours for a visit to the museum.

University of Texas, 2400 Trinity St. © **512/471-1604.** www.texasmemorialmuseum.org. Free admission (donations appreciated). Mon–Thurs 9am–5pm; Fri 9am–4:45pm; Sat 10am–4:45pm; Sun 1–4:45pm. Closed major holidays. Bus: UT shuttle.

## EAST SIDE

**French Legation Museum** ★     Occupying 2½ acres on a hilltop above downtown, this small museum with attractive grounds is a good place to pass the odd moment and explore Austin's French connection. The only difficulty is making sure the moment falls within the museum's limited hours. The main attraction is the original house dating from 1841, the oldest surviving house in Austin still standing in its original location. Its builder was Count Alphonse Dubois de Saligny, France's representative to the fledgling republic of Texas. He sold the house to the Robinson family in 1848, and it remained in their possession for close to 100 years. It represents a simple house of its era in both the construction methods and floor plan, which makes for interesting viewing. The house is furnished with antiques dating from the 1840s to 1870s. Some of the pieces actually belonged to Count Dubois and the Robinsons. At the rear of the house is a reconstructed kitchen of the era, the original having burned down. The tour takes 45 minutes and is quite enjoyable, as you'll probably have a guide all to yourself.

802 San Marcos St. © **512/472-8180.** www.frenchlegationmuseum.org. Admission $5 adults, $3 seniors, $2 students/teachers, free for children 5 and under. Tours Tues–Sun 1–4pm. Bus: 4 and 18 stop nearby (at San Marcos and Seventh sts.). Go east on Seventh St., then turn left on San Marcos St.

# Green Spaces

**Zilker Botanical Garden** ★ ☺ There's bound to be something blooming at the Zilker Botanical Garden from March to October, but no matter what time of year you visit, you'll find this a soothing outdoor oasis in which to spend some time. The Oriental Garden, created by the landscape architect Isamu Taniguchi when he was 70 years old, is particularly peaceful. Be sure to ask someone at the garden center to point out how Taniguchi landscaped the word "Austin" into a series of ponds in the design. A butterfly garden attracts gorgeous winged visitors during April and October migrations, and you can poke and prod the many plants in the herb garden to get them to yield their fragrances. Dinosaur tracks that are 100 million years old, discovered on the grounds in the early 1990s, are part of the 1.5-acre Hartman Prehistoric Garden, which includes plants from the Cretaceous Period and a 13-foot bronze sculpture of an ornithomimus dinosaur. Allow a half-hour to tour the Botanical Garden.

2220 Barton Springs Rd. ℂ **512/477-8672.** www.zilkergarden.org. Free admission. Grounds dawn-dusk. Garden center Mon–Fri 8:30am–4pm; Sat 10am–5pm (Jan–Feb 1–5pm); Sun 1–5pm (sometimes open earlier Sat–Sun for special garden shows; call ahead). Bus: 30.

**Zilker Park** ★ ☺ Comprising 347 acres, the first 40 of which were donated to the city by the wealthy German immigrant for whom the park is named, this is Austin's favorite public playground. Its centerpiece is Barton Springs Pool (see "The Top Attractions," earlier in this chapter), but visitors and locals also flock to the Zilker Botanical Garden, the Austin Nature and Science Center, and the Umlauf Sculpture Garden and Museum. See also the "Especially for Kids" and "Staying Active" sections for details about the Austin Nature and Science Center, the Zilker Zephyr Miniature Train, and Lady Bird Lake canoe rentals. In addition to its athletic fields (nine for soccer, one for rugby, and two multiuse), the park hosts a 9-hole disk (Frisbee) golf course and a sand volleyball court.

2201 Barton Springs Rd. ℂ **512/476-9044.** www.ci.austin.tx.us/zilker. Free admission. Daily 5am–10pm. Bus: 30.

## Especially for Kids

The **Bob Bullock Texas State History Museum** (p. 312) and the **Texas Memorial Museum** (p. 315), are child-friendly, but outdoor attractions are still Austin's biggest draw for children. There's lots of room for children to splash around at **Barton Springs,** and even youngsters who thought bats were creepy are likely to be converted on further acquaintance with the critters.

In addition, kids enjoy the **Austin Children's Museum** ★★, Dell Discovery Center, 201 Colorado St. (ℂ **512/472-2499;** www.austinkids.org), a rambling state-of-the-art facility with everything from low-key but creative playscapes for tots to studio soundstage replicas for teens. Bats, bees, and crystal caverns are among the subjects of the Discovery Boxes at the 80-acre **Austin Nature and Science Center** ★, Zilker Park, 301 Nature Center Dr. (ℂ **512/327-8181**), which also abounds with interactive exhibits involving rescued animals. The "Dino Pit" is a lure for budding paleontologists. The scenic 25-minute ride on the narrow-gauge **Zilker Zephyr Miniature Train,** 2100 Barton Springs Rd., just across from the Barton Springs Pool (ℂ **512/478-8286**), goes at a leisurely pace through Zilker Park along Barton Creek and Town Lake.

## Organized Tours

The aquatically inclined might consider taking one of the electric-powered **Capital Cruises** (ℂ **512/480-9264;** www.capitalcruises.com), which ply Town Lake from

March through October. Options include bat-viewing cruises, fajita dinner cruises, and afternoon sightseeing excursions. Similar itineraries are offered by **Lone Star River Boat** (© 512/327-1388), but they go farther upstream and add narration. Both companies depart from the dock near the Hyatt Regency Hotel. Can't decide between sea and land? Board one of the six-wheel-drive amphibious vehicles operated by **Austin Duck Adventures** (© 512/4-SPLASH [477-5274]; www.austin ducks.com). After exploring Austin's downtown and scenic west side, you'll splash into Lake Austin. Tours board in front of the Austin Convention and Visitors Bureau, 209 E. 6th St.

## Walking Tours

You won't find better guided walks than the informative and entertaining **tours** ★★ offered free of charge by the **Austin Convention and Visitors Bureau** (ACVB; © 866/GO-AUSTIN [462-8784] or 512/454-1545; www.austintexas.org) from March to November. The 90-minute tours of the historic Bremond Block leave every Saturday and Sunday at 11am; Congress Avenue/East Sixth Street is explored for 1½ hours on Thursday, Friday, and Saturday starting at 9am, and Sunday at 2pm. The hour-long capitol grounds tour is conducted on Saturday at 2pm and Sunday at 9am. All tours depart promptly from the south entrance of the capitol, weather permitting. Be warned, though: Arrive even a few minutes late and you'll miss out.

# STAYING ACTIVE
## Outdoor Fun

**BIKING**   Austin has various city bike routes for the benefit of local bike commuters and visitors who want to pedal around town. If you want to ride on trails, you have a choice of the mellow Hike and Bike Trail around Lady Bird Lake (10 miles), or the more challenging Barton Creek Greenbelt (7.8 miles). Contact **Austin Parks and Recreation,** 200 S. Lamar Blvd. (© 512/974-6700; www.ci.austin.tx.us/parks), for more information on these and other bike trails. There is also a paved **Veloway,** a 3.1-mile paved loop in Slaughter Creek Metropolitan Park, in far south Austin. It is devoted exclusively to bicyclists and in-line skaters.

You can rent bikes and get maps and other information from **University Cyclery,** 2901 N. Lamar Blvd. (© 512/474-6696; www.universitycyclery.com). A number of downtown hotels rent or provide free bicycles to their guests. For information on weekly road rides, contact the **Austin Cycling Association,** P.O. Box 5993, Austin, TX 78763 (© 512/282-7413; www.austincycling.org). For rougher mountain bike routes, try the **Austin Ridge Riders.** Their website will have the latest contact information (www.austinridgeriders.com).

**CANOEING**   You can rent canoes at **Zilker Park,** 2000 Barton Springs Rd. (© 512/478-3852; www.fastair.com/zilker), for $10 an hour or $40 per day (daily Apr–Sept; Sat–Sun and holidays, weather permitting, Oct–Mar). **Capital Cruises,** Hyatt Regency boat dock (© 512/480-9264; www.capitalcruises.com), also has hourly rentals on Town Lake.

**GOLF**   For information about Austin's five municipal golf courses and to set up tee times, log on to www.ci.austin.tx.us/parks/golf.htm. All but the 9-hole Hancock course offer pro shops and equipment rental, and their greens fees are reasonable. The **Hancock** course was built in 1899 and is the oldest course in Texas. The **Lions**

course is where Tom Kite and Ben Crenshaw played college golf for the University of Texas.

**HIKING**  Austin's parks and preserves abound in nature trails. Contact the **Sierra Club** (☎ **512/472-1767;** www.texas.sierraclub.org/austin) if you're interested in organized hikes. **Wild Basin Wilderness Preserve** (☎ **512/327-7622;** www.wildbasin.org) is another source for guided treks, hosting periodic "Haunted Trails" tours along with its more typical hikes.

**SWIMMING**  The best known of Austin's natural swimming holes is **Barton Springs Pool** (see "The Top Attractions," earlier in this chapter), but it's by no means the only one. Other scenic outdoor spots to take the plunge include **Deep Eddy Pool,** 401 Deep Eddy Ave. at Lake Austin Boulevard (☎ **512/472-8546**).

For lakeshore swimming, consider **Hippie Hollow** on Lake Travis, 2½ miles off FM 620 (www.co.travis.tx.us/tnr/parks/hippie_hollow.asp), where you can let it all hang out in a series of clothing-optional coves, or **Emma Long Metropolitan Park** on Lake Austin (☎ **512/346-1831** or 346-3807).

# Spectator Sports

College sports are very big, particularly when the **University of Texas (UT) Longhorns** are playing. The most comprehensive source of information on the various teams is www.texassports.com, but you can phone the **UT Athletics Ticket Office** (☎ **512/471-3333**) to find out about schedules and **UTTM Charge-A-Ticket** (☎ **512/477-6060**) to order tickets.

**BASEBALL**  The **University of Texas** baseball team goes to bat February through May at Disch-Falk Field (just east of I-35, at the corner of Martin Luther King, Jr., Blvd. and Comal). Many players from this school have gone on to the pros.

Baseball Hall of Famer Nolan Ryan's **Round Rock Express,** a Texas Rangers farm club, won the Texas League championship in 1999, their first year in existence (they now compete in the Pacific Coast League). See them play at the Dell Diamond, 3400 E. Palm Valley Rd., in Round Rock (☎ **512/255-BALL** [2255] or 244-4209; www.roundrockexpress.com), an 8,688-seat stadium where you can choose from box seats or stadium seating—and an additional 3,000 fans can sit on a grassy berm in the outfield. Tickets range from about $6 to $12.

**BASKETBALL**  The **University of Texas** Longhorn and Lady Longhorn basketball teams, both former Southwest Conference champions, play in the Frank C. Erwin, Jr., Special Events Center (just west of I-35 on Red River btw. Martin Luther King, Jr., Blvd. and 15th St.) November through March.

**FOOTBALL**  It's hard to tell which is more central to the success of an Austin Thanksgiving: the turkey or the UT–Texas A&M game. Part of the Big 12 Conference, the **University of Texas** football team often fills the huge Darrell K. Royal/Texas Memorial Stadium (just west of I-35 btw. 23rd and 21st sts., E. Campus Dr., and San Jacinto Blvd.) during home games, played August through November.

**FORMULA 1 RACING**  The Grand Prix circuit might again include the U.S., and if it does, the race will be held in Austin. It's not by any means a done deal, but the process has been moving forward at a brisk clip to get Formula 1 racing here by 2012. The track would be built south of Bergstrom Airport on a large parcel of undeveloped land. This would be the first track built in the U.S. specifically for Formula 1. Check www.formula1unitedstates.com for current information.

**GOLF**   Initiated in 2003 and boasting a $1.6-million purse, the **Triton Financial Classic** (☏ **512/732-2666**) is part of the PGA's Champions Tour, and is held at the Hills Country Club at Lakeway Resort in late April.

**HOCKEY**   The **Austin Ice Bats** hockey team (☏ **512/927-PUCK** [7825]; www. icebats.com) has been getting anything but an icy reception from its Austin fans. This typically rowdy team plays at the Travis County Exposition Center, 7311 Decker Lane (about 15 min. east of UT). Tickets, which run from $10 to $35, are available at any UTTM outlet or from **Star Tickets** (☏ **888/597-STAR** [7827] or 512/469-SHOW [469-7469]; www.startickets.com). The team generally plays on weekends mid-October through late March; a phone call will get you the exact dates and times.

**ROLLER DERBY**   Reincarnated in Austin in 2001, women's roller derby has become a popular pastime in Austin, and it also has spread to other cities. If you want to see some Austin quirkiness and celebrate low-brow culture in a tongue-in-cheek fashion, you can check out the **Lonestar Rollergirls** website (www.txrd.com) for upcoming action. Events are usually held every other Sunday at the Convention Center. There is also a flat-track league called the **Texas Rollergirls** (www.txroller girls.com). Their season lasts from March to August, with bouts taking place at the Playland Skate Center at 8822 McCann Blvd., close to the intersection of Hwy. 183 and Burnet Road.

# SHOPPING

## The Shopping Scene

Visitors to Austin don't really come for the shopping, but the opportunistic shopper can be rewarded with some wonderful discoveries. Folk art, arts and crafts, music, books—these are the areas where Austin excels. It's got the rest of the material world pretty well covered, too.

## Shopping Areas

In central Austin, the best concentration of shops and galleries is to be found along **East Sixth Street** near Congress Avenue, **West Sixth Street and Lamar Boulevard, West Second Street** near Congress Avenue, and **South Congress Avenue** (or "**SoCo**"). SoCo has gotten quite a bit fancier in the past few years. The funkier, less expensive shops moved on to lower-rent **South First Street** and **South Lamar Boulevard.** There is also a cluster of stores in the vicinity of the intersection of **North Lamar and 38th Street.** Many stores on the **Drag**—the stretch of Guadalupe Street between Martin Luther King, Jr., Boulevard and 26th Street, across from the University of Texas campus—are student-oriented, but a wide range of clothing, gifts, toys, and, of course, books can also be found here.

   If you're looking for a shopping center, the growth area seems to be in the northwest, where several upscale shopping centers vie for customers: the **Arboretum,** the **Arboretum Market,** the **Gateway Shopping Centers** (consisting of Gateway Courtyard, the Gateway Market, and Gateway Square), and the **Domain** have earned the area the nickname "South Dallas."

## The Goods A to Z

### ART

Austin's commitment to music makes it a perfect location for **Wild About Music,** 115 E. 6th St. (☏ **512/708-1700**; www.wildaboutmusic.com), a gallery and shop

# FIRST thursdays

As if there weren't already enough street theater in Austin, the merchants on South Congress Avenue decided a few years back to start hosting a monthly street festival. They began keeping their doors open late and providing food, drinks, and, entertainment on the first Thursday of every month. Soon, impromptu open-air markets sprang up, and jugglers, drum circles, and, of course, live bands performed indoors, outdoors, and in between.

First Thursdays have become quite popular for their mix of shopping, entertainment, people-watching, and the surprise factor—you never know what you're going to meet up with. It's also a way for locals to celebrate the approach of the weekend. The street festival occupies about 8 blocks along both sides of South Congress. Traffic along the avenue is not cordoned off, but everyone drives slowly because of the crowds crisscrossing the avenue. It starts around 6pm and runs until about 10pm. To find out more, check www.firstthursday.info.

strictly devoted to arts and crafts with a musical theme. **Women & Their Work,** 1710 Lavaca St. (℃ **512/477-1064;** www.womenandtheirwork.org), highlights more than visual art—it also promotes and showcases women in dance, music, theater, film, and literature. "Outsider" art, created in the rural South, usually by the poor and sometimes by the incarcerated, is the focus of **Yard Dog Folk Art,** 1510 S. Congress Ave. (℃ **512/912-1613;** www.yarddog.com). Folk art and crafts from Latin America and around the world can be found at several stores: **Tesoros Trading Company,** 1500 S. Congress Ave. (℃ **512/447-7500;** www.tesoros.com); **Eclectic,** 700 N. Lamar Blvd. (℃ **512/477-1816**); and **Ten Thousand Villages,** 1317 S. Congress Ave. (℃ **512/440-0440;** www.austin.tenthousandvillages.com).

## FOOD

To see the ultimate in supermarkets, visit **Central Market,** 4001 N. Lamar Blvd. (℃ **512/206-1000;** www.centralmarket.com), and the flagship store of **Whole Foods Markets** at 525 N. Lamar Blvd. (℃ **512/476-1206;** www.wholefoods.com).

In addition to hosting some of the nation's most lavish grocery stores, Austin also has an abundance of farmers' markets. Perhaps the most notable of them is **Austin Farmers' Market,** held downtown at Republic Square Park, Fourth Street at Guadalupe, every Saturday from 9am to 1pm March through November (℃ **512/236-0074;** www.austinfarmersmarket.com). It features not only food products, but also live music, cooking demonstrations, kids' activities, and workshops on everything from organic gardening to aromatherapy.

## MUSIC

Carrying a huge selection of sounds, **Waterloo Records and Video,** 600A N. Lamar Blvd. (℃ **512/474-2500;** www.waterloorecords.com), is always the first in town to get the new releases. The store has a popular preview listening section, offers compilation tapes of Austin groups, and sells tickets to all major-label shows around town.

## RUNNING GEAR

Owned by the footwear editor for *Runner's World* magazine and serving as the official wear-test center for that publication, **Run-Tex,** 422 W. Riverside Dr. (℃ **512/472-3254;** www.runtex.com), has a huge inventory of shoes and other running gear. It also does everything it can to promote healthful jogging practices, even offering free running classes and a free injury-evaluation clinic. The store is right near Austin's favorite jogging trail, which encircles Lady Bird Lake.

## TEXAS SOUVENIRS

The gift shop at the **Capitol Visitors Center,** 112 E. 11th St. (© **512/305-8400;** www.texascapitolvisitorscenter.com), sells all kinds of Texas memorabilia, including paperweights made from reproductions of the capitol's Texas seal, doorknobs, bookends, and local food products. There is also a variety of educational toys and an excellent selection of historical books.

## WESTERN WEAR

Name notwithstanding, **Allen's Boots,** 1522 S. Congress Ave. (© **512/447-1413**), sells a lot more than footwear. Come here too for hats, belts, jewelry, and other boot-scootin' accouterments (bring the kids, too). **Heritage Boots**, 1200 S. Congress Ave. (© **512/326-8577**), sells only boots, and these are beautifully made, all by hand, using the old ways of craftsmanship.

# AUSTIN AFTER DARK

Entertainment in Austin starts with live music. In fact, you might get your first taste of it before you even pick up your bags at the airport, where 11 concerts are held each week to serenade travelers. Live music is what this city is known for. A lot of musicians live here, and you can run into them anywhere. Austin's music scene is fluid; there's a lot of mixing of styles and genres, some well known, such as country and rock hybrids, others more incongruous, such as punk and bluegrass. It all makes the music scene here really rich and worth exploring. The level of virtuosity is impressive. Many famous musicians, such as the Dixie Chicks and Shawn Colvin, call Austin home and frequently perform here. But there is also a large number of lesser known but great performers, who for one reason or another are content to stay in Austin and enjoy a comfortable and modest level of success, which they supplement occasionally by going on tour, just to pay the bills.

Another aspect of the live music scene here is that it's inexpensive. Some really good bands play for tips on weekdays and for starving-artist pay at other times. This has been true for years, and it makes you feel that the city is getting a lot more from this arrangement than it puts out. That's not to say that Austin doesn't try to support its local musicians. Social groups organize benefit concerts, and the city and some companies offer lots of free concerts to promote the local talent.

Keep an eye out for performances by checking out the *Austin Chronicle* and *XLent,* the entertainment supplement of the *Austin-American Statesman.* Both are available in hundreds of outlets every Thursday.

For information about what's happening in the other performing arts, you should check out the website www.nowplayingaustin.com. This site is a joint project of the Austin Creative Alliance and the city. It has a comprehensive, well-organized calendar of events for all the performing arts, and includes museum shows as well. At this site, you can get information and buy tickets through its "Austix" link. If you would rather use the phone, call the **Austix Box Office** (© **512/474-8497**). Whether you buy online or by phone, the tickets can be picked up at the event, or at the Austix office, in the city's visitor center at 209 E. 6th St. Sometimes Austix offers discount tickets and sometimes half-priced, last-minute tickets. There is a small fee for using the service, which goes to support the performing arts.

9

# The Performing Arts

The **Long Center for the Performing Arts** (℗ 512/457-5500; www.thelong center.org) is Austin's venue for its symphony orchestra, opera, and ballet, and for visiting performance companies as well. The hall, set on the south shore of Lady Bird Lake, was designed to take advantage of its location. A raised terrace framed by a circular colonnade looks out over the lake, to the downtown skyline. The grand concert hall, named after Michael and Susan Dell, seats 2,400 people. There's also a studio theater for smaller size performances.

The University of Texas's **Performing Arts Center (PAC;** ℗ 512/471-2787; www.utpac.org) attracts major shows, including Broadway musicals, pop singers, and classical music ensembles. It has six theaters and the largest one, Bass Hall, has undergone major renovations. It also is the venue for performances by university theater and dance groups.

## OPERA & CLASSICAL MUSIC

A resident in Austin since 1911, the **Austin Symphony,** 1101 Red River St. ℗ 888/4-MAESTRO [462-3787] or 512/476-6064; www.austinsymphony.org), performs most of its classical works at Bass Concert Hall. The city's first professional opera company, **Austin Lyric Opera,** 901 Barton Springs Rd. (℗ 512/472-5992 for box office; www.austinlyricopera.org), presents three or four productions annually. The **Austin Chamber Music Center,** 4930 Burnet Rd., Ste. 203 (℗ 512/454-7562 or 454-0026; www.austinchambermusic.org), features an "Intimate Concert" series, held at private residences, and hosts visiting national and international artists.

## THEATER

Austin's oldest theater, incorporated in 1933, the **Zach Theatre** (℗ 512/476-0541 [box office] or 476-0594; www.zachscott.com) makes use of two adjacent venues at the edge of Zilker Park: the John E. Whisenhunt Arena at 1510 Toomey Rd., and the theater-in-the-round Kleburg at 1421 W. Riverside Dr.

## DANCE

The two dozen professional dancers of **Ballet Austin** (℗ 512/476-2163 [box office] or 476-9051; www.balletaustin.org) leap and bound in such classics as *The Nutcracker* and *Swan Lake,* as well as in the more avant-garde pieces of the trendsetting "Director's Choice" series. The latter pairs the work of various contemporary choreographers with the music of popular local Latin musicians and singer-songwriters. When in town, the troupe performs at the Long Center.

# The Club & Music Scene

Music was always important to life in Austin, but it became a big deal in the early '70s with the advent of progressive country (also known as redneck rock). Local boy Willie Nelson became its principal proponent, along with several other Austin musicians. The Armadillo World Headquarters, a music hall known for hosting all the '60s rock bands, became the center of events and symbolized the marriage of country with counterculture. The city has since become an incubator for a wonderfully vital, crossbred alternative sound that mixes rock, country, folk, blues, punk, and Tejano. Although the Armadillo is now gone, live music in Austin continues to thrive in bars all across central Austin.

While **Sixth Street** (btw. Congress Ave. and Red River St.) is well known to many outsiders and home to some good bars, just as popular but less famous is the

**Warehouse District** (just west of Congress Ave. btw. Second and Fifth sts.), with more glitz than grunge. For those wanting exposure to more of the local sound, there are cheap dives just off Sixth, on **Red River Street** (btw. Sixth and 10th sts.). There also are the many venues that don't fall inside these districts, like the Continental Club and the Saxon Pub. There's a lot to explore.

## FOLK & COUNTRY

**Broken Spoke** ★★, 3201 S. Lamar Blvd. (© **512/442-6189;** www.broken spokeaustintx.com), is one of the great country music dance halls. It dates back to 1964 when this level of South Lamar was the edge of town. People would come out here to two-step across the large wood-plank floor. It hasn't changed much, except for the occasional busload of tourists that stops by. This is Austin, so you don't have to be all duded up for dancing here. Granted, boot-scootin' is nice to do with real boots, but lots of people show up in sneakers and Hawaiian shirts. You can eat in a large, open room out front (the chicken-fried steak can't be beat), or take your longnecks back to a table overlooking the dance floor. Cover charges range from $5 to $15.

## JAZZ & BLUES

**Antone's,** 213 W. 5th St. (© **512/320-8424;** www.antones.net), has been synonymous with the blues. Stevie Ray Vaughan used to be a regular, and when major blues artists like Buddy Guy or Etta James venture down this way, you can be sure they'll be either playing Antone's or stopping by for a surprise set. The **Elephant Room,** 315 Congress Ave. (© **512/473-2279;** www.elephantroom.com), is an intimate space that's as dark and smoky as befitting a jazz den.

## ROCK

Austin's last word in alternative music, **Emo's,** 603 Red River St. (© **512/477-EMOS** [3667]; www.emosaustin.com), draws acts of all sizes and flavors, from Gang Green to Green Day. It primarily attracts college kids, but those of any age won't really feel out of place. Another good representative of the hot new music scene along Red River north of Sixth Street, the **Red-Eyed Fly,** 715 Red River St. (© **512/474-1084;** www.redeyedfly.com), showcases Texas's top hard-rock, pop, and punk bands—as well as national touring acts—at its great outdoor stage. Inside, the jukebox rocks with local sounds.

## SINGER/SONGWRITER

A small, dark cavern with great acoustics and a fully stocked bar, the **Cactus Cafe,** Texas Union, University of Texas campus (24th and Guadalupe; © **512/475-6515;** www.utexas.edu/student/txunion/ae/cactus), is singer/songwriter heaven. The attentive listening vibes attract the likes of Alison Krauss and Suzanne Vega, along with well-known acoustic combos.

## ECLECTIC

A terrific sound system and a casual country atmosphere have helped make **the Backyard,** Tex. 71 W. at R.R. 620, Bee Cave (© **512/263-4146**), one of Austin's hottest venues. Since it opened in the early 1990s, the Allman Brothers, Elvis Costello, Norah Jones, k.d. lang, and Bonnie Raitt have all played the terraced outdoor amphitheater. An Austin classic, **La Zona Rosa,** 612 W. 4th St. (© **512/263-4146;** www.lazonarosa.com), has departed from its funky roots a bit to feature bigger names and bigger cover charges than in the past. But this renovated garage filled with kitschy memorabilia is still a prime spot to listen to good bands. Within the rough limestone walls of **Stubb's,** 801 Red River St. (℃ **512/480-8341;** www.stubbs austin.com), you'll find great barbecue, three friendly bars, and terrific music ranging from singer/songwriter solos to hip-hop open mics to all-out country jams. Out back, the Waller Amphitheatre hosts some of the bigger acts. The Sunday gospel brunches are fast becoming an Austin institution. The **Saxon Pub,** at 1320 S. Lamar Blvd. (℃ **512/448-2552;** www.thesaxonpub.com), is a longtime local favorite. The crowd is older and more laid-back, and the volume is lower than at most of the Sixth Street bars. Check the calendar on the club's website, and you'll find performers who rarely play in such a small venue.

## The Bar Scene

### A HISTORIC BAR

Since 1866, when Councilman August Scholz first opened his tavern near the state capitol, every Texas governor has visited **Scholz Garten,** 1607 San Jacinto Blvd. (℃ **512/474-1958;** www.scholzgarten.net), at least once (and many quite a few more times). An extensive menu combines barbecue favorites with traditional bratwurst and sauerkraut; a state-of-the-art sound system cranks out polka tunes; and patio tables and a few strategically placed TV sets help Longhorn fans cheer on their team. All in all, it's a great place to drink in some Austin history.

### GAY & LESBIAN SCENE

Its name notwithstanding, **Oilcan Harry's,** 211 W. 4th St. (℃ **512/320-8823;** www.oilcanharrys.com), attracts a clean-cut, upscale Warehouse District crowd, while the **Rainbow Cattle Co.,** 305 W. 5th St. (℃ **512/472-5288;** www.rainbow cattleco.com), is Austin's prime gay country-and-western dance hall. It's about 75% male, but also attracts a fair share of lesbian two-steppers, especially on Thursday, which is Ladies Night.

### LOCAL FAVORITES

The **Cedar Door,** 201 Brazos St. (℃ **512/473-3712;** www.cedardooraustin.com), remains Austin's favorite neighborhood bar, drawing a group of potluck regulars ranging from hippies to journalists and politicos.

# HILL COUNTRY SIDE TRIPS FROM AUSTIN

The following destinations in Texas's Hill Country, one of the state's prettiest regions, can be visited on day trips from Austin, but you really should stay overnight in the area. Trips to the locations detailed here can easily be combined with those described in the "Hill Country Side Trips from San Antonio" section, in chapter 8. To locate these towns, see the "South-Central Texas" map on p. 233.

## Fredericksburg ★

Fredericksburg is a town of 10,000 inhabitants located just about 75 miles from either San Antonio or Austin. (All the towns mentioned until now are closer to San Antonio.) Fredericksburg is a town noted for its picturesque main street—old-time storefronts with sidewalk canopies, in the tradition of small-town Texas. It's also known for its German heritage, as it once was the center of a large German farming community. These days, the farmers are known for the peaches they grow (available at orchards and roadside stands May–July), and more recently their vineyards. Fredericksburg is the hub of the Hill Country wineries.

The town serves as a weekend escape for city dwellers in San Antonio and Austin. It has lots of bed-and-breakfasts and guesthouses, as well as hotels and motels. Many visitors come for the shopping and to relax, and perhaps taste some wine. Others come to explore the surrounding countryside, including nearby Enchanted Rock, the Hill Country's most famous geological feature.

## SEEING THE SIGHTS

The **Visitor Information Center,** 302 E. Austin St., Fredericksburg, TX 78624 (© 888/997-3600 or 830/997-6523), can direct you to the many points of interest in the town's historic district. These include a number of little **Sunday Houses,** built by German settlers in distant rural areas because they needed a place to stay overnight when they came to town to trade or attend church.

On the town's main square, called Market Square, is an unusual octagonal **Vereins Kirche (Society Church).** It's actually a replica (built in 1935) of the original 1847 building. The original was the first public building in Fredericksburg. It was built to be a church where both Lutheran and Catholic Germans could hold services and, as such, was a symbol of unity for the early pioneers. Inside is a history exhibit of the town, which can be viewed in a half-hour. It's open 10am to 4pm Monday to Saturday, and 1 to 4pm Sunday. The Vereins Kirche is operated by the Historical Society, which also maintains the **Pioneer Museum Complex,** 309 W. Main St. Admission to either museum is valid for the other. The cost is $5 for adults, $3 for students ages 6 to 17, and free for children 5 and under. The Pioneer Museum consists of the 1849 Kammlah House (which was a family residence and general store until the 1920s), as well as the barn and the smokehouse. Later, other historical structures were moved onto the site. These include a one-room schoolhouse and a blacksmith's forge. The complex is open Monday to Saturday 10am to 5pm, and Sunday 1 to 5pm. For information on both places and on the other historical structures in town, call © 830/997-2835 or log on to www.pioneermuseum.com.

The 1852 Steamboat Hotel, originally owned by the grandfather of World War II naval hero Chester A. Nimitz, is now part of the **National Museum of the Pacific War ★★**, 311 E. Austin St. (© 830/997-4379; www.nimitz-museum.org), a 9-acre Texas State Historical Park and the world's only museum focusing solely on the Pacific theater. It just keeps expanding and getting better. In addition to the exhibits in the steamboat-shaped hotel devoted to Nimitz and his comrades, there is also the Japanese Garden of Peace, a gift from the people of Japan; the Memorial Wall—the equivalent of the Vietnam War Memorial in Washington, D.C., for Pacific War veterans; the life-size Pacific Combat Zone (2½ blocks east of the museum), which replicates a World War II battle scene; and the George Bush Gallery, where you can see a captured Japanese midget submarine and a multimedia simulation of a bombing raid on Guadalcanal. Indoor exhibits are open daily from 9am to 5pm. Admission is $7 adults; $6 seniors, military, and veterans; $4 students; and free for children 5 and under.

### Nearby

North of town is **Enchanted Rock State Natural Area ★★** (© 325/247-3903; www.tpwd.state.tx.us/park/enchantd), a 640-acre site with a dome of solid-pink granite that was pushed up to the surface by volcanic uplifting. Take FM 965 north for 18 miles. You'll know when you get there. It's a stark sight that shares nothing in

## Luckenbach: Where Everybody's Somebody

Originally founded as a trading post by German immigrant Jacob Luckenbach in 1849, Luckenbach almost faded away until the late John Russell "Hondo" Crouch entered the picture. A political commentator, swimmer, writer, goat farmer, and humorist, Crouch bought the entire town in 1971, primarily so he would have a place to drink beer.

Declaring himself mayor, Crouch set to work establishing as many wacky traditions as possible, including women-only chili cook-offs and no-talent contests. The outdoor stage emerged as a favorite venue of Willie Nelson, Jerry Jeff Walker, Waylon Jennings, and other legends, and the catchphrase, "Everybody's Somebody in Luckenbach," caught on and became the subject of bumper stickers and T-shirts.

Centered on the old general store to this day, Luckenbach remains one of the best places to catch live music in all of Texas (there are shows 7 days a week; tickets are often free, but can run up to about $20). Souvenirs, food, and ice-cold beer are available. Hondo passed away soon after pushing for the Non-Buy Centennial as his personal protest against the commercialization of the bicentennial of the Declaration of the Independence in 1976. His memorial is on-site.

Luckenbach (© 888/311-8990 or 830/997-3224; www.luckenbachtexas.com) is located about 10 miles southeast of Fredericksburg.

common with the surrounding hills. The dome is almost 600 feet high. To hike up and down on the trail takes about an hour. Though the park is fairly large, the parking lot is not, and as soon as it fills, no more visitors are admitted. On weekends, if you get there by 10am, you shouldn't have a problem. The park is open daily 8am to 10pm; day-use entrance fees are $6 adults and free for children 12 and under.

## WHERE TO STAY

Fredericksburg is well known for having more than 300 bed-and-breakfasts and *Gästehauses* (guest cottages). Guesthouses are more private than the typical B&B. Either breakfast is provided the night before—the perishables are left in a refrigerator—or guests are given coupons to enjoy breakfast at a local restaurant. *Gästehauses* run anywhere from $120 to $200. Most visitors reserve lodgings through one of the main booking services: **First Class Bed & Breakfast Reservation Service,** 909 E. Main St. (© 888/991-6749 or 830/997-0443; www.fredericksburg-lodging.com); **Gästehaus Schmidt,** 231 W. Main St. (© 866/427-8374 or 830/997-5612; www.fbglodging.com); and **Main Street B&B Reservation Service,** 337 E. Main St. (© 888/559-8555 or 830/997-0153; www.travelmainstreet.com). Specializing in the more familiar type of B&B is **Fredericksburg Traditional Bed & Breakfast Inns** (© 800/494-4678; www.fredericksburgtrad.com). For something less traditional, consider the **Roadrunner Inn** (© 830/997-1844; www.theroadrunnerinn.com), a modern B&B above a boutique at 306 E. Main St. It has very large, uncluttered rooms furnished with a mix of modern, vintage, and industrial elements. Rates range from $130 to $190 double.

If you would rather stay in a hotel, the **Hangar Hotel,** 155 Airport Rd., Fredericksburg, TX 78624 (© 830/997-9990; www.hangarhotel.com), has large, comfortable rooms. It banks on nostalgia for the World War II flyboy era. Located, as the name suggests, at the town's tiny private airport, this hotel hearkens back to the

1940s with its clean-lined, art moderne–style rooms, as well as an officer's club (democratically open to all) and retro diner. The re-creation isn't taken too far: Rooms have all the modern conveniences. Rates—which include one $5 "food ration," good at the diner, per night—run from $120 to $170 double. For bargain rates, the old **Frederick Motel** (© **800/996-6050;** www.frederick-motel.com), at 1308 E. Main St., has rates from $40 to $100 double, which includes a full breakfast on weekends.

## WHERE TO DINE

Fredericksburg's dining scene is diverse, catering to the traditional and the trendy alike. For breakfast or lunch, a jewel of a place is **Rather Sweet Bakery & Cafe,** 249 E. Main St. (© **830/990-0498**). Rebecca Rather, the owner, is a noted cookbook author, who makes everything from scratch using the freshest ingredients, including homegrown herbs and vegetables. The bakery is open Monday through Saturday until 5pm, but the cafe stops serving lunch at 2pm. For breakfast takeout, you should try **Hilda's Tortilla Factory** (© **830/997-6105**) at 149 Tivydale Rd. (at S. Adams St.). This place serves good tacos on freshly made flour tortillas. "El Especial" has poblano, eggs, beans, bacon, and tomatoes. Be sure to ask for a couple of packs of green sauce. Often there's a line stretching out the door, but it moves quickly. If you've come to Fredericksburg for German food, you can try **Altdorf Biergarten,** 301 W. Main St. (© **830/997-7865**), open Wednesday to Monday for lunch and dinner, Sunday for brunch.

If you don't mind driving 10 miles, a great place to go for dinner (or for lunch on the weekend) is the **Hill Top Cafe** (© **830/997-8922;** www.hilltopcafe.com), on Hwy. 87 to Mason. This was an old country gas station that was converted into a restaurant by John and Brenda Nichols. John used to be a member of a legendary Austin band called Asleep at the Wheel. He usually plays music on Friday and Saturday evenings. Brenda runs the kitchen, and the food is well prepared—American with a smattering of Greek and Cajun dishes. Reservations are highly recommended.

## Lyndon B. Johnson Country

Just 50 miles west of Austin is Johnson City, where the forebears of the 36th president settled almost 150 years ago. A visit to LBJ's boyhood home (in Johnson City) and the sprawling ranch that became known as the Texas White House (14 miles farther west, near Stonewall), and other attractions can take a whole day. Even if you're not usually drawn to the past, you're likely to be intrigued by the depictions of LBJ and his origins at these sites.

From Austin, take U.S. 290 to **Johnson City,** a pleasant agricultural town named for founder James Polk Johnson, LBJ's first cousin once removed. The modest white clapboard **LBJ Boyhood Home ★**, where Lyndon was raised after age 5, is the centerpiece of this unit of the national historical park. Before exploring, stop at the **visitor center** (© **830/868-7128**)—take F Street to Lady Bird Lane and you'll see the signs—to see an educational film and to get details about touring the Boyhood Home. The Boyhood Home and visitor center are open from 8:45am to 5pm daily; admission is free.

From Johnson City, take U.S. 290 W. for 13 miles to the entrance of the **Lyndon B. Johnson State and National Historical Parks at LBJ Ranch ★**, near Stonewall, jointly operated by the Texas Parks and Wildlife Department (© **830/644-2252;** www.tpwd.state.tx.us/park/lbj) and the National Park Service (© **830/868-7128;** www.nps.gov/lyjo). To visit the ranch, you need to stop at the park and get a permit. The ranch, which is just the other side of the Pedernales River, was used by LBJ as a second White House, and Lady Bird lived here until she died in 2008. After her death, the park service began giving tours of the 7,500-square-foot ranch house. The tour of the house is the only thing that costs money ($2). So far, five rooms can be viewed, but there are plans to include more rooms once they are ready (which means refurnishing them to look as they did around 1965). With more of the house opened up for the tour, expect the entry fee to rise a little. The tour really brings home what a colorful character LBJ was and how different the 1960s were from present times.

## WHERE TO EAT & STAY

Johnson City doesn't have a lot of good food. The surest bet is **Ronnie's Ice House Barbecue,** 211 Hwy. 281, just south of U.S. 290 (© **830/868-7553**)—but he usually runs out of food by 1pm. Your next best bet is the **Silver K Café** (© **830/868-2911**), at the corner of Main and F streets. For lunch, they serve soups, salads, and sandwiches, and for dinner, there's a full menu. Prices range from moderate to expensive. If you prefer to get takeout, visit **Whittington's,** 602 Hwy. 281 S. (© **877/868-5501**), known for its beef and turkey jerky.

The area's top place to dine—and to bed down—is about 16 miles to the west. You'll drive down a rural back road to reach **Rose Hill Manor,** 2614 Upper Albert Rd., Stonewall, TX 78671 (© **877/ROSEHIL** [767-3445] or 830/644-2247; www.rose-hill.com), a reconstructed Southern manse. Light and airy accommodations—four in the main house, six in separate cottages, and two in a carriage house—are beautifully and comfortably furnished with antiques. All have porches or patios and great Hill Country views. Rates run from $155 to $250 double, including a full breakfast. The inn's New American cuisine, served Wednesday through Sunday evenings in an ultra-romantic dining room, is outstanding. Reservations are essential.

# New Braunfels & Gruene

New Braunfels sits at the junction of the Comal and Guadalupe rivers. German settlers were brought here in 1845 by Prince Carl of Solms-Braunfels, the commissioner general of the Society for the Protection of German Immigrants in Texas, the same group that later founded Fredericksburg. Although Prince Carl returned to Germany within a year to marry his fiancée, who refused to join him in the wilderness, his colony prospered. By the 1850s, New Braunfels was the fourth-largest city in Texas after Houston, San Antonio, and Galveston. Although you have to look a little to find its quainter side today, this is a good place to enjoy a bit of Germanic history—and a lot of watersports.

## EXPLORING NEW BRAUNFELS

At the **New Braunfels Chamber of Commerce,** 390 S. Seguin St., New Braunfels, TX 78130 (© **800/572-2626** or 830/625-2385; www.nbjumpin.com), you can pick up a pamphlet detailing the 40-point **historic walking tour** of midtown. Highlights include the Romanesque-Gothic Comal County Courthouse (1898) on Main Plaza; the nearby Jacob Schmidt Building, 193 W. San Antonio St., built on the site where William Gebhardt, of canned chili fame, perfected his formula for chili powder in 1896; and the 1928 Faust Hotel, 240 S. Seguin St., believed by some to be haunted by its owner.

Several small museums are interesting. In the 11-acre **Heritage Village** complex, 1370 Church Hill Dr. (© **830/629-6504;** www.nbheritagevillage.com), the **Museum**

**of Texas Handmade Furniture** ★, sheds light on local domestic life of the 19th century with its beautiful examples of Texas Biedermeier by master craftsmen. The pieces are displayed at the gracious 1858 Breustedt-Dillen Haus. The complex also includes an 1848 log cabin and a barn with a replica of a cabinetmaker's workshop.

## HISTORIC GRUENE

Get a more concentrated glimpse of the past at Gruene (pronounced "Green"), 4 miles northwest of downtown New Braunfels. First settled by German farmers in the 1840s, Gruene was virtually abandoned during the Depression in the 1930s. It remained a ghost town until the mid-1970s, when two investors realized the value of its intact historic buildings and sold them to businesses rather than raze them. These days, tiny Gruene is crowded with day-trippers browsing specialty shops in the wonderfully restored structures, which include a smoked-meat shop, lots of cutesy gift boutiques, and several antiques shops.

The **New Braunfels Museum of Art & Music** ★, 1259 Gruene Rd., on the river behind Gruene Mansion (℃ **800/456-4866** or 830/625-5636), focuses on popular arts in the West and South (as opposed to, say, high culture and the classics). Subjects of recent exhibits, which change quarterly and combine music and art components, have included Texas accordion music, central Texas dance halls, and cowboy art and poetry. Live music throughout the year includes an open mic on Sunday afternoons, and the recording of *New Braunfels Live* radio show of roots music on Thursday evenings. A brochure detailing the town's retailers, restaurants, and accommodations is available from the New Braunfels Chamber of Commerce (see above) or at local shops.

## WATERSPORTS

Gruene also figures among the New Braunfels area's impressive array of places to get wet, most of them open only in summer. Outfitters who can help you ride the Guadalupe River rapids on a raft, tube, canoe, or inflatable kayak include **Rockin' R River Rides** (℃ **800/553-5628** or 830/629-9999; www.rockinr.com) and **Gruene River Company** (℃ **888/705-2800** or 830/625-2800; www.toobing.com), both on Gruene Road just south of the Gruene Bridge. You can go tubing too, at **Schlitterbahn** ★, Texas's largest water park and one of the best in the country, at 305 W. Austin St. in New Braunfels (℃ **830/625-2351;** www.schlitterbahn.com). Those who like their water play a bit more low key might try downtown New Braunfels's **Landa Park** (℃ **830/608-2160**), where you can either swim in the largest spring-fed pool in Texas or calmly float in an inner tube down the Comal River.

## WHERE TO STAY IN NEW BRAUNFELS & GRUENE

The **Prince Solms Inn,** 295 E. San Antonio St., New Braunfels, TX 78130 (℃ **800/ 625-9169** or 830/625-9169; www.princesolmsinn.com), was built to be a small hotel. It has been in continuous operation since 1898. A prime downtown location, tree-shaded courtyard, and florid, High Victorian–style sleeping quarters have put this charming bed-and-breakfast in great demand. Three Western-themed rooms in a converted 1860 feed store next door work for families, and there's an ultra-romantic separate cabin in the back of the main house. Rates range from $125 to $195 double.

The **Faust Hotel,** 240 S. Seguin St. (℃ **830/625-7791;** www.fausthotel.com), has standard from $69 to $99 double. Rates go up when there's a festival in town. This is, in many ways, a classic old hotel with an ornate lobby and welcoming brewpub.

For a bed-and-breakfast experience, consider the **Gruene Mansion Inn,** 1275 Gruene Rd., New Braunfels, TX 78130 (© **830/629-2641;** www.gruene mansioninn.com). The barns that once belonged to the opulent 1875 plantation house were converted to rustic yet elegant cottages with decks; some also have cozy lofts (if you don't like stairs, request a single-level room). Accommodations cost from $170 to $240 double per night, including breakfast served in the plantation house. Two separate lodges, suitable for families, are available, too ($260–$340).

If you're planning to come to town during the Wurstfest sausage festival (late Oct to early Nov), be sure to book well in advance, no matter where you stay—that's high season here.

## WHERE TO DINE IN NEW BRAUNFELS & GRUENE

For my money, the **Huisache Grill,** 303 W. San Antonio St. (© **830/620-9001;** www.huisache.com), has the best food in town. The American menu has classic and original dishes. The pecan-crusted pork chop, the mixed grill, and the blue-cheese steak are among my favorites. Lunch and dinner are served daily; prices are moderate to expensive. The restaurant is divided into several different dining areas, each with its own character. To find it, take West San Antonio from the courthouse and take the first driveway to the left after you cross the tracks. The **New Braunfels Smokehouse,** 140 Hwy. 46 S., at I-35 (© **830/625-2416;** www.nbsmokehouse.com), opened in 1951 as a tasting room for the meats it started hickory-smoking in 1943. Savor the meat in platters or on sandwiches, or have it shipped home as a savory souvenir.

In Gruene, the **Gristmill River Restaurant & Bar,** 1287 Gruene Rd. (© **830/ 625-0684;** www.gristmillrestaurant.com), a converted 100-year-old cotton gin, includes burgers and chicken-fried steak as well as healthful salads on its Texas-casual menu. Kick back on one of its multiple decks and gaze out at the Guadalupe River.

## NEW BRAUNFELS & GRUENE AFTER DARK

Lyle Lovett and Garth Brooks are just a few of the big names who have played **Gruene Hall ★★,** Gruene Road, at the corner of Hunter Road (© **830/629-7077;** www.gruenehall.com), the oldest country-and-western dance hall in Texas and still one of the state's most outstanding spots for live music.

# WEST TEXAS

by Eric Peterson

This is the real Texas: vast open spaces; longhorn cattle; pickup trucks lined up in front of roadside honky-tonks; and deeply tanned cowboys with sweat-stained hats, slim-cut jeans, and muddy boots. While most of Texas has become quite metropolitan—the vast majority of the state's residents live in cities—the plains of West Texas retain much of the Old West flavor. Communities here are generally small and far apart, residents seldom lock their doors, and even the region's biggest city, El Paso, feels like an overgrown small town. For those willing to take the time and effort, this area is filled with gems: a wide range of people, attractions, and activities amid a landscape that's alternately bleak and beautiful, and sometimes both.

The region's history and culture come alive at numerous museums and historic sites, such as Spanish missions from the 17th and 18th centuries, several restored frontier forts, and the combination courtroom and saloon used in the late 1800s by Judge Roy Bean, the self-styled "Law West of the Pecos." West Texas also offers some surprises, including one of America's most beautiful caves; the state's oldest winery; a replica of William Shakespeare's famed Globe Theatre; an avant-garde installation art complex in the much-hyped town of Marfa; and numerous lakes, including 67,000-acre Lake Amistad, a national recreation area along the U.S.-Mexico border, which is a joint project of both countries.

## EL PASO

43 miles SE of Las Cruces, New Mexico; 564 miles NW of San Antonio; 617 miles W of Dallas

Here, in the sun-swept, mountainous desert of Texas's westernmost corner, is El Paso, the state's sixth-largest city. Built between two mountain ranges on the shores of the Rio Grande, the city is an urban history book, with chapters dedicated to Spanish conquistadors, ancient highways, gunfighters, border disputes, and modern sprawl.

El Paso's rich history is a result of its geography. The Franklin Mountains, which now border the downtown area and occupy the city's heart, offered natural defense for the American Indians who inhabited the area for more than 10 millenniums; the Rio Grande offered water. The mountains slope into a vast canyon, so the Spanish explorers who first crossed the Rio Grande in the 16th century saw it as an ideal north-south route, one that soon became known as the "Camino Real" (or "King's Highway") and served as a principal trade route for nearly 300 years.

With the 17th century came an influx of Catholic missionaries, a group that established numerous missions that survive today. But Spain saw its grip weaken, and a Mexican flag flew over El Paso when independence was established in 1821. This era was short-lived, as Mexico ceded the land north of the Rio Grande to the United States following the Mexican-American War (1846–48). After the railroad arrived in 1881, El Paso became a commercial center and also earned the nickname "Sin City," thanks to the saloons, brothels, and casinos that lined every major street. Many notorious gunfighters—including Billy the Kid and John Wesley Hardin—called the city home.

El Paso boomed in the early–20th century and again following World War II, entrenching itself as a center for agriculture, manufacturing, and international trade, as well as the military: On the east side of town, Fort Bliss is one of the U.S. Army's largest bases, now poised for more growth. El Paso's relationship with Ciudad Juárez has been symbiotic for centuries, even more so since the resolution of a century-old border dispute in the 1960s and the signing of the North American Free Trade Agreement in 1994. Unfortunately, increased border security and a wave of drug-related violence in Juárez have put a damper on the sister cities' relationship in recent years.

Nevertheless, in comparison with the relative wealth and glitz of Santa Fe or Tucson, El Paso is in many ways the authentic Southwest—unpolished, undiluted, and honest. Separated by a swath of the Rio Grande, El Paso and Ciudad Juárez each represent their country's largest border city, and the local culture, a fusion of Mexican and American traditions, is distinct and unique in comparison to the way of life in eastern Texas. A day or two of exploration is worthwhile; take the time to wander downtown, enjoy a meal at one of the city's terrific Mexican restaurants, and gain a better understanding of what a border town is all about.

## Essentials

### GETTING THERE

**BY PLANE** More than 125 commercial flights arrive and depart daily from **El Paso International Airport (ELP),** located a mile north of I-10 via Airway Boulevard on the city's east side (© **915/780-4749;** www.elpasointernationalairport.com). **American, US Airways, Delta, Continental,** and **United** all serve El Paso.

The major car-rental agencies are represented here; see "Getting Around," below. **Juárez El Paso Shuttle Service** (© **915/740-4400;** www.juarezelpasoshuttle. info) offers shuttle service to and from the airport (a 15-min. trip each way); a one-way trip downtown costs about $25.

**BY CAR** The main artery to the east and west is I-10, bisecting El Paso between downtown and the Franklin Mountains.

From Carlsbad Caverns (160 miles from El Paso) and Guadalupe Mountains National Parks to the east (about 130 miles), visitors arrive via U.S. 62/180 (Montana Ave.), which eventually skirts the north side of downtown El Paso. For those arriving from Alamogordo, New Mexico (80 miles to the north), U.S. 54 (also known as the Patriot Fwy.) runs through El Paso's east side to the Bridge of the Americas, which crosses the Rio Grande and connects El Paso with Ciudad Juárez, Mexico.

*Note:* Expect to be asked your citizenship when leaving the city at checkpoints on major highways.

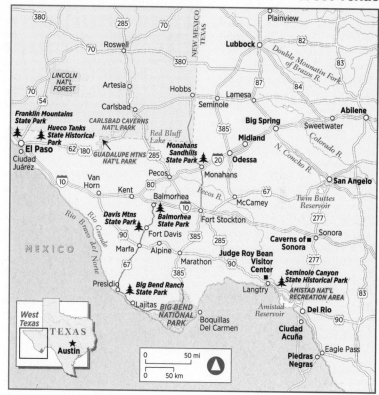

**BY BUS** Interstate and intrastate bus service is provided by **Greyhound,** 200 W. San Antonio Dr. (✆ **915/532-2365;** www.greyhound.com).

**BY TRAIN** Amtrak (✆ **800/872-7245;** www.amtrak.com) offers westward rail service on Tuesday, Thursday, and Saturday and eastward rail service on Monday, Thursday, and Saturday. Trains go east to Chicago (via San Antonio) and west to Los Angeles; other major cities on the routes include Houston and Tucson. The depot is located downtown at 700 W. San Francisco St.

## GETTING AROUND

Two natural features—the Rio Grande and the Franklin Mountains—have guided the urban development of El Paso for more than 400 years, so getting around can be a bit tricky for the newcomer. The city is essentially U-shaped, with the Franklin Mountains occupying the center and the downtown area at the bottom.

While El Paso has a public bus system, cars are the norm. Parking is rarely an issue, even downtown.

**BY CAR** There are numerous car-rental agencies in El Paso, clustered primarily around the airport in the east and North Mesa Street on the city's west side, including

# El Paso

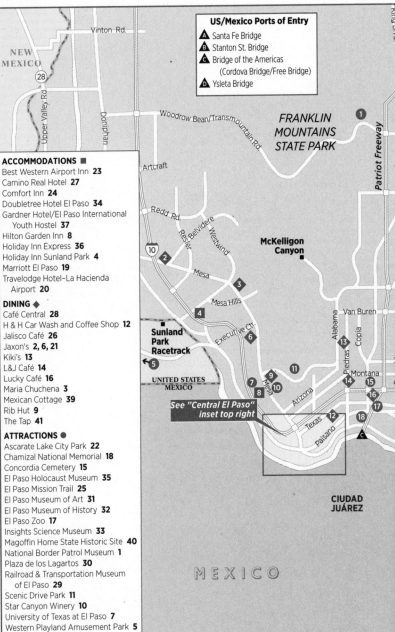

**US/Mexico Ports of Entry**

- **A** Santa Fe Bridge
- **B** Stanton St. Bridge
- **C** Bridge of the Americas
  (Cordova Bridge/Free Bridge)
- **D** Ysleta Bridge

**ACCOMMODATIONS** ■

Best Western Airport Inn **23**
Camino Real Hotel **27**
Comfort Inn **24**
Doubletree Hotel El Paso **34**
Gardner Hotel/El Paso International
  Youth Hostel **37**
Hilton Garden Inn **8**
Holiday Inn Express **36**
Holiday Inn Sunland Park **4**
Marriott El Paso **19**
Travelodge Hotel–La Hacienda
  Airport **20**

**DINING** ◆

Café Central **28**
H & H Car Wash and Coffee Shop **12**
Jalisco Café **26**
Jaxon's **2, 6, 21**
Kiki's **13**
L&J Café **14**
Lucky Café **16**
Maria Chuchena **3**
Mexican Cottage **39**
Rib Hut **9**
The Tap **41**

**ATTRACTIONS** ●

Ascarate Lake City Park **22**
Chamizal National Memorial **18**
Concordia Cemetery **15**
El Paso Holocaust Museum **35**
El Paso Mission Trail **25**
El Paso Museum of Art **31**
El Paso Museum of History **32**
El Paso Zoo **17**
Insights Science Museum **33**
Magoffin Home State Historic Site **40**
National Border Patrol Museum **1**
Plaza de los Lagartos **30**
Railroad & Transportation Museum
  of El Paso **29**
Scenic Drive Park **11**
Star Canyon Winery **10**
University of Texas at El Paso **7**
Western Playland Amusement Park **5**

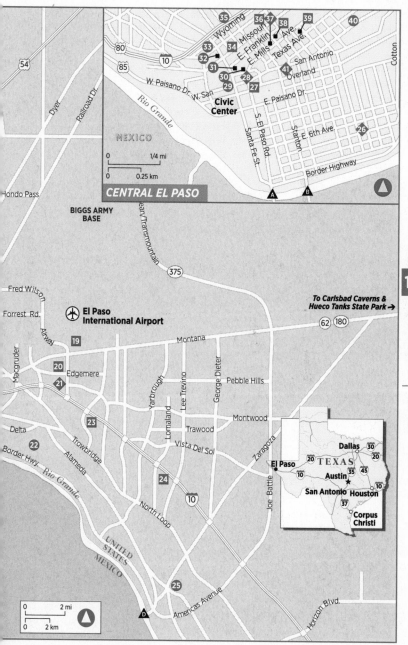

CENTRAL EL PASO

Avis (© 915/779-2700), **Enterprise** (© 915/779-2260), **Hertz** (© 915/772-4255), and **Dollar** (© 915/778-5445). The **American Automobile Association (AAA)** maintains an office in El Paso at 655 Sunland Park Dr. (© **800/765-0766** or 915/778-9521; www.aaa.com), open Monday through Friday from 9am to 6pm and Saturday from 9am to 1pm.

Street parking is free almost everywhere in El Paso except downtown, where the meters must be fed 25¢ per half-hour. The covered garages downtown typically charge $5 to $10 per day.

**BY BUS** El Paso's bus system, **Sun Metro** (© 915/533-3333; www.elpasotexas.gov/sunmetro), operates one of the world's largest fleets of natural gas–powered buses. The main transfer station is downtown on Franklin Street between Mesa and Santa Fe streets. There are also trolleys that run between the University of Texas at El Paso (UTEP) campus and downtown. Buses run from about 5am to 9pm on weekdays, with shorter hours on weekends and holidays; the fare is $1.50 for adults; $1 for children, students, and those with disabilities; and 30¢ for seniors. Day passes are $3.50.

**BY TAXI** **United Independent** (© 915/590-8294), **Border Cab** (© 915/533-4245), and **Sun City Cab** (© 915/544-2211) offer 24-hour service in El Paso and the surrounding area.

**BY FOOT** Downtown El Paso is well suited for a walking tour, and pedestrians can use the Santa Fe Bridge into Ciudad Juárez. *Note:* Be sure to carry your passport with you if you cross the border. While photo ID has been traditionally sufficient for reentry into the United States, all land crossings into Mexico now require a passport upon your return into the United States.

## VISITOR INFORMATION

The **El Paso Convention & Visitors Bureau** is located at One Civic Center Plaza, next to the El Paso Convention and Performing Arts Center (© **800/351-6024** or 915/534-0601; www.visitelpaso.com), and also operates an information center at the airport. *El Paso: The Official Visitor's Guide* is a good publication to request before your trip.

There is also a **Texas Travel Information Center,** with an excellent selection of brochures, maps, and other visitor resources located 20 miles northwest of El Paso in Anthony (I-10, exit 0), at the Texas–New Mexico border.

# [FastFACTS] EL PASO

**American Express** **Sun Travel American Express,** 3100 N. Mesa St. (© **915/532-8900;** www.suntvl.com), offers American Express services Monday through Friday from 7:30am to 6pm and Saturday from 9am to 2pm.

**Babysitters** Front desks at major hotels often can make arrangements on your behalf.

**Dentists** Contact **1-800-DENTIST** (336-8478).

**Doctors** Call **El Paso County Medical Society** (© **915/533-0940**).

**Drugstores** **Walgreens Drug Stores** has a 24-hour prescription service at 1831 N. Lee Trevino Dr. (© **915/594-1129**).

**Emergencies** For police, fire, and medical emergencies, call © **911.** To reach the **West Texas Regional Poison Center,** call © **800/222-1222.**

**Hospitals** Full-service hospitals, with 24-hour emergency rooms, include **Sierra Medical Center,** 1625 Medical Center Dr. (© **915/747-4000;** www.sphn.com), just northwest of downtown, and **Del Sol Medical Center,** 10301 Gateway W. (© **915/595-9000;** www.delsolhealth.com), on the east side of the city.

The *El Paso Times* (www.elpasotimes.com) is the city's only daily English-language newspaper, and an El Paso edition of *El Diario de Juárez* (www.diario.com.mx) is published in Spanish daily. *El Paso Scene* (www.epscene.com) is the city's free monthly arts-and-entertainment paper.

**Post Office** The main post office, located downtown at 219 E. Mills Ave., is open Monday through Friday from 8:30am to 5pm, Saturday from 8:30am to noon.

**Safety** While El Paso has among the lowest crime rates of any major U.S. city, it is far from crime-free, and drugs and auto theft are two preeminent problems. It's important to keep aware of your surroundings at all times and ask at your hotel or a visitor center about the safety of a given neighborhood, especially after dark. *Note:* When visiting Mexico, it is important to remember that Ciudad Juárez is one of the world's most active drug-smuggling centers, and recently it has been especially bad for drug-related violence. However, crime against tourists has remained relatively rare. Nonetheless, I do not recommend driving across the border or crossing alone.

**Taxes** In the city of El Paso, the total sales tax is 8.25% and 15.5% for lodging.

**Time Zone** El Paso is in the Mountain Standard Time zone, like nearby New Mexico, but unlike the rest of Texas, which is in the Central Standard Time zone. Set your clock back 1 hour if you enter El Paso from the east.

# What to See & Do
## THE TOP ATTRACTIONS

**Chamizal National Memorial** ★ When the Mexican-American War ended in 1848, the two countries agreed on a border: the center of the deepest channel of the Rio Grande. However, as historian Leon C. Metz once wrote, "Rivers are never *absolutely* permanent. They evaporate, flood, change channels, shrink, expand, and even disappear. Rivers are, by nature, capricious." After the war, the Rio Grande gradually shifted southward, resulting in a diplomatic stalemate between Mexico and the United States over the boundary's location. This impasse lasted until 1964, finally ending when presidents Lyndon B. Johnson and Adolfo López Mateos signed the Chamizal Treaty. Parcels of land were exchanged, residents and businesses were uprooted, and a permanent, concrete channel was constructed to signify a more predictable boundary.

Commemorating the dispute's peaceful resolution, the 55-acre park at the Chamizal National Memorial commemorates the dispute's settlement with a bevy of facilities: 2 miles of foot trails, an outdoor amphitheater and indoor theater that host many free concerts and other events, and a visitor center with a museum, three galleries, and a bookstore (expect to spend an hour touring the museum and galleries). It's a nice open space that's more accessible and greener than the Franklin Mountains and larger than the other municipal parks. There is also a walkway to the adjacent Bridge of the Americas leading to the memorial's Mexican counterpart, **Parque Chamizal,** with an anthropology museum and an amusement park in Ciudad Juárez.

800 S. San Marcial Dr., at Paisano Dr. and U.S. 54 (Patriot Fwy.). © **915/532-7273.** www.nps.gov/cham. Free admission, with fees for some events in the amphitheater. Park daily 5am–10pm. Visitor center Tues–Sat 10am–5pm.

**El Paso Mission Trail** ★ First established in the 17th and 18th centuries, three historic Spanish missions provide a link to El Paso's colonial past. All three are among the oldest continually active missions in the country, and warrant a visit for their architectural and historic merit. But if you have time to hit only one, drive out to San Elceario; unlike Ysleta and Socorro, it's removed from the modern urban development and still feels like it's from a different era and culture.

From I-10, exit Zaragoza Road (exit 32) and head south 3 miles to **Mission Ysleta,** 9501 Socorro Rd. at Zaragoza Road (© **915/859-9848;** www.ysletamission.org), established in 1682 in what was then Mexico. The silver-domed chapel here was built in 1851 after floods shifted the Rio Grande and washed away all of the previous structure, save the foundation.

Heading southeast on Socorro Road for 3 miles takes you to **Mission Socorro,** 328 S. Nevarez Rd. (© **915/859-7718**), established in 1682, 1 day after Mission Ysleta. The original adobe chapel (1692) was washed away by a flood in the 1740s, rebuilt, destroyed again in 1829, and finally replaced in 1843 by the current restored structure.

The most impressive of the three, **Presidio Chapel San Elceario** (© **915/851-2333** for administration or 915/851-1682 for tour information) was established at its present location in 1789 as a Spanish military outpost 6 miles south of Mission Socorro on Socorro Road. Parishioners built the present-day church in 1877 as the centerpiece of the village plaza, which retains its historical charm to this day. This structure is the largest of the three missions, and an excellent example of the merging of American Indian and Spanish architectural styles with majestic arches and a pressed-tin ceiling. The surrounding village has been gaining fame in recent years as the site of the "First Thanksgiving," said to have taken place in 1598, 23 years before the Plymouth Thanksgiving.

Visitors are welcome to tour the missions on their own; expect to spend at least 3 hours if you visit all three. Tours are available from the **El Paso Mission Trail Experience** (© **915/851-6012;** www.missiontrailexperience.com) and cost $5 to $8 for 4-hour trips.

An 8-mile stretch of Zaragoza and Socorro roads, southeast of downtown El Paso via I-10. Call the CVB at © **915/534-0630** for more information. Free admission.

**El Paso Museum of Art ★★**   Once regarded as lacking a regional focus, the El Paso Museum of Art has finally turned that criticism on its head: The stunning landscapes and personal portraits on display here evoke the region's look, and more important, its feel. Of the five permanent galleries, three are dedicated to the cultures that have commingled in El Paso for the past 400 years: One is dedicated to Mexican art of the 17th to 19th centuries, one to European art from the 13th to 18th centuries, and one to American works dating from 1800 to the mid-1900s. Seasonal exhibits often feature edgier contemporary works. A hidden treasure, the museum begs for an unhurried hour of your time.

1 Arts Festival Plaza. ℭ **915/532-1707.** www.elpasoartmuseum.org. Free admission; fees charged for special exhibits (usually $5–$10). Tues–Wed and Fri–Sat 9am–5pm; Thurs 9am–9pm; Sun noon–5pm.

## MORE ATTRACTIONS

Oenophiles will want to take a side trip to **Zin Valle Vineyards,** 7315 Hwy. 28, Canutillo (ℭ **915/877-4544;** www.zinvalle.com), where the tasting room is open from noon to 5pm Friday to Monday and by appointment at other times. In town in the Kern Place neighborhood, **Star Canyon Winery,** 2601 N. Stanton St. (ℭ **915/544-7000;** www.starcanyonwinery.com), has a tasting room that's open Tuesday to Thursday from 1 to 7pm and Friday and Saturday from 1 to 8pm. Railroad buffs will want to pay a visit to the **Railroad & Transportation Museum of El Paso,** 400 W. San Antonio Ave. (ℭ **915/422-3420;** www.elpasorails.org), open Tuesday through Saturday 11am to 5pm and Sunday 1 to 5pm.

**Ascarate Lake City Park** Centered on a 44-acre artificial lake, this municipal park consists of 400 acres of undeveloped terrain crisscrossed by trails. While swimming in the lake is prohibited, recreational opportunities include fishing (the lake is stocked with channel catfish and rainbow trout) and golfing at the park's 27-hole golf course. There's also an aquatics center with an indoor Olympic-size pool and ball fields.

6900 Delta Dr., btw. Alameda Ave. and Border Hwy. ℭ **915/772-5605.** Free admission to park, although there is a $1 fee for vehicles Fri–Sun and some attractions have fees, including the golf course. Daily dawn–dusk.

**Concordia Cemetery** El Paso's "Boot Hill," Concordia is the final resting place of numerous infamous outlaws who met their maker in the city's wilder days. The gravestones here, which mostly date to the second half of the 19th century, remain haunting reminders of El Paso's storied past. Near the northern gate, the most notable grave is that of notorious John Wesley Hardin, known as "the Fastest Gun in the West." After his 1895 assassination in downtown El Paso, Hardin was put to rest here alongside other gunslingers (including Hardin's killer) and a generation of law-abiding citizens. Hardin's grave is said to be El Paso's most-visited attraction.

Copia St. and I-10. ℭ **915/562-7062.** Free admission. Daily during daylight hours. Immediately north of I-10 via Copia St. (exit 22A).

**El Paso Holocaust Museum** ★ Moving into a permanent downtown location in 2008, the powerful El Paso Holocaust Museum does an excellent job telling a story that's alternately grim and life-affirming. The chronologically arranged exhibits

---

**Live by the Gun . . .**

Notorious gunslinger John Wesley Hardin, who claimed to have killed 40 men, was shot in the back of the head in a saloon in 1895. At the time, Hardin was planning to embark on a law career (he had even gone as far as printing business cards), despite the fact that he spent more than three-quarters of his last 20 years in prison.

---

include timelines, anti-Semitic Nazi propaganda, a replica of Auschwitz, stories of the resistance and liberation, and a memorial room. Allow 1 hour.

715 N. Oregon St. ✆ **915/351-0048.** www.elpasoholocaustmuseum.org. Free admission; donations accepted. Tues–Fri 9am–4pm; Sat–Sun 1–5pm. Closed major holidays.

**El Paso Museum of History** ★ Opened in 2007, the El Paso Museum of History is worthy of its subject, a major improvement on its shuttered predecessor on the city's east side. Of the five galleries, one features a permanent exhibit: "The Changing Pass," covering the area's evolution from the Ice Age to modern day. The remaining galleries feature regularly rotating exhibits on topics of all kinds; the museum serves as one of three U.S. hosts for the exclusive exhibit of Spanish colonial antiquities, "Threads of Memory," in 2011. Allow 1 hour.

510 N. Santa Fe St. ✆ **915/351-3588.** www.elpasotexas.gov/history. Free admission. Tues–Wed and Fri–Sat 9am–5pm; Thurs 9am–9pm; Sun noon–5pm. Closed city holidays.

**El Paso Zoo** ★ ☺ Home to some 1,700 animals from 240 different species in natural habitat exhibits, the El Paso Zoo is one of the state's best. The focus is on American and Asian wildlife, with a monkey island, reptile house, "Asian Grasslands" exhibit, and "Americas Aviary." Among the crowd favorites are sun bears, black jaguars, tigers, and Asian elephants. There is also a restaurant, a gift shop, and the "Paraje," a replica of the 16th-century equivalent of a rest stop on the Camino Real. Allow at least 1 hour.

4001 E. Paisano Dr. (across from the El Paso County Coliseum). ✆ **915/521-1850.** www.elpasozoo.org. Admission $10 adults, $7.50 seniors 60 and over, $6 children age 3–12, free for children 2 and under. Mon–Fri 9:30am–4pm year-round; Sat–Sun 9:30am–4pm winter, 9:30am–5pm summer. Closed Thanksgiving, Dec 25, and Jan 1.

**Magoffin Home State Historic Site** Built in 1875 for Joseph Magoffin, a pioneer leader who helped guide the city through its chaotic Wild West days, this is El Paso's only historic house museum open to the public. A recommended hour-long tour for the history buff, the house is a prime example of Territorial architecture, with an adobe structure and Greek revival accents. Many original furnishings are still in place: The Victorian parlor is unique due to its Mexican accents, the oldest part of the home still sports a viga ceiling (thatched and exposed), and one bedroom is outfitted with a 13-foot half-canopy bed from New Orleans.

1120 Magoffin Ave. ✆ **915/533-5147.** www.visitmagoffinhome.com. Admission $4 adults, $3 students, free for children 5 and under. Tues–Sun 9am–5pm; tours given on the hour 9am–4pm. Closed major holidays.

**National Border Patrol Museum** The only museum dedicated to the U.S. Border Patrol, this facility does a good job presenting displays on all aspects of the federal agency, founded in El Paso in 1924. Allow about a half-hour to peruse such highlights as the "Lady Liberty" exhibit, a Statue of Liberty replica and text and diaries about the immigrant experience; and two former Border Patrol aircraft: a Piper Super Cub plane and a Hughes OH-6A helicopter. There are also exhibits on Border Patrol dogs, electronics, and ground vehicles.

4315 Transmountain Dr. ✆ **915/759-6060.** www.borderpatrolmuseum.com. Free admission (donations accepted). Tues–Sat 9am–5pm. Closed major holidays.

## ESPECIALLY FOR KIDS

**Insights Science Museum** ★ ☺ This downtown museum is a winner for young minds curious about the inner workings of nature. There are interactive exhibits on

Located high above downtown atop the cliffs of the Franklin Mountains, this municipal park (on Scenic Dr. btw. Rim Rd. and Alabama Ave.) has amazing views, day and night. With the naked eye or coin-op telescopes, you can see downtown El Paso, across the Rio Grande to Juárez, and even parts of New Mexico.

topics ranging from energy and optics to health and biology. Kids get a big jolt of fun out of the Tesla coil that courses with 500,000 volts several times a day. Another favorite is the exhibit on sound, with an echo tube and displays on sonic waves. A comprehensive tour requires about an hour.

505 N. Santa Fe St. ✆ **915/534-0000.** www.insightselpaso.org. Admission $6 adults; $5 students, seniors, and military; $4 children 4–11; free for children 3 and under. Tues-Sat 10am–5pm; Sun noon–5pm.

**Western Playland Amusement Park** ☺ In 2006, the longtime local amusement park relocated to Sunland Park, New Mexico (about 8 miles northwest of El Paso), taking with it the Bandido roller coaster and opening several new thrill rides. Concession stands and picnic areas fill the needs of the hungry and thirsty.

1249 Futurity Dr., Sunland Park, NM, across from Sunland Park Race Track and Casino. ✆ **575/589-3410.** www.westernplayland.com. Admission $16 for a pass for unlimited rides. Mid-Feb to Oct; call or check the website for hours, which vary throughout the season.

## ORGANIZED TOURS

**Si! El Paso Tours** (✆ 915/533-5454; www.bordersights-tours-of-elpaso.com) offers a variety of tours of El Paso and vicinity for $45 adults, $20 children 18 and under. The **El Paso CVB** (✆ 915/534-0600; www.visitelpaso.com) can provide travelers with informative brochures that detail self-guided historic walking tours.

## OUTDOOR ACTIVITIES

At nearly 24,300 acres, **Franklin Mountains State Park** is the largest urban wilderness park in the United States and a favorite destination of El Pasoans looking to hike, bike, or climb. Rugged and speckled by cacti and ocotillos, the mountains are populated by small mammals, birds, reptiles, deer, and the occasional mountain lion. At 7,192 feet, the summit of North Franklin Mountain is about 3,000 feet higher than the city below.

The mountains, the final southern ridge of the geological phenomenon that created the Rocky Mountains, are home to about 50 miles of developed hiking and mountain biking trails; floods in 2006 washed out many trails, so call for current information. The hikes are primarily moderate to difficult; try the 1.2-mile round-trip to the Aztec Caves or the more difficult 9.2-mile round-trip to the peak of North Franklin Mountain.

If you don't want to break a sweat, take the **Wyler Aerial Tramway** (✆ 915/566-6622) to the summit of Ranger Peak ($7 adults, $4 children 12 and under). Beyond the trails and the tram, the park is also a renowned rock-climbing spot and home to an outdoor amphitheater (see "The Performing Arts," p. 347).

It takes about 20 minutes to reach the park by car from downtown El Paso. There are numerous primitive campsites, but no water or electricity in the park. Fees are $4 for day use (free for children 12 and under) and $8 for camping, and the park is open

**10**

**WEST TEXAS** | El Paso

from 8am to 5pm year-round (campers receive a combination to the locked gate so they can come and go after day-use hours). For more information, contact Franklin Mountains State Park, 1331 McKelligon Canyon Rd., El Paso, TX 79930 (© **915/566-6441;** www.tpwd.state.tx.us).

**Hueco Tanks State Park & Historic Site,** located 32 miles northeast of El Paso via U.S. 62/180 and RM 2775, is another popular rock-climbing destination. It is a world-class bouldering site, among the best on the planet. Centered on three small, rocky outcroppings that loom above the surrounding desert, the park gets its name from the *huecos* (depressions) that catch rainwater and attract life. Many of the rocks are marked by lively pictographs, the work of native tribes over the past 10,000 years. Tours of these fragile sites are offered Wednesday through Saturday at 9 and 11am in the summer and 10:30am and 2pm in the winter; reservations are recommended. Birding, bouldering, and biking tours are also available.

Other than climbing, hiking and camping are popular activities at the park. There are 6.5 miles of trails and a campground with 20 back-in sites (3 with water only, 17 with water and electricity) and showers. Campsite availability is dependent on volunteers; call ahead to see if the campground is open. The park charges $5 for day use and $12 to $16 for campsites. Bikes are not permitted. For more information, contact Hueco Tanks State Park & Historic Site, 6900 Hueco Tanks Rd. #1, El Paso, TX 79938 (© **915/857-1135;** www.tpwd.state.tx.us).

**GOLF**   The Tom Fazio–designed **Butterfield Trail Golf Course,** 1858 Cottonwoods Dr. (© **915/772-1038;** www.butterfieldtrailgolf.com), has been ranked as one of the top public courses in the state. Greens fees are $40 to $80, cart included. At the 27-hole **Painted Dunes Desert Golf Course,** located 9 miles northeast of I-10 via U.S. 54 at 12000 McCombs St. (© **915/821-2122;** www.painteddunes. com), nonresident greens fees range from $20 to $34 with cart or $10 to $21 without cart. Twilight rates are also available. Lee Trevino began his illustrious professional golf career at **Emerald Springs Golf and Conference Center,** 20 miles east of town at 16000 Ashford St. (© **915/852-9110**). Greens fees are $22 to $35, cart included. Other options include **Ascarate Golf Course** in Ascarate Lake City Park (© **915/772-7381**), with greens fees of $14 to $31, cart included; and **Lone Star Golf Club,** 1510 Hawkins Blvd. (© **915/591-4927;** www.lonestargolfclub.net), with greens fees of $25 to $42 with cart.

**HIKING**   The top hiking areas in and around El Paso are at **Franklin Mountains State Park** and **Hueco Tanks State Park & Historic Site** (see above).

**MOUNTAIN BIKING**   **Franklin Mountains State Park** (see above) is by far the most popular mountain biking destination in the El Paso area. There are about 40 miles of bike-accessible trails.

## SPECTATOR SPORTS

**BASEBALL**   The **El Paso Diablos,** an independent team in the Central League, play a May-to-August schedule at 10,000-seat Cohen Stadium, 9700 Gateway Blvd. N. Single-game tickets are $7 to $8. Call © **915/755-2000** or visit www.diablos. com for schedules.

**BASKETBALL**   The University of Texas at El Paso (UTEP) fields a Conference USA team, the **Miners,** that plays from December to March at the Don Haskins Center, 2801 N. Mesa St. Tickets range from $14 to $29 for single games. Call © **915/747-5234** or visit www.utepathletics.com to purchase tickets or for more information.

**FOOTBALL**   The **UTEP Miners** football squad plays a Conference USA schedule from September to December on campus at the Sun Bowl. Single-game tickets are about $20 to $40. Also, the stadium hosts the second-oldest New Year's bowl game in the nation. Call ✆ **915/747-5234** or visit www.utepathletics.com for schedules or to purchase tickets.

**HORSE RACING**   There is live horse racing just outside of western El Paso (actually in New Mexico) at **Sunland Park Racetrack and Casino,** 1200 Futurity Dr. (✆ **575/874-5200;** www.sunland-park.com). The racing season runs from December to April (simulcast racing from around the country is featured year-round). There are also restaurants, lounges, and a casino on-site.

**RODEO**   The **Southwestern International PRCA Rodeo** is held every September at Cohen Stadium, 9700 Gateway N. Call ✆ **915/755-2000** or visit www.elprodeo.com for schedules and ticket information.

## SHOPPING

El Paso's main shopping district is downtown—targeting both Mexican and American shoppers with all sorts of bargains—and there are several enclosed malls scattered around the city. The area is known for Western wear, Southwestern art, and Mexican imports.

The three-story **Galeria San Ysidro,** 801 Texas Ave. (✆ **915/544-4444**), is more than just an antiques store, housing an impressive selection of art, furniture, and decor from all over the world. **Cowtown Boots,** 11451 Gateway W. (✆ **915/593-2929;** www.cowtownboots.com), claims to be the world's largest Western wear store, with 40,000 square feet of boots (alligator to ostrich), jeans, clothing, and accessories. If you want some custom boots that are leather works of art, make an appointment at **Rocketbuster Boots,** 115 S. Anthony St. (✆ **915/541-1300;** www.rocketbuster. com), but you'll need at least $750 for a pair. For just about everything else—saddle blankets to yard art to painted longhorn skulls—check the huge, 2-acre showroom of **El Paso Saddleblanket,** 6926 Gateway E. (✆ **800/998-8608;** www.saddleblanket.com).

Shopping centers include **Sunland Park Mall,** 750 Sunland Park Dr. (✆ **915/833-5596**), and **Cielo Vista Mall,** 8401 Gateway W. (✆ **915/779-7071**). Located where Pancho Villa and General Pershing once negotiated, **Placita Santa Fe,** 5034 Doniphan Rd., features 20 quaint shops, specializing in art, designer clothing, antiques, and jewelry.

# Where to Stay

You'll find numerous hotels and motels in El Paso, but little in the way of B&Bs and resorts. Most of the accommodations are chain franchises, with a few exceptions, located either near the airport or adjacent to I-10. The city's room taxes add about 15.5% to lodging bills.

In addition to the properties described below, there are numerous hotels and motels located off I-10 near El Paso International Airport, including **Best Western Airport Inn,** 7144 Gateway E. (✆ **800/528-1234** or 915/779-7700), at $60 to $80 double, and **Comfort Inn,** 900 Yarbrough Dr. (✆ **800/228-5150** or 915/594-9111), at $69 to $89 double. Downtown, the **Holiday Inn Express** at 409 E. Missouri Ave. (✆ **888/465-4329** or 915/544-3333), has rates of $89 to $149 double. Adjacent to (and blending into) the UTEP campus, the **Hilton Garden Inn,** 111 W. University Ave. (✆ **915/351-2121;** www.elpaso.stayhgi.com), is a solid choice, with rates of

$89 to $169 double. In the Sunland Park area, the pick of the litter is the **Holiday Inn Sunland Park,** 900 Sunland Park Dr. (© **800/658-2744** or 915/833-2900), at $99 to $179 double.

## EXPENSIVE

**Camino Real Hotel** ★★  El Paso's finest hotel—and one of a handful downtown—is the only Camino Real hotel or resort outside of Mexico. However, it's just 6 blocks north of the border, adjacent to the El Paso Convention and Performing Arts Center and within easy walking distance of all of the downtown attractions. Listed on the National Register of Historic Places, the hotel effortlessly meshes El Paso's past and present. Formerly known as the Hotel Paso del Norte, the property first opened in 1912, awing guests with its lavish marble and cherrywood lobby under a stunning glass dome from Tiffany's in New York. In 1986, a modern 17-story tower was built next to the old Paso del Norte, expanding the lobby and more than doubling the hotel's capacity. Tastefully decorated with reproductions and contemporary furnishings, the oversize rooms have two doubles, two queens, or one king, and the decor accentuates the great downtown views.

101 S. El Paso St., El Paso, TX 79901. © **800/769-4300** or 915/534-3000. Fax 915/534-3024. www.caminoreal.com. 357 units. $99–$160 double; $170–$1,500 suite. AE, DC, DISC, MC, V. Parking $6. **Amenities:** 2 restaurants; bar; free airport transfers; exercise room; outdoor heated pool; room service; sauna. *In room:* A/C, TV, hair dryer, Wi-Fi (free).

**Doubletree Hotel El Paso** ★★  By completely renovating an abandoned downtown building into a first-rate hotel, the Doubletree El Paso turned a negative into a winning positive when it opened in 2009. The 17-floor hotel, with striking 360-degree city views from its uppermost level, stands out because of its attention to the details, such as attractive local artwork, movies projected onto a pool deck wall in summer, and contemporary desert-influenced design. Decorated in subtle earth tones, the rooms are some of the city's best, featuring one king bed or two queen beds, along with a cozy chair and ottoman. The location, within 2 blocks of four museums, is enviable. The hotel targets business travelers, but it's also a good choice for vacationers.

600 N. El Paso St., El Paso, TX 79901. © **915/532-8733.** Fax 915/532-8732. http://doubletree1.hilton.com. 296 units. $159–$219 double ($89–$109 on weekends). AE, DISC, MC, V. Free parking. **Amenities:** Restaurant; 2 bars; exercise room; Jacuzzi; outdoor heated pool; room service. *In room:* A/C, TV, hair dryer, Wi-Fi (free).

**Marriott El Paso** ★  Nicely renovated in 2008, this modern chain property is a solid lodging option for those flying in or out of El Paso. The thick-walled rooms are colorful, comfortable, and contemporary, featuring flatscreen TVs, black-and-white desert photos, and nifty LED reading lights. There is also a great courtyard pool, with several rooms opening onto it. There is a locally popular sports bar, **Pitchers,** as well as the **Red Rim Bistro,** serving breakfast and lunch. While the hotel is aimed at the business traveler, it more than fills the needs of tourists and is a bargain on weekends.

1600 Airway Blvd. (¼ mile south of El Paso International Airport), El Paso, TX 79925. © **800/228-9290** or 915/779-3300. Fax 915/779-4591. www.marriott.com. 296 units. $199–$219 double ($89–$125 on weekends). AE, DC, DISC, MC, V. Free parking. **Amenities:** Restaurant; bar; executive-level rooms; exercise room; Jacuzzi; 2 heated pools (1 indoor, 1 outdoor); room service; spa. *In room:* A/C, TV, hair dryer, Wi-Fi ($2–$40 per day, depending on usage).

## MODERATE

**Travelodge Hotel—La Hacienda Airport** ★ ☺ 🍴  Some roadside motels surprise you with their attention to detail—this is definitely one of them. Situated northeast of downtown off busy Montana Avenue, the grounds here are a world apart, centered on a shady courtyard surrounding a seasonal swimming pool. The rooms are housed in 10 different brick buildings, with exterior entry through hand-painted wooden doors. Some of the accommodations in the older buildings are on the small side, albeit well maintained and comfortable, while the larger rooms in the newer structures are a notch above the norm, with blue-and-white decor and exposed wood-beamed ceilings. I like the eight Jacuzzi rooms, featuring a picture window that separates the tub from the bedroom, and the family suites, amusingly decorated and with plenty of room.

6400 Montana Ave., El Paso, TX 79925. (C) **800/772-4231** or 915/772-4231. Fax 915/779-2918. www.travelodge.com/elpaso. 91 units. $49–$54 double; $69 suite; $74 Jacuzzi room. Rates include continental breakfast. AE, DC, DISC, MC, V. Pets $10 per night. **Amenities:** Restaurant; bar; outdoor pool; room service. In room: A/C, TV, fridge, hair dryer, Wi-Fi (free).

## INEXPENSIVE

**Gardner Hotel/El Paso International Youth Hostel** 🖋 A downtown mainstay since 1922, the Gardner Hotel has a storied history—infamous gangster John Dillinger stayed here in the 1930s while on the run. The public areas are well kept, especially the attractive lobby, which has been restored to its original condition with a marble staircase, mauve carpeting, and historical photographs. There are two shared hostel rooms—one for males and one for females—each with two bunk beds and desks. There is also a wide range of private accommodations—some with no frills, some with the original antique furnishings. Hostel guests share bathrooms and an equipped kitchen, and also have access to a basement lounge with a television and pool table, and a pay Internet kiosk. The private rooms have TVs, phones, and private bathrooms. The hotel also has a world-cuisine restaurant, **Pot-au-Fau.**

311 E. Franklin St., El Paso, TX 79901. (C) **915/532-3661.** www.gardnerhotel.com. 50 units. $23 dormitory bunk; $34–$69 double in private rooms. MC, V. **Amenities:** Restaurant; bar. In room: Fans, Wi-Fi (free).

## CAMPING

Several primitive campsites are available at Franklin Mountains State Park, and there are also some tent and RV sites at Hueco Tanks State Historic Site; see "Outdoor Activities," above.

**El Paso–West RV Park** Located just west of the Texas–New Mexico state line, this clean campground is nicely accentuated with trees, a rarity in the desert. It has laundry facilities, free cable TV and Wi-Fi, handicapped-accessible showers, and a small store with groceries and RV supplies. An 18-hole golf course is located right across the street.

1415 Anthony Dr., Anthony, NM 88021. (C) **800/754-1543** or 575/882-7172. 100 sites with full hookups, including 70 pull-throughs. $29–$33 nightly. MC, V. 10 miles west of El Paso city limits (I-10, exit 162 in New Mexico).

# Where to Dine

W. Park Kerr, founder of the El Paso Chile Company and self-described "ultimate El Paso food insider," labels the local culinary tradition as "border regional cuisine." It isn't quite Tex-Mex, nor is it authentic Mexican; it has notes of New Mexican and loads of first-rate chili. There are many great hole-in-the-wall eateries in El Paso. Among the recommended restaurants are **Kiki's,** 2719 N. Piedras St. ((C) **915/565-6713**); **Jalisco Café,** 1029 E. 7th Ave. ((C) **915/532-7174**); **Mexican Cottage,** 904 Texas Ave. ((C) **915/546-9816**); and **Lucky Cafe,** 3831 Alameda Ave. ((C) **915/532-2834**). *Note:* Smoking is not allowed in El Paso's restaurants.

## EXPENSIVE

**Café Central** ★★ CONTEMPORARY SOUTHWESTERN   Worth the splurge, Café Central is an anomaly in a town dominated by Tex-Mex—a sleek urban bistro serving sophisticated international cuisine. There are three seating areas: a gracious dining room, a sleek lounge, and a breezy patio out front. The menu changes daily, but always offers a wide range of standout fare (most notably the creative Southwestern interpretations of traditional Continental dishes). On a given night, you might start with Dos Equis–steamed clams with tomatoes, garlic, jalapeños, and cilantro; follow with a cup of cream of green-chile soup; and then enjoy a tantalizing main course of sautéed calamari and shellfish on a capellini bed, a grilled white veal chop with a revelation of a side dish in the green-chile risotto, or possibly luscious Guaymas shrimp with a zesty tequila-cilantro sauce. The award-winning wine list is one of the city's best, with more than 300 bottles, and the desserts include the best *leches* (Mexican milk cakes) in all of Texas.

109 N. Oregon St., in the lobby of the Texas Tower (One Texas Court). ⓒ **915/545-2233.** www.cafe central.com. Reservations recommended. Main courses $10–$14 lunch, $13–$35 dinner. AE, DISC, MC, V. Mon–Thurs 11am–10:30pm; Fri–Sat 11am–11:30pm. Bar open later. Closed major holidays.

**Maria Chuchena** ★ CONTEMPORARY MEXICAN   From the salsa (prepared tableside to your liking) to the slick decor (featuring contemporary light fixtures and Mayan-inspired artworks), Maria Chuchena is a standout restaurant on El Paso's trendy east side. Using traditional ingredients like squash blossoms, *xoconosostle* (sour prickly pear), and *epazote* (the herb known as Mexican tea), the menu incorporates equal parts contemporary American and traditional Mexican, with plenty of seafood (the Imperial salmon in chipotle cream sauce stands out) as well as beef and poultry. Traditionalists will like the Tampiqueña steak served with guacamole, enchilada, and refried beans—not to mention the attentive, Juárez-style service.

5860 N. Mesa St., Ste. 133. ⓒ **915/581-9511.** www.mariachuchena.com. Reservations recommended. Main courses $7–$11 breakfast, $7–$25 lunch, $9–$25 dinner. AE, DISC, MC, V. Daily 8am–11pm. Closed major holidays.

## MODERATE/INEXPENSIVE

The local microbrewery, **Jaxon's,** has three locations: 1135 Airway Blvd. (ⓒ **915/778-9696**), 4799 N. Mesa St. (ⓒ **915/544-1188**), and 7410 Remcon Circle (ⓒ **915/845-6557**). **The Tap,** 408 E. San Antonio St. (ⓒ **915/532-1848**), might just be the best deal in town, serving huge Mexican plates for under $10.

**H&H Car Wash and Coffee Shop** ★ 🍴 MEXICAN   A dinky coffee shop straight out of the 1960s, the H&H is a bit weathered, noisy, and not much to look at. It doesn't matter—the place is home to some of the best inexpensive Tex-Mex in town, using only the freshest ingredients and sticking with tradition. The place is packed with locals from open to closing times, as they scarf down such specialties as *carne picada* (diced sirloin with jalapeños, tomatoes, and onions), *huevos rancheros,* and chiles rellenos. For hungry road-trippers with dirty cars and tight budgets, you can't get any more convenient than the H&H: Gas up, get your car washed, and have a bite to eat, all in one fell swoop. The car wash operates from 9am to 5pm during the week and from 9am to 3pm on Saturdays, charging $12 to $25 for a complete hand cleaning, inside and out.

701 E. Yandell Dr. at Ochoa St. ⓒ **915/533-1144.** Reservations not accepted. Main courses $5–$8. AE, DISC, MC, V. Mon–Sat 7am–3pm. North of I-10, exit 20 at Cotton St.

**L&J Café ★★ MEXICAN** Nicknamed "the Old Place by the Graveyard" because of its proximity to the Concordia Cemetery (p. 339), the L&J is an El Paso landmark. Owned and operated by the Duran family since it first opened in 1927, the L&J served as a casino and speakeasy during Prohibition. Today, it packs in customers to its bustling bar and quieter dining room for transcendental "border regional cuisine." I'm hooked on the chicken enchiladas, which approach perfection, but the *huevos rancheros* (Mexican eggs), chili con queso, and *caldillo* (beef and potato stew with a green chile–and-garlic kick) are as good as you'll find anywhere. There are also healthy versions of many entrees, prepared with less cheese, and tortillas that aren't fried. It doesn't hurt that the salsa is spicy, the beer is cold, and the service is quick and friendly, even when the place is filled to capacity—as it is most of the time.

3622 E. Missouri Ave. © **915/566-8418.** www.landjcafe.com. Reservations accepted only for parties of 6 or more. Main courses $6–$15. AE, DISC, MC, V. Mon–Wed 10am–8pm; Thurs–Fri 10am–9pm; Sat 9am–9pm; Sun 9am–8pm. Bar open later. Just north of I-10, exit 22A at Copia St.

**Rib Hut BARBECUE** A favorite hangout for students from the nearby University of Texas at El Paso, the Rib Hut bustles day and night. You can't miss this A-shaped roof on North Mesa, and you can't beat the daily specials—especially the $1.75 rib nights on Mondays and Wednesdays. The menu includes sandwiches, combo plates, and other platters, primarily barbecue beef, pork, and chicken, but also fried catfish and steak. Beer is available, including—of course—cold Shiner Bock.

2612 N. Mesa St. © **915/532-7427.** www.ribhutelpaso.com. Reservations not accepted. Main courses $7–$15. AE, DISC, MC, V. Mon–Sat 11am–10pm; Sun noon–8pm.

# El Paso After Dark

El Paso's entertainment scene is spread throughout the city, and remarkably diverse. The El Paso Performing Arts Center, the beautifully restored **Plaza Theatre** (www.plazatheatre.org), the McKelligon Canyon Amphitheatre, the outdoor and indoor stages at Chamizal National Memorial, and the facilities at the University of Texas at El Paso all host regular performances. Fans of rock, country, Tejano, and jazz will likely find what they're looking for at the city's bars and clubs. The UTEP college scene is centered on Mesa and Cincinnati streets.

The free monthly *El Paso Scene* and its online counterpart, **www.epscene.com**, are the best places to start for exploring arts-and-entertainment opportunities. The Friday *El Paso Times* (www.elpasotimes.com) also features performance listings, as does *The Prospector*, UTEP's student newspaper. Tickets for many events are available through **Ticketmaster** (© **915/544-8444**; www.ticketmaster.com).

## THE PERFORMING ARTS

**El Paso Opera,** 310 N. Mesa St., Ste. 601 (© **915/581-5534** or 915/231-1100 for tickets; www.epopera.org), produces spring and fall shows annually, with a Thursday and Saturday performance of each show held at the Abraham Chavez Theater downtown. Spanish and English subtitles are projected for every performance. Tickets run $20 to $90 for a single event. **El Paso Pro-Musica,** 6557 N. Mesa St. (© **915/833-9400;** www.elpasopromusica.org), presents several concerts a year, including the El Paso Chamber Music Festival every January. Concerts are held at numerous locations with ticket prices of $5 to $25. **El Paso Symphony Orchestra,** 1 Civic Center Plaza (© **915/532-3776;** www.epso.org), puts on about a dozen different concerts annually. Tickets for single performances run between $10 and $40, with discounts for children and seniors. At Franklin Mountains State Park, the outdoor **McKelligon**

# THE copper CANYON

El Paso is often a jumping-off point for trips to the Copper Canyon in northwestern Mexico. If you are interested in seeing a rugged and beautiful land; or in taking one of the most remarkable train trips in the world; or in hiking or riding horseback through remote areas to see an astonishing variety of flora and fauna; or if you're curious about a land still populated by indigenous people living pretty much the way they have for centuries, the Copper Canyon is the place to go.

Most often, when people say "Copper Canyon," they are referring to a section of the Sierra Madre known commonly in Mexico as the Sierra Tarahumara (after the Indians who live there). The area was formed through violent volcanic uplifting, followed by a slow, quiet process of erosion that carved a vast network of canyons into the soft volcanic stone.

Crossing the Sierra Tarahumara is the famed **Chihuahua al Pacífico (Chihuahua to the Pacific)** railway. Acclaimed as an engineering marvel, the 390-mile railroad has 39 bridges (the highest is more than 1,000 ft. above the Chinipas River) and 86 tunnels. It climbs from Los Mochis, at sea level, up nearly 8,000 feet through some of Mexico's most magnificent scenery—thick pine forests, jagged peaks, and shadowy canyons—before descending again to its destination, the city of Chihuahua.

It's easier than ever to get to the region, but it's trickier than ever to travel through it on your own—hotel rooms can be hard to come by, and there have been numerous changes in the operation of the Copper Canyon train. Consequently, this is not the place to do casual, follow-your-nose traveling. A number of tour operators and packagers book trips to the Copper Canyon. The easiest thing is to contract with an agency that will plan your trip from El Paso. Or you can take a bus to Chihuahua and contact a travel agency there that will book a trip into the canyon. This is the cheapest and most flexible way to do it.

Another option is to go with a custom tour operator; travel through these companies generally allows you more time in the canyon and a better experience. The best of the bunch is **Canyon Travel** (© 800/208-6244; www.canyontravel.com), which is pretty much in a class by itself. It has lined up some beautiful small lodges in the canyons and staffed them with talented local guides. Another operator that provides good service is the El Paso–based **Native Trails** (© 800/884-3107; www.nativetrails.com).

For more information on traveling in the Copper Canyon, pick up a copy of *Frommer's Mexico* or check out www.frommers.com/destinations/thecoppercanyon.

—*David Baird*

**Canyon Amphitheatre**, 2 McKelligon Canyon Rd., annually hosts **Viva! El Paso** (© **915/231-1165**; www.viva-ep.org) from mid-June to early August. Tickets are about $10 to $25; barbecue-style dinners are available.

The **El Paso Playhouse**, 2501 Montana Ave. (© **915/532-1317**; www.elpasoplayhouse.com), stages a new production almost every month. Recent productions include *Much Ado About Nothing* and Noel Coward's *Blithe Spirit*. Tickets are usually less than $10. The **University of Texas at El Paso Dinner Theatre,** Union Ballroom on the UTEP campus (© **915/747-6060** or 747-5234; www.utep.edu/udt), is a tradition, producing student musicals since 1983. Today, the theater presents plays Wednesday through Sunday at 7pm during the school year. Dinner might include prime rib, baked potato, and a cookie sundae. Recent productions have included *Singin' in the Rain, Urinetown,* and *The Sound of Music.* Tickets run about $30 to $40, except for Sunday matinees (2:30pm), which are $22 to $24, but don't include dinner.

## THE CLUB & LIVE MUSIC SCENE

The Union Plaza District on the west side of downtown has blossomed in recent years to emerge as the top club-hopping area in El Paso. The pick of the litter is **the Garden,** 511 Western St. (© 915/544-4400; www.thegardenep.com), with something for everybody, from great New American cuisine to an outdoor beer garden to a DJ-driven dance floor. **The Republic,** 200 Anthony St. (© 915/694-5330), is another Union Plaza standout, a hip nightclub complete with velvet rope.

## THE BAR SCENE

Downtown, the **Tap,** 408 E. San Antonio St. (© 915/532-1848), is a classic watering hole, serving plenty of cold beer and spicy Mexican dishes. **The Cincinnati Bar,** 207 Cincinnati St. (© 915/532-5592), is a rowdy haunt favored by the UTEP crowd. It's located amid a strip of bars and restaurants on Cincinnati Street, one of the city's livelier blocks at midnight. One of the most regal places in the Southwest to sip a cocktail, **Dome Bar,** 101 S. El Paso St. in the Camino Real Hotel (© 915/534-3000), is light-years beyond a typical hotel bar. **Rosa's Cantina,** 3454 Doniphan Dr. (© 915/833-0402), was made famous by country legend Marty Robbins in his 1959 hit "El Paso"—or perhaps merely inspired by it after the fact.

# SMALL TOWNS OF CENTRAL WEST TEXAS ★

Travelers crossing West Texas pass through a smattering of communities where they'll find a variety of roadside motels and restaurants. But those who only grab some Z's or a quick bite to eat will be missing out on some fun things to see and do. While most of the areas discussed in this section would not be my choice as a vacation destination in and of themselves, they are definitely worth a stop, and one could easily spend anywhere from a few hours to a few days in each place.

## Fort Davis & Davis Mountains State Park

205 miles SE of El Paso; 23 miles NE of Alpine; 110 miles NW of Big Bend National Park

A charming small town surrounded by dramatic scenery and steeped in Old West lore, Fort Davis is one of those rare places that can please both city and country types. The town itself is teeming with boutiques and B&Bs, and to the north, outdoors buffs will appreciate Davis Mountains State Park.

The town's origins are tied to Fort Davis, the identically named U.S. Army post established in 1854. The town was initially a ranching center, but the fort's 1891 abandonment and the railroads' decision to bypass the community led to an economic bust. After the fort was designated a National Historic Site in 1961, traffic increased and helped create the tourism-heavy landscape in place today.

## ESSENTIALS
### Getting There

Fort Davis is located on Tex. 17 between Balmorhea and Marfa. From the north, the town is accessed via I-10 by taking either exit 192 or exit 206 and driving south on the highway for about 40 miles. Tex. 118 also runs through the town, from Kent (on I-10) to the northwest and to Alpine to the southeast. The nearest major commercial airports are 170 miles north in Midland and 205 miles to the northwest in El Paso.

## Getting Around

Fort Davis is centered on the town square and historic courthouse. Most of the businesses, lodging establishments, and restaurants are located on Main Street (Tex. 118), which runs north-south through the town square. You can stroll around town, but the attractions discussed below are not easy to access by foot.

## Visitor Information

The **Fort Davis Chamber of Commerce,** 4 Memorial Square (Box 378), Fort Davis, TX 79734 (✆ **800/524-3015** or 432/426-3015; www.fortdavis.com), provides brochures, advice, and other information.

**FAST FACTS** **Big Bend Regional Medical Center,** 25 miles southeast of Fort Davis at 2600 Tex. 118 N. in Alpine (✆ **432/837-3447**; www.bigbendhealthcare. com), has 24-hour emergency services. The **post office,** located on the town square on Main Street, is open Monday through Friday from 8am to 4pm.

## WHAT TO SEE & DO
### The Top Attractions

**Fort Davis National Historic Site** ★   One of the best remaining examples of a frontier military post, Fort Davis was established in 1854, named after then-Secretary of War Jefferson Davis. Surrounded by geological formations that offered natural defense as well as beauty, the fort was first occupied by six companies of the Eighth U.S. Infantry to battle hostile Comanches, Kiowas, and Apaches. Confederate soldiers controlled the fort for a spell in 1861; afterward, the fort sat vacant until 1867. It rose again as a stronghold in the Indian wars of the late–19th century, pitting the U.S. Cavalry and other soldiers, many of whom were African Americans, against the Apaches, until it was abandoned once and for all in 1891. More than 20 structures have since been restored, with a number of them meticulously decorated in 1880s style. Most Texas forts are either run-down or sitting in the middle of a barren plain, so this one—well manicured with a stunning rocky backdrop—is a standout. Expect to spend a little more than an hour if you tour the entire fort. There are also numerous daily bugle calls and about 5 miles of hiking trails leading to overlooks on Sleeping Lion Mountain and Davis Mountains State Park.

Tex. 17/118, 1 mile north of Fort Davis. ✆ **432/426-3224.** www.nps.gov/foda. Admission $3 adults, free for children 15 and under. Daily 8am–5pm. Closed major holidays.

**McDonald Observatory** ★ ☺   Operated by the University of Texas and free from urban light pollution, McDonald Observatory is one of the word's leading astronomical research facilities. Start at the visitor center and take in the 12-minute orientation video: It will provide you with a perspective both historical and interstellar. Guided tours depart the center several times daily and last about an hour. Twice daily, the visitor center hosts solar-viewing activities, where guests can get a glimpse of sunspots, flares, and other solar activity. If your schedule allows, visit during a nighttime "Star Party" ($12 adults, $10 seniors, $8 children) held Tuesday, Friday, and Saturday at times determined by the season. These events allow guests to view celestial objects and constellations through the observatory's high-powered telescopes. There's a restaurant in the visitor center, and serious stargazers can join as members ($50 and up) in order to stay in the Astronomer's Lodge on-site ($70 per person per night, meals included).

Tex. 118 N., 16 miles northwest of Fort Davis. 🕐 **877/984-7827** for recorded information, or 432/426-3640. www.mcdonaldobservatory.org. Daytime pass (includes guided tour) $8 adults, $7 children age 6–12, free for children 5 and under, $30 maximum per family. Daily 10am–5:30pm. Guided tours 11am and 2pm daily.

## Outdoor Activities

Fort Davis's outdoor recreation is centered on **Davis Mountains State Park,** located 4 miles northwest of town via Tex. 118 (🕐 **432/426-3337** or 512/389-8900 for campsite reservations; www.tpwd.state.tx.us). The second-highest range in all of Texas, the Davis Mountains reach their pinnacle at the peak of the 8,382-foot Mount Livermore. Hiking is my activity of choice here; try the moderate, 8-mile round-trip that leads to the Fort Davis National Historic Site. On or off the trails, the park is a great place for wildlife viewing and bird-watching. It's one of the few places in the United States where you might spot a Montezuma quail, and javelinas (the wild boars that roam the Southwest), tarantulas, horned frogs, and pronghorn antelope also live in the park. The entrance fee is $4 to $5 for adults, free for children 12 and under. Campsites run $20 for full hookups, $15 for water and electric hookups only, and $6 to $10 for tent and primitive sites.

For travelers looking to "cowboy up" in this decidedly Western part of the state, north of the park off Tex. 118 is a trio of guest ranches with various activities. For horseback riding, mosey over to the **Prude Ranch** (🕐 **432/426-3202;** www.pruderanch.com), where 1-hour rides run $30 and accommodations and cabins are $73 to $89 double; the **R.M. Sproul Ranch** (🕐 **432/426-3097;** www.rmsproulranch.com), the most remote of the three, with a focus on hunting, and cabins and houses for $95 to $150 nightly; and the **Harvard Lodge** at the H.E. Sproul Ranch (🕐 **432/426-2500** or 432/426-2501; www.harvardhotelandlodge.com), also with an emphasis on hunting, with a terrific outdoor pool deck, an exercise room, 4×4 tours ($55), and well-kept rooms and a cabin with queen and bunk beds for $125 to $200.

## WHERE TO STAY

**Hotel Limpia** ★   Spread out over eight historic buildings, the individually decorated rooms at the Hotel Limpia are outfitted with quilted queen- and king-size beds, rocking chairs, and private bathrooms both modern and vintage. The gorgeous 1,100-square-foot master suite in the vine- and stone-clad main building opens from a glassed veranda into a delightful garden area, but if you're looking for privacy, try one of the secluded cottages, located nearly a mile away from the main buildings. There's also a great gift shop with Texas-flavored curios, books, and decor; the county's only bar; and a good restaurant.

101 Memorial Square (P.O. Box 1838), Fort Davis, TX 79734. 🕐 **800/662-5517** or 432/426-3237. Fax 432/426-3983. www.hotellimpia.com. 43 units, including 25 suites. $99–$125 double; $125–$189 suite. AE, DISC, MC, V. **Amenities:** Restaurant; bar; Wi-Fi (free, in lobby and some rooms). *In room:* A/C, TV, hair dryer, kitchen (in some units).

**Indian Lodge**   Located at the base of a gentle slope adjacent to Davis Mountains State Park, this hotel is actually a state park in and unto itself—Indian Lodge State Park. Built in the 1930s by the Civilian Conservation Corps, Indian Lodge's architects drew inspiration from Indian pueblos, resulting in 18-inch-thick adobe walls and thatched viga ceilings fashioned from river cane and wooden beams. The original rooms are decorated the same as the day the place opened, with hand-carved cedar chairs, dressers, and bed frames, all with engraved petroglyphs, as well as decorative fireplaces and ornate stonework. All of the rooms are set off from a sunny central patio with a wishing well and rock gardens.

Tex. 118 N., at Davis Mountains State Park (P.O. Box 1707), Fort Davis, TX 79734. © **432/426-3254** or 512/389-8982 for reservations. Fax 432/426-2022. www.tpwd.state.tx.us. 39 units, including 1 suite. $90-$125 double; $135 suite. DISC, MC, V. **Amenities:** Restaurant; outdoor heated pool; Wi-Fi (free). *In room:* A/C, TV.

**Old Schoolhouse Bed & Breakfast**   Situated in a pecan grove at the foot of Sleeping Lion Mountain, this B&B served as Fort Davis's schoolhouse from 1904 into the 1930s, then as a private residence until 1999, when Carla and Steve Kennedy converted it into a charming inn. The quaint rooms are outfitted with antiques and scholastically themed: The spacious Reading Room has a king-size bed, a sleeper sofa, and a private entrance; the smaller 'Riting and 'Rithmetic rooms share a bathroom. You won't want to skip breakfast, such as corn-tortilla quiche or apple-baked oatmeal. The Kennedys also rent the three-bedroom Hopes Ranch Guesthouse, 3 miles east of town on 40 isolated acres.

401 N. Front St. (P.O. Box 1221), Fort Davis, TX 79734. © **432/426-2050.** Fax 432/426-2509. www. schoolhousebnb.com. 3 units (2 with shared bathroom, 1 guesthouse). $93-$101 double; $195 guesthouse. Rates include full breakfast. DISC, MC, V. *In room:* A/C, hair dryer, no phone, Wi-Fi (free).

**The Veranda ★★**   A hotel or boardinghouse since it first opened its doors as the Hotel Lempert in 1883, the Veranda is named for its eponymous feature, lined with rockers. Behind the 18-inch adobe walls is a gem of a B&B, fronted by a 154-foot hallway with 12-foot ceilings. The rooms are tastefully decorated with antiques and have nice mountain views. Most are outfitted with one king bed, and a few have two beds and tub-showers. The walled courtyard is a peaceful outdoor retreat, with an orchard of peach trees—the fruit is used in the inn's preserves—and nicely manicured gardens. The two-bedroom carriage house is a nice option for families. The inn is entirely nonsmoking.

**10**

**WEST TEXAS** | **Small Towns of Central West Texas**

210 Court Ave., Fort Davis, TX 79734. © **888/383-2847** or 432/426-2233. www.theveranda.com. 13 units (including 3 suites, 1 house, and 1 cottage). $105 double; $125 suite; $115 cottage; $150 house. Rates include full breakfast. AE, DISC, MC, V. *In room:* A/C, fridge, hair dryer, no phone, Wi-Fi (free).

## WHERE TO DINE

If you're looking for a quick bite, your best bet is **Murphy's Pizzeria & Café,** at the junction of Tex. 17 and Tex. 118 on the south end of town (© **432/426-2020**), serving up better-than-expected pizzas ($8 and up), as well as pasta, sandwiches, and salads. The **Hotel Limpia Dining Room,** 100 State St. (© **432/426-3241**), is upscale; main courses are $10 to $26. Upstairs is Sutler's Club, the only watering hole in the traditionally dry county.

# Balmorhea State Park ★★

185 miles E of El Paso; 32 miles N of Fort Davis

One of the lesser seen jewels of the Texas State Park system (and one of the smallest, at 45 acres), **Balmorhea State Park,** 9207 Tex. 17 S. (© **432/375-2370**; www.tpwd.state.tx.us), is centered on a massive, 1¾-acre swimming pool that is fed by San Solomon Springs. It holds 3.5 million gallons of water at a fairly constant 74°F (23°C). Size aside, this is no ordinary pool: The water teems with fish, and the floor is covered in rocks. The Civilian Conservation Corps built the V-shaped pool in the 1930s, surrounding it with shady trees and a 200-foot circle of limestone and flagstone. Swimming is popular, as are snorkeling and scuba diving. You might see the occasional (nonpoisonous) water snake or turtle in it. A canal system crosscuts the park, leading from the pool to other areas, and providing a habitat for many native fish species, two of which—the Comanche Springs pupfish and Pecos Gambusia—are endangered. There are changing areas with showers and two diving boards at the pool, which is open daily from 8am to sunset. Next door, the **Toyahvale Desert Oasis,** 9225 Tex. 17 S. (© **432/375-2572**; www.toyahvale.com), provides swimwear, snorkeling and scuba diving equipment rentals and air fills from 10am to 6pm daily March through October and 10am to 6pm weekends (or by appointment) the rest of the year.

A reconstructed *cienega* (desert wetland) is another notable attraction in Balmorhea State Park. Located near the campground, the San Solomon Cienega is a good spot to look for native wildlife: You might see a Texas spiny soft-shelled turtle, a blotched water snake, or a green heron from the raised wooden platform, or spot a headwater catfish

---

# A SIDE trip TO CANDELARIA

West of Presidio, FM 170 continues for 48 miles as a paved road to Candelaria. The drive is scenic, off the beaten path, and highly recommended. The commercial operations are few and far between, save **Chinati Hot Springs,** Box 67 Candelaria Route, Marfa, TX 79843 (© **432/ 229-4165**; www.chinatihotsprings.com), a rustic resort centered on the 109°F (43°C) water of the eponymous springs. It costs $13 to soak ($6 for children 12 and under); camping ($15 per person, includes admission) and overnight lodging ($75–$115 double) are also available. Regardless, you'll find many photo opportunities and get a sense of the border as a real place and not an imaginary line.

through the underwater viewing window. A path system allows viewing of the fish, reptiles, and amphibians in the canals.

The park has 34 campsites, most with water and electrical hookups, for $11 to $17 a night, in addition to the $7 entrance fee. Additionally, there is a small motel on the park's grounds, with standard rooms for $60 to $75 double and rooms with kitchenettes for $80 nightly. For groceries, you'll need to head into town, as the gift shop at the visitor center stocks mainly souvenirs and books. The park is located 4 miles south of the town of Balmorhea on Tex. 17.

# Marfa

115 miles NW of Big Bend National Park; 193 miles SE of El Paso; 21 miles S of Fort Davis

Named after a character in Dostoevski's *The Brothers Karamazov* by a railroad exec's wife, this town of 2,000 residents is on the brink of one of the last American frontiers. Surrounded by rugged terrain, Marfa is, to say the least, remote. Once an Old West saloon-and-casino outpost, the predominantly Mexican town has evolved into a haven for contemporary artists, its nucleus being the avant-garde Chinati Foundation. This phenomenon makes for some interesting contrasts: 10-gallon hats and berets, wine bars and feed stores, cowboys and intellectuals, all co-existing in the same small town. There's a lot of buzz about Marfa being "the next Santa Fe," but it remains more than a little bit sleepy—and that's a big part of its charm.

## ESSENTIALS
### Getting There

Marfa is located at the junction of U.S. 67, U.S. 90, and Tex. 17, 60 miles north of Big Bend Ranch State Park. If you're arriving from the east, take I-10, exit 248, and proceed 82 miles on U.S. 67 through Alpine. From the west, Marfa is located 78 miles southeast of Van Horn on U.S. 90; from the north, it's 60 miles south of I-10, exit 206, on Tex. 17. The nearest major commercial airport is in Midland.

### Getting Around

Tex. 17 (Lincoln St.) is the main north-south artery, and U.S. 90 (San Antonio St.) is the main east-west route. The town square and Presidio County Courthouse are located at Lincoln and Highland streets. You can stroll around downtown Marfa, but in general, a car is necessary to check out the Marfa lights and other attractions.

### Visitor Information

Contact the **Marfa Chamber of Commerce,** 207 N. Highland Ave. in the Paisano Hotel (P.O. Box 635), Marfa, TX 79843 (© **800/650-9696** or 432/729-4942; www.marfacc.com), for visitor information.

**FAST FACTS** The nearest hospital is 35 miles west in Alpine, the **Big Bend Regional Medical Center,** 2600 Tex. 118 N. (© **432/837-3447**). The **post office,** 100 N. Highland Ave., is open Monday through Friday from 8am to 4:30pm.

## THE TOP ATTRACTIONS

Besides the attractions listed below, **Big Bend Ranch State Park ★★**, 60 miles south of Marfa (© **432/358-4444** or 512/389-8919 for reservations; www.tpwd.state.tx.us), is Texas's largest state park at over 300,000 acres. It rivals Big Bend as a scenic desert wonderland featuring both the river and mountains—except it only attracts about 10,000 visitors a year, many of whom raft the park's stretch of Rio Grande and never venture into the remote interior. There are primitive campsites and excellent hiking opportunities in and around El Solitario, a huge volcanic swelling in the eastern end of the park. Entrance fees are $3 for adults, and free for kids 11 and under. Campsites are $8 and backcountry camping is $5. Mountain bike rentals, tours, and horseback rides are available at the Sauceda visitor center in the park's interior. There is also lodging available at Sauceda for $25 to $100 per night.

You can catch a ride in that big, blue West Texas sky with **Marfa Gliders** (☎ **800/667-9464;** www.flygliders.com). Rides cost about $130 and last 15 minutes to over an hour, depending on wind conditions.

**Chinati Foundation ★★** 🎨 Housed in 15 buildings at a former U.S. Army post, this decidedly different arts facility is the centerpiece of Marfa's fertile contemporary arts scene. Founded in 1985 by the late Donald Judd, the permanent collection consists of numerous works of modernist, minimalist, and avant-garde art in mediums ranging from paper to steel, from fluorescent light to concrete. Defying artistic expectations, the pieces are all about context; each is strongly tied to architecture and landscape. There are also temporary displays and exhibitions by an international group of artists-in-residence. The entire permanent collection is accessible by guided tours only. Tours start at 10am, break for lunch at noon, then continue from 2 to 3:30pm. Reservations are recommended 3 days in advance for individuals and are required during holiday periods. A separate, 40-minute artillery sheds tour allows a glimpse at Donald Judd's untitled works in mill aluminum. Call for additional tours of the collection during spring break season, for private viewing or for group tours (reserve 2 weeks in advance). The foundation hosts a major open house every October. Marfa's population momentarily doubles during the event, selling out every hotel within a 100-mile radius.

U.S. 67 (½ mile south of Marfa). ☎ **432/729-4362.** www.chinati.org. Admission $10 adults, $5 students and seniors, free for children 11 and under. Wed–Sun 10am. Artillery sheds tour: $5. Thurs–Sun 3:45pm.

**Marfa and Presidio County Museum** Housed in the historic Victorian adobe Humphris-Humphreys House, this museum focuses on the area since 1883, with exhibits on ranching, mining, and military history. I recommend it mainly for the excellent collection of black-and-white photographs shot by Frank Duncan in the first half of the 20th century, and a natural history exhibit on the surrounding Chihuahuan Desert. Allow 1 hour.

110 W. San Antonio St. ☎ **432/729-4140.** Free admission, donations accepted. Tues–Sat 2–5pm and by appointment.

**Presidio County Courthouse** Built in 1885 for $60,000—and magnificently restored in 2001 for $2.5 million—this courthouse is one of West Texas's most impressive, with its magnificent domed roof and classical Victorian woodwork. The architectural style is Second Empire with Italianate details such as overhanging eaves, decorative brackets, and windows that delineate the floors. A "Statue of Justice" stands atop the dome, sans the traditional scales. According to local legend, a convicted cowboy shot the scales out of the statue's hands in the 1890s, proclaiming, "There is no justice in this country." If you have the time, climb to the fifth floor for the view of Marfa and the surrounding countryside.

Lincoln St. and Highland Ave. ☎ **432/729-4942.** Free admission. Building Mon–Fri 9am–5pm; grounds 24 hr.

## WHERE TO STAY

**Cibolo Creek Ranch ★★★** Tucked under the Chinati Mountains in some of the most wide-open country in all of Texas, this is a getaway for the most special of

## MARFA'S mystery LIGHTS

In 1883, an illumination flickered on the horizon east of Marfa, spooking a young cowhand by the name of Robert Ellison. Fearing the lights were Apache campfires, Ellison left behind the cattle he was herding and searched the terrain on horseback. He found nothing. Ever since, the **"Marfa Ghost Lights"** have puzzled thousands of eyewitnesses, as they appear, disappear, and reappear in an area where there are no roads, no houses, and no human inhabitants. Some observers insist the lights are the work of supernatural beings or visiting aliens, while others point to electrostatic discharge, car headlights, campfires, or swamp gas as the real cause, but no one has definitively solved the mystery.

There is a nifty viewing area 9 miles east of Marfa on U.S. 90. The lights are best viewed between 2 and 4 hours after sundown: Look to the northeast, just to the right of the mountains, along the horizon for the sporadic flickers of light. If there's a crowd, it's a scene straight out of *Close Encounters of the Third Kind*. If the lights really pique your interest, don't miss the annual **Marfa Lights Festival,** a Labor Day weekend celebration with a parade, street dances, concerts, and arts-and-crafts sales.

occasions, and accordingly priced. Situated on a 32,000-acre ranch that's a world away from the outside world (and home to mule deer, bison, elk, aoudad, and Texas longhorns), the ranch is centered on a restoration of a historic 1857 private fort, the domain of trader and cattle baron Milton Faver until the 1880s. The idyllic setting plays host today to a first-class resort, featuring picture-perfect guest rooms with red-tile floors, adobe walls, and sumptuous border decor. The recreation is as impressive as the scenery: Horseback rides and Humvee mountain tours are available for a fee. Trails crisscross the property. Natural springs feed canals that fill an idyllic lake, complete with fish to lure and paddle boats to paddle. Gourmet meals, served family style, are part of the package at the remote ranch.

Located 32 miles south of Marfa off U.S. 67 (P.O. Box 44), Shafter, TX 79850. ✆ **866/496-9460** or 432/229-3737. Fax 432/229-3653. www.cibolocreekranch.com. 32 units. $475 double; $75 per additional person. Rates include all meals and recreational activities. AE, DISC, MC, V. **Amenities:** Restaurant; bar; exercise room; Jacuzzi; outdoor heated pool; Wi-Fi (free). *In room:* A/C, no phone.

**El Cosmico ★** 🗡 Opening in 2009, El Cosmico is a unique establishment with a mix of campsites, yurts, safari tents, and—the most luxurious—restored vintage trailers complete with outdoor showers or tubs. Most of them date from the 1940s to the 1960s and have plenty of funky, nostalgia-laden personality. The 18-acre resort is centered on the Highland House, with a small shop, beer and wine, a record player and a nice stash of vinyl, and plenty of places to lounge. There is a shared kitchen and bathroom for campers and those staying in tents and yurts. For the Chinati-oriented visitor, you can't get much closer—the properties border one another.

802 S. Highland Ave. (U.S. 67), Marfa, TX 79843. ✆ **432/729-1950.** www.elcosmico.com. 15 trailers, 14 yurts and tents, 25 campsites. $95–$125 trailer; $65 yurt or tent; $20 campsite. Pets accepted ($10 per night). AE, DISC, MC, V. **Amenities:** Bikes; Wi-Fi (free). *In room:* Kitchenette (in trailers), no phone.

**The Hotel Paisano ★★** After years of semi-hibernation, this glorious 1930s-era hotel has reclaimed its former status as the premier hotel between El Paso and San Antonio. The building itself is stunning, a renowned hybrid of prairie and mission architecture that's listed on the National Register of Historic Places. Inside, the rooms balance history and modernity, with comfortable new furnishings and a myriad of arches, stained-glass windows, and other subtle details. And there's some serious Hollywood lore: The cast and crew of the epic *Giant* stayed here during production in the 1950s. James Dean's one-time room is the most popular, but Rock Hudson's corner suite, with a full kitchen and a massive balcony overlooking the courtyard pool, is my favorite.

Texas St. and Highland Ave. (P.O. Box Z), Marfa, TX 79843. (C) **866/729-3669** or 432/729-3669. Fax 432/426-3779. www.hotelpaisano.com. 41 units, including 9 suites. $99–$159 double; $159–$250 suite. AE, DISC, MC, V. **Amenities:** Restaurant; bar; outdoor heated pool. *In room:* A/C, TV, kitchen, no phone, Wi-Fi (free).

**The Thunderbird Hotel ★★**  This one-time roadside motel is now a hip work of minimalist art after a renovation. Centered on an outdoor pool and a gravel parking lot, the U-shaped structure has rooms that are starkly contemporary with Western details (for example, cowhide rugs atop painted concrete floors) and such modern perks as iPod docking stations. The pool and adjacent fire-pit area have Wi-Fi. Available for rental here: cruiser bikes ($20 a day), vintage record players ($10 a stay), DVDs from a well-chosen library ($3 a night), and a typewriter (free).

601 W. San Antonio St. and Highland Ave., Marfa, TX 79843. (C) **432/729-1984.** Fax 432/729-1989. www.thunderbirdmarfa.com. 24 units. $130–$180 double. AE, DISC, MC, V. **Amenities:** Bikes; outdoor heated pool. *In room:* A/C, TV/DVD, movie library, hair dryer, minibar, Wi-Fi (free).

## WHERE TO DINE

Beyond the greasy spoons, there are a few high-end restaurants in Marfa, including **Jett's Grill** at the Hotel Paisano, Texas Street and Highland Avenue ((C) **432/729-3838**).

# GALLERY hopping IN THE BIG BEND

Marfa might be one of the most buzzed-about art towns in the West, but—outside of the Chinati Foundation—it has only a handful of galleries. Art aficionados can cover Marfa's gallery scene proper in a few hours, but a day can be spent visiting galleries in not only Marfa, but Alpine and Marathon as well. Here are my favorites.

**Marfa**  I like **Ballroom Marfa,** an installation-oriented space at 108 E. San Antonio St. ((C) **432/729-3600;** www.ballroom marfa.org), which also hosts film screenings, lectures, and musical performances; and the minimalist-oriented **Exhibitions 2d,** 400 S. Highland Ave. ((C) **432/729-3000;** www.exhibitions2d.com).

**Alpine**  Keri Artzt's **Kiowa Gallery,** 105 E. Holland Ave. ((C) **432/837-3067**), is my favorite in the region, with an eclectic collection of mostly regional work, ranging from elegant to oddball. **Ivey's Emporium,** 109 E. Holland Ave. ((C) **432/837-7474**), has a wide range of artwork and gifts.

**Marathon**  **Baxter Gallery,** 209 W. U.S. 90 ((C) **432/386-0689;** www.baxtergallery. com), specializes in landscapes and wildlife sculptures by local artisans. The fine art photography at **James Evans Gallery,** 21 S. 1st St. ((C) **432/386-4366;** www.jevans gallery.com), is alternately sublime and stunning.

**Terlingua**  In Terlingua Ghost Town, Bryn Moore's **Leapin' Lizard** ((C) **432/371-2775;** www.leapinlizardterlingua.com) showcases local jewelry, paintings, and folk art. There is also a good deal of art at the **Terlingua Trading Post** ((C) **432/371-2234;** www.historic-terlingua.com).

Named after James Dean's character in *Giant*, the restaurant serves dinner only and features Continental fare spiced with a south-of-the-border twist. Most main courses run $10 to $20. Another upscale option is **Maiya's,** 103 N. Highland Ave. (© **432/729-4410;** www.maiyasrestaurant.com), offering a creative selection of northern Italian fare in a very sleek, very red space. It's open Wednesday through Saturday evenings, with most dishes between $15 and $30. For a quick, cheap bite, it's hard to beat the **Pizza Foundation,** 100 E. San Antonio St. (© **432/729-3377;** www.pizzafoundation.com), serving New York–style slices and pies from a (barely) converted garage.

## SHOPPING

The best bookstore in the entire region is the sophisticated **Marfa Book Co.,** 105 S. Highland Ave. (© **432/729-3906;** www.marfabookco.com), which features a coffee and wine bar and a deep inventory of art and architecture titles.

# Alpine

80 miles N of Big Bend National Park; 26 miles E of Marfa; 23 miles SE of Fort Davis

The home of Sul Ross State University, Alpine is nicknamed "the Hub of the Big Bend." Long the commercial center of vast Brewster County, this town of about 6,000 residents has numerous amenities that make it a good jumping-off point to Big Bend National Park, or a nice stopover while en route to other area destinations: a vibrant Main Street with plenty of galleries and funky retailers, excellent hiking in all directions, an active railroad depot on the Southern Pacific line, and festivals and museums that are pure West.

## ESSENTIALS

### Getting There

Alpine is located at the junction of U.S. 67/90 and Tex. 118, just 80 miles north of Big Bend National Park. If you're arriving from the east, take I-10, exit 248, and proceed 56 miles on U.S. 67. From the west, Alpine is located 55 miles south of Balmorhea (I-10, exit 206). **Amtrak** (© **800/872-2745;** www.amtrak.com) serves the train station at 102 W. Holland St., the closest depot to Big Bend National Park. The nearest major commercial airport is in Midland.

### Getting Around

U.S. 67/90 (Holland St.) is the main east-west artery and Tex. 119 (5th St.) is the main north-south route; downtown is centered on the intersection of the two. Rental cars are available through **Alpine Auto Rental** (© **800/894-3463** or 432/837-3463; www.alpineautorental.com).

### Visitor Information

Contact the **Alpine Chamber of Commerce,** 106 N. 3rd St., Alpine, TX 79830 (© **800/561-3712** or 432/837-2326; www.alpinetexas.com).

**FAST FACTS** The **Big Bend Regional Medical Center,** 2600 Tex. 118 N. (© **432/837-3447;** www.bigbendhealthcare.com), has the only 24-hour emergency room in the region. The **post office,** 901 W. Holland Ave., is open Monday through Friday from 8am to 4pm, and Saturday 10am to 1pm.

## THE TOP ATTRACTIONS

**Elephant Mountain Wildlife Management Area** While hiking and camping are available, the prime activity here is a 15-mile round-trip driving tour that provides excellent wildlife-viewing opportunities. The area is home to a herd of desert bighorn,

## 99 Luftballons over Alpine

Well, maybe not quite 99, but you can see at least a few dozen balloons launch near the Casparis Airport, 2 miles north of Alpine off Hwy. 118, during Labor Day weekend. The **Big Bend Balloon Bash** is 3 days of balloons and other aerial pursuits. Arrive before 9am to see the balloons, or go see them glow Saturday night. Call ✆ **432/837-7486** or log on to www.bigbend balloonbash.com.

as well as mule deer, javelinas, and dozens of reptile and bird species. Morning is the best time to spot the critters in this mountainous desert environment. There are primitive campsites with fire rings available at no cost.

26 miles south of Alpine via Tex. 118. ✆ **432/837-3251.** www.tpwd.state.tx.us. Free admission. Portions of the area are open year-round; driving tour May–Aug.

**Kokernot Field**    One of the crown jewels of minor-league stadiums, this baseball park was built by local rancher Herbert L. Kokernot, Jr., who spared no expense in modeling the place after Chicago's Wrigley Field. From the red granite walls to the ironwork, the park cost Kokernot $1.25 million to build in 1947. It's still an active stadium, with home games played by the independent Alpine Cowboys. Expect to spend a few minutes here—unless a game is scheduled.

E. Hendryx Dr. and Fighting Buck Ave. ✆ **432/837-2326.** Free admission; donations accepted. Grounds open 24 hrs., stadium open on game days and for special events.

**Museum of the Big Bend** ★    This excellent facility tracks the Big Bend region's history, from American Indian cultures (points that date back more than 3,000 years) to the European settlers in "Big Bend Legacy." Among the other highlights are replicas of pterosaur bones excavated from Big Bend National Park and a plane-size scale model of the real deal flying in the rafters—the critter had a 51-foot wingspan!—and an outdoor cactus garden. Expect to spend about an hour.

On the campus of the Sul Ross State University. ✆ **432/837-8143.** www.sulross.edu/~museum. Free admission; donations accepted. Tues–Sat 9am–5pm; Sun 1–5pm.

## WHERE TO STAY

Besides the options listed below, I also like the **Alpine Guest Lofts** (877/298-5638; www.alpineguestlofts.com), with four units with a queen and king, plus a hideaway or a futon for $105 to $195. One unit has a full kitchen.

**Holland Hotel**    Originally opening on Alpine's main drag in the 1920s, the Holland Hotel was completely renovated in 2008. No room here is exactly the same as another, from the newly retouched suites (with hardwood floors, antique reproductions, and jetted tubs) to the cozy fourth-floor penthouse, complete with a private hot-tub deck. Rooms may also be combined to create differently sized suites.

209 W. Holland Ave., Alpine, TX 79830. ✆ **800/535-8040** or 432/837-2800. www.thehollandhotel texas.com. 24 units. $80–$140 double; $140–$230 suite. AE, DISC, MC, V. **Amenities:** Bar. *In room:* A/C, TV, no phone (some rooms), Wi-Fi (free).

**Maverick Inn** ★    A retro-minded and upscale update of a roadside motel—down to its newer old-fashioned neon sign—the Maverick Inn took cues from the Gage Hotel and other historic desert tourist outposts. Studies in masculine Texas chic, the woody, adobe-walled rooms have Saltillo tile floors with cowhide rugs. The small, bean-shaped pool is an oasis, bordered by desert flora and a shaded patio.

1200 E. Holland Ave., Alpine, TX 79830. (© **432/837-0628.** Fax 432/837-0825. www.themaverickinn. com. 18 units. $70–$140 double. Rates include continental breakfast. Pets accepted. AE, DISC, MC, V. **Amenities:** Outdoor heated pool. *In room:* A/C, TV, fridge, Wi-Fi (free).

## WHERE TO DINE

Named for a ranch in *Giant*, the **Reata Restaurant,** 203 N. 5th St. (© **432/837-9232;** www.reata.net), serves regional Texan food and some of the best steaks in the Big Bend; main courses are $8 to $13 for lunch and $15 to $30 for dinner. **Alicia's,** 708 E. Gallego Ave. (© **432/837-2802**), is a standby for big burritos and hearty breakfasts (about $3–$8). **Texas Fusion,** 200 W. Murphy Ave. (© **432/837-1214**), is a favorite with locals, serving barbecue, Mexican dishes, burgers, and steaks; main courses are $5 to $16.

# MIDLAND & ODESSA

300 miles E of El Paso; 135 miles S of Lubbock

Welcome to oil country, where the ups and downs of the petroleum industry have long defined these twin cities, 21 miles apart on I-20. Midland-Odessa sits in the geographic center of the Permian Basin, the home of the country's richest oil fields—about 20% of the United States' reserves. Today, only Alaska produces more oil than the Permian Basin.

The area saw the first of several oil booms in the 1920s. However, less than a decade later, the Great Depression brought on the first of several busts. Production increased during World War II, but foreign competition brought on another bust by the 1970s. The pendulum again swayed in the boom direction until 1982, when the bottom suddenly fell out of the oil market: Wells were capped, new houses went unsold, and banks failed. In the time since, the industry has diversified and recovered, but Midland and Odessa remain the heart and soul of the Permian Basin's oil industry. As it goes, so do Midland and Odessa.

The one-time home of two presidents—George H. W. Bush and his son George W.—the cities are home to a handful of noteworthy attractions and offer an educational glimpse at the rewards and the ravages of a volatile, oil-heavy economy. While Midland and Odessa are by no means tourist destinations, they are two of the few actual cities in West Texas, and a good gateway to the Big Bend area.

## Essentials

### GETTING THERE

Midland is located on the north side of I-20, accessible via exits 136 and 138. Tex. 349 runs north-south through the city. Odessa is located 21 miles west of Midland on the north side of I-20, accessible via exits 112 through 121. U.S. 385 (Grant Ave.) bisects the city north-south, through downtown and to I-20.

**Midland International Airport,** located between Midland and Odessa at 9506 La Force Blvd. (© **432/560-2200;** www.flymaf.com), is the primary commercial airport in the area (and the closest major airport to Big Bend National Park), served by **American, Continental, Southwest,** and **United.** Car-rental companies are on-site.

# MIDLAND'S famous SON, GEORGE

Born in New Haven, Connecticut, on July 6, 1946, George Walker Bush—also known as Dubya—was on the plains of West Texas by the time he was 2 years old. His father (and the 41st president), George H. W. Bush, moved the family west to seek fortune in the oil business. The first stop was Odessa, but in 1950, the family moved to Midland, where they lived until 1959. It was this time—young George's formative years—that made the biggest impression on this president-to-be, and in 1975 he returned as an adult to Midland's oil business. The Bushes lived at 1412 W. Ohio Ave. between 1951 and 1955, and this home has been restored to its 1950s appearance and is open to the public Tuesday through Saturday 10am to 5pm and Sunday 2 to 5pm. For additional information, contact the **George W. Bush Childhood Home,** 1412 W. Ohio Ave. (© **432/682-1112;** www.bushchildhood home.org). Additionally, the **Presidential Museum** in Odessa (p. 363) relocated the Bush home in Odessa to its grounds and also restored it for the public.

## GETTING AROUND

Laid out on a fairly standard grid that parallels I-20, Midland is a relatively easy city to navigate by car. Most of the accommodations are located on the north and west sides of town. The main downtown thoroughfare is **Wall Street** (Business 20), which continues east through downtown. **Loop 250** circumnavigates the city.

Odessa's busiest street is **Grant Avenue** (U.S. 385, also known as Andrews Hwy.), which runs north-south through downtown. **42nd Street** becomes **Tex. 191** and continues east to Midland. **Loop 338** circles the city.

## VISITOR INFORMATION

The **Midland Convention and Visitors Bureau,** 109 N. Main St., Midland, TX 79701 (© **800/624-6435** or 432/683-3381; www.visitmidlandtexas.com), and the **Odessa Convention and Visitors Bureau,** 700 N. Grant Ave., Ste. 200, Odessa, TX 79761 (© **800/780-4678** or 432/333-7871; www.odessacvb.com), can provide additional information on the cities. There is a visitor center in Midland just north of I-20 at exit 136.

**FAST FACTS** Midland Memorial Hospital, 2200 W. Illinois Ave. (© **432/685-1111;** www.midland-memorial.com), has a 24-hour emergency room; Midland's **downtown post office** is at 100 E. Wall St. **Medical Center Hospital,** 500 W. 4th St. (© **432/640-4000;** www.mchodessa.com), is Odessa's largest full-service hospital; the **main post office** is located at 200 N. Texas St.

# What to See & Do

## THE TOP ATTRACTIONS

Fans of roadside kitsch surely will appreciate two Odessa landmarks: The world's largest jack rabbit is located on 8th Street and Sam Houston Avenue; and on the campus of the University of Texas of the Permian Basin at 4901 E. University Blvd. sits a 70% scale replica of Stonehenge.

**American Airpower Heritage Museum** ★ With a "ghost squadron" of more than 130 planes and choppers, this museum is home to numerous historic aircraft, as well as the world's largest collection of vintage World War II "nose art." It's worth an hour or two for aviation and history buffs. The planes are housed in an adjacent 60,000-square-foot hangar, with about 15 on display at any given time alongside several multimedia exhibits. The museum's operators sponsor the annual AIRSHO each October, featuring dramatic re-creations of World War II events.

9600 Wright Dr. at Midland International Airport. ☎ **432/567-3010.** www.airpowermuseum.org. Admission $10 adults, $9 teens and seniors, $7 children 6–12, free for children 5 and under. Mon–Sat 9am–5pm; Sun and holidays noon–5pm.

### The Globe of the Great Southwest 🎭 
This theater is a replica of London's Globe Theatre (William Shakespeare's old haunt), down to the octagonal design and jutting stage surrounded by seating. The resident company produces about eight plays annually; the emphasis is on Shakespeare. The theater also hosts touring productions and concerts.

2308 Shakespeare Rd., Odessa. ☎ **432/332-1586** or 432/580-3177. www.globesw.org. Admission $5. Tickets for performances $9–$20. Mon–Fri 10am–6pm. Tours available by appointment only.

### Museum of the Southwest ★ ☺ 
Occupying the stately Turner Mansion (1934), this museum does a nice job displaying art and archaeological artifacts. I was impressed by the quality of the museum's permanent collection, with pieces by several Taos Society members and a wide range of indigenous art. Also on-site: a children's museum, with interactive exhibits on art and science and a kid-size town; and a cutting-edge planetarium. Expect to spend an hour or two here.

1705 W. Missouri Ave., Midland. ☎ **432/683-2882.** www.museumsw.org. Free admission to museum (donations welcome); children's museum $3; call for planetarium shows, $3 or $4–$6. Tues–Sat 10am–5pm; Sun 2–5pm.

### Odessa Meteor Crater and Museum 
The second-largest meteor crater in the United States (bested only by Sunset Crater near Flagstaff, Arizona) is about 50,000 years old, born when a flaming hunk of asteroid collided with the West Texas plains. A National Natural Landmark, the crater was once 550 feet wide and 100 feet deep, but sediment has obscured it substantially. It's still big enough to encompass a short nature trail, marked with interpretive signs detailing the initial impact and the subsequent study. The museum houses chunks of the actual meteorite among its displays. Expect to spend 45 minutes here.

Meteor Crater Rd. (2 miles off I-10, exit 108). ☎ **432/381-0946.** Free admission. Museum Tues–Sat 10am–5pm, Sun 1–5pm; trail daily 9am–6pm.

### The Permian Basin Petroleum Museum 
Midland, being the center of both the Permian Basin (geographically) and the American oil business (economically), is the ideal location for a museum dedicated to "black gold." Requiring a little more than an hour of time to investigate, the displays here are a tad dated (the museum opened in 1975, and some exhibits may be original) and often come off as PR for the Texas oil industry. Nonetheless, the museum does a nice job explaining both the prehistoric basis for the rich oil field—West Texas was a tropical sea 230 million years ago—and the industry's modern history, plus it has a nice gallery of oil paintings portraying life in the oil fields. The Chaparral Gallery has first-rate exhibits on Chaparral race cars, which describe their pioneering history and the interdependence of petroleum and surface transportation.

1500 I-20 W. (exit 136), Midland. ☎ **432/683-4403.** www.petroleummuseum.org. Admission $8 adults, $6 youths 12–17 and seniors, $5 children 6–11, free for children 5 and under. Mon–Sat 10am–5pm; Sun 2–5pm.

## Fantasy Land Park: The Origin of Alley Oop

Alley Oop, the time-traveling caveman who starred in the longest-running comic strip ever, has roots in the Permian Basin. Creator V.T. Hamlin came up with him while working at the *Des Moines Register* in 1932, drawing on his experience working in the oil fields around Iraan (the town's founding couple's names, Ira and Ann, combined into one trisyllabic word). In the 1960s, locals decided to honor Hamlin and his comic strip, and they came up with the idea for Fantasy Land, a park with all sorts of rides and statues inspired by the comic strip. A statue of Alley Oop's tame dinosaur Dinny was dedicated in 1965, and Alley Oop's oversized mug, sporting a top hat and smoking a cigar, followed a few years later. Organizers never got around to any other statues of characters like Oola, the Grand Wizer, Dr. Elbert Wonmug, or Queen Umpateedle, but the park's resident museum has a scrapbook full of old comic strips and its fair share of artifacts and oddities.

Fantasy Land Park (© 432/639-2232) is located on Alley Oop Lane in Iraan, about 90 miles southeast of Odessa.

**The Presidential Museum ★**   Whereas many museums detail the life and times of one president, this is one of a few museums dedicated to the office of the U.S. presidency itself. There is a gallery of portraits including every president from Washington to Obama, and the collection of memorabilia is fascinating, with scores of buttons, bobbleheads, posters, and stickers. Expect to spend an hour or two.

4919 E. University Blvd., Odessa. © 432/363-7737. www.presidentialmuseum.org. $8 adults, $5 students and seniors, free for children 4 and under. Tues–Sat 10am–5pm. Closed major holidays.

## OUTDOOR ACTIVITIES & SPECTATOR SPORTS

Midland has two public golf courses: the 27-hole **Hogan Park Golf Course,** 3600 N. Fairground Rd. (© 432/685-7360; www.hoganparkgolf.com), with greens fees for 18 holes of $10 to $20, and carts for $18; and the 18-hole **Nueva Vista Golf Club,** 6101 W. Wadley Ave. (© 432/520-0500; www.nuevavistagolf.com), with greens fees of $16 to $28 and carts for $12 per rider. In Odessa, **Sunset Country Club,** 9301 Andrews Hwy. (© 432/366-1061), is an 18-hole course open to the public year-round. Greens fees are $19 to $24, and carts are $11. There's also **Ratliff Ranch Golf Links,** 7500 N. Grandview Ave. (© 432/550-8181; www.ratliffranch golfodessa.com), with greens fees for 18 holes of $15 to $24, and carts for $11.

Baseball fans can get their fix in the form of the **Midland RockHounds** (© 432/520-2255; www.midlandrockhounds.org), the AA Texas League affiliate of the Oakland Athletics. The RockHounds play 70 home dates from April to August at the Citibank Ballpark, 5514 Champions Dr. Tickets cost $5 to $10. The Central Hockey League's **Odessa Jackalopes** (© 432/552-7825; www.jackalopes.org) play an October-to-March schedule at the Ector County Coliseum, 42nd Street and Andrews Highway. Tickets run $12 to $25. But it's high-school football that is the sport of choice in Midland and Odessa, which provides the backdrop to the best-selling book (and popular TV show and movie) *Friday Night Lights*.

## Where to Stay

**Hilton Midland Plaza ★**   If you're looking for luxury at a reasonable price, look no further than this full-service hotel, located in the heart of the oil business in downtown Midland. The hotel consists of two 11-story towers on either side of a courtyard pool. The guest rooms are spacious and comfortable. Every room has plush chairs, a pair of two-line phones, and a 32- or 42-inch flatscreen television. Some of the rooms on the concierge level have balconies. The facilities are terrific, including restaurants serving three meals daily, a pair of bars, and a top-flight exercise room.

117 W. Wall St., Midland, TX 79701. ℰ **432/683-6131.** Fax 432/683-0958. www.midland.hilton.com. 249 units. $109–$229 double; $209–$350 suite. AE, DISC, MC, V. **Amenities:** 2 restaurants; 2 bars; concierge; executive-level rooms; exercise room; Jacuzzi; outdoor pool; room service. *In room:* A/C, TV, hair dryer, Wi-Fi (free).

**MCM Eleganté** ★   This former Radisson reopened as an independent in 2002 under the tag "tropical elegance in the desert." With a lobby boasting multihued floral carpeting, stained-glass chandeliers, and a large aquarium, the hotel is a bit over the top, but it hits the mark more often than not. The rooms have nice city views from wall-length windows, crown molding, and red-hued wood furnishings—beyond what you'd expect in a chain—with plenty of perks. (One example: The smallish bathrooms are stocked with bottled water—which is much appreciated once you get a taste of what's on tap.) The recreational facilities are dynamite, including a jogging track, a putting/chipping green, a seasonally domed pool area, and several sports fields.

5200 E. University Blvd., Odessa, TX 79762. ℰ **866/368-5885** or 432/368-5885. Fax 432/362-8958. www.mcmelegante.com. 191 units, including 4 suites. $99–$209 double; $279–$449 suite. AE, DISC, MC, V. **Amenities:** Restaurant; bar; executive-level rooms; exercise room; Jacuzzi; outdoor pool; room service; spa. *In room:* A/C, TV, hair dryer, Wi-Fi (free).

## Where to Dine

My pick for a quick bite in the area is **Manuel's Crispy Tacos,** 1404 E. 2nd St., Odessa (ℰ **432/333-2751**), a fun family joint known for its namesake dish. Main courses are $5 to $16. In Midland, my Mexican pick is **Gerardo's Casita,** 2407 N. Big Spring St. (ℰ **432/570-8012;** www.gerardoscasita.net), serving tacos, enchiladas, chiles rellenos, steaks, and margaritas since 1977. Also recommended is **the Bar,** 606 W. Missouri Ave., Midland (ℰ **432/685-1757;** www.thebarmidland.com), a taxidermy- and petroliana-laden establishment with burgers and pub fare.

**Wall Street Bar and Grill** ★  NEW AMERICAN   With an air of elegance, this restaurant caters to the wheelers and dealers of Midland's business community, but history buffs will find other things to gawk at while they dine. The 1910 building, originally a saddle shop, still features the original pressed-tin ceiling, and the cherry-stained mahogany bar and back bar received a commendation from the Texas Historical Foundation for their restoration. The menu, conversely, is contemporary, with tasty, creative dishes such as seafood rellenos with chipotle-tomatillo sauce, pecan-crusted trout, and charbroiled pork chops, not to mention excellent hand-cut steaks. The crawfish étouffée, rich and thick, is just about as good as it gets.

115 E. Wall St., Midland. ℰ **432/684-8686.** Main courses $9–$25. AE, DISC, MC, V. Mon–Fri 11am–2:30pm; Mon–Sat 5:30–10pm; Sun brunch 10:30am–2:30pm; Sun 5:30–9pm.

## Dune Sledding in Monahans Sandhills State Park

30 miles W of Odessa

When Spanish explorers first stumbled upon these sandhills in the mid–16th century, they labeled them "perfect miniature Alps of sand." Perpetually changing geologic and geometric wonders, the 3,840 acres of dunes at **Monahans Sandhills State Park,** I-20 exit 86 (© **432/943-2092;** www.tpwd.state.tx.us), represent the only public access to a 200-mile range of dunes that stretches from eastern New Mexico into the Permian Basin of West Texas.

Start at the visitor center, where you can watch a short orientation video, check out exhibits on all things sandy, and trek through the dunes on a .25-mile interpretive trail. The center rents plastic disks and toboggans for West Texas–style sledding on dune slopes that top out at 70 feet. Besides sledding the dunes, you can explore them on foot or horseback. (You'll need to bring your own horse to the 600-acre equestrian area; no stables are on-site.)

The dunes are far from barren. Many plants thrive here, including the shin oak, an unusually small oak with unusually large acorns. Other native inhabitants are deer, coyotes, possums, and bobcats. For the human guests, there are 24 back-in campsites with water and electricity for $14 a night; the day-use fee is $13 (free for children 12 and under). The park is open daily from 8am to 10pm.

If you're in the area, stop in at **Million Barrel Museum,** 400 Museum Blvd. in Monahans (© **432/943-8401**), home to a now-dry reservoir that once held a million barrels of oil. You can walk or even drive in it today, plus check out a variety of displays on the area's history. Rock-and-roll fans will want to check out the **Roy Orbison Museum,** 213 Hendricks Blvd. in the nearby town of Wink, about 15 miles northwest of Monahans. Call © **915/527-3441** for an appointment.

# SAN ANGELO

224 miles NW of Austin; 111 miles SE of Midland; 64 miles N of Sonora

First known as "the town over the river" from Fort Concho, San Angelo was the prototypical rollicking, gunslinging Wild West outpost during the late 1860s and 1870s. During these early days, the soldiers from the fort and cowhands from the field would cross the Concho River to get to the brothels, casinos, and saloons that dominated the town on the other side.

A city of about 100,000 residents, modern San Angelo is worthy of a stop on a cross-Texas road trip. Its rowdy past can be revisited in the form of historic Concho Avenue, now lined with boutiques and jewelers instead of casinos and bordellos, and old Fort Concho, a National Historic Landmark. The city is also one of the few oases of West Texas, with the Concho snaking through town and five reservoirs within 40 miles, and home to a noteworthy arts scene.

## Essentials

### GETTING THERE

The largest city in Texas not located on an interstate, San Angelo lies at the junction of three U.S. highways: 67, 87, and 277. U.S. 87 crosses I-20 at Big Spring, and U.S. 67 and U.S. 277 are both accessible from I-20 near Abilene. From the south, U.S. 67 diverges from I-10 at Fort Stockton and U.S. 277 crosses the interstate at Sonora.

**San Angelo Regional Airport/Mathis Field,** located about 8 miles south of the city at 7654 Knickerbocker Rd. (© **325/659-6409;** www.mathisfield.com), is the only commercial airport in the Concho River Valley and is served by **American.** Car rentals are available at the airport from **Avis, Budget,** and **Hertz.**

## GETTING AROUND

With the confluence of the north and south forks of the Concho River marking the city center, bridges seem to be everywhere and can often make navigation by car a bit tricky. **Bryant Boulevard** (U.S. 87/277) is the major north-south street, but it splits into two one-way streets (the northbound **Koenigheim St.** and southbound **Abe St.**) in the middle of the city. **Chadbourne Street,** just a few blocks east of Bryant Boulevard, runs through the historic part of the city, skirting downtown and historic **Concho Avenue** en route to Fort Concho and other attractions.

The **civic bus system** (© **325/947-8729**) operates five routes from the historic Santa Fe Depot at 703 S. Chadbourne St., from 6:30am to 5:30pm Monday through Friday and 9:30am to 5:30pm Saturday. Fare is $1 for adults, 50¢ for students and seniors, and free for any accompanying children 4 and under.

## VISITOR INFORMATION

The **San Angelo Convention and Visitors Bureau,** 418 W. Ave. B., San Angelo, TX 76903 (© **800/375-1206** or 325/655-4136; www.sanangelo.org), operates a visitor center, open Monday through Friday from 9am to 5pm, Saturday 10am to 5pm, and Sunday noon to 4pm.

**FAST FACTS**   There are 24-hour emergency rooms at **San Angelo Community Medical Center,** 3501 Knickerbocker Rd. (© **325/949-9511;** www.sacmc.com), and **Shannon Medical Center,** 120 E. Harris Ave. (© **325/653-6741;** www. shannonhealth.com). The **main post office,** 1 N. Abe St., is open Monday through Friday from 8am to 7pm and Saturday from 9am to 4:30pm.

# What to See & Do
## THE TOP ATTRACTIONS

Worth a peek is **Paint Brush Alley,** between Concho and Twohig avenues downtown, an imaginative reinvention of an alley as an urban gallery of murals by different artists. Also of note is **Miss Hattie's Bordello Museum,** 18½ E. Concho Ave. (www.misshatties.com). The restored brothel offers tours Friday and Saturday every hour from 1 to 4pm and Monday through Wednesday at 2 and 4pm; admission is $5 per person. Call **Legend Jewelers** (© **888/655-4367** or 325/653-0112) for a tour.

**Fort Concho National Historic Landmark**   Established in 1867 as a means of pioneer defense, Fort Concho provided the impetus for San Angelo's original development of 40 buildings on 1,000 acres. This U.S. Army post, once commanded by William "Pecos Bill" Shafter, was active until 1889, with African-American Buffalo Soldiers making up a considerable portion of the men stationed here. The post is now one of the jewels of the old Texas forts, with 17 original buildings and five rebuilt structures. Some of the buildings are fully furnished with period artifacts, including an 1870 barracks outfitted to a T, down to the last checker on the board. There are exhibits in two of the restored officers' quarters (one is a small museum on telephony, featuring one of Alexander Graham Bell's originals) and the old post headquarters. The former hospital now serves as the interesting **Robert Wood Johnson Museum of Frontier Medicine,** including a re-created ward, some interesting snake oil cure-alls, and the Victorian prototype for the TV-shopping mainstay of electrostimulation. Expect to spend a little more than an hour here.

630 S. Oakes St. © **325/481-2646.** www.fortconcho.com. Admission $3 adults, $2 seniors, $1.50 children 6-17, free for children 5 and under. Guided tour $5 adults, $4 seniors, $3 children 6-17, free for children 5 and under. Mon-Sat 9am-5pm; Sun 1-5pm. Guided tours Tues-Fri on the half-hour 10:30am-3:30pm.

**River Walk** ★ Thanks to the River Beautification Project, which kicked off in 1986, the Concho River is now a splendid centerpiece for the entire city of San Angelo. It sports a 4-mile walking/jogging trail, bountiful outdoor gardens and water displays, a great playground, a skate park, and even a 9-hole golf course (© 325/657-4485) on the River Walk's acres (greens fees: $8.75–$11). Celebration Bridge crosses the river behind the San Angelo Museum of Fine Arts (see below), right past a bronze statue of a mermaid, *"Pearl of the Conchos."* Between the bridge and the old downtown plaza (El Paseo de Santa Angela) sits the Bill Aylor, Sr., Memorial River-Stage, an outdoor venue that is a focus of San Angelo's performing arts scene. The River Walk provides easy access to the San Angelo Museum of Fine Arts, historic Concho Avenue, and Fort Concho.

Along the banks of the Concho River.

**San Angelo Museum of Fine Arts** ★ From its eye-catching home on the Concho River, this standout museum is a must-see for lovers of art and architecture, demanding a stop of 45 minutes or more. The permanent collection focuses on contemporary American ceramics, with about 150 such pieces. Every year from April to June, the museum features the country's top ceramics show, with a national competition in even-numbered years. Another nice perk: The museum has an open back office that allows visitors to see how the facility is managed and get a glimpse into the storage areas. The award-winning building is a work of art in itself, consisting of native limestone, in-grain mesquite flooring, and a curving, copper-clad roof.

1 Love St. on the Concho River. © **325/653-3333.** www.samfa.org. Admission $2 adults, $1 seniors, free for students and children. Tues–Sat 10am–4pm; Sun 1–4pm. Closed major holidays.

## OUTDOOR ACTIVITIES

When it comes to outdoor recreation, San Angelo residents are blessed with the Concho River, two reservoirs, and an excellent civic park system. The highlight is **San Angelo State Park** ★, 3900-2 Mercedes St. (© **325/949-4757** or 949-8935; www.tpwd.state.tx.us), at O.C. Fisher Lake on the city's northwest side, attracting mountain bikers, hikers, boaters, anglers, and equestrians. The park sits at the nexus of four distinct geographical areas—Hill Country, Trans-Pecos, the rolling plains to the east, and the high plains to the north—in an area that has been inhabited by humans for over 10,000 years. Admission to the park is $3 per adult and free for children 12 and under. The day-use hours are from 8am to 10pm.

### The Concho Pearl

The word *concho* pops out from every other corner in San Angelo, from Concho Avenue to Fort Concho to the Concho River. If you're not from the area, it probably doesn't mean much, but if you're a San Angelo jeweler, it means a great deal. The Concho River Valley is home to a dozen species of freshwater mussels in the *Unionacea* family that produce the rare concho pearl, tinted luminous pink, deep purple, or rich lavender by Mother Nature. Some of the earliest known examples of the pearls were Spanish crown jewels in the 16th century. If you want to try to harvest one yourself, you'll need a permit from the **Texas Parks and Wildlife Department** (© **800/792-1112;** www.tpwd.state.tx.us). You can avoid wading in the river, however, if you're willing to plunk down some cash at a local jeweler.

The park's trail system is one of the best in all of West Texas, with more than 50 miles of multiuse trails (hiking, biking, and horseback riding). Certain trails provide access to the only ride-in equestrian campsites between El Paso and San Antonio. The trails connect the north and south shores of the reservoir and range from flat and smooth to rocky and rugged; a detailed map is available at the entrance. There are ample opportunities for birding and wildlife-watching, with 300 avian and 50 mammal species (including pelicans, cormorants, Texas longhorn cattle, and buffalo), and a significant population of horned lizards. In season, hunting and fishing are popular.

On guided tours, visitors can take a look at the petroglyphs in the park, go on a 3-mile hike to fossilized footprints, or learn about the history of buffalo and Texas longhorns. The tours are informative, engaging, and offered on demand (fees are charged).

There are 85 campsites with water and electrical hookups here, and more than 100 tent sites. The campground on the north shore, shaded by massive pecan trees, is especially isolated and attractive, while the southern campgrounds are closer to the reservoir and playground. Nightly camping fees, in addition to park entrance fees, are $8 to $18. There are also a few simple cabins that can accommodate six guests for $36 to $45 a night.

Six miles south of downtown via Knickerbocker Road, the city-owned **Lake Nasworthy** is a fishing, hiking, and boating hot spot. Below the nearly 1,600 surface acres of fresh water, two non-native saltwater species (hybrid trout–corvina and red drum) have thrived alongside native bass and catfish. **Spring Creek Marina & RV Park,** 45 Fisherman's Rd. (© 800/500-7801 or 325/944-3850; www.springcreek marina-rv.com), has campsites with full hookups ($32–$43 nightly), tent sites ($27 nightly), cabins ($50–$110 nightly), fishing docks, and a convenience store. The **San Angelo Nature Center** at Lake Nasworthy, 7409 Knickerbocker Rd. (© 325/942-0121), is a small museum with a garden, a library, and a short interpretive trail system. The center is open Tuesday through Saturday from noon to 5pm.

The **Pictographs of Painted Rocks,** called a "museum, library, and art gallery" of ancient American Indians, is another noteworthy excursion near San Angelo. Located 22 miles southeast of the city near the town of Paint Rock, the site features a natural limestone wall adorned with more than 1,600 pictographs. On the winter solstice, rays of light reflect off an ornate, otherwise invisible painting known as "Sun Dagger." For information on tours ($6 adults, $3 children), call © 325/732-4376.

The municipal park system in San Angelo is a cut above average, with the **River Walk** (p. 367) and **Civic League Park,** West Beauregard and Park streets, featuring the International Water Lily Garden. This garden displays lily species from all over the globe, which bloom both day and night during the spring and summer. Call **San Angelo Park Headquarters** at © 325/657-4279 for additional information on the city's park system.

**BOATING & FISHING**   In addition to O. C. Fisher Lake and Lake Nasworthy (see above), there are three other reservoirs within a 40-mile radius of San Angelo: **Twin Buttes Reservoir** (© 325/657-4206), located immediately west of Lake Nasworthy; **Lake E. V. Spence** (© 432/267-6341), known for its striped bass, situated 35 miles north of San Angelo via Tex. 208 and Tex. 158; and **Lake O. H. Ivie** (© 432/267-6341), the largest body of water in the region at nearly 20,000 surface acres, located 40 miles east of the city via FM 765 and FM 2134.

**GOLF**   The 7,171-yard **Quicksand Golf Course,** 2305 Pulliam St. (© 325/482-8337; www.quicksandsanangelo.com), is one of Texas's best (and toughest) 18-hole courses, with greens fees around $23 to $44, cart included. There's also the 18-hole **Riverside Hills Golf Course,** 900 W. 29th St. (© **325/653-6130**), with greens fees of $16 to $27, cart included.

**HIKING**   The top hiking area in the region is **San Angelo State Park,** with 50 miles of trails. The trails are easy to difficult, with the loops between the north and south shores and the hike to the **Highland Range Scenic Lookout** (less than a mile) being the most popular.

**MOUNTAIN BIKING**   The most popular mountain biking spots in the San Angelo area are the trails at **San Angelo State Park** and around **Twin Buttes Reservoir.** Bike rentals are not available in town, but **Concho Bike Shop,** 2015 Austin St. (© **325/655-6850;** www.conchobikeshop.com) offers repairs and advice.

## SPECTATOR SPORTS

The **San Angelo Colts** (© **325/942-6587;** www.sanangelocolts.com) play in the AA Central Baseball League from early May to early September at Foster Field, 1600 University Ave. Single-game tickets are $6 to $9. The **San Angelo Stock Show and Rodeo Association** (© **325/653-7785;** www.sanangelorodeo.com) organizes several annual roping and rodeo events, including the San Angelo Rodeo in February.

## SHOPPING

**Historic Concho Avenue,** downtown between Oakes and Chadbourne streets, is a melting pot of boutiques, jewelers, and antiques shops. Among its highlights are **J. Wilde's,** 20 E. Concho Ave. (© **325/655-0878**), a boutique with fashions and furnishings best described as Western chic (which doesn't quite do them justice); and **Legend Jewelers,** 18 E. Concho Ave. (© **888/655-4367** or 325/653-0112; www. legendjewelers.com), purveyors of the luminous concho pearl. The top shopping center is **Sunset Mall,** 4001 Sunset Dr., at Loop 306 (© **325/949-1947**).

San Angelo is home to a vibrant arts community, typified by the Texas hippie vibe at the **Old Chicken Farm Art Center ★,** 2505 N. Martin Luther King Blvd. (© **325/653-4936;** www.chickenfarmartcenter.com), a local landmark since 1971. Formerly an abandoned chicken farm, this funky artist's compound is home to 12 studios that are open at various times, displaying a wide range of pottery, metalwork, and paintings. The main **StarKeeper Gallery** houses the contemporary handmade ceramics of Roger Allen, the center's founder and proprietor; it's open Tuesday through Saturday from 10am to 5pm. The art center hosts resident artists' openings on the first Saturday of each month. There's also an on-site B&B, the **Inn at the Art Center** (see below).

# Where to Stay

San Angelo has a nice variety of lodgings, with a handful of B&Bs and numerous chain motels and hotels. Most of the properties are located along Bryant Boulevard or near the convention center on Rio Concho Drive. Of the chains, I recommend the **Best Western San Angelo,** 3017 W. Loop 306 (© **800/780-7234** or 325/223-1273), with double rates of $79 to $99.

**Inn at the Art Center ★ 🛏**   If you like your B&B a bit on the unusual side, look no further. In place of Victorian architecture and antiques, you'll find rooms in what once were chicken coops and feed silos at the Old Chicken Farm Art Center (see above). My favorite: the Artist's Loft, situated within two cylindrical silos (the bedroom in one, a sitting area and bathroom in the other) connected via arched doorways and decorated with interesting murals and mosaics. There are also the Santa Fe– and French-themed rooms in the old coop, as well as a nicely stocked guest kitchen. Outside, you can get a firsthand look at artists at work or relax in one of the many shady nooks and crannies on the property, including a sculpture-laden courtyard and a covered patio. The restaurant, the **Silo House** (© **325/658-3333**), serves prix-fixe dinners by reservation on Thursday, Friday, and Saturday evenings.

2503 N. Martin Luther King Blvd., San Angelo, TX 76903. © **325/659-3836.** www.innattheartcenter. com. 3 units. $75–$125 double. AE, DISC, MC, V. **Amenities:** Restaurant. *In room:* A/C, TV/VCR, Wi-Fi (free).

**Inn of the Conchos** Located on the north side of town, this solid property is reliable and convenient, and a good deal. While the inn won't win any awards for seclusion, the rooms are surprisingly quiet for their location on the main drag, and they are nicely outfitted with amenities and well maintained. The property has an outdoor pool to beat the summer heat, and a bar and grill located in the parking lot makes for an easy overnight stopover for the cross-Texas traveler.

2021 N. Bryant Blvd., San Angelo, TX 76903. © **800/621-6041** or 325/653-2811. Fax 325/653-7560. www.inn-of-the-conchos.com. 123 units. $70 double. AE, DISC, MC, V. **Amenities:** Outdoor heated pool; Jacuzzi. *In room:* A/C, TV, fridge, Wi-Fi (free).

## CAMPING

The best campgrounds are at **San Angelo State Park** (© **325/949-4757**) and **Spring Creek Marina and RV Park** (© **800/500-7801** or 325/944-3850) at Lake Nasworthy. See "Outdoor Activities," above.

# Where to Dine

**Armenta's** ★ 🎁 TEX-MEX  The proprietors of this festive eatery did not hold back one iota when it came to decoration, transforming a once-standard diner into a feast for the eyes with an armada of colorful parrot sculptures, tie-dyed drapes, and Mexican pottery. They don't hold back with the first-rate food, either, served inside or on an attached shady patio, and every bit as spicy as the scenery. Specialties include *enchiladas veracruzanas* with a creamy jalapeño sauce; fiery *guiso,* sautéed beef with onions, tomatoes, and peppers; and the *camarones a la diabla,* shrimp spiced for the most inflammable of taste buds. The homemade salsa packs a similar punch.

1325 S. Oakes St. (1 mile south of downtown). © **325/653-1954.** Breakfast tacos $1–$2; lunch and dinner main courses $7–$14. DISC, MC, V. Mon–Sat 7:30am–10pm; Sun 8am–9pm. Closed major holidays.

**Miss Hattie's Café and Saloon** STEAK/SEAFOOD  Named after the infamous proprietor of one of San Angelo's now-defunct bordellos, Miss Hattie's is one of the city's culinary standouts. Housed in a brick edifice that dates from 1884, the dining room is full of Victorian frills and antiques, with lace-sheathed tables under the original pressed-tin ceiling. The cuisine is a nice match for the atmosphere: tender steaks, daily seafood specials, salads, and pastas. My recommendation: Start with the corn fritters as an appetizer and move on to the Southwestern Carpetbagger (a rib-eye stuffed with spiced crabmeat) for the main course. The lunch menu sports a nice selection of gourmet sandwiches and salads, and heartier fare such as meatloaf and chicken with dumplings.

26 E. Concho Ave. © **325/653-0570.** www.misshatties.com. Main courses $6–$13 lunch, $10–$25 dinner. AE, MC, V. Mon–Thurs 11am–9pm; Fri–Sat 11am–10pm.

## San Angelo After Dark

San Angelo has a strong performing arts culture for a city its size. The **San Angelo Symphony** performs about a half-dozen classical and pops shows a year at various venues (© **325/658-5877;** www.sanangelosymphony.org). Single tickets are usually $20 for adults and $6 to $8 for children and students. The **Angelo Civic Theatre,** 1936 Sherwood Way (© **325/949-4400;** www.angelocivictheatre.com), the oldest community theater in the state, produces about five musicals, comedies, and dramas each year at its 230-seat playhouse. Tickets run $14 to $16. The city is also home to the **Cactus Music Series** (© **325/653-6793;** www.sanangeloarts.com) at the historic Cactus Hotel, 36 E. Twohig Ave.

## A Side Trip to the Caverns of Sonora

Hidden in the middle of nowhere, some 75 miles from San Angelo, are the delightful **Caverns of Sonora.** Designated a Registered Natural Landmark by the National Park Service in 1966, these truly magnificent caves are privately owned and can be explored only on guided tours. You'll see glistening draperies, miles of puffy popcorn, millions of helictites and soda straws, and reflecting pools, plus all the usual stalagmites and stalactites in a wildly fascinating collage of formations. The caverns' signature formation is an unusual helictite shaped like a butterfly. The tour is 2 miles long and takes about 2 hours; admission is $20 adults, $16 children 4 to 11, and free for kids 3 and under.

The caverns are open daily from 8am to 6pm March through Labor Day, and from 9am to 5pm the rest of the year, but are closed on Christmas. From San Angelo, go south on U.S. 277 for 64 miles to the small town of Sonora, then 8 miles west on I-10 to exit 392, then follow signs south to the caverns. For additional information, contact **Caverns of Sonora** (© **325/387-3105;** www.cavernsofsonora.com).

Campsites in an attractive, tree-shaded campground are available at the caverns. Other than that, the nearest lodging, dining, and other services are in Sonora. For information, contact the **Sonora Chamber of Commerce,** 205 U.S. 277 (P.O. Box 1172), Sonora, TX 76950-1172 (© **888/387-2880** or 325/387-2880; www.sonora tx-chamber.com).

# DEL RIO & AMISTAD NATIONAL RECREATION AREA ★

156 miles S of San Angelo; 154 miles W of San Antonio; 268 miles NW of Corpus Christi; 392 miles SW of Dallas

For my money, this pleasant little city of about 35,000 people is the nicest border town you'll find from Texas to California. Situated along the U.S.-Mexico border across the Rio Grande from Ciudad Acuña, Del Rio is a great base for watersports enthusiasts visiting Amistad National Recreation Area, and also has an excellent museum where you can learn about Judge Roy Bean, one of the most colorful judges in the history of the American West, who became both famous and infamous as "the Law West of the Pecos."

The site of Del Rio was originally called San Felipe del Rio by Spanish missionaries, who unsuccessfully tried to start a mission here in 1635, but were thwarted by hostile American Indians. The name survived, however, and was in use in the mid-1800s when the reliable water source of San Felipe Springs helped the area begin to develop as a farming community. The springs also were a watering stop for the short-lived U.S. Army Camel Corps, for which camels imported from North Africa were used on the Western frontier as a substitute for horses. The name of the community was shortened to Del Rio in 1883.

In the late 1960s, a dam was built on the Rio Grande near Del Rio, creating a 67,000-acre lake that provides flood protection and irrigation water, as well as a huge water playground in what is generally an arid, rocky land of cactus and sagebrush.

## Essentials

### GETTING THERE

Del Rio is located at the junction of U.S. 90 and 277/377, along the U.S.-Mexico border. The **Amtrak** station is at 100 N. Main St. (© **800/872-2745**; www.amtrak. com), along the Sunset Limited route. **Del Rio International Airport,** 1104 W. 10th St. (© **830/774-8538**) is served by **Continental.**

### VISITOR INFORMATION

The **Del Rio Chamber of Commerce,** 1915 Veterans Blvd., Del Rio, TX 78840 (© **830/775-3551**; www.drchamber.com), operates a visitor center and can mail information before your trip. In Ciudad Acuña, **OCV Acuña** (© **877/717-9966**; www.ocvacuna.com) is your best source of tourism information and advice.

**FAST FACTS** **Val Verde Regional Medical Center,** 801 Bedell Ave. (© **830/ 775-8566**; www.vvrmc.org), has a 24-hour emergency room. The **post office,** 2001 N. Bedell Ave., is open Monday through Friday from 8:30am to 4:30pm, Saturday from 10am to noon.

### THE TOP ATTRACTIONS

In addition to the attractions discussed below, there are some handsome, **historic buildings** in Del Rio. A free brochure, which describes and locates some three dozen buildings constructed between 1869 and 1929, is available at the chamber of commerce's visitor center (see "Visitor Information," above). At **San Felipe Springs,** enjoy a nice walk along crystal-clear water; the best access point is at the **Creekwalk** at Moore Park, Calderon Boulevard and De La Rosa Street, where you'll find a spring-fed swimming pool and a small amphitheater.

Many visitors to Del Rio take an excursion across the border to **Ciudad Acuña,** a small Mexican city with a main street lined with shops selling a variety of leather goods, pottery, woven items, jewelry, and other products, plus a number of good restaurants. As with most border towns, American currency is welcome at practically all businesses in Ciudad Acuña. Driving isn't a problem, but walking is a bit of a struggle,

**Creature of the Night**

In 1963, groundbreaking disc jockey **Wolfman Jack** got his start at XERF, a superpowerful 500,000-watt radio station in Ciudad Acuña, after he helped commandeer the station during a gunfight. From there, the Wolfman offered mainstream America its first taste of black music: A. B. B. King record was his first spin, and James Brown once paid a visit and climbed XERF's legendary tower.

Del Rio & Amistad National Recreation Area

WEST TEXAS

especially on hot days. *Note:* Be sure to carry your passport if you cross the border. As of 2008, passports are required for re-entry into the U.S.

**Alamo Village**  Built by John Wayne and company for his epic 1959 film *The Alamo*—and used for dozens of Westerns since—this attraction meshes Western and Hollywood history into one fun attraction. Beyond the mock-up of the Alamo, there is an entire Wild West village, complete with a roving herd of Texas longhorns.

FM 674, 7 miles north of Brackettville (30 miles east of Del Rio via U.S. 90). ⓒ **830/563-2580.** www.alamovillage.com. Admission $10, free for children 5 and under. Thurs–Sat 10am–3pm.

**Fort Clark Springs**  A notable army and cavalry post from 1852 to 1946, Fort Clark has since evolved into a unique oasis: a gated resort and leisure living community with good amenities for the traveler. There are 1,600 acres of wilderness here, populated by whitetail deer and wild turkeys, crosscut by miles of nature trails, and featuring a behemoth spring-fed swimming pool (Texas's third largest) and a golf course. There's also a museum, a basic motel ($50–$65 double), a tent campground ($10 per night), and an RV park (about $22 for a site with full hookups).

U.S. 90, Brackettville (30 miles east of Del Rio). ⓒ **830/563-2493.** www.fortclark.com. Free admission. Activity prices vary. Open daily year-round.

**Val Verde Winery**  Established in 1883 by Italian immigrant Frank Qualia, Val Verde Winery, the state's oldest bonded winery, is now the pride and joy of third-generation vintner Thomas Qualia. Using grapes from the adjacent vineyards and other Texas vineyards, the winery produces from six to eight varieties of wine, including its award-winning Don Luis Tawny Port, which is aged in French oak barrels for 5 years. Short, informative guided tours are available at no charge, followed or substituted by free tastings. Wines are available by the bottle (typically $10–$30). Allow 20 minutes for your visit.

100 Qualia Dr. (near its intersection with Hudson St.). ⓒ **830/775-9714.** www.valverdewinery.com. Free admission. Mon–Sat 10am–5pm.

**Whitehead Memorial Museum** ★ ☺  This above-average small-town museum really does have something for everyone in the family. Covering more than 2 acres, exhibits include a furnished log cabin, a blacksmith shop, a 1919 American LaFrance fire engine, and the early-20th-century office of Dr. Simon Rodriguez, the community's first Hispanic physician, who is credited with delivering more than 3,000 babies in the area. The graves of Judge Roy Bean and his son Sam are also on the property. The star of the museum, however, is the fantastic Cadena Nativity—a 32×20-foot Nativity scene that contains more than 600 figurines of people and animals, plus another 600-plus miniature buildings, trees, bushes, and the like. Allow 1 to 2 hours.

1308 S. Main St. ⓒ **830/774-7568.** www.whiteheadmuseum.org. Admission $5 adults, $4 seniors, $3 youths 13–18, $2 children 6–12, free for children 5 and under. Tues–Sat 9am–4:30pm; Sun.1–5pm. Closed major holidays.

## Where to Stay & Dine in Del Rio

Veterans Boulevard, the main drag through town (U.S. 90/277/377), is lined with chain motels. Choices here include **Best Western Inn of Del Rio,** 810 Veterans Blvd. (ⓒ **800/336-3537** or 830/775-7511), with rates of $69 to $79 double; **Hampton Inn,** 2219 Bedell Ave. (ⓒ **830/775-9700**), with rates of $99 to $199 double; and **Ramada Inn,** 2101 Veterans Blvd. (ⓒ **800/272-6232** or 830/775-1511), with rates in the range of $89 to $119 double. Room tax adds 13%.

As with lodging, you'll find scads of fast-food chains located along Del Rio's Veterans Boulevard. You'll be better served (in more ways than one) by seeking out one of Del Rio's locally owned restaurants, such as **the Herald Steakhouse & Martini Bar ★**, 321 S. Main St. (© **830/774-2845**). The former headquarters for the town's daily paper, the *News-Herald,* the swankiest eatery in downtown Del Rio specializes in sandwiches and soups for lunch and steaks and martinis at dinner. Also recommended are several Mexican eateries: **La Hacienda,** 330 Pecan St. in Pecan Street Station (© **830/774-7094**); **Chinto's Super Taco,** 400 E. 6th St. (© **830/774-1592**); and **Manuel's Steakhouse,** 1312 Veterans Blvd. (© **830/488-6044;** www.manuelssteakhouse.com).

If you want to get a true (and inexpensive) taste of the region, head south to Ciudad Acuña. My picks: **Crosby's,** Hidalgo #195 (© **011-52/87-72-20-20**), a tourist-oriented bar with a place in country music history thanks to a mention in George Strait's "Blame it on Mexico"; **Manuel's,** Morelos #130 (© **011-52/87-72-59-15**), an upscale Mexican restaurant with good steaks and chiles rellenos; **La Cabañita,** Galena #267 E. (© **011-52/87-72-14-67**), a fun, funky space with a menu for meat lovers; **Hosteria de Santa Marie,** Lerdo #200 (**011-52/87-72-38-00**), featuring traditional *burria* (spicy meat stew), paella, and *cuitlacoche* (corn truffles) dishes; and the local favorite, **Tacos Grill,** Guerrero #1490 S. (© **011-52/87-72-40-41**). There's also a legendary watering hole, the **Corona Club,** 2 blocks south of the downtown crossing bridge at Hidalgo #200 (© **011-52/87-72-51-08**). A location in the movie *Desperado,* this classic border dive opens into a spectacular courtyard.

# Amistad National Recreation Area ★

A beautiful spot for boating, fishing, water-skiing, scuba diving, and swimming, this is a rare international reservoir, created by the United States and Mexico with the construction of a 6-mile-long dam across the Rio Grande at the international border. Amistad Reservoir—*amistad* is Spanish for "friendship"—provides electricity generation, water storage, flood control, and, most important to anglers and watersports enthusiasts, a huge lake as a U.S. National Recreation Area.

The water here is a beautiful blue color, caused by the lake bed's limestone character and lack of loose soil. The 67,000-acre lake is actually at the confluence of three rivers, and runs 74 miles up the Rio Grande, 24 miles up the Devils River, and 14 miles up the Pecos River. The shoreline measures 890 miles: 540 miles in Texas and the rest in Mexico.

There are about a dozen boat ramps spread throughout the recreation area, with three developed boat-launching areas. **Diablo East** is 10 miles northwest of Del Rio via U.S. 90, **Rough Canyon** is 23 miles north of Del Rio via U.S. 90 and U.S. 277/377, and **Pecos** is 44 miles northwest of Del Rio via U.S. 90. Boat and slip rentals and sales of supplies are available at Diablo East and Rough Canyon. Motorized-boat use passes cost $4 per day or $40 per year.

At Diablo East, **Lake Amistad Marina,** HCR-3 U.S. 90, P.O. Box 420635, Del Rio, TX 78842 (© **800/255-5561** or 830/774-4157; www.lakeamistadresort.com), rents a variety of boats, ranging from fishing boats and runabouts costing $225 per 8-hour day to luxurious 70-foot houseboats that sleep 10 and rent for more than $1,000 a night in summer.

There is a swimming area (no lifeguards) at Governors Island, and swimming is permitted in most undeveloped areas. Water temperatures range from a chilly 54°F (12°C) in winter to a pleasant 86°F (30°C) in summer. Water-skiing is permitted in

# THE legend OF ROY BEAN

Judge Roy Bean, the self-styled "Law West of the Pecos," was by all accounts an eccentric character, and definitely the stuff of which legends are made. Born Phantly Roy Bean in Kentucky, probably around 1825, as a teenager he followed his two older brothers west, to California and then New Mexico. Although his brothers were mostly successful and respectable, Roy always seemed to be in trouble, usually related to gambling and women, and occasionally would leave town just a few steps ahead of the hangman.

During the Civil War, Bean reportedly smuggled supplies from Mexico to Confederate troops in Texas. After the war he ended up in San Antonio, where he cemented his already dubious reputation. There he married and had four children before abandoning the family about 16 years later, when he followed a rail-construction crew west to Vinegarroon. It's believed Bean then opened a saloon in a tent, before somehow getting appointed as the local justice of the peace in 1882.

Several years later, Bean moved north to a small settlement along the railroad tracks that came to be called Langtry. Bean claimed he had named the town after the beautiful English actress of the day, Lillie Langtry, with whom he was quite infatuated, although the town likely garnered its name earlier from a construction foreman. Bean wrote to Miss Langtry several times, asking her to visit the town "named in her honor."

Bean was elected and re-elected as justice of the peace on and off for about 20 years—he reportedly was briefly thrown out of office when it became evident that he had received more votes than there were eligible voters. Bean's Langtry courtroom, which he called the Jersey Lillie after Miss Langtry, was also his saloon and home, and he often chose his juries from the saloon's customers.

Numerous stories about Bean's sometimes bizarre rulings have been told, and it's often difficult to tell fact from fiction. When a railroad worker was charged with killing a Chinese laborer, Bean said that although it was against the law to kill your fellow man, he could find no law against killing a "heathen Chinaman," so the case was dismissed. The killer was, however, required to pay for the funeral. Another generally accepted story is the case of a dead man found to have a gun and gold coins worth about $40 in his pockets. Bean promptly fined the corpse $40 for carrying a concealed weapon. But he gained perhaps his greatest notoriety for staging a heavyweight championship fight in 1896. At the time, prizefighting was illegal in Texas as well as in Mexico, so Bean staged the fight on a sandbar in the Rio Grande, a no man's land between the two. He also made a tidy profit at his saloon selling drinks to the spectators.

Although there are also stories of Bean being a "hanging judge," there is no proof that he ever sentenced anyone to hang. But then, Bean kept no records at all of what transpired in his courtroom. Bean died in his saloon on March 16, 1903, supposedly after a binge of heavy drinking in Del Rio. A few months later, Lillie Langtry, who was performing in the region, finally made it to Langtry, spending 30 minutes there during a train stopover.

To learn more about Bean, drive out to Langtry (60 miles west of Del Rio via U.S. 90) to Bean's restored saloon at the **Judge Roy Bean Visitor Center** (© **432/291-3340**), where dioramas and displays in this official state visitor center tell the story of Bean's life. The visitor center and saloon are open daily from 8am to 5pm and admission is free. Allow about an hour.

open water (away from mooring areas, channels, and swimming beaches) during daylight hours only.

Forty-pound catfish have been pulled from the lake, as have record striped bass. Among other species caught are largemouth bass, yellowbelly and bluegill sunfish, white and black crappie, and alligator gar. Fishing is permitted from boats and from shore anywhere except in marinas, at boat ramps, and at designated swimming beaches. There are also fishing docks and fish-cleaning stations at several locations. A Texas fishing license (available at convenience stores and most shops along U.S. 90) is required on the U.S. side of the border. A list of licensed fishing guides is available at the headquarters.

Among the wildlife you're likely to see are white-tailed deer, javelina (also called collared peccaries), black-tailed jack rabbits, rock squirrels, and nine-banded armadillos. Campers might also see ringtails, which usually venture out only at night. The recreation area is also home to poisonous snakes, including several species of rattlesnakes, plus poisonous scorpions, spiders, and stinging insects. Birds to watch for include white-winged doves, sandpipers, great blue herons, great egrets, American coots, killdeer, roadrunners, black vultures, ravens, and an occasional bald or golden eagle. One particularly good spot to bird-watch is the San Pedro Campground, where you're also likely to see a lot of butterflies. Rangers lead morning birding walks every other Saturday; the group meets at the park visitor center at 8am.

American Indian peoples are believed to have come to this area about 12,000 years ago; however, it was not until about 4,000 years ago that creation of the spectacular rock art began, and it's visible today in several areas in and near the recreation area. These pictographs—designs painted on rocks using colors created from ground iron ore and other minerals mixed with animal fat—are difficult to get to, but well worth the effort.

One of the best rock art sites is **Panther Cave,** at the confluence of the Rio Grande and Seminole Canyon, which is usually accessible by boat and a steep climb up stairs. It has numerous figures that resemble humans or animals, including what looks like a 9-foot panther. Another good site, accessible by boat at average lake levels and by a strenuous hike through tall brush at low-water levels, is **Parida Cave,** located on the Rio Grande. See also the section on Seminole Canyon State Park & Historic Site, below.

The recreation area has four campgrounds, with a total of about 60 primitive sites. Campgrounds are generally open, with brush and some low trees, but little shade, and have vault toilets, covered picnic tables, and grills. **Governors Landing Campground,** with 15 sites overlooking the lake, is the only campground with drinking water (water is available along the Diablo East entrance road, where there is also an RV dump station). **San Pedro Campground** has 35 sites, and **Spur 406, 277 North,** and **Rough Canyon** campgrounds have 17, 8, and 4 sites, respectively. There is also a dispersed camping area at Spur 406 with rooms for about a dozen sites. Camping is first come, first served, and is limited to 14 consecutive days, or 60 days in a 12-month period. Backcountry camping from boats is permitted along the lakeshore, except at marinas and other developed areas. Camping costs $4 to $8 per night.

Rangers present a variety of programs, including evening programs at the amphitheater at the visitor center; and kiosks with displays on natural history, recreation, and water safety are scattered throughout the recreation area. Pets are permitted, but must be leashed at all times. Rangers warn that limestone, which is abundant along

## The Mouth of the Pecos

On the east rim of the 300-foot cliffs above the Pecos River, there is an overlook before the U.S. 90 bridge over the Pecos that is one of the region's best photo opportunities. Heading west on the highway from Del Rio, take the left immediately before the bridge for the most scenic views of the vast surrounding badlands and the untamed Pecos snaking into the Rio Grande below.

the shore, can cut the pads of dogs' feet, and they add that pets need to be protected from fleas, ticks, and heartworm (spread by mosquitoes) at the lake.

Admission to the park, which is open 24 hours, is free. About 10 miles west of Del Rio off U.S. 90, the park visitor center, with information, a small bookstore, and a few displays, is open daily from 8am to 5pm, except Thanksgiving, Christmas, and New Year's Day. The first lake access is about 10 miles west of the visitor center. For information, contact **Amistad National Recreation Area,** 4121 Veterans Blvd., Del Rio, TX 78840 (© 830/775-7491; www.nps.gov/amis).

*Note:* While Amistad has been free of the violence that has wracked much of the U.S.-Mexico border in recent years, in 2010 pirates murdered an American tourist on Falcon Lake, which straddles the border downriver near Laredo, and numerous other incidents have taken place. Take special care to pay attention to your surroundings while boating or fishing on Lake Amistad.

## SEMINOLE CANYON STATE PARK & HISTORIC SITE

Adjacent to Amistad National Recreation Area, about 45 miles northwest of Del Rio via U.S. 90, Seminole Canyon State Park provides opportunities for guided hikes to see what many consider the best pictographs in North America, possibly 4,000 years old. In addition, Seminole Canyon offers a short nature trail, camping, hiking through a rugged limestone terrain, wildlife viewing and bird-watching, and a museum.

Although it is believed that humans lived in this area at the end of the last ice age, some 12,000 years ago, they left few signs of their presence. Then, about 7,000 years ago, other peoples arrived, and within 3,000 years, they began to paint designs on sheltered rock walls. State park rangers lead hiking tours to several of the rock-art sites.

The **Fate Bell Cave Dwelling Tour** is offered Wednesday through Sunday at 10am year-round and also at 3pm from September through May. Cost is $5 per person for age 8 and over, and reservations are not required. This is a moderately rated 2-mile round-trip hike that leads into Seminole Canyon to a huge rock shelter where participants will see hundreds of pictographs. The state park also has two guided tours that are offered only about a half-dozen times a year, by advance reservation through the park office (see below). The 1.75-mile round-trip **Upper Canyon Tour,** which costs $12 per person and takes 2 hours, leads to a normally closed area of the park in the upper section of the canyon to see pictographs and some railroad sites from 1882; and the 8-mile round-trip **Presa Canyon Tour,** which costs $25 per person, is an all-day hike into the lower canyon to see rock-art sites that are normally off limits to the public. The **Rock Art Foundation** (© 888/525-9907; www.rockart. org) takes visitors on a 2-hour tour to the White Shaman site's hallucinogenic pictographs for $10, as well as other tours.

The park has a 6-mile round-trip **hiking/biking trail** along the top of the canyon that leads to a bluff from which you can see Panther Cave, and its namesake painted panther, across Lake Amistad (see the section on Amistad National Recreation Area, above). Bring your binoculars for a better view. The trail has little elevation change, but is rocky with little shade. No one is allowed to go down into the canyon except on guided tours.

The **Windmill Nature Trail,** just behind the visitor center/museum, is an easy, although not shaded and therefore hot, .7-mile loop. It meanders through a harsh environment of ocotillo, cacti, yucca, juniper, Texas mountain laurel, and other desert plants to its namesake windmill—actually the remains of two windmills, one from the 1890s and one from the 1920s.

The species of birds and animals to watch for in the park are much the same as at the adjacent Amistad National Recreation Area, and include birds such as great blue herons, black and turkey vultures, scaled quail, killdeer, white-winged and mourning doves, greater roadrunners, and northern mockingbirds. Also watch for great-tailed grackles, northern cardinals, pyrrhuloxia, ash-throated flycatchers, ladder-backed woodpeckers, and black-chinned hummingbirds. Mammals here include desert cottontails, black-tailed jack rabbits, coyotes, raccoons, white-tailed deer, striped skunks, and javelina.

The small campground, with 31 sites, sits on an open knoll covered with mesquite, creosote bush, yucca, cacti, and other desert plants. There are hot showers and a dump station. Sites with water only cost $12 per night, and those with water and electricity cost $17 per night.

The park is open 24 hours a day year-round, except for 1 week in November and 1 week in December when it is open only to properly licensed hunters. The visitor center, with its excellent museum containing exhibits on the area's ancient inhabitants as well as its more recent history, is open daily from 8am to 5pm. Admission to the park costs $3 adults, free for children 12 and under. For information, contact **Seminole Canyon State Park & Historic Site,** P.O. Box 820, Comstock, TX 78837 (© **432/292-4464;** www.tpwd.state.tx.us).

# BIG BEND & GUADALUPE MOUNTAINS NATIONAL PARKS

by Eric Peterson

Y ou'll find Texas's most spectacular mountain scenery, as well as absolutely wonderful opportunities for hiking and other forms of outdoor recreation, at Big Bend and Guadalupe Mountains national parks. These parks also have an abundance of wildlife and both prehistoric and historic sites. Big Bend National Park is bounded by the Rio Grande, as it defines the U.S.-Mexico border, while Guadalupe Mountains National Park boasts the highest peak in Texas and a canyon with perhaps the prettiest scenery in the state, especially in the fall.

In addition to these two national parks in Texas, a third, Carlsbad Caverns National Park, is just over the state line in New Mexico. This easy side trip from Guadalupe Mountains National Park will lead you to some of the world's most beautiful cave formations, and, if you're so inclined, the thrill of a true caving experience, as you crawl belly to rock through dirty, narrow, and dark underground passages.

## BIG BEND NATIONAL PARK ★★

Vast and wild, Big Bend National Park is a land of extremes—and a few contradictions. Its rugged terrain harbors thousands of species of plants and animals—some seen practically nowhere else on earth—and a visit here can include a hike into the sun-baked desert, a float down a majestic river through the canyons, or a trek among high mountains where bears and mountain lions rule.

Millions of years ago, an inland sea covered this area. As it dried up, sediments of sand and mud turned to rock; mountains were created and volcanoes roared. The resultant canyons and rock formations that we marvel at today—red, orange, yellow, white, and brown hued—make for one of the most spectacular landscapes in the Southwest. This is not a fantasyland of delicate shapes and intricate carvings, like Bryce Canyon National Park in Utah, but a powerful and dominating terrain. Although the greatest natural sculptures are in the park's three major river canyons—the Santa Elena, Marsical, and Boquillas—throughout Big Bend you'll find spectacular and majestic examples of what nature can do with this mighty yet malleable building material we call rock.

Visitors to Big Bend National Park will also discover a wild, rugged wilderness, populated by myriad desert and mountain plants and animals. Box turtles, black-tailed jack rabbits, piglike javelinas, powerful black bears, and mountain lions are all known to roam here. The park is also a birder's paradise, frequented by more bird species than any other national park. It's also a wonderful spot to see wildflowers and the delightfully colorful display of cactus blooms.

For hikers, there are all kinds of trails, from easy walks to rugged backcountry routes that barely qualify as trails at all. There are also opportunities to let the Rio Grande do the work as it carries rafts, canoes, and kayaks among canyons carved through 1,500 feet of solid rock. Drivers of 4×4s enjoy exploring the backcountry roads, and history buffs find a number of historical attractions and cultural experiences. Because of the vastness of this park, you'll need to schedule at least 2 full days here, though 3 or 4 would be better.

## Essentials

**GETTING THERE** Big Bend National Park is not really close to anything except the Rio Grande and Mexico. There is no public transportation to or through the park, so to get to the park you'll need a car. Park headquarters is 108 miles southeast of Alpine via Tex. 118, and 69 miles south of Marathon via U.S. 385. From El Paso, 328 miles northwest of the park, take I-10 E. 121 miles to exit 140, follow U.S. 90 southeast 99 miles to Alpine, and then turn south on Tex. 118 for 108 miles to park headquarters.

The closest train and bus service is in Alpine, where the nearest hospital is located. For information, contact the **Alpine Chamber of Commerce** (© **800/561-3712** or 432/837-2326; www.alpinetexas.com).

The nearest commercial airports are **Midland International (MAF)** (© **432/560-2200;** www.flymaf.com), 235 miles north, and **Del Rio International Airport (DRT)** (© **830/774-8538**), about 250 miles southeast. From Midland-Odessa, take I-20 W. about 50 miles to exit 80 for Tex. 18, which you follow south about 50 miles to Fort Stockton. There take U.S. 385 S. 125 miles through Marathon to park headquarters. From Del Rio, you take U.S. 90 W. 175 miles to Marathon, and U.S. 385 S. 70 miles to park headquarters.

**VISITOR INFORMATION** For advance information, contact the **Superintendent,** P.O. Box 129, Big Bend National Park, TX 79834 (© **432/477-2251,** or 477-1183 for the weather hot line; www.nps.gov/bibe).

Books, maps, and videos are available from the **Big Bend Natural History Association** (© **432/477-2236;** www.bigbendbookstore.org). The free park newspaper, *The Big Bend Paisano,* published seasonally by the National Park Service, is a great source of current information on special programs, suggested hikes, kids' activities, and local facilities, with telephone numbers inside and outside the park.

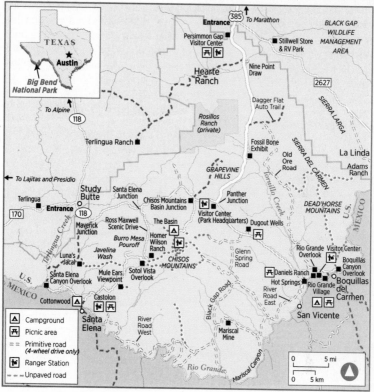

There are five visitor centers in the park: **Panther Junction Visitor Center** (open year-round) is centrally located at park headquarters; **Persimmon Gap Visitor Center** (open year-round) is at the North Entrance to the park on U.S. 385; **Rio Grande Village Visitor Center** (open Nov–Apr) is on the river in the eastern part of the park; **Castolon** (open Nov–Apr) is near the river in the southwestern end of the park; and **Chisos Basin Visitor Center** (open year-round) is in the Chisos Mountains in the middle of the park, at 5,401 feet in elevation. All visitor centers provide information, backcountry permits, books, and maps, and have exhibits; there is an impressive display on mountain lions at Chisos Basin and informative exhibits focusing on the park's cultural history at Castolon. Bulletin boards with schedules of ranger programs, notices of animal sightings, and other information are located at each of the visitor centers.

**FEES, REGULATIONS & PERMITS**  Entry into the park for up to a week costs $20 per passenger vehicle, and $5 per person on foot or bicycle. A $10 camping permit, available at any visitor center, is required for all backcountry camping and good for 2 weeks; permits are also required for all river-float trips (see "Camping" and "River Running," later in this chapter).

Wood or ground fires are prohibited in the park, and caution is advised when using camp stoves, charcoal grills, and cigarettes. Smoking is prohibited on all trails in the Chisos Basin. Check at the visitor centers for current drought conditions and any restrictions that may be in effect when you visit. Horses are not permitted on any paved roads in the park.

**WHEN TO GO**   Weather here is generally mild to hot, although because of the vast range of elevations—from about 1,800 feet at the eastern end of Boquillas Canyon to 7,825 feet on Emory Peak in the Chisos Mountains—conditions can vary greatly throughout the park at any given time. Essentially, the higher you go, the cooler and wetter you can expect it to be, although no section of the park gets a lot of precipitation.

Summers are hot, often well over 100°F (38°C) in the desert in May and June, and afternoon thunderstorms are common July through September. Winters are usually mild, although temperatures occasionally drop below freezing, and light snow is possible, especially in the Chisos Mountains. Fall and spring are usually warm and pleasant.

Average annual visitation is just over 300,000. Although the park is relatively uncrowded much of the year, there are several periods when lodgings and campgrounds are full: college spring break (usually the second and third week in Mar), Easter weekend, Thanksgiving weekend, and the week between Christmas and New Year's Day. Park visitation is generally highest in March and April, and lowest in August and September.

Although the park's visitor centers, campgrounds, and other developed facilities may be taxed during the busy season, visitors can still be practically alone simply by seeking out lesser used hiking trails. Those seeking solitude should discuss their hiking skills and expectations with rangers, who can offer suggestions on the best areas to escape the crowds.

**SAFETY**   Watch for wild animals along the roads, especially at night, when they may be blinded by your vehicle's headlights and stunned into standing still in the middle of the road. Feeding wildlife is strictly prohibited—not only to minimize the risk of injuries to park visitors, but also because it's bad for the animals.

The **Basin Road Scenic Drive** into the Chisos Mountains has sharp curves and steep grades and is not recommended for trailers longer than 20 feet or motor homes longer than 24 feet. The **Ross Maxwell Scenic Drive** to Castolon is fine for most RVs and trailers but might present a problem for those with insufficient power to handle the steep grade. These roads require extra caution by all users—drivers of motor vehicles, pedestrians, and bicyclists alike.

Desert heat can be dangerous. Hikers should carry at least 1 gallon of water per person per day; wear a hat, long pants, and long sleeves; and use a good sunscreen. Don't depend on springs as water sources, and avoid hiking in the middle of the day in summer. Early mornings and evenings are best. Talk to rangers about your plans before heading out; they can help you plan a hike in accordance with your ability and time frame. They can also advise you on expected weather conditions—sudden summer thunderstorms are common and can cause flash flooding in usually dry washes and canyons.

Swimming is not recommended in the Rio Grande, even though it may look tantalizingly inviting on a hot summer day. Waste materials and waterborne microorganisms have been found in the river and can cause serious illness. Also, strong undercurrents, deep holes, and sharp rocks in shallow water are common.

**RANGER PROGRAMS & SPECIAL EVENTS** Park ranger naturalists offer a variety of programs year-round. Illustrated evening programs take place at the 5,400-foot **Chisos Basin amphitheater** year-round. From November to April, evening programs are held regularly in the amphitheater at **Rio Grande Village** and occasionally at Cottonwood Campground. Subjects include the park's geology, plants, animals, and human history. The ranger-led **nature walks ★★** are especially good, and rangers occasionally lead driving tours. Workshops are also planned, on subjects such as adobe construction or photography. Look for weekly schedules on the bulletin boards scattered about the park. **Personal ranger-guided tours** are also available for $35 an hour with a 4-hour minimum. Call © **432/477-1108** for reservations or to check on availability.

The park has a **Junior Ranger Program** for children of all ages. Kids learn about the park through a variety of activities, and earn stickers, certificates, badges, and patches. Pick up Junior Ranger Activity Books ($2) at any visitor center.

## What to See & Do
### EXPLORING THE HIGHLIGHTS BY CAR

The park has several paved roads. In addition, there are several unimproved roads requiring high clearance or 4×4 vehicles.

There are two scenic drives in the park, both with sharp curves and steep inclines and not recommended for certain RVs and trailers (see "Safety," above).

The 7-mile **Chisos Basin Drive,** which takes at least a half-hour, climbs up Green Gulch to Panther Pass before dropping down into the basin. Near the pass, there are some sharp curves, and parts of the road are at a 10% grade. The views are wonderful any time of the year, and particularly when the wildflowers dot the meadows, hills, and roadsides. The best months for wildflowers are March and April, and even later on the highest mountain trails.

When you've breathed your fill of clear mountain air, head back down and turn west toward the **Ross Maxwell Scenic Drive** through the Chihuahuan Desert and finally to the Rio Grande. This drive, which will take an hour or so plus stops, winds through the desert on the west side of the Chisos Mountains, providing a different perspective. Afterward, it passes through Castolon, and then continues along and above the river to **Santa Elena Canyon.** Here you should park and hike the trail, which climbs above the river, allowing for great views into the steep, narrow canyon (see "Hiking," below).

Another worthwhile drive, recommended for all vehicles, begins at **Panther Junction Visitor Center** and goes to Rio Grande Village. Allow a half-day. From the visitor center, head southeast through the desert toward the high mountains that form the skyline in the distance. The first half of the drive passes through desert grasses, finally making a comeback after severe overgrazing in the decades before the establishment of the park in 1944. Recovery is slow in this harsh climate, but the area is beginning to vegetate again.

As the elevation gradually decreases, you progress farther into the desert, and the grasses give way to agave lechuguilla and ocotillo, cacti, and other arid-climate survivors. Off to the south is the long, rather flat **Chilicotal Mountain,** named for the chilicote, or mescal-bean bushes, growing near its base. The chilicote's poisonous red bean is used in Mexico to kill rats. Several miles farther, the River Road turns off and heads southwest toward Castolon, more than 50 miles away. This is a primitive road for high-clearance vehicles only.

## Don't Cross the Rio Grande!

Increased national security following the September 11, 2001, terrorist attacks has put a stop to the once-popular informal trips to Mexico that many visitors to Big Bend National Park used to make. Although there are no authorized border crossing points within the national park, for years Mexican citizens would use rowboats to ferry park visitors across the Rio Grande to several small Mexican villages, where the Americans could shop and eat genuine Mexican food. But Homeland Security officials have announced that those informal border crossings are no longer permitted, and anyone entering the United States from Mexico in the park is subject to a fine of up to $5,000 and imprisonment of up to 1 year.

If you feel adventurous, take the **Hot Springs** turnoff about a mile beyond the Tornillo Creek Bridge. The road follows a rough wash to a point overlooking the convergence of Tornillo Creek and the Rio Grande. A trail along the riverbank leads to several springs. The foundation of a bathhouse is a remnant of the town of Hot Springs, which thrived here about 20 years before the park was established.

Back on the paved road, you'll soon pass through a short tunnel in the limestone cliff, beyond which is a parking area for a short trail to a view point overlooking **Rio Grande Village.** It's just a short drive from here to Rio Grande Village, your destination, where you can take a .75-mile nature trail ending at a high point above the Rio Grande, providing terrific views up and down the river.

## HISTORIC SITES

There is evidence that prehistoric American Indians and later Apaches, Kiowas, and Comanches occupied this area. Throughout the park, you can find **petroglyphs, pictographs,** and other signs of early human presence, including ruins of **stone shelters.** There are pictographs along the Hot Spring Trail (see "Hiking," below), and along the river. Watch for **mortar holes** scattered throughout the park, sometimes a foot deep, where Indians would grind seeds or mesquite beans.

Also within the park boundaries are the remains of several early-20th-century communities, a mercury mine, and projects by the Civilian Conservation Corps.

The **Castolon Historic District,** located in the southwest section of the park just off the Ross Maxwell Scenic Drive, includes the remains of homes and other buildings, many stabilized by the National Park Service, that were constructed in the early 1900s by Mexican-American farmers, Anglo settlers, and the U.S. Army. The first is the **Alvino House,** the oldest surviving adobe structure in the park, dating from 1901. Nearby is **La Harmonia Store,** built in 1920 to house cavalry troops during the Mexican Revolution, but never actually used by soldiers because the war ended. Two civilians converted it into a general store and then purchased the building, calling it La Harmonia for the harmony and peaceful relations they hoped to encourage among area residents. The store continues to operate, selling snacks, groceries, and other necessities.

The village of **Glenn Springs,** located in the southeast section of the park and accessible by dirt road off the main park highway, owes its creation to having a reliable water source in an otherwise arid area. It was named for rancher H. E. Glenn, who grazed horses in the area until Indians killed him in the 1880s. By 1916 there were several ranches, a factory that produced wax from the candelilla plant, a store, a post office, and a residential village divided into two sections—one for the Anglos and the other for the Mexicans. But then Mexican bandit revolutionaries crossed the border and attacked, killing and wounding a number of people, looting the store, and partially destroying the wax factory. Within 3 years, the community was virtually deserted. Today, the spring still flows, and you can see the remains of several adobe buildings and other structures.

Remains of a small health resort can be seen at the **Hot Springs,** accessible by hiking trail or dirt road, along the Rio Grande west of Rio Grande Village in the park's southeast section. Construction of the resort began in 1909 under the auspices of J. O. Langford, who was forced to leave during the Mexican Revolution. However, Langford returned and completed the project in the 1920s, advertising the Hot Springs as "the Fountain of Youth that Ponce de León failed to find." Today, you'll see the ruins of a general store/post office, other buildings, and a foundation that fills with natural mineral water, at about 105°F (41°C), creating an almost natural hot tub—except when the river rises above 4½ feet in depth.

To get to the **Marsical Mine,** you will likely need a four-wheel-drive or high-clearance vehicle. Located in the south-central part of the park, it is most easily accessed by River Road East, which begins 5 miles west of Rio Grande Village. The mine operated on and off between 1900 and 1943, producing 1,400 76-pound flasks of mercury, which was almost one-quarter of the total amount of mercury produced in the United States during that time. Mining buildings, homes, the company store, a kiln, foundations, and other structures remain in what is now a National Historic District.

Also in the park, you can see some excellent examples of the work done by the **Civilian Conservation Corps** in the 1930s and early 1940s. These include stone culverts along the Basin Road, the Lost Mine Trail, and several buildings, including some stone-and-adobe cottages that are still in use at the Chisos Mountains Lodge.

## OUTDOOR ADVENTURES

Local companies that provide equipment rentals and a variety of guided adventures in both the park and the general area include **Desert Sports** (© 888/989-6900 or 432/371-2727; www.desertsportstx.com), located on FM 170, 5 miles west of the junction of FM 170 and Tex. 118; **Big Bend River Tours,** FM 170 just west of Tex. 118 (© **800/545-4240** or 432/371-3033; www.bigbendrivertours.com); and **Far Flung Outdoor Center ★**, FM 170 just west of Tex. 118 (© **800/839-7238** or 432/371-2633; www.ffoc.net).

### Bird-Watching & Wildlife Viewing ★★

There is an absolutely phenomenal variety of wildlife at Big Bend National Park. About 450 species of birds can be found here over the course of the year—that's more than at any other national park and nearly half of all those found in North America. At latest count, there were also about 75 species of mammals, close to 70 species of reptiles and amphibians, and more than three dozen species of fish.

This is the only place in the United States where you'll find the Mexican long-nosed bat, listed by the federal government as an endangered species. Other **endangered species** that make their homes in the park include the black-capped vireo and a tiny "mosquito fish"—the Big Bend gambusia—which I hope prospers and multiplies because its favorite food is mosquito larvae.

Birders consider Big Bend National Park a key bird-watching destination, especially for those looking for some of America's more unusual **birds.** Among the park's top bird-watching spots are Rio Grande Village and Cottonwood campgrounds, the Chisos Basin, and the Hot Springs. Species to watch for include the colorful golden-fronted woodpecker, which can often be seen year-round among the cottonwood trees along the Rio Grande; and the rare colima warbler, whose range in the United States consists solely of the Chisos Mountains at Big Bend National Park. Among the hundreds of other birds that call the park home (at least part of the year) are scaled quail, spotted sandpipers, white-winged doves, greater roadrunners, lesser nighthawks, white-throated swifts, black-chinned and broad-tailed hummingbirds, acorn woodpeckers, northern flickers, western wood-pewees, ash-throated flycatchers, tufted titmice, bushtits, cactus and canyon wrens, loggerhead shrikes, Wilson's warblers, and Scott's orioles.

**Mammals** you may see in the park include desert cottontails, black-tailed jack rabbits, rock squirrels, Texas antelope squirrels, Merriam's kangaroo rats, coyotes, gray foxes, raccoons, striped skunks, javelinas (wild desert pigs), mule deer, and white-tailed deer. There are occasional sightings of mountain lions, usually called panthers here, in the Green Gulch and Chisos Basin areas. Four attacks on humans have occurred at the park, with no fatalities. Black bears, which were frequently seen in the area until about 1940, were mostly killed off by area ranchers who saw them as a threat to their livestock. However, with the protection provided by national park status, they began to return in the mid-1980s and have now established a small population.

There are a number of **reptiles** in the park, including some poisonous snakes, such as diamondback, Mojave, rock, and black-tailed rattlesnakes, plus the Trans-Pecos copperhead. Fortunately, it is unlikely you will see a rattler or copperhead, since they avoid both the heat of the day and busy areas. You are more apt to encounter nonpoisonous western coachwhips, which are often seen speeding across trails and roadways. Sometimes called "red racers," they're reddish, sometimes bright red, and among America's fastest snakes. Other nonpoisonous snakes that inhabit the park include Texas whipsnakes, spotted night snakes, southwestern black-headed snakes, and black-necked garter snakes.

Among the **lizards** you may see scurrying along desert roads and trails is the southwestern earless lizard—adult males are green with black-and-white chevrons on their lower sides, and often curl their black-striped tails over their backs. You'll also see various whiptail lizards in the desert, but in the canyons and higher in the mountains, watch for the crevice spiny lizard, which is covered with scales and has a dark collar. Although rare, there are also **western box turtles** in the park, as well as several types of more common water turtles.

## Hiking ★★★

Big Bend National Park is a wonderful park for hikers, with a wide variety of trails, most of which are easy or moderate. There are a number of short, easy interpretative nature walks, with either booklets available at the trail heads or signs along the trail. One example is the **Panther Path,** outside the Panther Junction Visitor Center, which is a 50-yard round-trip walk through a garden of cacti and other desert plants. I also enjoy the **Window View Trail,** which is a .3-mile round-trip and is accessible via the Chisos Basin trail head. This level, paved, and wheelchair-accessible self-guided nature trail runs along a low hill and has beautiful sunset views through the Window, a V-shaped opening in the mountains to the west. The **Rio Grande Village**

**Nature Trail** ★ .75-mile round-trip starts at the southeast corner of Rio Grande Village Campground across from site 18 and is a good choice for sunrise and sunset views. It climbs from the surprisingly lush river flood plain about 125 feet into desert terrain to a hilltop with excellent panoramic vistas.

Those who want to see historic structures should try the easy 1-mile **Hot Springs Trail,** which is at the end of an improved dirt road to Hot Springs, off the road to Rio Grande Village. An interpretive booklet available at the trail head describes the sights, including a historic health resort and homestead (see "Historic Sites," above), along this loop. Fairly substantial ruins remain of a general store/post office, other buildings, and a foundation that fills with natural mineral water at about 105°F (41°C), creating an inviting hot tub. Also along the trail are pictographs left by ancient Indians, and panoramic views of the Rio Grande and Mexico.

Among other easy hikes is the **Tuff Canyon Trail** (.75 mile round-trip), which is accessed from the Ross Maxwell Scenic Drive, 5 miles south of the Mule Ears Overlook access road. This walk leads into a narrow canyon, carved from soft volcanic rock called tuff, and provides several canyon overlooks. The 1.6-mile **Chisos Basin Loop Trail** (access at the Chisos Basin trail head) is a fairly easy walk that climbs about 350 feet into a pretty meadow and leads to an overlook with good views of the park's mountains, including Emory Peak, the highest point in the park at 7,825 feet; more adventurous hikers can continue here to the breathtaking South Rim for a 12-mile round-trip. The easy **Grapevine Hills Trail,** which is 2.2 miles round-trip, begins about 6 miles down the unpaved Grapevine Hills Road. It has an elevation change of about 240 feet as it follows a sandy wash through the desert, among massive granite boulders, ending at a picturesque balancing rock.

Among shorter, moderately rated trails, I heartily recommend the .8-mile one-way **Santa Elena Canyon Trail** ★★★, which you'll find at the end of Ross Maxwell Scenic Drive. You may get your feet wet crossing a broad creek on this trail, which also takes you up a series of steep steps; it's one of the most scenic short trails in the park, leading along the canyon wall, with good views of rafters on the Rio Grande, and down among the boulders along the river. Interpretive signs describe the canyon environment. Beware of flash flooding as you cross the Terlingua Creek, and skip this trail if the creek is running swiftly. Another good moderate hike is the **Boquillas Canyon Trail** ★, which is 1.4 miles round-trip and starts at the end of Boquillas Canyon Road. This hike begins by climbing a low hill and then drops down to the Rio Grande, ending near a shallow cave and huge sand dune. There are good views of the scenic canyon and the Mexican village of Boquillas, across the Rio Grande.

Among longer trails, I suggest the moderately rated, 3.8-mile round-trip **Mule Ears Spring Trail** ★, which you'll find at the Mule Ears Overlook parking area along the Ross Maxwell Scenic Drive. This relatively flat desert trail crosses several arroyos and then follows a wash most of the way to Mule Ears Spring. It has great views of unusual rock formations, such as the Mule Ears, and ends at a historic ranch house and rock corral. At 4 miles round-trip, the moderate **Pine Canyon Trail** takes you from desert grasslands dotted with sotols into a pretty canyon with dense stands of pinyon, juniper, oak, and finally bigtooth maple and ponderosa pine. At the higher elevations (it climbs 1,000 ft.), you'll also see Texas madrones—evergreen trees with smooth reddish bark that is shed each summer. At the end of the trail is a 200-foot cliff, which becomes a picturesque waterfall after heavy rains. This trail is located at the end of unpaved Pine Canyon Road (check on road conditions before going).

There are additional hiking opportunities in the even lesser visited **Big Bend Ranch State Park,** located between Terlingua and Presidio via FM 170. See p. 354 for more information.

## Horseback Riding

Horses are permitted on most dirt roads and many park trails (check with rangers for specifics), and may be kept overnight at many of the park's primitive campsites, although not at the developed campgrounds. The **Government Springs Campsite,** located 3½ miles from Panther Junction, is a primitive campsite with a corral that accommodates up to eight horses. It can be reserved up to 10 weeks in advance (© 432/477-2241). Those riding horses in the park must get free stock-use permits, which should be obtained in person up to 24 hours in advance at any of the park's visitor centers.

Although there are no commercial outfitters for guided rides in the park as of this writing, there are opportunities for rides just outside the park on private land, such as nearby Big Bend Ranch State Park and across the river in Mexico. **Lajitas Stables** (© 800/887-4331 or 432/371-3066; www.lajitasstables.com) offers a variety of guided trail rides, lasting from 2 hours to all day. Some trips follow canyon trails; others visit ancient Indian camps and ghost towns. Typical rates are $60 to $70 for 2 hours, $90 to $100 for 4 hours, and $150 for a full day. A cattle drive in Big Bend Ranch State Park is also offered twice a year.

## Mountain Biking

Bikes are not permitted on hiking trails, but are allowed on the park's many established dirt roads. Mountain bikes are available for rent from **Desert Sports** (see above), at a cost of $35 per day, $150 for 5 to 7 days, and $20 for each additional day after 7 days. The company also offers 1-day and multiday guided trips, including a combination hiking/mountain-biking/float trip in the park—3 days for $550.

## River Running ★

One of the first rivers designated by Congress as part of the Wild and Scenic River System, the Rio Grande follows the southern edge of the park for 118 miles, and extends another 127 miles downstream. The river allows for mostly calm float trips, but it does have a few sections of rough white water during high-water times. It can usually be run in a raft, canoe, or kayak. You can either bring your own equipment or rent equipment near the park (none is available in the park), but for novices it's safest to take a trip with one of several river guides approved by the National Park Service.

Those planning trips on their own must obtain $10 permits at a park visitor center, in person only and no more than 24 hours before the trip. Permits for the lower canyons of the Rio Grande Wild and Scenic River are available at the **Persimmon Gap Visitor Center,** and a self-serve permit station located there when the visitor center itself is closed. Permits for the section of river through Santa Elena Canyon can also be obtained at the **Barton Warnock Environmental Education Center,** 1 mile east of the community of Lajitas, Texas, about 20 miles from the park's West Entrance. Park rangers, however, strongly advise that everyone planning a river trip check with them beforehand to get the latest river conditions. A river-running booklet with additional information is available at park visitor centers and from the **Big Bend Natural History Association** (see "Visitor Information," earlier in this chapter).

Rafts, inflatable kayaks, and canoes can be rented from **Desert Sports** (© 888/989-6900 or 432/371-2727; www.desertsportstx.com). Rafts cost $30 per person per day or $425 for 5 to 7 days. Inflatable kayaks cost $40 to $50 per day, and canoes cost $45 to $50 per day, with discounts for multiday rentals. The company also provides shuttle services and offers guided 1-day and multiday canoe and raft trips, where you can either grab a paddle and take an active role, or sit back and let your boatman and the river do the work. Typical prices are $315 per person for 2 days on the river through Santa Elena Canyon; and $550 per person for 3 days on the river through Marsical Canyon, considered the most remote canyon in the national park. Desert Sports also offers trips that combine a float trip with hiking or mountain biking. Also see "Mountain Biking," above.

Another recommended outfitter on the Rio Grande is **Far Flung Outdoor Center** (© **800/839-7238** or 432/371-2633; www.ffoc.net), offering raft and canoe trips for $140 per person for a full-day canyon float. Multiday trips range from $325 per person for an overnight trip to $1,800 for a 10-day expedition. Rentals run $59 per day for canoes and kayaks; other gear rentals and shuttles for river trips are available. The company also provides jeep and ATV tours of the region and several wilderness first aid courses a year.

Guided trips on the Rio Grande are also available through **Big Bend River Tours** (© **800/545-4240** or 432/371-3033; www.bigbendrivertours.com), which has daily raft trips year-round. Trips range from a delightful half-day float for about $72 per person to 10-day excursions for about $2,000 per person. Among the company's most popular trips is the 21-mile float through beautiful Santa Elena Canyon, which can be explored on a day trip (about $150 per person), a 2-day trip (about $300 per person), or a 3-day trip (about $500 per person), with varying rates based on the number of people making the trip. The longer trips include a stop in a side canyon with waterfalls and peaceful swimming holes. Big Bend River Tours also offers guided canoe and inflatable kayak trips, a shuttle service, and equipment rentals.

## Where to Stay

This is an isolated area, so don't expect to find your favorite chain motel or restaurant right around the corner. Make lodging reservations well in advance, especially in winter—the high season here—when rates are highest.

### IN THE PARK

**Chisos Mountains Lodge** ★ The best place to stay while exploring Big Bend, Chisos Mountains Lodge offers a variety of accommodations, ranging from simple motel rooms to the historic stone cottages. Built by the Civilian Conservation Corps in the 1930s, these six delightful cottages have a rustic feel that fit the setting, with stone floors, wooden furniture, three double beds, and covered porches. Book as far in advance as possible.

The Emory Peak units are also a bit on the rustic side, with one double and one single bed, wood furnishings, and painted brick walls with Western art. The lodge's motel rooms come in two flavors: The Rio Grande rooms are small and simply decorated, with two double beds and terrific views of the Chisos Mountains, and the Casa Grande units have larger and more modern motel rooms with private balconies. All rooms are nonsmoking.

Chisos Basin, Big Bend National Park, TX 79834. © **432/477-2291.** Fax 432/477-2352. www.chisos mountainslodge.com. 72 units. $120–$160 double. AE, DISC, MC, V. **Amenities:** Restaurant. *In room:* A/C (in motel and Casa Grande units), fridge, no phone, Wi-Fi (free; not available in the cottages and Emory Peak rooms).

## THE STUDY BUTTE–TERLINGUA AREA

Just outside the national park's West Entrance, this is the closest community to the park with lodging and other services. Here you'll find **Big Bend Resort & Adventures,** at the junction of Tex. 118 and FM 170 (P.O. Box 336), Terlingua, TX 79852 (© 800/848-BEND [2363] or 432/371-2218; www.bigbendresortadventures.com), offering simple but comfortable, well-maintained, modern motel rooms, with rates of $69 to $135 double, about $159 to $199 for two-bedroom apartments with kitchenettes, and $299 for a three-bedroom house. A restaurant and convenience store are on-site. In Terlingua Ghost Town, the formerly abandoned **Holiday Hotel,** behind the Terlingua Trading Company (© 888/371-2234; www.bigbendholidayhotel. com), has been nicely restored and has four rooms with rates of $115 to $200 double. The proprietors also have numerous historic homes for rent in the area. There's also the **Las Ruinas Camping Hostel** on Terlingua Ghost Town Road (© 432/498-6792; www.lasruinashostel.com), with pitch-your-own tent sites for $6 nightly or canvas tents for $10. An old school bus has been converted to a funky lounge here, and there's Wi-Fi and a bar on-site.

About 20 miles west of Terlingua, **Lajitas Golf Resort,** HC 70 (© 877/525-4827 or 432/424-5000; www.lajitasgolfresort.com), offers double rooms and suites for $149 to over $300 double, including use of an 18-hole golf course, a spa, and an outdoor pool. A wing of stylish rooms is located in a former cavalry post once under the command of "Black Jack" Pershing.

**La Posada Milagro** ★   Built on the site of a former ruin that is now incorporated into the structure, La Posada Milagro overlooks Terlingua Ghost Town and is a terrific place to hang your hat in the Big Bend region. Featuring distinctive West Texas touches—thatched ceilings, corner hearths, and great patio seating areas—three smaller rooms share a full bathroom and a half bathroom. A fourth room, the Chisos Honeymoon Suite, is larger and has a private bathroom. Also available is a nearby guesthouse, La Casita.

100 Milagro Rd., Terlingua Ghost Town, Terlingua, TX 79852. © **432/371-3044.** 5 units, 3 with shared bathroom, including 1 guesthouse. $145–$195 double with shared bathroom; $210 double with private bathroom; $350 guesthouse. AE, MC, V. *In room:* A/C, no phone, Wi-Fi (free).

**Las Casitas at Far Flung Outdoor Center** ★   New in 2010, longstanding local river outfitter Far Flung built six comfortable and modern cabins, with plans for six more. Centered on a nicely landscaped courtyard that's a hummingbird haven, the cabins are comfortable and functional, featuring two queen beds, kitchenettes, and plenty of peace and quiet. The convenience factor is also worth mentioning, especially if you're going on an expedition with Far Flung—you'll meet your guide in the parking lot—and the location is within easy walking distance of a Mexican restaurant and a liquor store.

FM 170 just west of Tex. 118 (© **800/839-7238** or 432/371-2533. www.ffoc.net. 6 units. $99–$135 double. DISC, MC, V. *In room:* A/C, TV, fridge, no phone, Wi-Fi (free).

**Ten Bits Ranch** ★   Located about 10 miles north of Study Butte, this isolated lodging is one of a kind, a re-creation of an old Western town, replete with boardwalks and storefronts masking the stylish guest rooms. Hosting their first guests in late 2004, the individually decorated units—the Bank, the Gunsmith, the Schoolhouse, and the General Store—are named for their corresponding storefronts, and decorated with a sense of desert chic, featuring private bathrooms and patios. The ranch is environmentally sustainable and off the grid—you can really get away from it all here.

390

Owners Jennifer and Steve Wick are well acquainted with the Big Bend area as a former travel agent and park ranger, respectively. The Wick's Big Bend Expeditions (www.biggbendexpeditions.com) offers guided hikes and 4×4 tours of the area.

6000 N. County Rd. (P.O. Box 293), Terlingua, TX 79852. © **866/371-3110.** www.tenbitsranch.com. 4 units. $129–$199 double, with a 2-night minimum stay Sept–May. Rates include continental breakfast. AE, DISC, MC, V. **Amenities:** Wi-Fi (free). *In room:* No phone.

## MARATHON

**Gage Hotel** ★★  Located 50 miles north of the park boundary, the historic Gage Hotel opened in 1927 as the social hub for area ranchers and miners, but fell into shambles under the desert sun in the ensuing decades. But that period is long over: The current owners restored the old redbrick's many charms in the early 1980s, melding history and an eye for Texas chic. The historic rooms have cow-skin rugs, hardwood floors, Navajo blankets, and oodles of personality; those with shared bathrooms are a bit on the smallish side, but those with private bathrooms are my personal favorites. With outdoor entrances closer to the magnificent pool and courtyards, the larger Los Portales rooms are part of an addition completed in 1992 and have adobe floors and expanded amenities (coffeemakers, phones, hair dryers, and irons). The restaurant, Café Cenizo, serves steaks and gourmet Southwestern cuisine.

U.S. 90 (P.O. Box 46), Marathon, TX 79842. © **800/884-GAGE** [4243] or 432/386-4205. www.gage hotel.com. 39 units (9 with shared bathroom), including 1 suite and 2 guesthouses. $107 double with shared bathroom; $137–$156 double with private bathroom; $218–$320 suite; $333–$363 guesthouse. AE, DISC, MC, V. **Amenities:** Restaurant; bar; exercise room; Jacuzzi; outdoor heated pool; spa. *In room:* A/C, no phone, Wi-Fi (free, most rooms).

# Where to Dine

## IN THE PARK

The restaurant at **Chisos Mountains Lodge** (see "Where to Stay," above) is your only dining option within park boundaries. It serves three meals a day, including a breakfast buffet.

## THE STUDY BUTTE–TERLINGUA AREA

For authentic Mexican food, hit **Los Jalapenos** at the Terlingua Store between Terlingua Ghost Town and the intersection of FM 170 and Tex. 118 (© **432/ 371-2487**).

**La Kiva** ★ BARBECUE  One of my favorite bars in the West is also an excellent place for a bite to eat. The cavelike La Kiva has personality to spare and all sorts of lowbrow touches, from faux dinosaur fossils of questionable taste embedded in the craggy walls to tree-stump bar stools. The menu features steaks, barbecue platters, burgers, and—my favorite—a fried-chicken sandwich. The dining room opens up to a courtyard with a stage on Terlingua Creek, and the management doesn't mind if you pitch a tent and camp out back.

FM 170 at Terlingua Creek. © **432/371-2250.** www.lakiva.net. Main courses $9–$15. DISC, MC, V. Sun-Fri 5pm–midnight; Sat 5pm–1am.

**Starlight Theatre** ★★ MEXICAN/NEW AMERICAN  A 1930s movie palace abandoned when the mines in Terlingua went bust, the Starlight Theatre (named for what was formerly visible through a hole in the ceiling) was reborn as an eatery and watering hole in 1991. Now bedecked with murals, artful tables, and longhorn skulls, the theater still has a stage, but the silver screen takes a back seat to the food (especially the trademark chili and filet mignon, as well as a number of vegetarian and seafood options), drink (namely Texas beers and prickly pear margaritas), and desserts (including a very good *tres leches*). Briefly shuttered in 2010, the Starlight still occasionally hosts movie nights, as well as plays and live music.

In Terlingua Ghost Town, off FM 170. © **432/371-4300.** www.starlighttheatre.com. Main courses $9–$30. AE, MC, V. Daily 5–10pm. Bar open later.

## CAMPING

A $10 camping permit, available at any visitor center, is required for use of the primitive backcountry roadside and backpacking campsites. All are open year-round.

### In the Park

There are three developed campgrounds run by the National Park Service (no showers, laundry facilities, or RV hookups; $14 per night), and an RV park run by a concessionaire. A limited number of campsites in Rio Grande Village and the Chisos Basin campgrounds accept reservations from November 15 to April 15; call © **877/444-6777** or visit **www.recreation.gov**.

**Rio Grande Village Campground** is the largest, with 100 sites, flush toilets, running water, and a dump station. It has numerous trees, many with prickly pear cacti growing up around them, and thorny bushes everywhere. Sites are either graveled or paved and are nicely spaced for privacy. Sites are often taken by 1pm in winter (the busy season). One area is designated a "No Generator Zone." Separate but within walking distance is **Rio Grande Village Trailer Park** (© **800/386-4383** or 432/477-2293), a concessionaire-operated RV park with 25 sites with full hookups. It looks like a parking lot in the midst of grass and trees, fully paved with curbs and back-in sites (no pull-throughs). Cost is $29 per night for two people. Tents are not permitted. A small store has limited camping supplies and groceries, a coin-operated laundry, showers for a fee, propane, and gasoline.

**Chisos Basin Campground** ★★, although not heavily wooded, has small pinyon and juniper trees and 65 well-spaced sites. The highest-elevation campground in the park at 5,400 feet, it's nestled around a circular road in a bowl below the visitor center. There is a dump station, along with flush toilets and running water. The access road to the campground is steep and curved, so take it slowly. The campground is not recommended for trailers over 20 feet or motor homes over 24 feet.

**Cottonwood Campground** is named for the huge cottonwood trees that dominate the scene. The 31 first-come, first-served sites in this rather rustic area are spacious and within walking distance of the river. There are pit toilets, and generators may not be used.

### Near the Park

About 7 miles east of the park's North Entrance on FM 2627 is **Stillwell Store and RV Park,** HC 65, Box 430, Alpine, TX 79830-9752 (© **432/376-2244;** www.stillwellstore.com), a casual RV park in desert terrain that's open year-round. There are two areas across the road from each other. The west side has full hookups, while the east has water and electric only, but the east side also features horse corrals and plenty of room for horse trailers. There are 80 RV sites ($16–$19 per night) plus almost unlimited space for tenters, who are charged $5 per person. There's a dump station, showers, a self-serve laundry, and a public phone. The RV park's office is at the Stillwell Store, where you can get groceries, limited camping supplies, and gasoline. There is also a small museum (donations accepted), with exhibits from the Stillwell family's pioneer days.

In Terlingua, the **Las Ruinas Camping Hostel** is a good spot for tent campers ($6–$10) and **Big Bend Resort & Adventures** has RV sites for $27 to $32 and 415 tent sites, with discounts for longer stays. For more information on both properties, see "Where to Stay," above.

# GUADALUPE MOUNTAINS NATIONAL PARK

Once a long reef below the ocean's surface, then a dense forest, Guadalupe Mountains National Park is today a rugged wilderness of tall Douglas firs and lush vegetation rising out of a vast desert. Here, you will find varied hiking trails, panoramic vistas, the highest peak in Texas, plant and animal life unique to the Southwest, and a canyon that many believe is the prettiest spot in all of Texas.

As you approach from the north, the mountains seem to rise gradually from the landscape, but seen from the south they stand tall and dignified. El Capitan, the southern tip of the reef escarpment, watches over the landscape like a sentinel. In the south-central section of the park, Guadalupe Peak, at 8,749 feet the highest mountain in Texas, provides hikers with incredible views of the surrounding mountains and desert.

Within its 86,416 acres of land, the park has several hubs of human activity and distinct ecological zones. Park headquarters and the visitor center are at Pine Springs, along the park's southeast edge, where you'll also find a campground and several trail heads, including one with access to the Guadalupe Peak Trail, the park's premier mountain hike. Nearby, a short dirt road leads to historic Frijole Ranch, with a museum and more trail heads. A horse corral is nearby for those traveling with their steeds. The McKittrick Canyon section of the park, near the northeast corner, gets my vote as the most beautiful spot in Texas, especially in the fall when its oak, maple, ash, and walnut trees produce a spectacular show of color. A day-use area only, McKittrick Canyon has a delightful although intermittent stream, a wide variety of plant and animal life, several trail heads, and historic buildings. Along the park's northern boundary, practically in New Mexico, is the secluded and forested Dog Canyon.

Particularly impressive about Guadalupe Mountains National Park is its vast variety of flora and fauna. You'll find species here that don't seem to belong in West Texas, such as the maple and oak, which produce the wonderful fall colors in McKittrick Canyon. Scientists say these seemingly out-of-place plants and animals are leftovers from a time when this region was cooler and wetter. As the climate changed and the desert spread, some species were able to survive in these mountains, where conditions remained somewhat cooler and moister. At the base of the mountains, at lower elevations, you'll find desert plants such as sotol, agave, and prickly pear cactus; but as you start to climb, especially in stream-nurtured canyons, expect to encounter ponderosa pine, ash, walnut, and oak trees, and ferns. Wildlife abounds, including mule deer, elk, all sorts of birds, and the occasional snake.

It takes several days to fully explore this park, but just a half-day trip to McKittrick Canyon would be well worth your time.

## Essentials

**GETTING THERE**   Located on the border of New Mexico and Texas, the park is 55 miles southwest of Carlsbad, New Mexico, along U.S. 62/180. From El Paso, drive east 110 miles on U.S. 62/180 to the Pine Springs Visitor Center.

Air travelers can fly to **Cavern City Air Terminal** (© **575-887-3060**), at the south edge of the city of Carlsbad, which has commercial service from Albuquerque with **New Mexico Airlines** (© **888/564-6119;** www.flynma.com). The nearest major airport is **El Paso International Airport** (© **915/780-4749;** www.elpaso internationalairport.com) in central El Paso just north of I-10, with service from most major airlines and car-rental companies; see chapter 10 for more information.

**VISITOR INFORMATION** Contact **Guadalupe Mountains National Park,** 400 Pine Canyon Rd., Salt Flat, TX 79847 (© **915/828-3251;** www.nps.gov/gumo). Books and maps can be ordered from the **Carlsbad Caverns Guadalupe Mountains Association,** 727 Carlsbad Caverns Hwy. (P.O. Box 417), Carlsbad, NM 88221 (© **575/785-2486;** www.ccgma.org).

Park headquarters and the main visitor center are located at Pine Springs just off U.S. 62/180. There are three other access points along this side of the park: Frijole Ranch, about a mile east of Pine Springs and a mile north of the highway; McKittrick Canyon (day use only), about 7 miles east and 4 miles north of the highway; and Williams Ranch, about 8 miles south of Pine Springs and 8 miles north of the highway on a four-wheel-drive road. (**Note:** Keys to locked gates can be checked out at park headquarters.)

The **Pine Springs Visitor Center,** open daily year-round except Christmas, has natural history exhibits, a bookstore, and an introductory slide program. **McKittrick Canyon** has an intermittently staffed visitor contact station with outdoor exhibits and an outdoor slide program on the history, geology, and natural history of the canyon. On the north side of the park is the year-round **Dog Canyon Ranger Station** (© **575/ 981-2418**), at the end of N.M. 137, about 70 miles from Carlsbad and 110 miles from park headquarters. Information, restrooms, and drinking water are available.

**FEES, REGULATIONS & PERMITS** Entry into the park runs $5 per person. Backcountry camping is free, but a permit is required. Corrals are available for those who bring their horses to ride in the park; although use is free, permits are required. All permits are available at the Pine Springs Visitor Center and Dog Canyon Ranger Station and must be requested in person, either the day before or the day of use. Horses are prohibited in the backcountry overnight.

Visitors to McKittrick Canyon, a day-use area, must stay on the trail; entering the stream is not permitted. The McKittrick Canyon **entrance gate** opens at 8am daily, and closes at 4:30pm Mountain Standard Time and at 6pm Mountain Daylight Time. Neither wood nor charcoal fires are allowed anywhere in the park.

**WHEN TO GO** In general, summers in the Guadalupe Mountains are hot (highs in the 80s and 90s/upper 20s and 30s Celsius, and lows in the 60s/upper teens Celsius) and winters are mild (highs in the 50s and 60s/teens Celsius and lows in the upper 20s and 30s/around 0 Celsius), but there can be sudden and extreme changes in the weather at any time. In winter and spring, high winds can whip down the mountain slopes, sometimes reaching 100 mph; on hot summer days, thunderstorms can blow up quickly. The sun is warm even in winter, and summer nights are generally cool no matter how hot the afternoon. Clothing that can be layered is best, comfortable and sturdy walking/hiking shoes are a must, a hat and sunscreen are highly recommended, and plenty of drinking water is essential for hikers.

Overall, Guadalupe Mountains National Park is one of America's less visited national parks, with attendance of only about 225,000 each year. This is partly

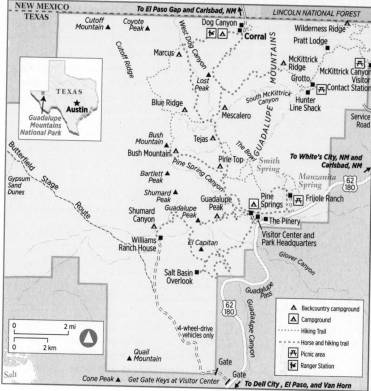

**Map legend:**
- ▲ Backcountry campground
- ▲ Campground
- ..... Hiking Trail
- •••• Horse and hiking trail
- ⊞ Picnic area
- ▮ Ranger Station

Scale: 0 — 2 mi / 0 — 2 km

because it is primarily a wilderness park, where you'll have to tackle rugged hiking trails to get to the best vistas, but also because of its isolation. The only time the park might be considered even slightly crowded is during spring-break time, usually in March, when students from area colleges bring their backpacks and hit the trails. Quite a few families visit during the summer, but even then the park is not usually crowded; and visitation drops considerably once schools open in late August.

An exception is McKittrick Canyon, renowned throughout the Southwest for its beautiful fall colors, at their best in late October and early November. The one road into McKittrick Canyon is a bit busy then, but once you get on the trails, you can usually walk away from the people.

**SAFETY** This is extremely rugged country, with sometimes unpredictable weather, and hikers need to be well prepared, with proper hiking boots and plenty of water. Because the park's backcountry trails often crisscross each other and can be confusing, rangers strongly recommend that hikers carry topographical maps.

**RANGER PROGRAMS** In March, summer, and fall, rangers lead a variety of programs and activities. Check at the visitor center for the current schedule.

# What to See & Do
## EXPLORING THE HIGHLIGHTS BY CAR

This is not the place for the vehicle-bound visitor. There are no paved scenic drives traversing the park; roads here are simply a means of getting to historical sites and trail heads.

## HISTORIC SITES

**The Pinery** was 1 of 200 stagecoach stations along the 2,800-mile Butterfield Overland Mail Coach Route. The stations provided fresh mules every 20 miles and a new coach every 300 miles, in order to maintain the grueling speed of 5 mph for 24 hours a day. John Butterfield had seen the need for overland mail delivery between the Eastern states and the West Coast, so he designed a route and the coaches, and acquired a federal contract to deliver the St. Louis mail to San Francisco in 25 days. In March 1857, this was a real feat, and the remaining rock walls at the ruins of the Pinery, which you can see on the Pinery Trail (see "Hiking," below) commemorate Butterfield's achievement.

Located in McKittrick Canyon and accessible by a 4.8-mile round-trip hike, **Pratt Cabin** was built by Wallace E. Pratt in 1931 and 1932, of stone quarried from the base of the Guadalupe Mountains, using heart-of-pine from east Texas for rafters, collar beams, and roof supports. Pratt, a geologist for the Humble Oil Co. (now Exxon-Mobil), and his family came for summer vacations when the heat in Houston became unbearable. He finally retired here in 1945. In 1957, the Pratts donated 5,632 acres of their 16,000-acre ranch to the federal government to begin the national park. In addition to the grand stone lodge, there are several outbuildings, stone picnic tables, and a stone fence.

**Williams Ranch House** rests at the base of a 3,000-foot rock cliff on the west face of the Guadalupe Mountains. The 7½-mile access road, navigable only by high-clearance 4×4s, follows part of the old Butterfield Overland Mail Route for about 2 miles. The road crosses private land and has two locked metal gates, for which you must sign out keys at the visitor center.

History is unclear about exactly who built the house and when, but it's believed to have been built around 1908, and it is fairly certain that the first inhabitants were Henry and Rena Belcher. For almost 10 years, they maintained a substantial ranch here, at times with close to 3,000 head of longhorn cattle. Water was piped from Bone Spring down the canyon to holding tanks in the lowlands. James Adolphus Williams acquired the property around 1917, and with the help of an Indian friend, ranched and farmed the land until moving to New Mexico in 1941. After Williams's death in 1942, Judge J. C. Hunter bought the property, adding it to his already large holdings in the Guadalupes.

Another historic site is **Frijole Ranch,** which was a working ranch from when it was built in the 1870s until 1972. Inside the ranch house is a museum with exhibits on the cultural history of the Guadalupe Mountains, including prehistoric Indians, the later Mescalero Apaches, Spanish conquistadors, and ranchers of the 19th and 20th centuries. On the grounds are several historic buildings, including a schoolhouse.

## OUTDOOR ADVENTURES
### Hiking ★★

This is a prime hiker's park, with more than 80 miles of trails that range from easy walks to steep, strenuous, and sometimes treacherous adventures. Among shorter trails, try the **Indian Meadow Nature Trail ★**, with access from Dog Canyon Campground (walk south from the water fountain). This exceptionally easy, .6-mile round-trip stroll follows a series of numbered stops keyed to a free brochure, available at the trail head. You'll learn about the native vegetation and cultural history of the area as you ramble along this virtually level dirt trail. The name comes from early settlers, who told of seeing Indian tepees in this lovely meadow. The **McKittrick Canyon Nature Trail ★**, rated moderate due to a rocky trail, is .9-mile round-trip, and begins at the McKittrick Canyon contact station. A great way to discover the variety of plants and animals that inhabit the canyon, this trail, which has some steep climbs, posts numerous educational signs along the path telling you why rattlesnakes are underappreciated and how the cactus supplies food and water for wildlife.

The easy .75-mile round-trip **Pinery Trail** (paved and accessible by wheelchair) gives visitors a brief introduction to the low-elevation environment at the park. Interpretive signs discuss the plants along the trail and the history of the area. About .25 miles from the visitor center, the trail makes a loop around the ruins of an old horse-changing station, left over from the Butterfield Stage Route (see "Historic Sites," above). The trail head is by the Pine Springs Visitor Center, or from the parking area on U.S. 62/180, located 1 mile north of the visitor center entrance road.

Among the park's longer trails, my favorite is the moderate-to-difficult **McKittrick Canyon Trail ★★★**, which is about 5 miles one-way, with access at the McKittrick Canyon Trail trail head. McKittrick Canyon is perhaps the most beautiful spot in all of Texas, and this trail explores the length of it. The first 2.4 miles to the Pratt Cabin are moderate because of rocky trail conditions; the following mile to the Grotto gains 340 feet in elevation and is also considered moderate; and the strenuous climb to the Notch rises nearly 800 feet in just 1.3 miles. Even so, this is one of the most popular hikes in the park, though not everyone makes it to the Notch.

The canyon is forested with conifers and deciduous trees. In fall, the walnut and ash trees burst into color, painting the world in bright colors set off by the brown of the oaks and the rich variety of the evergreens. The stream in the canyon, which appears and disappears several times in the first 3 miles of the trail, is permanent, with reproducing trout. Hikers may not drink from, wade in, or disturb the stream in any way.

The first part of the trail is wide and seems quite flat, crossing the stream twice on its way to Pratt Cabin, which is wonderfully situated at the convergence of North and South McKittrick canyons. About a mile from the lodge, a short spur veers off to the left to the Grotto, a recess with odd formations that look like they belong in an underground cave. This is a great spot for lunch at one of the stone picnic tables. Continuing down the spur trail to its end, you reach the Hunter Line Cabin, which served as temporary quarters for ranch hands of the Hunter family. Beyond the cabin, South McKittrick Canyon has been preserved as a Research Natural Area with no entry. Return to the main trail and continue toward the Notch, or head back down the canyon to your car. In another .5 mile, the trail begins switchbacking up the side of South McKittrick Canyon for the steepest ascent in the park, until it slips through the Notch, a distinctive narrow spot in the cliff. Sit down and rest while you absorb the incredible scenery. The view down the canyon is magnificent and quite dazzling in autumn. You can see both Hunter Line Cabin and Pratt Lodge in the distance. Remember to start down in time to reach your car well before the gate closes (see "Fees, Regulations & Permits," above).

To stand at the highest point in Texas, hike the strenuous **Guadalupe Peak Trail ★★**, which goes 4.2 miles from the trail head in Pine Springs Campground to the top of 8,749-foot-high Guadalupe Peak, where the magnificent views make the almost 3,000-foot climb worthwhile. If you have only 1 day to explore this park, and you are an average or better hiker, this is the hike you should choose. Start early, take plenty of water, and be prepared to work. When you've gone about halfway, you'll see what seems to be the top not too far ahead, but beware: This is a false summit. Study the changing life zones as you climb from the desert into the higher-elevation pine forests—this will take your mind off your straining muscles and aching lungs. A mile short of the summit, a campground lies in one of the rare level spots on the mountain. If you plan to spend the night, strongly anchor your tent, as the winds can be ferocious up here, especially in spring.

From the summit, the views are stupendous. To the north are Shumard Peak and Bush Mountain, the next two highest points in Texas, with respective elevations of 8,615 and 8,631 feet. The Chihuahuan Desert stretches to the south, interrupted only by the Delaware and Sierra Diablo mountains. This is one of those "on a clear day you can see forever" spots—sometimes all the way to 12,003-foot-high Sierra Blanca, near Ruidoso, New Mexico, 100 miles north.

## Horseback Riding

About 60% of the park's trails are open to horses for day trips, but horses are not permitted in the backcountry overnight. There are **corrals** at Frijole Ranch (near Pine Springs) and Dog Canyon (see "Visitor Information," above). Each set of corrals contains four pens that can accommodate up to 10 horses. There are no horses or other pack animals available for hire in or near the park. Park rangers warn that horses brought into the park should be accustomed to steep, rocky trails.

## Wildlife Viewing

Because of the variety of habitats here, and also because these canyons provide some of the few water sources in West Texas, Guadalupe Mountains National Park offers excellent opportunities for wildlife viewing and bird-watching. **McKittrick Canyon** and **Frijole Ranch** are considered among the best wildlife viewing spots, but a variety of species can be seen throughout the park. Those spending more than a few hours will likely see mule deer, and the park is also home to a herd of some 50 to 70 elk, which are sometimes seen in the higher elevations or along the highway in winter. Other **mammals** include raccoons, striped and hog-nosed skunks, gray foxes, coyotes, gray-footed chipmunks, Texas antelope squirrels, black-tailed jack rabbits, and desert cottontails. Black bears and mountain lions also live in the park, but are seldom seen.

 **Leaf Peepin'**

McKittrick Canyon's beautiful display of fall colors usually takes place between late October and early November. It varies, though, so call before going.

About two dozen varieties of **snakes** make their home in the park, including five species of rattlesnakes. There are also numerous **lizards,** which are usually seen in the mornings and early evenings. These include the collared, crevice spiny, tree, side-blotched, and Texas horned lizards, and Chihuahuan spotted whiptails. The most commonly seen is the prairie lizard, identified by the light-colored stripes down its back.

More than 200 species of **birds** are known to spend time in the park, including peregrine falcons, golden eagles, turkey vultures, and wild turkeys. You are also likely to encounter rock wrens, canyon wrens, black-throated sparrows, common night-hawks, mourning doves, rufous-crowned sparrows, mountain chickadees, ladder-backed woodpeckers, solitary vireos, and western scrub jays.

## Where to Stay & Dine

There are no accommodations or restaurants within the park. The closest communities with lodging include **Carlsbad,** New Mexico, 55 miles north of the park, discussed below in the section on Carlsbad Caverns National Park. **Van Horn,** Texas, is another option, 45 miles south of the park. Newly restored to its 1930s grandeur, **Hotel El Capitan,** 100 E. Broadway (© **877/283-1220** or 432/283-1220; www.hotelelcapitan.net), is easily the most distinctive lodging near the park. Rates range from $69 to $149 double.

### CAMPING
### In the Park

There are two developed vehicle-accessible campgrounds in the park. Both are open year-round, cost $8 per night, and have restrooms and drinking water, but no showers or RV hookups. **Pine Springs Campground** ★ is near the visitor center and park headquarters just off U.S. 62/180. There are 19 spaces for RVs, 20 very attractive tent sites, and two group campsites (call park headquarters for information). About a half-mile inside the north boundary of the park is **Dog Canyon Campground,** accessible from N. Mex. 137. Here, there are nine tent sites and four RV sites. Although reservations are not accepted, you can call ahead to check on availability of sites (© **915/828-3251**). Camp stoves are allowed, but wood and charcoal fires are prohibited.

The park also has 10 designated **backcountry campgrounds,** with from five to eight sites each. Be sure to pick up free permits at the Pine Springs Visitor Center or Dog Canyon Ranger Station on the day of or day before your backpacking trip. Water is available at trail heads, but is not available in the backcountry. All trash, including toilet paper, must be packed out. Fires are strictly prohibited; use cookstoves only. You can camp only in designated campgrounds.

# A SIDE TRIP TO CARLSBAD CAVERNS NATIONAL PARK

One of the largest and most spectacular cave systems in the world, Carlsbad Caverns National Park comprises more than 100 known caves that snake through the porous limestone reef of the Guadalupe Mountains. Fantastic and grotesque formations fascinate visitors, who find every shape imaginable (and unimaginable) naturally sculpted in the underground—from frozen waterfalls to strands of pearls, soda straws to miniature castles, draperies to ice-cream cones. Plan to spend a full day.

Formation of the caverns began some 250 million years ago, when a huge inland sea covered this region. Then, about 20 million years ago, a reef that was once under-sea moved upward, ultimately breaking free of thousands of feet of sediment enshrouding it. As tectonic forces pushed the buried rock up, erosion wore away softer minerals, leaving behind the Guadalupe Mountains. Brine from gas and oil deposits mingled with rainwater, creating sulfuric acid that dissolved limestone and created cave passages.

Once the caves were hollowed out, nature became artistic, decorating the rooms with a vast variety of fanciful formations. Very slowly, water dripped down through the rock into the caves, dissolving more limestone and absorbing the mineral calcite and other materials on its journey. Each drop of water then deposited its tiny load of calcite, gradually creating the cave formations we see today.

Although American Indians had known of Carlsbad Cavern (the park's main cave) for centuries, it was not discovered by settlers until ranchers in the 1880s were attracted by sunset flights of bats emerging from the cave. The first reported trip into the cave was in 1883, when a man supposedly lowered his 12-year-old son into the cave entrance. A cowboy named Jim White, who worked for mining companies that collected bat droppings for use as a fertilizer, began to explore the cave in the late 1800s. Fascinated by the formations, White shared his discovery with others, and soon word of this magical, below-ground world spread.

Carlsbad Cave National Monument was created in October 1923. In 1926, the first electric lights were installed, and in 1930, Carlsbad Caverns gained national park status.

Underground development at the park has been confined to the famous Big Room, one of the largest and most easily accessible of the caverns, with a ceiling 25 stories high and a floor large enough to hold six football fields. Visitors can tour parts of it on their own, aided by a state-of-the-art portable audio guide, and explore other sections and several other caves on guided tours. The cave is also a summer home to about 300,000 Mexican free-tailed bats, which hang from the ceiling of Bat Cave during the day, but put on a spectacular show each evening as they leave the cave in search of food, and again in the morning when they return for a good day's sleep.

## Essentials

**GETTING THERE**    The main section of Carlsbad Caverns National Park, with the visitor center and entrance to Carlsbad Cavern, the park's main cave, is located about 35 miles from Guadalupe Mountains National Park. From Guadalupe Mountains National Park, take U.S. 62/180 northeast to White's City, and turn left onto N. Mex. 7, the park access road. You enter the boundary of Carlsbad Caverns National Park almost immediately and reach the visitor center in about 7 miles. From the city of Carlsbad, head 30 miles southwest on U.S. 62/180 and then 7 miles on N. Mex. 7 to the visitor center.

For airport information, see the "Getting There" section under "Guadalupe Mountains National Park," earlier in this chapter.

**VISITOR INFORMATION**    Contact **Carlsbad Caverns National Park,** 3225 National Parks Hwy., Carlsbad, NM 88220 (© **575/785-2232;** www.nps.gov/cave). Books and maps can be ordered from the **Carlsbad Caverns Guadalupe Mountains Association,** 727 Carlsbad Caverns Hwy. (P.O. Box 417), Carlsbad, NM 88221 (© **575/785-2486;** www.ccgma.org).

The visitor center is open daily from 8am to 7pm from Memorial Day to Labor Day; and self-guided cave tours can be started from 8:30am to 5pm. During the rest of the year, the visitor center is open from 8am to 5pm, with self-guided cave tours from 8:30am to 3:30pm. Tour times and schedules may be modified during slower times in the winter. The park is closed on Christmas Day.

At the visitor center are displays depicting the geology and history of the caverns, bats and other wildlife, and a three-dimensional model of the caverns. You can get

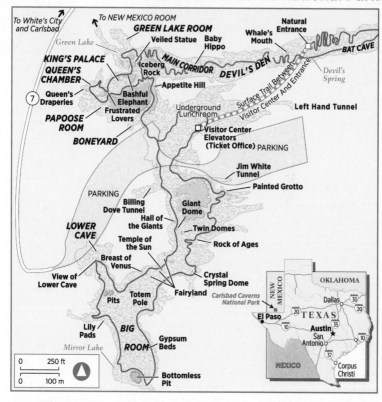

information about the tours available and other park activities, both above- and below-ground. There is also a well-stocked bookstore, a restaurant, and a gift shop.

**FEES**   Admission to the visitor center and aboveground sections of the park is free. The basic cavern entry fee, which is good for 3 days and includes self-guided tours of the Natural Entrance and Big Room, is $6 for adults and free for children 15 and under. Annual passes and senior passes are good for the entry of four adults.

A general cave admission ticket is required in addition to tour fees for all guided cave tours except those to Slaughter Canyon Cave and Spider Cave. Reservations are required for all guided tours. Holders of annual and senior passports receive 50% discounts on tours. The Kings Palace guided tour costs $8 for adults, $4 for children ages 6 to 15, and is free for children ages 4 and 5 with an adult—younger children are not permitted. Guided tours of Left Hand Tunnel, limited to those age 6 and older, cost $7 for adults and $3.50 for children 6 to 15. Guided tours of Spider Cave, Lower Cave, and Hall of the White Giant are limited to those 12 and older, and cost $20 for adults and $10 for youths 12 to 15. Slaughter Canyon Cave tours, for those 6 and older, cost $15 for adults and $7.50 for children 6 to 15. You can make reservations for cave tours up to 3 months in advance by phone or online (*C* **877/444-6777;** www. recreation.gov).

**REGULATIONS & PERMITS**   As you would expect, damaging the cave formations in any way is prohibited. What some people do not understand is that they should not even touch the formations, walls, or ceilings. This is not only because many of the features are delicate and easily broken, but also because skin oils will both discolor the rock and disturb the mineral deposits that are necessary for growth.

All tobacco use is prohibited underground. In addition, food, drinks, candy, and chewing gum are not allowed on the underground trails. Those making wishes should not throw coins or other objects into the underground pools.

Cave explorers should wear flat shoes with rubber soles and heels, because of the slippery paths. Children 15 and under must remain with an adult at all times while in the caves. Although strollers are not allowed for younger children, child backpacks are a good idea, but beware of low ceilings and doorways along the pathways.

No photography is permitted at the evening "Bat Flight" programs without a special permit.

Pets are not permitted in the caverns, on park trails, or in the backcountry, and because of the hot summer temperatures, pets should not be left unattended in vehicles. There is a kennel (*C* **575/785-2281**) available at the visitor center. It has cages in an air-conditioned room, but no runs, and is primarily used by pet owners for periods of 3 hours or so while they are on cave tours. Pets are provided with water, but not food, and there are no grooming or overnight facilities. Reservations are not necessary; cost is $5 per pet.

Free permits, available at the visitor center, are required for all overnight hikes into the backcountry.

**WHEN TO GO**   The climate aboveground is warm in the summer, with highs often in the 90s (mid-30s Celsius) and sometimes exceeding 100°F (38°C), and evening lows in the mid-60s (teens Celsius). Winters are mild, with highs in the 50s and 60s (teens Celsius) in the day and nighttime lows usually in the 20s and 30s (around 0°C). Summers are known for sudden intense afternoon and evening thunderstorms; August and September see the most rain. Underground it's another story entirely, with a year-round temperature that varies little from its average temperature of 56°F (13°C), making a jacket or sweater a welcome companion.

Crowds are thickest in summer, and on weekends and holidays year-round, so visiting on weekdays between Labor Day and Memorial Day is the best way to avoid them. January is the quietest month.

Visiting during the park's off season is especially attractive because the climate in the caves doesn't vary regardless of the weather on top, where the winters are generally mild and summers warm to hot. The only downside to an off-season visit is that you won't be able to see the bat flights. The bats head to Mexico when the weather starts to get chilly, usually by late October, and don't return until May. There are also fewer guided cave tours off season, although those tours will have fewer people. The best time to see the park might well be in September, when you can still see the bat flights, but there are fewer visitors than during the peak summer season.

**RANGER PROGRAMS**   In addition to the cave tours, which are discussed below, rangers give a talk on bats at sunset each evening from mid-May to October at the cavern's Natural Entrance (times change; check at the visitor center or call *C* **575/ 785-3012**). Rangers also offer a variety of demonstrations, talks, guided nature walks, and other programs daily. Especially popular are the climbing programs, where rangers demonstrate caving techniques. In recent years, there has also been a series of stargazing programs presented by graduate students from New Mexico State University. The park also offers a **Junior Ranger Program,** in which kids can earn badges by completing various activities. Details are available at the visitor center.

On the second Thursday in August (usually), a "bat flight breakfast" from 5 to 7am encourages visitors to watch the bats return to the cavern after their night of insect hunting. Park rangers prepare breakfast for early-morning visitors for a small fee and then join them to watch the early-morning return flight. Call the park for details.

## What to See & Do

### EXPLORING THE HIGHLIGHTS BY CAR

No, you can't take your car into the caves, but for a close-up as well as panoramic view of the Chihuahuan Desert, head out on the **Walnut Canyon Desert Drive,** a 9½-mile loop. You'll want to drive slowly on the one-way gravel road, both for safety and to thoroughly appreciate the dramatic scenery. Passenger cars can easily handle the tight turns and narrow passage, but the road is not recommended for motor homes or cars pulling trailers. Pick up an informational brochure at the visitor center bookstore.

### CAVING ADVENTURES ★★★

Carlsbad Cavern (the park's main cave), Slaughter Canyon Cave, and Spider Cave are open to the general public. All guided tours must be reserved and have individual fees in addition to the general cave entry fee (see "Fees," above). Guided tours are sometimes fully booked weeks in advance, so reserve early.

Most park visitors head first to Carlsbad Cavern, which has elevators, a paved walkway, and an underground rest area. A 1-mile section of the Big Room self-guided tour is accessible to those in wheelchairs (no wheelchairs are available at the park), though it's best to have another person along to assist. Pick up a free accessibility guide at the visitor center.

The Big Room Tour, Natural Entrance Route, and King's Palace Guided Tour are the most popular trails, and all of them are lighted and paved, and have handrails. However, the Big Room is the only one of the three that's considered easy. The formations along these trails are strategically lit to display them at their most dramatic. This also means that today's visitors can see much more of the cave than early explorers, who were limited by their weak lanterns.

The **Big Room Self-Guided Tour ★★★** is an easy 1-mile loop that you access by taking the visitor center elevator to the Underground Rest Area or via the Natural Entrance Route (see below). Considered the one thing that all visitors to Carlsbad Caverns National Park must do, this easy trail meanders through a massive chamber—it isn't called the Big Room for nothing—where you'll see some of the park's most spectacular formations and likely be overwhelmed by the enormity of it all. Allow about 1 hour.

The **Natural Entrance Route,** also 1 mile, is considered moderate to difficult, and is accessed outside the visitor center. This fairly strenuous hike takes you into Carlsbad Cavern on the same basic route used by its early explorers. You leave the daylight to enter a big hole, and then descend more than 750 feet into the cavern on a steep and narrow switchback trail, moving from the "twilight zone" of semidarkness to the depths of the cave, which would be totally black without the electric lights conveniently provided by the Park Service. The self-guided tour takes about 1 hour and ends near the elevators, which can take you back to the visitor center. However, I strongly recommend that from here you proceed on the Big Room Self-Guided Tour if you have not already been there.

The **King's Palace Guided Tour ★★** is a moderate 1-mile loop that you access by taking the visitor center elevator to the underground rest area. This 1½-hour ranger-led walk wanders through some of the cave's most scenic chambers, where you'll see wonderfully fanciful formations in the King's Palace, Queen's Chamber, and Green Lake Room. Watch for the delightful Bashful Elephant formation between the King's Palace and Green Lake Room. Along the way, rangers discuss the geology of the cave and early explorers' experiences. Although the path is paved, there is an 80-foot elevation change.

## Ranger-Led Cave Tours

In addition to the popular self-guided and guided tours discussed above, there are a number of ranger-led tours to less developed sections of Carlsbad Cavern, which provide more of the experience of exploration and genuine caving than the above-mentioned tours over well-trodden trails. These caving tours vary in difficulty, but all include a period of absolute darkness or "blackout," which can make some people uncomfortable. Because some tours involve walking or crawling through tight spaces, people who suffer from claustrophobia should discuss specifics with rangers before purchasing tickets.

**Left Hand Tunnel** starts in the visitor center near the elevator. The easiest of the caving tours, in this one you actually get to walk (rather than crawl) the entire time! Hand-carried lanterns (provided by the Park Service) light the way, and the trail is dirt but relatively level. You'll see a variety of formations, fossils from Permian times, and pools of water. Open to those 6 and older, this tour takes about 2 hours. The moderate **Lower Cave Tour,** which is 1-mile round-trip, starts at the visitor center near the elevator. This 3-hour trek involves descending or climbing over 50 feet of ladders, and an optional crawl. It takes you through an area that was explored by a National Geographic Society expedition in the 1920s, and you'll see artifacts from that and other explorations. In addition, you'll encounter a variety of formations, including cave pearls, which look a lot like the pearls created by oysters and can be as big as golf balls. This tour is open to those 12 and older only. Four AA batteries are required for the provided headlamp; sturdy hiking boots and gloves are recommended.

The **Hall of the White Giant Tour,** which starts at the visitor center, is only .5 mile (one-way), but it is strenuous and will take 3 to 4 hours as you crawl through narrow, dirty passageways and climb up slippery rocks. The highlight is, of course, the huge formation called the White Giant. Only those in excellent physical condition should consider this tour; children must be at least age 12. Four AA batteries for the provided headlamp and sturdy hiking boots are required; and kneepads, gloves, and long pants are strongly recommended.

## More Cave Tours

It takes some hiking to reach the other caves in the park, so carry drinking water, especially on hot summer days. All children 15 and under must be accompanied by an adult; other age restrictions apply as well. Each tour includes a period of true and total darkness, or "blackout."

The **Slaughter Canyon Cave Tour ★★** is 1.25 miles round-trip and is considered moderate. The parking area is about a 45-minute drive from Carlsbad and is reached via U.S. 62/180, going south 5 miles from White's City to a marked turnoff that leads 11 miles to the parking lot. Discovered in 1937, this cave was mined for bat guano (used as fertilizer) until the 1950s. It consists of a corridor 1,140 feet long with many side passageways. This highly recommended guided tour lasts about 2 hours, plus at least another half-hour to hike up the steep trail to the cave entrance. No crawling is involved, although the smooth flowstone and old bat guano on the floor can be slippery, so hiking boots are recommended. You'll see a number of pristine cave formations, including the crystal-decorated Christmas Tree, the 89-foot-high Monarch, and the menacing Klansman. The tour is open to children 6 and older; participants must bring their own flashlights.

The 4-hour tour of **Spider Cave** is a very strenuous, 1-mile loop (plus a .5-mile hike to and from the cave). Meet at the visitor center and follow a ranger to the cave. This tour is ideal for those who want the experience of a rugged caving adventure as well as some great underground scenery. Highlights include climbing down a 15-foot ladder, squeezing through very tight passageways, and climbing on slick surfaces—all this after a fairly tough, .5-mile hike to the cave entrance. But it's worth it. The cave has numerous beautiful formations—most much smaller than those in the Big Room—and picturesque pools of water. Children must be at least 12 years old. Participants need four AA batteries for the provided headlamps and good hiking boots. Kneepads, gloves, and long pants are strongly recommended.

## BATS, BIRDS & OTHER WILDLIFE VIEWING

At sunset, from mid-May to October, a crowd gathers at the Natural Entrance to watch hundreds of thousands of **bats** take off for a night of insect hunting. An amphitheater in front of the Natural Entrance provides seating, and ranger programs are held each evening (exact times vary; check at the visitor center or call ✆ **575/785-3012**) during the bats' residence at the park (the bats winter in Mexico). The most bats will be seen in August and September, when baby bats born earlier in the summer join their parents and migrating bats from the north on the nightly forays. Early risers can also see the return of the bats just before dawn.

However, bats aren't the only wildlife at Carlsbad Caverns. The park has a surprising number of **birds**—more than 300 species—many of which are seen in the Rattlesnake Springs area. Among species you're likely to see are turkey vultures, red-tailed hawks, scaled quail, killdeer, lesser nighthawks, black-chinned hummingbirds, vermilion flycatchers, northern mockingbirds, and western meadowlarks. In addition, each summer, several thousand cave swallows usually build their mud nests on the ceiling just inside the Carlsbad Cavern Natural Entrance (the bats make their home farther back in the cave).

Among the park's **larger animals** are mule deer and raccoons, which are sometimes spotted near the Natural Entrance at the time of the evening bat flights. The park is also home to porcupines, hog-nosed skunks, desert cottontails, black-tailed jack rabbits, rock squirrels, and the more elusive ringtails, coyotes, and gray fox. These are sometimes seen in the late evenings along the park entrance road and the Walnut Canyon Desert Drive.

## Where to Stay & Dine

There are no accommodations within the park, but there are two concessionaire-operated restaurants (✆ **575/785-2281**). A family-style full-service restaurant at the **visitor center** serves three meals daily in the $5-to-$10 range. The restaurant is open from 8:30am to 5pm most of the year, with extended hours from Memorial Day to mid-August and on Labor Day weekend. The **Underground Rest Area,** located inside the main cavern 750 feet below ground, has a cafeteria-style eatery with snacks and box lunches. Its hours are coordinated with cave hours.

The closest recommended services are in and near the city of Carlsbad, 30 miles northeast of the turnoff to the park on U.S. 62. Here, you'll find several chain and franchise motels and a number of independent and chain restaurants. Motels on the southwest edge of the city, on the road to Carlsbad Caverns, include **Best Western Stevens Inn,** 1829 S. Canal St. (© 800/730-2851 or 575/887-2851), with rates of $89 to $99 double. Also in this area is the **Days Inn,** 3910 National Parks Hwy. (© 800/325-2525 or 575/887-7800) with similar rates to the Best Western; and **Super 8 Motel,** 3817 National Parks Hwy. (© 800/800-8000 or 575/887-8888), with rates of $55 to $60 double.

For more information, contact the **Carlsbad Chamber of Commerce,** 302 S. Canal St., Carlsbad, NM 88220 (© 575/887-6516; www.carlsbadchamber.com).

## CAMPING

There are no developed campgrounds or vehicle camping of any kind in the national park. Backcountry camping, however, is permitted in some areas; pick up free permits at the visitor center.

There are numerous commercial RV parks on National Parks Highway on the way to the park, as well as in Carlsbad.

# THE PANHANDLE PLAINS

by Eric Peterson

A wide-open sea of prairie, the High Plains of northern Texas might well be the nation's crossroads: The small-town charm of the Great Plains, the spice of the Southwest, and the polite twang of the South are all present in equal measure. Beyond this cultural intersection, highways have crisscrossed the region since the 1930s, fostering a brood of cheap motels and kitschy roadside Americana.

---

Inhabited by nomadic tribes for much of the past 12,000 years, the Panhandle Plains are distinguished by a high mesa—3,000 feet above sea level—that tapers downhill to the south and east, bordered by spectacular canyons and unique geological formations. In 1541, when Vásquez de Coronado ventured north in his quest for the fabled Seven Cities of Gold, he pounded stakes into the ground to claim the land for Spain—as well as mark his route for a return trip through the mostly featureless flatlands. Thus, the "Llano Estacado," Spanish for "staked plains," was born. Today, Lubbock inhabits the center of the mesa that Coronado staked out; Amarillo sits on its northern edge.

The late–19th century brought significant change to the area: Ranchers began to graze cattle here, railroads crisscrossed the mesa in all directions, and agriculture took hold as the predominant industry. Million-acre ranches became the norm. During the fall and winter of 1874 and 1875, the indigenous tribes battled the U.S. Army in the Red River War, culminating with the dispersal of Comanches, Kiowas, and Southern Cheyennes to reservations in Oklahoma.

The landscape was irrevocably altered again by the discovery of oil in the 1920s, when ranchers found themselves sitting on "black gold." The Dust Bowl days of the 1930s dampened development, but the area recovered and saw tremendous growth following World War II.

At first glance, the Panhandle Plains might appear monotonous, but the region is actually worth a closer look than you'll get from behind the wheel. The magnificent palette of Palo Duro Canyon, the lively nightlife in Lubbock, and Amarillo's ranching heritage—from cattle to Cadillacs—are unexpected diversions that make this area a worthy stopover on a cross-country trip.

# AMARILLO

122 miles N of Lubbock; 267 miles E of Albuquerque, New Mexico

The commercial center of the Texas Panhandle, Amarillo arose when the Fort Worth and Denver City Railway started laying track in the area in 1887, a decade after ranchers began to graze their cattle on the buffalo grass–speckled plains. When the town was formally incorporated, the name Amarillo—meaning "yellow" literally and "wild horse" figuratively—was adopted from a nearby lake. In a little over a decade, the combination of the railroad and the ranchland led to the establishment of Amarillo's long-standing status as a cattle-shipping capital. To this day, the city "smells like money" most when the Amarillo Livestock Auction is in full swing.

While its agricultural roots remain the cornerstone of the local economy, Amarillo's location on a major east-west highway—Route 66 until 1970 and I-40 thereafter—has long made it a popular stopover for tourists, with a plethora of motels and restaurants catering to the cross-country crowd. Amarillo is fairly low-key and nondescript at first glance, but it's a pleasant, inexpensive spot for an overnight stay. Several of its attractions are must-see tourist traps, namely the roadside kitsch of Cadillac Ranch and the Big Texan steakhouse. As a destination, Amarillo can be a fun place to spend a weekend, especially for those with a taste for cowboy culture.

## Essentials

### GETTING THERE

**BY PLANE**   More than 50 commercial flights take off or land daily from **Rick Husband Amarillo International Airport (AMA)** (© 806/335-1671), off I-40 exit 76 (Lakeside Dr.) at 10801 Airport Blvd., 7 miles east of downtown. Airlines serving Amarillo include **American, Continental, Delta, Southwest,** and **United.** Car rentals are available from **Avis** (© 806/335-2313), **Hertz** (© 806/335-2331), **Enterprise** (© 806/335-9443), and **National** (© 806/335-2311).

**BY CAR**   Coming from east or west, Amarillo can be accessed via I-40, exits 62 (Hope Rd.) through 75 (Lakeside Dr.). The primary downtown exit is 70 (Taylor/Buchanan sts.), and the airport is located northeast of exit 75. Coming from the north by car, you'll likely enter Amarillo via U.S. 87/287, which takes you through downtown and continues south to Canyon and Lubbock as I-27. If you are coming from the northwest, Texas FM 1061 can be used as a shortcut from U.S. 385; it becomes Tascosa Road as it enters Amarillo. U.S. 60 is the primary route northeast to Pampa and southwest to Hereford, and U.S. 287 veers east beyond the city, to Childress, and, beyond that, Wichita Falls and Fort Worth.

### ORIENTATION

I-40 cuts through the heart of Amarillo, skirting the south side of downtown. The city's primary north-south artery is U.S. 87, which splits into four one-way, north-south streets in the downtown area. (From the west, these streets are Taylor, Fillmore, Pierce, and Buchanan.) South of I-40, U.S. 87 becomes I-27, which leads to Canyon and Lubbock. The northern boundary of downtown is 1st Avenue, the southern boundary I-40. The Route 66 Historic District begins at 6th Avenue and Georgia Street and continues west along 6th Avenue for a mile to Western Street. Amarillo Boulevard is a major east-west route through the northern stretch of the city. Along with Georgia Street, Ross-Mirror and Washington streets are among the busiest

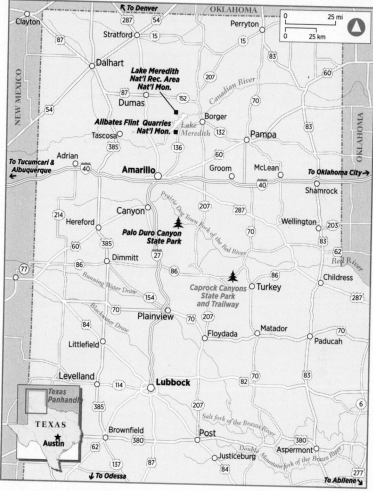

north-south roads in Amarillo. Loop 335 comprises four roads (Soncy Rd., FM 1719, Lakeside Dr., and Hollywood Rd.) that circumnavigate the city.

## GETTING AROUND

Aside from some one-way streets downtown, Amarillo is a snap to navigate by car, with relatively little traffic. (Instead of a rush hour, locals like to say they have a "rush minute.")

**Amarillo City Transit** (*©* 806/378-3095) operates a bus system Monday through Saturday from 6:30am to 6:30pm. The main transfer point is located downtown at 3rd Avenue and Fillmore Street. Eight different routes run from downtown to the major shopping centers and Harrington Regional Medical Center. Ride tickets are 75¢ for adults, 60¢ for children ages 6 to 12 and students, and 35¢ for seniors and travelers with disabilities.

Taxi service is provided by **Ace's Taxi** (© 806/676-7263), **Airport Taxi** (© 806/358-8350), and **Bob's Taxi** (© 806/373-1171).

## VISITOR INFORMATION

Contact the **Amarillo Convention & Visitor Council,** 1000 S. Polk St. (© 800/692-1338 or 806/374-8474; www.visitamarillotx.com). The CVC operates a **visitor information center** open daily at 401 S. Buchanan St. For statewide information, visit the **Texas Travel Information Center** on the city's east side; it's located on the south frontage road just west of I-40, exit 75.

**FAST FACTS** The **Northwest Texas Hospital,** 1501 S. Coulter Dr. (© 806/354-1000; www.nwtexashealthcare.com), and **Baptist St. Anthony,** 1600 Wallace Blvd. (© 806/212-2000; www.bsahs.org), are Amarillo's two largest hospitals. The main **post office** is located at 2301 S. Ross St. and is open Monday through Friday from 7:30am to 6pm and Saturday from 9am to 2pm.

## What to See & Do
### THE TOP ATTRACTIONS

**American Quarter Horse Hall of Fame & Museum** ★ ☺ Dedicated to the history of the equine breed named for its speed when racing a quarter-mile, this facility provides a comprehensive look at the animals and the culture surrounding them. The museum is geared toward horse lovers and kids—who will no doubt be delighted by the interactive exhibits and a fiberglass quarter horse replica you can climb aboard. Start with the orientation show in the modern Kenneth Banks Theater. Next, investigate the galleries, featuring an engaging chronological history of the American Quarter Horse and a look at the physiology of these impressive beasts. If the subject matter piques your interest, expect to spend an hour or more here.

2601 I-40 E. at Quarter Horse Dr. © **806/376-5181.** www.aqhhalloffame.com. Admission $6 adults, $5 seniors 55 and over, $2 children 6–18, free for children 5 and under. Mon-Sat 9am–5pm.

**Cadillac Ranch** ★ One of the more recognizable and inexplicable roadside attractions in the country, Cadillac Ranch consists of 10 vintage Cadillacs (dating 1949–64) buried up to their back seats in a wheat field west of Amarillo, rising out of the earth at the same angle as the Cheops Pyramid in Egypt. Conceived and funded by Amarillo's Stanley Marsh 3, the eccentric grandson of one of the Panhandle's most successful oilmen, Cadillac Ranch was constructed in 1974 by the Ant Farm, a San Francisco–based art collective, and relocated west in 1997 to its present site to escape the shadow of Amarillo's growth. Cadillac Ranch is also interactive: Marsh freely allows visitors to add their creative touches with spray paint, a marker, or a key. (For more on Stanley Marsh 3's artistic exploits in the Amarillo area, see "Unanticipated Rewards," p. 413.)

I-40 W., on the south frontage road btw. exits 60 (Arnot Rd.) and 62 (Hope and Holiday roads). Free admission. Daily 24 hr.

**Route 66 Historic District** This colorful area west of downtown Amarillo preserves about a mile of old Route 66, also known as the Mother Road. Once a suburb accessible by trolley car, the district has evolved into a hub for the city's nightlife and shopping. Buildings that once housed drugstores and theaters are now home to eateries, antiques stores, and specialty shops. The area is a bit run-down in spots, but it's

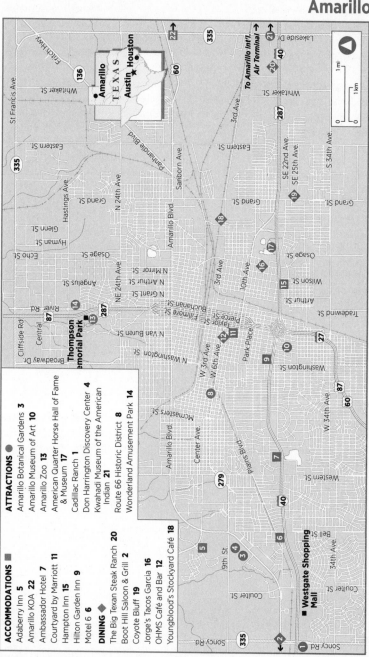

## ACCOMMODATIONS ■

Adaberry Inn **5**
Amarillo KOA **22**
Ambassador Hotel **7**
Courtyard by Marriott **11**
Hampton Inn **15**
Hilton Garden Inn **9**
Motel 6 **6**

## DINING ◆

The Big Texan Steak Ranch **20**
Boot Hill Saloon & Grill **2**
Coyote Bluff **19**
Jorge's Tacos Garcia **16**
OHMS Café and Bar **12**
Youngblood's Stockyard Café **18**

## ATTRACTIONS ●

Amarillo Botanical Gardens **3**
Amarillo Museum of Art **10**
Amarillo Zoo **13**
American Quarter Horse Hall of Fame & Museum **17**
Cadillac Ranch **1**
Don Harrington Discovery Center **4**
Kwahadi Museum of the American Indian **21**
Route 66 Historic District **8**
Wonderland Amusement Park **14**

not all that touristy and it's fun as a glimpse into the glory days of Route 66. The surrounding neighborhood, known as Old San Jacinto, might have once been a suburb, but, in many ways, it is now the heart of the city. During the summer, the district hosts several festivals, with street dances, live entertainment, and art displays.

6th Ave. btw. Western and Georgia sts. Call the Amarillo CVC at ✆ **800/692-1338** for additional information. www.amarillo66.com.

## MORE ATTRACTIONS

**Amarillo Botanical Gardens** 🎁 Dedicated to the art, science, and enjoyment of horticulture, these outdoor gardens feature displays on flora indigenous to the High Plains region and provide a pleasant spot to take a 30-minute break from the road. Of special note is a "scent garden" designed for patrons with sight impairments, and an attractive tropical conservatory.

1400 Streit Dr., at Harrington Regional Medical Center. ✆ **806/352-6513.** www.amarillobotanical gardens.org. Free admission. Outdoor gardens daily dawn–dusk; indoor exhibits Tues–Fri 9am–5pm year-round; Sat 9am–5pm Apr–Nov; Sat 1–5pm Dec–Mar.

**Amarillo Museum of Art** The only accredited art museum within a 260-mile radius, this institution houses a worthwhile collection of paintings, photographic exhibits, and sculptures in its galleries. Requiring about 30 minutes to peruse, the permanent collection includes a good deal of regional 20th-century art and a nice Asian exhibit, thanks to a local patron with a passion for Far Eastern works. The museum hosts nearly 20 changing exhibits annually in its six galleries; past programs have included works by Georgia O'Keeffe (a former area resident), pop-art retrospectives, and displays that used art as a lens to explore the area's colorful history.

2200 S. Van Buren St., on the campus of Amarillo College. ✆ **806/371-5050.** www.amarilloart.org. Free admission. Tues–Fri 10am–5pm (until 9pm the third Thurs of each month); Sat–Sun 1–5pm. Closed major holidays.

**Amarillo Zoo** ☺ Home to more than 60 species, this small accredited zoo excels at preserving and displaying the High Plains' indigenous animals, termed "Texotic." The highlight is a 20-acre range populated by grazing bison; the mustang, the feral horse of the American West, is here, as are mountain lions, Texas longhorns, snakes, and spider monkeys. There's also a herpetarium for the zoo's reptilian and amphibious inhabitants. In all, the zoo is a good hour-long stop for families with children who've been cooped up in the back seat for far too long.

NE 24th and Fillmore sts., Thompson Memorial Park, about 1 mile north of downtown on U.S. 287. ✆ **806/381-7911.** www.amarillozoo.org. Admission $3 adults, $2 seniors 62 and up, $1 children 3–12, free for children 2 and under (free on Mon). Daily 9:30am–5pm. Closed major holidays.

**Don Harrington Discovery Center** ☺ The Texas Panhandle's preeminent children's science museum, the Discovery Center is home to more than 60 permanent displays, including an eye-popping exhibit on turbulent weather patterns and "Amazing Bodies," dedicated to human and animal biology and physiology. The center is also home to the innovative Space Theater, an all-digital system that shows a variety of productions. Out front is the space-age Helium Monument, composed of four helium-filled steel columns.

1200 Streit Dr. ✆ **806/355-9547.** www.dhdc.org. Admission $7 adults, $5 children 3–12 and seniors 60 and up, free for children 2 and under. Tues–Sat 9:30am–4:30pm; Sun noon–4:30pm. Closed major holidays.

**Kwahadi Museum of the American Indian** At once a museum and a dance theater, this attractive facility presents the story of the people native to the Panhandle

# UNANTICIPATED rewards

**Cadillac Ranch** (p. 410) is just the tip of Amarillo's public art iceberg, which is in large part the product of the fervent imagination of Stanley Marsh 3 (he favors the Arabic "3" over the Roman "III").

The grandson of an early Texas oil millionaire, Marsh is also the man behind 200 signs on display at Amarillo homes and businesses. Looking very much like colorful municipal signs, they don't dispense traffic or parking rules, instead offering a variety of offbeat slogans. One reads "Strong drink." "What is a village without village idiots?" asks another. "'Either the well is very deep,' thought Alice, 'or I'm falling very slowly,'" reads yet another. While the signs are spread out around Amarillo and the surrounding towns, Old San Jacinto is the neighborhood where you'll see them in the highest concentration. The ever-enigmatic Marsh explained the signs, saying, "They are to be looked at. The signs are just there, like the Rock of Gibraltar or the Statue of Liberty. They are a system of unanticipated rewards."

Beyond Cadillac Ranch and the signs, Marsh's eccentric public art vision extends to the southern fringes of Lubbock, to the rural junction of I-27 and Sundown Lane, where a sculpture of a pair of disembodied legs greets passerby. (An absurd plaque explains that they are all that remains of a great statue of Ozymandias, "damaged by students from Lubbock after losing to Amarillo in a competition.") There's also "Floating Mesa," hundreds of sheets of plywood painted the color of a blue sky on the side of a mountain. Unless it is overcast, the resulting impression is that the summit is floating. It is located about 8 miles northwest of Amarillo on the west side of Tascosa Road.

While many are amused by the creations of Stanley Marsh 3, not every Amarillo resident finds them in good taste. Those disgusted by their presence have decried them as eyesores with little or no artistic value. In response, Marsh was once quoted as saying, "Art is a legalized form of insanity, and I do it very well."

through art and culture. Inside a Pueblo-inspired building, author and artist Thomas Mails's collection of paintings and artifacts is presented; out front, the Kwahadi Dancers take to the stage for regular performances. Most performances are on summer weekend nights at 7:30pm with ticket prices of $4 to $9, but there are also less regular shows in fall and winter.

9151 I-40 E. © **806/335-3175.** www.kwahadi.com. Admission $5 adults, $3 children. Summer Wed-Sun 1am-5pm; winter Sat-Sun 1-5pm; open until 10pm on show days. Call for the current schedule of the Kwahadi Dancers.

**Wonderland Amusement Park** ☺ An Amarillo landmark since the glory days of Route 66, Wonderland is the Panhandle's top amusement park, featuring more than 25 different nostalgic rides on a 15-acre chunk of Thompson Park. The amusements include three roller coasters, six water rides, a carousel, and several kiddie rides. My favorites: the double-loop "Texas Tornado" coaster and the "Shoot the Chute" water ride. There is also a minigolf course and an arcade.

2601 Dumas Dr., at Thompson Memorial Park. © **800/383-4712** or 806/383-3344. www.wonderland park.com. Individual rides $1.50 each plus a $5 gate admission fee. Unlimited rides $13-$16 weeknights, $18-$22 weekends. Apr to Labor Day Sat-Sun 1-10pm; also May Tues and Thurs-Fri 6:30-9:30pm and June to mid-Aug Mon-Fri 7-10pm.

## OUTDOOR ACTIVITIES

Amarillo offers many opportunities for outdoor recreation, in the form of in-city golf courses, pools, and parks, as well as several lakes, reservoirs, and state parks in the surrounding area. The best recreation spot is **Palo Duro Canyon State Park** (see "Canyon & Palo Duro Canyon State Park," later in this chapter), about 27 miles southeast of the city.

The **Lake Meredith National Recreation Area** (© 806/857-3151; www.nps. gov/lamr), located 38 miles northeast of Amarillo via Tex. 136, is another outdoor hot spot, featuring opportunities for boating, fishing, hunting, horseback riding, camping, hiking, swimming, scuba diving, wildlife and bird viewing, and four-wheeling, although the low water level shut down much of the boating in 2010. The site is also home to **Alibates Flint Quarries National Monument** (www.nps.gov/alfl), the point of origin for a significant percentage of arrowhead points and flint tools found throughout the Great Plains. While the monument is closed to most recreational activity, guided tours are offered at 10am and 2pm by **reservation** (© 806/857-3151). Aside from boat-launching fees, access to Lake Meredith is free to the public.

**Wildcat Bluff Nature Center,** 2301 N. Soncy Rd. (© 806/352-6007; www. wildcatbluff.org), is the best spot for hiking and wildlife viewing in the city itself, with more than 2 miles of moderate trails on its 600 acres of cottonwood-shaded hills. The center's wildlife population includes mule deer, horned toads, coyotes, and turkey vultures. The center is open Tuesday through Saturday 9am to 5pm; trails are open during daylight hours. Admission is $3 adults, $2 for kids and seniors, and free for kids 2 and under.

The major city parks in Amarillo include **Thompson Memorial Park,** at Dumas Drive and 24th Avenue, home to Wonderland Amusement Park and the Amarillo Zoo, as well as two 18-hole golf courses, 1 mile of jogging/walking trails, a heated outdoor pool (open seasonally), ball fields, picnic sites with grills, and fishing ponds; **John S. Stiff Memorial Park,** at SW 48th Avenue and Bell Street, with ball fields, three indoor and eight outdoor tennis courts, an outdoor heated pool, and picnic sites; and **Southeast Regional Park,** at SE 46th Avenue and Osage Street, with an outdoor heated pool, ball fields, fishing ponds, and picnic areas. For more information on Amarillo's city parks, contact the Parks and Recreation Department at © 806/378-3036 or visit **www.amarilloparks.org**.

**BOATING**   **Lake Meredith National Recreation Area** is the Panhandle's top watersports destination, but it's notably dry at press time. When full, the main lake occupies 12,000 of the area's 46,000 acres and draws in boaters, windsurfers, water-skiers, and even scuba divers. Powerboat rentals are available from **Forever Resorts** (© 806/865-3391; www.marinaatlakemeredith.com) at the marina at Lake Meredith National Recreation Area. To launch a boat of any size into Lake Meredith, a $4 day-use fee is required ($10 for 3 days).

**FISHING**   Catfish and bass are the fish of choice for anglers in the Texas Panhandle, and several spots in and around Amarillo are quite popular. For no fee outside of the cost of a Texas state fishing license, visitors can fish in several ponds in Amarillo's city park system, including **Thompson Memorial Park** at Dumas Drive and 24th Avenue, **Martin Road Park** at NE 15th Avenue and Mirror Street, **Southeast Regional Park** at SE 46th Avenue and Osage Street, and **Harrington Regional Medical Center Park** at SW 9th Avenue and Wallace Street. **Lake Meredith National Recreation Area** is another popular fishing spot for the Panhandle. At the lake's **marina** (© 806/865-3391), patrons find basic fishing supplies, concessions, and a heated and cooled fishing house ($5 adults for 12 hr., $2 kids and seniors). Fishing licenses can be obtained at local Wal-Marts and sporting-goods stores, including Big 5 Sporting Goods, 8004 I-40 W. (© 806/356-8115).

**GOLF**   The City of Amarillo Parks and Recreation Department manages four golf courses: two at **Comanche Trail,** 4200 S. Grand St. (© 806/378-4281; www. comanchetrail.com), with greens fees for 18 holes of $13 to $17; and two at **Ross Rogers Golf Course,** 722 NE 24th Ave. in Thompson Memorial Park (© 806/378-3086; www.amarilloparks.org), with greens fees of $17 to $23. At both courses, carts are $26 for 18 holes.

**HIKING**   Aside from the hiking opportunities at **Wildcat Bluff Nature Center,** there are two hiking trails at **Lake Meredith National Recreation Area.** The Devil's Canyon Trail is a moderate one-way trail that leaves from Plum Creek on the north side of the lake and continues into the canyon for 1.5 miles. In city limits, the **Rock Island Rail Trail** runs from Coulter Street on the west side to 7th and Crockett streets near downtown, 4 miles of jogging/biking/walking terrain in all. The area's best hiking destination is **Palo Duro Canyon State Park** (see "Canyon & Palo Duro Canyon State Park," later in this chapter), about a half-hour drive southeast of Amarillo.

**HORSEBACK RIDING**   There are several horse-friendly trails in **Lake Meredith National Recreation Area,** in McBride Canyon and alongside Plum Creek on the lake's north side. The National Park Service provides corrals at the Plum Creek and Mullinaw campgrounds, but riders need to bring their own horses. **Palo Duro Canyon State Park** also has horse trails and stables (see "Canyon & Palo Duro Canyon State Park," later in this chapter).

**MOUNTAIN BIKING**   The closest mountain biking trails to Amarillo are 27 miles away in **Palo Duro Canyon State Park** (see "Canyon & Palo Duro Canyon State Park," below). The 3-mile Devil's Canyon Trail at **Lake Meredith National Recreation Area** (see "Hiking," above) is also accessible to mountain bikers.

## SPECTATOR SPORTS

**FOOTBALL**   The **Amarillo Venom** play in the Indoor Football League, with home games at the Amarillo Civic Center's Cal Farley Coliseum, 401 S. Buchanan St. (© 806/378-4297; www.govenom.com), from February to June. Walk-up ticket prices are $10 to $40.

**HOCKEY**   The **Amarillo Bulls** play in the North American Hockey League at the Cal Farley Coliseum (also known as The Bull Pen), 401 S. Buchanan St. (© 806/242-1122; www.amarillobulls.com). The schedule runs from September to March, with single-game ticket prices ranging from $9 to $18.

**RACING**   Motor-sports enthusiasts can get a fix of racing action at **Route 66 Motor Speedway,** located about 10 miles east of downtown Amarillo at 3601 E. Amarillo Blvd. (© 806/383-7223; www.route66motorspeedway.com). The oval dirt track is a half-mile long. Races are held on Saturday nights from April to September; admission is $8 to $25.

**RODEO**   The Working Ranch Cowboys Association (WRCA) holds its annual **World Championship Ranch Rodeo** in Amarillo during the second week of November. Real working cowboys compete in such events as wild-cow milking, bronco riding, and team penning at the Amarillo Civic Center, 401 S. Buchanan St. (© **806/378-3096** for tickets; www.wrca.org). In October, there's the **Cowboy Mounted Shooting Association World Finals** (© **888/960-0003**; www.cowboy mountedshooting.com), with marksmen on horseback testing their skills. Several other major equestrian events are held in town during the fall and winter; contact the **Amarillo CVC** (© **800/692-1338**) for details.

## SHOPPING

Amarillo's biggest enclosed shopping center is the **Westgate Shopping Mall,** 7701 I-40 W., between the Coulter Drive and Soncy Road exits (© **806/358-7221;** www. westgatemalltx.com). The mall's stores include Dillard's, Gap, and Sears, as well as a movie theater and several restaurants. Westgate is open Monday through Saturday from 10am to 9pm, and Sunday from noon to 6pm. The **Historic Route 66 District** is an antiques buff's dream, with about 100 stores on West 6th Avenue between Georgia and Western streets. New upscale retailers have staked a claim to **South Soncy Road.** Western wear is also big in Amarillo; head to **Cavender's Boot City,** 7920 I-40 W. at Coulter Drive (© **806/358-1400**), for a huge selection of boots, along with hats, belt buckles, jeans, jewelry, and practically every other Western garment on the market.

# Where to Stay

Amarillo's location on I-40 makes it an ideal stopping point on cross-country trips. Several inexpensive mom-and-pop motels line Amarillo Boulevard (Loop 335) in northern Amarillo, but finding a good room in that area is a hit-or-miss proposition. A better bet is the I-40 corridor: You'll find dozens of chain motels located just off the interstate, including **Hampton Inn,** 1700 I-40 E. at exit 71 (© **800/426-7866** or 806/372-1425), with rates of $79 to $129 double; **Hilton Garden Inn,** 900 I-40 W. (© **800/321-3232** or 806/355-4400), with rates of $99 to $169 double; and **Motel 6,** 3930 I-40 E. at exit 72B (© **800/466-8356** or 806/374-6444), with rates of $40 to $60 double. Room taxes in Amarillo add about 15% to lodging bills.

**Adaberry Inn** ★★ ⛅   Constructed from scratch in 1997, the Adaberry Inn rose to national prominence when it served as Oprah Winfrey's home for 2 months in 1998 while she fought a defamation lawsuit brought on by Amarillo-area cattle ranchers. One look inside this thoroughly modern B&B and it's easy to see why the TV talk show star chose to stay here. The uniquely decorated rooms are each themed after a particular city: Missoula features a Western motif, with cowboy hats, barn doors under the sink, and a mountainous mural on one wall; Key West offers a more tropical setting with aquatic artwork, a latticed ceiling, and yellow walls. The best, though, is the Aspen suite (Oprah's room), which features a rock fireplace, a Jacuzzi for two, and ski-themed decorative touches. Seven of the rooms have private balconies or patios. There's also a game room with a putting green and a pool table downstairs, adjacent to a state-of-the-art home theater. The inn's main balcony is an ideal place to watch sunsets over the Lost Canyon, a quiet wildlife refuge with walking trails right in the Adaberry's backyard. Smoking and pets are not permitted inside of the inn.

6818 Plum Creek Dr., Amarillo, TX 79124. © **806/352-0022.** Fax 806/356-0248. www.adaberryinn. com. 9 units. $125 double; $195 suite. Rates include full breakfast, snacks, and beverages. AE, DISC, MC, V. Children 11 and under not permitted. **Amenities:** Exercise room. *In room:* A/C, TV/VCR, hair dryer, Wi-Fi (free).

**Ambassador Hotel** ★★   The 10-story Ambassador stands out on the I-40 strip as the city's best hotel. It provides a pleasant touch of class in cowboy country, featuring stately European interiors accented by Texan style, with plenty of basket-weave wood, granite, and tooled leather. The 9th and 10th floors make up the concierge level, with brass fixtures, minibars, and complimentary breakfast and cocktails. Many of the upper rooms have great views of the pleasantly treed cityscape below—those facing east are the best in this regard. Decorated with gallery-caliber art and maps, the lobby is striking—a five-story atrium with a sloping glass enclosure over an excellent cafe and a small pool—and the service and amenities are the best in town.

3100 I-40 W. (exit 68B on Georgia St.), Amarillo, TX 79102. ℂ **800/817-0521** or 806/358-6161. Fax 806/358-9869. www.ambassadoramarillo.com. 265 units, including 3 suites. $129–$169 double; $249–$499 suite. Rates include full breakfast (up to 2 per room). AE, DISC, MC, V. **Amenities:** 2 restaurants; bar; concierge; executive-level rooms; exercise room and access to nearby health club; Jacuzzi; indoor heated pool; room service. *In room:* A/C, TV, hair dryer, Wi-Fi (free).

**Courtyard by Marriott** ★ The only lodging in Amarillo's city center, the Courtyard by Marriott is located in the stately landmark Fisk Building (1927), totally renovated and reinvented as a hotel, opening in late 2010. The striking 10-story redbrick features a nice mix of old and new, including a terrific lobby mural of historic Polk Street. Rooms are comfortable and subtly contemporary, featuring sweeping city views and a variety of layouts. The downtown location is the real selling point, with numerous bars and restaurants on the surrounding blocks.

724 S. Polk St., Amarillo, TX 79101. ℂ **806/553-4500.** Fax 806/373-9101. www.cyamarillo.com. 107 units. $99–$169 double. AE, DISC, MC, V. **Amenities:** Restaurant; bar; exercise room and access to nearby health club; room service. *In room:* A/C, TV, fridge, hair dryer, Wi-Fi (free).

## CAMPING

Several camping options exist in and around Amarillo, with numerous RV campgrounds in the city as well as primitive camping opportunities at Lake Meredith National Recreation Area (see "Outdoor Activities," above). The recreation area does not have RV hookups, but it's free to stay here. See also "Canyon & Palo Duro Canyon State Park," below.

**Amarillo KOA** Located in a secluded spot near the airport on Amarillo's eastern fringe, this campground is well maintained and reliable. It has pull-through and back-in RV sites, tent sites, and cabins. Facilities include a pet walk, a heated outdoor pool, free Wi-Fi, a playground, a game room, and a gift shop with sundries and RV supplies.

1100 Folsom Rd., Amarillo, TX 79108. ℂ **800/562-3431** (reservations only) or 806/335-1792. www.amarillokoa.com. 124 sites. $29–$37 campsites; $57–$100 cabins. MC, V. Located east of Lakeside Dr. (I-40 exit 75) via U.S. 60.

# Where to Dine

There are numerous restaurants and bars in the 700 block of **South Polk Street** in Amarillo, serving food ranging from Mexican to Asian to pub grub. Burger buffs will want to hit the ramshackle **Coyote Bluff,** 2417 S. Grand Ave. (ℂ 806/373-4640), a dinky local landmark clad in rusty signs and featuring troughs of iced beer and some of the best half-pound hamburgers in the Panhandle. Main courses are $5 to $15 at lunch and dinner. In Vega, 35 miles west of Amarillo, I like **Boot Hill Saloon & Grill,** 909 Vega Blvd. (ℂ 806/267-2904; www.boothillvega.com), an eatery that looks as if it's straight from the Old West, but was built in 2007. The menu features both steaks and sandwiches, plus pastas, seafood, and baby back ribs ($10–$25).

**The Big Texan Steak Ranch** ★ ☺ STEAK It is next to impossible to miss the Big Texan when you drive across the Panhandle on I-40: You'll see the first billboards touting the legendary deal—EAT A 72-OUNCE STEAK DINNER IN AN HOUR AND GET IT FOR FREE!—hours before you get to the restaurant. Beyond the hype, the Big Texan is a unique attraction in itself, with a gift shop, a motel ($55–$90 double), horse corral, an old-fashioned shooting gallery, and an extensive collection of taxidermy and kitsch. Costumed cowboy musicians perform every night, dancing is a regular happening in the summer, and longhorn-bedecked limos will ferry you to and from motels on I-40.

With so much going on, you might forget that the Big Texan is a restaurant, but its legendary steaks are what put the place on the map: They're actually quite good. Beyond the 72-ouncer (which, not so incidentally, sports a $72 price tag if you don't finish it), the restaurant also serves juicy prime rib, rib-eye, New York strip, and other steaks in a dinner that includes salad, bread, and two side dishes. A smattering of seafood and barbecue dishes also delight diners. Breakfast and lunch are comparable: all-American and ultra-hearty.

For the record, more than 60,000 people have tried to eat the 72-ounce steak since its introduction in 1959, and about 9,000 have succeeded. One, a wrestler named Klondike Bill inhaled two of the dinners in the 1-hour time limit, and competitive eater Joey Chestnut finished one in 8 minutes, 52 seconds.

7701 I-40 E. © **800/657-7177** or 806/372-6000. www.bigtexan.com. Reservations accepted for large parties only. Main courses $5–$16 breakfast, $9–$40 lunch and dinner. AE, DISC, MC, V. Daily 7am–10:30pm.

**Jorge's Tacos Garcia** TEX-MEX   Jorge's proprietor, George Veloz II, dreamed of opening a Tex-Mex restaurant since he was in middle school. Fittingly, Jorge's Tacos Garcia is the spitting image of his childhood vision, right down to the fountain out front. The "West Texas Tex-Mex" and New Mexican recipes are time-tested at Jorge's, from a family that has been in the restaurant business for a half-century. I like the batter-free rellenos; the *enchiladas de chile verde,* made with blue-corn tortillas and topped with green chile; and the *taquitos de barbacoa,* grilled tacos loaded with "Mexican barbecue." Fans of the Mexican specialty *menudo* (traditional soup) can indulge themselves with Jorge's special recipe anytime the restaurant is open. There are also a dozen combination plates, seafood dishes, daily specials, and a kids' menu.

1100 S. Ross St. © **806/371-0411.** Reservations not accepted. Main courses $7–$15. AE, DISC, MC, V. Mon 10:30am–9:30pm; Tues–Sat 10:30am–10pm; Sun 10:30am–3:30pm.

**OHMS Café and Bar** ★★ NEW AMERICAN   This is my pick for a lunch spot. The chalkboard menu changes daily at this pleasant downtown eatery, which doubles as a gallery for local artists. (Incidentally, OHMS stands for "On Her Majesty's Service," so named by the former owner, a native of the United Kingdom.) Lunch is served cafeteria-style, with such regular dishes as a very British—and very good—shepherd's pie, linguine with fresh basil and brie, and herbed baked chicken, all with soup or salad (with tasty homemade dressings) and fresh bread. Served in the main dining room and an adjacent dim bar, dinner brings table service and higher prices, and healthier fare than the Amarillo norm; likely selections are sesame-crusted oysters, green chile macaroni, ginger-soy halibut, and beef tenderloin. The art on display changes monthly, and live acoustic music is featured on occasion.

619 S. Tyler St. © **806/373-3233.** www.ohmscafe.com. Reservations not accepted. Main courses $6–$10 lunch, $18–$42 dinner. AE, DC, DISC, MC, V. Mon–Fri 11:30am–1:30pm; Tues–Sat 5:30–10pm. Bar open later.

**Youngblood's Stockyard Cafe** 🍴 AMERICAN   Whereas the Big Texan is kitschy and Disney-esque, the Stockyard Cafe is the real deal: Diners just don't get any more cowboy than this. Tucked away at the site of one of the largest livestock auctions in the world, this restaurant is smoky, old-fashioned, and furnished with cowhides, burlap, and the requisite taxidermy. But it's the food that keeps those cattlemen coming, from the simple and fresh American breakfasts to the steaks, hamburgers, and sandwiches at lunch. Dinnertime in Amarillo means more steaks, and the Stockyard Cafe is no exception, serving the chicken-fried variety and 8-ounce sirloins, on Friday nights. Everything on the menu is fresh and Texas-size.

100 S. Manhattan St., in the Amarillo Livestock Auction Bldg. ✆ **806/374-6024.** Reservations not accepted. Main courses $7–$15. AE, DISC, MC, V. Mon–Sat 6:30am–2pm; Fri 5–8:30pm.

## Amarillo After Dark

### THE PERFORMING ARTS

The best places to check for performing arts events in Amarillo are **www. artsinamarillo.com** and **www.panhandletickets.com**.

**Amarillo Little Theatre,** 2019 Civic Circle (✆ **806/355-9991;** www.amarillo littletheatre.org), produces about 10 plays a year at two theaters southwest of downtown. The Mainstage focuses on musicals and lighter fare, whereas the Adventure Space produces edgier, adult-oriented fare. Recent productions have included *South Pacific, On Golden Pond,* and *Dirty Rotten Scoundrels.* Ticket prices range from $11 to $22.

The **Amarillo Opera** (✆ **806/372-7464;** www.amarilloopera.org) produces two main-stage operas annually, one each in the fall and spring, and an annual spirituals concert on the first weekend of every February. The performances take place at the Globe-News Center for the Performing Arts, 400 S. Buchanan St., and tickets are priced from $25 to $100. The **Amarillo Symphony** (✆ **806/376-8782;** www. amarillosymphony.org) performs classical and pops concerts year-round, also at the Globe-News Center; tickets for most concerts cost between $17 and $50.

**Lone Star Ballet** (✆ **806/372-2463;** www.lonestarballet.org) presents a season of local and guest performances from October to April at the Globe-News Center. The local company produces *The Nutcracker* annually on the second weekend of December, and occasionally performs joint performances with the Amarillo Symphony. Tickets are $15 to $50.

### NIGHTCLUBS & BARS

The main nightlife district in Amarillo is **South Polk Street** downtown, between 7th and 8th avenues. **Bodega's,** 709 S. Polk St. (✆ **806/378-5790**), is a wine bar and jazz club. **Butlers Martini Lounge,** 703 S. Polk St. (✆ **806/376-8180**), and a music venue, the **Mayfair Club,** 701 S. Polk (✆ **806/367-9640**), are other standbys on the block. Rough and raw, the **Golden Light Cafe & Cantina,** 2908 W. 6th Ave. (✆ **806/374-9237;** www.goldenlightcafe.com), is a Route 66 landmark, open since 1946 with a grill and oodles of nostalgia. For country-and-western fans, there's **Midnight Rodeo,** 4400 S. Georgia St. (✆ **806/358-7083;** www.midnightrodeo amarillo.com), featuring a gargantuan dance floor centered on an oval bar. Another good venue for live music—primarily country—is the hubcap-laden **Route 66 Roadhouse,** 609 S. Independence St. (✆ **806/355-7399**), which also has pool tables and dartboards.

# CANYON & PALO DURO CANYON STATE PARK ★

16 miles S of Amarillo; 103 miles N of Lubbock

Founded as Canyon City in 1889, Canyon takes its name from the spectacular Palo Duro Canyon, which lies 12 miles to the west. The nomadic pre-horse tribes of Apaches first inhabited the region, but by the 18th century, Comanche and Kiowa horsemen used the canyon as a major campground. By the late–19th century, white ranchers began grazing cattle in the area: Charles Goodnight, the inventor of the chuck wagon, drove a herd into Palo Duro Canyon in 1876 and established the JA Ranch.

Today a city of roughly 15,000 residents, Canyon is known primarily as the gateway to Palo Duro Canyon State Park and the home of West Texas State A&M University. The town is a good base camp for those who want to explore Palo Duro Canyon, but don't want to spend their nights in a tent. The community also has a charming small-town vibe, and much of its colorful history is presented at the excellent Panhandle-Plains Historical Museum.

## Essentials

### GETTING THERE & GETTING AROUND

Canyon is located immediately south of the junction of I-27 and U.S. 87, about 16 miles south of downtown Amarillo. Once entering town, U.S. 87 becomes 23rd Street, one of Canyon's main commercial thoroughfares. Tex. 217, which runs east-west, becomes 4th Avenue in town and is accessible via I-27, exit 106; head west 2 miles to get to Canyon proper or east 10 miles to get to Palo Duro Canyon State Park.

Canyon's small size makes it impossible to get lost. The streets run north-south and begin at 1st Street at the west side of town. The avenues run east-west and begin numerically in the north.

### VISITOR INFORMATION

Open from 9am to 4:30pm weekdays, the **Canyon Chamber of Commerce,** 1518 5th Ave., Canyon, TX 79015 (© **806/655-7815;** www.canyonchamber.org), can provide visitors with information and maps.

**FAST FACTS**  The closest hospitals are located 16 miles north in Amarillo. The **post office** is at 1304 4th Ave., open Monday through Friday from 9am to 4:30pm.

## What to See & Do

### THE TOP ATTRACTIONS

**Palo Duro Canyon State Park ★★ 📷**  The 60-mile Palo Duro Canyon, sculpted by the Prairie Dog Town Fork of the Red River over the past 90 million years, presents a grand contrast to the ubiquitous treeless plains of the Texas Panhandle. Its 800-foot cliffs, striped with layers of orange, red, and white rock and adorned by groves of juniper and cottonwood trees, present a stark beauty that make this the preeminent state park in all of Texas. Simply put, it is the one "can't-miss" natural attraction in the region. Palo Duro, which is Spanish for "hardwood," is a geology buff's dream: The base of the canyon is walled by red shales and sandstones from the Permian period (ca. 250 million B.C.); these are topped by colorful Triassic shales and sandstones; and the top of the canyon is made of a pastiche of stones only a few

Over three million people have attended the musical drama *Texas!* since performances began in 1965, making it the nation's biggest outdoor drama. It's been updated as *Texas,* a spectacle of song and dance covering the Panhandle's storied past. Staged at Pioneer Amphitheatre in Palo Duro Canyon State Park, the 2-hour play takes place Tuesday through Saturday from early June to mid-August at 8:30pm. For tickets, call © 806/655-2181 or visit www.texas-show.com. Adult tickets range from $14 to $30; those for children 12 and under are $10 to $26. For an extra $17 ($13 for children), attendees can partake of a steak dinner at 6pm. The admission fee to the state park is waived at 5:30pm for ticket holders.

million years old. Of the 200 species of animals that venture into the canyon, you're most likely to see mule deer and wild turkeys. There's also the famed Pioneer Amphitheatre, the venue for the musical drama *Texas;* several hiking, biking, and horseback riding trails; and a visitor center/museum/bookstore with interpretive exhibits on the canyon's formation, history, and wildlife.

11450 Park Rd. 5, Canyon, TX 79015. © **806/488-2227.** www.paloduracanyon.com. Day use $5 adults, free for children 12 and under. Additional fees for campsites (see "Camping," below). Gates open daily 8am–10pm. 12 miles west of Canyon via Tex. 217.

**Panhandle-Plains Historical Museum** ★★ 🎁   The largest history museum in the entire state, the Panhandle-Plains Historical Museum is anything but a dusty collection of spurs and bits. Well thought out, engaging, and informative, the facility stands out as the top museum in the Panhandle (and all of West Texas, for that matter) because it comprehensively covers so many subjects under one roof. "People of the Plains" is a comprehensive history of the Panhandle's inhabitants, offering a glimpse into how people have adapted to the past and present challenges of water, food, and climate. The museum is largely hands-on and interactive: You can sit in a Mustang and listen to Buddy Holly tunes or try out a sidesaddle. Other wings cover the region's history in terms of petroleum, art, transportation, Western heritage, paleontology, geology, and American Indian art. Allow 1 to 2 hours.

2503 4th Ave., on the campus of West Texas State A&M University. © **806/651-2244.** www.panhandle plains.org. Admission $10 adults, $9 seniors, $5 children 4–12, free for children 3 and under. Sept–May Mon–Sat 9am–5pm; June–Aug Mon–Sat 9am–6pm; year-round Sun 1–6pm. Closed major holidays.

## OUTDOOR ACTIVITIES

**GOLF   Palo Duro Creek,** 50 Country Club Dr. (© **806/655-1106;** www.pdcgc. com), is an 18-hole course open to the public 365 days a year. Greens fees are $10 to $13 for 18 holes, and $24 for a cart.

**HIKING**   With 25 miles of trails, **Palo Duro Canyon State Park** is the best hiking spot in the entire Texas Panhandle. The most popular hike is to see the **Lighthouse,** an impressive "hoodoo" rock formation so named because of its towering appearance. The Lighthouse is accessible by two trails: Lighthouse Trail, a moderate 5.8-mile round-trip; or Running Trail, a more strenuous 11-mile round-trip that runs through gullies and flats, and over a ridge. Both trail heads begin near the Hackberry Camp Area.

# old ROUTE 66

The ghosts of speed demons behind the wheels of phantom hot rods, torching the highway between Chicago and Los Angeles, still cruise northern Texas's stretch of the fabled "Mother Road." However, the construction of I-40, completed in 1984 on a similar course as Route 66, irrevocably changed the landscape of cross-country travel. What was once Route 66 is now a patchwork of service roads, two-lane highways, and inaccessible stretches of dirt. As the interstate defined the course of the past several decades of development, many of the towns through which Route 66 once snaked lost a fair share of commercial traffic, but hordes of nostalgic travelers have given many of the old and offbeat roadside landmarks a much-needed boost in recent years.

## OLD ROUTE 66 HIGHLIGHTS

Established in 1890 by an Irish sheep rancher, **Shamrock,** 100 miles east of Amarillo via I-40, is home to the **U Drop Inn,** located at the junction of U.S. 83 and Old Route 66. Built in 1936, this service station/coffee shop is one of the earliest examples of Art Deco architecture on the Texas plains. The motel was totally restored and reopened in 2004 as the home of the **Shamrock Chamber of Commerce** (© 806/256-2501). Aside from the U Drop Inn, the **Pioneer West Historical Museum,** 204 N. Madden St. (© 806/256-3941), is the prime tourist stop, with 25 rooms in the restored Reynolds Hotel (1925) devoted to historical artifacts and other displays. It's open Tuesday through Friday from 10am to noon and 1 to 3pm, although hours are somewhat erratic; admission is free, but donations are accepted. Also, come March 17, Shamrock hosts a lively St. Patrick's Day celebration, with a street fair, a parade, and other festivities. Shamrock has a number of restaurants and motels, including the **Irish Inn,** 301 I-40 E. (© 806/256-2106), with rates of about $50 double, including breakfast.

**HORSEBACK RIDING**   Many of the trails in **Palo Duro Canyon State Park** are horse-friendly, including the aforementioned Lighthouse Trail. Several equestrian campsites can also be found in the park. For those who do not have a horse of their own, **Old West Stables,** located inside the park (© 806/488-2180; www.oldwest stables.com), offers 1-hour guided tours on horseback for $35 and half-day rides to the Lighthouse for $140, lunch included.

**MOUNTAIN BIKING**   Mountain bikes are permitted—and quite popular—on the myriad trails in **Palo Duro Canyon State Park.** Bike rentals are available in Amarillo from **Hill's Sport Shop,** 4021 Mockingbird Lane (© 806/355-7224; www. hillssport.com) for $35 a day.

## Where to Stay

Canyon has a few mom-and-pop motels and a few B&Bs. For reliability and convenience, I like the **Holiday Inn Express Hotel & Suites,** 2901 4th Ave. (© 800/465-4329 or 806/655-4445), which has an indoor pool and exercise room. Rates are $99 to about $150 double.

**Hudspeth House** ★★   This charming, three-story B&B was a "kit home" ordered from a company back East, assembled in 1909, then relocated to its present location in 1913. The inn takes its name from a teacher at the college that became West Texas

In the small town of **McLean,** 16 miles west of Shamrock, you'll find the **Devil's Rope Museum,** at the junction of Old Route 66 and Kingsley Street (© **806/ 779-2225;** www.barbwiremuseum.com), a converted Sears bra factory now home to displays on the history and evolution of both barbed wire and Route 66. It's open Tuesday through Saturday 10am to 4pm (shorter hours in inclement weather) with admission by donation.

The town of **Groom,** 25 miles west of McLean, is the home of one of the largest crosses in the world: the **Cross of Our Lord Jesus Christ,** located off of I-40, exit 119 (© **806/665-7788;** www. crossministries.net). With about 1,000 visitors stopping daily, the 190-foot, 1,250-ton cross is truly monolithic.

Just east of Groom is another Route 66 landmark: the **Leaning Tower of Texas,** a water tower intentionally built to slant with one set each of short and long legs and the last remaining vestige of a long-gone truck stop. As with the cross in Groom and Cadillac Ranch in Amarillo, fans of roadside attractions will want to stop for this peculiar photo op.

By far the biggest Texas city on Old Route 66, **Amarillo** still houses a nicely preserved stretch of the restored highway in its **Route 66 Historic District,** between Western and Georgia streets on West 6th Avenue (p. 410).

About 45 miles west of Amarillo is the tiny town of **Adrian,** known as the "Midpoint of Route 66" for its location 1,139 miles from both Chicago and L.A. The appropriately named **MidPoint Cafe** on Route 66 (© **806/538-6379;** www. midpointroute66cafe.com), a favorite of tourists, cowboys, and bikers alike, is a friendly diner open daily March through November (8am–4pm) and closed in winter. The cafe is bedecked with Route 66 memorabilia and shelves of souvenirs, and the menu includes hearty American breakfasts, burgers with the works, "Ugly Crust" pies, and daily specials, with most main courses coming in at $6 to $12.

State A&M University, Miss Mary Elizabeth Hudspeth, a friend of Georgia O'Keeffe who also taught at the school in the 1910s. (The famed artist was a frequent dinner guest at the house in her time.) Outside, a shady wraparound porch and colorful gardens invite guests into a lively and elegant parlor. All of the rooms are uniquely decorated; I like the spare woodsy charm of the Lone Star room, and the large and stylish comfort of the Loft.

1905 4th Ave., Canyon, TX 79015. © **800/655-9809** or 806/655-9800. www.hudspethinn.com. 7 units. $95–$145 double. Rates include full breakfast. DISC, MC, V. *In room:* A/C, TV, Wi-Fi (free).

## CAMPING

**Palo Duro Canyon State Park** The park offers a wide variety of camping options, from primitive backpacking sites accessible only by foot to standard RV sites with water and electrical hookups. Several of the camping areas have showers and restrooms, as well as a dump station. For more substantial supplies, you'll want to hit a grocery store in Canyon first. The seven rustic, mission-style cabins were built in the 1930s, and since renovated. They can sleep two to four people and have varied facilities; they have no kitchens, but there are grills out front. Pets are permitted at all sites, but they must remain leashed at all times.

11450 Park Rd. 5, Canyon, TX 79015. © **806/488-2227** for information or day-of reservations, or 512/389-8900 for advance reservations. 100 sites, including 7 pull-throughs, 75 back-ins, and 18 tent sites. Additional primitive sites, equestrian sites, and 7 cabins available. $12–$25 campsites; $60–$125 cabins. DISC, MC, V. Located 12 miles east of Canyon via Tex. 217.

## Where to Dine

Despite the name, it's hard to go wrong at **Feldman's Wrong Way Diner,** open daily for lunch and dinner at 2100 N. 2nd Ave. (© **806/655-2700;** www.feldmansdiner. com). This family-friendly place features a miniature train chugging along rails in the rafters and all manner of offbeat decor on the walls, not to mention some pretty tasty sandwiches and entrees. Try, if you dare, the decadent Tortugas Chicken, chicken-fried chicken smothered in *queso* (cheese) and *pico de gallo* (salsa). Another local favorite, **Pepito's,** 408 23rd St. (© **806/655-4736**), is a solid Tex-Mex restaurant with tiled, landscape-adorned tables and regional art. The specialties are fajitas, and the restaurant is open for lunch and dinner from Monday through Saturday. Most restaurants in Canyon don't serve alcohol, but allow you to bring your own.

A unique dining experience can be had with **Cowboy Morning** (© **806/488-2100;** www.theelkinsranch.com). The meals include a horse-drawn wagon ride to a canyon overlook and authentic chuck wagon cuisine. Cowboy Morning includes biscuits, scrambled eggs, sausage, potato casserole, cowboy coffee, and orange juice and is priced at $27 for adults, $23 for children.

# LUBBOCK

122 miles S of Amarillo; 100 miles SE of Clovis, New Mexico

When Capt. Randolph Marcy, one of the first Anglo explorers to happen onto the site of modern-day Lubbock, arrived, he was something less than impressed. "It was the dreaded Llano Estacado," he wrote, "a land where no man, either savage or civilized, permanently abides; it spreads forth into a treeless, desolate waste of uninhabited solitude, which has always been and must continue, uninhabited forever."

Certainly, Marcy would be in for a shock if he were to see Lubbock today: a city of about 250,000 residents, the home of a major university in Texas Tech, and the economic and cultural center of the surrounding South Plains. Self-labeled as "the nursery" for Austin's music scene, its musical heritage is legendary: Buddy Holly still reigns as the local king, but Tanya Tucker, Mac Davis, Waylon Jennings, and Dixie Chick Natalie Maines have also called the city home.

Named after Col. Thomas Lubbock, a Confederate officer, Lubbock was established in 1890 and grew rapidly, its economy built on cotton and cattle and, later, oil and gas. The city has long been a regional hub—hence the nickname, "Hub City." Look at a map and the moniker's appropriateness becomes crystal clear: Lubbock is surrounded by dozens of small agricultural towns.

A college town that's a bit rough around the edges, Lubbock is a fun stopover for a night because of its lively dining scene, laid-back vibe, and happening nightlife with plenty of good music.

## Essentials

### GETTING THERE

**BY PLANE** **Lubbock Preston Smith International Airport,** 5401 N. Martin Luther King Blvd. (© **806/775-2044;** www.flylia.com), sees 70 arrivals and departures daily. Four airlines serve the airport: **American, Continental, Delta,** and **Southwest.**

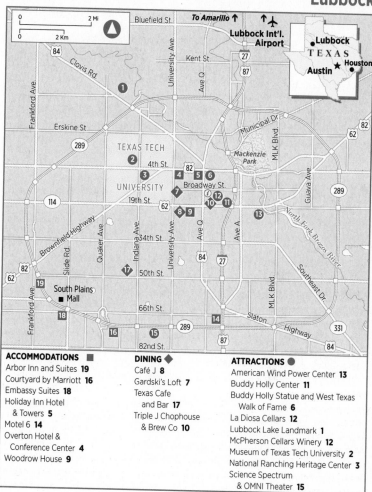

ACCOMMODATIONS ■
Arbor Inn and Suites **19**
Courtyard by Marriott **16**
Embassy Suites **18**
Holiday Inn Hotel
    & Towers **5**
Motel 6 **14**
Overton Hotel &
    Conference Center **4**
Woodrow House **9**

DINING ◆
Café J **8**
Gardski's Loft **7**
Texas Cafe
    and Bar **17**
Triple J Chophouse
    & Brew Co **10**

ATTRACTIONS ●
American Wind Power Center **13**
Buddy Holly Center **11**
Buddy Holly Statue and West Texas
    Walk of Fame **6**
La Diosa Cellars **12**
Lubbock Lake Landmark **1**
McPherson Cellars Winery **12**
Museum of Texas Tech University **2**
National Ranching Heritage Center **3**
Science Spectrum
    & OMNI Theater **15**

All the major car-rental agencies, including **Avis** and **Hertz,** have desks at the airport. **Royal Coach Towne Car Service** (© **806/795-3888**) offers airport transportation in Lincoln Town Cars into the city for $14 to $28.

**BY CAR**    Lubbock sits at the intersection of three major highways on the "Port to Plains" route; I-27 enters the city from the north and becomes U.S. 87 south of Lubbock. Cutting down from Clovis, New Mexico, northwest of the city, U.S. 84 continues southeast to I-20 near Abilene. U.S. 62/82 is the third major highway that runs through Lubbock, entering town from the southwest, where it is the primary route to and from Carlsbad and Roswell, New Mexico, and continuing through the plains to the east.

## GETTING AROUND

Getting around Lubbock is fairly stress-free: It is laid out on a standard grid with few anomalies, with I-27 bisecting the city north-south and Loop 289, a major highway, circling it. Downtown is located just west of I-27, accessible via either exit 3 (19th St.) or exit 4 (4th St.). The east-west streets in central Lubbock are numbered, beginning with 1st in the north, and the north-south streets surrounding I-27 are arranged alphabetically, from Avenue A on the east side of the highway and continuing to Avenue X on the west side of I-27.

**CitiBus** (✆ 806/712-2000; www.citibus.com), Lubbock's mass transit system, operates 11 routes Monday through Friday from 5:25am to 7:45pm and Saturday from 6:45am to 7:55pm. No service is offered on Sunday. The main downtown transfer station is located at the intersection of Broadway and Buddy Holly Avenue (the equivalent of Ave. H). Fares are $1.50 for adults, $1 for children ages 6 to 12, 75¢ for seniors and those with disabilities, and free for children 5 and under. A $3 day pass allows for unlimited rides.

Taxi service is provided by **Yellow Cab** (✆ 806/765-7777).

## VISITOR INFORMATION

**Visit Lubbock, the Convention and Visitors Bureau,** 1500 Broadway, sixth floor (✆ 800/692-4035 or 806/747-5232; www.visitlubbock.org), can provide visitors with local maps and information on lodging, dining, and attractions.

**FAST FACTS** The **University Medical Center,** 602 Indiana Ave. (✆ 806/775-8200; www.umchealthsystem.com), operates a 24-hour emergency room. The main **post office** is located downtown at 411 Ave. L and is open Monday through Friday from 8:30am to 5pm.

## What to See & Do

### THE TOP ATTRACTIONS

**Buddy Holly Center ★★** Named for Lubbock's legendary rock pioneer, this gem of a museum is a must-visit if you're a rock-'n'-roll fan, and at least worth a quick look if you're not. The permanent exhibit about the life and music of Buddy Holly is the centerpiece of this facility, which also houses an art gallery and the Texas Musicians Hall of Fame. Though Holly died in a plane crash at the age of 23, his impact on the development of rock is undeniable—he influenced everyone from Elton John to the Grateful Dead. The center's collection includes such memorabilia as Holly's trademark horn-rimmed glasses (the pair recovered from the crash site) alongside his guitars, personal mementos, and interactive exhibits. Visitors should also view the 20-minute Holly documentary, if time allows. The Lubbock Fine Arts Gallery features rotating exhibits of all kinds, and the Texas Musicians Hall of Fame gives perspective on Lubbock's deep musical heritage. Acting as a regional arts center, the B.H.C. also hosts numerous courtyard concerts, classes, and "Cultural Conversations" on topics of regional artistic interest. The museum's breadth dictates that guests spend a bit more than an hour here. If you crave more Holly, ask for their handout with directions to his grave, birthplace, and other places of interest.

1801 Crickets Ave. in the Depot Entertainment District. ✆ **806/775-3560.** www.buddyhollycenter.org. $5 adults, $3 seniors, $2 children 7–17 and students, free for children 6 and under. Tues–Sat 10am–5pm; Sun 1–5pm. Closed major holidays.

**Museum of Texas Tech University ★** Housing some three million objects and artifacts, this museum is a well-rounded facility that covers a diverse, if not terribly focused, mix of subjects: Visual arts, natural and social sciences, and the humanities are all represented by both permanent and regularly rotating exhibits. The ethnology and textiles collection is among the best you'll find anywhere, composed of objects made by people living in Texas, the Southwest, and the Great Plains. It also has galleries filled with Taos and sub-Saharan art, exhibits on wildlife, and full-size dinosaur skeletons. The temporary exhibits are routinely excellent. Also on-site is the Moody Planetarium (public shows are held daily for $2 adults, $1 students and seniors, free for children 4 and under). Expect to spend between 1 and 2 hours here if you want to scratch the museum's surface.

3301 4th St. at Indiana Ave. ✆ **806/742-2490.** www.depts.ttu.edu/museumttu. Free admission. Tues–Sat 10am–5pm (until 8:30pm Thurs); Sun 1–5pm. Closed major holidays.

**National Ranching Heritage Center**   As some of the country's largest and most storied ranches originated in the Panhandle area in the early 1900s, Lubbock is a natural for the home of a museum dedicated to preserving the history of ranching in the United States. However, the history buff short on time might skip this in favor of the more comprehensive Panhandle-Plains Historical Museum in Canyon (p. 421). The outdoor displays consist of nearly 40 relocated historic buildings; visitors can tour such structures as a vaquero corral (1783), a log cabin (1850), a "dugout" dwelling (1890), and the Victorian-style Barton House (1909). The center hosts several annual events, including a chuck wagon dinner and concert in the spring, fiddle dances in the summer, and "Candlelight at the Ranch" in December. Allow a half-hour to an hour.

3121 4th St. at Indiana Ave. ✆ **806/742-0498.** www.depts.ttu.edu/ranchhc. Free admission. Mon–Sat 10am–5pm; Sun 1–5pm. Closed major holidays.

## MORE ATTRACTIONS

**American Wind Power Center**    Between 1850 and 1920, more than 700 American companies manufactured windmills, but today only a handful of U.S. businesses make these iconic machines. Such statistics provided an impetus for this unique and worthwhile museum, which displays a collection of 200 water-pumping windmills. Windmills of every size, shape, and color are displayed in the main gallery and outside on the museum's grounds, including a rare twin-wheel windmill, with a pair of 12-foot wheels on a single tower, and a 164-foot Vestas wind turbine—with 77-foot blades. (It powers the museum as well as 60 homes.) Indoors, the center houses many more unusual windmills, an art gallery, and a gift shop. Allow 1 hour.

1701 Canyon Lake Dr. ✆ **806/747-8734.** www.windmill.com. Admission $5, or $10 per family. Tues–Sat 10am–5pm; Sun 2–5pm. Closed major holidays. Located 1 mile west of I-27 via 19th St.

> *At least the first 40 songs we wrote were Buddy Holly–influenced.*
> **—Former Beatle Paul McCartney**

**Buddy Holly Statue and West Texas Walk of Fame**   This shady urban isle just west of the Lubbock Civic Center pays tribute to Lubbock's most famous son, Buddy Holly, with an oversize statue of his likeness, guitar in hand. In 1979, Holly became the first inductee into the West Texas Walk of Fame that surrounds the statue. Other inductees include actor Barry Corbin (*WarGames*, "One Tree Hill," *Urban Cowboy*) and musicians Roy Orbison, Tanya Tucker, and Waylon Jennings. It's a pleasant spot to sit on a bench, enjoy the gardens, and reflect on the fleeting life and times of an American original.

Btw. 7th and 8th sts. at Ave. Q.

**Lubbock Lake Landmark**   A unit of the Museum of Texas Tech University, this 300-acre archaeological and natural history preserve is believed to be the only site in North America where a complete record of 12,000 years of human history has been uncovered. The nicely presented interpretive center features chronological displays on each group that has inhabited the region, from the nomadic hunters of the Paleo-Indian period to the pioneers of the late 1800s. The facility requires about 45 minutes to tour, and, if it's fresh air you're after, take an extra hour to explore 4 miles of nature trails and an outdoor sculpture garden with life-size bronzes depicting animals that once roamed the area, including a mammoth and a giant armadillo. Additionally, Lubbock Lake Landmark is home to an active archaeological program during the summer and children's programs throughout the year.

2401 Landmark Lane at Loop 289 and Clovis Hwy. (U.S. 84). ✆ **806/742-1116.** www.depts.ttu.edu/museumttu/LLL/index.html. Free admission (donation requested). Tues–Sat 9am–5pm; Sun 1–5pm. Closed major holidays.

**Science Spectrum Museum & OMNI Theater** ☺   This museum aims to educate children about science and technology, and hits the bull's-eye more often than not. With three floors and 200 exhibits that take 1 to 2 hours to explore, the subject matter runs the gamut from animals and aquariums to space and flight, and many of the displays are interactive. Also of note is the "Brazos River Journey," a permanent aquarium/terrarium exhibit detailing how the regional river ecosystem interacts with the hand of man, complete with rattlesnakes, largemouth bass, and sharks. The facility is also home to the OMNI Theater—with a 55-foot dome screen—and a gift shop.

2579 S. Loop 289 (btw. Indiana and University aves.). ✆ **806/745-2525.** www.sciencespectrum.com. Admission $7.50 adults, $6 seniors and children 3–12, free for children 2 and under. Additional tickets ($6.50–$8) necessary for the OMNI Theater; combo passes available. Mon–Fri 10am–5pm; Sat 10am–6pm; Sun 1–5pm. Closed major holidays.

## OUTDOOR ACTIVITIES

Within the city limits of Lubbock, the 248-acre **Mackenzie Park,** located east of I-27 at 4th Street (✆ **806/775-2687**), is the largest recreation area, with two golf courses (one traditional and one Frisbee); walking, jogging, and equestrian trails; and Prairie Dog Town, one of the few active colonies in the urban United States.

   **Caprock Canyons State Park and Trailway** ★ (✆ **806/455-1492;** www.tpwd.state.tx.us) is a 2½-hour drive from Lubbock, located to the northeast near Quitaque off Tex. 86. Like Palo Duro Canyon to the northwest, this 15,313-acre park provides a startling contrast to the plains in its jagged formations of red rocks and diverse vegetation. An abandoned railroad line was converted into a 65-mile trail system that travels along a canyon floor, through a one-time railroad tunnel, and up a steep incline onto the mesa of the High Plains. Hikers, bikers, and horses are permitted on the trail. Several other hiking opportunities exist in the park as well. Primitive backcountry campsites are available for $8 nightly, as well as tent sites for $12 to $14 and sites with partial RV hookups for $15 to $20. Additionally, boaters and fishers can take advantage of Lake Theo, located on the south side of the park. The park charges a $3 day-use fee per person (free for kids 12 and under).

**BOATING**   Two boat ramps access the spring-fed **Buffalo Springs Lake,** Tex. 835, 5 miles east of Loop 289 (✆ **806/747-3353;** www.buffalospringslake.net). Gate fees are $6 adults, $3 children 11 and under, $2 seniors, and $5 per watercraft and $10 per ATV. Boating is also allowed at **Lake Alan Henry** (✆ **806/775-2673;**

# A DIFFERENT kind OF TEXAS TEA

The images of herds of longhorn, oil pumps on the horizon, and endless cotton fields might be the enduring images of the northwestern Texas plains, but if the area's burgeoning wine industry has anything to do with it, the vineyard may just become another regional icon. The climate is close to ideal for the cultivation of grapes, with its moderate elevation, warm days, and cool nights. Within a 15-minute drive of Lubbock, there are five wineries that open their doors to tours.

Emerging from a grape-growing experiment on a shady Lubbock patio in 1976, **Llano Estacado Winery,** located 5 miles southeast of Lubbock at 3426 E. FM 1585 between U.S. 84 and U.S. 87 (**℃ 800/634-3854;** www.llanowine. com), is now one of the largest and best wineries in Texas: Its wines have won more awards than any other winery in the state. The tasting room is open from 10am to 5pm Monday through Saturday and from noon to 5pm Sunday. **Cap-Rock Winery,** 5 miles south of Lubbock at U.S. 87 S. and Woodrow Road (**℃ 806/863-2704;** www.caprock winery.com), uses vinifera grapes to produce chardonnays, cabernet sauvignons, and other wines. Free tours and samples are available from 10am to 5pm Monday through Saturday. **Pheasant Ridge Winery** on Route 3, 12 miles northeast of Lubbock via I-27 (**℃ 806/746-6033;** www.pheasantridgewinery. com), is located on the site of one of Texas's oldest vineyards and offers tours and tastings Friday and Saturday from noon to 6pm and Sunday from 1 to 5pm. In the Depot Entertainment District, visit **La Diosa Cellars,** 901 17th St. (**℃ 806/744-3600;** www.ladiosacellars.com). Its tasting room is actually a fantastic wine bar (serving tapas and featuring live acoustic music), open for lunch and dinner Tuesday through Saturday. The winery sources its fruit from Texas and produces about 2,000 cases a year. **McPherson Cellars Winery,** 1615 Texas Ave. (**℃ 806/687-9463;** www.mc phersoncellars.com), is the newest of the bunch, open from 11am to 6pm Monday through Saturday. Tastings are $5.

www.lakealanhenry.org), 65 miles southeast of Lubbock via U.S. 84 and FM 2458, a rugged-looking reservoir surrounded by a wildlife habitat area with several miles of hiking trails. Day-use fees are $6 to $8; boating fees are $5 to $8.

**GOLF** Lubbock has several public 18-hole golf courses, including **Shadow Hills Golf Course,** 6002 3rd St. (**℃ 806/793-9700;** www.shadowhillsgolf.com), with greens fees of $13 to $22 and carts for $14; **Rawls Golf Course,** 4th Street and Texas Tech Parkway on the campus of Texas Tech (**℃ 806/742-4653;** www.therawlscourse. com), with greens fees of $34 to $64, cart included; and **Meadowbrook Golf Course,** 601 Municipal Dr. in Mackenzie Park (**℃ 806/765-6679;** www.golf meadowbrook.com), with two 18-hole courses and greens fees of $17 to $36 with cart or $13 to $27 without. Nearby, the **Mackenzie Park Disk Golf Course** is free, although you'll need your own Frisbee. It is a 21-hole course that includes a 470-yard shot over the Brazos River from a cliff.

**HIKING** Four miles of nature trails snake around **Lubbock Lake Landmark** (p. 428), as well as the 65-mile trailway at **Caprock Canyons State Park** (see above). Several miles of walking and jogging trails, many of which are horse-friendly, are within the city limits at **Mackenzie Park,** 4th Street and I-27 (**℃ 806/775-2687**).

**MOUNTAIN BIKING** There are a few trails at **Buffalo Springs Lake,** Tex. 835, 5 miles east of Loop 289 (see "Boating," above), but Lubbock's hard-core mountain bikers head north to **Palo Duro Canyon State Park** (see "Canyon & Palo Duro Canyon State Park," earlier in this chapter) and **Caprock Canyons State Park** (see above).

**SWIMMING** Lubbock is home to four municipal pools, all outdoor and open from late May to early August: **Clapp Municipal Swimming Pool,** 4600 Ave. U; **Mae Simmons Community Center,** 2004 Oak St.; **Maxey Park,** 4007 30th St.; and **Montelongo,** 3200 Bates St. In season, each is open from 1 to 6pm daily with an admission fee of $2.50 for adults, and $2 for children 17 and under. For further information, call ☏ 806/775-2670. **Buffalo Springs Lake** (see "Boating," above) boasts two beaches that are open to swimmers year-round. Aside from the admission fee ($6 adults, $3 children 12 and under, $2 seniors), there is no additional fee to swim. A year-round indoor pool is located at the **YWCA,** 3101 35th St. (☏ 806/792-2723; www.ywcalubbock.org). Swimming costs $6 for a day pass for nonmembers.

## SPECTATOR SPORTS

The Lubbock home crowd roots for the **Texas Tech Red Raiders,** who compete in Big 12 football, baseball, and men's and women's basketball. Call ☏ 806/742-4412 or visit **http://texastech.cstv.com** for schedules and ticket information.

## SHOPPING

Lubbock is home to the region's largest mall, **South Plains Mall,** 6002 Slide Rd. at South Loop 289 (☏ 806/792-4653; www.southplainsmall.com), which houses about 150 stores, including Gap, Abercrombie & Fitch, and many other department stores, specialty shops, and restaurants. The mall's hours are from 10am to 9pm Monday through Saturday and from noon to 6pm Sunday. The **Antique Mall of Lubbock,** 7907 W. 19th St. (☏ 806/796-2166; www.antqmall.com), has West Texas's largest selection of antiques, open daily from 10am to 6pm.

# Where to Stay

You'll find Lubbock's greatest concentration of hotels and motels in three areas: downtown; off of I-27 between 50th Street and Loop 289; and in the city's southwest corner, off Loop 289 near Quaker and Indiana avenues. Rates are highest on the weekends that Texas Tech plays home football games and during graduation and other special events.

Among the city's chain properties are **Courtyard by Marriott,** 4001 S. Loop 289 (☏ 800/321-2211 or 806/795-1633), with rates of $129 to $149 double; **Embassy Suites,** 5215 S. Loop 289 (☏ 800/362-2779 or 806/771-7000), with suites for $109 to $259; and **Motel 6,** 909 66th St. (☏ 800/466-8356 or 806/745-5541), with rates of $42 to $52 double. In Post, 36 miles southeast of Lubbock via U.S. 84, the historic 1915 **Hotel Garza,** 302 E. Main St. (☏ 806/495-3962; www.hotel garza.com), offers individually decorated rooms and suites for $79 to $142 double, breakfast included. Room taxes in Lubbock add 13% to lodging bills.

**Arbor Inn & Suites** Opening in 2005, this independent property impressed me with its attention to detail and excellent service. The rooms are fresh and spacious, averaging about 500 square feet, and have great bathrooms, with granite counters and plenty of space. Functional and stylish, all rooms have a sleeper couch and many have balconies; the suites have complete kitchens as well. Ultimately, I was won over by the breakfast, featuring do-it-yourself waffle stations with premeasured batter and a Texas-shaped griddle, and the spectacular outdoor pool, with a faux beach, waterfall, and fountains.

5310 Englewood Ave., Lubbock, TX 79424. © **866/644-2319** or 806/722-2726. www.arborinnandsuites. com. 73 units, including 24 suites. $89–$109 double; $119 suite. AE, DISC, MC, V. **Amenities:** Exercise room; Jacuzzi; outdoor heated pool. *In room:* A/C, TV/DVD, fridge, kitchen (in suites), Wi-Fi (free).

**Holiday Inn Hotel & Towers**   The top downtown hotel in Lubbock, this early 1980s–era Holiday Inn is the city's largest lodging option, located adjacent to the Civic Center smack-dab in the middle of downtown. Well maintained and comfortable, the rooms are pleasant if unremarkable, with off-white walls and beige furnishings. I like the east tower, six stories of rooms surrounding a wide-open atrium. The suites with west-facing windows are the best—guests are greeted every morning by the Buddy Holly statue on the West Texas Walk of Fame below. Other rooms overlook a central courtyard with trees.

801 Ave. Q, Lubbock, TX 79401. © **800/HOLIDAY** (465-4329) or 806/763-1200. Fax 806/763-2656. www.holidayinn.com. 293 units, including 72 suites. $89–$99 double; $119–$139 suite. AE, DISC, MC, V. **Amenities:** Restaurant; bar; exercise room; small indoor pool; room service. *In room:* A/C, TV, hair dryer, Wi-Fi (free).

**Overton Hotel & Conference Center** ★★   The Overton immediately became the city's best hotel when it opened in 2009 as the anchor of a massive redevelopment on the eastern fringe of the Texas Tech campus. Exuding contemporary Texan elegance, the 14-story Overton features the most extensive facilities in the city, and has guest rooms to match, with one king or two queen beds, nice views, and creative, colorful flair. Some adjoin to comfortable hospitality suites. The hotel also serves as a hands-on classroom and home to a unique hospitality program at Texas Tech.

2322 Mac Davis Lane, Lubbock, TX 79401. © **806/776-7000.** www.overtonhotel.com. 303 units. $149 double; $179 suite. AE, DISC, MC, V. **Amenities:** Restaurant; bar; executive-level rooms; exercise room; Jacuzzi; outdoor heated pool; room service. *In room:* A/C, TV, hair dryer, fridge, Wi-Fi (free).

**Woodrow House** ★★   The Southern Colonial architecture (complete with white pillars and a redbrick exterior) of this urban bed-and-breakfast belies its age: Built in 1995, the Woodrow House combines Texas tradition with modern amenities. One suite here—a retrofit Santa Fe caboose in the backyard—is a real eye-catcher, and my favorite room in town. It has a queen-size bed framed by wrought iron and a foldout futon, as well as a kitchenette. The old engineers' seats are now great spots to sit and read. Inside, visitors enjoy an elegant parlor and six rooms. The Lone Star Room is a lot of fun: a framed Republic of Texas dollar, longhorn skulls, a Texas flag, and a king-size bed. New in 2010: a backyard pool and hot tub (featuring an adjacent checkerboard and Scrabble tiled into the cement) and a new building with three slick new suites.

2629 19th St., Lubbock, TX 79410. © **800/687-5236** or 806/793-3330. Fax 806/793-7676. www. woodrowhouse.com. 10 units. $99–$139 double; $119–$179 suite. Rates include full breakfast. AE, DISC, MC, V. **Amenities:** Babysitting; Jacuzzi; outdoor heated pool. *In room:* A/C, TV, hair dryer, kitchen or kitchenette (in suites), Wi-Fi (free).

## CAMPING

**Buffalo Springs Lake,** FM 835 (© **806/747-3353**), has one of the most scenic campgrounds in the area, with 33 shady sites and three tent areas. Camping fees are $15 for tents and $35 for full hookups. **Caprock Canyons State Park** (© **806/455-1492**) is another popular camping destination, with primitive backcountry sites ($8) and tent sites ($12–$14), as well as sites with partial RV hookups ($15–$20). Campsites are $8 to $10 at **Lake Alan Henry** (© 806/775-2673; www.lakealanhenry. org), 65 miles southeast of Lubbock. See "Outdoor Activities," above, for complete information on these parks.

## Where to Dine

**Café J** ★ MEDITERRANEAN/NEW AMERICAN   Hip yet homey, Café J has drawn raves for taking a fresh direction in Lubbock's dining scene. The menu includes a number of pastas and salads and a nice selection of lighter fare, including signature cream of green chile soup and grilled ahi tuna. More substantial entrees include a superlative beef tenderloin filet and tasty bacon-wrapped sea scallops served with pumpkin risotto. Thanks in part to its location directly across from the Texas Tech campus, the pair of bars here are among Lubbock's trendiest nightspots.

2605 19th St. © **806/743-5400.** www.cafejlubbock.com. Reservations accepted only for parties of 5 or more. Main courses $7–$15 lunch, $9–$30 dinner. AE, DISC, MC, V. Sun and Tues–Fri 11am–2:30pm; Tues–Thurs 5:30–10pm; Fri–Sat 5:30–11pm. Bars open later.

**Gardski's Loft** AMERICAN   A favorite of both students and businesspeople, this landmark eatery near the campus of Texas Tech University is actually a converted Victorian home, abandoned by its residents after a close call with a tornado in 1970. The place serves some mighty mean sandwiches—I can't resist the Smokin' Mad Jack, plump with smoked ham, brown sugar bacon, pepper jack, and red onions, with jalapeños on the side. A more upscale dinner menu includes lighter chicken and seafood plates, with down-home favorites such as meatloaf, catfish, chicken-fried steak, and good burgers.

2009 Broadway. © **806/744-2391.** www.gardskisloft.com. Reservations accepted for large parties only. Main courses $6–$10. AE, MC, V. Mon–Sat 11am–10pm; Sun 11am–9pm.

**Texas Cafe and Bar** BARBECUE   This rowdy, smoky roadhouse, affectionately called "the Spoon" by locals, is pure Texas, from the local color seated at the bar and weathered tables to the Lone Star neon signs, longhorn skulls, and politically incorrect wooden Indian. The menu, too, is 100% Texan: nachos; barbecued turkey, beef, and sausage; Texas beans; and big, juicy burgers. Everything here is spicy, hearty, and just plain good. There's a pool room in the back, and live music on weekends.

3604 50th St. © **806/792-8544.** www.texascafeandbar.net. Reservations not accepted. Main courses $6–$9. AE, DISC, MC, V. Daily 11am–10pm. Bar open later.

**Triple J Chophouse & Brew Co.** ★ STEAK   In the former domain of the Hub City Brewery, this eatery and microbrewery is more upscale than its predecessor, but still ranks near the top of my Lubbock list. There are tables in a long seating area, below brick walls adorned with horns and Texas photography of all kinds, and a slick bar, which sits directly in front of the glass-enclosed brewing area. The menu focuses on beef, but also offers seafood, wood-fired pizzas, and some good ol' Texan comfort food (potpies, rib tips, chicken-fried steak). The sides are creative (like Parmesan creamed spinach, sweet potato custard, and shoestring fries), but the terrific brews remain a key attraction, and there are typically 8 to 10 of them on tap. If you're feeling especially carnivorous, you can "grab the bull by the horns" and order a hand-cut steak to the thickness you indicate tableside.

1807 Buddy Holly Ave., in the Depot District. © **806/771-6555.** www.triplejchophouseandbrewco.com. Reservations not accepted. Main courses $7–$25. AE, MC, V. Mon–Thurs 11am–10pm; Fri–Sat 11am–midnight. Bar open later.

# Lubbock After Dark

## THE PERFORMING ARTS

Built in 1938, the beautifully restored **Cactus Theater,** 1812 Buddy Holly Ave. (✆ 806/762-3233 for information; www.cactustheater.com), is now the center-piece of Lubbock's performing arts scene. On Friday through Sunday, it features regular doo-wop and nostalgia shows, as well as other concerts and musicals. Popular productions include tributes to Buddy Holly and other music legends. Tickets run $15 to $40.

**Lubbock Symphony Orchestra,** 1313 Broadway, Ste. 2 (✆ 806/762-1688; www.lubbocksymphony.org), performs 10 classical concerts and one pops concert every year at the Lubbock Civic Center Theater (at 6th St. and Ave. O), often featuring guest conductors and musicians from around the world. Ticket prices range from $10 to $60.

Established in 1926, the **Texas Tech University Theatre,** on the Texas Tech campus on 18th Street between Boston and Flint avenues (✆ 806/742-3603; www. depts.ttu.edu/theatreanddance), has produced more than 1,000 plays since its founding. Recent productions include *Equus, The Rimers of Eldritch,* and *Footloose.* The theater also hosts ballets, experimental plays, and one-act play festivals. Tickets are $10 to $12.

## NIGHTCLUBS & BARS

Lubbock has a bustling nightlife, primarily due to the presence of 25,000 Texas Tech students. The vibrant **Depot Entertainment District,** located between Texas Avenue and I-27 around 19th Street, is where you'll find the highest concentration of clubs, including the **Blue Light,** 1806 Buddy Holly Ave. (✆ 806/762-1185; www. thebluelightlive.com), known for its live music and hip, young crowd. Also in the neighborhood, you can line dance and two-step to live country music at **Wild West,** 2216 I-27 (✆ 806/741-3031; www.wildwestlubbock.com). **Cricket's Grill and Draft House,** 2412 Broadway (✆ 806/744-4677), is a rowdy Texas Tech hangout with nearly 100 beers on draft. Just north of the campus, **Conference Cafe,** 3216 4th St. (✆ 806/747-7766), is another student favorite.

Many restaurants morph into bustling nightspots after sundown, including the **Texas Cafe and Bar** (p. 432) and **Café J** (p. 432). If you do imbibe in Lubbock, try the city's signature cocktail, the Chilton. Invented by a local doctor of the same name, the drink consists of vodka, fresh-squeezed lemon juice, and soda, in a salt-rimmed glass—the result is tart but refreshing.

# PLANNING YOUR TRIP TO TEXAS

by Neil Edward Schlecht

**13**

As everyone knows, Texas is big—bigger than most European countries. For travelers to the state, there isn't merely a lot of ground to cover, but a vast number of places to see and things to do, as well as varieties of climate, terrain, and even cultures. Given the state's sheer size, it's probably not a surprise that Texas is a true mix of urban and rural. It has three of the top 10 cities in the nation in terms of population, as well as some of the largest ranches and open spaces found in the country. Travel time by car or train can be very lengthy, so don't assume you can easily zip from Dallas to Austin and on to Houston and Galveston. Crossing the state takes a huge amount of time and effort, making regional vacations the way to go for most travelers.

---

As with any trip, a little preparation is essential before you start your journey to Texas. This chapter provides a variety of planning tools, including information on how to get there; tips on accommodations; and quick, on the ground resources. Also, check out the new interactive Texas Trip Planner offered online by Texas State Travel Guide (www.traveltex.com/plan-your-trip/trip-planner).

## GETTING THERE

### By Plane

The state's major airports are **Dallas/Fort Worth International (DFW), George Bush Intercontinental (IAH)** and **William P. Hobby (HOU)** in Houston, **San Antonio International (SAT),** and **El Paso International (ELP).** American Airlines has its hub in Dallas, Continental Airlines is based in Houston, and formerly regional and now national carrier Southwest Airlines is headquartered in Dallas. To find out which airlines travel to Texas, see "Airline Websites," p. 453.

### By Car

More than 3,000 miles of interstate highways crisscross this huge state, connecting four major urban areas to each other and to cities in nearby states. Some relevant mileages: Houston to New Orleans, 350 miles; Houston to Phoenix, 1,180 miles; Dallas to Little Rock, 320 miles; Dallas to Kansas City, 550 miles; and Dallas to Denver, 880 miles.

If you're planning a road trip, it's a good idea to join the **American Automobile Association** (© **800/336-4357;** www.ouraaa.com). In Texas, AAA regional headquarters is at 6555 Hwy. 161, Irving (© **469/221-6006**); there are also offices in many other cities, including Amarillo, Austin, Dallas, El Paso, Houston, and San Antonio. Members can get excellent maps, tour guides, and emergency road service; they'll also help you plan an itinerary. Members can get free emergency road service by calling **AAA's emergency number** (© **800/AAA-HELP** [222-4357]).

For information on driving, car rentals, and gas in Texas, see "Getting Around/By Car," below.

## By Train

**Amtrak** (© **800/USA-RAIL** [872-7245]; www.amtrak.com) operates three lines that travel through Texas. The **Sunset Limited** has stops at Beaumont/Port Arthur, Houston, San Antonio, Del Rio, Sanderson, Alpine, and El Paso on its New Orleans–to–Los Angeles run; the **Heartland Flyer** travels from Oklahoma City to Fort Worth (where it connects with the Texas Eagle); and the **Texas Eagle** runs from Los Angeles to San Antonio (where you can connect with the Sunset Limited) and on to Chicago, with stops at El Paso, Austin, Dallas, and Fort Worth. For the names and locations of various railway stations in major cities of Texas, see "Orientation" in the individual city chapters of this guide.

# GETTING AROUND

Texas is huge, so it's highly unlikely you'll try to see it all in one visit. Most visitors will explore either one or two cities or a relatively small section of the state. For those visiting major cities, it's easy to fly in, use public transportation, and then fly or take the train to the next city (see the individual city chapters for airline and rail information). However, those who plan to see a variety of Texas locales—within reasonable distance—will find that the most practical way to see Texas is by car.

## By Plane

A number of airlines offer flights between Texas's major cities; see "Getting There/By Plane," above, and "Airline Websites," later in this chapter.

Attention visitors to the U.S. from abroad: Some major airlines offer transatlantic or transpacific passengers special discount tickets under the name **Visit USA,** which allows mostly one-way travel from one U.S. destination to another at very low prices. Unavailable in the U.S., these discount tickets must be purchased abroad in conjunction with your international fare. This system is the easiest, fastest, cheapest way to see the country. Inquire with your air carrier.

## By Car

Driving is an excellent way to see Texas in small chunks—roads are well maintained and well marked, and a car is often the most economical and convenient way to get somewhere; in fact, if you plan to explore beyond the cities—which we highly recommend—it's practically the only way to get to some places. Of course, the main argument against driving is the distance between many destinations covered in this book.

Texas maintains 77,000 miles of roadways, including interstates, U.S. highways, state highways, and farm-to-market (designated FM on signs) roads.

Furthermore, it has some 48,000 bridges on public roads—the most in the nation.

Texas often has some of the lowest gasoline prices in the United States; although prices fluctuate, at press time regular unleaded gas ranged from $2.90 to $3.50 per gallon, with the lowest prices in the Gulf Coast area (for current prices, check out www.texasgasprices.com). Taxes are already included in the printed price. One U.S. gallon equals 3.8 liters, or .85 imperial gallons.

Major highways that crisscross the state include I-20 from West Texas to Dallas–Fort Worth and all the way to Louisiana; I-35 from the Oklahoma border to Dallas–Fort Worth, Austin, and San Antonio to the Mexican border at Nuevo Laredo; I-10 from El Paso to San Antonio; and I-45 from Houston to Dallas.

Access points into Texas include I-40 (from Oklahoma and New Mexico); I-10 (from New Mexico); U.S. 69/75 and I-44/U.S. 287 (from Oklahoma); U.S. 77 and I-35 (from Oklahoma); I-10 and I-20 (from Louisiana); I-30 (from Arkansas); and U.S. 77 and U.S. 83 (Harlingen/Valley border crossing). Expect delays (and leave plenty of time for) crossing into Texas from Mexico, especially now that the border area is problematic with drug and violence issues.

Once you leave the interstates, there is a veritable spider web of roads that will take you just about anywhere you want to go, at least until you venture into the vast emptiness of the southwest plains. This seemingly uncharted area contains two of the gems of the state, however: Big Bend and Guadalupe Mountains national parks. These two places make it worth the effort of finding a way to get there.

Traffic in major cities, such as Houston, Dallas, and Austin, can be very congested and frustrating, especially at rush hour, and distances are often great. Be sure to leave extra time for driving to places. Away from the cities, you'll often find the roads to be practically deserted.

Because much of Texas has a relatively mild climate, snow and ice are not usually a problem. However, those traveling to or through Amarillo and other northern sections of the state in winter should check weather reports frequently—being stranded by an ice storm is not unheard of.

All the major rental-car companies operate in Texas, including **Alamo, Avis, Budget, Dollar, Enterprise, Hertz, National,** and **Thrifty.** International visitors who plan to rent a car in the United States should keep in mind that foreign driver's licenses are usually recognized in the U.S., but you may want to consider obtaining an international driver's license. Note that insurance and taxes are almost never included in quoted rental car rates in the U.S. Be sure to ask your rental agency about additional fees for these. They can add a significant cost to your car rental. Many rental-car agencies have non-negotiable age requirements, both minimum-age (generally 25 or older) and upper-age limits (often 70 to 75 for certain vehicles); find out what the age limits are for rentals in Texas.

Check out **BreezeNet.com** (www.bnm.com), which offers domestic car-rental discounts with some of the most competitive rates around. Also worth visiting are

# Texas Driving Times & Distances

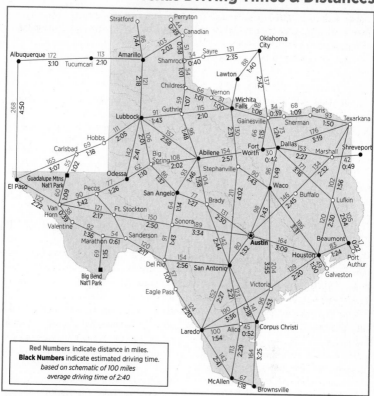

Red Numbers indicate distance in miles.
**Black Numbers** indicate estimated driving time.
based on schematic of 100 miles
average driving time of 2:40

Orbitz, Hotwire, Travelocity, and Priceline, all of which offer competitive online car-rental rates.

For anyone considering crossing into Mexico, the border region has received a lot of attention for violence, often drug-related. It's wise to acquaint yourself with the most recent information and warnings about Mexico and border crossings. Visit the U.S. Department of State at **www.travel.state.gov** for travel alerts and tips for traveling abroad. See also "Texas: Gateway to Mexico," below.

**INSURANCE**　If you hold a private auto insurance policy, you probably are covered for loss or damage to the rental car, and liability in case a passenger is injured. The credit card you used to rent the car also may provide some coverage.

Car-rental insurance probably does not cover liability if you caused the accident. Check your own auto insurance policy, the rental company policy, and your credit card coverage for the extent of coverage: Is your destination covered? Are other drivers covered? How much liability is covered if a passenger is injured? (If you rely on your credit card for coverage, you may want to bring a second credit card, as damages may be charged to your card and you may find yourself stranded with no money.)

# TEXAS: gateway TO MEXICO

Many travelers believe that a vacation in western or southern Texas would not be complete without an excursion across the border into Mexico, to visit the picturesque shops, dicker for colorful pottery and inexpensive jewelry, and sample genuine Mexican food. In our experience, the shopping is especially enjoyable—you really can get some bargains—and the food is often spectacular. Mexican border towns welcome tourists and almost universally accept U.S. currency—in fact, for many of these communities, tourism is the primary source of income.

However, remember that a trip across the border, even if you just walk across for the afternoon, constitutes a trip to a foreign country, and the laws of Mexico, not the United States, apply. In addition, these border towns are often hotbeds of drug smuggling, so stick to the main tourist areas, and, it should go without saying, never let anyone convince you to carry anything across the border for them.

U.S. and Canadian citizens must carry a passport if they plan on crossing back into the U.S. A Mexican tourist card (available from Mexican officials at the border) is required for those going beyond the border towns into Mexico's interior, or those planning to stay in the border towns for more than 72 hours. Other foreign nationals will need a passport and the appropriate visas.

Travelers driving cars beyond the border towns will need vehicle permits, available from Mexican officials at the border, and those driving cars across the border for any distance at all should first buy insurance from a Mexican insurance company (short-term insurance is available at the border and at travel clubs such as AAA). If you're only planning to cross the border, visit a few shops, maybe sample the Mexican food,

and then cross back into Texas, consider leaving your car on U.S. soil and walking. This will save the hassles of getting Mexican car insurance and the red tape if you are involved in an accident; of course, then you'll end up having to carry any purchases you make.

*Warning:* It is a felony to take any type of firearm or ammunition into Mexico (you could easily end up in jail and have your car confiscated). In addition, there are a number of regulations regarding taking pets across the border, plus fees, so it is usually best to board pets on the U.S. side.

When reentering the United States from Mexico, you will be stopped and questioned by U.S. Customs officials, and your car may be searched. U.S. citizens may bring back up to $800 in purchases duty-free every 30 days, including 1 liter of liquor, 100 cigars (except Cuban cigars, which are prohibited), and one carton of cigarettes. Duty fees are charged above those amounts, and Texas charges a tax of about $1 per liter on all alcoholic beverages. Items that may not be brought into the United States, or which require special permits, include most fruits and vegetables, plants, animals, and meat.

The above is just a brief summary of the complex laws related to traveling between the U.S. and Mexico. There are more details in the official state vacation guide available from the Texas Department of Transportation (see "Visitor Information" in "Fast Facts," later in this chapter); for complete information, contact **U.S. Customs** (© **202/354-1000;** www.cbp.gov) and the **Mexican Government Tourism Office** (© **800/446-3942** or 713/722-2581; mgtotx@ix. netcom.com). A good online source of information is **www.mexonline.com**.

**DRIVING RULES**   Texas law requires all drivers to carry proof of insurance, as well as a valid driver's license. Safety belts must be worn by all front-seat occupants of cars and light trucks; children 16 and under must wear safety belts regardless of where they are in the vehicle; and children 3 and under, or under 36 inches tall, regardless of where they're sitting, must be in approved child seats. The maximum speed limit on interstate highways is 70 mph; and the maximum on numbered non-interstates is 70 mph during daylight and 65 mph at night, unless otherwise posted. Motorcyclists are required to wear helmets, and radar detectors are legal.

**MAPS**   A good state highway map is available free at any state information center or by mail (see "Visitor Information" in "Fast Facts: Texas," later in this chapter). Maps can also be purchased at bookstores, gas stations, and most supermarkets and discount stores.

**ROAD CONDITIONS**   Texas roads are among the best in the western United States, and the state's generally moderate weather keeps snow closures to a minimum. However, icy roads are fairly common in the northern sections of the state during winter, and hurricanes can cause flooding in late summer and early fall along the Gulf Coast. A **24-hour hot line** (✆ **800/452-9292**) provides automated information on road conditions statewide; information is also available online at www.dot.state.tx.us/travel/road_conditions.htm.

For additional information, including charted routes, a mileage calculator, regional maps for download, driving tours, and travel information centers geared to road travel, visit www.traveltex.com/plan-your-trip/laws-highway-info. You can also call ✆ **800/452-9292** for other travel information and trip-planning assistance.

## By Train

More than a dozen towns and cities in Texas are linked by rail, with mostly daily service from Amtrak. See "Getting There," above, and "Orientation" in individual destination chapters for more information.

International visitors can buy a **USA Rail Pass,** good for 15, 30, or 45 days of unlimited travel on **Amtrak** (✆ **800/USA-RAIL** [872-7245] in the U.S. or Canada; ✆ **001/215-856-7953** outside the U.S.; www.amtrak.com). The pass is available online or through many overseas travel agents. See Amtrak's website for the cost of travel within the western, eastern, or northwestern United States. Reservations are generally required and should be made as early as possible. Regional rail passes are also available.

## By Bus

Bus travel is often the most economical form of public transit for short hops between Texas and U.S. cities, but it's certainly not an option for everyone (most travelers find Amtrak more comfortable and often similar in price). **Greyhound** (✆ **800/231-2222** in the U.S.; ✆ **001/214/849-8100** outside the U.S. with toll-free access; www.greyhound.com) is the sole nationwide bus line. Texas bus lines with service to and within the state include **Arrow Trailways of Texas, Kerrville Bus Co.** (www.iridekbc.com), and **Valley Transit Co.** (www.valleytransitcompany.com).

International visitors can obtain information about the **Greyhound North American Discovery Pass.** The pass, which offers unlimited travel and stopovers in the U.S. and Canada, can be obtained outside the United States from travel agents or through www.discoverypass.com.

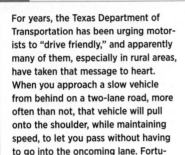

## The "Drive Friendly" State

For years, the Texas Department of Transportation has been urging motorists to "drive friendly," and apparently many of them, especially in rural areas, have taken that message to heart. When you approach a slow vehicle from behind on a two-lane road, more often than not, that vehicle will pull onto the shoulder, while maintaining speed, to let you pass without having to go into the oncoming lane. Fortunately, most Texas state highways have good, wide shoulders so there's little danger. We're not sure if this is technically legal or not, but everybody in rural Texas does it, including state troopers. However, road rage is not uncommon in Texas, and you should think twice before sending an obscene gesture the way of a driver who has just cut you off—especially if that driver is in a pickup truck with a gun rack on the back (also not uncommon in many parts of the state).

# TIPS ON ACCOMMODATIONS

Across the state, Texas offers a variety of lodging options, from typical American chain motels in convenient or airport locations to luxury hotels, historic hotels and bed-and-breakfast inns, as well as some pleasant and inexpensive mom-and-pop independent motels, cabins, and ranch-style resorts. A number of hotels really resonate with Texas flavor and charm. To make your lodging an integral part of your Texas experience, we recommend choosing a unique or historic property where available and/or choosing one in the neighborhood where you want to spend most of your time. Quite a few historic bed-and-breakfast inns are discussed in this guide and, especially considering the wonderful breakfasts prepared at most of them, the rates are fairly reasonable. Why spend $80 or more for a boring motel room and then another $10 to $15 for breakfast when, for just a bit more, you can instead sleep in a handsome inn, decorated with antiques, and be served a delightful, home-cooked breakfast?

The Texas Department of Transportation publishes the *Texas Accommodations Guide,* which is usually sent along with the official state vacation guide, or can be ordered separately at ✆ **800/452-9292.**

The nonprofit **Texas Bed & Breakfast Association** (✆ **800/428-0368;** www. texasbb.org) offers a free directory describing more than 100 member bed-and-breakfasts, country inns, unique hotels, and guesthouses. You can also get lodging information from the **Texas Hotel & Lodging Association** (✆ **800/856-4328;** www. texaslodging.com). Another good resource is **Bed & Breakfast Inns Online** (www. bbonline.com), where you can view interior and exterior photos of almost every property profiled, including several listed on the National Register of Historic Places. The site offers last-minute, midweek, and seasonal specials, besides a variety of other packages.

House swaps aren't for everyone—clean freaks and people with control issues may skip this section. However, you may find that staying in a private home while its owners stay in your home is a comfortable and cost-effective alternative to booking a hotel. **HomeLink International** (✆ **800/638-3841** or 813/975-9825; www.homelink.org) is an established house-swapping service. Home swaps in Dallas, Houston, Austin, and other Texas cities can be found through **Craigslist.org.** People over 50 may register their homes with **Seniors Home Exchange** (www.seniorshomeexchange.com).

**HomeAway** (www.homeaway.com), one of the nation's largest vacation rental sites (with home owners across the country offering both short- and long-term rentals) is based in Austin, and on the site, you'll find all kinds of listings for homes in the Texas Hill Country, Big Bend National Park area, the Gulf Coast, and major cities.

For tips on surfing for the best hotel deals online, visit Frommers.com.

# FAST FACTS: TEXAS

**Area Codes**    Major area codes in Texas are: Dallas (214, 972), Fort Worth (817), Arlington (817), Houston (713, 281), Austin (512), San Antonio (210, 830), El Paso (915), Waco (254), Corpus Christi (361), Galveston (409), east Texas (211, 936), and south Texas (956).

**Business Hours**    Offices are usually open weekdays from 9am to 5pm. Banks are open weekdays from 9am to 3pm or later, and sometimes Saturday mornings. Stores typically open between 9 and 10am and close between 5 and 6pm Monday through Saturday. Stores in shopping complexes or malls tend to stay open late, until about 9pm on weekdays and weekends, and many malls and larger department stores are open on Sundays. A growing number of discount stores (such as Wal-Mart) and grocery stores are open 24 hours a day.

**Car Rental**    See "Getting There/By Car," earlier in this chapter.

**Cellphones**    See "Mobile Phones," below.

**Crime**    See "Safety," later in this section.

**Customs**    For details regarding U.S. Customs and Border Protection, consult your nearest U.S. embassy or consulate, or **U.S. Customs** (www.cbp.gov). Also, see "Texas: Gateway to Mexico," above.

**Disabled Travelers**    Most disabilities shouldn't stop anyone from traveling in the U.S. Thanks to provisions in the Americans with Disabilities Act, most public places are required to comply with disability-friendly regulations. Almost all public establishments (including hotels, restaurants, museums, and so on, but not including certain National Historic Landmarks), and at least some modes of public transportation, provide accessible entrances and other facilities for those with disabilities.

**AbilityTrip** (www.abilitytrip.com/category/north_america/usa/texas) has destination reviews of Houston and Austin, detailing everything from airport, hotel, and restaurant facilities to wheelchair-accessible activities and arts facilities. On a very positive note, San Antonio inaugurated **Morgan's Wonderland** (② 877/495-5888; www.morgans wonderland.com), the world's first theme park for special-needs children and adults, in 2010.

The **America the Beautiful—National Park and Federal Recreational Lands Pass— Access Pass** (formerly the **Golden Access Passport**) gives persons who are visually impaired or permanently disabled (regardless of age) free lifetime entrance to federal recreation sites administered by the National Park Service (NPS), including the Fish and Wildlife Service, the Forest Service, the Bureau of Land Management, and the Bureau of Reclamation. This may include national parks, monuments, historic sites, recreation areas, and national wildlife refuges. The pass can be obtained only in person at any NPS facility that charges an entrance fee. You need to show proof of a medically determined disability. Besides free entry, the pass also offers a 50% discount on some federal-use fees charged for such facilities as camping, swimming, parking, boat launching, and tours. For more information, go to www.nps.gov/fees_passes.htm, or call the United States Geological Survey (USGS), which issues the passes, at ② 888/275-8747.

For more about organizations that offer resources to travelers with disabilities, go to Frommers.com.

**Doctors** See "Health," below.

**Drinking Laws** The legal age for purchase and consumption of alcoholic beverages is 21; proof of age is required and often requested at bars, nightclubs, and restaurants, so it's always a good idea to bring ID when you go out. Do not carry open containers of alcohol in your car or any public area that isn't zoned for alcohol consumption. The police can fine you on the spot. Don't even think about driving while intoxicated.

Minors can legally drink as long as they are within sight of their 21-or-older parents, guardians, or spouses. Where you can or cannot buy a drink, and what kind of drink, is determined in Texas by local option elections, so the state is essentially a patchwork of regulations. In most parts of the state, you can buy liquor, beer, and wine by the drink. However, there are a few areas where you can buy only beer (which Texas defines as having no more than 4% alcohol; anything higher is "ale"), and others where you can purchase beer or wine by the glass, but not liquor. There are also some areas that are completely dry—mostly in the Panhandle Plains and near the state's eastern border—and other confusing areas where one county will be "dry" (meaning you have to join private clubs—membership is normally free and immediately granted—to drink in restaurants, and liquor stores will stock beer and wine only) and the county right next to it will be "wet" (meaning you can drink in bars and restaurants).

**Driving Rules** See "Getting Around," earlier in this chapter.

**Electricity** Like Canada, the United States uses 110 to 120 volts AC (60 cycles), compared to 220 to 240 volts AC (50 cycles) in most of Europe, Australia, and New Zealand. Downward converters that change 220–240 volts to 110–120 volts are difficult to find in the United States, so bring one with you. Wherever you go, bring a **connection kit** of the right power and phone adapters, a spare phone cord, and a spare Ethernet network cable—or find out whether your hotel supplies them to guests.

**Embassies & Consulates** All embassies are in the nation's capital, Washington, D.C. Some consulates are in major U.S. cities, and most nations have a mission to the United Nations in New York City. If your country isn't listed below, call for directory information in Washington, D.C. (📞 **202/555-1212**) or check **www.embassy.org/embassies**.

The embassy of **Australia** is at 1601 Massachusetts Ave. NW, Washington, DC 20036 (📞 **202/797-3000;** www.usa.embassy.gov.au). Consulates are in New York, Honolulu, Houston, Los Angeles, and San Francisco.

The embassy of **Canada** is at 501 Pennsylvania Ave. NW, Washington, DC 20001 (📞 **202/682-1740;** www.canadainternational.gc.ca/washington). Other Canadian consulates are in Buffalo (New York), Detroit, Los Angeles, New York, and Seattle.

The embassy of **Ireland** is at 2234 Massachusetts Ave. NW, Washington, DC 20008 (📞 **202/462-3939;** www.embassyofireland.org). Irish consulates are in Boston, Chicago, New York, San Francisco, and other cities. See website for a complete listing.

The embassy of **New Zealand** is at 37 Observatory Circle NW, Washington, DC 20008 (📞 **202/328-4800;** www.nzembassy.com). New Zealand consulates are in Los Angeles, Salt Lake City, San Francisco, and Seattle.

The embassy of the **United Kingdom** is at 3100 Massachusetts Ave. NW, Washington, DC 20008 (📞 **202/588-6500;** http://ukinusa.fco.gov.uk). Other British consulates are in Atlanta, Boston, Chicago, Cleveland, Houston, Los Angeles, New York, San Francisco, and Seattle.

**Emergencies** Call 📞 **911** to report a fire, call the police, or get an ambulance anywhere in the United States. This is a toll-free call. (No coins are required at public telephones.) If you encounter serious problems, contact the **Traveler's Aid Society**

**International** (© 202/546-1127; www.travelersaid.org). The Texas office is at the Dallas/ Fort Worth International Airport (© 972/574-4420). This nationwide, nonprofit, social-service organization geared to helping travelers in difficult straits offers services that might include reuniting families separated while traveling, providing food and/or shelter to people stranded without cash, or even emotional counseling. If you're in trouble, seek them out.

**Family Travel**   Texas is a family-friendly state, with lots of things for all ages to enjoy. Throughout this guide, you'll find numerous attractions, lodgings, and even restaurants that are especially well suited to kids. These include places such as the Fort Worth Zoo, Six Flags Over Texas in Arlington, the Children's Museum of Houston, and the Zilker Zephyr Miniature Trail in Austin. See "The Best Family Adventures" in chapter 1, as well as "Especially for Kids" sightseeing sections in destination chapters.

To locate accommodations, restaurants, and attractions that are particularly kid-friendly, look for the "Kids" icon throughout this guide. For a list of more family-friendly travel resources, turn to the experts at Frommers.com.

**Gasoline**   See "Getting Around/By Car," earlier in this chapter.

**Health**   Vacationers in Texas generally don't need to take any extra health precautions beyond those they would take at home. It is worth noting, however, that visitors hiking in the drier parts of the state, such as in the deserts of West Texas or the mountains of Big Bend and Guadalupe Mountains national parks, should carry more water than they think they'll need, and drink it.

When heading into the great outdoors, keep in mind that Texas has a large number of poisonous snakes and insects, and you should be very careful where you put your hands and feet. If you're hiking, stick to designated hiking areas, stay on established trails, and carry rain gear. When boating, wear a life jacket.

Unless you're camping out in remote Big Bend and other areas, over-the-counter medicines are widely available, as are generic equivalents of common prescription drugs.

Contact the **International Association for Medical Assistance to Travelers** (**IAMAT;** © 716/754-4883, or 416/652-0137 in Canada; www.iamat.org) for tips on travel and health concerns and for lists of doctors. The United States **Centers for Disease Control and Prevention** (© 800/311-3435; www.cdc.gov) provides up-to-date information on health hazards by region or country and offers tips on food safety. The website **Travel Health Online** (www.tripprep.com), sponsored by a consortium of travel medicine practitioners, may also offer helpful advice on traveling abroad. You can find listings of reliable clinics overseas at the **International Society of Travel Medicine** (www.istm.org).

**Dietary Red Flags**   While Tex-Mex cuisine is generally milder than Mexican cooking, travelers who are unfamiliar with hot chiles and jalapeños or who have weak stomachs or ulcers should proceed with caution when eating Mexican food. Tap water is potable throughout the state, but not to everyone's liking. Texans are big meat eaters in general, but in larger cities, vegetarian-friendly restaurants are widely available.

**Bugs, Bites & Other Wildlife Concerns**   If you venture into the West Texas desert, snakes, spiders, and scorpions could be an issue, so it would be wise to carry appropriate medicines, especially if camping.

**Sun/Elements/Extreme Weather Exposure**   Perhaps the biggest health concern in Texas, with its big sky and blistering heat, is sun exposure. Travelers should make every attempt to protect themselves, including headgear, sunscreen, and sufficient hydration.

**Insurance**   Travel insurance is a good idea if you think for some reason you may be cancelling your trip. (Texas's occasional extreme weather can affect a trip.) It's cheaper than the cost of a no-penalty ticket and it gives you a safety net if something comes up, enabling you to cancel or postpone your trip and still recover the costs. For information on traveler's insurance, trip cancellation insurance, and medical insurance while traveling, visit www.frommers.com/planning.

**Internet & Wi-Fi**   The major nationwide Internet connectivity providers are present in Texas, including AT&T, Comcast, Time-Warner, and Verizon, as well as many smaller regional providers. There is free (or in a couple of cases, Boingo membership-required) Wi-Fi Internet access in all the major airports; in Austin's Bergstrom airport, kiosks offering free Internet service are stationed along the concourse and baggage claim. In addition, out on the road, Wi-Fi is available at all Texas Safety Rest Areas and Travel Information Centers.

To find Internet cafes in your destination, check www.cybercaptive.com or www.cybercafe.com. If you have your own laptop, every Starbucks in Texas has Wi-Fi. For a list of locations, go to www.starbucks.com/store-locator. To find other public Wi-Fi hotspots in your destination, go to www.jiwire.com; its Global Wi-Fi Finder holds the world's largest directory of public wireless hot spots.

Internet access and/or Wi-Fi is available is most hotels in Texas, either in the lobby, business center, or in-room. Most major hotels have Internet kiosks that provide basic Web access for a per-minute fee that's usually higher than cybercafe prices. Also, check out copy shops like FedEx Office (formerly Kinkos), which offers computer stations with fully loaded software (as well as Wi-Fi). Though convenient Internet access may not be present in the smallest towns, you may have the best luck at the local library.

**Legal Aid**   While driving, if you are pulled over for a minor infraction (such as speeding), never attempt to pay the fine directly to a police officer; this could be construed as attempted bribery, a much more serious crime. Pay fines by mail, or directly into the hands of the clerk of the court. If accused of a more serious offense, say and do nothing before consulting a lawyer. In the U.S., the burden is on the state to prove a person's guilt beyond a reasonable doubt, and everyone has the right to remain silent, whether he or she is suspected of a crime or actually arrested. Once arrested, a person can make one telephone call to a party of his or her choice. The international visitor should call his or her embassy or consulate.

**LGBT Travelers**   Texas is a largely conservative state and is one of only four (the others are Missouri, Kansas, and Oklahoma) that criminalize homosexual activity, with an anti-sodomy law that dates to the late 1800s. That law is occasionally enforced (two Houston men were arrested in 1998, spent a day in jail, and paid fines), but a gay-rights group is working to have the law overturned.

Despite the official policy, most gay and lesbian travelers will find that in most parts they are treated just like any other visitors to Texas, as Texans generally have a "live and let live" attitude. There are vibrant gay and lesbian communities in all of the larger cities, particularly Austin, Dallas, and Houston. Resources for gay and lesbian travelers include **GayTexas.com,** with city guides and a large database of gay-friendly businesses in major destinations; and

**Gay Texas Directory** (www.gaytexas.net), with links to online gay city chapters (Dallas, Austin and Houston) and organizations such as the Texas Gay Rodeo Association.

**Mail**   At press time, domestic postage rates were 28¢ for a postcard and 44¢ for a letter. For international mail, a first-class letter of up to 1 ounce costs 98¢ (75¢ to Canada and 79¢ to Mexico); a first-class postcard costs the same as a letter. For more information, go to **www.usps.com**.

If you aren't sure what your address will be in the United States, mail can be sent to you, in your name, c/o General Delivery at the main post office of the city or region where you expect to be. (Call © **800/275-8777** for information on the nearest post office.) The addressee must pick up mail in person and must produce proof of identity (driver's license, passport, and so on). Most post offices will hold mail for up to 1 month, and are open Monday to Friday from 8am to 6pm, and Saturday from 9am to 3pm.

Always include zip codes when mailing items in the U.S. If you don't know your zip code, visit www.usps.com/zip4.

**Medical Requirements** Unless you're arriving from an area known to be suffering from an epidemic (particularly cholera or yellow fever), inoculations or vaccinations are not required for entry into the United States. Also see "Health," above.

**Mobile Phones** Mobile (cell) phone and SMS texting service across Texas is generally good, with AT&T and Verizon generally faring best, and Sprint and T-Mobile lagging a bit behind. If you plan to use your phone a lot while in the U.S., it may be worthwhile to invest in an inexpensive "pay as you go" phone from a local outlet. Depending on the offer of the moment, you may get a generous credit for calls when you buy the phone—enough to last for your trip, perhaps, without having to add more calling time. Various calling plans are available, and although most no longer charge for roaming, additional costs for texting can add up. Definitely discuss the options to determine which one best suits your needs before making a commitment, and read the agreement to make sure you're not committing to a longer-term agreement than you need.

Keep in mind that your cellphone signal may be particularly weak in rural areas. If you need to stay in touch at a destination where you know your phone won't work, **rent** a phone that does from **InTouch USA** (© 800/872-7626; www.intouchusa.us) or a rental-car location, but beware: You'll pay $1 a minute or more for airtime. If you're venturing deep into national parks, you may want to

consider renting a **satellite phone** (satphone). It's different from a cellphone in that it connects to satellites rather than ground-based towers. Unfortunately, you'll pay at least $2 per minute to use the phone, and it works only where you can see the horizon (that is, usually not indoors). In North America, you can rent Iridium satellite phones from **RoadPost** (www.roadpost.com; © 900/446-2900 or 905/272-5665). InTouch USA offers a wider range of satphones, but at higher rates.

If you have a computer and Internet service, consider using a broadband-based telephone service (**Voice over Internet Protocol, or VoIP**) such as **Skype** (www.skype.com) or **Vonage** (www.vonage.com), which allow you to make free international calls from your laptop or in a cybercafe. Neither service requires the people you're calling to also have that service (though there are fees if they do not).

If you're not from the U.S., you'll be appalled at the poor reach of the **GSM (Global System for Mobile Communications) wireless network,** which is used by much of the rest of the world. Your phone will probably work in most major U.S. cities; it definitely won't work in many rural areas. To see where GSM phones work in the U.S., check out www.t-mobile.com/coverage. And you may or may not be able to send SMS (text messaging) home.

**Money & Costs** Frommer's lists exact prices in the local currency. The currency conversions provided in the table below are correct at press time. However, rates fluctuate, so before departing from home, consult a currency exchange website such as **www.oanda.com/currency/converter** to check up-to-the-minute rates.

In general, Texas is not overly expensive, especially compared to destinations on the East and West coasts of the United States. You'll find a wide range of prices for lodging and dining, and admission to most attractions is less than $10 (it's sometimes free, especially in the smaller towns). Prices in Dallas, Houston, and Austin are now firmly in

## THE VALUE OF THE U.S. DOLLAR ($) VS. OTHER POPULAR CURRENCIES

| US$ | A$ | C$ | € | NZ$ | £ |
|-----|-----|-----|-----|-----|-----|
| 1.00 | 1.00 | 1.00 | .70 | 1.30 | .60 |

| WHAT THINGS COST IN TEXAS | $ |
|---|---|
| Taxi from the airport to downtown Dallas | 25.00 |
| Double room, moderate | 125.00–175.00 |
| Double room, inexpensive | 75.00–125.00 |
| Three-course dinner for one without wine, moderate | 20.00–35.00 |
| Bottle of beer | 3.00–6.00 |
| Cup of coffee | 1.00–2.50 |
| 1 gallon of premium gas | 2.90–3.50 |
| Admission to most museums | 4.00–10.00 |
| Admission to most national parks | 10.00 |

line with those in large Southern cities such as Atlanta and Miami. Smaller cities and rural areas are much less expensive, while resort areas such as Corpus Christi can be a bit more expensive, especially during winter holidays. Traveler's checks and credit cards are accepted at almost all hotels, restaurants, shops, and attractions, plus many grocery stores; and ATMs are practically everywhere.

Beware of hidden credit card fees while traveling. Check with your credit or debit card issuer to see what fees, if any, will be charged for overseas transactions. Recent reform legislation in the U.S., for example, has curbed some exploitative lending practices. But many banks have responded by increasing fees in other areas, including fees for customers who use credit and debit cards while out of the country—even if those charges were made in U.S. dollars. Fees can amount to 3% or more of the purchase price. Check with your bank before departing to avoid any surprise charges on your statement.

For help with currency conversions, tip calculations, and more, download Frommer's convenient Travel Tools app for your mobile device. Go to www.frommers.com/go/mobile and click on the "Travel Tools" icon.

**Multicultural Travelers**   Texas has a lamentable history of race-related incidents, and bigoted and racist opinions are still found in some small towns and among some less cosmopolitan Texans. Regrettably, discrimination is still occasionally directed toward African Americans and Hispanics (and, more recently, people of Middle Eastern descent or appearance), as well as openly gay travelers. However, most travelers of color and ethnicity, and gays and lesbians, will likely encounter few (if any) problems. African-American travelers may want to be cautious, however, when traveling through the small towns of east Texas; see "Race Relations in East Texas," on p. 188. Also, around border towns, travelers of Hispanic descent or appearance may find that they are stopped by the border patrol more frequently than non-Hispanics, so be sure to carry a current, government-issued picture ID. See also "LGBT Travelers," above.

**Newspapers & Magazines**   The major daily newspapers in Texas are the *Dallas Morning News, Fort Worth Star Telegram, Austin American Statesman,* and *Houston Chronicle.* You will also find national editions of the *New York Times,* the *Wall Street Journal,* and *USA Today* in major hotels and kiosks. Texas-based magazines with local coverage include *Texas Monthly* and *D Magazine.* Alternative (free) newspapers include the *Austin Chronicle, Dallas Observer,* and *Houston Press.*

**Packing**  Texas's occasional extreme weather fluctuations may require you to pack for more than one season. Casual dress and Western wear are still seen in much of the state, but the big cities are more cosmopolitan and trendier than ever, and fashionable attire at restaurants, bars, and nightclubs is as much the rule in Dallas–Fort Worth, Houston, Austin, and San Antonio, as elsewhere in the country (even if many Texas women have a distinct style of overdressing). In some nightclubs and nicer restaurants, tennis shoes and (grungy) jeans are not welcome. For more helpful information on packing for your trip, download our convenient Travel Tools app for your mobile device. Go to www.frommers.com/go/mobile and click on the "Travel Tools" icon.

**Passports**  Virtually every foreign traveler entering the U.S. is required to present a valid passport. As of June 2009, U.S. citizens entering the United States by land or sea must present a passport or other Western Hemisphere Travel Initiative–compliant travel document such as a passport card, enhanced drivers license, or SENTRI card (see www.getyouhome.gov for details). The passport requirement is waived in some cases for minors.

**Entrance and Exit to Mexico:** In most cases, a visa or tourist permit is not needed to enter Mexico. Depending on their country of citizenship, length of stay in Mexico, and plans to travel outside of the border area, visitors may need to present a valid passport or proof of citizenship and fill out an immigration form for tourists at the point of entry. More information can be obtained from a Mexican consulate or at www.aduanas.gob.mx. For information about visiting Mexico, call **800/44-MEXICO** [446-3942] or visit www.visitmexico.com.

Canadians must carry a Canadian passport, enhanced driver's license/enhanced identification card, or a "trusted traveler card." Mexican citizens must present a passport with a nonimmigrant visa or a laser visa Border Crossing Card to cross the U.S. border. For the latest information about what documentation is needed to enter or re-enter the United States, visit www.getyouhome.gov.

*Warning:* Possession/importation of any type of firearm, weapon or ammunition is a felony in Mexico without advance written authorization from the Mexican Embassy in Washington, D.C., or from a Mexican consulate in the United States. It does not matter if you are licensed to carry the weapon in the United States, are a law enforcement or military official, or unintentionally transport it. Mexico has severe penalties for this offense, punishable by fines, confiscation of the weapon, and jail time. Ignorance of the law is not a defense. Even a few shotgun shells in the trunk can cause a big problem. Some cities, such as Nuevo Laredo, also have ordinances prohibiting the possession of knives of any kind or anything that might be considered a knife.

## PASSPORT OFFICES:

**Australia**  **Australian Passport Information Service** (℃ **131-232,** or visit www.passports.gov.au).

**Canada**  **Passport Office,** Department of Foreign Affairs and International Trade, Ottawa, ON K1A 0G3 (℃ **800/567-6868;** www.ppt.gc.ca).

**Ireland**  **Passport Office,** Setanta Centre, Molesworth Street, Dublin 2 (℃ **01/671-1633;** www.foreignaffairs.gov.ie).

**New Zealand**  **Passports Office,** Department of Internal Affairs, 47 Boulcott St., Wellington, 6011 (℃ **0800/225-050** in New Zealand or 04/474-8100; www.passports.govt.nz).

**United Kingdom**  Visit your nearest passport office, major post office, or travel agency or contact the **Identity and Passport Service (IPS),** 89 Eccleston Square, London, SW1V 1PN (℃ **0300/222-0000;** www.ips.gov.uk).

**United States**  To find your regional passport office, check the U.S. State Department website (http://travel.state.gov/passport) or call the **National Passport Information Center** (℃ **877/487-2778**) for automated information.

**Petrol**  See "Getting Around/By Car," earlier in this chapter.

**Police**  Dial ⓒ **911** for a police or medical emergency. In addition to local police, there are Texas state troopers, whom you are most likely to encounter on interstate highways, and the legendary **Texas Rangers,** the second-oldest state-level law enforcement agency in the United States. The Texas Rangers have statewide jurisdiction and have been involved in the investigation of major crimes, often across county lines (from murder and kidnapping to public corruption, narcotics violations, and organized crime) and been employed in border security operations and as riot police. (The Texas Rangers were created by Stephen F. Austin in 1823, when he deployed 10 men to protect some 700 newly arrived families after the Mexican War of Independence. A museum dedicated to the Texas Rangers is in Waco; visit www.texasranger.org/today/Coop.htm.)

**Safety**  Most areas of Texas are as safe as any other part of the U.S. However, large cities such as Houston, Dallas, and San Antonio have their share of big-city crime (a few years back, downtown Houston had a particularly dangerous reputation, as have certain neighborhoods, such as Deep Ellum, in Dallas). Border towns such as El Paso in particular have seen increased violence focused largely on drug (and in some cases, illegal immigrant) smuggling along the U.S.-Mexico border. To steer clear of stumbling into a drug transaction or police raid, avoid hiking alone in isolated areas along the border and stay in the major tourist areas in border towns. For more information, see "Texas: Gateway to Mexico" on p. 438, and visit **travel.state.gov** for updated travel advisories. Also, see "Multicultural Travelers," above, for discrimination issues and safety.

Avoid carrying valuables with you on the street, and don't display expensive cameras or electronic equipment. Place your wallet in an inside jacket or front pant's pocket. Consider using a money belt or other hidden travel wallet, and never leave valuables in the outside pocket of a backpack. Should you stop for a bite to eat, keep everything within easy reach—of you, not a purse snatcher. In congested areas, women might opt to carry purses on the shoulder away from the street or, better yet, to wear the strap across the chest instead of on one shoulder. Women with clutch bags should hold them close to their chest. And, of course, it's always a good idea to leave expensive-looking jewelry and other conspicuous valuables at home. If you're in doubt about which neighborhoods are safe, don't hesitate to inquire with the front desk staff at your hotel, or the local tourist office.

Remember that hotels are open to the public and that in a large property, security may not be able to screen everyone entering. Always lock your room door—don't assume that once inside your hotel, you're automatically safe.

If you must store belongings in a car, place them in the trunk. Burglaries of tourists' rental cars in hotel and shopping parking lots and major tourist sites are always a possibility. Park in well-lighted and well-traveled areas, if possible. Never leave any packages or valuables visible in the car. If someone attempts to rob you or steal your car, do not try to resist the thief or carjacker—report the incident to the police department immediately. Ask your rental agency about personal safety, and get written directions or a map with the route to your destination clearly marked.

Texas has some of the most lenient gun laws in the U.S., allowing concealed weapons (with a license) in many public and private places and in vehicles (at press time, a bill that would allow students to carry guns into buildings on college campuses appeared likely to pass). You're likely to see pickup trucks with gun racks and maybe even some folks "packing heat" (carrying a concealed firearm). Remember this while driving in traffic or potentially getting into an altercation; the other party might just have a gun.

**Senior Travel**   Many Texas hotels and motels offer discounts to seniors (especially if you're carrying an AARP card; see below), and an increasing number of restaurants, attractions, and public transportation systems do so as well.

Members of **AARP** (formerly known as the American Association of Retired Persons), 601 E St. NW, Washington, DC 20049 (© **888/687-2277;** www.aarp.org), often get discounts on hotels, airfares, and car rentals. AARP offers members a wide range of benefits, including *AARP The Magazine* and a monthly newsletter. Anyone over 50 can join.

The U.S. National Park Service offers an **America the Beautiful—National Park and Federal Recreational Lands Pass—Senior Pass** (formerly the **Golden Age Passport**), which gives seniors 62 years or older lifetime entrance to all properties administered by the National Park Service (NPS)—national parks, monuments, historic sites, recreation areas, and national wildlife refuges—for a one-time processing fee of $10. The pass must be purchased in person at any NPS facility that charges an entrance fee. Besides free entry, the America the Beautiful Senior Pass also offers a 50% discount on some federal-use fees charged for such facilities as camping, swimming, parking, boat launching, and tours. For more information, go to www.nps.gov/fees_passes.htm or call the United States Geological Survey (USGS), which issues the passes, at © **888/275-8747.**

Frommers.com offers more information and resources on travel for seniors.

**Smoking**   No statewide smoking ban exits in Texas. Many cities in Texas, including Austin, Corpus Christi, Dallas, El Paso, and Houston, have enacted a smoking ban in all enclosed work places, including bars and restaurants. Other cities, such as Arlington, Fort Worth, Galveston, and San Antonio, allow some exemptions (mostly bars and some restaurants).

**Student Travel**   The top spots for college students heading to Texas for spring break are **South Padre Island** for sun and fun and, to a lesser extent, **Big Bend National Park** for serious hiking, but all of the beach areas and parks are popular.

Check out the **International Student Travel Confederation (ISTC)** (www.istc.org) website for comprehensive travel services information and details on how to get an **International Student Identity Card (ISIC),** which qualifies students for substantial savings on rail passes, plane tickets, entrance fees, and more. It also provides students with basic health and life insurance and a 24-hour help line. The card is valid for a maximum of 18 months. You can apply for the card online or in person at **STA Travel** (© **800/781-4040** in North America, © 132 782 in Australia, or © 0871 2 300 040 in the U.K.; www.statravel.com), the biggest student travel agency in the world; check out the website to locate STA Travel offices worldwide. If you're no longer a student but are still 25 or under, you can get an **International Youth Travel Card (IYTC)** from the same organization, which entitles you to some discounts. **Travel CUTS** (© **800/592-2887;** www.travelcuts.com) offers similar services for both Canadians and U.S. residents. Irish students may prefer to turn to **USIT** (© **01/602-1904;** www.usit.ie), an Ireland-based specialist in student, youth, and independent travel.

**Taxes**   The United States has no value-added tax (VAT) or other indirect tax at the national level. Every state, county, and city may levy its own local tax on all purchases, including hotel and restaurant checks and airline tickets. These taxes will not appear on price tags.

Texans like to brag that the state is a great place to live because there is no state income tax. However, money for government services has to come from somewhere, and one of those sources is you, the traveler. Texas lodging taxes are among the highest in the region, ranging from the basic hotel rate of 6% to 17%, with the steepest rate in Houston. Sales taxes in Texas vary by county, but usually consist of the basic state sales tax of 6.25% plus an addition 2%, for a total of 8.25%, slightly higher than most surrounding states.

**Telephones** Generally, hotel surcharges on long-distance and local calls are astronomical, so you're better off using your **cellphone** or a **public pay telephone.** Many convenience stores and packaging services sell **prepaid calling cards** in denominations up to $50. Many public pay phones at airports now accept American Express, MasterCard, and Visa. **Local calls** made from most pay phones cost either 25¢ or 35¢. Most long-distance and international calls can be dialed directly from any phone.

**To make calls within the United States and to Canada,** dial 1 followed by the area code and the seven-digit number. **For other international calls,** dial 011 followed by the country code, city code, and the number you are calling.

Calls to area codes **800, 888, 877,** and **866** are toll-free. However, calls to area codes **700** and **900** (chat lines, bulletin boards, "dating" services, and so on) can be expensive—charges of 95¢ to $3 or more per minute. Some numbers have minimum charges that can run $15 or more.

For **reversed-charge or collect calls,** and for person-to-person calls, dial the number 0, then the area code and number; an operator will come on the line, and you should specify whether you are calling collect, person-to-person, or both. If your operator-assisted call is international, ask for the overseas operator.

For **directory assistance** ("Information"), dial 411 for local numbers and national numbers in the U.S. and Canada. For dedicated long-distance information, dial 1, then the appropriate area code plus 555-1212.

**Useful telephone numbers** include:

- Texas Parks & Wildlife Park Information ☏ **800/792-1112**
- Hunting information ☏ **512/389-4505**
- Fishing information ☏ **512/389-4505**
- Poison Center ☏ 800/**POISON-1** (764-7661)
- Road conditions hot line ☏ **800/452-9292**
- Weather hot line ☏ **512/232-4265**
- U.S. Department of State 24-hour Travel Advisory ☏ **202/647-5225**
- U.S. Passport Agency ☏ **202/647-0518**
- U.S. Centers for Disease Control international traveler's hot line ☏ **404/332-4559**

**Time** Almost all of Texas is in the Central Standard Time zone (CST); the only exception is the state's far western tip, which observes Mountain Standard Time (MST). The continental United States is divided into **four time zones:** Eastern Standard Time (EST), Central Standard Time (CST), Mountain Standard Time (MST), and Pacific Standard Time (PST). Alaska and Hawaii have their own zones. For example, when it's 9am in Los Angeles (PST), it's 7am in Honolulu (HST),10am in Denver (MST), 11am in Chicago (CST), noon in New York City (EST), 5pm in London (GMT), and 2am the next day in Sydney.

**Daylight saving time (summer time)** is in effect from 1am on the second Sunday in March to 1am on the first Sunday in November, except in Arizona, Hawaii, the U.S. Virgin Islands, and Puerto Rico. Daylight saving time moves the clock 1 hour ahead of standard time.

For help with time translations, and more, download our convenient Travel Tools app for your mobile device. Go to www.frommers.com/go/mobile and click on the "Travel Tools" icon.

**Tipping** Tips are a very important part of certain workers' income, and gratuities are the standard way of showing appreciation for services provided. (Tipping is certainly not compulsory if the service is poor!) In hotels, tip **bellhops** at least $1 per bag ($2–$3 if you have a lot of luggage) and tip the **chamber staff** $1 to $2 per day (more if you've left a big mess for him or her to clean up). Tip the **doorman** or **concierge** only if he or she has provided you with some specific service (for example, calling a cab or obtaining difficult-to-get theater tickets). Tip the **valet-parking attendant** $1 every time you get your car.

In restaurants, bars, and nightclubs, tip **service staff** and **bartenders** 15% to 20% of the check, tip **checkroom attendants** $1 per garment, and tip **valet-parking attendants** $1 per vehicle.

As for other service personnel, tip **cab drivers** 15% of the fare; tip **skycaps** at airports at least $1 per bag ($2–$3 if you have a lot of luggage); and tip **hairdressers** and **barbers** 15% to 20%.

For help with tip calculations, currency conversions, and more, download our convenient Travel Tools app for your mobile device. Go to www.frommers.com/go/mobile and click on the "Travel Tools" icon.

**Toilets**   You won't find public toilets or "restrooms" on the streets in most U.S. cities, but they can be found in hotel lobbies, bars, restaurants, museums, department stores, railway and bus stations, and service stations. Large hotels and fast-food restaurants are often the best bet for clean facilities. Restaurants and bars in resorts or heavily visited areas may reserve their restrooms for patrons.

**VAT**   See "Taxes" above.

**Visas**   The U.S. State Department has a **Visa Waiver Program (VWP)** allowing citizens of the following countries to enter the United States without a visa for stays of up to 90 days: Andorra, Australia, Austria, Belgium, Brunei, Czech Republic, Denmark, Estonia, Finland, France, Germany, Greece, Hungary, Iceland, Ireland, Italy, Japan, Latvia, Liechtenstein, Lithuania, Luxembourg, Malta, Monaco, the Netherlands, New Zealand, Norway, Portugal, San Marino, Singapore, Slovakia, Slovenia, South Korea, Spain, Sweden, Switzerland, and the United Kingdom. (Note: This list was accurate at press time; for the most up-to-date list of countries in the VWP, consult http://travel.state.gov/visa.) Even though a visa isn't necessary, in an effort to help U.S. officials check travelers against terror watch lists before they arrive at U.S. borders, visitors from VWP countries must register online through the Electronic System for Travel Authorization (ESTA) before boarding a plane or a boat to the U.S. Travelers must complete an electronic application providing basic personal and travel eligibility information. The Department of Homeland Security recommends filling out the form at least 3 days before traveling. Authorizations will be valid for up to 2 years or until the traveler's passport expires, whichever comes first. Currently, there is 1 US$14 fee for the online application. Existing ESTA registrations remain valid through their expiration dates.

***Note:*** Any passport issued on or after October 26, 2006, by a VWP country must be an **e-Passport** for VWP travelers to be eligible to enter the U.S. without a visa. Citizens of these nations also need to present a round-trip air or cruise ticket upon arrival. E-Passports contain computer chips capable of storing biometric information, such as the required digital photograph of the holder. If your passport doesn't have this feature, you can still travel without a visa if the valid passport was issued before October 26, 2005, and includes a machine-readable zone; or if the valid passport was issued between October 26, 2005, and October 25, 2006, and includes a digital photograph. For more information, go to **http://travel.state.gov/visa**. Canadian citizens may enter the United States without visas, but will need to show passports and proof of residence.

Citizens of all other countries must have (1) a valid passport that expires at least 6 months later than the scheduled end of their visit to the U.S.; and (2) a tourist visa.

For information about U.S. Visas, go to **http://travel.state.gov** and click on "Visas." Or go to one of the following websites:

**Australian** citizens can obtain up-to-date visa information from the **U.S. Embassy Canberra,** Moonah Place, Yarralumla, ACT 2600 (✆ **02/6214-5600**) or by checking the U.S. Diplomatic Mission's website at **http://canberra.usembassy.gov/visas.html**.

**British** subjects can obtain up-to-date visa information by calling the **U.S. Embassy Visa Information Line** (✆ **09042-450-100** from within the U.K. at £1.20 per minute; or ✆ **866/382-3589** from within the U.S. at a flat rate of $16 and is payable by credit card only) or by visiting the "Visas to the U.S." section of the American Embassy London's website at **http://london.usembassy.gov/visas.html**.

**Irish** citizens can obtain up-to-date visa information through the **U.S. Embassy Dublin,** 42 Elgin Rd., Ballsbridge, Dublin 4 (✆ 1580-47-VISA [8472] from within the Republic of Ireland at €2.40 per minute; **http://dublin.usembassy.gov**).

Citizens of **New Zealand** can obtain up-to-date visa information by contacting the **U.S. Embassy New Zealand,** 29 Fitzherbert Terrace, Thorndon, Wellington (✆ **644/462-6000; http://newzealand.usembassy.gov**).

**Visitor Information** Contact the **Texas Department of Transportation,** Travel Division, P.O. Box 141009, Austin, TX 78714-1009 (✆ **800/888-8TEX** [8839]; www.traveltex. com), for a free copy of the official state vacation guide, which includes a state map and describes attractions, activities, and lodgings throughout Texas.

The Texas Department of Transportation maintains a dozen excellent **Texas Travel Information Centers** around the state, offering free maps, brochures, and one-on-one travel counseling. Locations are as follows: **Amarillo,** I-40 East; **Anthony,** I-10 at the New Mexico state line; **Austin,** 112 E. 11th St., at the capitol complex; **Denison,** U.S. 75 at the Oklahoma state line; **Gainesville,** I-35 at the Oklahoma state line; **Harlingen,** U.S. 77 at U.S. 83; **Langtry,** off U.S. 90 on Tex. Loop 25; **Laredo,** I-35 North at U.S. 83; **Orange,** I-10 at the Louisiana state line; **Texarkana,** I-30 at the Arkansas state line; **Waskom,** I-20 at the Louisiana state line; and **Wichita Falls,** I-44 at U.S. 277/281. The centers are open daily from 8am to 5pm except on January 1, Easter Sunday, Thanksgiving Day, and December 24 and 25. For information, call ✆ **800/452-9292.**

The ever-expanding blogosphere is filled with blogs on things great and public as well as obscure and personal, and weblogs originating in Texas are no exception. Check out the resident blogs in *Texas Monthly* on Texas politics, food, and current events at www. texasmonthly.com/blogs. To sample a whole slew of Texas topics and musings, peruse the many blogs listed at www.networkedblogs.com/topic/Texas and www.ringsurf.com/ring/texasblogs.

**Water** Tap water is potable throughout Texas, though not to everyone's liking.

**Wi-Fi** See "Internet & Wi-Fi," earlier in this section.

**Women Travelers** The old macho cowboy culture still exists in some (usually less-urban) parts of Texas, and it's probably safe to say that Texans historically have a greater tolerance for sexist behavior and comments than in some other parts of the country. In bars and nightclubs, both men and women may act (and dress) in a more flirty manner than you might be used to. Brazen (although usually harmless) come-ons are not uncommon. Although that doesn't necessarily translate into danger for women going out alone at night, being accompanied by another female (or male, of course) will make you less of a target for unwanted advances.

# AIRLINE WEBSITES

## MAJOR AIRLINES

**Aeroméxico**
www.aeromexico.com

**Air France**
www.airfrance.com

**Air India**
www.airindia.com

**Air Jamaica**
www.airjamaica.com

**Air New Zealand**
www.airnewzealand.com

**Alitalia**
www.alitalia.com

**Alaska Airlines/Horizon Air**
www.alaskaair.com

**American Airlines**
www.aa.com

**Aviacsa (Mexico & Southern U.S.)**
www.aviacsa.com.mx

**British Airways**
www.british-airways.com

**China Airlines**
www.china-airlines.com

**Continental Airlines**
www.continental.com

**Delta Air Lines**
www.delta.com

**Emirates Airlines**
www.emirates.com

**Frontier Airlines**
www.frontierairlines.com

**Hawaiian Airlines**
www.hawaiianair.com

**Iberia Airlines**
www.iberia.com

**Japan Airlines**
www.jal.com

**JetBlue Airways**
www.jetblue.com

**Lan Airlines**
www.lan.com

**Lufthansa**
www.lufthansa.com

**Midwest Airlines**
www.midwestairlines.com

**North American Airlines**
www.flynaa.com

**Qantas Airways**
www.qantas.com

**Swiss Air**
www.swiss.com

**TACA**
www.taca.com

**United Airlines**
www.united.com

**US Airways**
www.usairways.com

**Virgin America**
www.virginamerica.com

**Virgin Atlantic Airways**
www.virgin-atlantic.com

## BUDGET AIRLINES

**AirTran Airways**
www.airtran.com

**Click Mexicana**
www.clickmx.com

**easyJet**
www.easyjet.com

**Frontier Airlines**
www.frontierairlines.com

**JetBlue Airways**
www.jetblue.com

**Jetstar (Australia)**
www.jetstar.com

**Ryanair**
www.ryanair.com

**Southwest Airlines**
www.southwest.com

**Spirit Airlines**
www.spiritair.com

**WestJet**
www.westjet.com

# Index

## A

AAA (American Automobile
Association), 435
Aardvark (Fort Worth), 135–136
AARP, 449
AbilityTrip, 441
Academic trips and language
classes, 37
Accommodations, 440–441
best, 1–5
tipping at, 450–451
Actors Theater of San Antonio,
272
Adair's Saloon (Dallas), 97–98
Adrian, 423
Adventure and wellness trips,
37–38
African American Museum
(Dallas), 86
Agency Limousine (Dallas), 54
Ahab Bowen (Dallas), 94
AIA Sandcastle Competition
(Galveston), 197–198
Airline websites, 453
Airport Flyer (Austin), 284
Air travel, 434, 435
Alamodome (San Antonio), 272
Alamo Fiesta (San Antonio), 269
Alamo Quarry Market (San
Antonio), 269
The Alamo (San Antonio),
259–260
Alamosa Wine Cellars (near
Lampasas), 281
Alamo Sightseeing Tours (San
Antonio), 266
Alamo Village (near
Brackettville), 373
Alan Henry, Lake, 428–429
Alibates Flint Quarries National
Monument, 414
Allen's Boots (Austin), 321
*Alley Oop,* 363
Alley Theatre (Houston), 182, 183
All in One Tour Services
(Dallas), 89
Alpine, 358–360
Alvino House (Big Bend National
Park), 384
Amarillo, 408–419
accommodations, 416–417
getting around, 409–410
nightlife, 419
orientation, 408–409
outdoor activities, 414
post office, 410
restaurants, 417–419
shopping, 416
sights and attractions,
410–416
spectator sports, 415–416
temperatures, 32
visitor information, 410

Amarillo Botanical Gardens, 412
Amarillo Bulls, 415
Amarillo Little Theatre, 419
Amarillo Museum of Art, 412
Amarillo Opera, 419
Amarillo Venom, 415
Amarillo Zoo, 412
American Airpower Heritage
Museum (Odessa), 361–362
American Automobile
Association (AAA), 435
American Express
Dallas, 62
El Paso, 336
Fort Worth, 105
American Indians
Alibates Flint Quarries
National Monument, 414
Amistad National Recreation
Area, 376
history of, 17–18
Kwahadi Museum of the
American Indian (Amarillo),
412–413
pictographs and petroglyphs
Amistad National
Recreation Area, 376
Big Bend National Park,
384, 387
Hueco Tanks State Park
& Historic Site (near El
Paso), 342
Pictographs of Painted
Rocks (San Angelo),
368
Seminole Canyon State
Park and Historic Site,
377
Witte Museum (San
Antonio), 262
Pictographs of Painted Rocks
(San Angelo), 368
American Institute of Architects
(AIA) Sandcastle Competition,
197–198
American Institute of Architects
Sandcastle Competition
(Galveston), 34
American Quarter Horse Hall of
Fame & Museum (Amarillo),
410
American Wind Power Center
(Lubbock), 427
American Yellow Checker Cab
(Austin), 284, 287
America the Beautiful—National
Park and Federal Recreational
Lands Pass—Access Pass, 441
America the Beautiful—National
Park and Federal Recreational
Lands Pass—Senior Pass, 449
Amistad National Recreation
Area, 371, 374–377
Amon Carter Museum of
Western Art (Fort Worth), 125
Amtrak, 435, 439
Alpine, 358
Austin, 284

Dallas/Fort Worth, 56
Del Rio, 372
El Paso, 333
Houston, 140
Anderson Fair (Houston), 185
Angelina National Forest,
188–189
Angelo Civic Theatre (San
Angelo), 371
Antique Colony (Fort Worth),
132
Antique Mall of Lubbock
(Lubbock), 430
Antone's (Austin), 323
Aquariums
Children's Aquarium at Fair
Park (Dallas), 87
Dallas World Aquarium, 88
Downtown Aquarium
(Houston), 169
Texas State Aquarium
(Corpus Christi), 206
Aransas National Wildlife
Refuge, 209, 212, 213
Area codes, 441
Arkey Blue & the Silver Dollar
Bar (Bandera), 282
Arlington, 89, 99–101
Armstrong, Lance, 27
Arneson River Theatre (San
Antonio), 271
Arrow Trailways of Texas, 439
Art Car Parade and Ball
(Houston), 34
Artfunkles Vintage Boutique
(Dallas), 94
Art galleries
Austin, 319–320
Marfa, 357
San Angelo, 369
San Antonio, 269
Art Museum of South Texas
(Corpus Christi), 208
ArtPace (San Antonio), 269
Arturo's Sports Bar & Grill (San
Antonio), 273
Ascarate Golf Course, 342
Ascarate Lake City Park (El
Paso), 339
Ashton Villa (Galveston), 195
Asian Cultures Museum (Corpus
Christi), 208
Atalanta (Jefferson), 189
AT&T Center for the Performing
Arts (Dallas), 95–96
AT&T Center (San Antonio), 272
AT&T Championship (San
Antonio), 268
AT&T Cotton Bowl Classic (&
Parade; Dallas), 33
AT&T Performing Arts Center
(Dallas), 80
Aura Lounge (Dallas), 99
Austin, 41, 283–330
accommodations, 288–299
family-friendly, 298
arriving in, 283–284
bats, 310

doctors, 287
drugstores, 287
emergencies, 287
food trucks, 308
getting around, 286–287
grocery stores, 303
Hill Country side trips, 324–330
hospitals, 287
Internet access, 288
layout of, 285
neighborhoods in brief, 285
newspapers and magazines, 288
nightlife, 321–324
organized tours, 316–317
outdoor activities, 317–318
police, 288
post office, 288
restaurants, 299–309
family-friendly, 305
safety, 288
shopping, 319–321
sights and attractions, 309–317
spectator sports, 318–319
taxes, 288
transit information, 288
visitor information, 284–285
weather, 288
*Austin American-Statesman* Bat Hot Line, 310
Austin-Bergstrom International Airport, 283–284
Austin Cab, 287
Austin Chamber Music Center, 322
Austin Children's Museum, 316
*Austin Chronicle* Hot Sauce Festival, 34
Austin Convention and Visitors Bureau, walking tours, 317
Austin Cycling Association, 317
Austin Duck Adventures, 317
Austin Farmers' Market, 320
Austin Ice Bats, 319
Austin Lyric Opera, 322
Austin Museum of Art—Downtown, 312–313
Austin Nature and Science Center, 316
Austin Ridge Riders, 317
Austin Symphony, 322
Austin Visitor Center, 284
Austix Box Office, 321
Australia
embassy of, 442
passports, 447
visas, 452
Auto racing
Amarillo, 415
Dallas, 91
Fort Worth, 130
Autry, Gene, 27
Autumn, 32
Average, precipitation, 32

## B

The Backyard (Austin), 323
Balcony Club (Dallas), 97
Ballet Austin, 322
Ballroom Marfa, 357
Balmorhea State Park, 353–354
Bandera, 279
Bandera Beach Club Kayak & Tube Rental, 279
Bandera County Convention and Visitors Bureau, 279
Bandera Saloon, 282
Barbecue (BBQ), 30
Bar Belmont (Dallas), 98
Bar Céline (Dallas), 98
Barton Springs Pool (Austin), 310–311, 318
Barton Warnock Environmental Education Center (Big Bend National Park), 388
Baseball
Austin, 318
Corpus Christi, 208
Dallas, 91
El Paso, 342
Houston, 179
Kokernot Field (Alpine), 359
Midland, 363
San Angelo, 369
Basin Road Scenic Drive, 382
Basketball
Austin, 318
Dallas, 91
El Paso, 342
Houston, 179–180
San Antonio, 268
Bass Performance Hall (Fort Worth), 123–124, 133
Bastrop, 36
Bat Conservation International (Austin), 310
Bats
Austin, 310
Carlsbad Caverns National Park, 400, 402, 403, 405
Battleship *Texas* (Houston), 170–171
Bayfest! (Corpus Christi), 34
Baylor University Medical Center (Dallas), 63
Bayou Bend (Houston), 176
Bayou Place (Houston), 184
Beachcombing
Padre Island National Seashore, 221–222
Port Aransas, 217
Beach cruising, 217
Beaches. *See also specific beaches*
Brazosport, 203
Galveston, 194–195
Port Aransas, 217
South Padre Island, 227–228
Bean, Roy, 375
Bear Creek Golf Club (Dallas), 90
Beaumont, 186

Beaumont Ranch (Grandview), 38
Becker Vineyards, 281
Bed & Breakfast Inns Online, 440
Bed & breakfasts (B&Bs), best, 3–4
Beer Can House (Houston), 176–177
Believe It or Not! Odditorium (Arlington), 100
Bellaire Boulevard (Houston), 182
Belle Starre Carriages (Dallas), 89
Bell Mountain Vineyards (near Fredericksburg), 281
Bermuda Triangle (San Antonio), 274
Beverages, 30–31
Big Balls of Cowtown (Fort Worth), 135
Big Bend Balloon Bash (Alpine), 359
Big Bend National Park, 41, 44, 379–393
accommodations, 389–391
exploring the highlights by car, 383–384
fees, regulations and permits, 381–382
historic sites, 384–385
outdoor adventures, 385–389
ranger programs and special events, 383
restaurants, 391–392
safety, 382
seasons, 382
security concerns, 384
traveling to, 380
visitor information, 380–381
Big Bend Natural History Association, 380
Big Bend Ranch State Park, 354–355, 388
Big Bend River Tours (Big Bend National Park), 385, 389
Big Easy Social and Pleasure Club (Houston), 184
Big Room Self-Guided Tour (Carlsbad Caverns National Park), 403
Big Thicket National Preserve, 186
Biking and mountain biking
Amarillo, 415
Austin, 317
Big Bend National Park, 388
Dallas, 89
El Paso, 342
Fort Worth, 129
Franklin Mountains State Park, 341
Houston, 178–179
Lubbock, 430
Palo Duro Canyon State Park, 422
Port Aransas, 217

**Biking and mountain biking**
  **(cont.)**
    San Angelo, 369
    San Antonio, 267
    Seminole Canyon State Park
      and Historic Site, 378
**Billy Bob's Texas**
    Dallas, 97
    Fort Worth, 134, 136
**Bird Island Basin, 222**
**Bird-watching**
    Aransas National Wildlife
      Refuge, 209, 213
    Big Bend National Park,
      385–386
    Brazosport area, 202
    Carlsbad Caverns National
      Park, 405
    Goose Island State Park, 214
    Guadalupe Mountains
      National Park, 398–399
    Padre Island National
      Seashore, 222
    San Angelo, 368
    South Padre Island, 226
    Texas Gulf Coast, 201
    whooping crane tours, 212
      Aransas National Wildlife
        Preserve, 209
**Bishop Arts District (Dallas), 93**
**Bishop's Palace (Galveston), 195**
**Blanco's (Houston), 185**
**Blanton Museum of Art (Austin),
  311**
**Blue Light (Lubbock), 433**
**Blue Star Arts Complex (San
  Antonio), 269**
**Blue Star Bike Shop (San
  Antonio), 267**
**Blue Star Brewing Company
  (San Antonio), 273**
**Board House Surf & Skate Shop
  (Port Aransas), 218**
**Boating (boat rentals). See also
  Canoeing; Kayaking; Rafting;
  Sailing**
    Amarillo, 414
    Amistad National Recreation
      Area, 374
    Big Bend National Park,
      388–389
    Caddo Lake, 190
    Lubbock, 428–429
    New Braunfels and Gruene,
      329
    Padre Island National
      Seashore, 222
    San Angelo, 368
**Boat tours and cruises**
    Austin, 316–317
    Caddo Lake, 190–191
    Corpus Christi, 208–209
    Galveston, 195
**The Bob Bullock Texas State
  History Museum (Austin), 312**
**Bob Wills and the Texas
  Playboys, 23**

**Bodega's (Amarillo), 419**
**Boerne, 277–279**
**Bohlin Custom Shop (Dallas), 94**
**Bolla Bar (Dallas), 98**
**The Bone (Dallas), 96**
**Bonham Exchange (San
  Antonio), 274**
**Booger Red's Saloon (Fort
  Worth), 133**
**Books, recommended, 26**
**Boot Hill (San Antonio), 270**
**Boot Town (Dallas), 93**
**Boquillas Canyon Trail (Big Bend
  National Park), 387**
**Botanical gardens**
    Amarillo, 412
    Austin, 316
    Dallas, 84–85
    Fort Worth, 125
    San Antonio, 265
**Brackenridge (San Antonio), 267**
**Brackenridge Park (San
  Antonio), 267**
**Brays Bayou (Houston), 179**
**Brazoria County Historical
  Museum, 200–201**
**Brazoria National Wildlife
  Refuge, 202**
**Brazosport, 199–205**
**Broken Spoke (Austin), 323**
**Brooklyn (Dallas), 97**
**Buddies II (Dallas), 99**
**Buddy Holly Center (Lubbock),
  426**
**Buddy Holly Statue and West
  Texas Walk of Fame
  (Lubbock), 427**
**Buffalo Bayou (Houston), 179**
**Buffalo Creek Golf Club
  (Rockwall), 90**
**Buffalo Springs Lake, 428, 430**
**Bum Steer (Fort Worth), 132**
**Bush, George H.W., 21**
**Bush, George W., Childhood
  Home (Midland), 361**
**Bush, George W., 27**
**Business hours, 441**
**Bus travel, 439**
**Butlers Martini Lounge
  (Amarillo), 419**
**Butterfield Trail Golf Course (El
  Paso), 342**
**Byron Nelson Championship
  (Dallas), 91**
**Byzantine Fresco Chapel
  Museum (Houston), 176**

**C**

**Cactus Cafe (Austin), 323**
**Cactus Music Series (San
  Angelo), 371**
**Cactus Theater (Lubbock), 433**
**Caddo Grocery (Uncertain), 191**
**Caddo Lake, 189**
**Caddo Lake State Park, 190**
**Caddo Lake Steamboat Co., 190**

**Cadillac Bar & Restaurant (San
  Antonio), 274**
**Cadillac Ranch (Amarillo),
  410, 413**
**Calendar of events, 33–35**
**Camping and RV parks**
    Amarillo, 417
    Amistad National Recreation
      Area, 376
    Big Bend National Park, 392
    Big Bend Ranch State Park,
      355
    Big Thicket National Preserve,
      186
    Carlsbad Caverns National
      Park, 406
    Caverns of Sonora, 371
    Corpus Christi area, 210
    El Paso, 345
    Guadalupe Mountains
      National Park, 399
    Palo Duro Canyon State Park,
      423–424
    Quintana, 203–204
    San Angelo, 368, 370
**Canada**
    documents needed for entry,
      447
    embassy of, 442
    passports, 447
**Candelaria, 353**
**Canoeing**
    Austin, 317
    Big Bend National Park,
      388–389
    Big Thicket National Preserve,
      186
    Caddo Lake, 190, 191
**Canyon, 420–424**
**Canyon Amphitheatre (El Paso),
  348**
**Canyon Springs (San Antonio),
  267**
**Canyon Travel, 348**
**Capital Cruises (Austin), 316–317**
**Capital Metro Transit (Austin),
  284**
**Capitol Visitors Center (Austin),
  284, 313, 321**
**Caprock Canyons State Park
  and Trailway (near Lubbock),
  428**
**Cap-Rock Winery (near
  Lubbock), 429**
**Captain Clark's Flagship (Corpus
  Christi), 208**
**Capt. Tommy Moore (Rockport),
  214**
**Caravan of Dreams (Fort Worth),
  135**
**Carlsbad Caverns National Park,
  399–406**
**Car rentals, 436–437**
**Car travel, 434–440**
**Casa Mañana Theater (Fort
  Worth), 133**
**Casa Ramírez (Houston), 181**

Casa Salazar (San Antonio), 269

Castolon Historic District (Big Bend National Park), 384

Castolon Visitor Center (Big Bend National Park), 381

Castroville, 278

Cattle Raisers Museum (Fort Worth), 129

Cavender's Boot City (Amarillo), 416

Cavender's Boot City (Dallas), 93

The Cavern (Dallas), 97

Caverns of Sonora, 371

Caves and caverns
  Carlsbad Caverns National Park, 399–405
  Caverns of Sonora, 371
  Cave Without a Name (Boerne), 277
  Fate Bell Cave Dwelling Tour (Seminole Canyon State Park and Historic Site), 377
  Panther Cave (Amistad National Recreation Area), 376
  Parida Cave (Amistad National Recreation Area), 376

Cave Without a Name (Boerne), 277

Cedar Creek (San Antonio), 267

Cedar Door (Austin), 324

Cellphones, 445

The Center for the Arts & Sciences (Brazosport), 201

Centers for Disease Control and Prevention, 443

Central Market (Austin), 320

Central Texas Oil Patch Museum (Luling), 276

Central Tickets (Dallas), 91, 95

Chamizal National Memorial (El Paso), 337

Chicken-fried steak, 29

Chihuahua al Pacifico (Chihuahua to the Pacific) railway, 348

Chihuahuan Desert, 403

Children, families with, 443
  Austin
    hotels, 298
    restaurants, 305
    sights and attractions, 316
  best family adventures, 13–14
  Dallas
    attractions, 88–89
    hotels, 71
    restaurants, 77
  El Paso area attractions, 340–341
  Fort Worth
    attractions, 128–129
    hotels, 113
    restaurants, 116

Houston
  hotels, 157
  restaurants, 166
  sights and attractions, 178

Junior Ranger Program
  Big Bend National Park, 383
  Carlsbad Caverns National Park, 403
  Padre Island National Seashore, 220

San Antonio
  accommodations, 247
  restaurants, 258
  sights and attractions, 266

suggested itinerary, 47–49

Children's Aquarium at Fair Park (Dallas), 87

Children's Medical Center of Dallas, 63

Children's Museum of Houston, 172–173

Chili, 29–30

Chilicotal Mountain, 383

Chinati Foundation (near Marfa), 355

Chinati Hot Springs (Candelaria), 353–354

Chinatown (Houston), 181

Chisos Basin amphitheater (Big Bend National Park), 383

Chisos Basin Campground (Big Bend National Park), 392

Chisos Basin Drive (Big Bend National Park), 383

Chisos Basin Loop Trail (Big Bend National Park), 387

Chisos Basin Visitor Center (Big Bend National Park), 381

Christmas, Galveston, 198

Christmas in the Stockyards (Fort Worth), 35, 121

Cielo Vista Mall (El Paso), 343

The Cincinnati Bar (El Paso), 349

City Market (Luling), 276

City of San Antonio Visitor Information Center, 232

City Streets (Fort Worth), 132

Ciudad Acuña (Mexico), 372–373

Civic League Park (San Angelo), 368

Civilian Conservation Corps (Big Bend National Park), 385

Civil War, 19

Clapp Municipal Swimming Pool (Lubbock), 430

Cliburn, Van, 28

Climate, 31–32

Colonial Invitational (Fort Worth), 130

Comanche Trail (Amarillo), 415

Comfort Cellars Winery, 280

Commemorative Air Force Annual AIRSHO (Midland), 35

Concepción (San Antonio), 263

Concho Bike Shop (San Angelo), 369

Concho pearls, 367

Concordia Cemetery (El Paso), 339

Conference Cafe (Lubbock), 433

Conjunto music, 273

Conservation International, 36

Contemporary Arts Museum (Houston), 173

Continental Club (Houston), 184

Cool Arrows (San Antonio), 273

Copper Canyon, 348

Corpus Christi, 205–211
  temperatures, 32

Corpus Christi Convention & Visitors Bureau, 206

Corpus Christi Hooks, 208

Cottonwood Campground (Big Bend National Park), 392

Cowboy boots, 28–29. See also Western wear and gear

Cowboy Cab
  Dallas, 54, 62
  Fort Worth, 105

Cowboy Cool (Dallas), 94

Cowboy hats, 29. See also Western wear and gear

Cowboy Mounted Shooting Association World Finals (Amarillo), 416

Cowboys Golf Club (near Dallas), 90

Cowboys Red River Dancehall (Dallas), 97

Cowboy Store (Bandera), 279

Cowboy Walking Tour (Fort Worth), 129

Cowtown Boots (El Paso), 343

Cowtown Cattlepen Maze (Fort Worth), 122, 128

Cowtown Coliseum (Fort Worth), 121, 130

Cowtown Marathon (Fort Worth), 129

Craigslist.org, 440

Crawford, Joan, 27

Credit cards, 446

Creekwalk (Del Rio), 372

Crew's Inn (Dallas), 99

Cricket's Grill and Draft House (Lubbock), 433

Cross-Eyed Moose (Fort Worth), 132

Cross of Our Lord Jesus Christ (Groom), 423

Crú (Dallas), 98

Cultural District (Fort Worth), 104, 121
  accommodations, 112–114
  restaurants, 118–120
  shopping, 131
  sights and attractions, 124–128

Currency exchange, 446

Customs regulations, 441

# D

**Da Camera of Houston,** 183
**Dallas,** 52–101
  accommodations, 63–71
    family-friendly, 71
  arriving in, 53–56
  babysitters, 63
  car-rental agencies, 62
  Deep Ellum, 57, 93
    nightlife, 96
  dentists, 63
  doctors, 63
  downtown, 57
    accommodations,
    64–65
    restaurants, 72–74
  drugstores, 63
  exploring, 80–92
  getting around, 60, 62
  hospitals, 63
  Internet access, 63
  layout of, 57
  maps, 63
  neighborhoods in brief, 57, 60
  newspapers and magazines,
  63
  nightlife, 95–99
    gay and lesbian scene,
    99
  North Dallas, 60
    accommodations, 69–70
    restaurants, 74–80
  organized tours, 89
  outdoor activities, 89–91
  picnic places, 80
  police, 63
  post office, 63
  restaurants, 71–80
    family-friendly, 77
  safety, 63
  shopping, 92–95
  spectator sports, 89, 91–92
  taxes, 63
  taxis, 54, 62
  temperatures, 32
  transit information, 63
  uptown, shopping, 93
  Uptown and Oak Lawn, 57
    restaurants, 74–80
  uptown & oak lawn, 66
  visitor information, 56–57
  weather, 63
**Dallas Alley,** 97
**The Dallas Arboretum &**
**Botanical Garden,** 85
**Dallas Area Rapid Transit**
**(DART),** 53–54, 60
**Dallas Arts District,** 57
**Dallas Children's Theater,**
**88,** 96
**Dallas Convention & Visitors**
**Bureau,** 56
**Dallas County Historical Plaza,** 81
**Dallas Cowboys,** 91
**Dallas Cowboys Cheerleaders,** 91
**Dallas Desperados,** 91
**Dallas Farmers' Market,** 94

**Dallas/Fort Worth International**
**Airport (DFW),** 53–55
  accommodations near, 70–71
**Dallas-Fort Worth Metroplex,**
**40–41,** 56
**Dallas Heritage Village,** 85
**Dallas Mavericks,** 91
**Dallas Museum of Art,** 82–83
**Dallas Opera,** 95
**Dallas Stars,** 91–92
**Dallas Surrey Services,** 89
**Dallas Tourist Information**
**Center,** 56
**Dallas Visitors Center,** 81
**The Dallas World Aquarium,** 88
**Dallas Zoo,** 88
**DART (Dallas Area Rapid**
**Transit),** 53–54, 60
**Davis Mountains State Park,**
**349–353**
**Davy Crockett National Forest,**
**189**
**Daylight saving time (summer**
**time),** 450
**Dealey Plaza (Dallas),** 82
**Deep Eddy Pool (Austin),** 318
**Deep Ellum (Dallas),** 57, 93
  nightlife, 96
**Dell, Michael,** 27
**Del Rio,** 371–378
**Depot Entertainment District**
**(Lubbock),** 433
**Desert Sports (Big Bend**
**National Park),** 385
**Devil's Rope Museum (McLean),**
**423**
**DFW Airport,** 53–55
  accommodations near, 70–71
**DFW Gun Club & Training Center**
**(Dallas),** 90
**DFW Towncars (Dallas),** 54
**Diablo East (Amistad National**
**Recreation Area),** 374
**Dickens on the Strand**
**(Galveston),** 35, 197
**Dietary red flags,** 443
**Dining**
  best, 5–7
  tipping at, 451
**Disabled travelers,** 441–442
**Discover Houston Tours,** 178
**Discovery Architectural Antiques**
**(Gonzales),** 275
**Dixie Dude Ranch (Bandera),** 38
**Dog Canyon Campground**
**(Guadalupe Mountains**
**National Park),** 399
**Dog Canyon Ranger Station**
**(Guadalupe Mountains**
**National Park),** 394
**Dolphin-watching and dolphin**
**tours**
  Port Aransas, 217
  Rockport area, 214
  South Padre Island, 226
**Dolphin Watch (Port Aransas),**
**217**

**Dome Bar (El Paso),** 349
**Don Harrington Discovery Center**
**(Amarillo),** 412
**Don McLeland Tennis Center**
**(Fort Worth),** 130
**The Door (Dallas),** 96
**Double Wide (Dallas),** 96
**Downtown Aquarium (Houston),**
**169**
**Downtown Fort Worth Rail**
**Market (Fort Worth),** 131
**Downtown Tunnel System**
**(Houston),** 170
**Dragonfly (Dallas),** 98
**Drinking laws,** 442
**The Driskill (Austin),** 313
**Driving rules,** 439
**Dry Comal Creek Vineyards**
**(between New Braunfels and**
**Bulverde),** 280
**Duck Tours (Galveston),** 195
**Dude, Sweet (Dallas),** 94
**Dune sledding, in Monahans**
**Sandhills State Park,** 365
**Dyeing o' the River Green and**
**Pub Crawl (San Antonio),** 33

# E

**East Beach (Galveston),** 194
**East Dallas,** 60
  accommodations, 69–70
  restaurants, 74
**East Texas,** 41, 186–191
  race relations, 188
**Eating and drinking,** 29–31
**Eatzi's (Dallas),** 80
**Eclectic (Austin),** 320
**Ecotravel.com,** 36
**EJ's (Houston),** 185
**Elderhostel (Road Scholar),**
**36,** 37
**Electricity,** 442
**Electronic System for Travel**
**Authorization (ESTA),** 451
**Elephant Mountain Wildlife**
**Management Area (near**
**Alpine),** 358–359
**Elephant Room (Austin),** 323
**Elisabet Ney Museum (Austin),**
**314**
**El Mercado (San Antonio),** 270
**El Paso,** 331–349
  accommodations, 343–345
  American Express, 336
  doctors and dentists, 336
  drugstores, 336
  emergencies, 336
  getting around, 333, 336
  hospitals, 336–337
  for kids, 340–341
  newspapers and magazines,
  337
  nightlife, 347–349
  organized tours, 341
  outdoor activities, 341–342
  post office, 337

restaurants, 345–347
safety, 337
shopping, 343
sights and attractions, 337–341
spectator sports, 342–343
taxes, 337
time zone, 337
traveling to, 332
visitor information, 336
**El Paso Convention & Visitors Bureau, 336, 341**
**El Paso Diablos, 342**
**El Paso Holocaust Museum, 339–340**
**El Paso Mission Trail, 337–338**
**El Paso Mission Trail Experience, 338**
**El Paso Museum of Art, 338–339**
**El Paso Museum of History, 340**
**El Paso Opera, 347**
**El Paso Playhouse, 348**
**El Paso Pro-Musica, 347**
**El Paso Saddleblanket, 343**
*El Paso Scene,* **347**
**El Paso Symphony Orchestra, 347**
*El Paso Times,* **347**
**El Paso-West RV Park, 345**
**El Paso Zoo, 340**
**El Solitario, 354–355**
**Embassies and consulates, 442**
**Emerald Springs Golf and Conference Center (near El Paso), 342**
**Emergencies, 442–443**
**Emma Long Metropolitan Park (Austin), 318**
**Emo's (Austin), 323**
**Empire Theatre (San Antonio), 271**
**Enchanted Rock State Natural Area (near Fredericksburg), 325–326**
**Ensemble Theatre (Houston), 183**
**E-Passport, 451**
**Ernest Tubb's Record Shop (Fort Worth), 132, 135**
**Escapade 2009 (Dallas), 99**
**ESTA (Electronic System for Travel Authorization), 451**
**E. V. Spence, Lake, 368**
**Excelsior House (Jefferson), 190**
**Exchange Avenue (Fort Worth), 132**
**ExecuCar (Dallas), 54**
**Exhibitions 2d (Marfa), 357**
**Extreme weather exposure, 443**
**Eyeopener Tours (Houston), 178**

**F**
**Fair Oaks (Dallas), 91**
**Fair Park (Dallas), 86, 88**

**Fair Park Passport (Dallas), 85**
**Families with children, 443**
Austin
  hotels, 298
  restaurants, 305
  sights and attractions, 316
best family adventures, 13–14
Dallas
  attractions, 88–89
  hotels, 71
  restaurants, 77
El Paso area attractions, 340–341
Fort Worth
  attractions, 128–129
  hotels, 113
  restaurants, 116
Houston
  hotels, 157
  restaurants, 166
  sights and attractions, 178
Junior Ranger Program
  Big Bend National Park, 383
  Carlsbad Caverns National Park, 403
  Padre Island National Seashore, 220
San Antonio
  accommodations, 247
  restaurants, 258
  sights and attractions, 266
suggested itinerary, 47–49
**Famous Texans, 26–28**
**Fantasy Land (Iraan), 363**
**Far Flung Outdoor Center (Big Bend National Park), 385, 389**
**Farmer's markets**
  Austin, 320
  San Antonio, 270
**Fate Bell Cave Dwelling Tour (Seminole Canyon State Park and Historic Site), 377**
**Fawcett, Farrah, 27**
**FC Dallas, 92**
**Festivals and special events, 33–35**
**Fiesta Cab (Houston), 148**
**Fiesta San Antonio, 33–34**
**Fiestas Navideñas (San Antonio), 35**
**Fiestas Patrias (Houston), 34**
**Films, 25**
**Finesilver Gallery (San Antonio), 269**
**Fins to Feathers Photo Safaris (South Padre Island), 226**
**Firearms, 90**
**Fire Station No. 1/150 Years of Fort Worth Exhibit, 124**
**First Thursdays (Austin), 320**
**Fisherman's Wharf (Port Aransas), 217**

**Fishing**
  Amarillo, 414–415
  Amistad National Recreation Area, 374, 376
  Brazosport area, 202–203
  Corpus Christi, 208
  Goose Island State Park, 214
  Lake Nasworthy, 368
  Padre Island National Seashore, 222
  Port Aransas, 217
  Rockport area, 213
  San Angelo, 368
  South Padre Island, 227
**Fitzgerald's (Houston), 184**
**Five Sixty (Dallas), 98**
**Flat Creek Vineyards, 281**
**Flatonia, 276**
**Floore's Country Store (San Antonio), 272**
**Flying Saucer Draught Emporium (Fort Worth), 133–134**
**Foley's (Houston), 180**
**Food and wine trips, 38**
**Football**
  Amarillo, 415
  Austin, 318
  Dallas, 91
  El Paso, 343
  Houston, 180
**Forest Park (Fort Worth), 129·**
**Forever Resorts (Amarillo), 414**
**Formula 1 Racing (Austin), 318**
**Fort Clark Springs, 373**
**Fort Concho National Historic Landmark (San Angelo), 366**
**Fort Davis, 349–353**
**Fort Davis Chamber of Commerce, 350**
**Fort Davis National Historic Site, 350**
**Fort Sam Houston (San Antonio), 235**
**Fort Worth, 102–136**
  accommodations, 106–114
  babysitters, 105
  Cultural District, 104, 121
    accommodations, 112–114
    restaurants, 118–120
    shopping, 131
    sights and attractions, 124–128
  doctors and dentists, 105
  drugstores, 105–106
  exploring, 121–130
  getting around, 104
  hospitals, 106
  Internet access, 106
  layout of, 103
  maps, 106
  neighborhoods in brief, 103–104
  newspapers and magazines, 106
  nightlife, 132–136
  organized tours, 129
  outdoor activities, 129–130

**Fort Worth** *(cont.)*
police, 106
post office, 106
restaurants, 114–120
safety, 106
shopping, 131–132
spectator sports, 130
taxes, 106
transit info, 106
visitor information, 103
weather, 106
**Fort Worth Botanic Gardens, 125**
**Fort Worth Convention & Visitors Bureau, 103, 121**
**Fort Worth Herd, 122**
**Fort Worth Museum of Science and History, 125, 128**
**Fort Worth Stock Show & Rodeo, 122, 127, 129**
**Fort Worth Tours and Trails, 129**
**Fort Worth Transportation Authority, 106**
**Fort Worth Water Gardens, 124**
**Fort Worth Zoo, 125–126**
**Forty Five Ten (Dallas), 93**
**Four Seasons Resort and Club (Dallas), 91**
**Four-wheeling, Padre Island National Seashore, 222**
**Franklin Mountains State Park, 341, 342**
**Fredericksburg, 324–327**
**Fredericksburg Winery, 280**
**Fred's Texas Café (Fort Worth), 134**
**French Legation Museum (Austin), 315**
**Fretz Park (Dallas), 91**
**Friedrich Wilderness Park (San Antonio), 267**
**Frijole Ranch (Guadalupe Mountains National Park), 396, 398**
**Frisco Rough Riders (Dallas), 91**
**Frito pie, 30**
**Front Gate Tickets (Dallas), 95**
**Frontiers of Flight Museum (Dallas), 55**
**Fulton Mansion (Rockport), 214**

**G**
**Galería Ortiz (San Antonio), 269**
**Galeria San Ysidro (El Paso), 343**
**Galleria area (Houston), 146**
shopping, 181
**Galleria (Dallas), 95**
**Galveston, 192–199**
**Galveston Harbour Tours, 195**
**Garcia Art Glass (San Antonio), 269**
**The Garden (El Paso), 349**
**Gateway Gallery (Dallas), 89**
**Gays and lesbians, 444**
Austin, 324
Dallas, 99
Houston, 185
San Antonio, 274

**Gay Texas Directory, 444**
**George, Phyllis, 27**
**George Bush Intercontinental Airport (Houston), 138–139**
accommodations near, 158–159
**George Ranch Historical Park (Richmond), 177**
**George W. Bush Childhood Home (Midland), 361**
**Ghostbar (Dallas), 98**
**Gilley's Dallas, 97**
**The Ginger Man (Dallas), 98**
**Glenn Springs, 384–385**
**Gliders, 355**
**The Globe of the Great Southwest (Odessa), 362**
**Glossary of Texan words, 20**
**Golden Light Cafe & Cantina (Amarillo), 419**
**Gold Spoon Charters (Rockport), 213**
**Golf.** *See also specific courses*
Amarillo, 415
Austin, 317–319
Canyon, 421
Dallas, 89–91
El Paso, 342
Fort Worth, 129–130
Houston, 179, 180
Lubbock, 429
Midland, 363
Port Aransas, 217
San Angelo, 368–369
San Antonio, 267, 268
**Gonzales, 275**
**Good Records (Dallas), 94**
**Goose Island State Park, 214**
**GORPtravel, 37**
**Government Springs Campsite (Big Bend National Park), 388**
**Governors Landing Campground (Amistad National Recreation Area), 376**
**Governor's Mansion (Austin), 313–314**
**Granada Theater (Dallas), 97**
**Grand Trolley Tours (San Antonio), 266**
**Gran Fiesta de Fort Worth, 34**
**Grape Creek Vineyard (near Fredericksburg), 281**
**Grapefest (Fort Worth), 34**
**Grapevine Hills Trail (Big Bend National Park), 387**
**Grapevine Opry, 135**
**Grapevine Vintage Railroad (Fort Worth), 123, 128**
**Grapevine Visitor Information Center, 135**
**Grasslands Nature Trail, 223**
**Gratitude Vintage Apparel & Nostalgia (Dallas), 94**
**Gray Line/Coach USA (Dallas), 89**
**Gray Line Tours, 38**
**Greater Houston Convention and Visitors Bureau (GHCVB), 140**

**Great Texas Mosquito Festival (Clute), 34**
**Great Texas Wildlife Trails, 36**
**Green Hornet Fishing Guide Service (Rockport), 213**
**Greenville Avenue (Dallas), 60**
restaurants, 74
shopping, 93
**Greenway Plaza (Houston), 146**
**Greyhound, 439**
**Greyhound North American Discovery Pass, 439**
**Groom, 423**
**Gruene, 328–330**
**Gruene Hall, 330**
**Gruene River Company, 329**
**GSM (Global System for Mobile Communications) wireless network, 445**
**Guadalupe Cultural Arts Center (San Antonio), 271**
**Guadalupe Mountains National Park, 41, 44, 393–399**
**Guadalupe Peak Trail (Guadalupe Mountains National Park), 398**
**Guadalupe River, 329**
**Guadalupe River State Park (near Boerne), 268**

**H**
**Haby's Alsatian Bakery (Castroville), 278**
**Half Price Books Records & Magazines (Dallas), 94**
**Hall of State (Dallas), 86**
**Hall of the White Giant Tour (Carlsbad Caverns National Park), 404**
**Halloween (Austin), 35**
**Harbor Lights Celebration (Corpus Christi), 35**
**Hardin, John Wesley, 339**
**Hard Rock Cafe (Houston), 184**
**Harrington Regional Medical Center Park (Amarillo), 414**
**Harrison's Landing (Corpus Christi), 209**
**Harry Ransom Humanities Research Center (Austin), 314–315**
**Harwin Drive (Houston), 182**
**Health concerns, 443**
**The Health Museum (Houston), 173**
**Hello-Lucky (Houston), 181**
**HemisFair Park (San Antonio), 265**
**Heritage Boots (Austin), 321**
**Heritage Society at Sam Houston Park (Houston), 170**
**Heritage Village (New Braunfels), 328**
**Hermann Park (Houston), 174**
golf course, 179

**Highland Park Village (Dallas),** 95
**Highland Range Scenic Lookout,** 369
**Highland Village (Houston),** 181
**Hiking.** *See also specific trails*
  Amarillo, 415
  Austin, 318
  Big Bend National Park, 383, 386–388
  Big Thicket National Preserve, 186
  Caprock Canyons State Park and Trailway (near Lubbock), 428
  El Paso, 342
  Franklin Mountains State Park, 341
  Guadalupe Mountains National Park, 396–398
  Houston, 178–179
  Lubbock, 429
  Padre Island National Seashore, 223
  Palo Duro Canyon State Park, 421
  Sam Houston and Davy Crockett national forests, 189
  San Angelo, 369
  San Antonio, 267
  Seminole Canyon State Park and Historic Site, 378
**Hill Country,** 277–282
  side trips from Austin, 324–330
  suggested itinerary, 49–51
**Hill's Sport Shop (Amarillo),** 422
**Hippie Hollow (Austin),** 318
**Historical attractions, best,** 12–13
**Historic Concho Avenue (San Angelo),** 369
**Historic Route 66 District (Amarillo),** 416
**History of Texas,** 17–22
**Hobby Airport (Houston),** 139
**Hobby Center for the Performing Arts (Houston),** 182
**Hockey**
  Amarillo, 415
  Austin, 319
  Dallas, 91–92
  Fort Worth, 130
**Hogan Park Golf Course (Midland),** 363
**Holidays,** 32
**Holly, Buddy,** 24
  Buddy Holly Center (Lubbock), 426
  Statue (Lubbock), 427
**HomeAway,** 441
**HomeLink International,** 440
**Hook Line & Sinker (Rockport),** 213
**Horseback riding**
  Amarillo, 415
  Bandera, 282
  Big Bend National Park, 388

  Davis Mountains State Park, 351
  Fort Worth, 129, 130
  Guadalupe Mountains National Park, 398
  Palo Duro Canyon State Park, 422
  San Angelo, 368
**Horse racing, El Paso,** 343
**Hotels,** 440–441
  best, 1–5
  tipping at, 450–451
**Hot Springs (Big Bend National Park),** 384, 385
**Hot Springs Trail (Big Bend National Park),** 387
**House of Blues Dallas,** 96
**House of Blues (Houston),** 184
**Houston,** 41, 137–191
  accommodations, 149–159
  area codes, 148
  arriving in, 138–140
  doctors and dentists, 148
  downtown, shopping, 180
  downtown/midtown, 141
    accommodations, 149–151
    restaurants, 159–161
  drugstores, 148
  East End, 141, 146
    accommodations, 151
    restaurants, 162
    shopping, 181
    sights and attractions, 170–172
  Galleria area, 146
    shopping, 181
  getting around, 147–148
  hospitals, 148
  Internet access, 148
  Kirby District, 176–177, 181
    accommodations, 155
    restaurants, 165
  layout of, 140–141
  maps, 148
  Montrose/The Heights, 146
    accommodations, 153–154
    restaurants, 162–165
    shopping, 181
    sights and attractions, 175–176
  Museum District. *See* South Main/Museum District *below*
  neighborhoods in brief, 141, 146
  newspapers and magazines, 148–149
  nightlife, 182–185
  police, 149
  post office, 149
  restaurants, 159–169
    family-friendly, 166
    fast food, 161
  safety, 149
  shopping, 180–182
  side trips to East Texas, 186–191

  sights and attractions, 169–178
    for kids, 178
    organized tours, 178
  South Main/Museum District, 146
    accommodations, 152–153
    sights and attractions, 172–175
  southwest, shopping, 182
  spectator sports, 179–180
  sports and outdoor activities, 178–179
  taxes, 149
  taxis, 148
  temperatures, 32
  transit information, 149
  Uptown, 146
    accommodations, 155–158
    restaurants, 168–169
    shopping, 181
  visitor information, 140
  weather, 149
**Houston Astros,** 179
**Houston Ballet,** 183
**Houston Dynamo,** 180
**Houston Grand Opera,** 183
**Houston Livestock Show and Rodeo,** 33, 180
**Houston Metro,** 138–139, 147
**Houston Museum of Natural Science,** 174
**Houston Rockets,** 179–180
**Houston Ship Channel,** 171
**Houston Symphony,** 182
**Houston Texans,** 180
**Houston Zoological Gardens,** 174
**Hueco Tanks State Park & Historic Site (near El Paso),** 342
**Hughes, Howard,** 27
**Hurricane Ike,** 194
**Hy O Silver (Bandera),** 279

**I**

**IAMAT (International Association for Medical Assistance to Travelers),** 443
**Indian Meadow Nature Trail (Guadalupe Mountains National Park),** 397
**InfoHub,** 38
**In-line skating**
  Dallas, 89
  Fort Worth, 129
**Insights Science Museum (El Paso),** 340
**Institute of Texan Cultures (San Antonio),** 265
**Insurance,** 443–444
**Intermodal Transportation Center (ITC; Fort Worth),** 56
**International Association for Medical Assistance to Travelers (IAMAT),** 443

The International Ecotourism Society (TIES), 36
International Festival (Houston), 33
International Society of Travel Medicine, 443
International Student Identity Card (ISIC), 449
International Student Travel Confederation (ISTC), 449
International Youth Travel Card (IYTC), 449
Internet and Wi-Fi, 444
InTouch USA, 445
Ireland
   embassy of, 442
   passports, 447
   visas, 452
ISIC (International Student Identity Card), 449
ISTC (International Student Travel Confederation), 449
Itineraries, suggested, 44–51
   for families, 47
   Hill Country, 49–51
   in 1 week, 44–46
   in 2 weeks, 46–47
Ivey's Emporium (Marfa), 357
IYTC (International Youth Travel Card), 449

**J**

Jack's Backyard (Dallas), 99
James Evans Gallery (Marfa), 357
Jasper, 188
Jefferson, 189–190
Jiménez, Flaco, 24, 273
Jimenez, Luis, 338
Jim's Travel Link (Dallas), 62
Jogging
   Dallas, 89
   Fort Worth, 129
   Houston, 178–179
John F. Kennedy Memorial (Dallas), 81
John Neely Bryan Cabin (Dallas), 81
Johnson, Lyndon B., 21
   Boyhood Home (Johnson City), 327
   Lyndon B. Johnson State and National Historical Parks at LBJ Ranch (Stonewall), 327–328
Johnson City, 327
John S. Stiff Memorial Park (Amarillo), 414
Jones, George, 23
Jones Hall (Houston), 182
Joplin, Janis, 24
Josephine Theatre (San Antonio), 272
J. R.'s Bar and Grill (Dallas), 99
Jubilee Theatre (Fort Worth), 133

Judge Roy Bean Visitor Center (Langtry), 375
Jump-Start Performance Company (San Antonio), 272
Juneteenth Festival, 34
Junior Ranger Program
   Big Bend National Park, 383
   Carlsbad Caverns National Park, 403
   Padre Island National Seashore, 220
J. Wilde's (San Angelo), 369

**K**

Katy Mills (near Houston), 180
Kayaking
   Big Bend National Park, 388–389
   Corpus Christi, 209
   Rockport area, 213–214
Keeton Park Golf Course (Dallas), 90
Kemah Boardwalk (Houston), 171
Kerrville Bus Co., 439
The Kessler (Dallas), 96
Kids, 443
   Austin
      hotels, 298
      restaurants, 305
      sights and attractions, 316
   best family adventures, 13–14
   Dallas
      attractions, 88–89
      hotels, 71
      restaurants, 77
   El Paso area attractions, 340–341
   Fort Worth
      attractions, 128–129
      hotels, 113
      restaurants, 116
   Houston
      hotels, 157
      restaurants, 166
      sights and attractions, 178
   Junior Ranger Program
      Big Bend National Park, 383
      Carlsbad Caverns National Park, 403
      Padre Island National Seashore, 220
   San Antonio
      accommodations, 247
      restaurants, 258
      sights and attractions, 266
   suggested itinerary, 47–49
Kimbell Art Museum (Fort Worth), 126
King's Palace Guided Tour (Carlsbad Caverns National Park), 404

King William Historic District (San Antonio) , 234, 260
   accommodations, 240, 246–247
   restaurants, 255–256
Kiowa Gallery (Alpine), 357
Kirby District (Houston), 146, 176–177, 181
   accommodations, 155
   restaurants, 165
Kirby Drive (Houston), 141
Kitchen Dog Theater Company (Dallas), 96
Kline Saddlery (Bandera), 279
Kokernot Field (Alpine), 359
Kowbell Rodeo (Fort Worth), 130
Kristofferson, Kris, 23
Kwahadi Museum of the American Indian (Amarillo), 412–413

**L**

La Carafe (Houston), 185
La Diosa Cellars (Lubbock), 429
Lady Bird Johnson Wildflower Center (Austin), 311
Laguna Madre, 222
Laguna Madre Nature Trail (South Padre Island), 226
La Harmonia Store (Big Bend National Park), 384
Lajitas Stables (Big Bend National Park), 388
Lake Alan Henry, 428–429
Lake Amistad Marina, 374
Lake Austin Spa Resort, 37–38
Lake E. V. Spence, 368
Lake Meredith National Recreation Area (Amarillo), 414, 415
Lake Nasworthy, 368
Lake O. H. Ivie, 368
Lake o' the Pines, 190
Landa Park (New Braunfels), 329
Landing (San Antonio), 272–273
Landmark Inn State Historic Site (Castroville), 278
Las Posadas (San Antonio), 35
Latino Cultural Center (Dallas), 96
La Villita National Historic District (San Antonio), 260–261
La Zona Rosa (Austin), 323
LBJ Boyhood Home (Johnson City), 327
LBJ Library and Museum (Austin), 312
Leaning Tower of Texas (near Groom), 423
Leapin' Lizard (Terlingua), 357
Leddy's Ranch at Sundance (Fort Worth), 131
Left Hand Tunnel (Carlsbad Caverns National Park), 404

Legal aid, 444
Legend Jewelers (San Angelo), 366, 369
Legends of the Game Baseball Museum (Arlington), 91
Le Midi (San Antonio), bar at, 274
Leon Springs Dancehall (San Antonio), 272
Lexington, USS, Museum on the Bay, 206, 208
LGBT travelers, 444
    Austin, 324
    Dallas, 99
    Houston, 185
    San Antonio, 274
Liberty Cab (Houston), 148
Lighthouse (Palo Duro Canyon State Park), 421
Lighting Ceremony and River Walk Holiday Parade (San Antonio), 35
Little's Boots (San Antonio), 270
Livestock Exchange Building (Fort Worth), 121
Lizard Lounge (Dallas), 99
Llano Estacado Winery (near Lubbock), 429
The Loft (Dallas), 96
Log Cabin Village (Fort Worth), 126–127
Lola's Sixth Street (Fort Worth), 136
Lone Star Ballet (Amarillo), 419
Lone Star Flight Museum (Galveston), 197
Lone Star Golf Club (El Paso), 342
Lone Star River Boat (Austin), 317
Lonestar Rollergirls (Austin), 319
Long Center for the Performing Arts (Austin), 322
Longwood Golf Club (Cypress), 179
Los Lonely Boys, 24
Louie's Backyard (South Padre Island), 230
Louis Tussaud's Wax Works & Ripley's Believe It or Not (San Antonio), 266
Love Field (Dallas), 55
Love's Antique Mall (Bandera), 279
Lower Cave Tour (Carlsbad Caverns National Park), 404
Lubbock, 413, 424–433
    accommodations, 430–432
    getting around, 426
    nightlife, 433
    outdoor activities, 428–430
    restaurants, 432
    shopping, 430
    sights and attractions, 426–428
    spectator sports, 430
    traveling to, 424–425
    visitor information, 426

Lubbock Lake Landmark, 428
Lubbock Symphony Orchestra, 433
Lucchese Gallery (San Antonio), 270
Luckenbach, 326
Luling, 276–277
Lyndon B. Johnson Country, 327–328
Lyndon B. Johnson State and National Historical Parks at LBJ Ranch (Stonewall), 327–328

M
McAllister Park (San Antonio), 267
McDonald Observatory (Fort Davis), 350–351
McFarlin Tennis Center (San Antonio), 268
McGonigel's Mucky Duck (Houston), 184–185
McKelligon Canyon Amphitheatre (El Paso), 347
Mackenzie Park Disk Golf Course (Lubbock), 429
Mackenzie Park (Lubbock), 428, 429
McKinney Avenue Streetcar Service (M-Line Trolley; Dallas), 60
McKittrick Canyon (Guadalupe Mountains National Park), 398
McKittrick Canyon Nature Trail (Guadalupe Mountains National Park), 397
McKittrick Canyon Trail (Guadalupe Mountains National Park), 397
McKittrick Canyon Visitor Center (Guadalupe Mountains National Park), 394
McLean, 423
McPherson Cellars Winery (Lubbock), 429
Macy's (Houston), 180
Mae Simmons Community Center (Lubbock), 430
Magik Theatre (San Antonio), 272
Magoffin Home State Historic Site (El Paso), 340
Mail, 444–445
Main Street (Houston), 140–141
Majestic Theatre (San Antonio), 271
Malaquite Beach, 220
Marathon, accommodations, 391
Marathon Baxter Gallery (Marfa), 357
Mardi Gras (Galveston), 33, 197
Marfa, 354–358
Marfa and Presidio County Museum, 355
Marfa Book Co., 358
Marfa Ghost Lights, 356

Marfa Gliders, 355
Marfa Lights Festival, 34, 356
Marfreless (Houston), 185
Marion County Chamber of Commerce, 190
Marion Koogler McNay Art Museum (San Antonio), 262
Market Square (San Antonio), 261
Marsh, Stanley, 413
Marsical Mine (Big Bend National Park), 385
Martin, Steve, 27
Martin Road Park (Amarillo), 414
Matagorda Bay, 204
Matagorda Island State Park and Wildlife Management Area, 204
Maverick (Fort Worth), 131
Maxey Park (Lubbock), 430
Mayan Dude Ranch (near Bandera), 38
Mayan Ranch (Bandera), 282
Mayfair Club (Amarillo), 419
Meadowbrook Golf Course (Lubbock), 429
Meadowbrooks Golf Course (Fort Worth), 129
Meadows Museum of Art (Dallas), 87
Meat Loaf, 27
Mecom Fountain (Houston), 141
Medical District (Fort Worth), 104
Medical requirements for entry, 445
Medina River Company (Bandera), 279
Memorial Park (Houston), 178–179
Memorial Park Golf Course (Houston), 179
Menger Bar (San Antonio), 273–274
Menil Collection (Houston), 175–176
Mesquite Championship Rodeo (near Dallas), 92
Metropolitan Transportation Authority (Metro; Houston), 138–139, 147
Mexican-American War, 19, 226
Mexic-Arte Museum (Austin), 314
Mexico
    documents needed for entry, 447
    driving to, 438
    history of Texas and, 18–19
Midland, 360–365
Midland RockHounds, 363
Midnight Rodeo (Amarillo), 419
MidPoint Cafe (Adrian), 423
Million Barrel Museum (Monahans), 365
Miss Hattie's Bordello Museum (San Angelo), 366
Mission Socorro (near El Paso), 338

Mission Trails (San Antonio), 267
Mission Ysleta (near El Paso), 338
Miss Texas USA Pageant (Lubbock), 34
M. L. Leddy's (Fort Worth), 131
Mobile phones, 445
Modern Art Museum of Fort Worth, 127
Molly the Trolley (Fort Worth), 104
Monahans Sandhills State Park, 365
Money and costs, 445–446
Montelongo (Lubbock), 430
Monte Vista Area (San Antonio), 234–235
    accommodations, 240, 247–248
    restaurants, 256
Montrose & the Heights (Houston), 146
    accommodations, 153–154
    restaurants, 162–165
    shopping, 181
    sights and attractions, 175–176
Montrose Boulevard (Houston), 141
Moody Gardens (Galveston), 197
Moody Mansion (Galveston), 195
Morgan's Wonderland, 441
Morton H. Meyerson Symphony Center (Dallas), 95
Mountain biking. See Biking and mountain biking
Movies, 25
Movie Tavern at West 7th Street (Fort Worth), 133
Moyers, Bill, 27
Mule Ears Spring Trail (Big Bend National Park), 387
Multicultural travelers, 446
Museo Alameda (San Antonio), 264
Museum District (Houston), 146
    accommodations, 152–153
    sights and attractions, 172–175
Museum of Fine Arts, Houston (MFAH), 174–175
Museum of Natural Science
    Brazosport, 201
    Houston, 174
Museum of Nature and Science (Dallas), 87, 88
Museum of Science and History (Corpus Christi), 208
Museum of Texas Handmade Furniture (New Braunfels), 328
Museum of Texas Tech University (Lubbock), 426–427
Museum of the American Railroad (Dallas), 86
Museum of the Big Bend (Alpine), 359
Museum of the Southwest (Midland), 362
Museums, best, 8–9

Museums of Port Isabel (South Padre Island), 226
Museum Store + Café (Dallas), 82
Music, 22–25
Music Hall at Fair Park (Dallas), 96
Mustang Island State Park, 217
Mystique Tours, 191

N

Nanette Richardson Fine Art (San Antonio), 269
Nasher Sculpture Center (Dallas), 83–84
Nasworthy, Lake, 368
National Border Patrol Museum (El Paso), 340
National Cowboys of Color Museum & Hall of Fame (Fort Worth), 123
National Cowgirl Museum and Hall of Fame (Fort Worth), 127–129
National forests, Big Thicket area, 186–189
National Museum of Funeral History (Houston), 177
National Museum of the Pacific War (Fredericksburg), 325
National Ranching Heritage Center (Lubbock), 427
Native Americans
    Alibates Flint Quarries National Monument, 414
    Amistad National Recreation Area, 376
    history of, 17–18
    Kwahadi Museum of the American Indian (Amarillo), 412–413
    pictographs and petroglyphs
        Amistad National Recreation Area, 376
        Big Bend National Park, 384, 387
        Hueco Tanks State Park & Historic Site (near El Paso), 342
        Pictographs of Painted Rocks (San Angelo), 368
        Seminole Canyon State Park and Historic Site, 377
        Witte Museum (San Antonio), 262
    Pictographs of Painted Rocks (San Angelo), 368
Native Trails (El Paso), 348
Natural attractions, best, 11–12
Natural Entrance Route (Carlsbad Caverns National Park), 403–404
Nautical Wheelers (Port Aransas), 217
Neiman Marcus (Dallas), 93

Neotropical Bird Sanctuary (Quintana Beach), 202
New Braunfels, 328–330
New Braunfels Museum of Art & Music (Gruene), 329
Newport Dunes (Port Aransas), 217
Newspapers and magazines, 446
New Zealand
    embassy of, 442
    passports, 447
    visas, 452
Nightlife, best, 10–11
1901 Cotton Belt Train Depot (Grapevine), 135
Nokia Live Center (Dallas), 97
North Dallas, 60
    accommodations, 69–70
    restaurants, 74–80
NorthPark Center (Dallas), 94
North Star Mall (San Antonio), 269–270
Nueva Vista Golf Club (Midland), 363

O

Oak Cliff, 60
Oak Lawn (Dallas), 57
    restaurants, 74–80
Ocean Star (Galveston), 196
Odessa, 360–365
Odessa Jackalopes, 363
Odessa Meteor Crater and Museum, 362
O'Hair, Madalyn Murray, 27
O. H. Ivie, Lake, 368
Oilcan Harry's (Austin), 324
Old Chicken Farm Art Center (San Angelo), 368
Old City Park (Dallas), 88
The Old Monk (Dallas), 98
Old Red Courthouse (Dallas), 81
Old Route 66, 422–423
Old West Stables (Palo Duro Canyon State Park), 422
150 Years of Fort Worth Exhibit, 124
The Orange Show (Houston), 171–172
Orbison, Roy, 27
Orbison, Roy, Museum (Wink), 365

P

Packing tips, 447
Padre Island National Seashore, 219–223
Padre Island Park Company, 220, 222
Paint Brush Alley (San Angelo), 366
Painted Dunes Desert Golf Course (El Paso), 342
Palestine, 190
Palladium (Dallas), 96

Palo Duro Canyon State Park, 420–421
Palo Duro Creek (Canyon), 421
The Panhandle Plains, 44, 407–433
Panhandle-Plains Historical Museum (Canyon), 421
Panther Cave (Amistad National Recreation Area), 376
Panther Junction Visitor Center (Big Bend National Park), 381, 383
Panther Path (Big Bend National Park), 386
Parida Cave (Amistad National Recreation Area), 376
Paris Hatters (San Antonio), 270
Park Cities, 60
Parque Chamizal (El Paso), 337
Paseo del Río (The River Walk; San Antonio), 261
Passports, 447
Pawnee Bill's Wild West Show (Fort Worth), 130, 136
Pearl's Dancehall & Saloon (Fort Worth), 134, 135
Pecan Valley (San Antonio), 267
Pecan Valley Golf Course (Fort Worth), 129
Pecos, 374
Pecos River, 377
Pegasus (San Antonio), 274
Performing Arts Center (Austin), 322
The Permian Basin Petroleum Museum (Midland), 362
Persimmon Gap Visitor Center (Big Bend National Park), 381, 388
Peters Brothers Hats (Fort Worth), 131
Pete's Dueling Piano Bar (Dallas), 98–99
Pete's Dueling Piano Bar (Fort Worth), 136
Petticoat Junction (San Antonio), 274
Pheasant Ridge Winery (near Lubbock), 429
Pictographs and petroglyphs
    Amistad National Recreation Area, 376
    Big Bend National Park, 384, 387
    Hueco Tanks State Park & Historic Site (near El Paso), 342
    Pictographs of Painted Rocks (San Angelo), 368
    Seminole Canyon State Park and Historic Site, 377
    Witte Museum (San Antonio), 262
Pier 21 Theater (Galveston), 196
Pillar Bluff Vineyards (near Lampasas), 281
Pine Canyon Trail (Big Bend National Park), 387

The Pinery (Guadalupe Mountains National Park), 396
Pinery Trail (Guadalupe Mountains National Park), 397
Pine Springs Campground (Guadalupe Mountains National Park), 399
Pine Springs Visitor Center (Guadalupe Mountains National Park), 394
Piney Woods, 186
Pinto Ranch (Houston), 181
Pioneer Days (Fort Worth), 34
Pioneer Museum Complex (Fredericksburg), 325
Pioneer Village (Gonzales), 275
Pioneer West Historical Museum (Shamrock), 422
Placita Santa Fe (El Paso), 343
Planetarium, Brazosport, 201
Planet Earth Adventures, 37–39
Planning your trip, 434–453
    accommodations, 440–441
    area codes, 441
    business hours, 441
    customs regulations, 441
    disabled travelers, 441–442
    drinking laws, 442
    electricity, 442
    embassies and consulates, 442
    emergencies, 442–443
    gays and lesbians, 444
    getting around, 435–440
    getting there, 434–435
    health concerns, 443
    insurance, 443–444
    Internet and Wi-Fi, 444
    legal aid, 444
    mail, 444–445
    mobile phones, 445
    money and costs, 445–446
    multicultural travelers, 446
    newspapers and magazines, 446
    packing tips, 447
    police, 448
    safety concerns, 448
    senior travel, 449
    student travel, 449
    telephones, 450
    time zones, 450
    tipping, 450–451
    toilets, 451
    visas, 451–452
    visitor information, 452
    women travelers, 452
Plano Balloon Festival (Dallas), 89
Playa de Rancho Nuevo (Tamaulipas, Mexico), 221
Plaza de los Lagartos (El Paso), 338
Plaza Theatre (El Paso), 347
PM Nightlife Lounge (Dallas), 98
Police, 448
Ponder Boot Company (Fort Worth), 131

Poor David's Pub (Dallas), 97
Port Aransas, 216–219
Port Isabel Historical Museum (South Padre Island), 226
Port Isabel Lighthouse State Historic Site (South Padre Island), 226
Pratt Cabin (Guadalupe Mountains National Park), 396
Presa Canyon Tour (Seminole Canyon State Park and Historic Site), 377
Presbyterian Hospital of Dallas, 63
Presidential Museum (Odessa), 361, 363
Presidio Chapel San Elceario (near El Paso), 338
Presidio County Courthouse (Marfa), 355
The Prospector (El Paso), 347
Prude Ranch (Davis Mountains State Park), 351
Pumpjack Tour (Luling), 276

Q
Quarry (San Antonio), 267
Quicksand Golf Course (San Angelo), 368–369
Quintana Beach County Park, 202, 203–204

R
Rafting, Big Bend National Park, 388–389
Railroad & Transportation Museum of El Paso, 339
Rainbow Cattle Co. (Austin), 324
Ranch-hand style, 28
Rangers Ballpark in Arlington, 91, 100
Rather, Dan, 27
Ratliff Ranch Golf Links (Odessa), 363
Rawls Golf Course (Lubbock), 429
Red Cat Jazz Café (Houston), 184
Red-Eyed Fly (Austin), 323
Regions in brief, 40–44
Renfield's Corner (Dallas), 97
The Republic (El Paso), 349
Republic of Texas, 19
Responsible travel, 35–36
Restaurants
    best, 5–7
    tipping at, 451
Retro Cowboy (Fort Worth), 131
Return of the Chili Queens (San Antonio), 34
Reunion Tower (Dallas), 82
Richmond Hall (Houston), 176
Rich's (Houston), 185
Ridglea Theater (Fort Worth), 135
Rienzi (Houston), 177

Rio Grande Village (Big Bend National Park), 383, 384

Rio Grande Village Campground (Big Bend National Park), 392

Rio Grande Village Nature Trail (Big Bend National Park), 386

Rio Grande Village Trailer Park (Big Bend National Park), 392

Rio Grande Village Visitor Center (Big Bend National Park), 381

Rio San Antonio River Cruise, 266

Rio Taxi Service (San Antonio), 236

Ripley's Believe It or Not (San Antonio), 266

Ripley's Grand Prairie (Arlington), 100

Rivercenter Mall (San Antonio), 270

River Oaks Shopping Center (Houston), 181

River running, Big Bend National Park, 388

Riverside Hills Golf Course (San Angelo), 369

River Walk (San Angelo), 367, 368

River Walk Mud Festival (San Antonio), 33

The River Walk (Paseo del Río; San Antonio), 261

Road conditions hot line, 439

Road Scholar (Elderhostel), 36, 37

Robert Wood Johnson Museum of Frontier Medicine (San Angelo), 366

Rock art (pictographs and petroglyphs)

Rock Art Foundation, 377

Rocketbuster Boots (El Paso), 343

Rockin' R River Rides (Gruene), 329

Rock Island Rail Trail (Amarillo), 415

Rockport, 211–216

Rockport Adventures, 214

Rockport Center for the Arts, 214

Rockwood Golf Course (Fort Worth), 129

Rodeo Exchange (Fort Worth), 135

Rodeos and livestock shows, 343
    Amarillo, 415–416
    Dallas, 92
    Fort Worth, 122, 127, 130, 136
    Houston, 180
    San Angelo, 369
    San Antonio, 268

Rogers, Ginger, 27

Rogers, Kenny, 23

Roller derby, Austin, 319

Rosa's Cantina (El Paso), 349

Rose Marine Theater (Fort Worth), 133

Ross Maxwell Scenic Drive (Big Bend National Park), 382, 383

Ross Rogers Golf Course (Amarillo), 415

Rothko Chapel (Houston), 176

Rough Canyon (Amistad National Recreation Area), 374

Round Rock Express (Austin), 318

Round-Up Saloon (Dallas), 99

Route 66, Old, 422–423

Route 66 Historic District (Amarillo), 423

Route 66 Motor Speedway (near Amarillo), 415

Route 66 Roadhouse (Amarillo), 419

Route 66 Historic District (Amarillo), 410, 412

Roy Orbison Museum (Wink), 365

Running gear, Austin, 320

Running-R Guest Ranch (Bandera), 38

Run-Tex (Austin), 320–321

Rusk, 190

RV parks. See Camping and RV parks

## S

Sabine National Forest, 189

Safety concerns, 448

Sailing, Corpus Christi, 209

The Saint (San Antonio), 274

St. Stanislaus (Bandera), 279

Salute! (San Antonio), 273

Sambuca (Dallas), 97

Sambuca Jazz Café (Houston), 184

Sam Houston National Forest, 188–189

San Angel Folk Art (San Antonio), 269

San Angelo, 365–371

San Angelo Colts, 369

San Angelo Convention and Visitors Bureau, 366

San Angelo Museum of Fine Arts, 367

San Angelo Nature Center, 368

San Angelo Regional Airport/Mathis Field, 365

San Angelo State Park, 367–370

San Angelo Stock Show and Rodeo Association, 369

San Angelo Symphony, 371

San Antonio, 41, 231–282
    accommodations, 237–250
        family-friendly, 247
    Alamo Heights, 235
        restaurants, 258–259
        sights and attractions, 262–263
    arriving in, 232
    doctors and dentists, 237
    downtown, 234
        accommodations, 240–246
        restaurants, 252–254
        shopping, 268
        sights and attractions, 264–265
    drugstores, 237
    getting around, 235–237
    hospitals, 237
    hot lines, 237
    King William Historic District, 234, 260
        accommodations, 240, 246–247
        restaurants, 255–256
    layout of, 233–234
    Monte Vista area, 234–235
        accommodations, 240, 247–248
        restaurants, 256
    neighborhoods in brief, 234
    newspapers and magazines, 237
    nightlife, 270–274
    North Central (near the Airport), 235
        accommodations, 250
    northwest, 235
        accommodations, 248–250
        attractions, 263–264
    parking, 236
    police, 237
    restaurants, 250–259
        family-friendly, 258
    safety, 237
    shopping, 268–270
    sights and attractions, 259–266
        for kids, 266
        organized tours, 266
    South Side, 234
        sights and attractions, 263
    Southtown, 234
        restaurants, 255–256
    spectator sports, 268
    sports and outdoor activities, 267–268
    taxes, 237
    temperatures, 32
    visitor information, 232
    West, 235
        accommodations, 248–250

San Antonio Arts & Cultural Affairs, 271

San Antonio Botanical Gardens, 265

San Antonio Children's Museum, 266

San Antonio Conservation Society, 260

San Antonio IMAX Theater Rivercenter, 266

San Antonio Missions National Historical Park, 263

San Antonio Museum of Art, 261–262

San Antonio Stock Show and Rodeo, 268

San Antonio Symphony, 271

San Antonio Visitor Information Center, 259

San Felipe Springs (Del Rio), 372

San Fernando Cathedral (San Antonio), 264–265

San Francisco de la Espada (San Antonio), 263

San Jacinto Festival and Texas History Day (West Columbia), 33

San Jacinto Monument & Museum (Houston), 170–171

San Jacinto Plaza (El Paso), 338

San José (San Antonio), 263

San Juan Capistrano (San Antonio), 263

San Pedro Campground (Amistad National Recreation Area), 376

Santa Elena Canyon (Big Bend National Park), 383

Santa Elena Canyon Trail (Big Bend National Park), 387

Satellite phones, 445

SATRANS (San Antonio), 232

Saxon Pub (Austin), 324

Scenic Drive Park (El Paso), 341

Schlitterbahn Beach Waterpark (South Padre Island), 227

Schlitterbahn Galveston Water Park, 197

Schlitterbahn (New Braunfels), 329

Scholz Garten (Austin), 324

Schultze House Cottage Garden (San Antonio), 265

Science Spectrum Museum & OMNI Theater (Lubbock), 428

Sea Center Texas (Lake Jackson), 202

Sea kayaking
Big Bend National Park, 388–389
Corpus Christi, 209
Rockport area, 213–214

Seasons, 31–32

Sea Turtle, Inc., 227

Sea turtles
South Padre Island, 227
Texas Gulf Coast, 221

SeaWorld of Texas (San Antonio), 263–264, 267

Selena, 24

Seminole Canyon State Park and Historic Site, 377–378

Seniors Home Exchange, 440

Senior travel, 449

Shadow Hills Golf Course (Lubbock), 429

Shamrock, 422

Shell Houston Open, 180

Shiner, 275–276

Shopping, best, 9–10

Shops at Houston Center, 180

Shops at La Cantera (San Antonio), 269, 270

Shops at Legacy (Plano), 92

Sid Richardson Museum (Fort Worth), 124

Si! El Paso Tours, 341

Sierra Club, 318

Silver Dollar (San Antonio), 274

Silver Spur Guest Ranch (Bandera), 282

Singing Water Vineyards (near Comfort), 280

Sister Creek Vineyards (between Boerne and Fredericksburg), 280

Sí Texas Tours, 38

Six Flags Fiesta Texas (San Antonio), 264

Six Flags Hurricane Harbor (Arlington), 100

Six Flags Over Texas (Arlington), 100

Sixth Floor Museum at Dealey Plaza (Dallas), 81–82

Skype, 445

Slaughter Canyon Cave Tour (Carlsbad Caverns National Park), 404–405

Sleepy Hollow Country Club (Dallas), 90

Slick Willie's (Houston), 184

Smith, Jaclyn, 27

Smoking, 449

Soccer
Dallas, 92
Houston, 180

Social (Dallas), 98

Society for the Performing Arts (SPA; Houston), 182

Sons of Hermann Hall (Dallas), 96

South by Southwest (Austin), 33

Southeast Regional Park (Amarillo), 414

Southern Pacific Station (Houston), 140

South Main (Houston), 146
accommodations, 152–153
sights and attractions, 172–175

South Padre Island, 223–230

South Padre Island Birding and Nature Center, 37

South Padre Island Convention and Visitors Bureau, 224

South Padre Island Kite Festival, 35

South Plains Mall (Lubbock), 430

Southwestern Exposition and Livestock Show and Rodeo (Fort Worth), 33

Southwestern Exposition and Livestock Show & Rodeo (Fort Worth), 130

Southwestern International PRCA Rodeo (El Paso), 343

Space Center Houston, 172

Spacek, Sissy, 27

Spanish Governor's Palace (San Antonio), 265

Special events and festivals, 33–35

Spider Cave (Carlsbad Caverns National Park), 405

SplashTown, Spring, 177–178

Splashtown, San Antonio, 266

Spoetzl brewery (Shiner), 275–276

Spring, 31

Spring Creek Marina & RV Park (San Angelo), 368, 370

Stagecoach Ballroom (Fort Worth), 134–135

Stampede (Bandera), 279

Stanley Korshak (Dallas), 93

Star Canyon Winery (El Paso), 339

StarKeeper Gallery (San Angelo), 369

Star Tickets (Austin), 319

Star Tickets (Dallas), 91, 95

State Capitol (Austin), 309–310

State Fair of Texas (Dallas), 34

Statehood, 19

STA Travel, 449

Steves Homestead Museum (San Antonio), 260

Stewart Beach (Galveston), 194

Stillwell Store and RV Park (Alpine), 392

Stock Show and Rodeo (San Antonio), 33

Stockyards Championship Rodeo (Fort Worth), 136

Stockyards Museum (Fort Worth), 122

Stockyards National Historic District (Fort Worth), 103
accommodations, 108–110
restaurants, 114–115
shopping, 131
sights and attractions, 121–122, 128

Stockyards Station (Fort Worth), 121
shopping, 131, 132

Stockyards Station Livery (Fort Worth), 130

Stockyards Wedding Chapel (Fort Worth), 132

Stubb's (Austin), 324

Student travel, 449

Studios at Las Colinas (Dallas), 89

Study Butte-Terlingua Area (Big Bend National Park)
accommodations, 390–391
restaurants, 391–392

Sue Ellen's (Dallas), 99

Summer, 31–32

Sundance Square (Fort Worth), 103, 131, 132

Sunday Houses (Fredericksburg), 325
Sun exposure, 443
Sunland Park Mall (El Paso), 343
Sunland Park Racetrack and Casino (near El Paso), 343
Sunset Country Club (Odessa), 363
Sunset Mall (San Angelo), 369
Super Bull (Amarillo), 33
Super Shuttle
  Austin, 284
  Dallas/Fort Worth, 54
  Houston, 138
Surfing
  Padre Island National Seashore, 223
  Port Aransas, 217-218
Sustainable tourism, 35-36
Swig (San Antonio), 274
Swimming
  Austin, 318
  Lubbock, 430
  Padre Island National Seashore, 223
  South Padre Island, 227-228
Swiss Avenue Historic District (Dallas), 88
Sycamore Creek Golf Course (Freeway), 129

**T**

Tap (El Paso), 349
Taxes, 449
TCU Tennis Center (Fort Worth), 130
Tejano Conjunto Festival (San Antonio), 34, 273
Telephones, 450
  area codes, 441
  useful telephone numbers, 450
Television shows, 25-26
Temperatures, 32
Tenison Golf Course (Dallas), 90
Tennis
  Dallas, 90-91
  Fort Worth, 130
  Houston, 179
  San Antonio, 268
Ten Thousand Villages (Austin), 320
Terlingua, 357
Terlingua Trading Post, 357
Teskey's Uptown (Fort Worth), 131-132
Tesoros Trading Company (Austin), 320
Texan style, 28
*Texas Accommodations Guide*, 440
Texas Aviation Hall of Fame (Galveston), 197
Texas Bed & Breakfast Association, 440
Texas Brahmas (Fort Worth), 130

Texas Cowboy Hall of Fame (Fort Worth), 122-123
Texas Gulf Coast, 41, 192-230
Texas Hill Country Wine and Food Festival (Austin), 33
Texas Hotel & Lodging Association, 440
Texas International Fishing Tournament (TIFT; South Padre Island), 227
Texas Jazz Festival (Corpus Christi), 35
Texas Legato (Pillar Bluff), 281
Texas Maritime Museum (Rockport), 215
Texas Memorial Museum (Austin), 315
Texas Motor Speedway (near Fort Worth), 130
*Texas* (musical drama), 421
Texas Outfitters and Guides Association, 37
Texas Parks and Wildlife Department, 37
Texas Rangers, 91, 448
Texas Rollergirls (Austin), 319
Texas Seaport Museum (Galveston), 196
Texas Stadium (Irving), 91
Texas State Aquarium (Corpus Christi), 206
Texas State Travel Guide, 39
Texas Tech Red Raiders (Lubbock), 430
Texas Tech University Theatre (Lubbock), 433
Texas Tickets (Fort Worth), 133
Texas Toast Culinary Tours, 38
Texas Town (Fort Worth), 128
Texas Travel Information Center (El Paso), 336
Texas Travel Information Centers, 452
Texas Twisters (Dallas), 99
Texas Wine Tours, 38
Tex-Mex cooking, 30
Tex's Grill (San Antonio), 274
Theatre Under the Stars (Houston), 183
Thistle Hill House Museum (Fort Worth), 128
Thompson Memorial Park (Amarillo), 414
Ticketmaster
  Dallas, 91
  El Paso, 347
  Fort Worth, 133
  San Antonio, 271
Ticket Stop (Houston), 179
TIES (the International Ecotourism Society), 36
Time zones, 450
Tiny Texas Houses (Luling), 276
Tipping, 450-451
Together Green, 38
Toilets, 451
Torian Log Cabin (Grapevine), 135

Torre di Pietra, 281
Tour 18 Dallas, 90
Tour 18 Houston, 179
Tourist information, 452
Tournament Players Course at the Woodlands (near Houston), 179
Tours, 37-39
Tower of the Americas (San Antonio), 265
Toyahvale Desert Oasis, 353
TPC at the Four Seasons Resort and Club (Dallas), 89
Trader's Village (Arlington), 101
Trains and railways, 435, 439. *See also* Amtrak
  Atalanta (Jefferson), 189
  Chihuahua al Pacifico (Chihuahua to the Pacific) railway, 348
  Grapevine Vintage Railroad (Fort Worth), 123, 128
  Museum of the American Railroad (Dallas), 86
  Rusk-Palestine train ride, 190
Trammell & Margaret Crow Collection of Asian Art (Dallas), 84
Travel CUTS, 449
Traveler's Aid Society International, 442-443
Travel Health Online, 443
Travel insurance, 443-444
Treasures of the Gulf Museum (South Padre Island), 226
Trees (Dallas), 96
Trevino, Lee, 28
Trinity Park (Fort Worth), 129
Trinity Railway Express (TRE; Dallas/Fort Worth), 56, 104
Trinity River Trails (Fort Worth), 129
Triton Financial Classic (Austin), 319
Tubing, 268, 282, 329
Tuff Canyon Trail (Big Bend National Park), 387
Twin Buttes Reservoir, 368, 369

**U**

U Drop Inn (Shamrock), 422
Uncertain, 190
Underwater Expeditions (Brazosport), 203
United Cab (Houston), 148
United Kingdom
  embassy of, 442
  passports, 447
  visas, 452
University Cyclery (Austin), 317
University of Texas at El Paso (UTEP)
  Dinner Theatre, 348-349
  Miners, 342, 343
University of Texas (UT; Austin), sports teams, 318

University Park Village (Fort Worth), 132
Upper Canyon Tour (Seminole Canyon State Park and Historic Site), 377
Urban cowboys, 28
USA Rail Pass, 439
USIT, 449
USS *Lexington* Museum on the Bay, 206, 208
The Usual (Fort Worth), 134

**V**

Valero Texas Open (San Antonio), 268
Valley Transit Co., 439
Val Verde Winery (Del Rio), 373
Veloway (Austin), 317
Vereins Kirche (Society Church; Fredericksburg), 325
Verizon Wireless Amphitheater (San Antonio), 272
Verizon Wireless Theater (Houston), 184
VIA Metropolitan Transit Service (San Antonio), 236
Vidor, 188
Villa Finale (San Antonio), 260
The Village (Houston), 181
Village Station (Dallas), 99
Visas, 451–452
Visa Waiver Program (VWP), 451
Visitor information, 452
Visitor Information Center (Fredericksburg), 325
Visit USA, 435
Viva! El Paso, 348
Voice over Internet Protocol (VoIP), 445
Volunteer and working trips, 38
Vonage, 445

**W**

Wahoo Saloon (South Padre Island), 230
Walking Arts District Strolls (Dallas), 89
*Walking Sculpture* brochure (Dallas), 84
Walking tours, 39
Walking Tours of the Stockyards (Fort Worth), 129
Walnut Canyon Desert Drive, 403
Wanna-Wanna (South Padre Island), 230
Water, drinking, 452
Waterloo Records and Video (Austin), 320
Watermelon Thump (Luling), 276
Watersports. *See also specific sports*
   New Braunfels area, 329
   San Antonio, 268
The Wave (South Padre Island), 224

Weather, 31–32
Websites, best, 14–15
West End Bicycles (Houston), 179
West End Historic District (Dallas), 57
West End MarketPlace (Dallas), 92
Western Mercantile show (Fort Worth), 131
Western Playland Amusement Park (Sunland Park), 341
Western Warehouse (Dallas), 93–94
Western wear and gear, 29
   Austin, 321
   Bandera, 279
   Dallas, 93–94
   El Paso, 343
   Fort Worth, 131–132
   Houston, 181
   San Antonio, 270
Western Wear Exchange (Fort Worth), 132
Westgate Shopping Mall (Amarillo), 416
Westheimer Road (Houston), 141
Westin La Cantera (San Antonio), 267
West Lake (near Austin), 286
West 7th Street Corridor (Fort Worth), 104, 131
West Texas, 41, 331–378
   small towns of central, 349–360
   wildfires of 2011, 352
West Village (Dallas), 93
White Elephant Saloon (Fort Worth), 133
Whitehead Memorial Museum (Del Rio), 373
White Rock Lake (Dallas), 89
Whole Foods Market
   Austin, 320
   Dallas, 80
Whooping cranes, 212
   tours
      Aransas National Wildlife Preserve, 209
      Rockport area, 214
Wild About Music (Austin), 319–320
Wild Basin Wilderness Preserve, 318
Wild Bill's (Dallas), 93
Wildcat Bluff Nature Center (Amarillo), 414, 415
Wildlife Management Areas (WMA) of Texas, 36
Wildlife viewing. *See also* Bird-watching; Dolphin tours; Zoos
   Amistad National Recreation Area, 376
   Big Bend National Park, 385–386
   Brazosport area, 202
   Carlsbad Caverns National Park, 405

Elephant Mountain Wildlife Management Area (near Alpine), 358–359
Guadalupe Mountains National Park, 398
   health concerns, 443
Matagorda Island State Park and Wildlife Management Area, 204
Padre Island National Seashore, 222
San Angelo, 368
Wildcat Bluff Nature Center (Amarillo), 414
The Wild West, 19
Wild West (Lubbock), 433
William P. Hobby Airport (Houston), 138–139
Williams Ranch House (Guadalupe Mountains National Park), 396
Will Rogers Memorial Center (Fort Worth), 130
Windmill Nature Trail (Seminole Canyon State Park and Historic Site), 378
Window View Trail (Big Bend National Park), 386
Windsurfing
   Corpus Christi, 209
   Padre Island National Seashore, 223
   South Padre Island, 228
Wineries and vineyards, 31
   El Paso area, 339
   Lubbock area, 429
   between New Braunfels and Boerne, 280–281
Wine tours, Grapevine, 135
Wine Tours of Texas, 38
Wings over Houston Airshow, 35
Winspear Opera House (Dallas), 80, 95
Winter, 32
Witte Museum (San Antonio), 262–263
Wolfman Jack, 372
Women & Their Work (Austin), 320
Women's Museum: An Institute for the Future (Dallas), 86
Women travelers, 452
Wonderland Amusement Park (Amarillo), 413
Woodrose Winery, 281
Woody's Sports Center (Port Aransas), 217
World Birding Center, 37
World Championship Ranch Rodeo (Amarillo), 415–416
World Legacy Awards, 36
Worldwinds Windsurfing, 222, 223
Wortham Center (Houston), 182
Wrangler Walking Tour (Fort Worth), 129

WWOOF (World-Wide Opportunities on Organic Farms), 36
Wyler Aerial Tramway (El Paso), 341–342
Wyly Theater (Dallas), 80, 96

## Y

Yard Dog Folk Art (Austin), 320
Yellow Cab, Houston, 148
Yellow Checker Cab, San Antonio, 236–237

Yellow Checker Shuttle "Airporter" (Dallas), 54
Yellow Checker Taxi
  Dallas, 54, 62
  Fort Worth, 105
YWCA (Lubbock), 430

## Z

Zach Theatre (Austin), 322
Z. Boaz Golf Course (Fort Worth), 129
Zilker Botanical Garden (Austin), 316

Zilker Park (Austin), 316, 317
  Tree Lighting, 35
Zilker Zephyr Miniature Train (Austin), 316
Zinc (San Antonio), 274
Zin Valle Vineyards (Canutillo), 339
Zoos
  Amarillo, 412
  Dallas, 88
  El Paso, 340
  Fort Worth, 125–126
  Houston, 174